A LIFE
IN LABOR LAW

BENJAMIN AARON, c. 1955

A LIFE
IN LABOR LAW

THE MEMOIRS OF
BENJAMIN AARON

UCLA INSTITUTE FOR RESEARCH ON LABOR AND EMPLOYMENT

2007

Printed in the United States of America

A Life in Labor Law: The Memoirs of Benjamin Aaron / Benjamin Aaron
Library of Congress Control Number: 2007938851
ISBN: 978-0-89215-003-8

♾ The paper used in this publication meets the minimum requirements of the American
National Standard for Information Sciences—Permanence of Paper for Printed Library
Materials, ANSI Z39-48-1994.

UCLA Institute for Research on Labor and Employment
10945 Le Conte Avenue
Suite 2107
Los Angeles, CA 90095-1478

CONTENTS

ACKNOWLEDGMENTS

The number of persons to whom I am indebted for assistance in writing this book is considerable. To name each of them would be impracticable, but to all of those who aided me I express my sincere thanks. A relatively few persons, dear friends all, dedicated untold hours reading and criticizing each chapter of my manuscript and provided constant encouragement.

My bonds of friendship and affection for Howard Block, Richard Mittenthal, and Rolf Valtin are unbreakable, and my debt to each of them can never be repaid.

I am similarly indebted to Willard Wirtz, whose friendship and assistance have so frequently influenced and advanced my career. My brother, Daniel Aaron, reviewed the first few chapters of my manuscript and gave me much helpful though deflating criticism of my writing style.

I am especially grateful to Professor Michael Schill, Dean of the UCLA School of Law, who made available to me all of the school's facilities despite my non-teaching emeritus status, and who constantly encouraged me to complete this ambitious undertaking.

Ruth Milkman, Professor of Sociology and Director of UCLA's Institute for Research on Labor and Employment (formerly the Institute of Industrial Relations), generously made available to me the part-time services of Rebecca Frazier, an experienced editor, whose wise editorial corrections and suggestions greatly improved the readability of the book.

My law school assistant, Tal Grietzer, without whose help in so many different ways I probably would never have completed this project, was solely responsible for reproducing and keeping track of innumerable versions of each chapter of the manuscript as well as for preparing the manuscript for publication.

Finally, my beloved wife, Eleanor, despite her disappointment that I did not elect to write a relatively short volume that would have been limited to those matters primarily of interest to our two daughters and other family members, loyally accepted my decision to write a larger work and never ceased to support and encourage me.

I remain solely responsible for any factual errors.

Benjamin Aaron
9 July 2007

INTRODUCTION

This volume does not conform to the conventional style of memoirs. The events covered are not recounted in chronological order; they frequently overlap in time. Most conclude with a meditation on what I have learned from the described experience. The work was conceived of as a relatively brief response to suggestions by my wife, Eleanor, and our two daughters, Judith and Louise, that I recount the activities that engaged so much of my time when "the girls," now middle-aged ladies, were young. But before the project got under way a number of friends in organizations in which I had played an active role, together with some of my colleagues in the UCLA School of Law—my academic home since 1960—began urging me to record all of my professional activities dating back to 1942, particularly those within the University of California and similar institutions. After considering the matter for some time, I made the fateful decision, which I have sometimes regretted, to undertake the larger work.

Another preliminary decision that had to be made was whether to confine myself to an account of my professional activities or to include a number of autobiographical details relating to my relations with my immediate family. My decision was to report solely on the former, not only because I feel uncomfortable about publicly discussing family matters but also because extending my account beyond my purely professional activities would expand the book to an unacceptable length.

It has always been my practice to keep detailed records of my various activities, but, unfortunately, I have been deprived of the use of some of my most important records. For example, three cabinets of files on matters arising in the 1940s and 1950s in which I was deeply involved were lost in

Editor's note: Professor Aaron passed away before completing the process of preparing this manuscript for publication. He drew many of the quoted passages from his notes and his recollections; many of these are so noted. Some quoted passages, however, remain unattributed. Professor Aaron had planned to write his memoirs in two volumes: this first volume is dedicated to his professional activities. He was in the early stages of drafting the second volume, which was to cover his academic career, when he died. Vic Telesino of the UCLA Law School was instrumental in preparing the manuscript.

a flood in the basement of the UCLA campus building in which they were stored. Others were misplaced over the years and have never been recovered. Luckily, most of my professional activities were matters of public record, so I have been able to verify important names, events, and dates by referring to the print media. Nevertheless, many of my recollections of events are based entirely on my all too fallible memory.

In "War and Memory," Tobias Wolfe made an observation that applies to my memories of my professional career:

> We tend to think of memory as a camera, or a tape recorder, where the past can be filed intact and called up at will. But memory is none of these things. Memory is a storyteller, and like all storytellers it imposes form on the raw mass of experience. It creates shape and meaning by emphasizing some things and leaving others out.[1]

Indeed, I have caught myself describing events that actually never occurred or that happened quite differently from the way I remembered them. This disturbing discovery gives rise to fears that I may have unwittingly done an injustice to some persons about whose actions I have commented unfavorably or have misrepresented my own role in incidents I have described. In an effort to forestall such errors, I have carefully checked corroborative sources, where they exist, and thoroughly searched my memory. Certainly, I have not consciously altered the facts as I recall them in order to tell a better story.

Finally, to forestall criticisms of my use of the term *Negro*, instead of *Afro-American*, I offer the following explanation. I have always had a distaste for the concept of "hyphenated Americans," which seems to me unnecessary and demeaning; therefore, I have stuck to the word *Negro*. In so doing, I have followed the practice of two impeccable sources: Martin Luther King Jr. and my good friend and fellow member of the UAW Public Review Board, James E. Jones Jr., both of whom used the term *Negro*.[2]

---

[1] Tobias Wolff, "War and Memory," *The New York Times*, 28 April 2001.
[2] See his autobiography, *Hattie's Boy: The Life and Times of a Transitional Negro* (Madison: University of Wisconsin Law School, 2006).

CHAPTER 1

THE NATIONAL WAR LABOR BOARD, 1942–1945

LOOKING FOR A JOB

My narrative begins in the spring of 1941. Newly married, Eleanor and I arrived in Washington, D.C., in the latter part of April. Our total assets consisted of several thousand dollars worth of stock and what I had assumed was a firm promise of a job for me in the Office of the Solicitor of the U.S. Department of Labor. Unfortunately, the job offer turned out to have some strings attached. In those days, federal civil service appointments in the lower grades were subject to quotas: only so many for each state. When I showed up at the Department of Labor, I was informed that the quota for my home state, Illinois, was already full. Not to worry, however, the department's personnel man said; all I had to do was to claim Michigan, where I had attended college from 1933 to 1937, as my home state and get several of my friends there to confirm that I had voted in a Michigan election (which I had never done). This sort of misrepresentation, he told me, was routine—simply a harmless means to get around a silly bureaucratic roadblock.

Eleanor and I talked it over. Although I badly needed a job, we agreed that getting one by lying was no way to begin a career. Reluctantly, I declined, blessedly unaware that eight long months would elapse before I would find another position. Before I describe my agonizingly long search for employment, however, I need to provide a few personal background facts that will help to explain why I had such difficulty in finding a job.

Washington in 1941 was still a Mecca for recent law school graduates, most of whom found ready employment in the executive departments or the various administrative agencies established by Congress in the early days of the Roosevelt administration. But I did not fit the pattern of the average job seeker. My three-year record at the Harvard Law School, from 1937 to 1940, had been undistinguished. Looking back, I realized that I had decided to become a lawyer for no other reason than that my father, Henry J. Aaron, and two of his brothers, Charles and Ely, had chosen that profession. My father's highly successful career was cut short by a fatal disease when he was only 41 and I was six. My mother had died a year earlier. All my life I had heard him extolled by former friends and associates as a brilliant lawyer and a highly principled man of great integrity: an ideal role model. He was succeeded as head of our family by Charles ("Uncle Charlie" to all his nieces and nephews and their friends), cofounder of the Chicago firm of Henry J. and Charles Aaron. He was also my guardian, for whom I had great respect, admiration, and affection. So it was natural, I suppose, that I decided to become a lawyer.

When I arrived at Harvard, I realized almost at once that I was badly prepared for the rigorous law school curriculum. My academic performance at the University of Michigan had been creditable, but my notoriously soft sociology major, supplemented by courses I had taken in English, history, and philosophy, had not prepared me for the more rigorous discipline of the law. I had taken only one science course (chemistry), which I passed only after being tutored, no courses in mathematics, and only two or three in economics and political science. The standard law school aptitude test (LSAT), which is now one of the key determinants of admission to law school, was not in effect when I was admitted to Harvard, but it was given to all members of our first-year class on an experimental basis. I scored very high on questions testing use and comprehension of English and general information, but dropped nearly to the bottom of the curve on questions testing mathematical and related abilities. Had the test been required when I applied for admission to Harvard, I doubt that I would have been accepted.

Final examinations at the end of my first year of law school came as a terrible shock to me. Without any justification other than my largely irrelevant academic success at the University of Michigan, my family and I had assumed that I would do well in law school, but my first-year grades were barely passing. It was not that I did not understand the material;

rather, it was my inability to spot rapidly the issues in the examination questions and my fatal tendency to waste valuable time searching for just the right word or phrase to express my thoughts. In short, I proved to be an exceptionally bad exam taker, a failure that persisted through my entire law school career. I graduated in the bottom quarter of the class.

During my law school years I had begun to wonder whether I had made the right career choice. Most of the courses I took simply did not interest me. It was not until my third year that I was able to work up any enthusiasm for what I was learning. At one time I seriously considered becoming a specialist in the sociology of law, not remotely comprehending what that would entail or to what use I could put such expertise. An interview with Professor Max Rheinstein of the University of Chicago Law School, a noted authority on comparative law, brought me down to earth. He received me graciously and enthusiastically outlined a proposed course of study that I judged would require a minimum of an additional four years, plus the mastery of several foreign languages.

Eventually, I found my true calling: a career in labor law and industrial relations. My years at the University of Michigan had coincided with the rise of the Congress of Industrial Organizations (CIO) and of the United Auto Workers (UAW). From that time on, my sympathies were strongly for organized labor. In addition, through my acquaintance with a family friend, Max Meyer, a New York businessman, civic leader, and member of the New York State Mediation Board, I became interested in labor mediation and arbitration. Then, in my third year at Harvard, I took Dean James M. Landis's course in labor law—one of the few in which I did well—and Professor Paul A. Freund's seminar in problems of governmental litigation, for which I wrote a lengthy paper on the first National Labor Relations Board (NLRB) decision that the U.S. Supreme Court refused to enforce. Those experiences confirmed my resolve to practice labor law in one way or another. After graduation, in a burst of naive enthusiasm, I wrote to Richard Frankensteen, a vice president of the UAW with whom I had a casual acquaintance, offering my services to the union's legal department. He did not bother to reply. (A few years later, I mentioned this incident to Walter Reuther, whom I had come to know rather well. Walter laughed and told me that he had a whole drawer of job applications from Ph.D.s and law graduates, but that the union preferred to use rank-and-file members whenever possible.)

After graduating from law school, I spent the summer in Chicago, ostensibly preparing for the Illinois bar examination. By that time, however, I was engaged to Eleanor, whom I had met in my third year at Harvard, and my thoughts were concentrated on getting married and going to Washington to work for the government. For some incomprehensible reason, I decided that I didn't need to enroll in a bar preparation course. It would be enough, I thought, to buy a number of course outlines and to study on my own time. My "study" consisted of taking them to the lakefront on Chicago's south side, where I lay in the sun and skimmed through them without really concentrating on their content. Inevitably, I flunked the bar exam.

By this time my self-esteem had almost vanished. My uncles were sympathetic and supportive, but I sensed that they had begun to doubt whether I would ever succeed as a lawyer. While waiting to retake the bar exam, I registered as a graduate student at the University of Chicago Law School, not for the purpose of obtaining a graduate degree in law, but to do research under the supervision of Professor Charles O. Gregory, an authority in the field of labor law. Gregory later told me that he had never met anyone who appeared to have less self-confidence than I did when we first met.

My preparation for the bar exam the second time around was more disciplined. I studied several nights a week with a refugee couple from Europe and a young associate at our family law firm. We all passed the fairly rigorous two-day examination, and in May 1941, I returned to Cambridge to get married and to begin my assault on Washington.

Why did I choose government service over private practice? Probably for the same reasons that motivated the New Deal economist, Walter Salant, who recalled that the spirit of the Roosevelt Administration brought in young people and "generated ideas, fermentation, energy, a feeling that something was being done, that there was leadership when leadership was needed, and there was a relationship between the government and the people in which the government was the citizen's friend."[1]

With a position in the Department of Labor no longer available, I began my job search with the principal agency dealing with labor-management matters, the National Labor Relations Board (NLRB). Thanks to a letter of introduction from a now-forgotten source, I eventually obtained an interview with Robert B. Watts, the board's general counsel. After asking me the inevitable opening question—"Were you on the law review?"—and receiving a negative answer, he rather abruptly dismissed me with the statement that there were no jobs available. I encountered the same treatment everywhere I went, long after I had given up hopes of getting a job in a labor agency and was prepared to accept anything that was offered. It seemed that nobody was interested in an inexperienced applicant who had not achieved at least a measure of academic distinction in law school.

Eleanor, a skilled legal stenographer, was of course able to get a job immediately, first with a Washington law firm and then as secretary to a lawyer in the foreign funds division of the U.S. Treasury Department. We were thus able to keep our heads above water financially, but the psychological pressure upon me soon became unbearable. I was overwhelmed by feelings of shame and worthlessness because of my continuing inability to find work. These emotions were intensified every time we spent a social evening with friends or new acquaintances. The first ice-breaking question, invariably, was "Where do you work?" Each time I had to answer that I was still looking, and my embarrassment grew more painful.

A major problem for me was how to spend my time. At first, I used to stay in our little apartment in Arlington, Virginia, and wait for the mail, hoping against hope that it would bring a favorable response to one of my job applications. Eventually, this regime became intolerable. I could not bear staying home when I felt I should be out working or at least *doing* something. In desperation, I took to going each day to the Department of Justice library, a comfortable, quiet place, where I

---

[1] Obituary, *New York Times*, 3 May 1999, A24.

systematically read and took notes on U.S. Supreme Court and NLRB decisions in labor cases and descriptions of private arbitration systems for the settlement of labor-management disputes.

Throughout this long ordeal, several good friends never ceased their efforts to help me find a job. One of these was Max ("Moose") Isenbergh, a brilliant, many-talented lawyer, who had been a year ahead of me at Harvard and whom I came to know much better in Washington. He was then clerking for U.S. Supreme Court Justice Hugo Black. Although unable to place me anywhere, he did introduce me to Black and to a number of influential members of the government establishment. The person who ultimately succeeded in getting me a job was Ralph T. Seward, whom I met shortly after coming to Washington. At that time, Seward was working as a lawyer in the U.S. Immigration Service, then an agency of the Department of Justice. When we first met, he predicted that new opportunities would soon open up in the labor law field and told me to keep in touch.

In March 1941, President Roosevelt established the National Defense Mediation Board (NDMB) by executive order. The NDMB was created because of growing industrial unrest that threatened seriously to interfere with the rearmament program during the winter of 1940–41. Its jurisdiction was limited to those controversies that threatened to burden or obstruct the production or transportation of equipment or materials essential to national defense and that could not be adjusted by the U.S. Conciliation Service, an agency of the Department of Labor. The NDMB was primarily a mediation agency with the authority, in the event that it failed in its efforts to bring about voluntary agreement between the parties to the dispute, to make public recommendations for its settlement. If these means failed, the president could order military occupation of the plants, which he did in three instances. Seward was made an alternate public member of the NDMB, and shortly thereafter I went to see him. He assured me that although there were no jobs for which I could qualify at the NDMB, something suitable would soon become available.

In November 1941, the NDMB broke up after a majority of its tripartite membership (representatives of the public, industry, and the two labor federations[2]) refused to order the steel companies to agree to a union shop in their wholly owned, or "captive," coal mines. The members of the United Mine Workers (UMW) struck, the CIO members withdrew from the board, and the president was forced to intervene to maintain coal production.[3]

The urgent necessity for uninterrupted production to support the war effort led President Roosevelt to convene a conference of labor and management representatives to formulate means for eliminating strikes and lockouts in so-called defense industries. The conferees, who met in December 1941, quickly agreed that there should be no strikes or lockouts for the duration of the war, and that a war labor board should be established to deal with labor-management disputes that could not be resolved through collective bargaining. The major point of difference, which the conferees failed to settle, was the same issue on which the NDMB had foundered: the "union shop," or "union security." The employer representatives wanted existing practices to be frozen for the war's duration and strongly opposed intervention by the government in disputes over that issue. Representatives of the American Federation of Labor (AFL) and the CIO took the opposite position, asserting that disputes over union security should be resolved in the same way as those over wages and other matters. Typically, FDR finessed the impasse and "accepted "without reservation" the "covenants that there shall be no strikes or lock-outs and all disputes shall be settled by peaceful means." He then stunned the employer group by stating that the points agreed upon "cover of necessity *all disputes* that may arise from labor and management." The furious employers, outmaneuvered by the master politician, were left to find such comfort as they could in the president's concluding statement: "I have full faith that no group in our national life will take undue advantage while we are faced by common enemies."

[2] The American Federation of Labor (AFL) and the Congress of Industrial Organizations (CIO).

[3] The dispute was ultimately submitted to final and binding arbitration. The tripartite arbitration board, chaired by John R. Steelman, director of the U.S. Conciliation Service, granted the union's demand over the employer member's dissent, but the board's decision went almost entirely unnoticed because it was issued on 7 December 1941.

On 12 January 1942, Roosevelt issued Executive Order No. 9017, abolishing the NDMB and establishing the National War Labor Board (WLB). Along with several former NDMB members and staff, Seward, my guardian angel, moved over to the new agency as an associate public member. I soon went to see him, and this time he arranged an appointment for me with the WLB's vice chairman, George W. Taylor, a professor of economics from the Wharton School at the University of Pennsylvania.

My first meeting with this man, who was to have such a lasting influence on my career, was one I shall never forget. "Doctor" Taylor (a title used by everyone who addressed him) was short and rotund. He wore his hair slicked back, and his complexion was rather pasty. He seemed very good natured and laughed easily. After asking me a few preliminary questions, he raised the general subject of the arbitration of labor disputes. I warmed to this topic, hoping to impress him with my imagined expertise. Taylor let me talk and at least created the impression that he was interested in what I had to say. After a while he pronounced himself satisfied with my qualifications and told me I was hired.

That evening, describing the interview for Eleanor, I offered a preliminary assessment of Taylor that still makes me laugh when I recall it. He seemed to me, I said, to be a very nice man, but not as well informed as I was on the subject of our conversation. At that time, I was unaware that Taylor was one of the country's most outstanding figures in the field of labor-management relations. Among other things, he had served as impartial umpire for the full-fashioned hosiery industry in Philadelphia and for General Motors (GM) and the UAW. I would discover in due course that I had much to learn about arbitration.

My interview with Taylor effectively ended my eight-month search for employment—one of the worst experiences of my life. To this day, I cannot abide staying home during a regular working day. Even when forced on rare occasions to do so because of illness or some other unusual circumstance, I relive again the feelings of guilt and despair that overwhelmed me during that bad time in Washington.

EARLY DAYS AT THE WLB

Without doubt, the most vivid recollection I have of my entire four years at the WLB is of my first day at work.[4] The day following my interview with Taylor, I reported for work and spent the morning filling out forms. It was then that I learned that I would be paid $2,600 per year (the standard beginning salary for lawyers in the executive departments and the well-established administrative agencies was $2,000). I telephoned Eleanor at her place of work and told her, "We're rich!" We agreed to celebrate when I came home that evening. Having completed all the paper work, I reported to the board's assistant executive director, Lewis M. Gill. He said he would break me in gently by assigning me as assistant to a tripartite panel that was hearing a simple case involving a pay dispute.

I was much too excited to eat lunch, and at about one o'clock Gill took me into the hearing room and introduced me to the members of the panel. The neutral member and chairman was Fowler V. Harper, a law professor then at Indiana University (he subsequently moved to Yale), a noted civil libertarian, and the author of a leading treatise on tort law. His co-panelists were Dale Purves, treasurer of the J. B. Stetson Co., and Fred Hewitt, editor of the *International Association of Machinists' Journal*.

The company involved in the dispute was a well-known manufacturer, Babcock & Wilcox; the union was a small "federal labor union"—that is, one that was chartered directly by the AFL and was not affiliated with any of its national or international unions. The union representatives were completely inexperienced, whereas the company was represented by a major Pittsburgh management law firm. Its spokesman was a short, combative attorney named Donald Ebert, who suffered from ulcers and had a very bad disposition. From time to time during the afternoon he was forced to lie down on a sofa in the hearing room to ease his stomach pains.

The issue before the panel was to what extent the collective bargaining agreement between the parties could be reopened in mid-term for the

---

[4]I gave an abbreviated account of that day in a speech at the 46th Annual Meeting of the National Academy of Arbitrators in 1993; it appears in National Academy of Arbitrators, *Arbitration 1993: Arbitration and the Changing World of Work* (Washington, D.C.: Bureau of National Affairs, 1994), 291–303.

negotiation of a wage increase. The union argued that there was no limit on the increase that could be granted; it asked for 10 cents per hour. The company contended that the maximum wage increase permitted was two cents per hour. Harper, who dominated the proceedings, was obviously trying, so far without success, to mediate a settlement at a figure somewhere between two and 10 cents per hour. Minutes after I had entered the room, he announced, "Our counsel has just joined us. I'll get his opinion on whether the agreement permits reopening for more than two cents per hour." With that, he handed me a copy of the agreement and gave me a look, the meaning of which could not be misunderstood. I hurriedly read the disputed provision and then gave the answer I knew was expected: "It seems to me that the agreement is reopenable for more than two cents." The union representatives smiled; Ebert shot me a look of inexpressible contempt and lay down on the sofa.

The rest of the afternoon was spent in futile discussion, with Ebert immediately and emphatically rejecting every proposal offered by Harper. Undaunted, the chairman announced at about 6:00 p.m. that we would recess for dinner but would reconvene at about 8:00 p.m. in the company's suite at the Carlton Hotel. As we broke up, Harper and one of the company's representatives, also a Hoosier, engaged in some joking about who could drink the most bourbon whiskey, and they resolved to settle that dispute when the session resumed.

Harper, Purves, Hewitt, and I then repaired to the Carlton, then one of Washington's most elegant hotels, and Harper suggested that we wait in the bar until the company's representatives returned. No one seemed interested in dinner. The three panel members had several rounds of drinks, but I declined, not wishing to do anything that might add to the mental confusion I already felt. After a while, the company's representatives returned, each (except for Ebert) bearing a large paper sack full of booze. We all went up to their suite, and everyone, except Ebert and I, began to drink. At the same time, Harper and Ebert continued to argue about the amount of wage increase that was permissible under the agreement. I think Harper scored at least a technical victory over his fellow Hoosier in their drinking contest. The latter disappeared briefly and then returned clad only in his long underwear. He began racing noisily in and out of the room until his companions grew tired of his antics and locked him in a closet. This proved to be a mistake. He shouted, pounded on the door, and created such a rumpus that the hotel's front desk called to complain. About this time I noticed, to my bewilderment, that perfect strangers had wandered into the suite and were joining in the argument, which by then had become general, over the amount of an allowable wage increase.

Harper was now quite drunk, but he had not ceased pushing for a settlement of the dispute. Sometime after midnight he said to me, "I want you to type up a new proposal." I replied, "Sir, we don't have a typewriter." Unfazed, Harper told me to go to the reception desk and ask for the key to the apartment at the Carlton maintained by his friend, Oscar Ewing, an eminent New York attorney and prominent Democrat. He said there was a typewriter in the apartment that I could use. I told him that the desk clerk would almost certainly not give me the key, so Harper said he would come with me. We went to the reception desk and Harper, after introducing himself to the clerk as an associate public member of the WLB, asked for the key to Ewing's apartment. Hotel clerks in wartime Washington, when rooms were at a premium, were a class unto themselves: haughty, distant, disdainful, and downright rude. The one at the Carlton was no exception. He surveyed Harper with contempt and replied, "You, sir, are drunk. Go back to your room." Incensed, Harper rejoined, "Do you mean to tell me that you are defying the power of the president as commander in chief in time of war?" But the clerk had the last word, saying, "If you don't go back to your room, I'll call the police." So we went back upstairs—but Harper had another idea. He handed me a paper on which he had written a settlement proposal for a five-cent wage increase and told me to take a cab to the Washington Press Club, where there were lots of typewriters, and make 15 copies of it. He assured me that no one at the Press Club would bother me.

It was now about 2:30 a.m. Shaking like a leaf, I took a cab to the Press Club, which was open but deserted. I found paper and carbons and typed out the brief settlement proposal; then I returned to the Carlton and to the now disorderly company suite. I gave the typed copies to Harper, who staggered around the room, handing them to whomever would take one. Then he collapsed in a deep armchair. Ebert, cold sober, followed Harper around the room, retrieving each copy that had been handed out and tearing it up. At this point, Harper became violently ill and threw up all over himself. Ebert, seizing his opportunity, rapped on the mantelpiece and yelled, "Quiet, everybody!" Then he pointed to Harper and said, "Gentlemen, I give you the government's representative." That ended the session. Purves, Hewitt, and I cleaned Harper up a bit and put him in a taxi. Just before we closed the door, to my utter amazement, he grinned, winked at me, and said, "Don't worry, we'll get 'em tomorrow."

It was about 5:00 a.m. when I arrived at our apartment in Virginia, totally exhausted and reeking of whiskey and cigars, none of which I had touched. As I walked in the door, my wife called from the bedroom, demanding to know where I had been all night. "I've been mediating," I said, to which she replied, "You have not!" I tried to describe the ordeal I had gone through; she countered by telling me about the ruined celebratory dinner she had prepared, wasting precious "red points" on a roast.[5] At length, I admitted some doubts about my fitness for the career I had chosen. After a few hours' sleep, however, I arose, reinvigorated, and went to the office.

That afternoon the panel reconvened. Harper, chipper and confident, made no reference to the previous evening's debacle. He refloated his proposal of a five-cent wage increase and, true to his prediction, finally succeeded in obtaining the agreement of both sides. How he overcame Ebert's adamantine opposition I shall never know. Perhaps the latter's ulcers forced his surrender. More probably, however, the reservation at the Carlton had run out and he and his colleagues were unable to find any other place to stay—a common problem for visitors to wartime Washington. Whatever the reason, the case was settled on a triumphant note.

In the subsequent weeks I worked as Harper's panel assistant in a number of other cases, none as dramatic as the first. He proved to be

---

[5] Meat was rationed during wartime.

a charming and generous man, as well as an exceptionally able mediator from whom I learned a great deal. I remember him with gratitude and affection.

A few months later, I served as panel assistant in a case involving the shipbuilding division of Bethlehem Steel Corporation and the Industrial Union of Marine & Shipbuilding Workers, an affiliate of the CIO.[6] I remember this case not because it presented any novel or particularly interesting issues, but because of the personalities involved. The hearing was held in New York City at the offices of one of the city's most prominent law firms, Cravath, DeGersdorff, Swaine & Wood. When I arrived, I was met by no less a personage than Hoyt A. Moore, one of the firm's senior partners, who represented Bethlehem. He escorted me to a small private office, equipped with a telephone, legal tablets, and pens and pencils, which had been provided for my use during the hearing.

Moore was a gentleman of the old school. His manner was courtly but dignified, and he dressed conservatively. I seem to recall that he wore a Hoover collar. Once the hearing began, it became clear that he had not the slightest understanding of labor-management relations. The union's representative was a Philadelphia lawyer named M. H. Goldstein. He was an able and experienced attorney whose deep, strong voice, beady eyes, and little black moustache gave him a strong resemblance to Governor Thomas E. Dewey of New York. In speaking of Bethlehem's employees, Moore always used the French word "employés." Goldstein, on the other hand, called them "workers," to Moore's increasing annoyance. Finally, Moore could stand it no longer. In exasperated tones he said to his opponent, "Mr. Goldstein, would you please stop referring to our employés as workers; it sounds so communistic."

Another and even funnier exchange between the two men occurred when Goldstein accused the company of illegally firing several employees. Moore replied indignantly, "Mr. Goldstein, the Bethlehem Steel Corporation has never 'fired' any of its employés. From time to time, it has found it necessary to call in one of them and to explain that in their mutual best interests it is necessary to separate the employé from his

---

[6]National War Labor Board, *Report* 3 (1942): 17.

employment." This was too much for the panel's chairman, William L. Nunn. "Oh hell, Mr. Moore," he interjected, "you fired them."

This case serves as a reminder of how difficult it was for some employers and their attorneys (to say nothing of many judges) to come to terms with the new rules of collective bargaining, which were ushered in by the Wagner Act of 1935. From Moore's horrified perspective, Goldstein and his union clients must have seemed like the barbarian Goths preparing to sack Rome.

With the exception of a few holdovers from the NDMB, I think I was probably the first staff person taken on by the WLB, and it took some time before others were added. Consequently, for the first month after being hired, I worked very long hours. We seemed to be in perpetual round-the-clock mediation, and nobody got much sleep. At the end of this period, I was beginning to look like an advance man for a famine. Weighing only about 145 pounds when I took the job, I lost 15 pounds the first three weeks. Finally, George Kirstein, the board's executive director, ordered me to go home and not return until I had gained some weight. Reluctantly, I complied, but I could stand it for only two days, after which I reported back to work. By that time, Kirstein was occupied with more pressing concerns. Nobody challenged my return and I resumed my constantly changing duties.

As previously noted, the WLB was tripartite in structure; it originally consisted of four representatives from each of three sectors: the public, employers, and employees. The term "employee member" was in fact a misnomer; "union member" would have been more accurate, except that independent unions—that is, those not affiliated with either the AFL or the CIO—had no representatives on the board. The same is true of nonunion workers, who comprised the great majority of the labor force. There were also substitute and alternate members in each of the three categories; many of these became, in time, regular members. Finally, there were associate members in each category, a number of whom served on the tripartite mediation panels that initially heard the disputes submitted to the board for adjudication. At the bottom of the organizational totem pole was a small group of younger persons on the WLB staff who served as mediation assistants; they were initially assigned to assist the tripartite panels and later allowed to go into the field as mediation officers. Settlements obtained by panels or individual mediation officers were reported to the board and duly noted. In the case of unsuccessful mediation attempts, the facts of the dispute were reported to the board, together with a recommended settlement, which the board approved, modified, or replaced with a decision of its own.

Neither the panels nor the individual mediators had the power to impose a settlement on the parties. The function of a mediator is to persuade the disputants voluntarily to agree on a settlement and, to that end, he or she is permitted, and usually expected, to submit compromise proposals that differ from those offered by the parties themselves. When unresolved disputes came before the full WLB, it disposed of them by issuing decisions given the redundant title of "directive order." Actually, the board had no legal authority to compel acceptance by the parties of its decisions. Thanks in large part to the efforts of its employer and employee members, however, the board was able to achieve a high degree of compliance with its directive orders, even those reflecting a divided vote. In a few cases, when all efforts to achieve voluntary compliance failed, the dispute was referred to the president, who, exercising his powers as commander in chief of the armed forces in time of war, ordered the secretary of war to seize the facility involved.[7]

Each of the four original public members of the WLB contributed in special ways to the board's work. The chairman, William H. Davis, an eminent patent attorney, had previously served as chairman of the New York State Mediation Board and, more recently, of the NDMB. He was well trained in the classics and often quoted from the dialogues of Plato to make a point. In his occasional exchanges during board hearings with John L. Lewis, president of the UMW, he invariably topped Lewis's classical references, much to the latter's frustration. Davis believed profoundly in the superiority of persuasion over force. He was fond of remarking that "creation is the product of persuasion, except in the case of rape."

---

[7] The name of the Department of War was not changed to Department of Defense until after the conclusion of World War II.

Emphasizing the importance of gathering relevant data, he frequently observed that "reasonable men cannot be in disagreement about a fact; they can only be in ignorance of it."

A major element in the war effort was the stabilization of prices and wages. This task was entrusted to the Office of Price Administration (OPA) and the WLB. There was a tension between the policies and personnel of the two agencies, and Davis frequently found himself in disagreement with Leon Henderson, the director of OPA. Davis had little respect for the OPA economists and particularly objected to what he considered the vagueness of their pronouncements. They lacked, he said, the disciplined precision of, say, engineers. To illustrate his point, he posed the following hypothetical case, with tongue in cheek: "Suppose I told an engineer to go over to the White House and measure the height of the president, and the engineer subsequently reported that the president was exactly three feet, six inches tall. It would never occur to me to doubt the accuracy of his measurements; I would simply conclude that he had measured the wrong man."

Inevitably, the WLB was the target of criticism by both labor and management, as well as by certain public figures and the media. Most of it was centered on Davis. He bore all these attacks, some quite vicious, with equanimity and almost never replied in kind. His persistence in the pursuit of consensus through persuasion and his willingness to make hard decisions when such actions became unavoidable made him the moral as well as the titular leader of the board.

Frank P. Graham, who, like Davis, was a holdover from the NDMB, was president of the University of North Carolina. After the war, he served for one term as senator from North Carolina and, subsequently, as a United Nations mediator in the dispute between India and Pakistan over the status of Kashmir. Diminutive in stature, Graham was full of energy and good will. Like Davis, he had a deep faith in the democratic ideal and a strong liberal bent. Graham was noted for the painstaking way in which he explored the positions taken by employers on hotly disputed issues, such as union security. He would always listen carefully to their arguments and ask many questions designed to clarify their views. He often gave the impression during board hearings that he was sympathetic with the employers' positions, but more often than not, he ended up voting for the unions. As a consequence, he came to be known in management circles as "the sweetest little son of a bitch in Washington." Despite his short stature, Graham was amazingly strong. He loved to Indian wrestle and to challenge staff members to a contest. On a number of occasions when I encountered him in the hall, he would shout out, "Hey, ole Tool and Die Ben, want to wrestle?"[8] He usually won.

Wayne L. Morse was the public member I cared for the least. He seemed less congenial, less a "team player" than his colleagues, and he appeared to be preoccupied with his own, private agenda. A former dean of the University of Oregon Law School, he had established a reputation as an expert in labor-management relations. Among other things, he had served as the Pacific Coast umpire under the collective bargaining agreement between the Pacific Maritime Association and the International Longshoremen and Warehousemen and as the neutral in some major disputes arising under the Railway Labor Act. Morse was smart, aggressive, egotistical, and very ambitious. He was also very hard working, writing by far the most opinions for the board (118) during his two-year tenure. Many of these were dissents, notably in a case in which the WLB approved a wage settlement between the UMW and the U.S. Department of the Interior, even though the union had violated labor's no-strike pledge and the board's policy was to deny wage increases to the workers involved. Morse's opinions were forceful and usually quite long, including in many instances lengthy excerpts from his earlier opinions. In the last year of his service on the board, if not before, it became clear that Morse was looking to advance his career elsewhere. In 1944, he resigned to run, successfully, for the U.S. Senate, where he had a long and stormy career as a Republican, then an independent, and, finally, a Democrat.

I had relatively little contact with Morse during his tenure on the WLB, but after the war, when he was in the Senate, I had occasion to write or talk to him several times. In those instances he was warm, friendly, and gracious.

---

[8]This was a reference to my sometime position of chairman of the Detroit Area Tool and Die Commission (1942–1944).

Taylor, with whom I had the closest relationship (described in greater detail later in this account), was vice chairman of the board and the dominant figure in the development of its wage stabilization policies. He was also the most knowledgeable public member about collective bargaining and a creative and ingenious problem solver. Our association continued without interruption after the war and became ever closer, until his death many years later.

Despite their different backgrounds and personalities, the four public members shared one characteristic: a protective attitude toward the board's junior staff members. Whether in their capacity of panel assistant or mediation officer, the latter occasionally incurred the wrath of one or more employer or employee representatives or board members who sometimes attacked them in WLB executive sessions. On those occasions, the public members always stood up for the defenseless staff members, who were in no position to protect themselves. Moreover, they were quick to praise any staff member who did anything, however slight, to merit favorable recognition. They seemed to take a genuine pleasure in helping us develop our skills and further our careers; they served not only as role models but also as confidence builders.

Employer members of the WLB, mostly top executives of large corporations, could not spend as much continuous time in Washington as could the public members; consequently, there were more public members, and they substituted for one another quite frequently. I do not recall who constituted the first four "regular" industry members. Among those frequently present at board meetings was Roger D. Lapham, chairman of the board of the American-Hawaiian Steamship Company. He was white-haired, florid of face, and addicted to brightly colored, flowery neckties. His genial personality had a soothing effect on some of his more combative colleagues, but on certain issues, such as maintenance of union membership, he would become quite exercised.[9] His face

[9] No issue presented to the WLB precipitated more furious debate than union security. The authority of the board even to act on the issue was challenged to the very end of its existence, although most employers, despite their dissenting positions, accepted the board's decisions on this issue. The unions demanded that the board require employers to continue the closed shop, which permitted the hiring of only union members, where it already existed, and in other cases to order the establishment

became even redder, his voice grew louder, and he frequently concluded his peroration by throwing his eyeglasses on the table. Often, they slid across to the employee members' side, and one of the members would return them with elaborate courtesy, to the general amusement of all those present.

Cyrus S. Ching was vice president of the U.S. Rubber Company and subsequently director of the Federal Mediation and Conciliation Service (FMCS), an independent agency established by the Labor-Management Relations (Taft-Hartley) Act of 1947 to replace the U.S. Conciliation Service in the Department of Labor. He was a Canadian by birth and had once worked as a streetcar conductor. A huge man (six feet, five inches tall) who puffed constantly on his curved-stem pipe, he was the soul of amiability and good humor and was universally liked.

The employee members were equally divided between representatives of the AFL and the CIO. Like the employer members, they had a fairly large roster and a changing presence on the board. Among the more colorful was Van A. Bittner, assistant to the president of the United Steelworkers. A veteran of countless organizational battles and strikes, he was an enthusiastic advocate. On one occasion the board was debating whether to adopt the recommendations of a single mediation officer. After speaking at length in favor of the recommendations, Bittner concluded, in part, that the officer "'has been out in the field and has met with the parties. He has listened to them carefully, weighed the facts, and submitted this excellent report. It is a unanimous report."

The standout among the AFL board members, and clearly the ablest labor representative from either federation, was George Meany, the

---

of a union shop, under which new employees must, as a condition of continued employment, join the union and remain members in good standing. The employers, on the other hand, insisted that the board simply require that the situation in respect of union security, or lack thereof, that existed at the time the WLB was established be continued without change.

The union security formula eventually worked out by the WLB public members was designed as a compromise between the sharply conflicting positions of the employer and employee board members. In essence, it required an initial "escape period" of 15 days, during which present union members could withdraw from the union without prejudice. Thereafter, all those who remained in the union, and any new employees who voluntarily joined the union, had to continue their membership in good standing as a condition of continued employment.

secretary-treasurer (and later president) of the AFL. He was also the most disagreeable. Although always well prepared and vigorous in setting forth his views, he was utterly humorless and customarily ill-tempered, frequently resorting to *ad hominem* attacks against those with whom he disagreed.

Not long after I was hired, James D. Ewing joined the board's staff. Jim and I shared an office and a secretary, a young lady from a small town in Ohio, where she had acquired some experience as a legal secretary. She quickly endeared herself to Jim and me by answering the telephone with the singsong greeting, "Aaron and Ewing." Jim and I got along well from the start. A graduate of Princeton University, who later taught classics for a time at the Taft School in Connecticut, he had no previous training in industrial relations, but he quickly brought himself up to speed at the board and became a successful mediator. He was extremely personable and had a wonderful sense of humor. What I admired most about him was his unshakable imperturbability, born of his innate self-confidence, which never, however, verged on conceit or arrogance.

Jim met his future wife, Ruth Dewing, while they were both working for the WLB. She was, I think, the first woman to be hired by the board as a mediator and, like Jim, she was a very good one. The field of labor relations in those days was completely dominated by men, and women were definitely not welcome. Ruth's success was noteworthy because she had to overcome the twin handicaps of sex and youth.

The first major case on which I worked as a panel assistant involved GM and two CIO affiliates, the UAW and the United Electrical Radio & Machine Workers (UE). The UAW represented over 200,000 workers employed at some 95 of the corporation's plants, which were situated in various parts of the country. The UE represented 25,000 workers employed at eight plants that made up the corporation's electrical division. The dispute grew out of negotiations between the unions and the corporation over the terms of new collective bargaining agreements. Mediation efforts by both the U.S. Conciliation Service and a panel appointed by the WLB resolved some of the issues between the parties, but a number of them, including maintenance of membership and hours of work and overtime pay, ultimately had to be decided by the board.

The issue of pay for overtime work led to some initial skirmishing between GM and the WLB. Under the corporation's collective bargaining agreements with the two unions, workers were entitled to time and a half for Saturday work and double time for work on Sundays and holidays. Following the entrance of the United States into the war, unions affiliated with the CIO publicly relinquished their contractual rights to time and a half and double time for Saturdays and Sundays, provided that a satisfactory formula to replace those provisions could be reached with the employers with which they had contractual relationships. The UAW and the UE, however, were unable to agree with GM on an acceptable formula. After a conference with the parties, the board issued an interim order on 1 May 1942, directing that the previously existing overtime pay practices be extended until 18 May. The corporation publicly refused to abide by this order, asserting that it had been made without granting GM due process. The WLB then held a public hearing on 7 May, at which time GM formally withdrew its charges against the board and agreed to abide by the terms of the interim order. Meanwhile, the board had appointed a panel to hear the dispute; it consisted of Harper, William H. Doran, vice president of a utility company in Reading, Pennsylvania, and Patrick T. Fagan, a member of the UMW. I was assigned as the panel assistant.

In the period immediately preceding the certification of this case to the board, I had been working with Taylor as a kind of unofficial assistant. He had assigned various tasks to me, including the drafting of the boilerplate sections of some of his opinions in other cases. He invariably revised my drafts, reducing all my compound sentences to simple declarative ones. I found his prose style regrettably pedestrian, and a few years later, in my review of his book, *Government Regulation of Industrial Relations*, I gently opined that "Skill in writing is not one of Dr. Taylor's outstanding abilities."[10]

---

[10] *Illinois Law Review* 44 (1949): 419, 421.

I rapidly fell under Taylor's spell. Our relationship became much closer. He obviously liked me, and in the course of our discussions of cases he elaborated his views on collective bargaining, tri-partitism, and many other matters. He did this easily, without the faintest hint of arrogance or pomposity and always with a leavening sense of humor. I quickly accepted him as a mentor in whose knowledge and good judgment I should put my trust. I also began to feel completely at ease in his company and to express my own views on some matters. This led to the single instance in our long association in which he felt compelled to put me in my place. The incident occurred during the early stages of the GM case, when the corporation engaged in its brief defiance of the board's interim order concerning overtime pay. This produced a good deal of concern at the WLB and eventually led to a public hearing on 7 May. I thought the corporation's behavior was outrageous and the board's temporizing little short of pusillanimity, and I foolishly made some grumbling comment to that effect to Taylor. His response was immediate and devastating, not so much because of what he said but because of how he said it. His flabby face congealed into a hard, cold mask, and his normally warm and friendly tone suddenly became harsh and distant. "Ben," he said, "I suggest that you stick to your assigned duties and leave the conduct of board affairs to those of us who have the responsibility for determining policy." Properly squelched, I immediately regretted my gratuitous criticism that threatened a cherished relationship. For the next few days, although I saw Taylor frequently, the coolness between us persisted. Eventually, however, sensing my unhappiness, Taylor took me aside and very kindly said something to the effect that all of us occasionally speak out of turn, even with the best intentions, and then we're sorry and should, of course, be forgiven. With that, he gave me a sunny smile and began to talk about the case as if nothing had happened between us.

The panel hearing in the GM case attracted a good deal of media attention and was somewhat more formal than those cases in which I had previously been involved. The GM team, led by Harry Anderson, vice president for industrial relations, had position papers on each of the issues in dispute. The paper on each issue was read by a different corporation representative. To me, their presentations seemed incredibly inept. The persons reading the papers seemed to be looking at them for the first time: they stumbled over syntax, mispronounced words, lost their place, and simply distracted the panel members who were trying to read the prepared texts handed to them. By contrast, the union spokesmen, Reuther for the UAW and James Matles for the UE, were remarkably effective speakers. Their extemporaneous but well organized presentations held the panel's undivided attention. A few days later, Doran, the employer member of the panel, suddenly unburdened himself to me. For years he had regarded GM as a model of industrial efficiency and leadership. Now this belief had been shattered by its pitifully ineffective presentation to the panel, and he was deeply disturbed. Eventually, despite tremendous pressure upon him by industry representatives, he concurred in the basic premise of the panel's recommendation on maintenance of membership, contrary to the position taken by GM.

After the formal presentations had been made by the parties, the mediation sessions began. These usually extended well into the evening. The weather was hot and humid, and the air conditioning in the Department of Labor Building, where the board's offices were located, went off promptly at 5:00 p.m. One of my most vivid recollections of those meetings is of a steaming, smoky room filled with sweaty men in shirtsleeves. In sharp contrast to all the others, Reuther wore a starched white shirt and a tie. He seemed totally unaffected by the heat and humidity, as if he were encompassed by a personal air-conditioning system. Other representatives on both sides became tired and irritable as the night wore on, whereas Walter remained cool as a cucumber and never gave the slightest indication of fatigue.

Although the UAW and the UE were presenting what appeared on the surface to be a coordinated front against GM, there were in fact fundamental differences in their respective approaches to some of the issues in dispute. In 1942, the UE, which was expelled by the CIO a few years later for being a "Communist-dominated organization," was at the very least following the Communist Party line. After originally opposing U.S. entry in the "imperialist" war in Europe, it reversed its position immediately after the Nazi invasion of Russia and became both a strong supporter of the war effort and a vigorous lobbyist for a second front to relieve the pressure on our "heroic Soviet allies." The reason for this sudden reversal of position was perfectly clear to the UAW and to most neutral observers, but GM, unwilling to look a gift horse in the mouth, did not question the sincerity of UE's miraculous change of heart and gladly accepted the bargaining concessions that it was now ready to make. The UE's political U-turn affected its bargaining stance on at least two of the most important issues in the GM case: overtime pay and incentive systems of payment. C. E. Wilson, president of GM (subsequently commonly referred to as "Engine Charlie" to distinguish him from C. E. Wilson, president of General Electric Corporation, known as "Electric Charlie"), was an engineer with little or no experience in industrial relations. One of his pet proposals to increase wartime production was to obtain the unions' consent to work 44 hours per week at straight time, despite the fact that the federal Fair Labor Standards Act of 1938 (FLSA) required the payment of time and a half after 40 hours. Even if one or both unions had agreed, this would have been legally impossible unless Congress amended the law, because the FLSA created individual, nonwaivable rights. The parties, however, did not concern themselves with the legal aspects of Wilson's proposal. On behalf of the UE, Matles said that its members would go along with it because it would enhance the war effort. Reuther, on the other hand, declared flatly that the UAW opposed GM's overtime scheme. He explained that the union movement had fought long and hard for the provisions embodied in the FLSAs and that the UAW would not betray members of the armed forces by waiving any of their rights while they were defending the country.

A similar split between the two unions occurred on the issue of incentive pay systems. Reuther opposed such methods of payment on the ground that they were too easily manipulated by management and led to speed-ups and favoritism. Matles again avowed the willingness of his members to cooperate with any arrangement that would further the war effort. The bizarre result of the differences between the unions was that

GM accused the UAW and Reuther (an outspoken anti-Communist, who had waged an unceasing battle against the Communist faction in his union) of giving aid and comfort to the country's enemies, while praising Matles and the UE for their patriotism.

Matles was not the first UE representative I had encountered at the WLB. Shortly after being hired, I became acquainted with Neil Brant, another official of the union, who served as the union's representative in several cases in which I acted as the panel assistant. Brant was well educated, personable, and a very smooth talker. In just about every case in which he was involved, the panel was able to mediate a settlement of all or most issues, aided in large part by his persuasive influence on the employers involved. More than once, at the successful conclusion of the case, the employer's spokesman would say to him, "Mr. Brant, I can assure you that if you had taken part in our initial negotiations at the plant, we would never have had to come to Washington." It was not always clear that the members of the union involved, on whose behalf Brant had made a number of concessions, were equally pleased, but for the most part he managed to soothe their doubts.

Brant was a strong "second-fronter," and he gave me a subscription to a Soviet newsletter, a highly sophisticated and well-written publication reporting on such topics as the Soviet war effort, Nazi atrocities, and the desperate necessity of opening up a second front in Europe. My sympathies throughout the war were with the Russian people, who were enduring frightful hardships and sustaining almost unimaginable losses. It was some time, therefore, before I realized that the newsletter was a very clever piece of propaganda and discounted its contents accordingly.

One evening Eleanor and I were invited by the Brants to dinner, ostensibly to enjoy his wife's paprika chicken, which Neil assured me was the best in Washington. Before dinner was served, he and I were playing chess in the living room while Eleanor was helping his wife in the kitchen. Suddenly, without any preliminary discussion, he asked me if I would like to join the Communist Party. So stunned I could hardly reply, I finally blurted out that under no circumstance would I ever consider becoming a party member. He dropped the subject immediately and we sat down to dinner. His boast about his wife's cooking was justified—the paprika chicken was delicious—but there was an underlying tension between us for the rest of the evening. We never returned the dinner invitation, and so far as I can recall, Brant never spoke to me again. Similarly, when I encountered Matles on an airplane a year or two after the war was over, he stared right through me and did not acknowledge my greeting.

Shortly after the conclusion of the GM case, I served as panel assistant in a much smaller one that, nevertheless, made a lasting impression on me. The parties involved were the Buckeye Cotton Oil Company, a wholly owned subsidiary of Proctor and Gamble, and Local 19, United Cannery, Agricultural, Packing and Allied Workers, an affiliate of the CIO. Buckeye operated two cottonseed oil plants in Memphis, Tennessee. Its employees were mostly black. In October 1941, the union had won representation elections in both plants and was trying to negotiate a collective bargaining agreement with the company. Negotiations began in December 1941, but got nowhere, and on 25 February 1942 the employees voted unanimously to strike. The strike threat was withdrawn two days later, however, when the dispute was certified to the WLB. Theodore W. Kheel, a WLB mediator, who later achieved considerable celebrity in New York as an arbitrator, mediator, labor lawyer, and consultant, went to Memphis and managed to settle all the issues between the parties except union security and wages. Those were then submitted to a WLB panel in Washington.

The file in this case was a real shocker. The first thing I looked at was the verbatim transcript of the hearing before Kheel. Under "Appearances," the names of each of the company's representatives was either preceded by "Mr." or followed by "Esquire," whereas the name of each of the union's representatives was simply followed by the word "colored." It got worse as I read through the transcript. The company's lawyer and witnesses refused to respond directly to any questions from the union side; instead, they spoke only to the hearing officer. The company's strategy was obviously designed to humiliate and frustrate the union's black leaders and members. The record also contained copies of news items appearing in the Memphis *Commercial Appeal*, attacking the union for threatening to strike and featuring statements by a spokesman for the minority of "loyal" skilled white workers who strongly opposed the union.

Hourly wages for most of the workers at the two plants were at an all-time high of 40 cents (up from 11 cents in 1933). The issues involved in the dispute included wages and union security. The company refused to grant either a general wage increase or any form of union security. Regarding the latter issue, the company asserted that if it granted any sort of union security the resulting prestige to a union composed mostly of Negro workers would "cause trouble" in the plants and might lead to a "couple of killings" or a wholesale quitting of all the skilled white workers.

A hearing by the WLB panel was held on 5 June 1942. Meanwhile, we had received two letters from the union—one forwarded from the president's office and the other sent directly to the "International War Labor Board"—expressing its frustration over the delay in processing its case.[11] The first asked the president "to call immediate actions by the War Labor Board concerning our case because the company is enforcing unfair labor practices and demstremulation and preditry against us by firing union members and replacing them with ununion members." The second letter demanded "complete action on this case without any further preliminary or investigation." "We feel," the letter said in part, "that we are being jived from 3 angles but we will prove that we are not jiving at a date that will not be mentioned regardless to what will be the results."

I confess with shame that my original reaction and that of my staff colleagues to these letters was one of great amusement. We were not yet familiar with the facts of the case, and we had a good laugh at the language used by these uneducated workers. Reading over the second letter 57 years later, I marvel that I paid so little attention to its final paragraph, which has a fervor that reminds me of some of the letters written from prison by Nicola Sacco. It reads in part:

---

[11] I sent copies of these letters to my brother Daniel, who saved them and later returned them to me. The quotations from them are therefore exact.

Once again we say to the International War Labor Board of the United States, that this is an organize constitutional government from the president through the senate and congress and from the highest to the lowest courts of the United States, to declare war against our enemies, had to be in a perform of organized activity, and any person or group of men or any managers of industries who do not believe in organization, they do not believe in their government. Therefore we are asking you to act quickly in completion of this case, or else we will act, because we are American citizens and is a part of the United States government. Remember organization and organize labor will win this war.

In the end, the board, with the employer members dissenting, ordered both a general wage increase somewhat less than what the union had requested and inclusion in the collective bargaining agreement of a maintenance-of-membership clause, as well as a check-off provision. The union thus achieved something of a moral victory, but I never learned whether, in that community atmosphere of open hatred and discrimination against Negroes, it was able to take advantage of it.

Sometime during this period I was promoted to the classification of mediation officer and dispatched on occasion to mediate cases in the field on my own. Most of the cases assigned to me were in the Midwest. Wartime travel for government workers presented something of a challenge. We were given a book of government travel requests ("TRs") with which to pay for transportation by train or plane. On overnight train trips we were allowed to buy a roomette instead of a berth, provided one was available. Pullman conductors had their own little racket: all the roomettes were taken, they would say, but they would keep an eye out for a last-minute cancellation. That was your cue to slip them five bucks, which usually did the trick. To meet most other expenses, including meals and hotels, we were allowed a *per diem* of six dollars, at that time adequate if not munificent; one could almost always get a comfortable room in a good hotel for three dollars a night. But three meals a day on three dollars was hard going, especially in the larger cities.

Shortly after arriving in Washington in May 1941, I had received my "greetings" from the draft board and reported for induction, only to be rejected and given a 4-F rating because of a large hole in my eardrum. The country was not yet at war, I had still not found a job, and I was elated by my good fortune. Once war was declared, however, I began to feel guilty about my exempt status. Good friends of mine were being drafted, their civilian careers interrupted. Some never returned. During my train travels in the field, I was sometimes asked by casual strangers why I was not in uniform. None of them ever seemed satisfied by my explanation, and this increased my discomfort with my 4-F status.

My first meetings with the parties to the disputes I had been assigned to mediate usually began the same way. In the summer of 1942 I was 27 years old and looked younger. When I entered the hearing room and identified myself, the employer and union representatives stopped talking and simply stared at me in disbelief and sometimes with ill-concealed anger. They could not understand why the WLB had sent a green kid to deal with their all-important problems, but by this time I had developed sufficient self-confidence to enable me to disregard their distrust and to proceed with the business at hand. My technique was simple enough. Both sides usually threw in as bargaining chips a few issues that they were prepared to settle or withdraw for a small consideration. I'd begin with these in order to create a common feeling of movement toward an overall settlement. Discussion of the tougher issues would be postponed until the parties were ready to make some serious compromises. Often, the real obstacle to agreement proved to be personality conflicts between a company and a union representative. These usually could be ironed out, or at least substantially diminished, through conciliation—that is, explaining the position of one to the other in such a way as to diminish mutual suspicions. This process, conducted by a neutral third party, tended to remove obstacles to agreement created solely by personal animosity. How many cases I handled as a single mediator, I don't recall, but I do remember that I was able to settle all the issues in most of them.

I learned a great deal from these forays into the field. Lawyers or consultants were almost never present in my mediation sessions. The men from both sides who participated (no women ever appeared) were usually inexperienced in collective bargaining and initially disinclined to retreat from their most extreme bargaining positions. It was often necessary to meet with the two sides separately, gain their trust, and gradually get them thinking about compromise proposals of my own. These sessions were completely informal and confidential. Eventually, both parties would reveal the real concerns underlying their stated positions and arrive at some mutually acceptable compromises. It was in these sessions, too, that I became familiar with the various mispronunciations, malapropisms, and mixed metaphors that enrich the dialogue of industrial relations: for example, "This greevyance raises the pacific question of whether management is granting the French benefits guaranteed by Article XV of the contract and other revelant provisions"; "As a result of the union's mechanations, this company finds itself caught in a jackpot"; "The red herring the employer has dragged through this entire case is made out of whole cloth."

In September 1942, Davis received a formal invitation from Meany, in his capacity of secretary-treasurer of the AFL, to attend the federation's 62nd annual convention in Toronto, Canada. As the guest of the AFL, he would have been invited to sit on the platform in the convention hall and to address the assembled delegates. Davis told Kirstein that he had no intention of going, and he instructed him to appoint someone in his stead. Kirstein fixed his cold eye on me and said, "Aaron, you're it." So Eleanor and I made the long and uncomfortable journey to Toronto on a train seemingly preserved from the Civil War era.

Toronto was then a far cry from the vibrant and beautiful city it now is. Everything seemed to shut down each evening about nine o'clock, and newspapers were not published on Sundays. The convention was being held at the Royal York Hotel, a gloomy Victorian structure that had about as much charm as a mausoleum. Shortly after we arrived, I was presented to Meany as the WLB's representative. He looked at me with obvious distaste, did not proffer his hand, and after acknowledging the introduction with a curt nod, walked away. I could hardly blame him for resenting the slight he must have felt, and I wondered afterward if that might explain at least in part his subsequent personal attacks against Davis. Needless to say, I was not invited to sit on the platform or to address the delegates.

The convention, which lasted from 5 to 14 October, was unspeakably boring and the delegates paid little or no attention to the speakers. I dutifully monitored the proceedings during the day; Eleanor and I spent our evenings drinking and playing poker with the labor reporters who were covering the convention. Among those I particularly remember were James Wechsler, then with the newspaper *PM* and later the editor of the *New York Post*, and Archie Robinson, who was working for the *Daily Labor Report*, which was published by the Bureau of National Affairs.

On the afternoon of the seventh day, the convention debated a resolution submitted by A. Philip Randolph and Milton P. Webster of the entirely black Brotherhood of Sleeping Car Porters. The resolution urged in part that the federation "set up a minorities committee composed of representatives of the various minority groups of the A. F. of L. such as Negroes, Jews, Catholics and others for the purpose of thoroughly exploring the question of discrimination practiced against minority groups by [AFL] unions and various industries." Although president of the union, Randolph had never been a Pullman porter. He had worked as an elevator operator, a janitor, and a ship's waiter, and he was a well-known civil rights agitator. His education had ended with a few courses at the City College of New York. But, as Murray Kempton put it, "he had absorbed Shakespeare and the Bible and his bass voice rumbled in periods which mixed the cadences of the King James Version with the accent of massive cultivation."[12] Randolph had made it a practice at a number of preceding AFL conventions to offer similar resolutions and to call attention to the discriminatory practices of some AFL affiliates. "He was a nuisance of enormous presence, impelling one afflicted delegate from the carpenters to complain that it wasn't fair for this Harvard man to come in and outtalk them."[13]

On this occasion, Randolph reminded his fellow unionists that 15 or 20 AFL affiliates had constitutional or ritualistic prohibitions against the admission of Negroes. Others, he pointed out, excluded Negroes by

---

[12] Murray Kempton, *Part of Our Time: Some Ruins and Monuments of the Thirties* (New York: Simon and Schuster, 1955), 244.

[13] Kempton, *Part of Our Time*, 246.

practice and custom, or admitted them as members but kept them from obtaining employment, or admitted them to membership only in separate auxiliaries without voice or vote in union affairs. He once again warned the delegates that "the question of racial discrimination strikes at the heart of the workers" and that as long as such discrimination persisted "there will be no peace, there will be no brotherhood of man, but we will be facing a conflagration even more catastrophic, even more disastrous, even more destructive than the world war in which we are now engaged."[14]

Randolph's eloquent speech met a fate similar to all his others at previous conventions. The committee on resolutions responded by voicing its approval of the recent executive order of the president, which was intended to accomplish "the praiseworthy elimination of racial distinction between the wage earners and the citizens of the United States [sic]," and recommended the adoption of this statement in lieu of separate action on the resolutions presented.[15] Randolph was no doubt disappointed by this outcome, but he could hardly have been surprised. "[H]is protests were after all matters doomed to interment in the record, because they were appeals to conscience where so faint a conscience existed."[16]

Randolph could scarcely have been prepared, however, for the savage reply to his remarks the following day by Daniel J. Tobin, president of the Teamsters Union, a dominating influence within the AFL, and a friend of President Roosevelt. Tobin began by characterizing Randolph's statements as "brutally untrue insofar as they relate to ninety per cent of the organizations affiliated here" and accused him of making "a very, very dangerous threat to his own people and to the people of the United States in general...[that] the black man is not going to take this any longer and if it continues then, 'We will find a way to stop it.'" Decrying "this stuff," which he said "is read in many of our largely populated colored districts," Tobin accused Randolph of arousing "entirely unjustified bitterness."

---

[14] American Federation of Labor, *Report of the Proceedings of the Sixty-Second Annual Convention of the American Federation of Labor* (American Federation of Labor, 1942): 579.

[15] American Federation of Labor, *Proceedings*, 575. The executive order, dated 25 June 1941, was signed reluctantly by President Roosevelt only after Randolph had threatened a march on Washington by 25,000 Negroes and their supporters to protest discrimination in employment.

[16] Kempton, *Part of Our Time*, 248.

"Some slight outrage," he continued, "may have been committed by a black man or a white man, but this is the kind of stuff that starts the fires, destruction and hatred and the unnecessary offering up of human lives in a foolish belief that they are fighting for something that really doesn't exist, against race prejudice." Sooner or later, Tobin concluded, "this kind of stuff will have to be stopped." He declared that in times like the present, inflammatory language tending to promote dissension and destruction among a large section of the population was an abuse of freedom of speech that should not be tolerated.[17]

Randolph attempted to reply, but AFL president William Green, who was presiding, refused to let him speak, saying that he had had his chance the day before and that the incident was now closed.

The foregoing quotations from the speeches by Randolph and Tobin are taken verbatim from the published convention proceedings, but I believe Tobin's was edited after delivery and before publication in at least one respect. Despite the passage of so many years, I distinctly recall Tobin saying substantially this: that the Teamsters had been influential in helping the Sleeping Car Porters obtain affiliation with the AFL, that his union had picked them out of the gutter, and that if these kinds of intolerable attacks continued, his union would kick them back into the gutter.

That evening I suggested to my reporter friends that the day's proceedings had surely provided a hot story for their respective newspapers. To my surprise and disappointment, Wechsler replied that he had no intention of reporting the incident. *PM* was pro-labor, he explained, and the unions were having enough brickbats thrown at them as it was. He would not report events that would subject them to further attacks. The others expressed similar sentiments.

Eleanor and I returned to Washington the day after the convention ended. We had an early breakfast in the hotel dining room and saw Green sitting by himself at a small table. A few reporters walked over and started asking him some questions. Green seemed warmed by their attention and began talking to them with more animation than he had exhibited during the convention. Suddenly, Meany appeared and began

---

[17] American Federation of Labor, *Proceedings*, 646–48.

walking slowly toward Green's table. The latter looked positively frightened; he abruptly stopped talking, got up, and left the room. Whatever his former achievements, at this stage of his career Green cut a sad figure. One could not help recalling Lewis's cruel comment: "Explore the mind of Bill Green? I have done a lot of exploring of Bill's mind, and I give you my word there's nothing there." The AFL, he said, "has no head; it has only a neck that grew up and haired over."

Several times in 1942, Lewis appeared in person before the board. Whenever he did so, WLB staff members who were not otherwise engaged would attend the hearing in order to see this formidable public figure in action. On these occasions his demeanor was usually defiant or disdainful and always lordly, that of a superior being pestered by lesser mortals.

I recall one appearance in which he had been summoned to explain why a number of wildcat (i.e., unauthorized) strikes were occurring in the coalfields. Everyone knew the true reason — the miners were striking not against the mine operators but in protest against a recent dues increase imposed upon them without their consent by the union leadership. Lewis chose to ignore it, however, and characterized the strikes as the result of the iniquitous and finally unbearable abuses heaped upon the suffering miners by the heartless operators. Responding to the observation of one board member that one word from Lewis would have sufficed to end the strikes, Lewis asked rhetorically, "Who ever heard of a general concerning himself with mere skirmishes in the field?"

During the noon recesses, Lewis never ate in the Department of Labor cafeteria but instead walked up to the Carlton Hotel, where the same table in the dining room was always reserved for him. He walked slowly with his hat thrust forward on his head. His entourage, including Tom Kennedy, vice president of the UMW, and Philip Murray, who eventually succeeded Lewis as president of the CIO, always kept several paces behind, not one of them presuming to walk by his side. With the exception of Reuther, no union leader I have ever observed had the dominating presence of Lewis. "Old bushy-eyebrows," as he was irreverently referred to by some WLB staffers, inspired fear and respect even among his enemies.

THE DETROIT AREA TOOL AND DIE COMMISSION

My first position with the WLB involving major responsibilities was that of chairman of the Detroit Area Tool and Die Commission.[18] As the United States accelerated its shift from peacetime to wartime production, critical problems developed in the relatively small but vitally important tool and die industry, especially in Detroit, home of the manufacturing giants GM, the Ford Motor Company, and Chrysler, as well as of smaller companies that supplied them with necessary parts. Retooling involved the service of highly skilled tool and die workers, then in short supply. These men were employed either in large tool rooms of the major manufacturers or in a number of independently owned tool and die job shops that varied in size and quality of equipment. Regardless of where the work was performed, it typically required maintenance of close tolerances, often measured in ten-thousandths of an inch.

The most highly skilled tool and die workers were employed by the job shops that had no maximum rates for tool and die classifications. Because these workers were in such short supply they were increasingly being pirated from one shop to another by offers of higher pay. This was not true generally for tool room employees of the manufacturing companies, all of which had established fixed maximum rates for the various tool and die classifications and offered more stable employment and better working conditions than did the job shops. Moreover, the loss of valuable but nonportable seniority rights attendant on any shift in employment discouraged employees of those companies from changing jobs.

In a case involving GM, Chrysler, the Automotive Tool and Die Association, and the UAW, the WLB issued an order in October 1942 that was designed to stabilize wages and employment in the Detroit tool and die industry.[19] Acting on recommendations by a special tripartite panel headed by William E. Simkin, a Taylor protégé who later became the director of the FMCS, the board established maximum rates for

---

[18] The background events leading to the establishment of the commission are set forth in detail in its first annual report, National War Labor Board, *Termination Report of the National War Labor Board: Industrial Disputes and Wage Stabilization in Wartime*, 3 vols. (Washington, D.C.: n.p., 1947–49), 1: 1134–63.

[19] National War Labor Board, *Report* 4 (1942): 33.

tool and die classifications in the job shops to arrest the upward spiral of wages. At the same time it increased by 10 percent per hour the wage rates paid to all tool room employees in the manufacturing companies in order to restore the historical differential in wages paid by the two groups of employers. The board also established fixed minimum rates for all tool and die classifications in both manufacturing companies and job shops. Finally, the board established the tripartite Detroit Area Tool and Die Commission to administer its order.

I can only dimly recollect that I served as assistant to the Simkin panel. I do remember, however, working with Bill Simkin, a calm, absolutely unflappable professional with whom I developed a lasting friendship. I suspect he was most responsible for my appointment as chairman of the commission.

In December 1942, Eleanor and I packed our few belongings and traveled by car to Detroit. En route, we passed through Pittsburgh, a city of surpassing ugliness that evoked William Blake's image of "dark Satanic Mills." Detroit was no improvement. I spent the first two weeks after we had found a place to live looking for suitable office space (the Detroit regional board was not yet in operation) and hiring a secretary. During that time I never once saw the sun, and the raw winter weather, coupled with the pervasive dreariness of the place, left me with an antipathy to Detroit that remains. There were bars aplenty and a wealth of professional sports events, but that was pretty much it. There was virtually no theater, and the struggling Detroit Symphony Orchestra was kept alive only by the beneficence of Weinstein's Cut-Rate Drugstores. The immensely wealthy families living in splendid isolation in the suburb of Grosse Pointe contributed little or nothing to support the city's civic projects.

The establishment of the Tool and Die Commission was prominently featured in Detroit's two leading newspapers, the *Free Press* and the *News*. The announcement of my appointment as chairman provoked some hostile comment. The press delightedly reported in detail the attack on me by the president of a small independent union, the Society of Tool and Die Craftsmen. This man, whose name I have forgotten, criticized the WLB's directive order stabilizing tool and die wages and creating the commission and dismissed me in a sentence that made the headlines: "Aaron knows about as much about tool and diemaking as a jack rabbit." He was absolutely correct. Up to that time I had never even been in a tool and die shop.

My first meeting with a large group of tool and die workers shortly after my arrival in Detroit was a stormy one. Chaired by Reuther, its purpose was to explain the WLB's stabilization order to several hundred members of two large UAW tool and die unions, Locals 155 and 157. After Reuther had outlined in a general way the provisions of the new order and had introduced me, John Anderson, president of Local 155, took the floor. An avowed Communist (he had run for governor of Michigan on the Communist Party ticket), Anderson denounced the order and the creation of the commission and ridiculed my lack of knowledge about the industry. He was an effective speaker, and his remarks drew much laughter and applause. Reuther, who was well acquainted with Anderson's performances, turned to me and smilingly asked if I would like him to reply on my behalf, but in this situation, I decided that valor was the better part of discretion and spoke for myself. Anderson had committed a major blunder: he had misrepresented some key provisions of the WLB's order with which I was thoroughly familiar. Taking the offensive, I pointed out his mistakes and told him he didn't know what he was talking about. To my surprise, my response was greeted with even more laughter and applause than Anderson had received. Only after I had gained greater insight into the political rivalries within the UAW did I realize that my friendly reception on this occasion was due more to the majority opposition to Anderson and the Communists than to my own performance. Nevertheless, that meeting got me off to a good start in my new role and ended public attacks against me.

A few weeks later, Anderson walked into my office. He grinned at me and said he really ought to have punched me out for "making me look like a fool" at the meeting. Then he declared that he bore me no grudge and congratulated me on the way I had handled myself. Thereafter, our relations remained friendly and he never gave me any trouble.

The commission differed from others established by the WLB in specific industries, such as meatpacking, telephone, and trucking, in that its employer and employee members were not full-time appointees. As the only permanent member of the commission, I was authorized to act in most wage cases by myself. In each dispute case, however, I designated *ad hoc* employer and employee members to serve on the commission's tripartite panel that conducted the hearing. I usually appointed the same two men: Chester A. Cahn, managing director of the Automotive Tool and Die Manufacturers Association, which represented job shops, and Joseph H. Piconke, a member of the UAW's skilled trades division. The latter was selected because the UAW represented a large majority of tool and die workers within the commission's jurisdiction. Cahn was urbane, sophisticated, and an effective spokesman for his constituents; Piconke lacked Cahn's smoothness and articulateness, but his practical experience as a skilled craftsman proved to be very helpful in dealing with some of the issues presented to the commission.

The two independent unions, the Society of Tool and Die Craftsmen and the Mechanics Educational Society of America (MESA), at first objected very strenuously to not being given regular representation on the commission. The former had very few members and was involved in only a minimal number of wage cases, most of which I decided by myself, but the MESA, a relatively small but militant union, played an important role in the commission's work. During the period 1935–1947, the NLRB discriminated against unions not affiliated with either the AFL or the CIO. This practice was probably due to the large number of so-called independent unions that were dominated or substantially assisted by employers during the years immediately following passage of the Wagner Act. Not until the adoption of the Taft-Hartley Act in 1947 was the NLRB prohibited from treating genuinely independent unions like the MESA differently from AFL or CIO affiliates. To a certain extent, the WLB was guilty of the same discriminatory practices. For example, the MESA, while properly excluded from participation in the proceedings leading to the WLB's wage stabilization order for the Detroit area tool and die industry because it was not a party to the cases then under consideration, did represent a significant number of tool and die workers affected by the order. Hence it should have been allowed official representation on the commission. We redressed that omission by permitting a MESA representative (usually its president, George White) to sit as a panel member on any case in which that union was the bargaining agent for the workers involved.[20]

Something of the distinctive character of the MESA is reflected in its bimonthly newspaper, the *MESA Educator*, then by far the most interesting of the union journals I had read. At its masthead appeared the following lines from a poem by James Russell Lowell:

> Let liars fear, let cowards shrink,
> Let traitors turn away,
> Whatever we have dared to think
> That dare we also say.

In addition to the usual news about strikes and organization drives, the paper carried articles attacking government labor policies, especially its insistence upon labor's no-strike pledge. It also included such things as a reprint of a lengthy book review in *The New Leader* of a collection of Thomas Jefferson's writings.

The dominant figure in the MESA was its elected national secretary, Matthew Smith. An Englishman and former member of the British Independent Labor Party who had emigrated to the United States in 1928, Smith resolutely refused to become an American citizen because he would not give his enemies "the satisfaction of badgering him into it."[21] His obduracy attracted the attention of the FBI, which kept a constant watch on his activities. As labor leaders go, Smith, a former toolmaker, was something of an anomaly: he opposed the closed shop and the check-off, and he once startled me by referring to seniority—the

---

[20] On 17 May 1944, the WLB announced adoption of a resolution submitted by the Independent Unions for Representation, which stated in part that it was the board's policy "to accord equality of treatment to all unions, whether affiliated or independent." The full text of the resolution, including its provisions for independent union representation in tripartite panels, is reprinted in National War Labor Board, *Termination Report*, 2: 579.

[21] Walter Davenport, "Unique Unioneer," *Colliers*, 13 May 1994, 14, 57; quoted in Harry Dahlheimer, *A History of the Mechanics Educational Society of America in Detroit From Its Inception in 1933 Through 1937* (Detroit: Wayne University Press, 1951), 47.

cherished union principle that preference in respect of promotions, layoffs, and various employment benefits should be based on length of service—as "that wretched doctrine." On behalf of his union, he also refused to give a no-strike pledge to the government. Indeed, in 1944, he called a strike of 25,000 MESA members in Cleveland, Toledo, and Detroit in protest against an NLRB decision to order a representation election requested by the UAW in a plant where the MESA had bargaining rights. He was about 50 years of age, a stocky man of medium height, and a constant smoker. Ashes from the cigarette ever present in his mouth used to fall all over the vest of the dark blue suit he customarily wore. He read widely and used to bring me books he thought important, telling me not to return them but to pass them on to someone else. Among those he gave me I remember particularly several novels by Ignazio Silone.

Smith and I became good friends. What he appreciated in me, I think, was my willingness to accord the MESA exactly the same treatment as that given to the UAW. Whatever the reason, he contributed greatly to my understanding of tool and die work and the interesting psychology of many of those who performed it. In February 1944, when I left the commission and returned to Washington, Smith, on behalf of the MESA, presented me with a set of the Encyclopedia Britannica as a token of the union's appreciation of the fairness with which I had administered the tool and die order. As a government servant, I could not accept this generous gift, so Smith and I agreed that it be sent to the Highlander Folk School in Tennessee, a favorite project of Mrs. Roosevelt and an organization about whose political philosophy the FBI remained deeply suspicious.

In the first few months of its existence the commission was virtually autonomous. Although it reported actions on wage cases to the WLB's regional director in Cleveland, it was under no supervision from that office.[22] Of course, the WLB in Washington could have reviewed the

---

[22] On 2 October 1942, Congress passed the Economic Stabilization Act, which controlled wage and salary increases for all workers. An executive order issued the next day assigned administration of the wage stabilization program to the WLB. The resulting surge of cases coming to the board led to the establishment in January 1943 of twelve tripartite regional boards (including one in Detroit) with

commission's decisions either on appeal or on its own motion, but it never had occasion to do so. Left largely to my own resources, I gradually worked out its policies and procedures. At first, I convened the full commission only in dispute cases, of which there were very few. Then, as the regular members came to know each other better, discussions and conferences became more frequent, and I eventually referred all questions of policy to the full group.

The board for region XI, with jurisdiction over the entire state of Michigan and situated in Detroit, was established in February 1943. At this time the commission moved into the regional board offices in the Penobscot Building and immediately became an administrative division of that board. Nevertheless, the commission continued for a time to act independently, largely because the WLB directive order establishing it had made no provision for the supervision of any of its activities by any other agency than the WLB. This situation was corrected in July 1943, when the WLB, acting on the joint recommendation of the regional board and the commission, amended its original directive order of 11 December 1942 to provide that the Detroit Area Tool and Die Commission was now the Tool and Die Commission of Region XI and subject to overall supervision by the regional board.[23]

In deciding the cases submitted to it, the commission frequently had occasion to visit the shops where the particular work involved was being performed. These visits were largely designed for my benefit, and I gradually acquired a familiarity with the functions of the various machine tools covered by the maximum wage schedule established by the initial WLB order.

The WLB's tool and die stabilization order did not put an end to the practice of pirating workers by some job shop employers. When the board issued its order to cap wage rates, a number of these workers were being paid wages that were higher than the maximum set for their

---

power to make initial decisions in all cases. These regional boards became operational early in 1943. Thereafter, the WLB functioned primarily as an appellate body and policy maker.

[23] For the text of the board's July 1943 order, see National War Labor Board, *Termination Report*, 1: 1142. A provision of that order providing that the regional board would appoint the chairman of the commission was never implemented, because I had been appointed to that position by the WLB.

classification. In accordance with the order, their rates were not reduced to the legal maximum. Subsequently, however, many of them transferred to other employers at the same or higher rates, thus threatening to destabilize the system established by the board. Consequently, on 1 April 1943, the commission issued a regulation providing that any tool and die worker being paid above the legal maximum rate who transferred to another employer without the commission's specific approval would have his rate at his new place of employment reduced to the legal maximum. The regulation also included a list of the principal reasons for which some transfers above the maximum would be deemed "in furtherance of the war effort" and therefore permissible.

The first of these—"When the worker is competent to perform higher skilled work than his current employer is able or willing to provide"—was relied upon in a surprising number of transfer applications submitted to the commission for approval.[24] The proposed moves frequently involved no increase in pay. The applicants, many of them highly skilled emigrants from central Europe, simply felt demeaned by the kind of work to which they were being assigned, and they wanted to go where they would be required to maintain extremely close tolerances. Although the commission's regulation allowed considerable flexibility in the administration of the general rule, we did reject a number of applications, and in spite of some undetected violations, the regulation substantially diminished the amount of labor pirating in the Detroit area tool and die industry.

The staff of the commission remained small: in addition to my secretary, it consisted of the deputy chairman, James Dunn, and a hearing officer, Kurt Anderson, both of whom were former NLRB field examiners, and an economist and statistician, Herbert R. Northrup. Northrup was then in the process of completing an outstanding book that documented his own extensive field research on the widespread discrimination by labor unions against Negroes in a variety of industries.[25] Whether because of his experiences while doing research on his book or for other reasons, Northrup, who became a leading advocate of a confrontational

[24] National War Labor Board, *Termination Report*, 3: 685.
[25] Herbert R. Northrup, *Organized Labor and the Negro* (New York: Harper, 1944).

approach toward unions by employers, developed a strong and abiding hostility toward organized labor. Taylor subsequently brought him to the Wharton School at about the same time that the school hired William Gomberg, a former official of the International Ladies Garment Workers and a militant unionist with a strong anti-management bias. Taylor told me at the time that he hoped these two very bright protagonists would "civilize" each other and jointly contribute to an improved climate of labor-management relations. Unfortunately, that didn't happen.

The first chairman of the Detroit Regional War Labor Board was Edwin E. Witte, an eminent labor economist from the University of Wisconsin. He had been intimately associated with John R. Commons, Selig Perlman, and other members of the "Wisconsin school," whose teachings and writings had dominated the field of labor economics and social legislation. His own book, *The Government in Labor Disputes* (1932), is a classic, and his various articles on labor history are standard sources for scholars in the field. He also had played a major role in the drafting and enactment of the Norris-LaGuardia Act of 1932 and the Social Security Act of 1935. Witte was an inveterate collector of newspaper reports of strikes, injunctions, and other matters involving workers and unions. He once told me that much of the data included in Felix Frankfurter and Nathan Greene's famous work on labor injunctions came from his personal files.[26]

Witte was a friendly, exuberant man with some endearing mannerisms. He was stocky and of medium height, and had a sort of waddling walk. I usually encountered him hurrying down the hall, holding several telegrams between his teeth and clutching an array of pens and pencils in both hands. In discussions he was wont to scratch his bald head absent-mindedly with a pen, leaving it covered with ink marks.

In his relations with other board members and the staff, Witte was considerate and even-tempered. The only time I ever saw him show real anger was after he had been made a public member of the WLB in Washington and had been falsely accused of some misconduct by the president of a small union in New York. Outraged by this attack on

[26] Felix Frankfurter and Nathan Greene, *The Labor Injunction* (New York: Macmillan, 1930).

his integrity, Witte searched for words to express his indignation and finally came out with "That man is a—a skunk!" He was also a workaholic; when not occupied with board matters, he could usually be found in a corner somewhere grading student exams or term papers. Ronald Haughton, his former assistant at the University of Wisconsin and the disputes director of the regional board, with whom he shared an apartment, used to try to lure Witte away from work by taking him for a sail on the Detroit River on weekends. But Witte always brought his work with him and sat in the stern of the boat grading his papers.

I came to know Witte much better during the years 1944–1945, when we were both in Washington. He had a keen intelligence and a comprehensive knowledge of labor-management relations, informed by years of research and practical experience. During hearings he had a disconcerting habit of sinking into semi-slumber with one eye closed and the other open. On one memorable occasion, a particularly important case was being argued before a panel of the WLB, and a number of staff members and reporters were present. The two public members on the panel were Witte and Graham. The attorney for the employer was a prominent New York lawyer of considerable pomposity. He noticed, as all of those present did, that Witte appeared to be asleep. The attorney therefore kept raising his voice until he was almost shouting, and he frequently interrupted his argument by saying, "I am especially anxious that the public members understand our position on this point." Graham, who was presiding, also assumed that Witte had fallen asleep and decided to try to wake him up by kicking him under the table. Graham was so short, however, that to accomplish his purpose he had to slide down in his chair. To the suppressed delight of the audience, he sank lower and lower until only the top of his head was visible. When he finally administered the awakening kick, Witte opened his closed eye and put one or two penetrating questions to the employer's attorney that left him utterly deflated and speechless.

While I was still in Detroit I became good friends with Harry Shulman, a professor and subsequently dean of the Yale Law School. Shulman had left the WLB staff in 1942 to become the first umpire under the labor agreement between Ford and the UAW. Umpires differ from the more numerous *ad hoc* arbitrators who are chosen by the parties to decide only a single case. By contrast, an umpire is selected to decide all the unresolved grievances arising under the collective bargaining agreement for a fixed term. Taylor once observed that an umpire "penetrates into the blood stream" of the industry in which he serves and gains a much more intimate knowledge of the nature of the relationship between the parties than an *ad hoc* arbitrator can possibly acquire. Shulman was the supreme exemplar of that dictum. This was confirmed to me in 1951, when I was interviewed by Ford and UAW officials who were seeking a successor to Shulman. I met with each side separately. One of the questions I asked was whether it was true that Shulman sometimes disposed of as many as 60 to 80 cases in a day, and if so, how did he do it? Both sides gave me identical answers. They described a procedure in which Shulman sat in a room with only one company and one union representative. He would then rapidly review the file in each grievance, asking questions as he did so. He usually spent no more than five minutes on each case. I expressed doubt that anyone could come so quickly to a decision but was told that in these sessions Shulman came to a final decision on almost none of them. Some he would reject as not yet ripe for decision; others he would reserve for later disposal in a short memorandum. A small number were scheduled for a formal hearing, followed by the issuance of a decision and opinion. Explaining how he could conduct this triage so expertly, each side told me, using almost identical words, "First, he knows more about this industry and this company than anybody on either side, and second, he can tell in five minutes which one of us is lying."

Shulman's decisions are generally recognized as classics. One of my most prized possessions is a bound volume of them for the years 1943–1946. What they reveal is the man's keen intelligence, his ability to analyze and explain complex issues in language that the workers could understand, the deft use of humor in appropriate circumstances, and above all, the application of contract terms in such a way as to preserve and implement the underlying purposes of the collective agreement.

During the time we spent together in Detroit, I had ample opportunity to observe Shulman's unique relationship with Ford and the UAW. He retained a suite in the Penobscot Building that served as both his office and his living quarters. In the evening he would usually hold court in the cocktail lounge on the top floor. After I gave up a hopeless effort to keep up with his consumption of martinis, I found it a most interesting and enjoyable experience to sit with him on a number of these evenings. He would regularly be approached by company or union representatives, with the full knowledge and approval of both sides. In violation of all the conventions observed by *ad hoc* arbitrators, Shulman would discuss with company and union people pending cases as well as those already decided, and those which, in his words, he had put under his desk blotter "to let them age and ripen" before he released them. He even occasionally advised union representatives about whether to file grievances involving certain matters, and sometimes he was consulted about purely personal problems. In short, he acted as a kind of father confessor for everyone who came to see him.

In this way Shulman established a remarkable rapport with the parties and gained their trust and respect. I suspect that his good friend, Supreme Court Justice William O. Douglas, had Shulman in mind when he described the function of an arbitrator in one of the cases comprising the *Steelworkers Trilogy*:

> The labor arbitrator is usually chosen because of the parties' confidence in his knowledge of the common law of the shop and their trust in his personal judgment to bring to bear considerations which are not expressed in the contract as criteria for judgment. The parties expect that his judgment of a particular grievance will reflect not only what the contract says but, insofar as the collective bargaining agreement permits, such factors as the effect upon productivity of a particular result, its consequences to the morale of the shop, his judgment whether tensions will be heightened or diminished.... The ablest judge cannot be expected to bring the same experience and competence to bear upon the determination of a grievance, because he cannot be similarly informed.[27]

This somewhat overblown description could not possibly apply to *ad hoc* arbitrators, who may be unknown to the parties at the time they are chosen. It could refer only to umpires, and not even to all of them. As is clear from Justice Douglas's opinion, however, which quoted freely from Shulman's famous Holmes Lecture at Harvard, "Reason, Contract, and Law in Labor Relations," it was Shulman's conception of his role as

---

[27] *United Steelworkers v. Warrior & Gulf Navigator Co.*, 363 U.S. 574, 582 (1960).

umpire that led to Douglas's incorrect assumption that most arbitrators function in that manner.[28]

In time, Ford and the UAW both tired of Shulman's ideas of his proper role as umpire. As I was subsequently informed, they wanted someone with a more "judicial" approach who would be less inclined to mediate. They also knew that he was seriously ill with cancer, and neither party wished to terminate him. Shortly after Shulman's death, they selected Harry H. Platt to succeed him. Platt was a very able umpire, but his style was more attuned to the changed approach preferred by both parties.

Like Taylor, Shulman had a profound influence on me. It was not only his wisdom and common sense that impressed me; it was also his broad humanity and the total absence of pettiness in his personality. I did sense a kind of loneliness in him, which became apparent in the last letter he wrote me very shortly before his death. Not quite sure how to reply, I delayed answering until it was too late, an act of omission I shall never cease to regret.

By the end of 1943, Eleanor and I had had our fill of life in Detroit, especially after the savage race riots of 1943. The amalgam of a wide variety of racial, ethnic, religious, and political groups lent a certain spice to the community culture, but also exacerbated racial and ethnic antagonisms.[29] The large black community clashed with white southerners, many of whom were members or supporters of the Ku Klux Klan. There was an explosive incident at the Packard Motor Company plant after three black women were promoted from the lowest labor grade to the one just above it. This seemingly inconsequential personnel action touched off a wildcat strike that shut down the plant for three days and led to a conflagration that engulfed the entire city. Looking out of my office window, I observed with horror and a terrible feeling of helplessness a group of white thugs armed with pieces of pipe chasing a single frightened young black man. Blacks and whites alike turned to violence and looting; the chief victims were small stores owned by Jews, who were

---

[28] For the Holmes Lecture, see *Harvard Law Review* 68 (1955): 999.

[29] I recall with pleasure the several evangelical Protestant churches that regularly advertised their Sunday services as entertainment spectaculars: "Come hear the 12 sanctified accordions. Grand climax: see 20-foot whale swallow Jonah."

accused, rightly or wrongly, of charging their primarily black customers prices above those authorized by the OPA.

In any case, I was anxious to go back to Washington and to start a new assignment. I discussed the matter with Taylor, and he agreed that I was due for a change. In February 1944, Eleanor and I returned to Washington, in mutual agreement that Detroit was not a place we would care to revisit soon.

THE NATIONAL AIRFRAME PANEL

On 2 April 1944, I took over as chairman of the tripartite National Airframe Panel. The jurisdiction of the panel encompassed all wage and nonwage disputes arising in some 30-odd companies that made up the airframe industry, which is defined as the manufacture and assembly of finished airplanes. The largest percentage of the panel's cases came from the Southern California aircraft industry, commonly referred to as the SCAI, which comprised principally five companies: Consolidated-Vultee Aircraft, San Diego; Douglas Aircraft, Santa Monica; Lockheed Aircraft, Burbank; North American Aviation, Inglewood; and Northrop Aircraft, Hawthorne. The panel was also empowered to make final rulings on voluntary wage and salary adjustments if and when the rulings were unanimous. Most of the cases coming to the panel involved disputes and were scheduled for hearing. Then the panel's recommendations, accompanied by an opinion by the chairman (and frequently by dissenting opinions by the employer or employee members) were submitted to the WLB for approval or modification. The panel consisted initially of only one public member, the chairman, two employers' representatives, and two employees' representatives, until the appointment of Philip S. Brayton, a lawyer and a WLB staff member, to serve as vice chairman. His modest and retiring manner masked a keen intelligence, and he possessed a dry and very funny sense of humor.

Although the employer members serving on the panel changed from time to time, the two regulars were Paul S. Chalfant, from Douglas, and R. Randall Irwin, from Lockheed. The former lived in the Westwood section of Los Angeles and was quickly dubbed "Westwood Pegler" by the panel's employee members because of his anti-labor attitude and right-wing political views, which he vociferously expressed at every opportunity.[30] Irwin was a quiet, thoughtful man and much more moderate in his attitudes toward unions. In a general way, each man mirrored the industrial relations philosophy of his own company.

The two principal employee members were Ed Hall of the UAW and Garry R. Cotton of the International Association of Machinists (IAM), an affiliate of the AFL. Hall, a veteran UAW member, was customarily belligerent in our discussions and also given to occasional outbursts of temper, but his bark was worse than his bite, and he was generally more willing to compromise than his AFL colleague. I remember him chiefly because of his own inimitable way with the English language. When Hall confronted what he regarded as an intractable problem, he pronounced himself "stymated." He could be heard to mutter darkly from time to time about someone he particularly disliked, "I've got a yen against that guy." Once, at a dinner at his house in a suburb of Los Angeles, he waxed poetic about the beauties of the "High Saharas" visible from his front porch.

Cotton was something else: he was by nature saturnine and rebarbative. A machinist, he had spent many years at his trade and was extremely knowledgeable about most of the job classifications in the airframe industry. Unlike the garrulous Hall, Cotton was taciturn and not given to small talk. He was virtually humorless and seldom laughed.

The dispute cases coming before the panel included the usual issues of union security, seniority, fringe benefits, and the like, but they were mainly concerned with wage questions involving the application of the SCAI job evaluation plan. All of the SCAI companies used pretty much the same job classifications, although the job titles varied somewhat. Most classifications were divided into three levels of difficulty—A, B, and C. In order to diminish, if not entirely eliminate, intercompany competition based on wages, the SCAI plan classified all jobs into ten labor grades, each grade

---

[30] Westbrook Pegler was a prominent newspaper columnist who began his career as a gifted sportswriter but eventually became a strident, embittered political commentator who espoused reactionary antilabor views.

carrying a fixed rate range. Thus, theoretically at least, an assembler, a utility worker, or a machinist would be paid the same rate at any of the SCAI companies. Although the SCAI plan did much to stabilize wages among its member companies, it was not entirely successful, and it certainly failed to reduce significantly the number of job-classification grievances filed by the unions. Disparities in wages paid by the individual companies to employees in the same jobs continued, largely reflecting the differing policies of the managements involved. To give but one illustration, Douglas classified most of its assemblers at the C level, the lowest labor grade, whereas Lockheed classified most of its assemblers at the A, or highest, level. North American pegged most of its assemblers at the B level.

Another prolific source of grievances was the use of rate ranges, instead of single rates, for each job, because the top of the range for, say, assembler C exceeded the bottom of the range for assembler B. Then, too, the evaluation of each job was based on a number of factors: mentality, responsibility, mental application, physical application, job conditions, and unavoidable hazards. Appraising these factors obviously involved subjective as well as objective judgments that were also repeatedly challenged. Some of the alleged distinctions between differing job evaluations contended for by the companies and the unions often bordered on the metaphysical and were the cause of endless argument among the panel members. I speedily grew weary of these types of cases, but almost in spite of myself I eventually acquired a reputation in the industry as an expert on the SCAI job evaluation plan.

Occasionally, we were presented with much more interesting problems. One of these was the issue of whether an employer should be directed over its strong objections to pay union stewards for some or all of their time spent in handling grievances. WLB policy on this question was to grant a union's request for such a contract provision only upon a positive showing that management was responsible for "unnecessary" and "unusual" delays in the handling of grievances or that the requested provision was "essential" for the proper functioning of the grievance procedure.[31]

---

[31] McQuay Norris, as quoted in National War Labor Board, *Report* 9 (1943): 538; and National War Labor Board, *Report* 14 (1944): 210.

In June 1944, the panel held hearings in a dispute between the Glenn L. Martin Co. of Baltimore, a manufacturer of military and naval aircraft, and the UAW.[32] At issue was employer payment to union stewards for time spent in handling grievances, which was regarded by both parties as by far the most important of those submitted to the panel. Because of the many issues involved, the hearings took three days and were attended by a large number of Martin employees.

There were several aspects of the *Martin* case that the union particularly emphasized: (1) the practice of paying union stewards for grievance time had been agreed to by virtually every other company in the industry; and (2) in the period before the Martin plant was organized, the company had voluntarily paid individual employees for minimal time spent in presenting their complaints to management. Nevertheless, after prolonged and bitter debate, a majority of the panel—myself and the employer members—voted to recommend against the union's proposal, but the employer members, who dismissed the union's arguments as wholly without merit, specifically disassociated themselves from the personal views expressed in my opinion and concurred only in the result. The board upheld the panel majority's recommendation, but referred the issue back to the parties for collective bargaining based on the policy announced in *McQuay-Norris*, the past practice of the company, and the contract grievance procedure.

Shortly after the panel's recommendations and the board's decision were made public, I received a note from Professor Sumner L. Slichter, the distinguished labor economist at Harvard. He said he was very interested in the issue of pay to union stewards for grievance time and suggested that we meet for breakfast at the Cosmos Club in Washington a few days later to discuss it. Slichter was a man of tremendous presence: with his short-cropped white hair, pale face devoid of wrinkles, and patrician features, he resembled a Roman senator. He was neatly dressed in a somewhat shiny but well-pressed serge suit and an immaculate white shirt that had been skillfully darned near the collar. In discussing the matter of pay to union stewards he displayed an encyclopedic knowledge

---

[32] National War Labor Board, *Report* 14 (1944): 263.

of various industry practices and of the policies of a number of different unions. He asked me a few questions about the UAW and the airframe industry, but I'm sure I learned much more from our conversation than he did. To my delighted surprise, he ended the meeting by inviting me to present a paper on the subject to his graduate seminar at Harvard. Naturally, I accepted, and I spent a number of evenings at home working on the project, for which I received an honorarium of $75.00—one of the few times in my career that I was paid for a specific piece of research.

A relatively novel issue considered by the panel was presented in a dispute between Lockheed and the IAM.[33] The union had proposed inclusion in the collective bargaining agreement of a statement of company policy permitting employees covered by the agreement to retain ownership of inventions they made during the course of employment. The company strongly opposed the union's proposal and presented as part of its submission the expert testimony of a well-known patent attorney.

The opinion I wrote on this issue, explaining the panel's majority recommendation to deny the union's proposal, was based not only on the lengthy submissions of the parties but also on my own research. It was one of the few occasions I had as chairman of the National Airframe Panel to engage in this kind of exercise, and I remember the satisfaction I derived from doing so. I also recall with pleasure my discussions of the issue with Davis, who was himself an eminent patent attorney.

Sometime during the spring of 1944, I made my first visit to Southern California in my official capacity. Several panel hearings had been scheduled, but the intervals between these gave me some time for other activities. I brought Eleanor with me—it was her first trip west of Chicago — and we enjoyed for the first and last time together a most pleasurable journey on the Santa Fe Chief, which even in wartime offered a kind of service never available on the airlines that soon displaced railroads as the prime means of long-distance passenger transportation in the United States.

Shortly after our arrival in Los Angeles, I received an invitation from Frank Lauerman, director of industrial relations for Consolidated-

---

[33] National War Labor Board, *Report* 27 (1945): 432.

Vultee, to have lunch with him at the California Club, an exclusive, very conservative institution that openly denied membership to women and tacitly excluded Jews, Negroes, and other ethnic and racial minorities. Lauerman, whom I came to know quite well, was an interesting and rather pathetic person. He had come to Consolidated-Vultee from Republic Steel and had been schooled in the industrial relations policies of that company's iron-fisted president, Tom Girdler, who was well known for his uncompromising opposition to unions. Lauerman hardly seemed the type: he was soft-spoken and unassertive, and always appeared to me to be frightened about something. During our frequent telephone conversations in the succeeding months, he almost invariably began with the question, "Are you alone?" As I came to know him better, I learned that Frank and his wife were devout Roman Catholics and had a son who was a priest. For some reason, he felt that it was necessary to conceal that fact from his business associates, and his willingness to talk to me about his son — always in lowered tones prefaced by the earnest request that I keep the information confidential — was a mark of his trust in me. Left to his own devices, I think Frank would have opted for a more cooperative attitude towards the IAM, which represented the company's employees in San Diego, but he had not forgotten Girdler's policy of firing any industrial relations director who got along well with the union, so Consolidated-Vultee's policy toward the IAM was basically one of containment.

At our initial lunch at the California Club, Lauerman invited me to inspect the company's plant in San Diego. Although at the time there was no case involving Consolidated-Vultee on the panel's docket, I accepted because I had not yet had the opportunity to visit an airframe plant and was eager to do so. In the course of our conversation, Lauerman mentioned that his company's new general counsel was Watts, the former general counsel of the NLRB. I responded jokingly that I hadn't seen Watts since he turned me down for a job at the NLRB. Lauerman's response to my casual remark was comical but also indicative of what I soon came to recognize as an innate feeling of insecurity: he choked, turned deeply pale, and began to stammer excuses, saying that he was sure I had been rejected because of some misunderstanding. He also repeatedly insisted that Watts bore me no ill will. I tried to reassure him, telling him that Watts had really done me a favor because routine work as an NLRB lawyer could not possibly be as satisfactory as the various experiences offered by employment with the WLB, but I could see that he remained upset.

A few days later, Eleanor and I flew down to San Diego. Lauerman met us at the airport and took us to the El Cortez Hotel, one of the best in San Diego. Watts was waiting for us there. I can only guess what Lauerman must have told him, but Watts greeted us in a manner that can best be described as obsequious. He had already checked us in and told us he would wait downstairs until we were ready to go to the plant. Upon going upstairs we discovered that instead of the room we had expected we had a large and luxurious suite. Prominently on display as we entered was a huge bouquet of flowers sent by the company. A moment later the telephone rang. It was Watts inquiring whether we found everything satisfactory. He could have easily been mistaken for the hotel manager.

When we arrived at the plant, Watts asked us if there was anything in particular we wanted to see. Before I could reply, Eleanor, who had never been inside any kind of plant, said, "Yes, I'd like to see a foreman." Revealing an unsuspected sense of humor, he told her to "look for the man with horns." That was the last time I ever saw Watts. He did not appear at any of the hearings involving Consolidated-Vultee, for what reason I can only surmise.

A reader of this account may naturally wonder why we accepted the hospitality of a company that I knew would undoubtedly be a party to disputes soon to come before the panel. Certainly, such conduct would be condemned today. I shall return to that question a little later. Meanwhile, I shall simply note that before going to San Diego, I told the other panel members of my plans and none of them objected.

After I returned to Los Angeles, the panel held hearings in two dispute cases involving, as I recall, Douglas and Lockheed. Prior to the Douglas hearing, we called upon the company's founder and president, Donald Douglas, at his office in the Santa Monica plant. We found him sitting at his desk, an English setter lying at his feet. He was dressed in expensive-looking tweeds and was smoking a pipe. He seemed to me more like an English country gentleman than an American captain of industry. After a few minutes of amiable chitchat, we were given the signal to depart by Chalfant, who rose and said, "Thank you, Mr. Douglas, for agreeing to see us. We'll stop cluttering up your office now and let you go back to work." I never saw Douglas again, but the memory of Chalfant's self-demeaning valediction still rankles.

I can't recall when or in what circumstances I met Robert Gross, Lockheed's president. Unlike Douglas's remote and rather cold manner, Gross's was warm, forthcoming, and energetic. I admit to having been predisposed in his favor because his attitude toward unions seemed the most enlightened in the industry. As one firmly committed to the national labor policy in favor of collective bargaining, I naturally approved of his acceptance of unions and his willingness to work cooperatively with them rather than simply holding them at arm's length.

Within a relatively short time I developed a friendship with several persons closely connected with the airframe industry that continued long after my service with the WLB had ended. By far the most important of these was Robert Canan, a labor relations specialist on the legal staff of Lockheed. He was a man of great integrity and solid common sense, an exceptionally able lawyer, and a loyal Democrat of liberal persuasion. Bob and I had a cordial professional relationship while I was with the WLB, and when Eleanor and I moved to Los Angeles after the war, we renewed our ties with Bob and his wife, Molly.

Gene Starkweather was the industrial relations director of North American and the principal representative of the SCAI industrial relations group. He was a conservative, no-nonsense type and also a man of great integrity, but he had little tolerance for the views of those who disagreed with him, and in his dealings with the UAW, which represented North American's employees, he remained fairly inflexible. He and I continued our friendship after the war, and he occasionally invited me for a spin in his airplane.

The man with whom I came most frequently in contact during my service with the National Airframe Panel was J. Stuart Neary, legal counsel for North American and representative of the SCAI companies in their joint dealings with the panel and the WLB. Stuart was a partner of the prominent Los Angeles law firm of Gibson, Dunn & Crutcher as well as the head of its labor department. His nickname was "Slugger," in token of his belligerent and combative tactics in NLRB, court, and arbitration proceedings. Stuart's self-described background was "shanty-Irish from the wrong side of the tracks." I believe he was born in South Dakota. He was educated in Catholic parochial schools and obtained his law degree from the Creighton University Law School. He obviously did not move in the same social circles as his partners at Gibson, Dunn, most of whom had been educated in prestigious universities and had studied law at Harvard or Yale. One must conclude that he had achieved his status in the firm solely on the basis of his ability.

Neary was a big man, a little over six feet tall and weighing well over 250 pounds. His normal speaking voice was low and rather soft, but when he became aroused, the decibel level would rise very quickly. He habitually worked, played, ate, drank, and smoked to excess. His chronic alcoholism frequently got out of control, usually with damaging consequences. On one occasion, the SCAI companies asked me to come to Los Angeles to discuss a proposed upgrading of the common labor classification, which would have required WLB approval. The matter was one of considerable importance to them because of their inability to attract a sufficient number of workers for that job at the currently approved rate. We scheduled a meeting in a downtown hotel for 10:00 a.m., and the industrial relations directors of all the companies showed up on time. The only person missing was Neary, who was to make the presentation on behalf of the industry. We waited and waited; still no Neary. White-faced with rage, Starkweather called Neary's home, office, and several other places, but to no avail. About 11:30 a.m. Stuart sauntered in, obviously drunk. He was clearly in no condition to present his case, but when I suggested that perhaps we should recess the meeting for a few hours, he turned nasty, uttered a few unpleasantries for my benefit, and walked out. Starkweather apologized and assured me that he was "going to fire that son-of-a-bitch." I urged him not to do so, and at length he reluctantly agreed to give Stuart another chance. We rescheduled the meeting for the following day. Stuart showed up on time and apologized to me and to his associates for his behavior the day before. His masterful presentation of the companies' proposal led to its approval by the WLB. He and I never discussed that incident, but he knew that I had saved him from losing a valuable client. We remained good friends until his untimely death.

Because of the high incidence of SCAI cases on its docket, some of which required on-site inspections at the various plants, the panel made a number of trips to Los Angeles. On these occasions, Brayton and I would stay at the Biltmore Hotel in the downtown area. The hotel manager, Eddie Bernard, was especially generous to all War Labor Board personnel. He would install us in an elegant three-room suite and would send up a complimentary bottle of booze and a basket of fresh fruit. For this he charged us only $3.00 per day. At first, I remonstrated with him, saying that we would be quite content with just a regular bedroom, but he explained that we were really doing him a favor, because if we weren't in the suite, he would probably have to rent it to some marines from Camp Pendleton, who would wreck the place.

On each of our visits, the public and the employer members of the panel would be invited to dinner by representatives of the SCAI companies. The employee members were also invited but routinely declined. We usually were taken to some nightclub like Earl Carroll's Vanities, where the liquor was plentiful, the food mediocre, and the parade of seminude showgirls ultimately tiresome. I was never able to figure out whether our hosts chose these places under the misapprehension that we wanted to go there or because they preferred them. At any rate, I remember those evenings primarily as occasions when everyone got drunk.

As I noted earlier, the fraternization by public servants with only one side of an essentially adversarial relationship would not be condoned today. Why did we do it? Any retroactive rationalization of our behavior is, of course, suspect, but I can say that these social occasions had no effect on our decisions and that both sides knew it. That is why the panel's employee members never objected and why the industry people scrupulously avoided talking about any matters either pending or likely to come before us. Moreover, everyone knew that the companies, all of which operated under cost-plus contracts, simply wrote off this entertainment as business expenses. Like many of our WLB colleagues who, as members of commissions and panels set up for other industries, were similarly regaled, we cynically referred to these occasions as "getting drunk on cost-plus."

By the time I was ready to leave the National Airframe Panel, Eleanor and I had decided to make our home in Southern California. Knowing of our plans, some of my friends in the airframe industry urged me to become their full-time arbitrator. They assured me that I would get more work than I could handle and that I would rapidly become the reigning neutral expert in the field. I must admit that I was tempted by these roseate predictions, but I had enough sense to seek the advice of Taylor, who had succeeded Davis as chairman of the WLB in March 1945. Taylor speedily dissolved this fantasy in a cold shower of common sense. He predicted, quite accurately, that within a few years of the end of the war some of the SCAI companies, all of which were operating under cost-plan contracts with the federal government, would be in deep financial trouble or out of business. In those that remained, he warned, both management and unions would place much more emphasis on winning each dispute, regardless of its significance, than they had during wartime. He further cautioned me that as the pressures increased I would find myself worrying that an arbitration decision for one side or another might result in my being fired by the losing party, and that inevitably my concern about protecting my standard of living would have at least a subconscious influence on the way I decided cases. Besides, he reminded me, one did not decide unilaterally to become a full-time arbitrator; that happened only after a substantial testing period had made clear that one had earned the trust and acceptance of the parties. Finally, he asked me why I wanted to become a full-time arbitrator anyway. By then he knew me very well, and he urged me to embark on an academic career and to practice arbitration merely as an avocation. Doing so would inform my teaching and research without making me dependent upon the self-interested decisions of others for my livelihood.

That was the single most valuable piece of advice concerning my career that I have ever received. In the succeeding years I have often given the same admonition to young men and women who have consulted me about choosing arbitration as a career. I have not sought to steer all of them into the academic life, but I have warned them of the dangers of starting out their arbitration practice with the intention of engaging in it full time. Regrettably, this advice has been more often rejected than accepted for reasons I shall discuss more fully later in this narrative.

THE DEATH OF ROOSEVELT AND THE CHANGING OF THE GUARD

Shortly after 5:00 p.m. on the afternoon of 12 April 1945, as I was driving from my Washington office to our apartment in Fairfax, Virginia, I became aware that the volume of the radios in the cars around me (I did not have a radio) was louder than usual. When I arrived at our apartment, Eleanor came running out to meet me. Crying, she told me that President Roosevelt had died suddenly after suffering a massive cerebral hemorrhage. The shock of this news was overwhelming. Like the majority of Americans, especially those of my generation who had been attracted to Washington by Roosevelt's New Deal policies, I had come to regard him uncritically as one who knew what was best for our country and had played the decisive role in guiding the allies to the impending victory over their Axis enemies. Although Eleanor and I had been deeply disturbed by the physical deterioration he had suffered during his years in office, like so many others we had refused to contemplate what might happen when he died. That his death had occurred at this critical juncture of human history was almost too much to comprehend.

That evening, some of our friends in the Park Fairfax subdivision where we lived came over to our place. We discussed this traumatic event in hushed tones, as if there had been a death in our immediate family. We talked about Roosevelt's political career and about what he had meant to us and to our country. Even then we were unwilling and unable to turn our minds to the question of what the new Truman presidency would be like.

Harry Truman was virtually unknown to the vast majority of Americans. True, before reluctantly yielding to Roosevelt's insistence that he accept the vice presidency, Senator Truman had established a reputation for rectitude and persistence; as chairman of the Senate Special Committee to Investigate the National Defense Program (which came to be known as the Truman Committee), he had ferreted out waste, inefficiency, and corruption in the federal government's procurement programs. But relatively few people not directly involved in these programs paid particular attention to the committee's activities. On the other hand, we at the WLB tended to take a rather dim view of the new president. As a senator from Missouri, he had routinely urged, unsuccessfully, the appointment of local political hacks to various positions on the regional board in Kansas City. Moreover, he was a close friend of Senator Lewis B. Schwellenbach of Washington, who became secretary of labor in Truman's cabinet. Schwellenbach was resentful of the way the board had taken over some of the department's functions, particularly those formally exercised by the U.S. Conciliation Service, and he wanted to get rid of the board as soon as possible. We therefore viewed the advent of the Truman presidency with considerable trepidation.

After the German surrender on 7 May 1945, followed by that of Japan on 14 August 1945, a national debate erupted over the appropriate policy of reconversion from war to peace. The confusion within the administration was described by the veteran White House correspondent for the old *New York Herald Tribune* in the following passage:

> Secretary of Labor Schwellenbach feuded with William Davis [whom Truman had appointed director of the Office of Economic Stabilization] and Dr. George W. Taylor, chairman of the War Labor Board, over the board's role. Schwellenbach also feuded with Davis over whether industry could afford wage rises. Henry Wallace [secretary of commerce] advocated limited wage and price increases across the board. Schwellenbach wanted decisions case by case.
>
> Secretary of Agriculture [Clinton P.] Anderson feuded with [Chester] Bowles [director of the Office of Price Administration] over farm subsidies and elimination of price controls on food. Bowles, who was mindful of consumers, feuded with [Julius ("Cap")] Krug, [chairman of the War Production Board], who was sympathetic with business, over removal of productions controls…. Bowles, fearing inflation, wanted to go slow on easing controls. [John] Snyder [director of the Office of War Mobilization and Reconversion], eager to restore free enterprise and spur business activity, considered Bowles impractical and wanted to remove controls more rapidly.[34]

---

[34] Robert J. Donovan, *Conflict and Crisis: The Presidency of Harry S. Truman, 1945–1948* (New York: Norton, 1977), 111.

During this tumultuous interlude, Taylor sent Truman a number of memoranda proposing ways to achieve a gradual relaxation of wage and price controls and to develop mechanisms for the orderly resolution of labor-management disputes. The president ignored them all, a decision he was subsequently to regret.

WLB personnel were particularly outraged by Truman's cruel dismissal of Davis. On 18 September 1945, while Davis was attending a meeting in another part of the White House, Truman, without telling him, at the secret instigation of Schwellenbach, announced at a press conference that the Office of Economic Stabilization would be absorbed by Snyder's Office of War Mobilization and Reconversion. When asked by a reporter what would happen to Davis, Truman replied, "Well, he won't have anything to do. John Snyder will take his job."

FINAL DAYS AT THE WLB

My last job at the WLB was that of executive director, which I assumed in October 1945. This was the top staff position in the agency, in which I served until the board was officially terminated at the end of December. At that time there were something like 2,600 persons employed in Washington and in 12 regional offices throughout the country. My principal duties involved preparations for the orderly closing down of the board's offices in anticipation of its termination. Although my term as executive director was short, a few incidents took place during those few months that remain fixed in my memory.

Upon taking over my new, rather large office, I noticed that it contained two desks besides my own. One was for my secretary, whom I had inherited from my predecessor, Kheel. She was a mature woman, a southerner, with long experience in government service in Washington. The other desk was reserved for a clerk-stenographer, a position currently vacant. Shortly after I assumed my duties, my secretary told me that she needed help and that I should hire a clerk-stenographer. I told her to check with personnel, review the list of possible candidates, and select a Negro with the necessary qualifications if one was available. I shall never forget her reaction. She became very upset and started to cry. When I asked what was wrong, she said she could not possibly work in the same room with a black person. Realizing that I could not persuade her to change her mind, I simply told her that in my view it was time to start providing equal employment opportunities without regard to race, creed, or color, and that she would have to conform to that policy. As it turned out there were no qualified black applicants for the vacancy—hardly surprising in Washington at that time—but thereafter my relations with my secretary were rather frosty. I mention this incident only because it gave me an inkling of what a long, hard road lay ahead before the principles of equal opportunity in employment would be accepted by a majority of those who had spent their lives in a political and social system in which a consistent discrimination against blacks and other minorities was an accepted way of life. Indeed, it was not until passage of the Civil Rights Act of 1964, including Title VII, which made it an unlawful employment practice to discriminate against present or prospective employees on the grounds of race, color, religion, sex, or national origin, that the effort to uproot the prejudices embedded in our society since before the adoption of the Constitution really got underway on a massive scale.

Throughout the war, the FBI had routinely investigated WLB employees and applicants for employment and sent the board reports of its findings. These activities continued without abatement until the board was terminated. As executive director, I had to review the reports sent to us. They included no formal findings or recommendations and consisted of what the FBI termed "raw data." It was obvious that no piece of information, no matter how speculative, vindictive, inane, or obviously delusional, was excluded from these files; indeed, as presented by the FBI, each was given the same weight as all the others. Merely to give the flavor of these reports, I shall describe one of them. The person under investigation, a suspected Communist Party member or sympathizer, was reported by an unnamed "Confidential Informant X" as having been seen entering his apartment building carrying a large paper-wrapped package, which said informant had "reliable cause" (unstated) to believe contained copies of the *Daily Worker*, a Communist Party newspaper (the publication of which was entirely legal). I never found anything in the dozen or so of these reports I reviewed to justify taking any adverse action against the person being investigated. Nevertheless, we were asked in each instance to advise the FBI what action the board was taking or contemplating on the basis of the reports submitted. My responses were undiplomatic in the extreme, a fact that is probably duly noted in my own FBI dossier.

Another vivid recollection I have is of a hearing of a subcommittee of the Senate Appropriations Committee, before which Lloyd K. Garrison, who had succeeded Taylor as chairman of the WLB about the time I had become executive director, and I appeared. We had been summoned ostensibly to explain our request for sufficient additional funds to complete the termination of the board's activities. The subcommittee was chaired by "the powerful, disagreeable, bulbous-nosed, squinting" Kenneth D. McKellar of Tennessee.[35] The other two members were Allan J. Ellender of Louisiana and Charles W. ("Curly") Brooks of Illinois. It was obvious from the beginning that McKellar, 76 years old at the time, was already in his dotage. He fell asleep almost immediately, but would wake up from time to time to ask what the board was doing about the "snooping wage and hour inspectors" who had apparently cited some of his more important constituents for violations of the Fair Labor Standards Act (FLSA). Each time Garrison, an old hand at this sort of thing, would patiently and politely explain that the WLB had nothing to do with the FLSA, which was administered by a division of the Department of Labor. McKellar would then resume his slumber, only to reawaken periodically and repeat his inquiry.

Meanwhile, the hidden agenda of the hearing gradually became apparent. Under regulations promulgated by the economic stabilization director in 1942, illegal wage or salary adjustments were to be disregarded by government agencies in calculating costs or expenses for income tax or other purposes. Specifically, the amount to be disregarded was the total wage or salary paid or accrued and not merely an amount representing only the increase itself. If literally applied, these regulations could have resulted in severe losses to employers that violated the law, whereas the

---

[35] Donovan, *Conflict and Crisis*, 27.

affected employees would have suffered only the prospective loss of the amount of the illegal pay increase. The WLB had no stomach for the strict enforcement of these rather draconian penalties, and it eventually obtained permission to modify them to fit the circumstance of each case. Practically, this meant that employers who acted out of ignorance or in good faith were not punished but were required only to rescind the illegal pay increases. In the relatively few cases, however, in which an employer had deliberately violated the law and sought to conceal the violation, the board strictly enforced the regulations.[36]

Brooks had a few constituents who had been found guilty of willful violations of the wage stabilization laws and assessed the full penalty. In various ways he intimated that his vote to approve or disapprove the board's request for supplementary funds would depend on whether it was willing to reconsider the penalties assessed against these employers. I forget exactly how Garrison handled the situation, but I think he made some sort of concession. At any rate, the board's request was approved by the subcommittee, although McKellar continued to complain about the activities of the meddlesome wage and hour inspectors in Tennessee. This was my first, but by no means last, experience with the games played by legislative committees and with the ways individual senators and representatives pursued their own private agendas while ostensibly dealing with broader public concerns.

On the final day of the WLB's existence, I attended the meeting at which the few remaining board members disposed of the last few cases on the docket. With that task completed, someone produced a bottle of whiskey, which we drank from paper cups. Garrison, a submariner in World War I, sang "old sailors never die, they just fade way," after which the board members fell to reminiscing about their shared experiences during the previous four years. They also talked about the future and of how the board was likely to be remembered. It was perhaps not the ideal time for such speculations. The board was then at the nadir of its popularity: the

---

[36] A fuller description of the board's enforcement program is set forth in Benjamin Aaron, "Enforcement," in *Problems and Policies of Dispute Settlement and Wage Stabilization during World War II*, ed. W. Ellison Chalmers, Milton Derber, and William H. McPherson (Urbana: Institute of Labor and Industrial Relations, University of Illinois, 1951), 350–80.

war was over and the nation was anxious to return to "normalcy," whatever that might be, and employers and unions alike wanted to escape from the onerous wartime wage and price controls. President Truman had placed the board under the jurisdiction of the Department of Labor, and as previously noted, Secretary Schwellenbach had made no secret of his desire to liquidate it as soon as possible. Witte, by nature an optimist, suggested that although the board was currently unpopular, in later years the public might conclude that its performance could have been far worse. The situation reminded him, he said, of the time when, as a member of the Wisconsin Industrial Commission, he had received a letter from the irate widow of a man killed in an industrial accident. Her claim for the statutory death benefit had been snarled in red tape and remained unpaid. Venting her frustration, she wrote: "I have had so much aggravation trying to collect this claim that I sometimes almost wish I had my husband back again."

Now, over 50 years later, I think back on my service with the WLB, which covered virtually the entire period of its existence, with gratitude for the priceless training I received in my chosen field of work and for the enduring friendships I formed with a few board members and some of my staff colleagues. I also recall leaving the board with a profound sense of obligation, tinged with a feeling of guilt. I had spent the war years working at a job that I loved and that met every personal expectation. I had been promoted rapidly from the bottom to the top while being rewarded with generous periodic salary increases, and my prospects for future employment were excellent. At the same time, many of my friends had had to put their careers on hold while they served in the armed forces. A few of them had lost their lives in combat. I have never been able entirely to overcome the feeling that my comparative good fortune was undeserved and had to be paid for in some way. Accordingly, in recognition of that debt, I accepted just about every request subsequently made of me to undertake various assignments for the federal, state, and local governments, sometimes at the cost of considerable sacrifice on the part of my family.

CHAPTER 2

MISSION TO JAPAN, 1946

In the waning days of 1945, I received an inquiry from the U.S. War Department: would I agree to join a Labor Advisory Mission specifically requested by General Douglas MacArthur to devise new labor legislation for Japan? This opportunity was a tempting one; I was eager for a new assignment after four years with the War Labor Board (WLB).[1] Moreover, I would be given the assimilated rank of a full colonel in the military government, with equivalent pay and privileges. As attractive as this invitation was, I was troubled by the knowledge that my acceptance would be hard on Eleanor. She was then well advanced in her first pregnancy, and the baby was expected sometime in April 1946. We had already decided to move to California as soon as the WLB ceased operations, and my sister, Ruth, and her husband, Oscar Auerbach, who had two small children of their own, had generously offered to let us stay with them until we could find a place to live. But if I went to Japan, our house hunting could begin only after my return. Although Ruth and Oscar declared that this would present no problem, Eleanor and I were both reluctant to impose on them for such a long time. Also, Eleanor obviously would have greatly preferred that I be with her in the final months of her pregnancy. Nevertheless, knowing how much I wanted to go to Japan, she generously agreed that I should take advantage of this exceptional opportunity, insisting only that I return before the birth of our baby. (I made that a condition of my acceptance and the War Department agreed.) This was but one of many occasions during our married life when Eleanor unselfishly subordinated her own preferences

---

[1] To refresh my faded recollections of this period, as well as to place some of the events I describe in their historical contexts, I have made use of accounts in several books dealing in whole or in part with the occupation of Japan: Herbert P. Bix, *Hirohito and the Making of Modern Japan* (New York: HarperCollins, 2000); John W. Dower, *Embracing Defeat: Japan in the Wake of World War II* (New York: Norton, 1999); Theodore Cohen, *Remaking Japan: The American Occupation as New Deal* (New York: Free Press, 1987); and Joe Moore, *Japanese Workers and the Struggle for Power, 1945–1947* (Madison: University of Wisconsin Press, 1983).

to mine—actions that I deeply appreciated but which, to my discredit, I rarely reciprocated.

In February 1946, most of the members of the mission left from Hamilton Field near San Francisco on the long flight to Japan. We traveled in a DC-4 operated by the Army Transport Command—a slow, unpressurized airplane that had a cruising ceiling of no more than 10,000 feet. We were joined on this flight by a group of young women who were going to Japan to work in various clerical jobs for the U.S. military government and who were greeted rapturously by the enlisted men at each one of our stops en route. The trip took several days, with stops at Honolulu, Johnson Island, Kwajalein, and Guam.

I no longer remember very much about the 10 other members of our mission. They included manpower specialists, economists (including my friend, William H. McPherson, from the University of Illinois), a comparative law scholar, and a journalist, Helen Mears, the only woman in the group. I think most of us approached our assignment with what J. K. Galbraith has termed, in a related context, "an arrogant certainty of high purpose," as well as with considerable naïveté. Mears was the exception: she reminded us of our ignorance of Japanese culture and institutions and warned that we were likely to do more harm than good by trying to impose American legislative models on the Japanese people. This did not make her very popular with her colleagues, but in retrospect I believe she, of all of us, had the clearest understanding of the situation.

Prior to our departure, we were favored with a long and solemn lecture on the dreadful consequences that might ensue if we were to drink or eat anything outside the army mess. In particular, we were warned against milk (all Japanese cows were tubercular and the milk was unpasteurized) and raw fish (the source of any number of fearsome parasites, which would find their way into the intestinal tract and wreak frightful havoc). On the evening of our arrival in Tokyo, our group was invited by the staff of the *Oriental Economist*, a scholarly journal, to a dinner in our honor that included milk and raw fish. We thus had to choose between disregarding the official warnings and offending our hosts. We decided to eat and drink whatever was put before us and fortunately experienced no ill effects. Thus encouraged, I continued to eat Japanese food whenever given the opportunity. (Ironically, the only illness I suffered during my time in Japan resulted from a compulsory flu shot administered by the army, which put me flat on my back for 48 hours.)

Among my recollections of Japan, none is more vivid than the shock I experienced at the first sight of the physical devastation of two of its principal cities: Tokyo and Yokohama. (I passed up the opportunity to fly over Hiroshima because I had grave reservations about the morality of dropping the first atomic bomb, and I could not bring myself to witness the horrible destruction it had produced.) In Tokyo, the precision bombing attacks by the U.S. Air Force had spared the emperor's palace and its environs, as well as a few buildings that later served as the headquarters of MacArthur, who held the position of Supreme Commander of the Allied Powers (SCAP), but a few heavy fire-bombing raids, exacerbated by high winds, had destroyed most of the rest of the city. In Yokohama, nothing was left standing; this large industrial seaport had been leveled to the ground as far as the eye could see. It seemed to me, when I first beheld it, more like a vast wasteland than the site of a once populous city.

As a civilian holding the assimilated rank of colonel, I was billeted in what had once been the guesthouse of a large mansion on the outskirts of Tokyo, which was owned by Baron Iwasaki, president of the Mitsubishi Corporation. The mansion had been virtually destroyed by bombs, but the guesthouse, reserved for field grade officers and their civilian equivalents, was intact, as was the adjoining formal English garden. Our living conditions were elegant. Although the cuisine was strictly American, we were waited upon by young women in *kimono*, the traditional Japanese dress, under the direction of a dignified butler who had once been the major domo at the Japanese embassy in London and who spoke perfect English. In addition, each of us was assigned a houseboy, who sat outside one's room all night long, in case he might be needed. I found this arrangement embarrassing, to say the least, but was told that I could do nothing about it. I used to get up quite early in the morning and go to the bathroom to shower and shave. By the time I returned, my bed would be made and the room tidied. I quickly discovered, moreover, that it was impossible to throw anything away. We sent our laundry out, and the shirts were returned neatly folded and pinned, with cardboard inserts. Every time I put the cardboard and pins in the wastebasket, they reappeared on the top of my dresser, neatly lined up in a row. When I commented on this to our butler, he explained that Japanese household staff members were acutely sensitive to the risk of being accused of theft.

There were no more than a dozen residents in our billet, and most of them were army officers. One naval officer and two or three civilians completed the group. The military men had all recently spent several years fighting the Japanese in the Pacific. They obviously had a low opinion of the civilians in their midst, but they mostly treated us politely, if not warmly. We dined together in the evening, but usually went our separate ways after dinner. Every morning, an army staff car would pick up my fellow civilians and me and drive us to the military government's Labor Division offices in the Forestry Building. The Daiichi Building next door housed the headquarters of SCAP. Every day, precisely at 12:00 noon, MacArthur would leave the building and invariably would be greeted by a crowd of cheering Japanese as he made his way to his car.

MacArthur had asked for our mission in a series of urgent cables to the War Department, so we not unreasonably assumed that we would meet with him at least once during our stay in Japan. That expectation proved to be an illusion. The general kept himself aloof from the rest of the world. No telephone was ever installed in his top floor office in the Daiichi Building; access to him was only through his military secretaries, and only General Courtney Whitney, the chief of his government section, was able to see him without an appointment. Thus, during our entire stay in Japan, MacArthur never acknowledged our presence. Our only contact with his headquarters consisted of a brief meeting with Major General William F. Marquat, chief of the economic and scientific section. Marquat was affectionately remembered by his close associates not only as a kind and compassionate man of unassailable common sense but also as a fast learner. Unhappily, none of these qualities was apparent in our brief session with him, which proved to be an utter disaster. However commendable Marquat's character and abilities, his ignorance of unions and labor matters in general was monumental. He began the meeting by asking a few questions about what we were doing. One of the projects mentioned by a member of our mission was establishment of a program of occupational training. Marquat responded, "Occupational training! Does this mean we're going to have the CIO over here?" The session concluded soon after, and we all left with grave doubts that our efforts were likely to influence SCAP policy.

My particular assignment was to develop legislation to reform the salary structure and retirement system for employees in the civil service. I can no longer remember the details, but I do recall that the existing arrangements struck me as bizarre. Like wages and salaries in the private sector, those in government employment had nothing to do with efficiency, but were determined by such factors as age, seniority, number of children, and, in the case of public servants, social status. Once a government employee reached retirement age, he (there were no women in these positions) and his wife were given one-way train tickets to their native village. It was presumed that their children would then assume the responsibility for taking care of them.

Another member of our group and I proposed, among other things, to rationalize this system by eliminating salary differentials based on social status, introducing efficiency of performance as at least one criterion in salary determination, and establishing minimum levels of retirement compensation. We negotiated with midlevel representations of the Japanese government, whose tactics can best be described as nonresisting resistance. The simple task of arranging meetings invariably resulted in Sisyphean frustration. Telephone service in Tokyo was a sometime thing, and even if contact was established, there was so much static that it was very difficult for the speakers to hear each other. Moreover, our ignorance of Japanese and our counterparts' limited ability to speak or understand English led to constant misunderstandings about the time, place, and agenda of meetings. In addition, because of the Japanese government's inefficient and discriminatory food distribution policies, all citizens, with the exception of the elite classes, had been reduced to a bare subsistence level, or lower, and even government employees spent a number of hours every day simply searching for food in the countryside. All of these circumstances were exploited by our Japanese counterparts to avoid reaching agreements on anything, while maintaining a façade of cooperation. Whether any of our specific proposals was ever adopted during the occupation, even in modified form, I do not know.

Nevertheless, I was not too upset by these tactics. I had come to Japan with no hatred of the Japanese people. During my teens I had attended Lowell High School in San Francisco, where many of my classmates and friends were Chinese and Japanese. I joined a Pacific Relations Club whose idealistic goal was to promote racial understanding and harmony. Even in the grim days following the attack on Pearl Harbor, I could not summon up the intensity of rage against Japan that I felt toward Germany. Rightly or wrongly, I believed that whereas most Germans openly or tacitly supported Hitler and his policies, the average Japanese citizen had little knowledge of or interest in the war aims of the country's militaristic leaders. My experiences in Japan in 1946 tended to confirm these views. It seemed to me that the Japanese bureaucrats with whom we negotiated were simply trying to survive under the opposing pressures of their conquerors and their own government superiors, who were resisting the proposed changes by every possible means. On the other hand, the attitude of the elite group of Japanese lawyers and other professionals with whom I occasionally came in contact was distinctly different. In the negotiations I observed, I was particularly impressed by the arrogance of the Japanese spokesmen, most of whom were lawyers who had gone to the best American universities and spoke perfect English, and by their barely concealed contempt for their American counterparts. One could imagine them asking themselves, "How did we ever lose the war against people such as these?"

The work of the Labor Advisory Mission was obviously affected by the activities of the resurgent Japanese labor unions. The Japanese labor movement was not born after the war, it was reborn. By 1936, seven percent of the nonagricultural labor force had been organized, and in the elections of 1937, the union-sponsored Social Masses Party had received one million votes and elected 37 out of 466 representatives in the lower house of the Diet. Even before the American occupation forces entered Japan, the remnants of the Japan Federation of Labor had begun a new organization campaign.

American policy on Japanese unions and collective bargaining was formulated in the United States in 1943-44. It was embodied in the "Trade Unions and Collective Bargaining Guide," which urged the establishment of a free, democratic labor movement in Japan, the encouragement of union organization, the permission of strikes (except those affecting occupation force security or objectives), and the complete exclusion of the police from labor affairs. The primary emphasis was on business trade unionism on the American model. Finally approved in late December 1944, the guide was sent to SCAP as official U.S. policy.

On 3 October 1945, SCAP Directive 93 removed restrictions on political, civil, and religious liberties, under which Communists, among others, had been imprisoned for almost two decades. This group included a number of labor activists, who immediately began a serious rivalry with democratic-minded labor leaders for control of the resurgent labor movement. Organization activities were well underway when our mission arrived in Tokyo. Given MacArthur's public endorsement of collective bargaining, Japanese employers were quick to respond, but some did so in a way that demonstrated that they were not entirely clear about the concept. When some members of our group visited small business establishments, they were often told by an apologetic proprietor that he did not yet have a union, but that one would be in place in a few weeks. Some unions took an extremely militant approach to collective bargaining. This militancy typically erupted during contract negotiations, which were sometimes held on a stage and witnessed by an audience of employees. Union spokesmen berated the employer or his representatives, often resorting to physical violence. In one case I recall, the union negotiators beat an employer so badly that he had to be hospitalized. His tormentors showed up at his bedside in the hospital and forced him to sign a contract, which he later repudiated.

I witnessed one profoundly important aspect of the contest for control between the Communist unions and their more moderate rivals: the labor tactic known as "production control" (*seisan kanri*)—worker seizure and operation of an enterprise—although at the time I was not fully aware of all its implications. Production control made sense from both the workers' and the public's viewpoint. Because people were starving and economic activity was at a very low level, it would have been useless for workers to engage in the conventional form of strike. Production control permitted continuation of the output of badly needed goods and services, while ensuring that workers lost no wages during the "strike." Initially, workers viewed production control as an effective dispute tactic, not as a revolutionary act. Participants were careful to stay within the limits of the law by keeping the locked-out management informed and by adhering to the existing production plan, often allowing company officials to continue making policy and operating decisions, subject to workers' review. The strikers did not challenge the fundamental legitimacy of managerial prerogatives based on the rights of private property, and they kept accurate records and accounts in anticipation of returning the enterprise to employer control after settlement of the dispute. Yet despite this apparent recognition of traditional management rights, production control, even in its earliest manifestation, called into question the most fundamental aspect of the capitalistic system: private property. It pointed toward a rapid erosion of the rights of management in hiring and firing, in supervision of the work force, and in making policy decisions on selection of goods to be produced and allocation of the firm's resources.

Resort to production control grew rapidly in the months I was in Japan. Despite urgent efforts by the Japanese government and leading industrialists to outlaw the tactic, MacArthur withheld his support, insisting that all questions involving the legality of production control should be resolved by the courts. Frustrated in their efforts to prohibit production control by law, the Japanese "Old Guard" sought to confine its scope and duration by denying the participants access to funds, supplies, and markets, hoping in this way to bring the workers to terms. But these efforts proved counterproductive and succeeded only in radicalizing the workers and leading to even more extensive demands against their employers. Indeed, in some cases the new objective, openly adopted by some communist unions, was to dispossess completely the capitalist owners and to institute permanent workers' control. Moreover, in the face of incontrovertible evidence of widespread corruption and incompetence in the government's handling of food distribution, large masses of Japanese citizens began forcibly to take over the control and disposition of food supplies. These events culminated in May 1946, when MacArthur finally issued a statement, in his typically orotund style, warning the Japanese people "that the growing tendency towards mass violence and physical processes of intimidation, under organized leadership, present a grave menace to the future development of Japan" and condemning "excesses by disorderly minorities." This marked the beginning of the end of what seemed to me to have been, at least in its earlier phases, an ingenious and socially useful union technique. The infrequent instances of mass violence and intimidation, the number of which were greatly exaggerated by the Japanese authorities and by SCAP, were actually provoked by the tactics resorted to by the employers, who apparently knew which buttons to push to produce the desired reaction by MacArthur. The history of the rise and fall of production control illustrated the inherent restraints on emergent, grassroots democratic initiatives in Japan by the American policy of imposing "democracy from above": when ordinary citizens embraced the new democratic ideals too enthusiastically, SCAP exposed the mailed fist within the velvet glove.

Perhaps the most significant development that began during my time in Japan was the adoption of a new national charter to replace the Meiji Constitution of 1890. I shall provide only a brief sketch of the principal events preceding the introduction of the American draft of the new charter and then add a few personal impressions of contemporary events, of which I was an interested but uninvolved observer.

In their Potsdam Declaration of 26 July 1945, the United States, Great Britain, and the Soviet Union announced the terms of surrender for Japan. This, together with some directives elaborating postsurrender policy prepared by the Joint Chiefs of Staff and sent to MacArthur in August 1945 established the principal objectives of the subsequent occupation. Among the conditions set forth in the Potsdam Declaration were that military forces would be "completely disarmed"; that the government would be required to "remove all obstacles to the revival and strengthening of democratic tendencies among the Japanese people" and to establish freedom of speech, religion, and thought, as well as respect for human rights; and that the occupation would be terminated when "there had been established in accordance with the freely expressed will of the Japanese people a peacefully inclined and responsible government." The other policy documents went further, making clear that disarmament and demilitarization were not merely to be "complete" but also "permanent." They also specified that the purging of individuals who advocated militarism or militant nationalism would be broader than might have been inferred from the Potsdam Declaration, extending even into the "economic field." Thus, the Washington policymakers called for dissolution of the large industrial and banking combinations that had exercised control of a great part of Japan's trade and industry.

Crucial to MacArthur's occupation strategy was his conviction that the concept of the emperor as the symbolic leader of the nation must be preserved, although in substantially altered form. No longer was the emperor to be regarded as a divine presence to whom all Japanese owed an absolute and unquestioning allegiance; instead, he was to become a constitutional monarch, on the English model, who reigned but did not rule, being subject to the will of the people as expressed by their freely elected representatives. The assumption underlying this strategy was that, in the wake of Japan's military defeat, the emperor alone retained sufficient prestige to unite the people behind the new policies imposed by the occupation.

In retrospect, one wonders why protecting the status of the emperor was deemed so important. From the fatal day—15 August 1945—when Emperor Hirohito addressed the nation by radio and, without once using the words "surrender" or "defeat," told his subjects that the war had not "turn[ed] in Japan's favor" and enjoined them to "endure the unendurable and bear the unbearable," his godlike image began to fade. There were increasing demands that he abdicate, that the entire imperial system be scrapped and replaced by a constitutional republic, and even that the emperor be tried as a war criminal—surely not an irrational proposal in light of the overwhelming evidence that Hirohito bore a major responsibility for beginning and continuing the war against the United States and its allies. Whether rightly or wrongly, however, MacArthur never retreated from or modified his insistence that the emperor should be absolved of all war guilt and should retain his position as head of state. Historians of the period have suggested that the real reason for MacArthur's obduracy in insisting that the imperial system be retained was his fear that if it were scrapped, the alternative adopted would be a leftist model not only obnoxious to him but also a threat to the objectives and the security of the occupation.

Another policy of SCAP was that the wide-ranging constitutional reforms it demanded must appear to be voluntarily adopted by the Japanese government. There were obvious reasons for this insistence. For one thing, the military government, like all occupying forces, was largely dependent upon the existing bureaucracy to carry out its directives. This process would be greatly facilitated if the directives came from the Japanese government itself. Moreover, SCAP's objective of imposing democracy from above would be more likely to succeed if it operated behind the scenes and made it appear that key decisions were being made by the Japanese authorities.

Accordingly, by October 1945, SCAP had privately and publicly conveyed to the Japanese government and people that constitutional reform was expected, but in the ensuing months it made no obtrusive efforts to interfere while awaiting the Japanese response. The public reaction came quickly. Both private groups and political parties drafted and publicized constitutional proposals, several of which were quite liberal. These developments, duly reported in the newspapers, were closely monitored by SCAP. The public discussion was in full swing when I arrived in Japan, and I followed it in the English-language Japanese newspaper. Also, I observed many open discussions at street corners and other public places. Although I could not understand what was being said, two aspects of these discussions impressed me particularly. One was their free-for-all character, reminding me of those I had witnessed in London's Hyde Park. The other was the active participation by newly enfranchised women.

The government's reaction to SCAP's prodding was, by contrast, slow and almost completely unresponsive. A cabinet committee had been established and its proposals were merely cosmetic in content; this was so obvious that they were greeted with public derision. Realizing that the government could not be relied upon to come up with credible proposals to revise the constitution along the lines laid down in the Potsdam Declaration, SCAP decided to convene its own, secret "constitutional convention." This enterprise, entrusted to the government section on 4 February 1946, was to be based on three principles that MacArthur had declared essential. Briefly summarized, they were (1) that the emperor remain as head of state with duties and powers exercised in accordance with the constitution and the basic will of the people; (2) that war as a sovereign right of the nation be abolished and that no Japanese armed forces ever be authorized or granted any rights of belligerency, even for preserving the country's security; and (3) that the feudal system in Japan be abolished and that the rights of peerage and patents of nobility be severely curtailed. Incredibly, the gigantic task of turning these sparse guidelines into a model constitution was to be accomplished in exactly one week. The apparent reason for this haste was the imminent formation of a multination Far Eastern Commission (FEC), which might issue its own policy decisions on constitutional reform. Moreover, MacArthur's directives on that issue would be subject to veto by any member of the four-nation Allied Council of Japan, which was scheduled to commence operations in Tokyo shortly after the FEC came into being. The prospect of his unlimited authority to make policy decisions on constitutional reform coming to a speedy conclusion thus convinced MacArthur of the need to conclude the drafting of a new constitution in one week's time. Yet another reason for urgency was SCAP's concern over the popularity of proposals being discussed publicly that would have altered the structure of the government, and especially the status of the emperor and the nobility, more radically than those contained in its own draft.

The constitution drafted by the government section within the prescribed time limit was an eclectic document that established a parliamentary government with a British-style cabinet system wrapped in an imperial dynasty, but it was also inspired by the political idealism of American democracy. It was by no means a replica of the U.S. Constitution; indeed, some of its provisions dealing with civil rights, for example, were more liberal. On 13 February 1946, it was handed to the Japanese prime minister and his cabinet with the clear indication that the draft, or something very close to it, must be adopted by the Japanese government. After desperately trying for a month to escape the inevitable, the government capitulated. On 6 March, a detailed outline of the document was made public, together with a written statement by the emperor giving his unreserved approval. To maintain the fiction that the proposed new constitution was the creation of the Japanese government, SCAP forbade U.S. government officials from making any reference to its own involvement, and the media were not allowed to speculate openly about the origins of the document. Public reaction was quite favorable on the whole, and I think most people must have assumed from the nature of the proposed reforms that it had been approved, if not actually written, by MacArthur's headquarters. I know that my American colleagues and I felt sure that the draft under discussion was a SCAP creation. In any case, open public debate over the contents of the new constitution ended rather abruptly, and on 3 May 1947 it finally went into effect, with a few modifications successfully bargained for by the Japanese government.

Having no knowledge of the background events, except for the Potsdam Declaration, or of the pressures on SCAP described above, I thought at the time that the American intervention in the constitutional reform process was heavy-handed and premature, if not totally unnecessary. With the information I later acquired, however, I am less ready to criticize SCAP's role. It is extremely doubtful that the left-liberal forces could have attained a majority in the Diet, and given the fanatical resistance to fundamental change put up by the "Old Guard," it is likely that, without resolute American intervention, the constitution would have remained essentially unchanged. As it turned out, the new one proved to be surprisingly durable: it has never been amended.

My official duties as a member of the Labor Advisory Mission did not usually bring me in contact with American military personnel. One such incident occurred, however, when I decided to telephone Eleanor. Inquiring about how to do this, I was told I would have to obtain the permission of the army chaplain. Somewhat mystified, I reported to the chaplain's office. A friendly middle-aged man, he greeted me courteously and invited me to sit down. After an exchange of pleasantries, he asked me the purpose of my visit. I explained that Eleanor was in the final trimester of her pregnancy, that I had been away from her for over a month, and that I just wanted to speak to her directly. The following colloquy, as best I can remember, then took place:

> Chaplain: I see. Your wife is worried about you and this is adversely affecting her health?
>
> Me: Oh, no. She seems to be doing fine.
>
> Chaplain: But *you* are worried about *her*, and this is distracting your attention and impairing your own job performance?
>
> Me [the light suddenly dawning]: Well, now that you mention it, I have been worried and I'm sure that once I have talked to her, I'll be greatly relieved and can do my work much better.
>
> Chaplain [with obvious relief]: Oh well, then, I'll give you permission to make the call.

Shortly thereafter, I was allowed to make my three-minute overseas call to Eleanor. Although our conversation was painfully brief, it meant a great deal to both of us and was, I concluded, its own justification for a few white lies.

The clearest recollections I have of my few months in Japan relate to my contacts with ordinary Japanese citizens, which, with a few exceptions, inspired feelings of pity for their terrible plight and admiration for their courage and stoicism in facing up to it. On the first day I was driven to work, our car passed a large area covered with metal scraps of varying sizes—all that remained after the bombing. One old man was beginning to sort them out. I remarked to my fellow passengers about the hopelessness of his efforts; his situation reminded me, I said, of fairy stories in which the evil witch gave the young prince an impossible physical task that had to be completed by nightfall, under pain of death. Only in this case the old man had no chance of succor by a supernatural being. I should have remembered that he also had no deadline for the completion of his labors. In the days that followed we watched his progress. Within a few weeks he had cleared the area and sorted the metal pieces into piles. Then, in the next few weeks, using a primitive compactor powered only by his own physical efforts, he reduced all of the metal rubble into a number of oblong blocks, which he piled neatly along the roadway. To me, this achievement was a perfect example of the indomitable spirit of the Japanese people in the face of military defeat and terrible destruction.

There were few nighttime diversions in Tokyo, or at least few that I knew about. There was, however, a nightly high-stakes poker game at the Daiichi Hotel, which I joined on only one occasion. The participants were mostly junior army officers who had accumulated large amounts of pay during the Pacific campaign and who thought nothing of betting hundreds of dollars on a single pot. Luckily for me, I emerged a heavy winner that night. I spent my winnings on a pair of beautiful sake pourers and small cups to match. The problem was how to send them home safely. I sought out our butler and asked if he could find me a box of suitable size and sturdiness, and he promised to see what he could do. Returning to the guesthouse that evening, I found my sake pourers and cups in a wooden box that had obviously been made to order and filled with some soft material to protect the contents. I asked the butler how he had obtained the box. He explained that he had found a man to make it, and that the man was waiting to see me. The box maker turned out to be a little man well past middle age with the face and demeanor of one who had suffered greatly. The butler explained that his wife and three children had been killed in the B-29 firebombing raids, which had also destroyed his house and all his possessions. Through the butler, I thanked the man for his kindness and praised the quality of his work. At the same time, I was trying to figure out how I could reward him for his services. Military regulations strictly forbade the giving of money or food to Japanese nationals; even if I had offered them, the man would have refused to accept either of these forms of payment. Having no alternative, I told the butler to ask him to look around my room and to tell me if he saw anything he fancied. Almost immediately, the man pointed to a beat-up brown fedora—a relic from my college days that I had occasionally worn during my winters in Washington—that Eleanor had insisted I take with me to Japan. After some conversation with him, the butler explained that one of the man's prize possessions destroyed in the bombing raids was a fine fedora, and that if I could bring myself to part with mine, he would feel richly rewarded. When I agreed, he took the hat, smiling for the first time, and after many bows, departed. In due course the box arrived safely in California, and the sake pourers are on display in our living room to this day. My pleasure in them is somehow diminished, however, whenever I think of the personal tragedy of the box maker.

Soon after my arrival in Tokyo, I made the acquaintance of Joe Goldstein, a young second lieutenant in the army's translation and interpretation section. The son of family friends in Los Angeles, he had graduated from the Japanese language school at the University of Michigan and spoke and read Japanese fluently. We hit it off well from the start and agreed to spend our weekends exploring the region outside Tokyo. By virtue of my assimilated rank, I was usually able to get a jeep out of the motor pool, and Joe served as driver and guide. Our first trip, which we subsequently repeated several times, was to a hot springs resort in the mountain town of Tona Sawa. We started late on a Friday afternoon and soon picked up a Japanese student who was thumbing a ride in our direction. Joe asked him if we were on the right road to Tona Sawa, and the student answered, incorrectly as it turned out, "Hai!" (yes). (This was my first experience with the Japanese reluctance to answer a question by saying No, which is considered rude.) We soon became hopelessly lost, although Joe felt that we were not too far from our destination. Eventually, the jeep got stuck in a rice paddy, and Joe left to summon help. The student and I were left together with virtually no means of communication: I spoke no Japanese and he had only a few words of

English. The evening was clear but quite cold. We got out of the jeep and walked along the ridges of the rice paddy to keep warm. Suddenly, he said to me, "You know 'Old Blocka Joe?'" I nodded, and he said, "We sing." So in the middle of the rice paddy, under a full moon, we linked arms and sang "Old Black Joe" at the tops of our voices. (I never learned how he came to know the words of the song.)

Before long, young white Joe returned, accompanied by a truck and driver from a nearby army base. The driver pulled us out of the rice paddy and we resumed our journey. After dropping off our passenger, we continued on to Tona Sawa, arriving close to midnight. By this time, Joe and I were very cold. Once in our modest room, we got out of our clothes and donned freshly laundered *kimono* (mine reached barely to my knees, to the considerable amusement of the young ladies who brought us tea and towels). Then, after fortifying ourselves with some whiskey I had brought from the United States, we went down to the hot springs—an underground grotto hollowed out of stone in which there was a good-sized pool of very hot water. Both the pool and the surrounding area covered by flat stones were enveloped in heavy clouds of steam, so one could barely discern the figures of other bathers. This was a great relief to me, because as I stood in the buff on the side of the pool, washing myself before entering it in accordance with the Japanese custom, a small group of naked Japanese ladies walked by. Used as they were to mixed bathing, they took no notice of me or the other man there and quietly occupied the far end of the pool. The hot water, once I became accustomed to it, was wonderfully soothing, but also enervating. When I got out, therefore, I doused myself with ice-cold water from a pipe in the wall. This act produced exclamations of amazement from the other men present, one of whom startled me by saying in English, "Wow, you must come from Minnesota!"

During this and subsequent visits, we exchanged our army rations for soup, fish, rice, and vegetables provided by our hosts. Although this was contrary to strict instructions issued by the military government, we could see no harm in it: we found our GI rations barely edible, but our hosts readily accepted them in exchange for the food they provided.

Unfortunately, because they had no soap with which to wash the dishes, everything they gave us tasted of fish, but we soon became used to that.

On several of our visits we encountered groups of Japanese businessmen. Typically, they would sit in the pool in a large circle and pass around bottles of sake. Their tolerance for alcohol was apparently quite low, because they all seemed to become tipsy very quickly and would then start giggling and singing. On one occasion, a member of the group appeared to be making a toast before taking a swig from the sake bottle. I asked Joe what he was saying, and Joe replied, "Loosely translated, it means 'Drink and be merry, because tomorrow we may be purged.'" This was a reference to SCAP's forced dissolution of the giant conglomerates owned by the business oligopolies known as *zaibatsu*.

I guess the greatest culture shock I experienced during my time in Japan also occurred at the Tona Sawa hot springs. While there one weekend, Joe and I encountered the Japanese government official with whom I had been negotiating about the reform of civil service pay and retirement policies. He was accompanied by a male friend and two young ladies. The government man (whose name I have forgotten, but whom I shall call "Kanju") greeted me warmly and rather obsequiously. Given the nature of our professional relationship, I was at first reluctant to do anything but exchange greetings, but he refrained from discussing business matters and just seemed to be trying to be friendly. At length, after a brief conference with his male companion, he absolutely floored me by offering to loan the two ladies to Joe and me for the night. We both declined—I with embarrassment, and Joe, who though younger than I was more sophisticated in these matters, coolly and with some amusement. He later assured me that this was a not uncommon practice among Japanese males and was regarded by them merely as a friendly gesture.

The following week, Kanju invited Joe and me to have dinner at his house. My initial reaction was to decline, but my reluctance gave way to curiosity and the realization that this would probably be my only opportunity to visit a Japanese home. Accordingly, Joe and I showed up at the appointed time and were greeted at the door by Kanju and his wife. The latter was dressed more like a kitchen helper than the lady of the house.

Instead of *kimono* she wore baggy trousers and a blouse, and she had what looked like a sweatband around her head. She did not speak, but kneeled down and touched her head to the floor; then she disappeared into the kitchen. Our host then brought us into his western-style parlor and introduced us to the other guests, all of whom were Japanese. I experienced another shock when I recognized one of them as the lady friend we had met in Tona Sawa and realized that she was acting as hostess for the evening. With obvious pride, Kanju showed us his bar and the bottles of champagne and whiskey on display. Apparently, these were intended only for visual enjoyment, because he offered us nothing to drink.

The dining room was Japanese-style: we all sat cross-legged around a low table. As was customary in that austere period, the room was very cold; the only warmth was provided by a few pieces of charcoal in a brazier by the table. The other male guests wore sweaters under their shirts. Lacking even an undershirt, I had some difficulty keeping my teeth from chattering, although the warm sake we drank with our dinner helped a little. Dinner was served by Kanju's wife and two kitchen helpers. She did not join us at the table, which was presided over graciously by the lady friend. Altogether, it was a strange and, for me, very uncomfortable evening. All the conversation was in Japanese, except for the occasional comment addressed to me by Kanju in his fractured English. That part of it translated for me by Joe seemed to consist of polite and rather stilted compliments and questions not designed to elicit any meaningful replies. Also, I was not used to sitting cross-legged for such a long time, and when the dinner ended I had considerable difficulty getting to my feet. Finally, it was time to leave. Once again, Kanju summoned his wife from the kitchen, and once again she kneeled, touched her head to the floor, and then silently disappeared.

Afterward, when I expressed to Joe my incredulity and disgust at the way Kanju had humiliated his wife by inviting his mistress to usurp her rightful place as hostess, he assured me that appearances could be deceiving and that the wife probably had a much higher status and a more secure position in the marriage than I imagined. Others to whom I described the dinner at Kanju's house made similar comments, but nothing anyone said reconciled me to what I regarded as an example of the intolerable abasement of Japanese women.

Shortly before I left Japan, I had the opportunity to observe a hearing before a panel of a tripartite labor commission created by the new trade union law that had been adopted at MacArthur's insistence. The panel's two public members were Izutarō Suehiro, former dean of Tokyo Imperial University Law School and the most eminent legal scholar in Japan, and Iwao Ayusawa, a former official of the International Labor Office in Geneva, who had a Ph.D. in labor economics from Columbia University and was the editor of the *Oriental Economist*. The issue before the panel was whether deck officers in the merchant marine had the right to organize and, if so, whether they were free to join the union representing merchant seamen. Spokesmen for the deck officers argued that the answer to both questions should be "Yes"; the shipowners' representations, declaring that the deck officers were an integral part of management, argued that the answer to both questions should be "No."

The eclectic approach to the problem taken by the panel was entirely new to me and had a lasting effect on my own thinking. The panel's judgment was given orally at the end of the hearing in separate statements by Suehiro and Ayusawa. Together, they comprised a comprehensive disquisition on comparative labor law in which the methods of handling this problem in a number of foreign countries, including the United States, were described. The solution adopted seemed eminently reasonable: the deck officers would be allowed to organize, but they would not be permitted to join the union representing the seamen whom they supervised. What impressed me most about the panel's approach was its willingness to inform itself about relevant policies of other countries before coming to its own independent decision. This was in contrast to the typical disinclination of American legislators, administrators, and courts to pay any attention to the policies and practices of other labor law systems. Some years later, when I began my own study of comparative labor law, I had occasion more than once to recall that hearing in Japan.

As previously arranged, my tour of duty with the Labor Advisory Mission ended before its work was completed. My departure was timed to bring me home just before the expected birth of our first child, Judith. Space on ATC flights to the United States was at a premium, but I reserved a place well in advance on one leaving Tokyo early in the morning. The night before I left, my colleagues had a party to send me off in style. It lasted into the early hours and we all got very drunk. Later that morning, after about two hours' sleep and suffering from a severe hangover, I showed up at the airport, only to learn that, by some mistake, my name had been left off the passenger list. I vented my rage against the hapless sergeant responsible for the error and informed him dramatically that because of his stupidity I would not be present when my child was born. Duly contrite, he promised to make amends and in fact managed to get me on a flight later that day.

The trip home was quite different from the one that took me to Japan. Instead of being a "plush job," that is, having commercial seats, the DC-4 had only "bucket seats," consisting of canvas spread over a metal frame along both sides of the aircraft. Except for me, the passengers were returning soldiers. The seats were extremely uncomfortable, and at night we all stretched out on the deck. It was a new experience for me to be wakened from an uneasy sleep by a GI's boot in my face. The upside was that we completed the trip to San Francisco in the record time (for then) of 55 hours. On the last leg of the flight, from Honolulu to San Francisco, the captain saw me sitting disconsolately in my bucket seat (I had elected to try sleeping sitting up rather than joining the pile of bodies on the deck) and invited me to take the copilot's seat while the latter was on his rest break. The roomy leather seat seemed to me the quintessence of comfort, and the black, velvety night sky was illuminated by the light of countless stars. The radio was tuned to dance music from the mainland. The captain let me stay with him in the cockpit until just before our landing at Hamilton Field, and I shall be forever grateful for those few hours of heavenly comfort at the end of my journey home. As it turned out, Judith decided not to be born until about a month after her scheduled appearance. In the meantime I had accepted a U.S. Labor Department appointment on a fact-finding board in a labor dispute. The hearings were conducted in San Francisco, and I did not return to Los

Angeles until a week after Judith's birth. Thank goodness the sergeant that I had so angrily bawled out never learned that his error was really quite inconsequential after all.

In the years since my trip to Japan, I have often recalled the experience with mixed emotions. With the benefit of hindsight, I have concluded that the mission of which I was a member must be judged to have been a failure. Knowing little of Japanese history and culture, we sought to impose changes in their governmental practices that reflected the American experience rather than an informed analysis of the situation in Japan. Few changes we introduced stood the test of time; the rest were either abandoned or substantially modified by the Japanese government as soon as its sovereignty was restored. The best that could be said of our efforts was that we probably did no lasting harm.

From a purely personal standpoint, my brief sojourn in Japan was richly rewarding. I witnessed the ways in which the Japanese people, responding to their emperor's admonition, "endured the unendurable and bore the unbearable." My observations enforced my previously held favorable views of the Japanese people, as distinguished from their political leaders. I also acquired some familiarity with Japanese customs, including some not mentioned in this account.

Some 56 years later, in November 1996, I returned to Japan at the invitation of Professor Kazuo Sugeno, University of Tokyo, to give the inaugural lecture in the special series by the Japan International Labor Law Forum (JILL) inviting "distinguished scholars to Japan and [sic] exchange opinions on labour and employment relations from a comparative viewpoint."[2] On this occasion, my wife and I were treated with the legendary courtesy of the Japanese. Our hosts, Professor Sugeno, his colleague on the University Tokyo law faculty, Professor Takashi Araki, and the late Professor Emeritus Kichiemon Ishikawa, also of the University of Tokyo and former chairman of the Japanese Central Labour Commission, and their wives, spared no efforts in making our visit a memorable one. Professor Ishikawa and his

---

[2] My lecture, "Industrial Relations and Labor Law in the United States: A Comparative View," was published in *Japan International Labor Law Forum Special Series No. 1* (1997).

wife insisted on accompanying Eleanor and me on a brief visit to the beautiful city of Kyoto.

The utterly devastated city of Tokyo that I remembered from my visit in 1946 had been replaced by a modern, crowded metropolis. Professor Sugeno was able, with the help of his son, an architect, to locate the site of the billet in which I was housed in 1946, which had been replaced by a management conference center. In fact, almost all vestiges of the Tokyo I remembered had vanished. But my memories of the country and warmth of the Japanese people were renewed by the kindness and generosity of our hosts in 1996; I shall remember them always with gratitude and affection.

CHAPTER 3

THE NATIONAL WAGE STABILIZATION BOARD, 1951–1952

The National Wage Stabilization Board (WSB) was in some respects similar to its World War II predecessor, the National War Labor Board (WLB). Both were established in response to wartime emergencies, and both were administered by a tripartite board. In each case the board was established primarily to stabilize wages but inevitably became involved, despite strong objections by employers, in the settlement of disputes over nonwage issues as well. The circumstances existing at the time the two agencies were established, however, were quite different. At the start of American participation in World War II the nation was just emerging from a prolonged depression and mass unemployment. Employers were predominantly anti-union, and labor organizations were comparatively weak. Still fighting for their existence, unions were willing to trade off wage increases for protection of institutional security and a few relatively low-cost fringe benefits. By contrast, when the Korean War began in 1950, unions had become much stronger, more responsive than formerly to their members' desire for wage increases, and less willing to trade such increases for the union shop and the check-off.

There were additional important differences between conditions at the outset of the two wars. From the start of the earlier conflict it was apparent that the nation was locked in a titanic struggle in which its total resources must be engaged. Sacrifices required by the war effort were supported by an overwhelming majority of the population. In the Korean War, on the other hand, the United States found itself involved in a dubious combat of limited scope but uncertain duration. Severe shortages of raw materials and finished goods, shifts in the structure of production, and manpower scarcities were much less extensive than in World War II. No great sacrifices were demanded of the civilian population; unions, for example, were not even asked to give a no-strike pledge, which was a key ingredient in the stabilization policies of World War II. The government's wage stabilization policies during the Korean War, therefore, lacked the urgency and comparative inflexibility of those promulgated in the earlier conflict.

Finally, the WSB got off to a much rockier start than had its World War II counterpart. North Korea invaded South Korean in June 1950, and the United States began its "military action" in support of South Korea almost immediately thereafter; yet it was not until mid-October that President Truman established the Economic Stabilization Agency (ESA) and appointed the nine-member, tripartite WSB to serve in an advisory capacity to the ESA administrator in planning and developing wage and salary controls. The chairman of the WSB was Cyrus Ching, who took temporary leave from his position of director of the Federal Mediation and Conciliation Service (FMCS) to head the new agency. Like Ching, the other two public members of the WSB were veterans of the WLB: John T. Dunlop, an economics professor from Harvard, had played a prominent role in the wage stabilization division of that board in Washington, and Clark Kerr, also an economics professor from the University of California, Berkeley, had been vice-chairman of the Seattle Regional Board. Each had achieved eminence in the field of labor economics and industrial relations, making important contributions to the literature. Both had also accumulated considerable practical experience in the field. Dunlop, in particular, had acquired an encyclopedic knowledge of the philosophy, structure, and internal practices of labor unions, especially the building trades.

It took the WSB some time to reach agreement on an appropriate wage stabilization policy for the current emergency. Industry and organized labor argued publicly about the relative importance of wage and price controls and their relation to each other. The board's first attempt to establish a policy ended in disaster. On 16 February 1951, it issued General Regulation No. 6, imposing a 10 percent limit on general wage increases. Drafted by Dunlop and Kerr, it was supported only by the public and employer members of the board. Outraged union representatives denounced their lack of input in wage-price stabilization policies and charged that industry was being allowed to dominate policy-determination for the entire defense effort. Shortly thereafter, following the resignation of labor members from the WSB, organized labor withdrew its representatives from positions in the six other defense agencies.

The furor resulting from the promulgation of General Regulation No. 6, which was approved on 27 February by Eric Johnston, administrator of the ESA, and the resignation of the labor members left the six remaining members of the WSB unable to develop wage stabilization policy any further. For the next six weeks, the board simply coasted, leaving the staff to process applications for the allowable 10 percent wage increase and to answer as best it could questions about how the regulation was to be applied.

Meanwhile, President Truman considered how to reconstruct the WSB and, in particular, whom to appoint to succeed Ching, who was scheduled to return to his position as director of FMCS. The person recommended by most of those he consulted was George W. Taylor. This presented a problem for Truman. As previously related, Taylor had succeeded William H. Davis as chairman of the WLB and was serving in that capacity when the war in Europe ended and planning began for a return to a peacetime economy. Truman had ignored all of Taylor's suggestions on that subject, and relations between the two men were anything but cordial. Now, in the crisis following the breakup of the WSB, Truman still could not bring himself to approach Taylor directly about returning to Washington as head of the reconstituted agency. Eventually, however, the president swallowed his pride, telephoned Taylor at his home in Philadelphia, and invited him to come to the White House for a personal meeting. Taylor accepted and ultimately agreed to serve as chairman of the new agency for a limited period on a part-time basis. Whatever bitterness remained between the two men was soon dissipated and replaced by mutual respect and admiration.

On April 1951, President Truman issued an executive order reconstituting the WSB with authority to handle disputes either voluntarily submitted by employers and unions or referred to it by the president. The new agency was tripartite and was enlarged to 18 members. In addition to Taylor, the public members were Kerr; William M. Hepburn, dean of the Emory University Law School; Nathan P. Feinsinger, professor of law, University of Wisconsin; Dunlop; and Frederick H. Bullen, executive secretary of the New York State Board of Mediation. On 3 May, the WSB resumed its deliberations, despite the active campaign spearheaded by the National Association of Manufacturers and the United States Chamber of Commerce to divest the board of its dispute-settlement functions. Their efforts led to hearings on this issue before subcommittees of the House Committee on Education and Labor and the Senate Committee on Labor and Public Welfare, but in the end the WSB's jurisdiction over disputes remained unchanged.

It was at this point that my service with the WSB began. In June 1951, while attending a labor education conference in Santa Cruz, California, I received a telephone call from Taylor. He asked if I would accept a presidential appointment as a public member of the WSB, effective immediately, to replace Kerr, who had recently resigned. His inquiry not only was totally unexpected but also came at an inconvenient time. In 1946, Eleanor and I had bought a house in Santa Monica, California, and I had joined the staff of the Institute of Industrial Relations at UCLA as a research associate. I was just beginning to feel comfortable in my new career. Recently, I had been appointed impartial umpire under the collective bargaining agreement between the B.F. Goodrich Rubber Company and United Rubber Workers, which covered some nine plants throughout the country, and had built up a growing practice as an *ad hoc* arbitrator.[1] I was also teaching courses in labor law under the auspices of the UCLA Department of Economics. Our two daughters, Judith and Louise, both born since our move to California at the end of 1945, were aged five and three, respectively. Nevertheless, without even consulting Eleanor about such an important decision, I told Taylor then and there that I would accept the appointment, which he assured

---

[1] An impartial umpire is appointed by the parties to hear all grievances arising under their collective bargaining agreements for a fixed term, which in some instances may be renewed for many years. An *ad hoc* arbitrator is appointed to hear only one grievance or a group of grievances. He or she may subsequently be recalled by the parties to serve again on the same basis, but more often the appointment is repeated, if at all, only at irregular intervals over time.

me the president was ready to make. Why did I act so irresponsibly? As mentioned earlier in this narrative, I had left the WLB after four exciting and rewarding years with a profound sense of obligation, a feeling that my good fortune, compared with the lot of some of my friends who had spent the same period in the armed forces, was undeserved and had to be paid for in some way. Now, Taylor was offering me the chance to honor that obligation. Joining the WSB would entail a family move to Washington and renting our newly decorated house on short notice at a time when we were just beginning to be really comfortable with our situation. This was, as Eleanor glumly commented when I broke the news to her, a payback with a vengeance. Nevertheless, despite her unhappiness with my decision, she subordinated her wishes to mine, as she had done in the past and would occasionally do again in the future. So when President Truman announced my appointment on 5 July, I hurried off to Washington, leaving Eleanor to cope with all the burdensome details of making our house ready for the two young bachelors who rented it (a disastrous choice of tenants forced by our need to rent the house quickly) and getting herself and our children to Washington. By the time they arrived, I had rented a roomy, two-story house in the northwest section of Washington.

Presidential appointment as a public member of the WSB brought certain perquisites, including a large office, my own secretary, and occasional invitations to White House receptions. There were other, less gratifying signs of my new status. At age 36, I was the youngest board member, but I was made to feel much older one morning when, as I mounted the steps outside the Social Security Building, two at a time as usual, I was suddenly passed by a young WSB staff member, who rushed to hold the door open for me and said "After you, sir." That incident depressed me for a week.

The main feature of the White House receptions was the long receiving line and the ritual handshakes with Harry and Bess Truman. As we drew close to them, a military aide would ask us our names and then repeat them in a loud voice. Mrs. Truman had developed an admirable technique for preventing her hand from being crushed while at the same time keeping the line moving. She would grab about three fingers of one's outstretched hand in an iron clasp, at the same time moving one forcefully to her right. My recollection is that she seldom smiled. One had the impression of a woman determined to do her duty but not enjoying it. Who could blame her? The president managed a smile and frequently a few words of greeting, and he gave the appearance of enjoying the occasion, but he, too, must have been bored to distraction. After attending several of these presidential levees, I concluded that the First Couple deserved to be excused from such dreary formalities.

On the whole, the body of work handled by the WSB was less interesting and varied than what I had been involved with at the War Labor Board. What I chiefly recall are the relatively few dispute cases referred to us either by the president or by the parties. The first of these was a wage dispute in the copper industry involving a number of different copper companies and the AFL and the CIO, as well as the independent Mine, Mill and Smelter Workers (MMSW) union. A strike was called by the MMSW, which had been expelled from the CIO in 1950 because of its alleged domination by the Communist Party. Following the practice adopted by the WLB in World War II, the WSB summoned all the parties to Washington for a hearing on 29 August 1951. In off-the-record discussions prior to that hearing that are not reflected in the transcripts of their executive meetings, members of the WSB debated whether to allow MMSW representatives to speak at the hearing. By this time, the so-called Cold War between the United States and the Soviet Union, their World War II alliance now hopelessly fractured, was well under way. The federal government's loyalty-security program, perhaps the most tragic mistake of the Truman administration, had been promulgated, and outright persecution of persons merely suspected of being Communists or Communist sympathizers was growing. Some employer and labor members of the WSB argued that no MMSW representatives should be allowed to address the board because they would use the occasion to spout their Communist propaganda and turn the proceedings into a publicity stunt. My contrary position, supported by my fellow public members, was that suppressing the voice of the MMSW at a hearing designed to elicit the views of all the parties to the dispute would be an obvious and insupportable denial of free speech and due process. During our debate one of the labor members waved his finger at me and said "Aaron, you and your do-gooder ACLU [American Civil Liberties Union] buddies are a bunch of Communist dupes." Fortunately, his view did not prevail, and a MMSW vice-president, Orville Larson, was allowed to speak at the hearing. He proved to be the most articulate among the various labor and industry representatives who addressed us. His statement was brief, unemotional, and well organized, his manner calm and dignified. But he refused to call off the strike until a satisfactory settlement of the wage dispute was effected. Next day, the WSB unanimously decided, again following WLB precedents, that it would not process the case while the work stoppage was in progress. Accordingly, it returned the dispute to the White House, and the president invoked the national-emergency provisions of the Taft-Hartley Act. The day following the public hearing, I couldn't resist asking the labor and employer members who had opposed allowing any MMSW representative to speak what they thought of Orville Larson's performance. The response of the chief employer spokesperson was, "Did you ever see a more perfect example of iron Communist discipline?"

During our time in Washington, Eleanor and I became friends with Arthur Goldberg, then the general counsel of the United Steelworkers, and his wife, Dorothy, an accomplished artist. On one occasion we were invited to their house for a Passover dinner, or seder. The other guests were mostly non-Jewish officials of the steel and automobile workers unions. It was a seder unlike any I had ever attended: we skipped the usual ritual and prayers and concluded with a rousing chorus of labor songs. Everyone had a wonderful time. On another occasion, we went with the Goldbergs to a place in Maryland for dinner and a dance recital by two former prima ballerinas of the Ballet Russe de Monte Carlo. Arthur drove and I sat next to him. A nonstop talker and a spectacularly bad driver, Arthur accentuated every point in his continuous discourse by pressing down on the brake pedal. The result was a ride of constant starts and stops that brought Eleanor and me to the verge of car sickness. (Dorothy, apparently accustomed to her husband's tempest-tossed style of driving, seemed unaffected by the experience.) In later years, especially after his appointment by President Kennedy, first as secretary of labor and then as an associate justice of the United States Supreme Court, Arthur acquired a not entirely undeserved reputation for egotism and pomposity, but to me he was always a generous and warm-hearted friend.

Because I was for some time the only public member of the WSB to establish a Washington residence—the others all returned to their respective homes elsewhere each weekend—I was more or less in charge of the store during their periodic absences. Thus, I was summoned to the White House on a few occasions when minor crises arose in which WSB input was required. Invariably, these involved strikes threatening to halt production of materiel destined for our armed forces in Korea. Most of those attending these sessions were representatives from the Department of Defense and the army, navy and air force, who routinely predicted that unless the strikes were halted immediately, our armed forces in the field, deprived of essential weapons, would face imminent danger of being overwhelmed by the enemy. It always turned out that the struck manufacturer was the sole producer of the necessary materiel. I kept asking why the award of contracts had not been diversified, and several times I pointed out that in some instances the company involved had a long history of bad labor relations frequently punctuated by work stoppages. The military men always reacted with irritation to these observations without deigning to reply, nor did they hesitate to urge approval of an impermissible wage increase in order to end a strike. These meetings were presided over by John R. Steelman, who liked to be referred to as "the" assistant to the president. The former director of the United States Conciliation Service (a division of the Department of Labor that had been abolished by the Taft-Hartley Act and replaced by the FMCS, an independent agency), Steelman was a big, hearty, genial man who radiated bonhomie and who was adept at putting together often ambiguous compromises that seemed to quiet, if not satisfy, contending parties. He loved to smoke expensive cigars—the kind that came enclosed in aluminum tubes—but always carried an additional supply of 15-cent White Owls, which he occasionally offered to all those present. After a few of these meetings I developed a deep distrust of the dire predictions of the military, as well as the conviction that in disposing of matters of this nature the policies of the WSB did not weigh heavily in the balance.

In September 1951, Taylor resigned from the WSB to resume his academic duties at the Wharton School. Feinsinger, the vice-chairman, was appointed to succeed him, and he in turn was succeeded as vice-chairman by Bullen. Feinsinger and Bullen made the arrangements for a farewell dinner given in Taylor's honor by his fellow WSB members. A date was set, but inquiries about arrangements elicited only the vaguest replies. The day before the dinner, which was to be held at the Statler Hotel at 16th and K Streets, we were told that we must be there at 6:00 p.m. sharp. When I got home that evening I expressed my irritation to Eleanor, asking rhetorically, whoever heard of a celebratory occasion like this starting so early? She replied that there could be only one explanation: the president was coming sometime during the evening. That was absurd, I said. The president was much too preoccupied with the war and a number of pressing domestic concerns to take time off for such a relatively minor event.

As usual, Eleanor was right. Cocktails were served promptly at 6:00, followed shortly thereafter by dinner. Those present besides Taylor and his wife, Edith, were the 18 members of the WSB and a few of their wives. The meal was served rather rapidly and somewhat inexpertly by (as we learned later) members of the secret service detail assigned to the president. (Security had been greatly enhanced since the attempted assassination of the president by Puerto Rican nationalists in November 1950.) All cutlery was speedily removed from the table as soon as we finished. Then Feinsinger rose and began a somewhat rambling tribute to Taylor, during which he constantly turned to glance at the doorway to our private banquet room. Suddenly, the door opened and in walked the president and a small entourage, including Steelman and his wife, David Stowe, who was another presidential assistant and a good friend of the public members, and a few others. Truman was introduced to all those present and seemed in the best of spirits. If he was worn down by the cares of his office, he gave no sign of it. One of the employer members, an avowed "Dixiecrat" strongly opposed to Truman and his policies, played the clown and, draping a napkin over his arm, asked the president if he could serve him a drink. Truman obligingly ordered a bourbon and water.

A few minutes later, the president rose to speak. No one was prepared for what followed. Truman's inadequacies as a public speaker had been widely noted and often derided. His delivery was customarily monotonous, his gestures wooden. But on this occasion he spoke in an entirely different manner. After paying a warm and obviously sincere tribute to Taylor, praising his self-sacrifice in accepting the chairmanship of the WSB and the skill with which he had performed his duties, the president began to speak with unanticipated eloquence about the need to prevent a third world war and to ensure a lasting peace among nations. The effect of his remarks on the small audience was almost palpable. There was a brief silence when he concluded, then a burst of applause that was anything but perfunctory. At this point Mrs. Steelman approached Eleanor and asked if she could play "For he's a jolly good fellow." Surprised, Eleanor nevertheless said she would and proceeded to do so on the small upright piano in the room. Everyone joined in the singing, after which, to Eleanor's barely concealed amusement, Mrs. Steelman, her eyes of full of tears, came up to her and gushed, "Oh, that was beautiful!"

Members of the board then began asking Truman for his autograph. Eleanor nudged me and told me to get autographs for our two daughters. I was disinclined to do so, but Edith Taylor supported my wife and told me that Truman really enjoyed giving autographs. Accordingly, I approached the president and told him I had two daughters who were still too young to appreciate the honor but would cherish his autograph when they grew old enough to comprehend its significance. While signing the two slips of paper I handed him, Truman said, "This isn't good enough for your little girls. You know," he continued with almost childlike enthusiasm, "at the White House, we have these little stiff cards with white bows on them. That's what we need for little girls." He then called over Stowe and told him to get the names of our daughters and remind him the next day to sign the cards. Dave gave me an exasperated look but made a note of our daughters' names.

As we drove home from the party, Eleanor asked me if I intended to call Stowe the next day to remind him of what the president had said. I told her to forget it and reminded her that there was a war going on and that the president was far too busy to be bothered with such petty matters. Once again I was proven wrong. The next afternoon a messenger from the White House delivered to my office a neat package that enclosed two white cards with bows, which were inscribed to Judith and to Louise and signed "Sincerely, Harry S Truman." When I called Stowe to thank him, he exploded over the telephone, saying, "You son of a bitch, you almost got me in a lot of trouble! It's lucky I was wearing the same suit I had on last night, with the names of your daughters on a piece of paper in my pocket, because the first thing the boss said to me this morning was, 'Have you got the names of those two little girls?'"

Truman's loyalty to his associates and appointees was legendary. A few years after he had left the presidency, he gave a speech to the Town Hall of Los Angeles, a civic organization. At a small reception preceding the speech he was introduced to members of the organization's board of governors by its executive secretary and my good friend, William B. Miller. When he came to me, Miller said to Truman, "Of course you remember Mr. Aaron, one of your appointees to the Wage Stabilization Board." Both Bill and I knew that Truman probably had not the faintest recollection of who I was, but with this prompting, he grabbed my hand and said loudly, "Of course I remember Mr. Aaron. He made outstanding contributions to the work of the board and was one of my best appointees." Although I knew this was but the automatic response of a seasoned politician, I couldn't help feeling pleased about it.

With Taylor's departure, Feinsinger assumed the chairmanship of the WSB. He brought to his task exceptional skills: a keen, analytical but flexible intellect and enormous powers of concentration, together with considerable experience as an arbitrator and a well-deserved reputation as perhaps the most successful mediator of difficult labor disputes in the country. His was quite a different temperament from Taylor's. He possessed a tremendous, unquenchable vitality, undiminished by a near-fatal automobile accident in 1950 that left him partially crippled and in constant pain for the rest of his life. Characteristically, Feinsinger treated this piece of bad luck almost as an irrelevancy. A born fighter and optimist, he never gave up, never wasted time in self-pity, and continued to look for solutions to problems that his associates found hopelessly intractable. As chairman of the WSB, he presided impartially over a tripartite board of prima donnas, commanding their respect and affection, if not always their agreement. Each Friday marked a time of organized chaos, as he prepared to return, if only for a few hours, to his beloved Aspen, Colorado. He regularly booked numerous alternative reservations on various airlines, canceling or reconfirming a trip up to the last minute. Like Antaeus, he needed to renew his energy by contact with his particular piece of ground. After each visit to Aspen, he returned refreshed and ready for new battles.

Another feature of Friday afternoons at the WSB, particularly in the later stages of Feinsinger's chairmanship, was the gathering in his office of the public members. A bottle of booze was passed around while we listened to Feinsinger, who was keeping a diary, dictate the week's events to his secretary. Stomping up and back and across the room with his cane, he described private meetings with various functionaries, revealing what was said by whom, and also including salty comments about the persons involved. We listened in appreciative silence to these monologues, which were interrupted only by his constant changes of airline reservations. He invariably delayed his departure for the airport until the last possible minute.

Feinsinger inspired a fierce loyalty and deep affection in those of us privileged to work with him. Outwardly brusque, he concealed a genuine concern for the welfare of his friends under a layer of humorous badinage, yet on many occasions he showed a sympathetic sensitivity to the emotional needs of others. When the big crunch came in the steel case of 1952, he was a constant source of strength and support for all of us.

One of the very few events in the WSB's brief and turbulent history that is still remembered is its biggest case: the dispute between the United Steelworkers of America and various steel and iron ore companies. The last complete collective bargaining agreement between the parties had been negotiated in 1947 and was due to expire on 31 December 1951. It was widely assumed that in negotiations over the new agreements the union would attempt, among other things, to force wage concessions in excess of what WSB regulations permitted. Thus, for example, on 12 December 1951, Joseph A. Beirne, president of the Communications Workers of America (CWA) and a labor member of the WSB, declared that his and other unions were counting on the Steelworkers to break "the rigid WSB wage increase formula."[2] Even before bargaining commenced, industry spokesmen and President Truman's political opponents in and out of Congress were voicing dark speculations about a possible deal being hatched between Truman and Philip Murray, the Steelworkers president, which would break the existing governmental wage regulations in return for organized labor's support in the presidential election of 1952.

The print media, in particular, faithfully reported these rumors, thus building expectations that the steel case would present the ultimate test of the WSB's willingness and determination to administer the wage stabilization rules in a fair and consistent manner, despite outside pressure from organized labor and the White House to help out the Steelworkers. Some newspapers made up their minds well before the steel negotiations had even begun. In a speech to an industry conference on 7 December 1951, Feinsinger had indicated that the WSB might consider developing regulations governing wage adjustments for increased productivity. Indeed, he appointed a WSB committee, with me as chairman, to look into the matter. The committee sponsored an all-day meeting, open to the public, to discuss the topic. As I recall, we spent the day listening to a lengthy presentation on how productivity is measured by Ewan Clague, the widely respected commissioner of labor statistics. I don't think we scheduled any further meetings, and we issued no report to the board as a whole. This was due in large part to the opposition by the industry members to the

---

[2] BNA, *Daily Labor Report*, no. 241 (12 Dec. 1951): A-1–A-3.

development of any productivity policy that might lead to further permissible wage increases. Shortly after the all-day meeting, I was approached by a young Washington reporter of the *Wall Street Journal*, whose beat included the WSB. I remember only his first name, Steve. We had had a number of talks on previous occasions, and he had impressed me as bright and conscientious. Steve asked me whether there was any truth in the rumor that the establishment of the WSB productivity committee was a planned step in the direction of establishing a way to give the Steelworkers a greater wage increase than was allowable under existing regulations. I assured him that the rumor was without foundation and reminded him that the parties had not yet even begun serious bargaining and that no one knew in what posture the case would reach the WSB, if it ever did. He took notes of my response, thanked me, and left. The next day I read a piece in the *Journal*, under Steve's byline, repeating the rumor and omitting any reference to my denial. When I saw him shortly thereafter, I informed Steve that in view of his unprofessional behavior, I would grant him no further interviews. He apologized profusely and explained that he had written the story featuring my denial, but that his supervisors in New York had rewritten it for their own political purposes. He seemed genuinely upset, and I believed him. My faith in his honesty and integrity was subsequently vindicated. Some months later, Congressman Ralph W. Gwinn, a Republican from New York, attacked the WSB public members by name in a telegram to President Truman, accusing them of having accepted fees from CIO and AFL sources and of being beholden to unions. The Gwinn wire was quoted in a full-page advertisement, signed by the Committee for Constitutional Government, that appeared in a number of metropolitan newspapers. Referring to me, he stated: "Benjamin Aaron, another public member, appointed to work solely in the interest of the public, is beholden to union bosses for part of his income." Steve came to my office to get my response. I explained that Gwinn must have referred to my income as a labor arbitrator. I informed him that when I became a public member, I ceased all activity as an arbitrator, including my service as impartial umpire for Goodrich and the Rubber Workers union. I also pointed out that any payments for arbitration services paid to me by unions were matched in exactly equal amounts by employers. Finally, I assured him that the facts were essentially the same for the other public members. Steve said he knew all that already, but had been told by his New York editors to ask me about the story. A few days later he returned and handed me a teletype from the *Journal's* offices in New York. It read, "Looks like the public members have clean shirts on this one but keep digging. We're sure you'll find some dirt sooner or later." Steve said, "Now, maybe you'll believe my version of the earlier story on productivity." He went on to express his disgust with the *Journal's* efforts to slant various stories to support its editorial opinions and said he was thinking of resigning. I don't know whether he ever did. I do know that these two experiences left me with a deep distaste for *The Wall Street Journal* that I have never completely lost.

Throughout December 1951, bargaining negotiations in the steel industry continued. The Steelworkers submitted some 22 demands ranging from a general wage increase to such issues as union security, contracting out, seniority, local working conditions, and a guaranteed annual wage. No real progress was made, and the union threatened to call an industry-wide strike on 31 December. On 22 December, President Truman referred the dispute to the WSB and urged both parties to continue production while the board considered the case. The steel companies immediately assented to the president's request; the union agreed only to postpone the strike for 45 days, but later extended that time for an additional 28 days. The WSB first met with the parties on 7 January 1952. A special tripartite panel, which was appointed by the board to hear the presentations of the parties and to prepare an outline of the issues and a summary of the parties' positions, held hearings in Washington and New York in January and February. It submitted its report on 13 March. Feinsinger again asked the parties to continue work and production during the period of the board's consideration of the issues and the preparation of its own report and recommendations; both sides agreed to do so.

The WSB issued its report and recommendations, together with the opinion of the public members, on 20 March 1952. Separate opinions by the industry and the labor members were released the next day. Few people now remember or care about what the board recommended, and the events that followed are of interest only to a limited group of historians, constitutional lawyers, law professors, and specialists in labor-management relations. I shall limit my account to the process by which the board arrived at its majority recommendations and a brief discussion of two of the most controversial issues: the general wage increase and union security.

In retrospect, the week between the submission of the tripartite steel panel's report and the issuance of the WSB's report and recommendations to the president and the parties had a phantasmagoric quality. For one thing, the public members, at least, got almost no sleep during that time. Days were divided between board executive sessions to discuss and vote on the issues and numerous private discussions with both the labor and industry members of the board and various spokesmen for the steel companies and the Steelworkers. Nights were devoted to discussions among the public members and further informal meetings with the parties and the industry and labor members, during which we tried to build some consensus on the issues. Relations between the industry and labor members of the board were strained almost to the breaking point, and the public members, striving to effect some kind of compromise between the parties on the most contentions issues, were having no success. The tension was so great that Bullen and I sought relief several times during that week by sneaking off for a half-hour at noon to an empty office and playing the children's game "Battleship."

Faced with the obdurate refusal of the parties to compromise on any of the pay issues, as well as with the unwillingness of the industry members to offer meaningful counterproposals to the union's demands, the public members became increasingly frustrated. At one point, I remember thinking that it might be better to advise the president of our failure to achieve consensus and throw the whole case back to the parties for further collective bargaining. To do so, however, would have meant shirking our responsibility to make recommendations to the president and to the parties. Moreover, Feinsinger, ever the optimist, continued his negotiations with the industry and labor members and the parties themselves, never conceding that we could fail.

On the issue of wages, the Steelworkers were asking for a general increase of 18.5 cents per hour. The steel companies rejected this demand, taking the position that the best solution was no wage increase and no price increase. They made no other counterproposal. There was a sharp disagreement between the labor and industry members of the board over how much of an increase was allowable under existing regulations. The public members disagreed with the estimates of both the other groups, but were much closer to those of the labor members. Opinion among the public members was not at first unanimous. Indeed, as late as the evening of 19 March, we had reached no consensus on the amount of a wage increase to recommend. At that time we were considering a proposal of a general wage increase of 12.5 cents per hour, plus two additional increases of 2.5 cents, effective at successive six-month intervals. Goldberg, the Steelworkers' general counsel, was present during this discussion and, like everyone else, was showing the strain of the protracted negotiations. He warned that Murray had become so angry and frustrated that he was on the verge of calling a strike to compel acceptance of the union's demands. At this point, Dunlop made a suggestion that the proposed 17.5-cent increase be the only general rate adjustment for a period of 18 months, instead of the usual 12 months. Goldberg seized upon this proposal at once, saying that he accepted it on behalf of the union. When Feinsinger inquired whether Murray himself would concur, Goldberg said, "Leave that to me; I'll take care of Phil."

The union security issue was equally contentious but far less complicated. The union wanted the union shop; the steel companies, supported by the WSB industry members, insisted on maintaining the status quo (maintenance of membership and the check-off) and contended that regardless of the merits, a recommendation by a government board in favor of the union shop would be contrary to public policy. The public members believed that the union shop, or some variation thereof, would be an appropriate recommendation in this case. Under this form of union security, an employer and a duly authorized union may agree that employees represented by the union must join the union as a condition of continued employment. In the Taft-Hartley Act of 1947 and amendments to the Railway Labor Act in 1951, Congress had specifically legalized such agreements. The U.S. Supreme Court subsequently put its own gloss on the statutory language by ruling in 1963 that required membership in a union meant only an obligation to tender regular union dues and fees. The WSB's findings of fact included the following:

The record in this case indicates that of a total of 2,200 contracts with this Union covering production and maintenance units in basic steel and fabricating plants, union shop provisions have been agreed to by employers in 994 (45 per cent). It also appears that of 66 companies operating basic steel plants with which the Union had contracts in October 1951, 27 had agreed to either the full union shop or some modification thereof beyond maintenance of membership. Furthermore, while most of the major steel producing companies have not agreed to the union shop in their contracts with this Union, several of them have included such clauses in agreements with other labor organizations.[3]

But, as is true today, the federal law only permitted the union shop; it did not compel it, and therein lay the rub. As early as 18 February 1952, a former industry member of the WSB, G. Maynard Smith, had publicly challenged the board's "moral or legal right" to take jurisdiction of the union shop issue in the steel case. One week later, a Republican congressman from Illinois, Leo Allan, submitted a resolution calling on the House Committee on Labor and Education to investigate whether the WSB was exceeding its authority and contravening national public policies in dealing with nonwage issues, especially the union shop. In addition, anti-union groups around the country organized a letter-writing campaign to the individual public members of the WSB, opposing, among other things, the union shop. Between 22 December 1951 and 20 March 1952, I personally received 1,350 of these communications, which I saved and later analyzed in a journal article.[4] What they revealed was widespread confusion and ignorance about union security

---

[3] *Opinion of the Public Members, in the Matter of Basic Steel Industry and United Steelworkers of America (C10)*, case No. D-18-C.

[4] "Public Opinion and the Union Shop," *The Southern Economic Journal* 20 (1953): 74–80.

in general and the union shop in particular, as indicated in the following representative comments:

1. It is "unconstitutional," "un-American," "undemocratic," "fascistic," "communistic," "socialistic," "pure slavery," and "illegal" (violates anti-trust laws).
2. It is a closed shop under another name.
3. It is necessary only when an employer is trying to cheat his employees.
4. It will result in "the type of labor-socialist movement which destroyed the British empire and enslaved the British worker."
5. It has fostered the growth of "union monopolies."
6. It is bad for retail stores, which need prompt and courteous sales people.

A great many of these communications came in the form of identically worded postcards obviously prepared by someone other than the signer. The largest number of these came from jewelry stores in small towns—a group unlikely to be organized, let alone confronted by the demands for a union shop.

In the conclusion to my article, I alluded to the current debate over the role of government in disputes over union security issues and expressed the opinion that until that question was resolved, it was unlikely that general agreement on an acceptable form of union security could be secured. Today, 50 years later, considerable resistance to this form of union security remains. Indeed, under the Taft-Hartley Act, state laws forbidding union security arrangements take precedence over federal laws permitting them.

Although it was clear that the WSB could not order the steel companies to include a union-shop provision in their agreements with the Steelworkers, the public members were convinced that the board had not only the legal authority but also the duty to make some recommendation on the issue of union security. After describing a number of union-security arrangements, including variations of the union shop, that had been adopted by many large employers and unions, they recommended that the parties "include a union-shop provision in their new contracts, the exact form and condition thereof to be determined by them in their forthcoming negotiations." The opinion accompanying this recommendation, which I wrote, included the following explanation:

> The Public Members would have preferred a different recommendation, one which would have returned the matter to the parties for collective bargaining, with the Board to be prepared to consider further recommendations in the event the parties failed to resolve the issue. But a majority of the Board could not be obtained to support this position. When the Labor Members moved for a recommendation of the union shop, the Public Members voted in the negative, stating that they did so because they believed that the parties should be given another chance to bargain on the issue, since their prior bargaining had been so unsatisfactory. The Public Members then moved their proposal and this was rejected by both the Labor and Industry Members. The latter took the position that retention of jurisdiction would imply that, if the parties failed to agree, the Board might then make the recommendation, whereas the Board should not recommend the union shop in any case. The Public Members were then left with only the alternative of recommending the union shop or agreeing that the Board would not do so in any case. Under the necessity of choosing between these alternatives, the Public Members concluded that reason, fairness, and equity required the former.[5]

Having finally assured that the board could issue majority recommendations on all issues in the steel case, the public members spent the night of 19 March writing their accompanying opinion, which was preceded by an introductory statement by Feinsinger. Dunlop was in charge of coordinating our efforts, each of us having been assigned responsibility for drafting various parts of the opinion. In the early hours of 20 March, I was hurrying to complete the section on union security. My secretary, completely exhausted, had gone home many hours earlier, and I was writing my draft in longhand. Dunlop came to my office and asked how I was doing. I held up a number of handwritten pages and told him that I would soon be through but that I needed a typist. Dunlop had always struck me as being more of a lone wolf than a team player, but in this instance he grabbed my manuscript, sat down at my secretary's desk, and began typing. Some time on the morning of 20 March the board's report and recommendations were completed and released.

---

[5] *Opinion of the Public Members, in the Matter of Basic Steel Industry and United Steelworkers of America (CIO), Case No. D-18-C.*

Public reaction was immediate and overwhelmingly negative. Attention focused almost exclusively on the wage recommendation, which was pronounced by the great majority of commentators as having far exceeded what was allowable under the WSB's regulations. Leading the pack, C.E. ("Engine Charlie") Wilson, head of the defense mobilization agency, declared that the board's recommendations would destabilize the entire economy. The critics ignored the extension of the contract between the parties to 18 months and the delay in the two 2.5 cent-per-hour increments in addition to the initial 12.5 cent general increase for three and six months, respectively. Instead, they reported that the board had recommended a general increase of 17.5 cents per hour, just one cent lower than the Steelworkers' demand.

All members of the board were besieged by the media for interviews. As the only public member in town (all the others had left immediately after the release of our report and recommendations), I was asked to appear the evening of 20 March on "Capital Cloakroom," a radio program broadcast nationwide. Three reporters questioned me about the WSB's recommendations in the steel case, concentrating almost entirely on the wage increase. Although they treated me courteously, it was apparent that they all thought the increase was excessive and contrary to the board's regulations. I did my best to explain and defend the board's decision, but the effort failed insofar as my interrogators—and presumably most of those listening to the program—were concerned. At the conclusion of the broadcast, I felt completely drained. Eleanor and I joined the reporters for drinks at a nearby bar, after which we went home and I fell into bed, exhausted. The following morning, a Saturday, I slept late; then I puttered around for the rest of the day, not doing much of anything. In the afternoon I fell asleep on the living room sofa until Eleanor woke me at five for our customary cocktail hour. When she roused me, I sat up and then realized I could not see. My initial reaction was sheer panic, but then I recalled a visit a few weeks earlier to a noted eye specialist in Washington, to whom I had complained about increasing bouts of blurred vision. He examined my eyes and then asked me what sort of work I did. The steel case was than approaching its climax, and

I explained that I was working very long hours—16 to 20 a day. He responded that there was nothing organically wrong with my eyesight, but that the great strain I was putting on myself was causing the symptoms of which I complained. His advice was to slow down; if I did so, he said, my eyesight would return to normal. So on that terrible afternoon several weeks later, when I suddenly experienced total blindness, I tried to quiet my anxiety by recalling my ophthalmologist's diagnosis. Eleanor comforted me and assured me that my condition was only temporary. We had our drinks, I relaxed a little, and a few hours later my eyesight began gradually to return. The experience remains vividly in my memory as one of the scariest in my life.

The opinions of the labor and industry members, which were released about a day after the report and recommendations of the public members, contained no surprises. The labor members expressed their disappointment with the WSB's majority recommendations, especially with those relating to wages, which they termed inadequate and unfair, and also with the board's failure to recommend improvements in working conditions or to deal substantively with the Steelworkers' demand for a guaranteed annual wage. They justified their concurrence with the public members' recommendations in the following self-serving statement: "Nevertheless, in keeping with labor's traditional sense of social responsibility and its devotion to the overriding needs of our country, we voted for most of the resolutions offered by the Public Members of the Board." Stripped of its sanctimony, the labor members' opinion amounted to an admission that even though the Steelworkers had not received everything they had asked for, they could live with the board's recommendations.

For their part, the industry members vigorously attacked the majority recommendations regarding wages and the union shop, declaring that the former far exceeded the amount permissible under existing regulations and that the latter should not have been the subject of any recommendations. In addition, they declared that the majority recommendations as a whole "reflect a conscious and admitted effort to recommend terms of settlement which the union could accept," and complained that "no similar effort was made to ensure that the terms would be acceptable to the companies involved." Finally, the industry members asserted that the board majority had "refused to make clear and positive recommendations on several issues of great importance to the companies [for example, affirmation of the steel companies' rights to manage their plants] because they were complex and could not be intelligently handled before the deadline imposed by the union for Board action."

Not content with this expression of their dissenting views, three industry members, including one who had not participated in the steel case, issued an additional public statement on 25 March 1952 that contained a number of highly provocative statements, including the following:

> Recent actions of the [Wage Stabilization] Board in its recommendations in the steel case...show that...rather than resolving disputes it is creating more disputes; rather than combating inflation, it is creating more inflation....In the steel dispute case, the collective bargaining process was by-passed, and the original union demands, which would certainly have been considerably reduced in collective bargaining, were brought directly through the...Board. The majority of the Board disregarded Board regulations in this dispute and recommended an increase greater, in our opinion, than would have resulted from collective bargaining....We, therefore, feel that the... Board no longer serves a useful purpose.[6]

At least one newspaper, the *New York Herald Tribune*, reported that the industry members had decided to resign from the board, a story repudiated by the industry members the next day.

At the executive meeting of the board the following day, a bitter dispute erupted that briefly seemed to threaten the continued existence of the WSB. Elmer Walker, a member of the International Association of Machinists and the principal spokesman for the AFL labor members, angrily denounced the statement and declared that if the industry members felt that the board no longer served a useful purpose, they should resign. In this he was fully supported by the CIO labor members. Walker also paid his disrespects to Wilson, saying that he knew "as much about the Steel Case and the deliberations of this Board as a hog knows about Sunday." George Armstrong, president of the Lone Star Steel

---

[6] The full text of this statement is quoted in the transcript of the executive meeting of the WSB for 26 March 1952.

Company of Texas (a non-unionized company not a party to the steel case) and the chief spokesman of the industry members participating in the steel case, defended the statement, but he sought to soften its effect by suggesting that although he believed the statement to be true when it was made, it did not necessarily have to continue to be true. Feinsinger joined in by exposing the patent inaccuracies of some parts of the industry members' statements, strongly urging them to issue a public modification of that document. After a long and rancorous discussion, the industry members agreed to consider Feinsinger's proposal. On 27 March, they issued another public statement in which they said that their previous statement had apparently "given rise to some misinterpretation" and declared that they had no plans to walk off or withdraw from the board's activities. Rather, they intended to "continue their efforts to persuade a majority to their point of view as to the proper action to take in matters coming before it." Their statement concluded: "However, Industry Members regard themselves, like all other members of the Board, as being free either individually or collectively to express their views on the Board's activities."

This second statement was no more acceptable to the labor members than the first, and they continued to question the allegiances of the industry members to the board and the objectives of the president's executive order that created it. Nevertheless, although relations between the labor and industry members remained strained, the board stayed intact and gradually resumed its normal routine.

During the ensuing weeks, criticism of the board's recommendations and personal attacks against President Truman and the WSB public members by representatives of the steel companies and their political allies in Congress became increasingly vituperative. On 31 March, Wilson resigned, accusing Truman of breaking a promise to grant price relief to the steel industry to offset the WSB's recommended wage increases. Faced with the industry's refusal to accept the board's recommendations, the Steelworkers called a strike for 9 April. On 8 April, Truman ordered seizure of the steel mills, while at the same time blasting the industry for demanding a price increase. On 16 April, Clarence B. Randall, president of Inland Steel Company and the spokesman for the industry, denounced the seizure as "an evil deed without precedent in history" that discharged "a political debt to the CIO." The "actors in this corrupt political deal," Randall charged, were "the so-called public members of the Wage Stabilization Board." Shortly thereafter, Admiral Ben Moreell, board chairman of Jones & Laughlin Steel, sent a telegram to each of the public members, asking whether the member had ever worked for a union, ever been paid by a union, ever represented a union, ever accepted fees from a union (other than split arbitration fees), or ever had any other connection with a union. He demanded a detailed reply to each of these questions.

My resentment against these unfair personal attacks had been growing ever since Representative Gwinn, as previously mentioned, had publicly charged the public members with being "beholden to union 'bosses' for part of their income." When I received Moreell's telegram, I just blew up and, in true American fashion, looked around for someone to sue. I persuaded Feinsinger, Bullen, and Dunlop to join me in consulting a lawyer. Thanks to the assistance of Ralph Seward, we got an appointment with Paul Porter, a partner in the prestigious Washington firm of Arnold, Fortas & Porter. Porter introduced us to another partner, Abe Fortas, later to become an associate justice of the U.S. Supreme Court, who took over the interview. He proceeded to tell us, gently but firmly, the facts of life. We should not, he advised, take these attacks personally. Even though they were ostensibly aimed at us, their real target was President Truman. As for suing Gwinn for libel, as I proposed, because his statements were made in a telegram to President Truman and thus not protected by the immunity provided by the Speech or Debate Clause in Article 1, Section 6, of the Constitution, Fortas told us to forget it. Such a suit, he explained, would be welcomed by Gwinn and his financial backers, who had unlimited funds to defend the action. It would have to be brought in federal court, he went on, because of the diversity of citizenship of the parties, and this would involve lengthy pretrial discovery during which, he assured us, any incident in our lives that might be considered at all discreditable would inevitably be exposed.

More important, he pointed out, even if we could afford to maintain the suit, it would probably take two or three years before it came to trial, by which time no one would remember or care about the facts on which it was based. Finally, he doubted our ability to prove that we had suffered any financial damage. Fortas told us that he had given the same advice to a number of other government employees outraged by unfair attacks on their integrity. His firm, he said, took only those libel cases it knew it could win and obtain very large damage awards. As an example, he cited a case then in progress in which a widely circulated book had stated that many sales personnel at a Dallas department store were call girls. Those charges had also been reported on CBS, and Fortas predicted that the money damages would be immense. (The risk of bringing even the most promising libel suits was demonstrated when this one subsequently proved to be unsuccessful.) Well, we asked, what kind of a reply should be made to Moreell? Have the board's secretary send him a "bedbug letter #3" response, Fortas advised, and that is what we did.

In addition, Feinsinger issued a statement on behalf of the public members, from which I quote in part:

> The charges against the Public Members have now taken on a broader aspect. Persons who profess to be genuinely concerned with the charges, though admitting no personal knowledge of the facts, have called upon the Public Members to affirm or deny the charges. They have not called upon the complainants and asked them to explain their charges and to supply the evidence. Instead, they have asked us to disprove the charges. They add sophomoric catch questions designed to elicit any comment which could possibly be tortured into an admission of wrongdoing by some facile mind. Such questions are designed simply to set up straw men to shoot at should the baselessness and baseness of the original charges be exposed....
>
> We are under no illusions that the Public Members are the real game being hunted. What is involved is an attack on the whole stabilization program and on the whole concept of effective government intervention, in the public interest, to prevent and settle labor disputes which would impair the defense of our country. Whether these critics realize it or not, they are weakening the fabric of the democratic institutions and practices to which they profess allegiance. I urge them to reconsider their course before the damage already done becomes irreparable.
>
> I am reminded by these attacks of the advice given by an old teacher of trial practice to his law classes. He was a wise but cynical ex-practitioner. His instructions were these: "If you have a bad case on facts, attack the law. If you have a bad case on

the law, attack the facts. If you have a bad case on the law and on the facts, attack the Judge." This, I think, is a fair analysis of what is gong on today.

One's honesty and impartiality are not matters which one debates. They are matters established by one's record over his lifetime. There is no Public Member of this Board who would hesitate to be judged by the public on that record.[7]

From then on, things seemed to go rapidly downhill. In a widely publicized speech to the Industrial Relations Research Association, Sumner Slichter declared that the WSB recommendations in the steel case violated the "reality and spirit" of wage stabilization and asked, more in sorrow than in anger, "How could such good men produce such a bad decision?"

On 29 April, the steel seizure was held unconstitutional by a federal district court, and the Steelworkers responded by calling an immediate industry-wide strike. At President Truman's request, however, Murray ordered them back to work on 2 May.

Hearings by the House Committee on Education and Labor pursuant to the resolution to investigate the WSB commenced on 6 May. Wilson, the leadoff witness, testified that in his opinion, implementation of the board's recommendations in the steel case would go "well beyond the limits of proper wage and price stabilization policy." He also proposed stripping the WSB of authority to make recommendations in labor disputes certified by the president and creating a new board composed of all-public members chosen from persons "who have had business contacts, that have been businessmen, and lawyers, and that had…a reasonable understanding of the problem."[8]

Along with Feinsinger and Tom Coman, a public member who had not participated in the steel case, I also testified before the House committee. My principal purpose in doing so was to refute the charges of being "beholden to union bosses" made by Gwinn, who was a member of that committee. I gave my testimony on 3 June, about a week after President Truman had appointed me vice-chairman of the board to

---

[7]BNA, *Daily Labor Report*, no. 77 (17 April 1952): A-3–A-4.

[8]Hearings before the House Committee on Education and Labor on H.Res. 532, 82d Cong., 2d Sess., 6 May 1952, 49.

replace Bullen, who had resigned. After giving a brief resume of my background, I adverted to Gwinn's charges and stated:

> I wish to take this opportunity, therefore, categorically to deny those charges. I have never been on the payroll of any company or union, nor have I received money from any union or employer except as a fee for my services as an arbitrator jointly selected by both parties; and I have never received a fee from one party in an arbitration case which exceeded the fee paid by the other party in the same case.
>
> Finally, since I assumed my present position as a public member of the Wage Stabilization Board, I have not received 1 penny of income from any source other than the United States Government.[9]

Gwinn led off the questioning by members of the committee and by its general counsel, John S. Forsythe. Revealing his total ignorance of the arbitration process in collective bargaining, he repeatedly attempted to get me to concede that I was principally indebted to presidents of the AFL and the CIO for my appointments as arbitrator in various labor disputes. Apparently not persuaded by my reiterated explanations that those two gentlemen had probably never even heard of me until I joined the WSB, and that my appointments were made by agreement between local employer and union officials, he kept returning to this point before finally giving up. The rest of the questions asked by various members of the committee dealt mostly with the WSB's wage recommendations in the steel case and a few others, as well with the union shop. On the latter issue, the questions were all designed to expose the alleged inequities of the union shop and to obtain my admission that the public members were philosophically committed to recommending that form of union security in every case in which that possibility was presented. I did my best to defend the board's recommendations in the steel case, after repeating in substance the answers Feinsinger had given to the same questions posed by the same committee a month before. A few members of the committee used their time to make general statements opposing in principle not only the union shop but also the idea of allowing a government agency to make any recommendations on the issue, and then asked whether I agreed. (In most instances I disagreed, and said so.)

---

[9] Hearings on H.Res. 532, 3 June 1952, 846.

Toward the end of the hearing, which lasted all day, I finally got the question that I had been expecting. In January 1952, I had received a letter from my older brother, David, who was then practicing law in California. He said he was coming to Washington in a few days to testify as a former Communist and friendly witness before the House Un-American Activities Committee (HUAC). My shock at the news, of which I had not the slightest inkling, was overwhelming. For most of his life David had held and volubly expounded extremely conservative views on questions of economic and social policy. After a brief marriage that ended in divorce and service in the army during the World War II, he settled in California and, in 1946, got a job as an attorney with the regional office of the National Labor Relations Board (NLRB) in Los Angeles. In 1948, he left the board and established an office and residence in Orange County, California. Shortly thereafter, he remarried and acquired a new set of friends, most of whom were conservative Republicans. Although I had met some of his friends and associates at the NLRB, whom I thoroughly disliked and guessed were at least fellow travelers if not members of the Communist Party, I never dreamed that David would join the party, which in fact he did in November 1948, shortly after leaving the NLRB.

Upon receipt of his letter, I wrote to him and told him that Eleanor and I wanted him to stay at our house while he was in Washington. That same evening, I also went to see Feinsinger and told him the news. Given the virtual hysteria then sweeping the country over the alleged infiltration of our government by Soviet agents, and the common practice of finding persons disloyal purely on the basis of their association with others suspected of being Communist sympathizers, every government agency was extremely apprehensive of possible charges that persons of doubtful loyalty were in its employ. Unpopular ones like the WSB were particularly vulnerable. Accordingly, I told Feinsinger that if he felt that I should resign, I would immediately do so. A day or so later, he convened a meeting of the board, which I of course did not attend, and related to them what I had told him. He advised me later that the members of the board had unanimously concluded that there was no occasion for my resignation, that the disclosure was all that was necessary, and that they would support me if any challenge were raised concerning my own fitness to continue to serve as a public member. Subsequently, individual labor and industry members came to me and told me the same thing. Later that month, the White House Loyalty Board for Presidential Appointees sent Feinsinger a letter saying that having received the information submitted by the FBI, it "has been determined that on all the evidence there is no reasonable doubt as to Mr. Aaron's loyalty to the Government of the United States."

When David arrived, we spent an evening discussing his involvement with the Communist Party. He told me that during the period 1946–1948 he had had a vague sense that something was wrong with our society, but that he had joined the party primarily because he was lonely and unhappy, and because some members of the NLRB regional staff and others who were friendly and kind to him were also members and had urged him to do so. It was clear from what David told me and from what he said in his testimony before HUAC, which I subsequently read, that he had been a fish out of water among the party faithful. Asked at the committee hearing what the party meetings were devoted to, he replied "Lots and lots of talk…[about] literature, pamphlets, periodicals, books, articles; most of which was completely over my head." He had left the party at the end of 1948. Explaining his decision, he said, "the more I saw how it operated and actually what was going on, that is what just made me quit.…It sounds nice on paper, but…it doesn't work.…You begin to realize that what you would end up with is a system where you would not be governed by law, but by men, and that is just the opposite of everything that I have been brought up to believe."[10]

I was certainly glad that David had left the Communist Party, and I could understand why he had felt it necessary to protect his future career by cooperating with the FBI and HUAC. What I could not understand at the time, however, was why he had decided to name all those with whom he had been associated while still a party member. I had nothing

[10] Hearings before the House Committee on Un-American Activities, 82nd Cong., 2nd Sess., 23 Jan. 1952, 2515, 2517.

but contempt for HUAC, because I believed that it and similar groups outside of Congress were trying to suppress wholly legal opinions and activities with which they disagreed in ways that denied law-abiding citizens the rudimentary elements of due process. My brother's willingness to name others as party members and his endorsement during his testimony of the committee's activities hurt me a great deal and caused an estrangement from him on my part that lasted for several years. In retrospect, I think my judgment of him was unduly harsh. Although I had said nothing to him about my feelings, he sensed my disapproval. Moreover, he knew that the publicity about our relationship had been an embarrassment if not a serious threat to my status as a member of the WSB, a fact that caused him great pain and remorse. Fortunately, the affectionate bond between us, which grew stronger in later years, overcame my distaste for his testimony before HUAC. David returned to his earlier conservative views and by mutual agreement we steered clear of political discussions when we got together at family gatherings. He spent the last years of his life as a dedicated and very popular municipal court judge. I loved him and miss him.

So when Richard Vail, a Republican from Illinois, asked me first whether I knew a man named David Aaron and then, after I had said he was my brother, "Is he now or has he been a member of the Communist Party?," I briefly told him David's history. When I had finished, I asked if Vail or any other member of the committee had any questions concerning my loyalty or fitness to serve on the WSB. Vail replied: "I do not think any question has been raised with respect to your own background, Mr. Aaron. We are simply establishing the relationship. That is all."[11] But that, clearly, was not all. The next day, the Hearst papers throughout the country, and perhaps others as well, featured stories that the brother of a public member and vice-chairman of the WSB had been a member of the Communist Party.

A day or two prior to my appearance before the House Labor Committee, the Supreme Court had issued its decision in *Youngstown Sheet & Tube Co. v. Sawyer*, holding that the president had exceeded his

---

[11] Hearings on Un-American Activities, 924.

powers in seizing the steel mills in the absence of legislative authorization.[12] Declaring that his members would not work without a contract, Murray called an industry-wide strike. At the end of June, Truman "reluctantly" signed the Defense Production Act Amendments Act of 1952, which drastically cut the WSB's budget and removed its authority to settle disputes. I held a news conference in which I charged that the action of the House in reducing the board's budget from $15 million to $7.5 million amounted to a "fraud on the public," because it would force the board to shut down all its regional offices and to eliminate or sharply curtail many of its essential activities. I concluded that it would be better not to have a wage stabilization program at all than to pretend to carry one out with the knowledge that to do so was impossible.[13]

In the latter part of July, the steel strike was settled on terms very similar to what the WSB had recommended. The added crucial element was that the steel companies received a price increase of $5.20 a ton for carbon steel. This made clear what we had known all along: the concern of the steel industry had been focused not so much on the WSB recommendations as on its demands for a compensating price increase, over which the board had no jurisdiction. The Steelworkers approved the strike settlement, hailing it as a "mighty victory." In an effort to initiate an era of improved labor-management relations, Benjamin Fairless, president of U.S. Steel, and Murray agreed to tour all of U.S. Steel's plants together and to discuss local problems with labor and union leaders at each plant.

At the end of the July, Truman created a new Wage Stabilization Board, with Archibald Cox as chairman, and the old board went out of existence with neither a bang nor a whimper. There was no final, nostalgic meeting such as the one that had taken place on the last day of the War Labor Board seven years earlier; the public members simply packed up and went home. Most of the industry and labor members continued to serve on the new board.

---

[12] 343 U.S. 579 (1952).

[13] The text of my statement appears in BNA, *Daily Labor Report*, no. 128 (30 June 1952): A-3.

The contrast between my return from service on the WLB in 1945 and from the WSB in 1952 could scarcely have been greater. In 1945, I was on top of the world, with greatly enhanced prestige in my own field and with roseate hopes for the future. In 1952, I returned to UCLA and to an academic and local professional community that regarded me with some suspicion because of my role on the unpopular Wage Stabilization Board. It took me a full year before I began to be chosen again as an arbitrator; even then I was regarded by some faculty members at UCLA and some business groups as pro-union and anti-business.

Prior to becoming a member of the WSB, I had believed that an ideal arrangement for a person such as myself would be to return periodically for fairly short tours of duty with the federal or state government, during which I could employ some of the ideas and skills acquired from my teaching and research. Upon my return to academic life, I reasoned, I could put to use in my teaching and research what I had learned in government service. My experience with the WSB caused me to reconsider this assumption but not to reject it, and I continued to accept government appointments, although for much shorter periods.

CHAPTER 4

EMERGENCY DISPUTES, 1960–1992

Peaceful relations between employers and unions do not constitute news, and they rarely register on the public's consciousness. On the other hand, serious breakdowns that result in disruptions affecting broad areas of the economy are highlighted in the media and are likely to produce demands in and out of Congress for enactment of various schemes to prevent them, even though there are already two statutory procedures in place to deal with such situations. In the period from 1960 through 1992, I served as a member or chairman of several emergency boards under the Railway Labor Act (RLA), a board of inquiry under the Labor Management Relations (Taft-Hartley) Act (LMRA), and an arbitration board created by an act of Congress. The substantive issues in most of these disputes would be of interest chiefly to specialists, but the procedures themselves—a subject that periodically vexes the nation—are, I believe, worthy of description and analysis.

EMERGENCY PROCEDURES UNDER
THE RAILWAY LABOR ACT

Under the RLA, procedures for handling emergency disputes apply to railroads and airlines involved in "major" disputes—that is, those over proposed changes in collective bargaining agreements. The appointment of an emergency board has two steps. First, the National Mediation Board (NMB), the agency that administers the RLA, notifies the president of the United States of any dispute that, in its judgment, "threatens substantially to interrupt interstate commerce to a degree such as to deprive any section of the country of essential transportation services." It does so only after its efforts to mediate the dispute have failed and the parties have rejected the option of voluntary arbitration. In that event the NMB refers to the president almost every case in which a strike is imminent, the assumption apparently being that any railroad or airline strike is likely substantially to interrupt interstate commerce and deprive some section of the country of essential transportation services. Second, the president appoints an emergency board. Whether to do so is entirely within his discretion, but a president has never failed to appoint a board in any case officially referred to him by the NMB because the latter never sends a case to the White House without first ascertaining that the president will refer it to an emergency board.

Traditionally, RLA emergency boards consist of three persons who have no interest in the dispute. In recent years, members have tended to be well-known arbitrators of labor-management disputes. Once appointed, a board must investigate the facts of the controversy and report its findings to the president within 30 days from the date the board was established. Frequently, however, emergency boards seek and obtain one or more extensions of time in which to complete their assignments. Although the statute speaks only of a "report" to the president, emergency boards have traditionally made recommendations as well as findings of fact. The standard practice is for a board to present its report and recommendations directly to the president, after which the White House transmits them to the parties and makes them public. During a 30-day period following issuance of the board's report and recommendations, no change except by agreement may be made by the disputants in the conditions out of which the controversy arose. At the expiration of the 30 days, they are free to strike or lock out unless Congress intervenes.

Immediate acceptance by all parties of an emergency board's recommendations is rare, but the recommendations have provided the foundation for the ultimate settlement of a majority of emergency disputes in the railroad industry without any disruption of work. In a number of important cases, however, they failed to achieve that result. Thus, in the airline industry between 1936 and 1940, emergency board recommendations were rejected by unions in over 40 percent of the cases, and between 1959 and 1966 union rejections increased to over 60 percent and strikes occurred in all the principal cases.

The railroad world has been described by Lloyd Garrison as "a state within a state." It has a substantial although diminishing population, lives to a considerable extent according to rules of its own making, and has its own customs and specialized vocabulary. Some years ago, for example, the following bulletin was issued by the superintendent of the Southern Pacific Railway in San Jose, California, to all yardmasters: "Effective date, all yardmen in cannonball service bringing drags in yard from outside points will bleed and cut own cars." Until relatively recently, most of the parties in the railroad industry, as well as their lawyers and consultants, argued that the procedures before emergency boards were eminently sensible and fair and should not be changed. These procedures had the familiarity and the sanctity of tradition, which rules this industry as it does no other. Beginning in the 1960s, however, the emergency disputes procedures of the RLA were subjected increasingly to criticism by neutrals who had served on emergency boards, as well as by knowledgeable outsiders who had studied the process. The principal objections were that the procedures were unduly time-consuming, inefficient, and frustrating.

I was first introduced to the mysteries of RLA emergency board procedures in April 1960, when President Eisenhower appointed me to serve on the three-man Emergency Board No. 130, which was headed by my old friend and colleague, John Dunlop. The third member was Arthur W. Sempliner, a stranger to both me and Dunlop. The dispute was a big one, involving approximately 200 railroads and terminal switching companies and over half a million workers represented by 11 cooperating non-operating railway labor organizations.[1] The issues concerned wages, health and welfare benefits, vacations, and holidays. The official record in this case was substantial, although not unusual by emergency board standards: 18 bound volumes, consisting of 2,800 pages of transcript, 76 exhibits running to thousands of pages, and 388 pages of pre- and post-hearing briefs.

Hearings were held at the Masonic Temple on east Randolph Street in Chicago's Loop. The large square room in which we met was illuminated

---

[1] Railroad unions are of two general types: the operating unions, whose members are employed in the actual operations of trains (for example, engineers, firemen, conductors, and brakemen), and the nonoperating unions, or "nonops" (shop employees, maintenance of way employees, and telegraphers). Collectively, the unions are referred to as the organizations; the railroad companies, as the carriers.

by approximately 86 light bulbs in the ceiling (I counted them many times during the lengthy, and boring, proceedings). Morning sessions began at 9:00 a.m. and continued, as a rule, until 1:00 p.m. On occasion we began at 1:00 p.m. and continued until about 5:00 p.m. To make sure that the parties were allowed approximately the same amount of time to make their presentations, each side appointed an official timekeeper. At the end of each session, the two timekeepers would march together up to the front of the room and present their respective computations—in hours, minutes, and seconds!—of the time consumed by each party. The theory was that at the end of the hearings each side would have taken approximately the same amount of time in the presentation of its case. A team of stenographic reporters, working in five-minute shifts, recorded and transcribed the proceedings and usually were able to deliver to board members a copy of the record of the day's work by late afternoon or early evening.

The procedures for presenting evidence and argument, formal in the extreme, were initially outlined in pre-hearing briefs and then repeated in lengthy opening statements by highly experienced attorneys who specialized in RLA cases. Then came the presentation of testimony, which was unique in the sense that most of it was not the usual Q and A, but was in narrative form—that is, the witness simply read, with virtually no interruption, from a lengthy manuscript. At the conclusion of this performance, which in the case of some witnesses consumed several days, opposing counsel would cross-examine.[2] All the exhibits were printed and bound, and most had been used in several previous cases. The economic data in support of the organizations' demands were usually presented by their chief economist, Eli Oliver, an extremely able and experienced expert witness on railway economic issues, whose performance on the witness stand was positively stupefying. He testified in a low monotone, discussing each exhibit *in extenso* and emphasizing

---

[2] Carriers' witness, James M. Symes, chairman of the board of the Pennsylvania Railroad, for example, testified almost without interruption for three days of hearings, reading from a large looseleaf notebook and discussing in exhaustive detail a single 155-page exhibit. This was apparently as traumatizing an ordeal for him as it was for the board: a few days after completing his testimony he suffered a heart attack.

specific items in each that were perfectly apparent. The soporific effect of this lengthy testimony, only rarely broken by a question from the organizations' attorney, was almost irresistible. Cross-examination by one of the carriers' experts would then begin. It was quite apparent that Oliver and his cross-examiner had been through this same performance involving the same exhibits many times. Members of the board occasionally interrupted with questions of their own, but the sheer mass of data dropped in our laps made it difficult to question the witness.

At one of the recesses during the month-long hearings, I expressed to my two board colleagues my dissatisfaction with the way evidence was being presented. Why not, I suggested, receive the pre-hearing briefs and all the exhibits at the start, which would take no longer than a day or two, then take a recess for one week to study the exhibits and note any questions we might have. After that, we could call the parties back into session and take testimony on those aspects of the case that we felt needed to be explored further. I was overheard by Howard Neitzert, the lead attorney for the carriers, who spent almost all his time preparing and presenting their cases before emergency boards. Coming over to me, Neitzert gripped my arm and asked, "Ben, Ben, what are you trying to do, deprive me of my livelihood?" He laughed uneasily as he spoke, but he was in dead earnest. I still think my suggestion was worthy of further consideration, but it failed to resonate with the parties and was never raised again.

The final day of hearings was devoted to closing statements. Counsel for each side presented very lengthy summations, repeating what they had told us in their opening statements, only in greater detail, and commenting on the testimony and evidence submitted by both parties. The carriers also filed a post-hearing brief.

On 8 June 1960, Emergency Board No. 130 issued its report, including recommendations that, as Dunlop explained in the introduction, were not intended to write the precise language of the collective bargaining agreement or to determine the exact terms of settlement of the disputes between the parties. Rather, he noted, they were designed to suggest a relatively narrow area of settlement, which the parties should explore constructively. He went on to remind the parties of a further responsibility of the board:

"to clarify the public interest in the private collective bargaining between these parties in this vital transportation industry."

Although the RLA itself certainly didn't require it, custom decreed that the members of the emergency board present their report and recommendations to the president in person. Eisenhower apparently felt, not without reason, that his time was too valuable to be spent on this formality; instead, we were directed to present our report to his chief of staff, General Wilton Persons. Accordingly, we showed up at the White House, held a press conference, and then sought out Persons to obtain his approval of the press release we had prepared. The general, who obviously had not read the report, was totally unfamiliar with the railroad industry. Although over 200 railroads and switching terminals were involved in the case, the presidential order establishing the emergency board referred to them as the "Akron & Barberton Belt Railroad and Other Carriers." The Akron & Barberton was the first on the alphabetical list of carriers, but it was a small industrial railroad with only a few dozen miles of track at most and, naturally, we did not refer to it specifically in our press release. Persons glanced at the text and then indignantly tossed it back to us, complaining that it made no reference to "the principal railroad involved in this case." Dunlop, never one to suffer fools gladly, could hardly restrain his incredulity and exasperation. In barely civil tones, he informed the general of the utter insignificance of the Akron & Barberton in this case. Although Persons remained unconvinced that we were not committing a major blunder, he apparently concluded, after another heated exchange with Dunlop, that the easiest way to get rid of us was to approve the press release as we had written it.

My experience with emergency boards under the RLA, together with impressions formed by reading about a number of other cases, left me with a sense of profound dissatisfaction. In a paper delivered in 1963 to a meeting of the Industrial Relations Research Association in Toronto, Canada, I summarized my criticism in part as follows:

> The emergency board procedures of the Railway Labor Act have grown increasingly formal, cumbersome, expensive, and unproductive. The ritual of presenting the case to the board is as stylized as the courtship dance of the great crested grebe. The board,

immobilized by hours of hearings during which prepared testimony is literally read into the record, and smothered by an avalanche of printed exhibits and briefs, has no time for open, forthright mediation; at best it can make only a few tentative, sometimes clandestine, efforts to bring the parties together. Genuine collective bargaining seldom begins until after the board's report and recommendations have been released.[3]

An even harsher judgment on the weakness of RLA emergency dispute procedures was pronounced in 1964 by the members of Emergency Board No. 161, headed by Richardson Dilworth, the former mayor of Philadelphia. In its report, the board deplored the preference of the parties for "lengthy, formal hearings, of a quasi-judicial nature, in which… mountains of exhibits are filed by each side to the dispute." In this case, the board noted, "the printed exhibits alone total 75, and when piled on top of one another come to a height of almost 7 feet." While praising the attorneys for both sides as "men of much ability, with great knowledge of every phase of the railroad industry," the board also commented dryly on their "persistent determination to explore every facet of labor relations in the industry since the first steam engine made its appearance." Observing that every witness appearing before it in this case had testified in many earlier emergency proceedings, the board declared it had "the distinct impression that this was, to a great extent, a repeat performance of an even longer run than 'My Fair Lady,' with each side knowing exactly what the other side would present." The parties, the board concluded, "appear to regard the Board as an audience to an elaborate ritual—something like the Japanese Kabucki [sic] Theater."[4]

Strictures such as these led to a panel discussion on procedures under the RLA at an annual meeting of the National Academy of Arbitrators in 1965.[5] Moderated by Howard G. Gamser, chairman of the NMB, the panel consisted of James R. Wolfe, general attorney for the National Railway Labor Conference (NRLC), a carriers organization; Oliver, of the Labor Bureau of the Midwest; and arbitrators Saul Wallen, James C. Hill, Lewis M. Gill, and Ronald W. Haughton, all of whom had served

---

[3] "Observations on the United States Experience," *Labor Law Journal* 14 (1963): 746–47.
[4] *Report to the President by Emergency Board No. 161* (Washington, D.C., 1964), 2.
[5] National Academy of Arbitrators, *Proceedings of the Eighteenth Annual Meeting of the National Academy of Arbitrators*, ed. Dallas L. Jones (Washington, D.C.: BNA, 1965), 27–65.

on a number of emergency boards under the RLA. Wallen reiterated the animadversions against emergency board procedures originally expressed in the Report of Emergency Board No. 161. Gill and Hill added some additional criticisms, though less caustically phrased. In reply, Wolfe and Oliver vigorously defended the procedures and insisted that their detractors lacked a detailed knowledge of the railroad industry and familiarity with its problems and practices. Wolfe's comments were biting, but politely expressed. Oliver was not similarly restrained; he denounced the conduct of members of some of the emergency boards as "iniquitous, vicious, and destructive of the collective bargaining process in the railroad industry." He opined that any failure in emergency board procedures in recent years should be attributed to the personnel of those boards, not to the procedures as such, and urged that future appointments of emergency board members should be from a select panel of names approved by labor and management groups within the railroad industry.

Despite the industry's adamantine resistance to change, emergency board procedures involving railroads tended in subsequent years to become shorter and more flexible.

RLA emergency procedures involving airlines were not nearly so rigid as those for railroad cases, as I discovered in 1961, when President Kennedy appointed me to serve on Emergency Board No. 136 in a dispute between Northwest Airlines and the International Association of Machinists (IAM). They could be almost as time-consuming, but they were blessedly free from all the special rituals dear to the hearts of the railway carriers and labor organizations. My two fellow members on the board were Paul N. Guthrie, who served as chairman, and Paul D. Hanlon; both were prominent arbitrators. The board was established on 24 February and hearings began on 6 March in St. Paul, Minnesota, continuing with some interruptions until the end of that month. As usual, the transcribed record was a large one: 1,200 pages of testimony and argument and about 175 exhibits. Because of the length of the proceedings, it was necessary to secure two extensions of the statutory time limit. The board finally submitted its report to the president on 24 May 1961.

Some nine issues were submitted to the board by the parties, but the "elephant in the living room" was not mentioned in any of the formal notices filed. Nevertheless, the board reported that the key issue was that of the proper cockpit crew complement on turbojet aircraft, which were being brought into commercial use, and the necessary qualifications for the occupant of the "third seat" (the flight engineer). The problem for Northwest was that the pilots were represented by the Air Line Pilots Association (ALPA) while the flight engineers were represented by the IAM. Federal Aviation Agency (FAA) rules at the time required the occupant of the third seat on all turbojet aircraft to possess a valid flight engineer's certificate. The critical question was whether the occupant of the third seat should have additional qualifications and, if so, what they should be. Northwest insisted that this person should also have a commercial pilot's certificate with instrument rating. Although not objecting to that particular qualification, the IAM insisted upon the further requirement of an airframe and power plant (A&P) license, which was held by all flight engineers on Northwest who were represented by IAM. The issue was complicated by the fact that for some months prior to the hearing of this dispute, Northwest's turbojet aircraft had been flown by crews made up of three pilots represented by ALPA, one of whom had a flight engineer's certificate but no A&P license. The board found no evidence that those flight operations had fallen below acceptable standards of safety or efficiency because no member of the flight crew possessed an A&P license. At the same time, the board concluded that the IAM flight engineers presently employed by Northwest were highly qualified and competent, and that their background of mechanical training and experience, represented in part by the A&P license, had undoubtedly enhanced their value to Northwest, particularly in respect of propeller-driven aircraft.

Faced with these conflicting considerations, the board made what I think was an eminently fair recommendation. It concluded that the possession of an A&P license for the occupant of the third seat on turbojet aircraft, although not a matter of safety or efficiency, was a valid criterion of job preference. Therefore, the board recommended that possession of an A&P license by flight engineers presently employed by Northwest should guarantee those who also had a commercial pilot's certificate with instrument rating a special priority for the third seat on turbojet aircraft. The board also recommended, however, that Northwest not be required to impose the requirement of an A&P license on new hires to fill the third seat or on pilots presently employed who elected to acquire a flight engineer's certificate and to bid for the third seat on turbojet aircraft.

The issues in the Northwest case encompassed most of the problems dealt with in the report made by the president's commission on the air lines controversy, headed by Nathan Feinsinger, which had been created on 21 February 1961 "to consider differences that have arisen regarding the performance of the flight engineer's function, the job security of employees performing such function, and related representation rights of the unions, namely, the Flight Engineers' International Association and the Airline Pilots Association on the following carriers: Pan American World Airways, American Airlines, Trans World Airways, Eastern Airlines, National Airlines and Flying Tigers." Both the board's and the commission's reports were presented to the president at the same time. Immediately prior to that event, Arthur Goldberg, secretary of labor in the Kennedy cabinet, had asked the members of the board and the commission whether we would object to submitting our respective reports to him for transmittal to the president. We unanimously objected, reminding him of the long-standing practice of having emergency boards present their reports directly to the president. Although Arthur jealously guarded his special relationship with Kennedy, he withdrew his suggestion and accompanied us to the president's office, making sure, however, that he had a few minutes alone with Kennedy first.

I had met Kennedy during his campaign for the presidency. Although a devoted supporter of Adlai Stevenson, I was quite impressed by his young rival. Eleanor and I had attended the 1960 Democratic convention in Los Angeles as guests of Goldberg, and once Kennedy was nominated we became strong supporters of his candidacy. The meeting with President Kennedy on the morning of the 24 May 1961 did nothing to diminish my high opinion of him. That day seemed to be an unusually busy one, even for the White House. The president was scheduled to address Congress about one-half hour after our meeting with him. Vice President Lyndon Johnson had just returned from a trip to Africa and was waiting to report to the president. Treasury Secretary Douglas Dillon was hanging around in the president's outer office, trying to persuade his appointments secretary to let him in for a few minutes before Kennedy left for the hill. The president received us standing up, and we all remained standing throughout the 10 minutes or so we spent with him. He was cordial, unhurried, and seemed totally focused on the matters about which we were reporting, displaying what was to me a surprising grasp of the issues. Doubtless he had been briefed by Goldberg during the few minutes before we met with him; nevertheless, I was deeply impressed by his performance. (I was also surprised, as I reported to my family later, to observe unmistakable evidence of dandruff on the collar of the President's elegantly tailored jacket.) Our interview ended when Goldberg ushered us out of the office, only to return for a last-minute conversation with Kennedy before the latter left to tend to more important business.

About 30 years elapsed before my next and final experience on an RLA emergency board. This time I was appointed by President George H. W. Bush as chairman of three emergency boards to deal with over 150 issues. These boards heard disputes between the NRLC, which represented most of the country's Class I line haul railroads and terminal and switching companies, and the IAM (Emergency Board No. 220); the Consolidated Rail Corporation (Conrail) and the Brotherhood of Maintenance of Way Employees (BMWE) (Emergency Board No. 221); and the National Railroad Passenger Corporation (Amtrak) and 10 railway labor organizations that collectively represented most of Amtrak's employees (Emergency Board No. 222). Presidential executive orders created the boards effective 3 April 1992, and each order specified that the board must report to the president 30 days later, on 3 May. My fellow board members were arbitrators Preston J. Moore, Eric J. Schmertz, David W. Twomey, and Arnold M. Zack, all highly experienced. Schmertz and Twomey were appointed members of all three boards; Moore and Zack were appointed members of Emergency Boards Nos. 221 and 222. We decided, however, that all five of us would hear all three cases, although only Schmertz, Twomey, and I would sign the report of Emergency Board No. 220.

The magnitude of our task was considerable. We held hearings in Washington, D.C., from 6 to 22 April, compiling a record consisting of over 2,000 pages of transcript and almost 8,000 pages of exhibits. Although the parties, under our urging, sped up their presentations, the number of unions involved made a short hearing impossible. Well before the conclusion of the hearings, it became clear to the board members that we could not deal with the multiple issues in the three cases in a thorough and professional manner within the time limit set by the executive orders. We therefore sought and obtained from each of the parties involved their agreement to request an extension of 25 days, from 3 to 28 May, to submit our report and recommendations. Each of the parties also agreed to maintain the status quo until 24 June 1992. Accordingly, I submitted the request for a time extension to the NMB, whose chairman, Patrick J. Cleary, forwarded it to C. Boyden Gray, the counsel to the president.

Such requests had often been made and granted in previous emergency dispute cases, but ours met with immediate and vigorous resistance. In a series of telephone calls with my contacts in the White House and, ultimately, with Andrew H. Card, Bush's secretary of transportation, I was told that the longest extension that would be granted was 21 days, to 24 May. This condition was being imposed by Representative John Dingell in the House, who, correctly as it turned out, feared that the parties would not accept the emergency boards' recommendations and wanted to impose a legislative settlement, thus preventing any work stoppages, before the House adjourned early in July. After consulting with my fellow board members, I informed Secretary Card, much to his surprise and indignation, that we respectfully declined to agree to submit our report by 24 May and that if our requested extension to 28 May were denied, we would all resign. So far as I am aware, no previous emergency board had presented the administration with such a threat. In any case, it worked: we were finally granted the full extension we had requested, and we submitted the reports and recommendations in each of the three disputes on 28 May 1992.

In the ensuing month, the parties to the three cases were unable to agree on a settlement of the issues based on the boards' recommendations. Congress then adopted a joint resolution requiring the parties to continue negotiations for a specified period and, failing agreement, to submit to arbitrators of their choosing a final offer in the form of a complete proposed agreement. The arbitrators were given authority to select one offer or the other, and their decisions were to be final unless disapproved by the president. (The parties in the case involving the NRLC and the IAM were persuaded by their arbitrator, Richard Mittenthal, to bargain out a settlement, which they then asked him to embody in an award signed by him, thereby allowing him to take the blame from their dissatisfied constituents.) President Bush allowed the arbitrators' awards in all three cases to stand. Subsequently, Mittenthal told me that an IAM vice president involved in the presentation of its case to Emergency Board No. 220 had commented that despite his intense dissatisfaction with the wage recommendation in that case, he had admired my defiance of the White House and the Congress on the issue of the time extension. "That took real balls!" he exclaimed.

EMERGENCY PROCEDURES UNDER THE TAFT-HARTLEY ACT

Emergency dispute procedures under the Taft-Hartley Act differ substantially from those under the RLA. They may be invoked by the president whenever in his opinion a threatened or actual strike or lockout "affecting an entire industry or a substantial part thereof" would "imperil the national health or safety." In that event he may appoint a board of inquiry that is vested with subpoena power, is authorized to hold hearings, and is charged with the duty to report the facts and the issues in dispute. The board is expressly forbidden, however, to make recommendations. Upon receipt of the board's report, the president may, and usually does, direct the attorney general to petition a federal court for an injunction, which it grants in almost every case. After the injunction has been granted, the board of inquiry is reconvened, and if the dispute remains unsettled, the board must submit another report at the end of a 60-day period that sets forth the efforts made to resolve the dispute, the current positions of the parties, and the employer's last offer. At no point in this process, however, is the board officially involved in mediation efforts, which are the sole responsibility of the Federal Mediation and Conciliation Service (FMCS).

Within 20 days following submission of the board's second report, the NLRB polls the employees by secret ballot on their acceptance or rejection of the employer's last offer and certifies the vote to the attorney general. Whatever the outcome of the vote, the injunction must be discharged. At this point the president is required to submit to Congress a full and comprehensive report of the proceedings in the dispute up to that point, together with any recommendations for further action he may see fit to make. It is then up to Congress to decide what to do.

I was involved in only one emergency dispute arising under the Taft-Hartley Act, but the circumstances of that case reveal some of the sillier aspects of the statutory procedure. The principal parties to the case were the Boeing Company and its Vertol Division and the IAM, but the Rohr Corporation, a supplier of aircraft and missile components, and the United Auto Workers (UAW), the United Welders, and the Operating Engineers were also involved. Negotiations over the terms of new collective bargaining agreements began in July 1962. The main issues were wages, health and welfare benefits, and union security. In August the unions voted to authorize strikes, but no strike date was set, pending a vote on Boeing's final offer. Despite mediation efforts by the FMCS, no settlement was reached, and on 13 September President Kennedy appointed a fact-finding board of three neutrals to supplement the efforts of the FMCS. After its initial meeting with the parties, the board reported that the union security issue was the chief impediment to a settlement. Continuing efforts by the board and the FMCS failed to achieve a settlement. In December, the NLRB announced that in a non-binding poll Boeing employees favored a union shop by nearly three to one. On 2 January 1963 the board reported to the president that efforts to head off a strike scheduled for 15 January had failed because of management's resistance to the union demand for a union shop. It recommended that the company reconsider its position on the union security provision over and above the present maintenance of membership clause. It also recommended that the wage issue be settled in conformance with the company's offer. Strike action was postponed pending results of balloting on Boeing's latest offer. The offer was rejected, and the IAM ordered a strike to begin on 26 January.

At this point, President Kennedy, stating that a work stoppage at Boeing would be a serious threat to the nation's defense effort, invoked the emergency procedures of the Taft-Hartley Act and appointed a three-man board of inquiry to investigate the dispute. On 23 January I was advised of my appointment as chairman of the board (the two other members were economists Lloyd Ulman and J.B. Gillingham) and told that our report had to be on the president's desk by the morning of 25 January. It took the rest of that day for the board and the parties to assemble in Seattle, thus leaving only one day to complete our work. There was obviously no time to explore the present status of the dispute. Our job was simply to compile the respective statements of the parties on each issue. This proved to be more difficult than one might suppose and could not have been accomplished without the exceptional cooperation of all parties concerned. For example, the representatives from Boeing's Vertol Division in Wichita, Kansas, were delayed en route to Seattle by bad weather and had to abort their trip, so the union obligingly telephoned in its positions on the various issues. In the end, the so-called inquiry boiled down to a frantic cut-and-paste job that assembled the written position statements of the parties on each issue. We finished just in time to give our report, indicating that a strike appeared to be imminent, to a FMCS representative, who caught a red-eye flight to Washington that night and delivered it to the White House the next morning, on 25 January.

Upon receipt of the report, President Kennedy ordered the Justice Department to seek an injunction against the threatened strike, and a temporary injunction was issued by a federal district judge in Seattle that same day. On 1 February the court extended the injunction for 86 days, thus blocking any strike until 15 April. Negotiations between the parties resumed on 19 February, and on 24 March the board of inquiry reconvened in Seattle and received reports on the current positions of all parties to the dispute. On 26 March the board made its final report to the president: the parties remained deadlocked on the major issues, despite mediation efforts by the FMCS in 11 sessions between 19 February and 22 March. On 8 April the NLRB announced that unofficial returns of balloting indicated that the union had rejected the company's final offer. On 15 April, just hours before the expiration of the injunction, the parties announced a tentative agreement on the terms of a new contract. In Seattle union members voted to accept the contract, but those at Cape Canaveral, Florida, rejected it, and employees in Wichita also voted it down. On 29 April the union announced timetables for progressive walkouts at Boeing operations across the country. After the company had submitted some new proposals on 1 May, President Kennedy urged the union to postpone the strike action and to submit the new proposals to its membership for a vote. In response, A. J. Hayes, the IAM's international president, advised all locals that strike sanctions were being temporarily withdrawn pending results of this vote. Finally, on 10 May, union members ratified the new collective bargaining agreement, ending 10 months of negotiations.

As a result of my experience in this case and of my study of previous Taft-Hartley emergency dispute cases, I made a number of specific criticisms of the statutory procedures in a paper delivered in 1967 to a labor institute sponsored by the Southwestern Legal Foundation.[6] The first of these concerned the function of boards of inquiry in general. They are, in practice, purely ministerial; one competent clerk can perform their duties more promptly and just as efficiently. Their initial task is not to inform the judgment of the president but to provide support for a presidential decision, already made, to declare that an emergency as defined by the statue exists and to seek an injunction against an existing or threatened strike

---

[6] *Labor Law Developments, 1967* (New York: Bender, 1967), 185–208.

or lockout. Because time is always of the essence in these situations, great pressure is put on the boards to report the facts and issues of the dispute as promptly as possible. This they are usually able to do only because of the cooperation of the disputants, who know the decision to seek an 80-day injunction has already been made and who have formed their strategies accordingly. Inasmuch as the boards lack sufficient time to explore issues in depth and are not permitted to make recommendations for the settlement of disputes, the practice of appointing three experienced neutrals to each board is pointless. The same observations apply to the second report that these boards must submit at the end of 60 days.

I then criticized the required employee vote on the employer's last offer. It represents a triumph of hope over contrary experience that, if given the opportunity to vote by secret ballot, workers will reject the advice of their leaders and will respond affirmatively, prompted by either government appeals to their patriotism, secret personal desires for freedom from organizational control, or bargaining offers from their employers. In the period from 1947 through 1968, the employer's last offer was rejected in each of the 14 disputes in which the workers were polled. Moreover, it is doubtful that some of the more complex issues involved in emergency disputes can be intelligibly reduced to a form permitting only a Yes or a No vote. Furthermore, the presentation of a "last" offer freezes bargaining at the very moment when even a relatively minor shift in position by either party might lead to a settlement. In short, the compulsory vote on the employer's last offer inhibits collective bargaining and wastes valuable time and considerable money. It also inspires cynicism about the law and makes government appear helpless.

My third point concerned the virtually automatic government request for an 80-day injunction in emergency cases. The policy has aroused the deep and lasting antagonism of organized labor, as well as the opposition of many neutral observers, on the grounds that it invariably aids the employer and hurts the union. Moreover, the inability of the executive arm of the government to compel a settlement of the dispute at the expiration of the 80-day injunction has perplexed and dismayed the average citizen. Powerless to act at the height of the crisis, the president can only refer the problem to Congress, which if it takes any action is likely to do so in haste and in anger—not a desirable climate for legislation.

THE RAILROAD WORK RULES DISPUTE

The biggest and certainly the most important emergency labor dispute in which I was involved was that between almost all the nation's major railroads and the five railroad operating unions commonly referred to as "the organizations": the Brotherhood of Locomotive Engineers (BLE), the Brotherhood of Firemen and Enginemen (BLFE), the Order of Railway Conductors and Brakemen (ORCB), the Brotherhood of Railroad Trainmen (BRT), and the Switchmen's Union of North America (SUNA). These unions represented approximately 200,000 train and engine service employees. One of the distinguishing features of this case was that, unlike most emergency labor disputes, it was not governed by the procedures of either the Taft-Hartley or the Railway Labor Act. Instead, it was referred by a joint resolution of Congress, Public Law 88-108, to compulsory arbitration by a seven-man, tripartite board, designated as Arbitration Board No. 282.

The issues in this dispute were particularly complex, and the parties were more than usually inflexible. The problem that confronted the loco-motive firemen, who were represented for the most part by the BLFE and to a lesser extent by the BLE, was created by perhaps the most fundamental and rapid technological change ever experienced by the railroad industry: the introduction in the 1920s of the diesel locomotive. Within a period of about 30 years it supplanted the steam locomotive in both passenger and freight service; by the 1960s the steam locomotive was rarely seen outside of railroad museums. Firemen on steam locomotives shoveled coal, made mechanical repairs, maintained a lookout on the left side of the locomotive, relayed hand signals from brakemen to the engineer, and actually relieved the engineer from time to time. The work was necessary and onerous. With the advent of the diesel engine, however, the fireman's job became far easier and relatively less important. No longer required to shovel coal, he occupied a comfortable seat on the left side of the cab. There was less need to make mechanical repairs en route, and the responsibilities for left-side lookout and the relay of hand signals were shared or taken over completely by a brakeman who rode in the cab. This new situation led increasingly to charges by the carriers that the continued employment of firemen in freight service was an egregious example of "featherbedding"—that is, the employment of unwanted and unneeded workers. Despite these attacks, the BLFE successfully negotiated individual agreements with various carriers to preserve the continued status of firemen, and in 1937 it joined with substantially all carriers in signing the National Diesel Agreement, renewed in 1950, which provided for the employment of firemen on practically all diesel locomotives. New technology and the introduction of labor-saving devices during this period had also lightened the traditional workload of train service crews and, according to the carriers, had left many trainmen with little or nothing to do.

The formal beginning of the work-rules case came in November 1959, when the carriers served the organizations with notices of proposed changes in many work and compensation rules, including those bearing on the continued use of firemen on diesel locomotives and the composition, or "consist," of train crews in road and yard service.[7] All the proposed changes were confined to freight services; passenger trains were not affected. What the carriers proposed was the virtual elimination of firemen in road or yard service and the abrogation of regulations fixing the size of train crews. In September 1960, the organizations served a series of counter-proposals on the carriers directed at continuing and even extending the use of firemen and at setting the crew-consist level at not less than one conductor and two brakemen, plus such additional trainmen as maximum safety demanded.

In November 1960, President Eisenhower appointed a commission, requested and agreed to by the parties, to inquire into the dispute. It was composed of 15 members, divided equally between carrier, organization,

---

[7] Collective bargaining agreements on the railroads, unlike those in virtually all other industries, are usually not for a fixed term. They are open-ended and remain in effect until one party or the other files a notice of a proposed change, in accordance with procedures specified in section 6 of the Railway Labor Act.

and public representatives. Directed to report its findings and recommendations, the commission devoted more than 13 months of study to the issues, holding extensive hearings, conducting independent investigations, and making field inspection trips on trains and at railroad installations. Failing in their efforts to mediate a settlement of the dispute, the five public members issued a report in February 1962 that contained detailed findings on every issue and far-reaching recommendations for the modification of many work rules, including those relating to the firemen and crew consist issues. In general, the carriers accepted the report's recommendations, but the organizations rejected them.

There followed a series of unsuccessful negotiations pursuant to the Railway Labor Act, an announcement by the carriers of their intention to put their rules changes into effect, and litigation by the organizations to forestall such actions. The legal jousting ended in March 1963, when the U.S. Supreme Court issued a decision holding that the parties had exhausted all the statutory procedures and that, accordingly, the organizations were free to strike and the carriers were free unilaterally to impose new work rules.

In April 1963, President Kennedy established Emergency Board No. 154, following an announcement by the carriers of their intention to activate their proposed rules changes and notice from the organizations that such action would be met by an immediate strike. The board devoted its efforts almost entirely to mediating the dispute. Its report, issued in May 1963, recommended guidelines and procedures that might serve as a framework for further collective bargaining, including the arbitration of unsettled disagreements. The carriers accepted the recommendations; the organizations declined either to accept or reject them, but conceded that the report could be "a useful tool in the search for a fair and suitable settlement."

Issuance of the board's report was followed by a period first of direct negotiations between the parties and then of intensive mediation by Secretary of Labor Willard Wirtz and Assistant Secretary James Reynolds, joined by the chairman and members of the NMB. During this time the president extended the 30-day period during which the status quo had to be maintained to 10 July. On 5 July, Wirtz proposed that the firemen and crew consist issues be settled according to the emergency board's recommendations. The carriers again accepted, but the organizations refused to go along. Then, on 9 July, the president proposed, undoubtedly at the instigation of Goldberg, who was now an associate justice of the U.S. Supreme Court, that all issues be submitted to Goldberg for final determination.[8] Once again the carriers agreed, but the organizations demurred.

At this stage President Kennedy was left with no alternative but to refer the dispute to Congress. On 22 July, he sent a special message to Congress, recommending in substance that for a two-year period the Interstate Commerce Commission should be given authority to rule on proposals for interim changes in work rules. He estimated that a nationwide railroad strike would force the almost immediate shutdown of all the industrial establishments that depended primarily on rail shipments, jeopardize fruit, vegetable, and grain crops, disrupt mail service and commuter traffic, and—if it lasted even 30 days—result in the layoff of some six million nonrailroad workers in addition to the 700,000 idled railroad employees. The result would be a rise in unemployment of 15 percent and a drastic decline in production and in the country's competitive position in foreign and domestic markets. Noting that the dispute over railroad work rules was part of a much broader national problem, Kennedy declared his intention to appoint a presidential commission on automation, which would be charged with the responsibility for, among other things, identifying and describing the major types of worker displacement, both technical and economic, likely to occur during the next 10 years and the effect on the economy, manpower, communities, families, and social structure and human values. (President Kennedy

---

[8] This singularly inappropriate suggestion was another indication of Goldberg's insatiable desire to play a key role in every labor dispute, founded on his unshakable conviction that he could always work out a formula for settlement. An even stranger manifestation of this tendency occurred a short time after he had succumbed to President Johnson's blandishments and traded his seat on the Supreme Court for the position of U.S. Ambassador to the United Nations. I met Arthur at a conference in Washington and asked him how he liked his new job. Ignoring my question, he referred to a threatened strike by musicians of the New York Philharmonic Orchestra and said, "If they'd only let me in on that dispute, I'm sure I could settle it!"

died before he could establish this commission, but President Johnson did so in 1965.)

Lengthy hearings were held on the president's legislative proposals by committees of the House and Senate, and the parties again agreed to extend the status quo, this time to 29 August. Wirtz undertook once again to mediate the dispute. Despite his heroic efforts, the parties remained deadlocked. Thus, by 28 August, after four years of collective bargaining, exhaustion of the mediation procedure of the Railway Labor Act, investigation and recommendations of two presidential commissions, and intensive mediation by the secretary and assistant secretary of labor and the NMB, the country was on the brink of a national railroad strike. Faced with this prospect, and despite the nation's traditional opposition to compulsory arbitration of labor disputes, Congress enacted Public Law 88-108, ordering arbitration.

The new law created an arbitration board to be composed of seven members, two each representing the carriers and the organizations, and three others selected by the president. The board was ordered to rule on the firemen and crew consist issues, and its award was to be "binding on both the carrier and organization parties to the dispute and…constitute a complete and final disposition" of those issues. Its award was to continue in force for a period determined by the board, but was not to exceed two years from the date it took effect, unless the parties agreed otherwise.

Some notion of the magnitude of the board's task is provided in part by the following: it held 29 days of hearings, received testimony of more than 40 witnesses recorded in almost 5,000 pages of transcript, and examined more than 200 documentary exhibits, together with a number of motion pictures, photographs, and charts; it made inspection trips to four railroad yards in the Chicago area; and it discussed the issues at length in executive sessions. But as the public members were to discover almost from the start of the proceedings, the most formidable—and ultimately insurmountable—barriers were the unyielding attitudes of the parties, whose positions remained unaltered during the entire course of the case.

My participation in this case was quite unexpected. Although I had been appointed by President Kennedy to serve on emergency boards on two previous occasions, I doubt that he had any recollection of who I was. I therefore attribute his designation of me as a public member of Arbitration Board No. 282 to the recommendation of my good friend, Secretary of Labor Wirtz. In September 1963, I was scheduled to deliver the national report on the subject of internal relations between unions and their members at the Fifth International Congress of the International Society for Labor Law and Social Legislation, as it was then known, in Lyon, France. I got as far as Paris, where I spent the night of 7 September on the town with friends, expecting to continue on to Lyon the following day. When I returned to my hotel early in the morning, I found a telegram from Assistant Secretary of Labor Reynolds, advising me that the president had officially named Ralph Seward, James J. Healy, and me as public members of the arbitration board, and that a meeting of the full board had been scheduled a few days hence. I spent that afternoon trying to change my return ticket in an unsuccessful attempt to triumph over the boorish indifference of the clerks at a Pan American Airways ticket office. I finally gave up and went out to the airport early the next day, where I was able, moments before takeoff, to secure the last seat on a flight to Washington.

The organizational meeting of the board was held on 11 September 1963. Although I was well acquainted with Seward and Healy, this was my first encounter with the four partisan members. The carrier arbitrators were J. E. Wolfe (universally referred to as "Doc"), chairman of the NRLC, and G. W. Knight, vice president of the Pennsylvania Railroad. The organization arbitrators were H. E. Gilbert, president of the BLFE, and R. H. McDonald, a representative of the BRT. A diminutive man, scarcely five feet tall, Wolfe was by far the shrewdest and the most dynamic of the partisan board members. Truly a legend in his own time, he had started working in the railroad industry at the age of 10, and his knowledge of all its intricacies was encyclopedic. Gilbert, an honest and sincere man, was simply no match for Wolfe in negotiating skills. Totally obsessed with pushing the demands of the locomotive firemen, Gilbert's attitude was one of unyielding stubbornness; the word *compromise* was simply not in his vocabulary. Knight and McDonald played subordinate roles, although each had considerable experience and expert knowledge about the issues in dispute.

Our first executive session provided a hint of what was to come. The joint resolution adopted by Congress provided that the president should appoint the public members of Arbitration Board No. 282 but said nothing about the designation of a chairman. President Kennedy assumed that he was to appoint the chairman and announced that Seward would head the board. At our first meeting the partisan members insisted that it was up to the board to name its own chairman. Having made their point, Wolfe, seconded by McDonald, moved that Seward be so designated and the motion carried unanimously. Although the joint resolution specifically directed that the arbitration board incorporate in its decision "any matters on which it finds the parties are in agreement,… resolve the matters on which the parties are not in agreement, and…give due consideration to those matters on which the parties are in tentative agreement," we spent several hours arguing over the scope of our inquiry, it being clear that both sides were reserving the right to challenge items reported by the secretary of labor to be in actual or tentative agreement.

Because time was of the essence, the parties agreed to schedule hearings five days a week. At my request, we agreed to meet Tuesday through Saturday. I had a particular reason for wanting Mondays free. For the first time since I joined the UCLA law faculty in 1960, I had been assigned to teach the basic course in labor law, which met Mondays, Tuesdays, and Wednesdays, from 9:00 to 10:00 a.m. I desperately wanted to continue teaching that course. A few months earlier, Derek Bok, the future dean of the Harvard Law School and president of Harvard University, but then a junior law professor, had been given a leave to do some research and had asked me if he could be provided a place to work at UCLA. I was able to make the necessary arrangements, and he was assigned an office close to mine. Imposing shamelessly on our friendship, I asked Bok if he could teach my course on Wednesdays for the duration of the arbitration board hearings. He generously agreed and we worked out the following schedule. Instead of meeting the class on Monday and Tuesday at 9:00 a.m., I would teach two hours on Monday, from 7:00 to 9:00 a.m. Bok would teach on Wednesday at the usual time. We also agreed that he would concentrate on that section of the course dealing with problems of recognition and certification of unions, a subject on which he was then writing an article, while I would cover the rest. There was considerable doubt in my mind that I could persuade more than a handful of the approximately 90 students enrolled in the course to show up at 7:00 a.m. To induce them to do so, I promised to take the first 15 minutes of each session to bring them up to date on the more interesting aspects of the railroad dispute as they unfolded in the arbitration hearings. To my great surprise, attendance at my Monday class was about the same as it would have been had we met at the previously scheduled time.

The downside of this arrangement was that it forced me to adhere to an exhausting schedule. Our Saturday hearings in Washington ended about 1:00 p.m., following which I rushed to the airport in time to catch a flight to Los Angeles that arrived in the evening. Sundays, I rose early and spent a large portion of the day at UCLA, attending to administrative matters at the Institute of Industrial Relations, of which I was the director, and preparing for my labor law class the next day. As soon as my Monday class was over, I went directly to the airport and flew back to Washington. Healy and I each had a room at the same hotel, which we kept for the duration of the hearings. In them we kept our individual copies of the daily transcripts and exhibits, and upon my arrival on Monday nights, I would review those in preparation for the next day's hearing.

Hearings before the board commenced on 24 September and concluded on 2 November 1963. Despite the urging by the public members that the presentation of testimony and documentary evidence be streamlined and concentrated on the key elements of disagreement over the firemen and crew consist issues, we were unable to achieve that result. As I recalled in a piece written about 15 years later, in their mutual desire to prevent the possibility that the public members would intrude too recklessly into the special world of the railroad industry, the partisan members of the board and counsel for both sides managed effectively to keep out of the record most of the critical information about industry practices that would have been most useful to the public members in formulating their decision.[9] Instead, they presented lengthy testimony and submitted countless exhibits, a great portion of which was irrelevant. Conversely, the board heard much too little that was relevant. Not until after the parties began reconvening the board following the issuance of its award and to raise questions of interpretation of its provisions did the public members begin to grasp fully the hidden complexities of the issues submitted to the board.

On 6 and 7 November, the public members, with the agreement of the parties, visited certain railroad yards in the Chicago area, where we observed, among other things, the astonishing spectacle of an automated marshalling yard in which freight cars were detached and then reassembled in different combinations—the entire operation being handled by one man sitting in a control booth. Rebuttal exhibits and written arguments were received on 9 November. This left the board with just 17 days to come to a decision and write its opinion. My notes show that the board met in executive session at various times between 12 and 20 November, thus allowing the public members only about two days to prepare the final drafts of their decision and opinion. By now it was clear that the opinion would represent the views of only the public members and that separate opinions by the partisan members would be filed.

The task of writing the public members' opinion was divided into three parts: Seward wrote the introduction, summarizing the lengthy history of the dispute and describing the board's approach to the firemen and crew consist issues, and Healy and I wrote the sections on crew consist and firemen, respectively.

Early on in the hearings it had become apparent even to the organization members of the board, whether they would admit it or not, that there would have to be some reduction in the number of firemen's jobs, and that there would also have to be readjustments in the consists of some train crews. It was necessary, therefore, to decide not only how

[9]Benjamin Aaron et al., "Voluntary Arbitration of Railroad and Airline Interest Disputes," in *The Railway Labor Act at Fifty: Collective Bargaining in the Railroad and Airline Industries* (Washington, D.C.: National Mediation Board, 1977), 129, 145.

many of those jobs should be eliminated, or "blanked," but also what to do with the present incumbents of those jobs. With that in mind, the public members had tentatively suggested that they would be greatly aided in deciding that question by private, separate discussions with the partisan members. To our surprise and disappointment, the suggestion was indignantly rejected by all the partisan members as soon as it was made. In fact, they insisted on formally adopting a motion forbidding the public members from meeting separately with either side without the other's express permission, which they assured us would never be granted. This response led me to the melancholy conviction that the only thing the disputants could agree upon was a decision likely to increase the risks for both in the outcome of the case.

On the fireman issue the public members ultimately decided on a procedure under which the carriers could blank all firemen's jobs and the organizations could veto management's decision for a certain percentage of those jobs. Such vetoes would be final and not subject to challenge. The critical question thus became the size of the percentage of firemen's jobs blanked by a carrier should the organization representing them be allowed to veto. The public members concluded that the record evidence justified a maximum of only 10 percent, but we also felt sure that a substantially larger figure would be acceptable to the carriers. We presented the general outline of our proposed award during the executive sessions following the end of the formal hearings, and we urged our partisan colleagues to give us some ideas of their own as to the percentage of blanked jobs the organizations should be allowed to veto. Once again our overtures were rejected. Continuing their obdurate refusal to consider any compromise, both groups stood firm, and we were left with no choice but to incorporate the 10 percent figure in our award. When we finally announced our decision on this point to the partisan members, Gilbert went into shock, saying that he had never imagined that we would set so low a figure. Wolfe and Knight, on the other hand, could scarcely conceal their great satisfaction with the outcome, thus seeming to confirm our belief that they would have accepted a substantially higher figure.

Rather than go into the specifics of the award, I shall simply quote the brief summary contained in the opinion of Circuit Judge Leventhal in *Brotherhood of Railroad Trainmen v. Akron & Barberton Belt R.R.*

> Award 282 held that the nearly 200 carriers involved could eliminate ninety percent of the firemen positions, and set forth a procedure for dismissal and attrition. It was a staggering blow to the BLFE. The award did not, however, authorize a single spasmodic discharge of thousands of firemen. Indeed, in some aspects it was "highly favorable to the employees" [citing the opinion of the federal district court]. Thus the Award guaranteed permanent employment for life, or until retirement or resignation [or dismissal for cause], for every fireman who had been in active service for more than ten years, with a comparable job insured for all with service of two years or more. Those firemen with less than two years seniority were accorded severance allowances, amounting in some cases to six months pay. Under the terms of this Award the carriers have pruned eighteen thousand firemen from their ranks, paid out some $36,000,000 in separation benefits, and provided comparable jobs to twelve hundred former firemen.
>
> On the crew consist issue, the Board determined that a single national standard would be inappropriate. It ruled that no change in crew consist be made except pursuant to the Award. Then it required that where existing rules provided more or less than two trainmen, any party might give notice of a proposed change. If after conferences were held by the local properties no agreement was forthcoming, the issue could be referred to a special board of adjustment created at the local level. The Award articulated a series of "guidelines" to be followed by these special boards in resolving particular disputes. Many crew consist agreements and special awards were made under this procedure.[10]

In addition, with further regard to the firemen issue, in recognition that the overall formula provided in the award might prove to be inadequate or unfair, the award also called for the establishment of a national joint board comprised of two representatives of the carriers and one each of the BLFE and BLE, who would be charged with the responsibility for making an intensive and continuing study of the experience in road freight and yard service with and without the employment of fireman during the period that the award remained in effect. As specified in the joint resolution, that period was a maximum of two years. During a three-month period prior to the expiration of the award, the national joint board was also directed to issue a report based on its study.

---

[10] 385 F.2d 581 (D.C. Cir. 1967), *cert. denied*, 390 U.S. 923 (1968).

As anticipated, the carrier members of the board signed the award, thereby creating the necessary majority. Although their separate statement expressed disappointment with a few of the award's provisions, they praised the public members for "the care and diligence which they have shown in their efforts to make a fair and just award." The reactions of the two organization members, each of whom filed a dissenting opinion, were another matter. The main thrust of Gilbert's lengthy dissent was that Arbitration Board No. 282 had disregarded congressional intent and the express wording of the joint resolution by not incorporating in its award matters on which the parties were in agreement and by limiting its own input to matters on which the parties remained in disagreement. He argued that in their final negotiations with the secretary of labor the parties had reached substantial agreement on a number of points and that it was sheer sophistry on the carriers' part to insist that because those understandings had not been reduced to writing, the points to which they applied were still in dispute. McDonald's shorter dissenting opinion complained that the compulsory arbitration procedure imposed by the joint resolution "was forced upon the employee parties unwillingly and without their consent" and without proof that a genuine emergency existed. He also joined Gilbert in charging that the board had misinterpreted and misapplied the joint resolution in reaching its decision.

The deadline for our award was Monday, 25 November, at which time we had an appointment at the White House to present the board's decision and opinion to the president, who was expected to be back by then from his trip to Dallas. On Friday, 22 November, Healy and I were putting the final touches on our respective sections of the public members' opinion. We finished about noon and decided to celebrate the event by giving ourselves an elegant lunch at Harvey's Restaurant, then considered one of Washington's best. After lunch we strolled back to the hotel. Healy said he had a few changes to make in his draft and returned to his room. I lingered in the lobby, intending to buy a cigar before going back to mine. The young woman behind the cigar counter was on the telephone to someone and sobbing convulsively. Suddenly she turned to me and cried, "Isn't it awful?" Seeing that I did not understand what she was talking about, she said, "The president's been shot!" At that, I turned and ran up three flights of stairs to my room and turned on the television, just in time to hear Walter Cronkeit announce in somber tones that President Kennedy was dead.

I don't suppose that anyone who was old enough to comprehend the enormity of President Kennedy's assassination will ever forget that terrible day, which plunged the nation into sorrow and despair. Everyone seemed to be in a state of shock. I spent that evening at the house of friends. We sat up until the early hours of the next day, mourning the abrupt termination of a life so full of promise and speculating fearfully on what the immediate future held for our country. Remembering how Truman had surpassed almost everyone's expectations when he succeeded to the presidency following Roosevelt's death in 1945, I resolved to withhold my personal judgment about Lyndon Johnson, whom I did not greatly admire, until he had had an adequate period in office to demonstrate his capabilities in his new role.

Seward reconvened the arbitration board in emergency session on Saturday, 23 November. In light of the crisis created by President Kennedy's death, the public members urged our partisan colleagues, in the public interest, to settle their dispute voluntarily, even if it meant ignoring or modifying some provisions of the award. Both sides remained adamant in their refusal to alter the positions they had previously taken. Reluctantly, we had to concede defeat and to deliver our decision and opinion to the White House.

I remained in Washington long enough to watch the dead president's cortege as it proceeded slowly from the White House to the Capitol, the flag-draped coffin mounted on a gun carriage, followed by a riderless black stallion. As the procession moved past where I was standing on Pennsylvania Avenue, an awful silence descended on the huge crowd gathered there. The recollection of that scene remains vividly with me still.

The aftermath of our decision in the railroad work rules dispute was as contentious and almost as long as the events preceding it. The organizations immediately sued in federal district court to impeach the award. The attack was two-pronged: first, they contended that the statute authorizing compulsory arbitration in this context was unconstitutional because it was beyond the power of Congress or, in the alternative, that it delegated power to an administrative body without adequate standards to govern its decision. Second, they argued that the award did not conform to the statute under which it claimed validity. Both of these arguments had been prefigured in the dissents of Gilbert and McDonald. In 1964, the district court rejected both challenges, approved the statute, and confirmed the award. The court of appeals affirmed, and the Supreme Court denied certiorari, thus putting an end to this aspect of the dispute.

But litigation continued. In subsequent months a number of suits were filed by the organizations and the carriers that presented issues involving the proper construction of the statute or award as it applied to individual fact situations. Instead of using the two-year period specified by Congress and the award to engage in negotiations looking toward long-range adjustments of the problems confronting them, the parties chose instead to be guided by speculations on whether the expiration of the award would leave them in a better position than they might achieve by returning to the bargaining table, where some concessions might have to be made by each side. Although the parties named representatives to serve on the national joint board established by the award to review the results of eliminating some firemen's jobs, the board never met. The organizations took the position that upon expiration of the award at the end of two years, the situation would return to the status quo ante and the National Diesel Agreement would once more control work rules. As a hedge, they served notices proposing in substance that on termination of the award, work rules substantially similar to the old rules, with relatively minor adjustments, would come into effect.

In sharp disagreement, the carriers argued that the status created by the award continued in effect even after the award itself expired. They also filed notices to preserve the benefits provided to them by the award. Suits and counter-suits filed in federal district court by both sides raised two basic issues: which set of rules were in force the day after the award expired, and whether the parties had a duty to bargain about changing

those rules and, if so, when that duty arose. In a guideline opinion underlying the subsequent rulings, the district court held in 1966 that even
though the award had formally terminated, it had created a "new plateau"
of work rules, which were to continue in force until changed pursuant
to the procedures of the Railway Labor Act. This holding was affirmed
by the court of appeals for the District of Columbia. The district court
also held that the notices filed by the parties while the award was still in
effect did not require negotiation until after the award terminated. This
holding was reversed by the court of appeals, which ruled that the parties
had an obligation to bargain over proposed changes to the rules during
the period before the expiration of the award in order to try to reach an
agreement that would become effective upon termination of the award.

Meanwhile, in 1965, seeking vindication of its position in another
forum, the BLFE invoked the legislative oversight jurisdiction of the
Senate Commerce Committee over Public Law 99-108 (the joint resolution) by filing charges that Arbitration Board No. 282 had not properly
carried out its functions under that law. The committee held 17 sessions
over a period from 2 August through 28 September and heard numerous
witnesses, including Gilbert, Wolfe, Seward, and me (Healy was unable
to attend because of other commitments). All of the issues in the case
were thoroughly rehashed, but the hearings led to no legislative action.

Under a provision of the Railway Labor Act applicable to the award
of Arbitration Board 282, any disputes over the meaning or application of the award could be referred back to the board for adjudication.
The parties to the work rules dispute took full advantage of this right.
Between November 1963 and October 1968, the board was reconvened
in Washington numerous times to resolve more than 300 such questions.
We public members of the board were eager, to put it mildly, to be rid of
our responsibilities, because the interruptions of our own work schedules were becoming increasingly onerous. Taking advantage of the first
time the NMB informed us that no requests for further interpretations
of the award were pending, we sent President Johnson a letter, dated 3
October 1968, informing him of that fact and stating that we considered our work to be completed and that this was an appropriate time to

terminate our service on the board. It took a while for the president to respond, but on 21 December 1968 he sent each of us a letter accepting our resignations and expressing his appreciation for our services.

The five years spent on this assignment meant, as the president acknowledged in his letter, "putting aside many professional and personal obligations," but that fact notwithstanding, I concluded in retrospect that the experience was worth it. The foremost truth emerging from this drawn out process was that disputes of such magnitude cannot be effectively resolved by a law or an arbitration award, even though governmental action might be needed to prevent a national emergency. The work rules dispute was finally settled by the parties themselves through collective bargaining. I have often wondered if this result would not have been achieved earlier if the joint resolution had simply required that the status quo be maintained by all parties until they mutually agreed on a new set of work rules. This would have put considerable pressure on both parties while depriving them of their most potent weapons: the organizations' right to strike and the carriers' right to make unilateral changes in work rules they felt were unduly burdensome. The procedure dictated by Congress did prevent a national stoppage of rail services, but in all other respects it was far from satisfactory. Restricted by the terms of the joint resolution as well as the incomprehensible (at least to the public members) decisions of the organization members of the board to resist all mediation efforts on our part and to cooperate with the carriers in pursuing a course leading ineluctably to disaster, we were compelled to issue an award that brought no quick end to the dispute and nearly destroyed the BLFE.

EMERGENCY LABOR DISPUTE TASK FORCE

Although there were only 29 instances between 1947 and 1968 when Taft-Hartley emergency disputes procedures were invoked (there were 88 occasions when RLA emergency boards were established in railroad or airline disputes in the same period), the high visibility of those cases contributed to a continuing quest for ways to improve the handling of emergency disputes under the Taft-Hartley and Railway

Labor Acts. Indeed, the introduction of new bills to repeal, revise, or supplement emergency dispute procedures under either or both statutes was as dependable as the annual return of the swallows to the mission at San Juan Capistrano. Concocting panaceas for dealing with emergency disputes became a popular indoor sport, and it was obvious from some of the goofier proposals advanced that expert knowledge of the problem was not a requirement of participation. The years 1966 through 1967, in particular, proved to be very embarrassing for President Johnson and his administration in this regard. In 1966, the IAM rejected the recommendations of RLA Emergency Board No. 166 (chaired by Senator Wayne Morse) in a wage dispute with five airlines, leading to mediation efforts by President Johnson himself that produced a tentative agreement on an increase somewhat higher than that recommended by the board and the administration's own wage guideposts. That agreement was rejected by the union membership, and a 43-day strike followed that shut down 60 percent of the domestic trunkline air industry. The ultimate wage settlement was higher than the previous tentative agreement. A similar fiasco occurred in 1967, when a dispute between six shop craft unions and most of the major railroads led to the unions' rejection of the recommendations of two boards and a two-day strike. Congress than passed a law ordering the strikers back to work and setting up a third board to decide the issues in dispute. This process was described as "mediation to finality," a transparent euphemism for compulsory arbitration.

In November 1966, President Johnson created an emergency labor dispute task force. I was asked to serve on it. The group was headed by Nicholas Katzenbach, the undersecretary of state, and included Bok; Dunlop; David Ginsburg, former general counsel of the Office of Price Administration in World War II and a well-known Washington lawyer and presidential adviser; Bernard Meltzer, University of Chicago Law School; J. Keith Mann, Stanford University Law School; and Assistant Secretary of Labor Reynolds.

My appointment as a member of the task force came in a letter dated 6 November 1966 from Joseph A. Califano Jr., special assistant to President Johnson, setting forth the purpose of the task force—to develop some practical alternatives for dealing with emergency labor disputes—and emphasizing that both the right to strike and the protection of the public interest must be preserved. He suggested that the task force focus initially on four questions: first, what tools, if any, should be given to the government to use after the expiration of "freeze" periods in existing legislation; second, what emphasis should be put on efforts to avert emergency disputes, either by improving mediatory and procedural aspects of existing legislation or by encouraging labor and management to improve the structure and procedures of collective bargaining; third, should federal legislation embrace state and local disputes, and if so, how; and fourth, should the test of any "emergency dispute" be redefined, and if so, should this extend to an attempt to deal with the problem of wage settlements that might be inflationary.

The letter arrived just a few months after I had begun a year's stay as a fellow at the Center for Advanced Study in the Behavioral Sciences in Stanford, California. It announced that the first meeting of the group would be held in Washington on 15 November. Mann and I arranged to travel to Washington together. Two days before our scheduled departure, I was coaxed against my better judgment and over Eleanor's strong protest into participating in a touch football game at a fellows' picnic on the campus of UC Santa Cruz. On the very first play I managed to fracture my ankle and was hauled off to a hospital, where a walking cast was put on my leg. Unfortunately, my ankle and leg swelled so much that walking was too painful to endure. So, armed with crutches and trundled to the gate in a wheelchair, I flew to Washington with Keith the next day.

The only member of the task force I did not know was our chairman, Katzenbach. Despite his lack of background in labor law or industrial relations, he proved to be an ideal choice. He was urbane, good-humored, and very skillful in running a meeting and keeping the discussion focused on the principal points. The members of the task force worked together easily and quickly. Each of us prepared a memorandum setting forth our responses to the questions raised in Califano's letter. After those were discussed over the course of several meetings, Bok was asked to prepare a draft report embodying our consensus conclusions. The rest of us reviewed his draft and suggested changes. The final report was a reasoned analysis of the perceived strengths and weaknesses of the existing Railway Labor Act and Taft-Hartley Act procedures for handling emergency disputes. It proposed only a few modest changes. Specifically, it recommended that the emergency procedures of the RLA be repealed and replaced by new ones that would be applicable to the longshore-maritime industry as well as to railroads and airlines, those being the three industries for which existing procedures had proved to be inadequate. Among the most important of these changes was the transfer of the responsibility of determining that a national emergency exists from the NMB to the secretary of labor, after consultation with the NMB and the FMCS. Although recognizing certain procedural defects in the Taft-Hartley emergency disputes procedures, the report concluded that it would be unwise to seek amendments to that statute. The report supported the idea that management and labor organizations in industries with special problems should explore the possibility of agreeing to their own procedures for resolving emergency disputes, but it endorsed no specific uniform plan for doing so. It opposed extending the federal power to deal with state and municipal emergency disputes and declined to recommend that states be relieved from the restrictions in the Taft-Hartley Act limiting states' ability to devise their own procedures to cope with disputes involving newspapers and privately owned utilities. Similarly, it opposed the suggestion to modify the definition of an emergency dispute to take into consideration inflationary wage demands by unions. Finally, citing the numerous previous studies, seminars, and articles on the subject of national emergency disputes, the report expressed the view that another broad, government-sponsored study of the issue would not contribute substantially to the resolution of those problems.

The task force report was completed and delivered to the president some time in December 1966. Our last meeting was held at the State Department, and because I was still on crutches, Keith and I were taken to the airport in a department limousine. The other passenger was Ellsworth Bunker, then U.S. ambassador to South Vietnam. He proved to be an elegant gentleman, every inch the diplomat, and very good company. By tacit agreement, Keith and I did not air our strong opposition to the war in Vietnam, which was probably just as well.

When it was all over, each of the task force members received a personal letter of thanks from President Johnson. It contained the formulaic paragraph included in all such communications: "Our nation is indeed fortunate that outstanding individuals such as you are willing to interrupt busy schedules and longstanding commitments to devote their talents and energies to the resolution of the complex problems we face." Of greater interest to me was his promise to study our report carefully, and his assurance that "your recommendations will be thoroughly considered as our programs are developed."

And that, so far as I know, was the last anyone ever heard of our report, which was apparently deep-sixed by the president. In fact, the report was never released to the press, although I saw in the BNA's *Labor Relations Reporter* for 30 January 1967 what purported to be a summary of the task force's recommendations, based on "interviews and inquiries." I can only surmise that what for a time the president and his advisers had judged to be a dangerous situation requiring some initiative by the White House had cooled down by the time the task force submitted its report, and that they had concluded that it was best to let sleeping dogs lie.

The steady decline in the size and influence of the American labor movement beginning in the 1970s, together with periods of recession and a general politicized tilt to the right in the Republican administrations of Ronald Reagan and George H. W. Bush, led to a continuing diminution in the number of national emergency disputes. As the latest free-market incarnation has gained ascendancy, bringing with it renewed attacks against collective bargaining as the keystone of national labor policy, political leaders and a majority of the American people seem to have accepted that labor laws such as the RLA and the NLRA are virtually irrelevant to the way business and industry are now conducted. These days, in the relatively rare instances in which national or regional emergency labor disputes involving airlines, for example, do arise, the tendency is immediately to invoke existing statutory procedures and then, if the parties cannot settle their dispute within the specified statutory period, order them to submit the issues to final and binding arbitration. Efforts continue to be made, it is true, to develop through so-called preventive mediation ways to prevent such disputes from arising or from getting out of hand, but so far the results are mixed.

Contrary to the current weight of opinion, and after reviewing the numerous proposals for dealing with emergency disputes that I have studied over the years, I still believe that the best way to deal with such disputes—either by prevention or by reducing their harmful impacts if and when they arise—is to support and strengthen the institution of collective bargaining. In this connection, I also support the idea, long promoted by Dunlop, among others, that in those industries in which emergency disputes have arisen most frequently, the collective bargaining parties should develop special settlement procedures designed to address the problems peculiar to each industry. Finally, I believe that responsible public officials should be less ready to denominate a strike or lockout a "national emergency" than they have been in the past. We can all agree that a nationwide stoppage of rail or air traffic is a national emergency, and there may be a few instances in which a regional or even local cessation of a critical public service also creates a true emergency. The common factor in these examples is that the disputants can hold out longer than the public they serve. In many other cases, however, the cessation of operations constitutes at most a severe inconvenience to the public. Any system that encourages the weaker party in a labor dispute to seek governmental intervention, rather than trying to achieve a settlement through collective bargaining, may prove in the long run to be detrimental to our society, because a predictable intervention by the state almost always gives one party an advantage over the other.

CHAPTER 5

THE NATIONAL COMMISSION ON TECHNOLOGY, AUTOMATION, AND ECONOMIC PROGRESS, 1964–1966

In 1963, President Kennedy announced his intention to establish a presidential commission on automation as part of his recommendations for settling the dispute over railroad work rules. He was assassinated before he could do so. Nevertheless, after holding extensive hearings over a seven-month period in 1963 on employment problems confronting the nation, Congress enacted Public Law 88-444 in August 1964, creating a National Commission on Technology, Automation, and Economic Progress. The commission was composed of 14 members appointed by the president, with the advice of the Senate, from persons outside the government who possessed the necessary competency. The commission, intended to be broadly representative, was to include at least four members drawn equally from labor and management. In addition, the law established a federal interagency committee that was jointly chaired by Secretary of Labor Willard Wirtz and Secretary of Commerce John T. Connor.[1]

The chairman of the commission was Howard R. Bowen, an economist and the president of the University of Iowa. A thoughtful, rather modest man, he proved quite adept at dealing with some of the more opinionated and temperamental members, besides contributing his own substantial proposals. The biggest stars, so far as I was concerned, were professors Robert M. Solow from MIT, who subsequently won a Nobel prize in economics; Daniel Bell, an influential sociologist then at Columbia; and Edwin H. Land, president and research director of the

---

[1] Other members of the committee were the heads of the Departments of Agriculture, Defense, and Health, Education, and Welfare, the National Aeronautical and Space Administration, the Council of Economic Advisors, the Office of Science and Technology, the Atomic Energy Commission, and the United States Arms Control and Disarmament Agency.

Polaroid Corporation and inventor of the revolutionary Polaroid camera. Other industry representatives were Patrick E. Haggerty, president of Texas Instruments; Thomas J. Watson Jr., chairman of the board of IBM; and Philip Sporn, chairman of the System Development Committee, American Electrical Power Company. Organized labor's representatives on the commission were Walter P. Reuther, president of the United Auto Workers; Joseph A. Beirne, president of the Communications Workers of America; and Albert J. Hayes, past president of the International Association of Machinists. The remaining members in addition to me were Whitney M. Young, Jr., executive director of the National Urban League; Anna Rosenberg, president of a consulting firm; and Robert H. Ryan, president of the Regional Industrial Development Corporation of Southwestern Pennsylvania. I have never asked Wirtz, to whom I obviously owed my appointment, why he nominated me. I assume he did so in part because of our close friendship and his trust in my judgment. That I was the only member of the commission with a background in law and industrial relations may also have had something to do with it. In any case, as the youngest and least well known of the members, I approached my assignment with considerable unease and diffidence.

The legislative charge to the commission was overly ambitious in my opinion.[2] In abbreviated summary, it included the following:

1. To identify and assess the past effects and the current and prospective role and pace of technological change.
2. To identify and describe the impact of technological and economic change on production and employment likely to occur during the next 10 years; the specific industries, occupations, and geographic areas most likely to be involved; and the social and economic effects of these developments on the nation's economy, manpower, communities, families, social structure, and human values.
3. To define those areas of unmet community and human needs toward which application of new technologies might most effectively be directed.

[2] Public Law, 88-444 (1964).

4. To access the most effective means for channeling technologies into promising directions, and assess the proper relationship between governmental and private investment in the application of new technologies to large-scale human and community needs.

5. To recommend, in addition to those actions which are the responsibility of management and labor, specific administrative and legislative steps which should be taken by the federal, state, and local governments in meeting their responsibilities (1) to support and promote technological change in the interest of continued economic growth and improved well-being of our people, (2) to adopt measures that will facilitate occupational adjustment and geographical mobility, and (3) to share the costs and help prevent and alleviate the adverse impact of change on displaced workers.

The commission met in monthly two-day sessions beginning in January 1965. It heard a great many witnesses, received reports from numerous organizations and individuals, and had the assistance of a highly competent and dedicated staff.[3] The first session was held at the White House and was attended for part of the time by President Johnson. This was my first personal contact with Johnson. He arrived shortly after the session got under way, looking much the worse for wear: his face was pale and drawn, and he was obviously suffering from a severe head cold. Sitting quietly, slumped in his chair, he evidenced no outward reaction to the ongoing discussion. When Wirtz, who chaired the session, asked him if he had anything he wanted to say to the group, the president responded with what I later came to recognize as a typical Johnson ploy. No, he said, in a tired, croaky voice, he had nothing to say; rather, he had come to listen and to learn. He humbly thanked the commission members, whom he described as learned and distinguished public servants, for selflessly taking time away from their busy schedules and important pursuits to help solve the weighty problems confronting the

---

[3] Those reports were published in 1966 by the U.S. Government Printing Office in six appendices to the commission's report: "The Outlook for Technological Change and Employment," "The Employment Impact of Technological Change," "Adjusting to Change," "Educational Implications of Technological Change," "Applying Technology to Unmet Needs," and "Statements Relating to the Impact of Technological Change."

nation. Then he walked around the table, shaking hands with each of us before making his exit. I confess to having been deeply impressed by this performance, not realizing at the time that it was no more than that.

For me, the subsequent meetings of the commission were like a continuing seminar, during the course of which I learned a great deal from my fellow commissioners and from some of our witnesses, but to which I had relatively little to contribute. Our principal emphasis, at least at the start, was on the impact of technology on employment. When Public Law 88-444 was passed, the national unemployment rate was 5.1 percent, compared to about 3 percent at the end of the Korean War. The United States and much of the rest of the world were experiencing a rapid increase in scientific and technological development. Stock phrases— "raging technology," "knowledge explosion," "second industrial revolution," "automation revolution"—reflected popular opinion. According to one extreme view, the world—or at least the United States—was on the verge of a glut of productivity sufficient to make obsolete our economic institutions and the very concept of gainful employment, with the economic role of individual citizens reduced to that of consumers of abundance. Labor unions, in particular, were inclined to blame the unrestrained impact of new technology for rising unemployment and the consequential decrease in union membership. It was not surprising, therefore, that this question was in the forefront of the commission's concerns. During the life of the commission, however, the situation changed dramatically: largely as a result of tax cuts and other fiscal policies adopted in early 1964, unemployment was reduced to 4 percent. The largest portion of the commission's deliberations and report therefore dealt with the other issues referred to in Public Law 88-444.

My tangible contributions to the commission's report were minimal, being restricted largely to the section on the adjustment to change for minority groups, which was based chiefly on a memorandum I prepared.[4] This section described and condemned various discriminatory employment practices by employers and unions against racial and ethnic

[4]See National Commission on Technology, Automation, and Economic Progress, *Technology and the American Economy* (Washington, D.C.: U.S. Government Printing Office, 1966), 67–79.

minorities and women. It called for the elimination of such practices and also for the adoption of affirmative action policies to aid minorities and women in obtaining more and better jobs. My memorandum included, in addition, a section that never made it into the commission's report. Noting that under common seniority provisions in collective bargaining agreements, those employees most recently hired were the first to be laid off when the labor force was reduced, I observed that because minority workers were usually last to be hired, the gains achieved by affirmative action programs would be largely nullified by the "last in, first out" rule. I therefore suggested that in some situations it might be advisable to suspend that rule and retain at least some of the recently hired minority workers when layoffs occurred. I subsequently came to realize that this suggestion, though well-intentioned, would probably have created more problems than it would have solved. In the event, it was immediately and violently denounced by the labor members of the commission. Speaking for all three labor members, Reuther launched into an emotional tirade about how union members had fought long and hard to establish the seniority principle as the chief protection against arbitrary and discriminatory practices by their employers, and he declared that they would never consent to any weakening of that principle for whatever reason. I had supposed that the employer members of the commission might endorse my proposal because none of the enterprises they headed was organized and they had nothing to lose. What I failed to appreciate at the time was that they were more concerned about winning the support of the union commission members for other recommendations in the report and thus were unwilling to risk incurring their displeasure.

The no-nonsense mood of the commission's monthly two-day sessions was occasionally relieved by some purely social events. I recall with particular pleasure a moonlight outing on the Potomac aboard the presidential yacht, Sequoia, during which I spent considerable time talking to Paul Hoffman, Anna Rosenberg Hoffman's husband, who had had a distinguished business career, including the presidency of the Studebaker automobile company. A sophisticated and urbane man with a delightful sense of humor, he was a welcome change from some of my more serious colleagues on the commission. On another occasion, we all dined together at a restaurant featuring a dance band. After refusing invitations to dance from several commission members, Anna suddenly jumped out of her seat, grabbed Young, who was black, and hauled him off to the dance floor, saying, "Come on, Whitney, let's integrate this joint!"

Discussions during commission sessions of the various issues under consideration were stimulating, often contentious, and occasionally, to me at least, entertaining when the considerable egos of the more active participants came into conflict. There was perhaps a little too much promotion of individual pet ideas and not enough constructive reaction to the proposals of others. Still, a number of the schemes put forward were imaginative and even exciting. To mention only one of these—a computerized nationwide service for matching work seekers to available jobs—was inspired by Land's curiosity about and study of the American Airlines passenger reservations system. Out of this emerged a commission recommendation to establish a nationwide job and manpower bank that would contain detailed information on the manpower requirements of job vacancies and the personal characteristics of job seekers. Although generally in favor of this innovation, I expressed reservations about possible invasions of the privacy of job seekers, who might not want to have specific items of information given to a prospective employer (e.g., draft status, police record) revealed to anyone else. Not to worry, I was told; either the employer or prospective employee could place any desired restriction upon use of the information supplied, and "appropriate safeguards" could be established to guard against invasion of privacy. The system would function like a safety deposit box: no information could be released without the simultaneous consent of job seeker and employer, just as a safety deposit box cannot be opened without the keys of both the depositor and the bank. Despite these assurances, I remained skeptical. Subsequently, during my year as a visiting fellow at the Center for Advanced Study in the Behavioral Sciences, I was told by one of the local experts on computer technology that it would be relatively easy for an outsider to break into electronic communications between job seekers and employers.

In the end, the commission's 108-page report, together with its major conclusions and recommendations, was virtually unanimous, although there were occasional reservations or outright disagreements (the word *dissent* was scrupulously avoided) noted by individual members on specific points. In general, the three labor leaders, Reuther, Beirne, and Hayes, sometimes joined by Young and Bell, favored endorsement of a more active role by the federal government in dealing with economic and social inequality in our society. The most frequent doubter and objector was Sporn, a rather prickly and uncollegial man, with whom I cannot recall having had even one personal exchange during the life of the commission. He was occasionally joined by Haggerty. These two espoused a policy based on a free market and the encouragement of individual business initiative and evinced a distrust of proposals for increased government planning and control. For example, the chapter of the commission's report on facilitating adjustment to change through public policy offered proposals for helping some regions of the country that were suffering from chronic unemployment, poverty, and hardship. The majority of the commission members recommended, among other things, that each Federal Reserve District establish an advisory council for economic growth composed of leaders from business, labor, government, the universities, and other groups within the district. The council's suggested activities would include the identification and interpretation of all factors affecting the economic well-being of the district, on the basis of which it would prepare comprehensive program and policy recommendations directed at both public and private institutions within the district. In response, Sporn, while recognizing that the problem of economically distressed regions merited a great deal of effort to find a solution, objected to "the superficial analysis and bromidic prescriptions...presented in this report."[5] His views on this and other matters on which he commented seem, in retrospect, to have had somewhat greater merit than I was willing to concede at the time.

---

[5] *Technology and the American Economy*, 57. Dissent from commission discussion of the problem of economically distressed regions and its proposals for facilitating regional adjustment.

It is not feasible to summarize here, even in broad outline, all of the commission's findings and recommendations. I shall limit this account, therefore, primarily to a brief description of those dealing with the pace of technological change and its effects on employment—the principal sources of public concern at the time. In its discussion of the pace of technological change, the commission noted that technological change does not proceed evenly over time, but it agreed with the popular impression that the near future, as well as the present, would likely be a time of rapid technological progress. It based this conclusion on the combination of increased expenditure on research and development, extended and deepened education, continued urbanization, and improved communications. At the same time, the commission professed an inability to know "whether the computer, nuclear power, and molecular biology are quantitatively or qualitatively more 'revolutionary' than the telephone, electric power, and bacteriology." Its broad conclusion was that the pace of technological change had increased in recent decades and might increase in the future, but that a sharp break in the continuity of technical progress had not occurred and was unlikely to do so in the next decade. A number of commission members filed additional comments to this section of the report. The three labor members, joined by Young and Rosenberg, regretted that the section lacked the "tone of urgency" that they felt was called for. They expressed the hope that the report would be read and understood as a call for "the full mobilization of America's resources in the building of a truly Great Society." By contrast, Sporn, joined by Haggerty, deplored the report's failure to give adequate emphasis to the positive contributions of technology. While recognizing that, largely because of the beneficial effects of technological progress, society was no longer willing to accept "the inevitability of the hardships and dislocations that often accompany the change characteristic of a dynamic society," they asserted that this did not constitute an indictment of technology; rather, it should be regarded only as "a challenge to the dynamism, strength, and adaptability of the nation's political, social, and economic institutions to develop and facilitate the widespread introduction of new technology and the wider dissemination of its benefits."[6]

---

[6] *Technology and the American Economy*, 7. General comment on report.

Despite these differences in emphasis, the commission members unanimously supported the conclusions reached in the chapter of the report devoted to technological change and unemployment;not one member filed even a comment on the text. The principal point emphasized in this chapter was that the general level of unemployment must be distinguished from the displacement of particular workers at specific times and places. The persistence of a high general level of unemployment in the years following the Korean War, the commission reported, was not the result of accelerated technological progress but was caused by the interaction between rising productivity, labor force growth, and the lack of a compensating growth of aggregate demand. "The basic fact," it concluded, "is that technology eliminates jobs, not work." Thus, the continuous obligation of economic policy is "to match increases in productive potential with increases in purchasing power and demand. Otherwise the potential created by technical progress runs to waste in idle capacity, unemployment, and deprivation."[7] That economic growth can offset the growth of productivity and the labor force and reduce unemployment, the commission pointed out, was evidenced by the sharp reduction in unemployment from 5.1 to 4 percent in the two years from 1964 to 1966. This proved, it concluded, that the high unemployment leading to the formation of the commission was caused by passive public policy and was not the inevitable consequence of the pace of technological change.

On the question of the influence of skill and education on unemployment, the commission observed that in a slack labor market employers must have some means of selecting among numerous job applicants, and that it was not surprising that educational attainment was often used as a convenient yardstick, regardless of its direct relevance to the requirements of the job. Using the metaphor of a giant "shape-up," the commission described the labor market as one in which those looking for work queued in order of their relative attractiveness to employers.[8] If the

---

[7] *Technology and the American Economy*, 9.

[8] A labor term to describe the assembly of workers at the beginning of the workday, from which some will be selected by the employer's or a union's representative and the others dismissed.

labor market operates efficiently, employers will start at the head of the line, selecting as many as they need of employees most attractive to them. Such choices may be based on objective standards relating to ability, or on invidious standards of race, sex, or age. Wage differentials may also be important and formal education may be used as a rough screening device. The total number of employed and unemployed depends primarily on the general state of economic activity. The unemployed tend to be those near the end. Only as demand rises will employers reach farther down the line in their search for employees, a fact reflected in the familiar aphorism, "A rising tide lifts all boats."

The commission drew particular attention to differential levels of educational attainment by age and color (sex discrimination in employment had not then reached the level of public concern that it later acquired). It quite properly characterized the disadvantage associated with color as "shocking": of all nonwhites in the labor force 18 years and older in 1965, 37.6 percent had only elementary school educations, 37.5 percent had completed high school, and only 7.00 percent had at least 4 years of college. The corresponding figures for white workers were 21.6, 60.0, and 12.2 percent. Those figures, bad as they were, concealed the equally shocking disparity between the quality of education available to nonwhite and white students in the largely segregated public and private schools. Included in the commission's 20 summary recommendations was the following statement, which seemed to me then, and even more so now, as more of a homily than an urgent call to action: "Growth patterns in both the economy and the labor force provide an important warning: Unless Negroes and, to a lesser degree, youth, are able to penetrate growing occupations and industries at a more rapid rate than in the past, their high unemployment rates will continue or even rise. Our society must do a far better job than it has in the past of assuring that the burdens of changes beneficial to society as a whole are not borne disproportionately by some individuals."[9]

It was inevitable that many of the commission's recommendations took the form of worthy but not very remarkable exhortations, of which

---

[9]"Summary of Major Conclusions and Recommendations," in *Technology and the American Economy*, 110.

the following are examples: "To facilitate adjustment to change as well as to improve the quality of life, adequate educational opportunity should be available to all"; and "Displacement, technological and otherwise, has been particularly painful to those blocked from new opportunity by barriers of discrimination. The Commission wishes to add its voice to others demanding elimination of all social barriers to employment and advocating special programs to compensate for centuries of systematic denial." Statements such as these reflected compromises among the commission's 14 members, who could agree on general goals but might disagree sharply on appropriate ways to achieve them. Nevertheless, unanimity was achieved on some specific and quite significant recommendations, as exemplified by the proposal of "a program of public service employment, providing, in effect, that the Government be an employer of last resort, providing work for the 'hard-core unemployed' in useful community enterprises." In calling for tax cuts and more government spending, the commission acknowledged that the Vietnam War "may temporarily drain" resources, but stated that if it did not, "major attention should be given to public expenditures." The report also rejected the idea that toleration of unemployment was "an acceptable way to relieve inflationary pressure."[10]

Other recommendations were included to forestall the labor members, who threatened to dissent to the entire report and to file a separate report. These recommendations included proposals of a negative income tax, or some other income maintenance device, to replace or supplement welfare programs by paying families whose breadwinners are unemployable, 14 years of free public schooling, and a commitment to provide every qualified person with a college education. During the course of its deliberations, the commission had received a special request from President Johnson to consider the question of "appropriate periods of work—daily, weekly, annually, and over a lifetime." This issue was hotly debated, but because of the widely divergent views held by various commission members, no consensus could be reached. Again in the interest of harmony, the members unanimously agreed that no useful

---

[10] *Technology and the American Economy*, 26.

purpose would be served by documenting their differences, and they refrained from making any recommendations. On a related matter, the commission called for labor and management to equalize fringe benefits among salaried and hourly workers and to pay all workers a weekly or monthly, rather than an hourly, salary.

Early in February 1966, the commission submitted its report to the president and the Congress. The *New York Times* summarized the report in its news columns and characterized it in an editorial as "an encouraging blueprint for national greatness, rather than an essay on gloomy foreboding" and "an avowal of faith in the nation's flexibility and imagination." The report, it concluded, "is a welcome addition to the nation's common fund of wisdom on the complexities of change."[11] In response to inquiries, the White House said the president was studying the report, but so far as I know he never commented on it publicly or took any action to ensure that any of its recommendations were acted upon by either government agencies or the Congress.

Indeed, the commission's report stimulated very little public discussion, suffering the same fate as that of another ambitious government undertaking, approximately 30 years later, by a star-studded Commission on the Future of Worker-Management Relations, which was headed by John Dunlop.[12] In a speech on the Dunlop commission report, I compared it with the earlier commission report on technology and the American economy and, borrowing an epigram from Don Marquis, observed that publishing both reports was like "dropping a rose-petal down the Grand Cañon and waiting for the echo."[13] I also endorsed the decision of both commissions not to propose precise statutory language to accomplish their recommended goals, recalling Russell Smith's observation that the launching of a statutory proposal on a Congressional voyage is fraught with the very real danger that the vessel, if it accomplishes the passage at

---

[11] "Facts on Automation," *New York Times*, 4 Feb. 1966, 30.

[12] See Commission on the Future of Worker-Management Relations, *Report and Recommendations* (Washington, D.C.: U.S. Department of Labor, 1994).

[13] Benjamin Aaron, "The Dunlop Commission Report: Where Do We Go From Here?" keynote address at the UC Davis 23rd Annual Employer-Employee Labor Relations Conference, Sacramento, 10 Feb. 1995.

all, will come to port with a 30-degree list, bottom leaking, and unwanted contraband aboard.[14] Although I predicted that the Dunlop commission's report and recommendations would be largely rejected or ignored in the short run, I also suggested that, like those of the earlier report on technology, they might well influence the thinking of employers, unions, elected government officials, academics, and others in the years ahead. For it is true that although the report of the National Commission on Technology, Automation, and Economic Progress had little immediate impact, a number of its major conclusions and recommendations kept resurfacing in later years and exercised some influence on both federal and state legislation. Writing to me many years later, Wirtz offered his appraisal: "The automation commission didn't change much of anything, but it was an example of the democratic system working at its best."

---

[14] "The Role of Law in Arbitration," in *Arbitration and the Law: Proceedings of the Twelfth Annual Meeting, National Academy of Arbitrators*, ed. Jean T. McKelvey (Washington, D.C.: BNA, 1959), 87–88.

CHAPTER 6

THE CALIFORNIA FARM LABOR PANEL, 1965

In an eight-month period partially overlapping my service as a member of the National Commission on Technology, Automation, and Economic Progress, I served as chairman of the California Farm Labor Panel, appointed by Secretary of Labor Willard Wirtz. The other two panel members were Arthur M. Ross and Daniel G. Aldrich Jr. Ross, an old friend, was professor of industrial relations and former director of the Institute of Industrial Relations at UC Berkeley. He was soon to be named head of the U.S. Bureau of Labor Statistics. Aldrich, whom I had not previously met, was chancellor of UC Irvine, the newest UC campus.

At the end of 1964, Public Law 78—the last in a series of federal laws that authorized the admission of Mexican nationals for temporary agricultural employment in California and other states—was allowed to expire. The Congress had concluded that, on balance, the law's undeniably negative economic and social effects outweighed its value to the growers. In a statement issued on 16 December 1964, Wirtz said in part:

> The explanation given for this program has been that the work *braceros*[1] do won't be done by U.S. workers....
>
> A good deal of this work is unquestionably hard and unpleasant. But this is only part of the story. The rest of it is that the wage rates which have been paid for those jobs have been less than the rates paid for other kinds of work which are just as hard and just as objectionable....
>
> There has been increasing complaint against the importation of these hundreds of thousands of foreign workers being paid wage rates as low as 60 cents an hour while about 4 million U.S. men and women are unemployed. There has also been accumulating evidence that U.S. workers will be available to do this work if decent working conditions are provided and if it is paid for on terms in line with those for other work that is usually hard and unpleasant.

---

[1] The word *bracero* applies to Mexican agricultural laborers permitted to enter the United States to work for a limited period of time.

Wirtz proposed a program for transition to a wholly domestic farm labor force; the program would carry out the will of Congress and, at the same time, allow for the harvesting of crops without undue loss to growers and processors. During the spring of 1965, he moved to assist agricultural employers make the transition by permitting limited importation of Mexican workers under Public Law 414. He also made it plain that chronic or large-scale importation of *braceros* through this device would subvert the intent of Congress and would not be countenanced. He emphasized that growers would be eligible for supplementary foreign labor only if they had made full use of available domestic labor and had cooperated fully with federal and state agencies in domestic recruitment. To provide a practical test of recruitment possibilities, "criteria" wage rates were established. The minimum hourly rate in California was $1.40, and Wirtz stipulated that piecework rates must provide at least that amount in hourly earnings before an application for Mexican labor could be considered. Additional criteria included provision for transportation, meals at cost, and written contracts. To help carry out the new policy, Wirtz established the California Farm Labor Panel and directed it to determine facts and make specific recommendations to him regarding applications and arrangements for supplemental foreign labor. The panel was also instructed to "make recommendations for any further procedures which will effectuate the purpose of serving fully all agricultural labor needs, of relying on domestic workers for this so far as they are available, and of maintaining adequate agricultural wages and living conditions."[2]

I readily confess that I did not come to this task with a completely open mind. I had for some time been interested in the working conditions of farm workers, particularly the seasonal migrant laborers, and I had been deeply affected by *After the Bracero*, a 1964 report by the UCLA Institute of Industrial Relations that was sent to the California Department of Employment. As director of the institute at the time, I was nominally the general director of the project, but I had not contributed to the report, which was written by Fred H. Schmidt, an institute staff member. Among the many points made in this outstanding study

---

[2] *Final Report of the California Farm Labor Panel* (1965), 5.

was that, historically, farm employers in California and elsewhere in the United States had justified their incessant demands for permission to import cheap farm labor by stating that no "white man" would consent to do such work and that urban workers in general were unwilling and unable to do it—a proposition, Schmidt noted, that the employers constantly emphasized. Schmidt's report, based on a number of surveys and questionnaires, found that there was a substantial potential supply of domestic farm laborers of all races among urban workers in Los Angeles available for both seasonal and year-round agricultural work, and that there were no cultural or psychological barriers that universally sealed off these workers from the acceptance of farm labor work. Rather, their reluctance to accept these jobs was basically economic in nature. The report concluded that the State of California could mitigate the conditions that discouraged domestic farm labor.

These and other findings predisposed me to support the cutoff of legalized importation of Mexican farm laborers and to concentrate on ways to raise the abysmally low wages paid for farm labor and to improve workers' often intolerable housing and working conditions. My sentiments were generally shared by Ross, who was an authority on the harvest labor market in California. We both assumed that Aldrich would have quite a different perspective on our assignment. A former director for many years of the university's highly regarded Agricultural Extension Service, he had been popular with the growers—his constituents—and was still in close personal touch with all the influential growers and their various organizations throughout the state. He was widely thought to be the growers' representative and advocate on the panel. A bluff, hearty man who made no secret of his conservative views on a variety of issues, he nevertheless assured Ross and me that he was approaching our assignment with a completely open mind and that in his view the burden of proving the necessity for importing more Mexican laborers rested with the growers. Neither of us really believed him.

The panel's initial meeting was on 17 April 1965. We decided that we should begin our inquiry by holding a series of public hearings in various parts of the state to obtain the views of interested parties. We conducted these hearings during April and May. On one of the first of these occasions, we scheduled hearings in widely separated cities in the state, starting early in the morning and ending late in the afternoon. Governor Pat Brown kindly made available an airplane leased by the state to get us from one place to another. At the end of the long day I arrived at the Claremont Hotel in Berkeley, exhausted and desperately in need of relieving myself. Immediately after checking in, I went into the bathroom and wearily settled myself on the throne, only to be interrupted by the jingling of the telephone on the wall beside me. I irritably picked up the receiver and learned that my caller was a reporter from a Sacramento newspaper, who asked if I would consent to a five-minute telephone interview. Pleading fatigue, I asked if we couldn't do it another time. His response was, for me, the highlight of the entire enterprise. "Professor Aaron," he said, "I wonder if you realize that at this moment you are sitting on the biggest news story in this state."

In addition to holding public hearings, panel members met with state and federal agriculture and employment officials and engaged in informal efforts with all parties concerned to gain acceptance of Wirtz's policy and to encourage and assist in its implementation. We also made occasional field trips to observe housing provided for *braceros* and conditions in the fields where they worked. A minority of farms we visited provided adequate housing and reasonably good meals for their workers. In the majority of instances, however, the quality of housing ranged from poor to disgraceful. I recall one farm where the so-called housing was so bad that if it had been used for animals, it would have been denounced by the ASPCA.

On the other hand, our meetings with growers brought greater appreciation on our part of the difficulties of recruiting domestic farm labor. They reported almost unanimously that domestic urban workers in particular tended to quit after one or two days' work and were generally shiftless and unproductive. They continued, however, to resist the suggestion that low wages might be an important reason why they were not able to attract a better group of urban workers. Nevertheless, the panel recognized that some of the growers' requests for foreign workers in addition to those allowed under Public Law 414 were meritorious. Over the eight-month period of its investigation, the panel recommended that Wirtz allow the importation of a total of 21,900 *braceros* to harvest particular crops—asparagus, strawberries, lettuce, tomatoes. He approved all our recommendations. At the same time, we refused in a number of instances to endorse requests for additional foreign workers that we felt were unnecessary or excessive.

Despite some difficulties, 1965 proved to be an excellent year for California agriculture. Crops were brought in with much less recourse to *braceros* than in previous years, and growers' gross revenues were generally higher. Tens of thousands of additional jobs were made available for domestic farm workers, who in 1965 accounted for 97.3 percent of the man-years of labor in California's seasonal hired agricultural employment, while contract foreign labor provided the remaining 2.7 percent. This was a huge improvement over the average for the preceding five years, which showed that domestic labor accounted for 73.7 percent of total seasonal man-years, with foreign labor providing 26.3 percent. The panel's report hailed the progress toward a wholly domestic farm labor force in California, noting that those who argued that no American would do stoop labor, or could climb trees, or work in high temperatures, had been proven wrong. Nevertheless, it concluded that agriculture was still not competitive with other industries for domestic labor. Although wage rates had risen, they were below the levels prevalent in other industries. Little had been done to augment family housing facilities, to provide for more stable employment throughout the harvest season, or to disseminate more reliable information on employment, earnings, and manpower. The panel's report also reviewed a number of existing programs and new policies aimed at building an able and adequate domestic farm labor force. These included intensified intrastate and interstate recruitment, a Department of Labor youth farm employment program during the summer for high school athletes, a program under the Manpower Training and Development Act to train workers for the field harvest, new agricultural work simplification devices and mechanization, especially for the harvesting of tomatoes, lettuce, and melons, and

a demonstration project for a limited number of low-cost housing units
for migrant families.

In the course of the time we spent together, I began to change my
initial assessment of Aldrich. He continued to put the growers' positions
in a sympathetic light, but he also demonstrated increasing impatience
and indignation with some of their practices and arguments. Totally
without subtlety or artifice, he stated his own views candidly and forthrightly. By the end of our association, I had developed great respect and
regard for him. He played only a minor part in the drafting of the panel's
report, which was done largely by Ross and me. Although we had both
come to like him personally, we nevertheless assumed that Aldrich would
dissent from some of our proposed recommendations and might even
file a separate statement explaining his reasons. To our considerable
surprise, he agreed to all of them, saying simply, "I told the growers that I
would support their positions only if they made a convincing case; they
didn't make it." In joining in the panel's unanimous recommendations to
Wirtz, Aldrich knew he would incur the wrath of the growers, would be
denounced as a traitor to their cause, and would see the end of valued
friendships with some of them. Showing the integrity that was an integral part of his character, he acted on the basis of the evidence, which in
his mind refuted the assumptions he had formerly held.

The panel's recommendations consisted of some general observations, followed by specific recommendations concerning wages, housing,
recruitment, legislative protection of farm workers, field sanitation, and
statistical reporting. Recognizing that, with the termination of Public
Law 78, California farmers had to look to the domestic labor force to
meet their requirements, the panel emphasized the need to make wages
and working conditions sufficiently desirable to attract an adequate
number of productive domestic workers. On this point the report
said, in part:

> Above all else, what is required is a change in the expectations and attitudes of the
> growers. Employer resistance to the Secretary of Labor's program to switch to an
> all-domestic supply of farm workers was a major, though by no means the exclu-
> sive, cause of some of the difficulties encountered this year. Specifically, a refusal to
> accept the full implications of the Congressional decision not to renew Public Law

78 has led some growers to keep wages unrealistically low, to delay in providing adequate housing, and to cooperate half-heartedly or not at all with various efforts to recruit domestic farm labor....Growers and processors have the right to expect aid and guidance from appropriate Federal and State agencies in the recruitment of their employees; they have no right, however, to continue to claim competitive advantages and special protection not available to others.[3]

On the subject of wages, the panel not only urged California growers to adopt a wage policy that would make California agriculture competitive for labor with other industries but also recommended that the federal government take the necessary steps to raise farm labor wages throughout the country. More specifically, it expressed the belief that hourly rates should not fall below those prescribed by federal or state minimum wage laws not otherwise applicable to farm labor, and that flexible piecework rates be set so as to insure substantially higher average hourly earnings for more productive workers.

With reference to housing, the panel declared that adequate housing must be provided for farm workers and their families. It urged that, where economically feasible and structurally possible, existing barracks housing should be converted to family units. It also called for tighter regulation and stricter enforcement of farm labor housing codes, as well as increased funding of existing federally sponsored farm housing programs such as those administered by the U.S. Office of Economic Opportunity and the Farmers Home Administration. In addition, the panel advocated more experimentation by all concerned with building techniques and arrangements, as well as with financing plans, so that the maximum amount of housing could be built at the minimum cost. If necessary, it recommended that new legislation should be enacted to make it possible for growers, assisted by state and federal governments, to build the requisite amount of new family housing.

On the related subject of field sanitation, the panel declared that higher and more rigidly enforced standards of field sanitation were essential to decent working conditions and should be provided. At the very least, it said, all farm workers, including adult males, should be

---

[3] Final Report of the California Farm Labor Panel, 40–41.

provided with the field sanitary facilities specified in a 1965 order of the California Industrial Welfare Commission, which was applicable to women and minors employed in agricultural occupations. These facilities included adequately screened and properly ventilated toilets and adequate washing facilities that were readily accessible to employees. The panel reported that these regulations had been widely ignored, even in respect of women and minors, as had been the requirement that each place of employment be supplied with potable drinking water, suitably cool and at locations convenient to employees. "Facilities such as these," the panel concluded, "are not 'frills'; they are absolutely essential to maintain minimum standards of health and decency. We regret the necessity, in the year 1965, to make so elementary a consideration the subject of a specific recommendation."[4]

With reference to the statutory protection of farm workers, the panel expressed its belief that farm workers should, like their counterparts in other industries, be covered by unemployment compensation for agricultural labor, as well as by the Fair Labor Standards (Wage and Hour) Act and the National Labor Relations Act, and that they should also be given improved coverage under the Social Security Act.

Declaring that present farm labor supervision, itself a product of the *bracero* system, was notoriously inadequate, the panel recommended more and improved training programs for farm labor supervisors.

In its report, the panel was highly critical of the existing interstate recruitment system. It recommended a complete reexamination of that system, with the goal of clarifying the appropriate roles and responsibilities of the government and the growers in such recruitment. So far as the growers were concerned, the panel urged that recruitment teams be sent to other states well in advance of the harvest season to interview and screen farm workers and to enter into firm contracts with them for employment for fixed periods during the harvest season. It specified that such contracts should include commitments regarding transportation, compensation, housing, and food.

---

[4] *Final Report of the California Farm Labor Panel*, 45.

Finally, the panel recommended improvements in statistical reporting, declaring that better information about labor requirements, hours worked, and wages earned must be collected and made available.

The panel's report was released on 1 December 1965 and received fairly wide coverage in the press. Wirtz hailed it and claimed that it supported his previously expressed views that domestic workers would perform onerous farm labor if they received adequate wages and were provided with acceptable working conditions. He predicted that no foreign labor would be needed in California in the next season. In reply, Senator George Murphy of California, a Republican, charged that the secretary's program had merely substituted one kind of Mexican labor for another: "35,000 extra Mexican green-card (temporary) workers— recorded as domestics for statistical purposes—and illegal entries ('wet backs') for those who came to the United States under the well-organized and properly supervised *bracero* program."[5] Somewhat surprisingly, the California Farm Bureau Federation, representing some 60,000 growers and owners, adopted a resolution pledging "all reasonable effort" to recruit domestic laborers and support better working conditions and housing for them.[6]

Regrettably, as of 2006, it appears that the roseate expectations of Wirtz's program, expectations that were encouraged by the panel's report, never came fully to fruition. The program's main objective—to eliminate the use of foreign farm labor—was only partially realized. Moreover, farm workers employed in California are still overwhelmingly Hispanic, although many of them are either American citizens or green-carders (aliens who have permission to work in the United States under specified conditions). Efforts to recruit substantial numbers of domestic urban workers to assist in harvesting crops have been unsuccessful. On the other hand, the California Agricultural Labor Relations Act of 1980 increased mechanization, and the organization of farm workers by the United Farm Workers and the International Brotherhood of Teamsters have had the combined effect of raising wages and improving working conditions.

---

[5] Murphy Charges Wirtz Eliminated Farm Jobs," *Los Angeles Times*, Dec. 15, 1965.
[6] "Farm Bureau Endorses Domestic Worker Use," *Sacramento Bee*, Dec. 2, 1965.

Employment of some foreign laborers is permitted each harvest season, but the numbers are considerably lower than they were under Public Law 78. I therefore look back on my experience on the California Farm Labor Panel as a worthwhile endeavor, one small step toward a goal that has not yet been achieved: to provide farm workers in the United States with the same statutory protections applicable to all other workers and thus to assure them fair wages and proper working conditions.

CHAPTER 7

THE LOS ANGELES SCHOOL TEACHERS' STRIKE, 1970

On 13 April 1970, approximately 14,000 out of about 25,000 certificated teachers in the Los Angeles Unified School District began a strike that continued for almost five weeks. It was the largest teacher walkout in the history of California public education. The strike effectively shut down the school district and created serious problems, especially for working parents who could not afford private day care for their children. The teachers were represented by a statutory negotiating council, theoretically composed of representatives of qualifying employee organizations (i.e., teachers unions), but in this case consisting entirely of representatives of the United Teachers-Los Angeles (UTLA), which represented about 22,000 of the 25,000 teachers in the district. UTLA was created by an uneasy alliance of two historic rivals: the Associated Classroom Teachers of Los Angeles (ACTLA), affiliated with the National Education Association (NEA), and the Los Angeles Teachers Union (LATU), affiliated with the American Federation of Teachers (AFT).

On the first day of the strike, Superior Court Judge Richard Schauer issued a restraining order against the walkout, which the teachers ignored. UTLA declared that it viewed the strike as a moral, not a legal, issue. On 16 April, school district officials went to court seeking contempt of court citations against four top UTLA officials for violating the restraining order. At a hearing on 8 May, Superior Court Judge Stevens Fargo denied the school district's request because of insufficient supporting data. He did issue another set of contempt citations against UTLA leaders for violating a preliminary injunction against the strike, which he had issued on 4 May and which was also disregarded by the teachers. At a subsequent hearing on the contempt charges several months after the strike had ended, the judge fined the UTLA and each of the four officers a total of $12,000 for violating the anti-strike injunction. He declined to impose jail sentences, however, saying he did not want to grant the leaders the cloak of martyrdom they obviously sought.

Many years later I learned more about Fargo's thinking from Leo Geffner, a prominent labor attorney, former student, and good friend, who represented the UTLA. Geffner told me that he had told Fargo that UTLA officers not only were willing to go to jail for contempt but also felt that by doing so they would unite their constituents and gain further adherents to their cause. Geffner warned the judge that no effective negotiations to end the strike could be held if UTLA officers remained in custody. Fargo took his point and solved the problem by setting the date to hear the contempt charges several months later, thus allowing sufficient time for the strike to be settled before he rendered his judgment.

My involvement in this dispute began on 22 April, about a week after the strike had begun. Thereafter, I kept a daily diary, fortunately still in my possession, in which I recorded the ups and downs (mostly the latter) of my mediation endeavors, as well as my own frustrations and comments on the behavior of the key participants in the negotiations. What follows is based on that record.

Negotiations over my appointment as mediator were themselves so complicated and mishandled that I came close to backing out before becoming involved. On the afternoon of 22 April, I received a telephone call from Geffner, who advised me that he was calling on behalf of himself and Lyman Powell, an attorney acting as the board of education's negotiator. Powell came on the line and Geffner introduced us to each other. I had never met Powell but knew of his reputation as a "union-buster." Geffner explained that it had been the parties' original intention to call in a mediator from the Federal Mediation and Conciliation Service (FMCS), but that certain difficulties had made that course impracticable; they had elected instead to engage a private mediator, and, he said, he and Powell had chosen me. Powell confirmed that fact. Neither told me at the time, but I subsequently learned from Geffner that their first choice had been Sam Kagel, an arbitrator and mediator in San Francisco, whose success in mediating major labor disputes was legendary. But Kagel could give them no firm commitment that he would be able to devote all his time to the effort, so they had turned to me. Many years later, Geffner told me that my name had originally been suggested by a mutual friend, Edmund D. Edelman, then a member of the Los Angeles City Council. Contemporary newspaper accounts reported that I had been recommended by both the FMCS and the California State Conciliation Service (CSCS).

Geffner asked me if I would accept the appointment and, if so, how soon I could begin my mediation efforts. I replied that I would serve and could start immediately, but only on the assumption that both sides, by accepting mediation, had indicated a willingness to recede to some degree from their respective positions in order to settle the strike. Powell stated that I should not assume that the board, by agreeing to mediation, was abandoning its position that it would not negotiate with the UTLA while teachers remained on strike. He added, however, that he naturally expected that any mediator would urge both sides to reconsider their positions. I replied that I did not expect either party to give up anything prior to the commencement of my mediation efforts. Geffner, Powell, and I then agreed that I should meet with UTLA representatives at the organization's offices that same evening, and that Powell and I would meet at his home the following morning. I explained that to keep these engagements I would have to cancel a number of appointments, and I asked if they planned to announce my entry into the case to the press. Geffner stated that as soon as our conversation terminated he would release the information to Harry Bernstein, the principal labor reporter for the *Los Angeles Times*.

About an hour later I received a call from Powell, who said he had some "rather confusing news" to report. In brief, he confessed that he had not had the authority to agree to my appointment, but assured me that he had no reason to doubt that the board would approve it. He said that things were now in something of a "bureaucratic snarl," but that if I would only be patient, everything could be worked out. He asked if I had told anyone of my appointment and I replied that I had unavoidably done so in the course of canceling a number of prior engagements, including an arbitration in Sacramento the next day. Trying to conceal my irritation, I told Powell I was willing to wait until the following day, but if by that time the board was still undecided on whether to appoint me as mediator, I would permanently withdraw my name from consideration. I also told him to call Donald R. Baer, UTLA's executive director and spokesman for its bargaining committee, and explain to him why I would not keep my appointment with him for that evening, and to telephone Geffner, who was by that time in Fresno, and tell him exactly what had occurred. Powell, full of apologies, promised to make both calls and did in fact do so. Early the following morning, 23 April, I called Geffner in Fresno and asked if he had heard from Powell. He confirmed that Powell had called the night before and then went on to tell me what had occurred.

On 21 April CSCS had rather insistently requested that its representatives be invited to mediate the teacher strike. Geffner responded that he was meeting Powell at noon on 22 April and that he would advise CSCS of any decision made at that meeting. To the surprise of both Geffner and Powell, two CSCS representatives showed up at the meeting in Geffner's office. After some discussion, Powell informed them that the parties would rather call in FMCS. The CSCS representatives objected, and a violent argument ensued. Finally, the CSCS representatives left, but only after telling Powell that their agency would not formally withdraw from the case nor would it authorize the FMCS to intervene. From previous conversations with Curtis Counts, director of the FMCS and a former student of mine, Geffner and Powell knew that the FMCS had no jurisdiction to intervene without the CSCS's express consent. By this time the CSCS had unsuccessfully attempted to recruit Kagel as the mediator. It was then that they had decided to appoint me.

Later on the morning of the 23 April, Powell telephoned me and again apologized for the confusing events of the previous day. He explained that the board would be meeting that afternoon and that he fully expected it to approve my appointment as mediator. He asked me if I would be willing to wait until then for a definite decision, and I agreed to wait until evening. I warned Powell, however, that if no answer were forthcoming by the end of the day, I would definitely withdraw my name from consideration. We then discussed for the better part of an hour the mediation procedures to be followed if I were appointed. Powell reiterated his statement of the previous day that by agreeing to mediate, the board was not necessarily retreating from its position that it would not resume negotiations with the UTLA unless the teachers ended their strike. I responded that I understood the board's position, but my first order of business would be to persuade it to abandon that stance, because obviously there could be no successful mediation unless it did so. I also told him that I planned to tell the UTLA representatives that the teachers would have to go back to work before a complete contract with the board could be executed, thus assuring him that both parties would be expected to recede from their polar positions. I asked Powell whether he objected to my dealing directly with some members of the board and with the superintendent of schools. He said no, but added that he hoped that I would keep him informed, would not do anything behind his back, and would not seek to undercut him. I assured him that I had no desire to undermine his authority.

Powell then said he was opposed to around-the-clock negotiations and would resist any suggestion that we "hole up in some hotel for 18 to 24 hours at a time." I told him that he ought to leave such decisions to me and to be ready to meet whatever schedule I set. Seeking to reassure him, I explained that I did not believe in the technique of mediation or negotiation by exhaustion, but that there might be times when it was important to keep going until we reached agreement on a specific issue. Powell next told me that the board was a very bureaucratic organization and moved very slowly. He described the pace of negotiations before the strike, and I inferred from his comments that he favored a schedule of conducting mediation sessions only two or three times a week. I told him that given the extreme urgency of the situation, such a schedule was absolutely out of the question and that mediation efforts must be more or less continuous, except for appropriate intervals for rest. Finally, Powell informed me that tentative agreements reached on specific issues would have to be referred back to the board for further consideration, and that if anyone tried to exercise any discretion that the board reserved to itself, "we might all be looking for new jobs." At this point I interrupted him to remind him that I neither had a job with the board nor was looking for one. I also told him that the old ways of doing things would simply not work in the present situation and that the board had to be prepared to change its procedures. I said that if I got the impression that the board did not really want a negotiated settlement and was using a mediator only as a means to gain time, I would resign and make a public statement saying why. Powell seemed momentarily upset by my comments and said he doubted that the board would agree to mediation if it might end with a public statement by the mediator denouncing the board. I told him that was certainly not my intention, but that, given the manifest importance of the dispute, the board could not prevent the mediator from discharging his duty to inform the public of the progress in negotiations or the lack thereof. Powell then conceded that a mediator had to have the power to "lean a little on the parties." Our telephone conversation ended about noon.

A few hours later, I was advised by Powell that my appointment as mediator had been announced. I told him that I would set up a meeting with UTLA's executive director, Donald Baer, and his committee for that evening, and I asked him to arrange an appointment for me with Arthur Gardner, board of education president, and Robert E. Kelly, acting superintendent of schools. That meeting having been fixed for the following day at 2:00 p.m., I called Powell and scheduled an additional meeting about an hour earlier with him and his staff.

I accepted this assignment with two primary goals in mind. The first was to bring an end to the strike as soon as possible. Although a firm advocate of teachers' right to strike and an opponent of an outright statutory ban against strikes by teachers and other public employees, I considered actual teachers' strikes to be counter-productive in most instances and to be avoided except in the most intolerable circumstances. Interrupting the normal educational process was detrimental to students and in a variety of ways placed great strains on the entire community. My second goal was to establish the basis of collective bargaining between the UTLA and the school board; this meant persuading the board to enter into a binding contract with the UTLA. If these two goals could be achieved, I felt, the noneconomic terms of that contract, with a few exceptions, would assume a secondary importance. Economic terms presented a more difficult problem. But the UTLA had shrewdly placed its emphasis on those expenditures that would improve the teaching environment and directly benefit students and had refrained from emphasizing a demand for an increase in teachers' salaries. It had seized upon a slogan—"Teachers want what students need"—that caught public attention and contributed to the surprising amount of support for the strike among many parents of the affected students. At no point in the ensuing negotiations did the issue of a pay increase for teachers figure significantly in the UTLA's strategy.

At my initial meeting with Baer and the members of his committee on 23 April, I asked him to acquaint me with the background of the dispute. Baer, whose negotiating skill, dedication, and integrity I came to admire greatly, responded by handing me a 67-page document titled "Negotiating Package between United Teachers–Los Angeles and the Los Angeles City Schools." He explained that this list of contract demands represented a codification of "thousands of pages" of board rules and regulations and added that the board had previously agreed that some codification was necessary. The list of proposals had been formulated in the fall of 1969. Pre-strike negotiations had lasted for only one month, during which period there were only eight negotiation sessions. Three additional meetings had been scheduled, but according to Baer, when the UTLA representatives had showed up, they were told that the board representatives were not ready to discuss anything. At the conclusion of those negotiations, the only item agreed to was related to bulletin boards. Moreover, at the eight negotiating sessions the parties had discussed only noneconomic issues. The one exception was a 5 percent wage increase unilaterally announced by the board. Baer said that the UTLA believed the board had deliberately stalled the negotiations to provoke a confrontation leading to a strike. He also complained that Powell demonstrably lacked authority to decide anything and had no real power to negotiate on behalf of the board.

Baer described the history of the Los Angeles School District over the previous eight years as one of continuing and rapid deterioration.

Class sizes in Los Angeles, he said, were the largest in the nation, and supporting services of all kinds had either been reduced substantially or eliminated altogether. The UTLA had responded to these developments by lobbying intensively for improvements at state and local levels, discussing the situation with Governor Ronald Reagan, and calling a two-day strike in 1969. The results of all this, according to Baer, were unfulfilled promises, budget cuts, and absolutely no improvements in the quality of education or in benefits to teachers.

I inquired about the current tax situation and was told that there were 26 special areas in which the board was free to raise taxes without approval of the electorate, areas that the UTLA regarded as a source of additional revenue to finance school improvements. Baer complained that the UTLA had been excluded from all budgeting sessions of the board and had not been consulted in any way. He pointed out, as an indication of how far the educational situation in Los Angeles had deteriorated, that Los Angeles presently spent approximately $700 per child per year, whereas New York spent $1,200 and Beverly Hills about $1,400.

Having received my briefing, I began to explore with Baer and the members of his committee what kinds of action could be taken to end the teachers' strike and resolve the current dispute. I asked that the UTLA refrain from making any statements to the press, indicating that I would make the same request to the board representatives. Baer did not give me a direct response, but I sensed from his attitude that the UTLA would cooperate on that point, at least for the present. I stressed the importance of mutual trust and good faith, and I made the usual mediator's commitment not to disclose any information given to me in confidence unless specifically authorized to do so. This drew no comment whatsoever from any member of the committee, confirming my impression that none of them cared much about such assurances; what they were looking for was some tangible proof of progress.

It was then time to deal with the real point I wished to make: namely, that the UTLA had to be prepared to recede at least in part from its position that the teachers would not end their strike until they had secured a full contract, signed, sealed, and delivered. Repeating the same admonition I had previously given to Powell, I told the committee that there could be no successful negotiations without such a move on their part, but I assured them that I would similarly ask the board to draw back from its position not to negotiate with the UTLA until all the strikers had returned to work. Again I drew a blank from Baer and the other committee members. Nevertheless, I continued to press the matter, suggesting that there must be some items in their proposed agreement that were more important than others and that the UTLA surely ought to be able to establish a list of priorities. All I wanted, I said, was a pledge from the UTLA that after negotiations had resumed and a certain amount of progress made, the amount to be determined by the UTLA itself, it would then ask its members to return to work so that the remainder of the negotiations could continue. It became quite clear, however, that nobody was ready to respond to my suggestion. I said I did not really expect an answer that evening, but would return to the question after the members of the committee had had a chance to talk things over among themselves. Baer expressed agreement with that approach. I left the meeting somewhat daunted by the formidable task of bridging the wide chasm between the respective positions of the parties.

Shortly after noon on Friday, 24 April, I met with Powell and the five staff members comprising his negotiating team at the offices of the board of education. The purpose of this meeting was simply to get acquainted with them and to explain the procedure I intended to follow. I asked them to make no public statements about the dispute and received their promise of complete cooperation. I also emphasized the importance of resuming negotiations with UTLA and the necessity of meeting fairly continuously and short-circuiting the lengthy clearance procedures that had provoked considerable criticism from the UTLA. At this juncture Powell again referred to the bureaucratic nature of the board and the handicap under which he labored because he had only recently become involved in the negotiations, as well as to the "heroic" efforts he had made to catch up with the well-prepared UTLA representatives. I replied that he would have to become an even greater hero, because his efforts to date had obviously not been good enough. Powell mentioned a contract between the Santa Maria, California, school district and a teacher organization, which he described as a brief document of only about six pages, listing most of the important items under the heading "to be discussed." He said this was the kind of contract he could easily enter into, but expressed doubt that the UTLA would even consider it. I replied that the Santa Maria contract had interesting implications and possibilities and asked him for a copy, which he agreed to provide.

I then moved on to a meeting with Gardner, Kelly, Powell, and Arthur Andreson, the deputy superintendent. I repeated my belief that to bring about a resumption of negotiations, both sides would have to retreat from their previously stated positions. The four men told me that efforts had been made to get the UTLA to agree to some kind of skeleton contract as a prelude to ending the strike, but that those efforts had failed. I remarked that communications between the two groups had apparently been very bad, a fact they readily confirmed, and that the UTLA believed the board had provoked the strike and was now trying to stall in the belief that the strike could be broken. Assuring them that I was not taking any position on the merits of UTLA charges, I told them that it was my impression that the strike was still quite solid. Gardner, who immediately impressed me as an intelligent and fair-minded man, said that in his view the worst calamity that could happen would be the failure of the strike, explaining that in that event the teachers would be in a state of anarchy and none of the issues confronting both sides could then be resolved. He added that, for obvious reasons, he could not make a public statement to that effect, but those were his true feelings. Andreson, on the other hand, emphasized several times the problems the board would have with the approximately 12,000 teachers who had remained at work if it made major concessions to the UTLA. He claimed that the division between those teachers and the ones who were on strike was far wider and deeper than those between the board and the UTLA.

Powell once again launched into a long complaint about the handicaps under which he labored and expressed the view that negotiations, if resumed, would fail because the UTLA intended to remain on strike until the end of the school term. He opined that the only real issue involved was union power and implied that the numerous issues raised by the UTLA were merely a smoke screen. Powell also reiterated that he really lacked authority to agree to anything without going back each time to the board, and he again stressed the importance of allowing sufficient time between negotiating sessions for him to report back to the board for instructions. My response was that if Powell had so little power, perhaps it would be necessary to have representatives from the board with sufficient authority to make decisions present at all sessions. Gardner interposed, saying that it would be a catastrophe if a single member of the board attended even one negotiating session, because if one member did, all would insist on doing so and the result would be a complete shambles. He added that he had asked Powell several times to give the board some idea of the extent of the authority he needed, and that if Powell would only do so, he (Gardner) would try to get him the necessary four votes (i.e., a majority of the seven-member board). To my utter amazement, Gardner went on to say that a majority of the board was willing to support final and binding arbitration of all grievances involving the interpretation or application of the contract, a prime UTLA objective, but that Powell had opposed arbitration as the final step. Powell interrupted with what I regarded as some rather silly remarks about the dangers of private arbitration. I told him that I did not want to debate the issue with him at the present time but did want to note my disagreement with his views. Andreson then voiced the opinion that the board had to act much more promptly than it had in the past on matters discussed in negotiations. He suggested, and the others agreed, that an executive session be scheduled at the end of each regular board meeting, so that the board could at that time consider any pressing matters brought up in negotiations and express its approval or disapproval.

The conversation turned next to a brief overview of the board's positions on the principal substantive issues raised in the prior negotiations. The chief sticking points appeared to be the following:

1. Recognition. The board's view was that it could not enter into a contract with the UTLA; it could do so only with a "negotiating council," as set forth in the Winton Act of 1965, a state law applicable solely to school district employees.

2. Exclusive representation. The board's position was that the Winton Act precluded it from granting exclusive representation rights to any one teachers' organization.

3. Money matters. The board claimed it had already explored all avenues for raising money, including the special taxing powers referred to by the UTLA representatives at our meeting the previous evening. On this point Gardner was adamant; he refused to consider the possibility of deficit financing or even setting up a hypothetical budget on the assumption that more money might become available later on.

Finally, we returned to the matter of resuming negotiations. Gardner said the board should not be involved in this at all and that he felt Powell and Kelly had sufficient authority to go ahead on their own. I got the distinct impression that Gardner would not oppose the informal resumption of negotiations with the UTLA on an exploratory basis, without any strings attached.

Following the conclusion of this meeting, I met privately with Powell to continue a discussion of some of the matters taken up with the larger group. I emphasized as strongly as I could the importance of the grievance and arbitration procedure that Gardner had indicated a majority of the board would support. Powell elaborated on his previously stated objection, revealing that his true reason was a reluctance to offer too much to the UTLA in his first proposal. Still, he said he was willing to do whatever a majority of the board directed. To my surprise, he also went along with my suggestion that we try to arrange for an informal negotiating session with the UTLA. I feared that he would begin to attach a number of unacceptable conditions if I explored this idea any further, so I let the matter drop, telling him that I would call him the next morning.

At my suggestion, Geffner and I had dinner together that evening. We discussed the events of the day, after which, at his urging, I called Baer and asked him to join us. The three of us talked until about midnight. Baer concurred with my proposal that Geffner and I should meet Powell for lunch the next day (Saturday) to discuss the ground rules for resuming negotiations. We all agreed that our biggest problem was Powell himself, because his feelings of inadequacy and insecurity were causing him to do a number of things that were counterproductive to successful negotiations. I told them I planned to meet with Powell before lunch on Saturday and to urge him to modify his behavior. Baer said he would cooperate by asking his people to discontinue their public criticism of Powell for a while.

On Saturday morning, 25 April, I telephoned Powell and told him I had arranged a luncheon meeting with Geffner for the purpose of setting the ground rules for resumption of negotiations on Monday, 27 April. He expressed satisfaction with the news. I also asked if I could come to his house beforehand to discuss other matters, and he agreed. When I arrived at his house, I told him the purpose of my visit was to give him some friendly advice. I said that a major purpose of my mediation efforts was to insure that the representatives of both sides came out looking like heroes, and that the only expendable person was myself. The reason, I explained, was that if a settlement could be achieved, the parties would be working together for some time, and it was important that their principal representatives emerge from the negotiations with enhanced prestige. Everything I was about to tell him, I continued, was in furtherance of that purpose, and he should learn to trust my judgment. Reminding him that he had repeatedly complained of the difficulties he had encountered to date, I suggested it was time to forget about his past troubles and to concentrate on getting this particular job done. I also cautioned him not to reject out of hand any proposals made during the forthcoming joint sessions that he considered totally unacceptable and advised him simply to respond that he would consider them. He agreed, but I sensed an underlying reluctance on his part. This was my last effort to involve Powell in a constructive way in the forthcoming negotiations.

The luncheon with Geffner a few hours later got off to a bad start. Powell began at once to complain about UTLA's "propaganda machine." Geffner replied that he preferred to think of it as a public relations effort. Powell then stated that he had something to say "just once"—namely, that in his view the UTLA did not want a settlement, had planned to take the teachers out three months before the end of the school term, to keep them on strike until the term ended, and then to confront the board with the threat that they would not return in the fall until all their demands had been met. He had said exactly the same thing to me during our conversation that morning, and I had told him that I thought his perception of the situation was completely wrong. Geffner listened quietly to Powell and then said he would refrain from making any comment despite his strong inclination to do so. I told Powell that we would hold him to his promise to make that kind of statement "just once." Two minutes later, he started to repeat it, but I interrupted, reminding him of his promise. About five minutes later, the same thing occurred. Finally, he dropped the subject.

The rest of our conversation was more productive. We agreed that I would hold a press conference on Sunday morning, 26 April, and announce the resumption of negotiations on Monday morning. I was to say that no concessions were being made by either party, that they were meeting at my request and in recognition of their responsibilities to the public. We also agreed that in order to pacify the CSCS I would ask one of its representatives, Ralph Duncan, to make the physical arrangements, and I would invite him to be present at the press conference. But when I suggested that another state conciliator, Lou Gilbert, also be invited to come, Powell flew into a rage and said that Gilbert was personally obnoxious to him; he stated that he would not agree to this invitation and expressed his doubt that the board would agree. Thoroughly fed up, I told Powell rather sharply that this was not a matter requiring either his or the board's approval and that I would make decisions of this kind. Powell subsided, saying reluctantly that he would go along with my decision, despite his disagreement.

When all the arrangements had been agreed to, Powell added, almost as an afterthought, that of course he would have to obtain the board's approval before anything more could be done. Geffner reacted with amazement and disbelief, and I asked Powell why he was taking that position, reminding him that only the day before Gardner had said that Powell was free to make procedural arrangements of this type without clearing them with the board. Powell replied that he had not so understood Gardner's remarks and that, anyway, Gardner could not speak for the entire board. I asked if he was talking about the necessity of taking up the matter at a regular board session (an obvious impossibility before Monday), and Powell said he needed only to "touch base" with each of the members. He added that he anticipated no objections. Geffner then asked him if he knew how to get in touch with Gardner, and to our bewilderment Powell replied that he did not know where Gardner was, but that he would talk to Andreson.

The meeting broke up in mid-afternoon, and I returned to my office. I telephoned Duncan, explaining what we planned to do, and asked him to make the necessary arrangements. We had agreed that the joint sessions would be held at the Statler Hotel in downtown Los Angeles, that three rooms would be reserved (a hearing room and two caucus rooms, one for each party), and that the parties would split the expense. Duncan expressed his satisfaction and said he would take care of the details.

I went home at about 5:00 p.m., and within a few minutes I received a call from Powell. He told me that he had talked to Andreson and that he wanted to report to me what Andreson had told him. Powell then repeated a statement he attributed to Andreson, which, in effect, was a thumbs down on the procedural agreement reached at lunch: the board could not agree to the resumption of negotiations, could not sign a contract with the UTLA, and could not agree to share the costs of meeting in a hotel. I made no comment but simply asked for Andreson's telephone number. Powell asked me why I wanted it. I replied that I intended to talk to Andreson myself. Powell asked if we could set up a conference call, and I told him that was unnecessary, that he had already talked to Andreson and reported back with a completely unacceptable answer, and that I was going to talk to Andreson without Powell's participation. Then I hung up on him.

When I reached Andreson, I repeated Powell's account of their conversation and said I did not understand it. He replied that he had not really comprehended what Powell had told him, and he suggested that we start again. I then explained the arrangements and what I planned to say at the press conference. Andreson said he had no problem with any of it, asking only that I describe the negotiations as "exploratory talks." When I read him a portion of my prepared statement, in which I spoke of my intention of meeting with the parties to "explore" the possibility of a settlement, Andreson said, "That's beautiful." He went on to say that he hoped I understood that the board could never sign a contract with the UTLA, a position he had taken at Friday's meeting, but when I pressed him, he conceded that he was not precluding the possibility of a contract with a "negotiating council." I suggested that we postpone a decision on this matter until later and that he should not be overly concerned about it. Andreson then stated his objection to paying half the expenses for the hotel rooms, but I interrupted him to say that I did not regard this issue as serious enough to warrant further discussion. He replied that I did not understand the problem, that the board was constantly being criticized for cutting necessary expenditures, and that if it agreed to pay half the costs of the hotel rooms, someone would say the money thus spent could have kept a superannuated maintenance man on the job. Rejecting his argument, I assured him that the public would regard this expenditure as one of the most sensible the board had made in some time. Andreson then said he was not afraid of being fired because he was planning to retire the following August. He agreed that he would try to get the board's retroactive approval of this expenditure, but that if things did not go well, he might have to blame it all on me. Telling him that I would cheerfully accept the blame and not to worry about it any more, I terminated the conversation. I immediately called Powell, and he asked me what had happened. I told him simply that Andreson had agreed to the arrangements, that there was nothing more to be said about it, and that I was going to hold the press conference on Sunday morning, accompanied by Geffner and, I hoped, by Powell. I told him, however, that the press conference would take place, with or without him. He assured me that he would be there.

On Sunday morning, 26 April, I held a press conference at the Sheraton Universal Hotel in Universal City. Radio, TV, and print media coverage was extensive. Geffner and Powell were present and sat on either side of me as I read my prepared statement, in which, among other things, I said that the willingness of the parties to meet with me was "evidence of their awareness of their responsibility to the public and a confirmation of their assurances, given to me at the outset, that they would cooperate with my efforts to bring about a resolution of the current impasse." In keeping with my promise to both sides, I cautioned that the agreement to resume negotiations involved no concessions by either side, and that because the many issues involved were important and difficult, it would be highly unrealistic to assume that all of them could be disposed of within a few days. Finally, I stated that I had asked the parties to refrain from commenting publicly on any matters relating to the negotiations, but that I would do my best to keep the public informed about any significant developments.

As soon as I had concluded my statement, the newsmen present began to question both Geffner and Powell. They concentrated on Powell, asking him if the board's agreement to resume negotiations did not represent a complete retreat from its earlier position that it would not negotiate unless and until the teachers returned to work. To my surprise and great relief, Powell handled their questions deftly and courteously. When they began to press him, I intervened, saying I thought it was unfair to question the parties about their positions prior to their joint session under my auspices. I reiterated that all information about the negotiations would come from me.

Sunday evening I telephoned Gardner at his home. By this time I had become convinced that I could not rely on Powell to transmit accurately to his superiors any arrangements tentatively agreed to, so I asked Gardner to have dinner with me on Monday evening and not to tell anyone we were meeting. I told him I would explain when we met. He readily agreed.

Joint talks began at the Statler Hotel in Los Angeles on Monday morning, 27 April. We immediately ran into a problem: the rooms that had been reserved were totally inadequate. Accordingly, arrangements were made to transfer to the Biltmore Hotel the following day. We spent all day Monday discussing the nondiscrimination clause in the proposed contract. The procedure I adopted at the outset was to meet with the parties jointly and then separately. Despite earlier indications of the difficulties involved in dealing with the board's committee, I was unprepared for what I actually encountered. Powell acted neither as a leader nor as a spokesman; he participated simply as one of a five- or six-man committee (the number fluctuated from day to day). As a group, the board committee did not come to the talks with any clear positions, and each proposal from UTLA resulted in endless discussion among the committee members, who frequently disagreed with one another. The day passed without agreement being reached on the text of the proposed nondiscrimination clause, something that should have been accomplished long before the day ended.

Emerging from the first day's negotiating session, I was surrounded by a number of newspaper, TV, and radio reporters demanding to know what progress, if any, had been made. I responded in a way I was later to regret, saying that on a scale of one to ten, I would give the session a four. In the succeeding days every question about the amount of progress made was prefaced by the words, "on a scale of one to ten." And as the days went by I had less and less to report on progress being made in the negotiations.

From that moment until the teachers ended their strike, I was the center of more media attention than I had imagined possible. I gave several radio and television on-the-spot interviews every day, and my face became recognizable to large numbers of people. In restaurants one or more persons would invariably approach me, either to inquire about the status of negotiations or to express hope that the teachers would soon return to work. Strangers on the street frequently accosted me, expressing support for the teachers and displeasure with the school board. I also received a number of telephone calls at my home and office, most expressing the caller's appreciation of my efforts to end the strike. One woman representing a small civic organization even inquired, to my amazement, whether I would consider running for governor.

That evening I met Gardner for dinner as previously agreed. We had a most satisfactory talk. Membership on the school board was only a part-time position; Gardner's regular job was as a pilot for Western Airlines.

He was a member of the Air Line Pilots Association and familiar with collective bargaining practices. His flight schedule dictated that most of our subsequent meetings be held in the evening, sometimes quite late. Gardner indicated that if arrangements could be made in complete secrecy, he would be willing to meet with Baer and me to discuss the terms of a settlement that might be acceptable to the board and sufficient to persuade the teachers to return to work. He made it clear that he would not disclose these contacts to the members of his board. I said I'd explore his suggestion with Geffner and Baer. After I got home, I telephoned Geffner, who agreed that Gardner's suggestion was a good idea; he promised to discuss it with Baer.

Meetings were resumed on Tuesday, 28 April, at the Biltmore Hotel, where the accommodations were somewhat better. Agreement was reached on the language of the nondiscrimination clause, and some progress was made toward agreement on a grievance and arbitration procedure. Nevertheless, the pace was terribly slow. Moreover, each time I met alone with the board's representatives I had to take on not only Powell but also several other members of his committee. All of them repeatedly stated that they lacked discretion to agree to specific provisions, notably final and binding arbitration of grievances, which they said could be approved only by the board itself. The fear they exhibited at the prospect of incurring the displeasure of the board or their immediate superiors was palpable. At length, I told them that if they lacked sufficient authority, they ought either to get it from the board or bring somebody to the negotiations who had it. This comment produced only deep resentment.

The UTLA representatives were more disciplined, but it was apparent that they were becoming restive. Each time I brought a proposal from the board representatives, I would be greeted by sarcastic references to "another big breakthrough." The day ended on a discouraging note.

That evening I had dinner with Geffner and Baer. In advance of a meeting with Gardner later that evening, which I had arranged the night before, I tried to sound out Baer on his willingness to proceed informally with Gardner in an effort to flesh out the substance of an agreement between the parties. Baer indicated his ready acquiescence, stating that he had great respect for Gardner. At the same time, he remained a little evasive about details. After dinner, we returned to Geffner's office, where Gardner was waiting. For the next five hours Baer and Gardner went through the first 32 of the 67-page packet of proposals originally submitted by the UTLA. They discussed only the noneconomic demands, and Gardner repeated several times that all of this work would go for nothing if the UTLA was unwilling to settle its economic demands on the basis of a "contingent budget." More specifically, he said that the board would never agree, nor would he personally, to a contract committing it to deficit financing. All of UTLA's economic proposals required the expenditure of substantial amounts of money, none of which was presently in hand. Gardner suggested, therefore, that the UTLA rank in order of their importance a list of specific projects that required the expenditure of money for the board's consideration. He insisted over and over again, however, that the UTLA must clearly understand that no money would be spent on any of these projects if the necessary funding was not provided.

The discussion of the noneconomic issues went extremely well. I limited my role to that of moderator, making only an occasional suggestion of my own. Geffner took notes on what was said and what was tentatively agreed to. We concurred that if these discussions could have taken place before the strike, which Baer insisted the UTLA had never desired, it probably could have been averted. The meeting broke up about 1:00 a.m., and we agreed to meet again that evening.

The joint sessions on Wednesday, 29 April, were largely unproductive. It became increasingly clear to me that very little was going to be accomplished through this technique. That evening I had dinner with Geffner and John Geagan, a representative of the Service Employees International Union (SEIU). Geagan told me that a strike that had been called on 24 April by a SEIU local representing classified employees of the school district to protest a projected cut in jobs for its members was a complete farce and that most of them were continuing to work. A similar stoppage called by the Building Trades Council was even more ineffectual, he said. Quite clearly, the teachers could expect no real support from either quarter. Geagan also told me that during his negotiations with Andreson and several other administrators he had been confronted by the assertion that the board could not legally enter into a contract with any of its employees. I knew that the board had received this advice from the office of the Los Angeles County counsel, John D. Maharg, but it was my understanding that the board had decided to ignore it. Geagan's news, therefore, was a disturbing surprise.

Later that evening, Geffner, Baer, Gardner, and I met again in Geffner's office, and the dialogue between Baer and Gardner continued. At the start of the meeting, I expressed the view that formal negotiations under my auspices between the two committees representing the parties would not result in a settlement and that whatever hopes for success we had lay in an informal agreement between Gardner and Baer that each could sell to his principals. For the first time, I explained the strategy I had in mind: submission to me of final proposals by each side, which would be used as a basis for drawing up my version of a proposed contract. Baer and Gardner seemed receptive, but they remained noncommittal. Gardner again emphasized that these discussions would lead nowhere unless the UTLA was prepared to accept a contingent budget. Although I joined Gardner in pressing Baer very hard on this point, he refused to commit himself. Gardner left, and Baer, Geffner, and I continued to talk. I again told Baer that Gardner's proposed solution seemed to be the only feasible one, but Baer responded that he did not know whether he could sell it to his committee. He expressed concern that he might be losing control of the committee.

There was some basis for Baer's worries. His committee included members of both the NEA and the AFT, organizations with quite different philosophies and bargaining histories. Generally speaking, the AFT was much the more militant and confrontational, and its representatives on the committee were more outspokenly critical of the slow pace and lack of progress in the negotiations. Moreover, the strike had attracted national attention and much was at stake. Both the AFT and the NEA had sent outside representatives from the east to assist and advise the UTLA, and I suspected that the pursuit of their own agendas created more of a hindrance than a help to Baer.

The joint and separate meetings with the parties on Thursday, 30 April, were again largely unproductive. Both committees were becoming increasingly restive, each complaining to me that the other was not contributing anything valuable to the discussions. The board representatives announced that they would have to leave at noon to brief some of the district's top administrators prior to an executive session preceding the public board meeting later that afternoon. Despite the UTLA committee's protests, I sided with the board committee. I spent the next two hours with UTLA committee members, discussing various matters, and it was apparent that Baer was having considerable difficulty in keeping them all in line. Shortly after my return to the university at about 2:00 p.m., I was summoned, at Gardner's request, to attend the board's executive session at 4:00 p.m. Besides the board members, Kelly, Andreson, Deputy Superintendent J. Graham Sullivan, and Jerry Halverson, the board's attorney, were present.

This was my first meeting with the board and the first opportunity to get an idea of what I was up against. As soon as I arrived, board member J.C. Chambers, who was a bitter foe of the teachers and who opposed all dealings with the UTLA, expressed his displeasure by walking out of the meeting. Gardner began by asking for my appraisal of the current situation. I said I thought one of the major barriers to progress was the board committee's actual or assumed lack of authority to make final decisions on noneconomic issues, such as recognition of the UTLA as the teachers' exclusive bargaining representative and a grievance and arbitration procedure. Referring to the injunction against the strike previously issued by Fargo and the subsequent contempt citation against UTLA leaders for defying it, I pointed out that it would be difficult to carry on negotiations in the following week if the principal UTLA representatives were in court as defendants in the contempt proceedings. Asked if a continuance was possible, Halverson said no, but added that it was not absolutely necessary that the defendants be in court. In response to my suggestion, the board said it would consider giving Powell more specific authority to bargain on the issues I had mentioned, although Gardner repeated his belief that Powell already possessed sufficient authority to agree to a grievance and arbitration procedure. A good deal of time was consumed by wrangling among board members. Richard Ferraro, a highly emotional man with an unconcealed bias against any dealings with the county's various labor organizations, was strongly in favor of refusing to deal with the UTLA and of vigorously prosecuting the contempt charges against its leaders. Julian Nava, a charismatic figure with political ambitions, and Robert Docter, an educator, were strongly pro-UTLA. Georgiana Hardy, a veteran school board member with a reputation as a liberal, and Donald Newman, about whom I knew nothing, asked a few questions but did not indicate their positions on the issues. Shortly before the session ended, Docter suggested that either a three-person committee of the board, or Gardner individually, be appointed to deal with the UTLA. Gardner responded that he was prepared to do whatever the board considered useful. The executive session ended shortly after 5:00 p.m., and the board held a public meeting, followed by yet another executive session. Newspaper accounts the next day reported that Chambers had stalked out of the second executive session shortly after it began, saying that what the board was doing made him so angry that he could not stay in the room. I later learned that the board had voted to disregard Maharg's advice and to enter into a contract with the UTLA if mutually agreeable terms could be negotiated.

After leaving the board meeting, I joined Geffner for dinner. While there, I received telephone calls from Bernstein and Gardner, each telling me what had happened after I left. Gardner offered to meet with Baer, Geffner, and me for a short time the next day if we thought that would be helpful. I told him I'd let him know. Geffner and I then discussed UTLA's position at some length. We recognized that the union's problem was that, even with a pretty good contract, it could not call off the walkout unless it achieved the principal objectives for which the strike had been called. Merely obtaining promises from the board in the form of a contingency budget would probably not be sufficient. Baer also reported increasing difficulty in keeping his committee in line, but Geffner and I concluded that his concern was largely fictitious and designed to maintain a strong bargaining position vis-à-vis Gardner.

The mediation sessions on Friday, 1 May, again went very badly. I spent most of the morning going through the various proposals submitted by the UTLA with the board's negotiating committee. All members of the committee were in a very bad mood. Powell and several of his colleagues individually told me with great feeling that they resented both the pressure I was putting on them and the lack of any modified UTLA proposals in response to the ones they had submitted. I heard them out and then suggested that we could save a good deal of time if, on the following day (Saturday) we had a joint session at which we would go through the entire list of UTLA proposals and they would indicate which were acceptable, which were unacceptable, and which might provide the basis for discussion leading to a modified proposal acceptable to both parties.

At this point Powell declared that he had no intention of meeting beyond noon on Saturday and that he saw no reason for doing so. He said he did not believe it was fair to disrupt the home lives of his colleagues and that he himself had made other plans for Saturday afternoon. I responded that at the very least we should meet a half-hour early on Saturday morning and then see what came of the meeting. Emphasizing the urgency of the situation, I said neither party had a right to refuse to meet if there was any possibility of making some progress.

Continuing with our meeting, we went through more of the UTLA's proposals. Then the committee members told me they needed some time by themselves to work out their position on the rest of them. Accordingly, I left them and met with the UTLA committee, which I found in a state of growing disorganization. Baer seemed to have less control, and the individual members of the committee were making speeches about what should be done. There was no agreement; indeed, there was a great deal of animosity among some of them. Asked what plans I had for future negotiations, I told them of my plan to hold a joint session on Saturday to run through the entire list of their proposals. I asked them to await the outcome of that procedure. Their general response was openly cynical.

Instead of rejoining the board committee, I asked to see Powell by himself. I told him that henceforth I would not meet with his committee but only with him. It seemed clear to me, I explained, that he was regarded by the other committee members as no more than first among equals and that I was tired of taking on each one of them separately. I also warned Powell that if he walked out of the Saturday session at noon, on the grounds that he did not want to disrupt the home lives of his committee members, nothing could save him from being crucified by the UTLA. Refusing to back down, Powell grudgingly promised to stay if it appeared that important progress was being made. I then released him and his committee for the rest of the day, had another painful session with UTLA representatives, and then released them, too.

That evening Eleanor and I gave a cocktail party at our house in honor of departing staff member Arthur Carstens of the Institute of Industrial Relations. I knew that Baer, Gardner, and Geffner were meeting in Geffner's office, and about 10:00 p.m. I telephoned to inquire what progress they were making. Geffner suggested that I join them as soon as possible. I left immediately, arriving at Geffner's office about a half-hour later. The discussion on the economic issues was not going very well. Everyone seemed tired and dispirited. Gardner continued to insist that the UTLA would have to accept that no money would be available except on a contingent basis, and Baer continued to stop short of agreeing to that condition. In contrast, all noneconomic issues seemed pretty well resolved. I told them that the joint negotiations were going so badly that I could see no real chance for substantial progress in the near future. Explaining my plans for the next day, I said I would probably have to act drastically to speed things up. The meeting broke up about 2:00 a.m.

The joint sessions on Saturday, 2 May, began at 9:30 a.m. at the Biltmore. As planned, we proceeded to go through each of UTLA's proposals in the original package, and Powell indicated those that were acceptable, those that he rejected outright, and those that might serve as the basis for further discussion. The number of rejected proposals far exceeded those in the other two categories. Baer rejoined with a short but bitter statement about the unacceptability of the board's response to UTLA's proposals, and then we terminated the session.

By this time it was clear beyond question that the joint sessions between the parties were largely unproductive and that something different had to be done to save the situation. Accordingly, I met privately with Baer and Powell and told them the time had come for me to inject my own ideas on how to reach a mutually agreeable settlement. I informed them that I was going to call a halt to these sessions and would ask each side to submit its final proposals to me in confidence, after which I would prepare a proposed contract for consideration by both parties. Powell said he would need until the following Wednesday to put his proposals together. Baer furiously opposed the delay, but I backed Powell. I assumed Baer's anger was mostly feigned, because he knew that I, too, would need the time to prepare my own proposals, which would be based very largely on what Baer and Gardner had already agreed to. Powell seemed relieved by this turn of events; it was plain that he had no taste for dealing any further with the UTLA committee.

At noon on Saturday I held a hastily convened news conference at which I read the following statement:

> After meeting more or less continuously with the parties in joint or separate sessions since April 23, I have concluded that such progress as we have made has been, and promises to continue to be, much slower than the urgency of the current dispute permits. Accordingly, I have resolved to speed up the resolution of the problem by introducing some proposals of my own.
>
> I have asked representatives of the school district and of United Teachers-Los Angeles to submit to me no later than Wednesday morning, May 6, a proposed contract which they would be willing to sign and which they believe has some possibility of acceptance by the other party. On the basis of those proposals, which each side has agreed to submit to me on condition that I not disclose it to the other, I shall prepare my own version of a contract which I think both parties might be willing to accept and, in my opinion, ought to accept. This I shall submit to both sides no later than Thursday, May 7. I shall not publicly reveal the substance of my proposals, but I shall expect a prompt response from both sides.
>
> Let me emphasize, once again, that neither party is under any legal obligation to accept my recommendations. I can only hope that they will be acceptable as submitted or, if not, that they will provide the basis for an immediate settlement.

Between now and next Wednesday, I shall continue to explore with each side possible grounds for an accommodation of their differences that will be mutually satisfactory.

Monday evening, 4 May, was probably the most critical time in the entire period of mediation. Geffner and I had dinner together. We invited Baer to join us, but he said that his committee members were so disturbed that he felt it important to remain with them as long as possible. He agreed to join us later in the evening at Geffner's office. Gardner had previously agreed to meet us there.

When we all gathered in Geffner's office, I opened the discussion by saying that the time had come for Baer forthrightly to state his position on the economic issues so that we would know whether there was any chance of working out a proposal that would be acceptable to both parties. But Baer did not comply with my request; instead, he responded by pointing out the extreme difficulties under which he was laboring. In brief, he said that the UTLA felt trapped. It had called the strike, not to secure important benefits for teachers personally or for their organization, but to obtain improvements in the educational program. If the UTLA agreed to end the strike after signing a contract providing it with a certain amount of institutional security but without including tangible economic improvements in the educational program, it would be regarded as having betrayed its constituency. Gardner replied that he understood UTLA's problem, but reiterated that the board was simply not in a position to guarantee benefits without money in hand to provide them. He renewed his warning that under no circumstances could or would the board consider deficit financing.

We continued to discuss the problem rather aimlessly until Geffner came up with an idea that Baer embraced immediately and Gardner appeared to support. What Geffner proposed was that the contract state that the board agreed to retain the teacher positions it had been preparing to eliminate because of the current $41 million deficit and to introduce a number of important educational improvements, such as a reduction in class size and the adoption of a special reading program. The contract would further state, however, that if monies to effectuate those agreed-upon objectives were not forthcoming by the commencement of the fall school term, the UTLA would be empowered to terminate the contract.

This proposed solution seemed to me an ingenious if somewhat deceptive way out of UTLA's dilemma. The contract would commit the board to a program of educational improvements, but if money to support the program was not forthcoming, the board would not implement it. The UTLA would then be free to terminate the contract and, presumably, to resort once again to a strike. The proposal was attractive to me because I was sure that UTLA would not be in a position to call another strike for some time, and I did not believe there was any real danger of its denouncing the contract in the fall. On the other hand, I hoped the contract language would be perceived by UTLA's membership as an important accomplishment because it bound the board, at least in principle, to the achievement of some of UTLA's primary goals. To my surprise, Gardner appeared to accept Geffner's proposal, but at this stage I was not inclined to look a gift horse in the mouth, and I did not attempt to probe Gardner's response in detail.

We turned next to a discussion of immediate economic benefits for teachers themselves. Baer had already told me privately that, if necessary, the UTLA would be willing to give up even the 5 percent salary increase offered by the board if by so doing it could obtain further educational improvements. I doubted that his membership was willing to make such a sacrifice, and Geffner, who was shocked by Baer's proposal, had urged me not to reveal it to Gardner. At this meeting, however, Baer asked for a salary increase in excess of the 5 percent previously offered by the board. Predictably, Gardner reminded Baer of UTLA's public stand that its strike was for educational improvements, not increases in teachers' salaries, and he asked if that had been simply a cynical ploy designed to fool not only the general public but its own membership. I said I thought that the teachers were entitled at least to a cost-of-living adjustment, which I calculated to be roughly seven percent. Gardner, although not accepting that specific figure, conceded that it was "in the ball park." Geffner, Baer, and I all took that as an indication that Gardner would support, or at least not oppose, a salary increase of approximately that amount if the matter should come before the board for action.

The next issue discussed was fringe benefits. The UTLA urged inclusion in the contract of certain improvements in the medical and dental program, specifically prescription drugs and eye care. Gardner's response to that proposal was lukewarm, but he did agree that something might be done to improve the retirement program. Other fringe benefits were also discussed, but it seemed to me that UTLA's position on all of these was highly unrealistic and created barriers to reaching some kind of practical accommodation. Nevertheless, by the time we concluded our meeting, which lasted well past midnight, I had the sense that we had worked out a general understanding of the terms of the contract I would recommend to the parties.

On Tuesday, 5 May, I spent the afternoon in Geffner's office with the UTLA negotiating committee. Baer was not present. The committee was, of course, unaware of the numerous prior meetings I had had with Baer and Gardner. Our discussion centered mainly on the economic issues, and it became immediately apparent that the committee members were far more concerned with economic betterment for the teachers in the form of salary increases than Baer had previously indicated. At the same time, there was no mistaking the tremendous emphasis the group put upon an improved educational program; indeed, they insisted that many more details of their initial set of proposals be addressed than had been covered in my prior discussions with Baer and Gardner. Continued sharp differences of opinion between former NEA and AFT members of the committee were also apparent. Later, in reviewing what had been accomplished during this meeting, I concluded that I had obtained a pretty good reading of the committee's emotional intensity, but very little help in putting together any concrete provisions in the proposed contract I was preparing. I spent the evening working on preliminary drafts of some of those provisions.

On Wednesday morning, 6 May, I picked up a copy of the board's proposed contract at Powell's house and then joined Geffner at his office, where we had decided to prepare my contract proposal. Geffner turned over his private office to me, and I worked almost without interruption from shortly before noon until about 7:00 p.m. In essence, I merely put into contract language what I understood Baer and Gardner had already agreed to. Whenever possible, I incorporated language from Powell's proposed contract, but most of it was unusable. In order to save time, Geffner and I did not go out to dinner but ate some sandwiches he ordered in. Shortly after 8:00 p.m., my secretary from the Institute of Industrial Relations, Joan Gusten, joined the two women working in Geffner's office, and the three of them worked on typing and duplicating for the rest of the night. Following our brief "dinner" break, Geffner and I invited Gardner to join us to read over the draft contract I had prepared, in order to avoid any misunderstandings or unpleasant surprises when he formally received the document. Gardner joined us about 9:30 p.m. and stayed for several hours. He carefully reviewed the text of my draft contract and suggested a number of changes, all of which were made. When he left, both Geffner and I were positive that he would do his best to gain board approval of the contract as submitted. Indeed, Geffner believed that Gardner had virtually guaranteed that a majority of the board would follow his lead, and he reported this to Baer.

The drafting, typing, and duplicating process was very time-consuming; we did not finish until 5:00 a.m. on Thursday, 7 May. I went home, slept for two hours, and then made arrangements to hold a news conference at noon at the Los Angeles Press Club. Representatives of the media attended in force. My prepared statement read in part:

> My draft agreement reflects a number of the proposals previously submitted by the parties to each other and to me, but it is more than an amalgam of provisions taken from the documents prepared by the two sides. As mediator, I have deemed it necessary and proper to include a few ideas of my own.
>
> I am not free at this time to discuss the contents of my proposed agreement, but I think it would be idle to assume that either the district or UTLA will receive the document with enthusiasm. Indeed, I anticipate that each party will be upset by some of the provisions I have included in my draft, as well as disappointed by my omission of other provisions. The best I can hope for is that neither side will reject the agreement without giving serious thought to its public responsibilities and to the consequences of such action, and that after reflection, both will conclude that the

proposed agreement represents an acceptable, if not entirely satisfactory, basis for settling their differences.

With the submission to the parties of my proposed agreement, my usefulness as a mediator in this dispute is about over. If they should decide to accept the proposal, there would happily be no further need for my services. If one or both of them reject it, I shall have failed in my efforts to bring them together, and I shall therefore withdraw immediately....

Whether or not my proposal provides an acceptable basis for settling the dispute, I fear we are all in trouble. I say "we" advisedly, because the problem transcends the specific differences between the district and UTLA. The entire educational system of the State of California is involved. The current dispute will be settled—if not now, then later; but regardless of how or when it is settled, the principal underlying problem will remain. That problem, in my opinion, is lack of sufficient financial support of local school districts by the state. I urge both parties to reach a prompt agreement and to join with others in this community and throughout the state in the concerted political action which alone can bring about a lasting solution.

After reading my statement, I answered questions for about 15 minutes and then called it quits for the day.

Although I was the principal draftsman of the contract submitted to the parties, its substantive provisions reflected not only my ideas but those of Geffner, Baer, and Gardner. It included the following principal items:

1. Cancellation of most of the $40 million in cutbacks proposed earlier in the dispute by Acting Superintendent Kelly. These included reducing the school day in junior and senior high schools by one class period, thereby eliminating 1,321 teaching positions; cutting a total of 3,000 school jobs, resulting in the layoff of hundreds of school employees; a cut of 66 percent in school health services; and sharp cutbacks in text book purchases, counseling services, building repairs, equipment maintenance, and groundskeeping.
2. Limits on class size at every grade level.
3. A requirement that the agreement be in contractual form, signed by the board and the negotiating council, which would be allowed to name UTLA as its negotiating agent.
4. A 7 percent salary increase for teachers.

5. A fully paid optical and drug program for teachers and their dependents.

6. Special classes for pupils behind in reading levels.

7. A special program for increased benefits for schools in poverty areas.

8. A grievance procedure, including binding arbitration by neutrals.

9. Appointment of faculty members by the negotiating council to serve jointly with administrators in determining a host of school-related matters, including textbook selection, pupil disciplinary policy, teacher promotions, and teacher assignments to school activities in general.

10. A proviso that if the board is unable to fund the costs of any of the contract provisions from state or other sources, the agreement could be "terminated by the negotiating council, and the no-strike clause incorporated in the proposed agreement will also be canceled."

Of the foregoing items, the most important from UTLA's point of view were numbers 2, 3, 8, 9, and 10. Limiting class sizes was one of its primary objectives. The provision for a signed contract between the board and the UTLA, or the recognized agent for the negotiating council, was designed to overcome the Winton Act's implied rejection of exclusive negotiating agency by any single teachers' organization. A grievance procedure, including arbitration by outside neutrals, was another of UTLA's cherished goals. I designed the provision establishing joint committees as a way of dealing with the teachers' demands to have a voice in a wide variety of administrative determinations, including such matters as the length of the school day, class assignments, teacher facilities, and staff meetings. Those committees were to be composed of an equal number of teachers and administrators. When I discussed this provision with members of the UTLA negotiating committee, they objected that the vote would always be evenly divided and asked what would happen then. My answer was, "Then you lose," but I went on to explain that the most they could hope for in their first contract with the board was acceptance of the principle that teachers be allowed to participate in these determinations. I also suggested that in time their views would become increasingly influential. The last item was included for psychological purposes only, as an answer to UTLA committee members who demanded to know what could be done if the money to fund the various benefits provided in the contract were not available. It was clear to me, however, that the teachers would be unable to mount another effective strike in the foreseeable future, so the assurance that if the necessary funds could not be found, they would be free to cancel both the contract and the no strike clause was simply "feel-good" language without any real effect. Nevertheless, it was of crucial importance in securing acceptance of the proposed contract.

After studying the proposed contract for only a day, UTLA's negotiating committee, by a divided vote, recommended its adoption, and the document was reviewed on Sunday, 10 May (Mother's Day), at a mass meeting at the Shrine Auditorium attended by about 7,000 teachers. Geffner recalls that he and his wife dropped in during the afternoon merely to observe the proceedings, but that when he appeared, he was greeted by UTLA's president with the angry inquiry, "Where the hell have you been?" Taken aback, Geffner asked why his presence was required and was told that he had to present and explain the contract, section by section, to the assembled teachers. He protested, saying that this would take hours, but his objections were overruled. He remembers that as he proceeded with his explanations, audible support for the proposed terms increased to the point where, as he concluded each part, the audience cheered. He knew then that the teachers were so anxious to return to work that they were in no mood to mount any serious challenge to any of the provisions of the proposed contract.

Meanwhile, a meeting of the board to consider the contract did not go smoothly. In fact, after hours of debate, the board adjourned its session without taking any action. Gardner had previously inquired whether I would be willing to meet with the board in executive session if it had any questions about the proposed contract. I said I would, provided that neither Powell nor members of his negotiating committee were present and that I would be permitted to explain my proposals rather than simply defend them. Gardner promised that only the board members and a few top district administrators would be present and that I would not be heckled, and he kept his word to the extent he was able.

On Monday morning, 11 May, I advised Baer that I would probably be called to the board's executive session some time that day and that it would be well if his committee could stand by to attend the final mediation sessions, which I anticipated would begin during the afternoon. He assured me that he and his committee would be ready. Geffner recalled that he and Baer were shocked by the news that the board had failed to approve the proposed contract and were particularly angry at Gardner, whom they felt had either misled or double-crossed them. Gardner's call came at noon, and he asked me to come downtown immediately. He explained that the entire area was crowded with demonstrating teachers and said he would send a car for me so that I could be driven in unnoticed. I entered the board of education building without any trouble, but ran into a huge pack of radio, television, and newspaper reporters just outside the entrance to the boardroom. I promised to keep them informed of ongoing developments.

As I recall it, my meeting with the board was a long and stormy one, with the two most determined opponents of the proposed contract being much more vocal than those who either supported it or were leaning in that direction. At one point, late in the evening, when it appeared that the board was deadlocked over whether to accept or reject the proposed contract, I remember picking up my briefcase and stating that I appeared to have failed in my mission and would therefore resign as mediator. As I started to leave, Gardner urged me to continue my efforts, stating his belief that some agreement between the parties was still possible. At the same time, Ferraro leaped to his feet and literally shrieked, "Let him go! Let him go, and good riddance!" But Docter, Hardy, and Nava joined Gardner in urging me to continue, so, much to the disgust of Ferraro and Chambers, I agreed to do so.

I have no clear recollection of what happened immediately after that. According to an article in *California Public Employee Relations*, negotiations resumed the next day under my auspices and continued for more than 19 hours, at the end of which the parties had reached a tentative agreement.[1] The new document eliminated or modified several of the more important provisions in my proposed contract but incorporated most of the rest, and it was approved by the board by a vote of four to two, on 12 May. It was then reviewed at another rally of seven thousand striking teachers at the Shrine Auditorium. After lengthy discussions, a motion calling for a formal vote by secret ballot, to be held the next day, was approved by a voice vote.

As reported in local newspaper accounts, at the beginning of the rally the chairman of UTLA's negotiating committee reported that its board of directors had just voted 72 to 26 to reject the tentative agreement with the school district. A little later, however, Docter and Nava addressed the gathering and urged them to accept the agreement, assuring them that it represented the most the board was willing to give. After four hours of debate, it became clear that a majority of the strikers was prepared to return to the classroom. The next day the teachers voted by secret ballot to accept the contract and to end the strike.

At one point during the rally, the teachers voted to include a proposition on the strike ballot urging the board to use the $18 million earmarked for the 5 percent salary increase (the board's original offer) for reading programs and reductions in class size. In the secret ballot vote the next day the proposal was adopted 4,964 to 3,714. The board held firm, however, arguing that the vote failed to take into account the wishes of the nonstriking teachers, who were not allowed to participate in the balloting, and that eliminating the salary increase would merely encourage the legislature to make further cuts in the board's budget. Although the board did not publicly acknowledge it, the fact that salary increases for school administrators were keyed to increases for teachers was the principal reason for its decision.

In any case, the battle was by no means over; it simply went into a new phase. On 13 May, Superior Court Judge John L. Cole, in response to two suits filed by taxpayer groups who had opposed the strike, issued a preliminary injunction prohibiting the board from signing the contract.

---

[1] David J. Bowen, "A Report on the Los Angeles Teachers' Strike, April 13-May 13, 1970," *California Public Employee Relations* 6 (1970): 19–23.

The court held, among other things, that the contract appeared to be in violation of the Winton Act, which did not specifically authorize school boards to enter into written contracts with any organization representing teachers. The court also questioned the legality of the provision naming the UTLA as sole bargaining agent of the negotiating council. The board's response was to announce its intention to embody the terms of the contract in Board Rule 3700, with the offending section naming the UTLA as the sole bargaining agent of the negotiating council deleted. But the Citizens League Defense Alliance successfully petitioned for a temporary restraining order against the board that gave individual teachers within the school system more time to study the proposed rule. Judge Schauer granted the order barring adoption of the rule for an additional week. Meanwhile, the UTLA filed an appeal from the injunction issued earlier by Cole. On 22 June, the Superior Court decided to consolidate all existing legal actions into one, and a hearing on the combined actions was scheduled for 20 July.

Pending a decision on the legality of the contract and on the board's adoption of the substance of the contract as its own regulation, Powell resigned amid rumors that the board had decided not to renew his contract for the coming year. In his waning days as the board's negotiator, Powell had fought strenuously against the adoption and then the implementation of the board's agreement with the UTLA. Following his resignation, he disappeared without a trace; I never saw or heard anything about him again. Finally, on 20 October 1970, Superior Court Judge Charles C. Stratton handed down a sweeping and precedent-setting decision that held that the agreement between the UTLA and the board was illegal because the board had unlawfully delegated its authority. Neither the Winton Act nor the state education code, Stratton declared, gave authority to either Los Angeles teachers or the board to bargain collectively or to strike. Moreover, he continued, the board lacked express statutory authority, or necessary implied authority, to enter into a binding bilateral agreement. Insisting that the provision in the education code directing the board to "fix and prescribe the duties to be performed by all persons in public school service" prohibited the board from sharing that and related responsibilities with the teachers, Stratton held that the section of Rule 3700 allowing binding arbitration of grievances by neutrals was clearly an invalid delegation of the board's authority. In summary, he indicated his general agreement with the county counsel's amicus brief, which argued that Rule 3700 was really part of an "attempt [by the board] to establish a 'collective bargaining relationship'" and would mean an abdication of its "statutory responsibility to control and manage the school district." Also implied in Stratton's decision was his belief that even if the agreement had been legal in other respects, because it was the direct result of the teachers' unlawful strike, it was contrary to public policy and must be struck down.

UTLA was outraged by Stratton's decision and immediately filed an appeal directly to the California Supreme Court. The board also voted four to three to appeal from Stratton's decision and authorized its attorney to seek a writ of prohibition restraining him from interfering with its claimed right to adopt Rule 3700. None of these efforts was successful. The board never was able to adopt Rule 3700, and Stratton's decision was never overruled.

I, too, was shocked by Stratton's decision, which I considered to be retrograde in its view of public employee rights and out of step with developments elsewhere in the country. I also entertained what turned out to be the unrealized hope that his ruling would be overturned on appeal. In April 1973, a California Appeals Court unanimously affirmed the lower court's decision, and the UTLA abandoned its efforts to obtain judicial relief.[2] Instead, it concentrated its energies on legislative reform.

Change came slowly, but it came. In 1975, following negotiations during strikes by teachers and other municipal employees, the San Francisco School District adopted a resolution and the municipality enacted an ordinance, both of which contained a salary schedule and other provisions. Two taxpayer suits challenged the validity of these actions, and the dispute eventually reached the California Supreme Court. This case was similar on its facts to *Grasko*.[3] The challenge was

---

[2] *Grasko v. Los Angeles City Board of Education*, 31 Cal.App.3d 390 (1973).

[3] *City and County of San Francisco v. Cooper*, 13 Cal.3d 898 (1975).

based primarily on the argument that enactment of the resolution and ordinance was caused by the illegal strikes. The California Supreme Court handed down a unanimous decision that rejected this contention. The court pointed out that throughout the strike, representatives of the employee associations and of the city and the school district had held "meet and confer" sessions, specifically authorized by the Winton Act, to resolve the dispute. Nothing in California's constitution or any state statute, the court continued, barred the public employers concerned from adopting a resolution embodying the terms of agreements reached in the course of those sessions. Citing the *Grasko* case and expressly rejecting its holding that an employment agreement entered into by a school district in response to an illegal employee strike was void as against public policy, the court concluded that the illegality of a strike did not necessarily taint any agreement entered into by a public employer to end it.

The California Supreme Court did agree, however, that a school board could not legally enter into a bilateral agreement with an employee association, which the Los Angeles County Board of Education had unsuccessfully attempted to do. This ultimate goal, which the UTLA had sought and would have been achieved under the proposed contract, thus remained legally out of reach.

It was only in 1975, five years after the Los Angeles teachers' strike, that the California legislature enacted the Educational Employment Relations Act (EERA), which finally granted rights that the UTLA and other teachers' organizations throughout the state had sought so long to obtain. Among other things, EERA guarantees to public school employees the right to form, join, and participate in the activities of organizations of their own choosing, and it grants exclusive representation rights to a recognized or certified employee organization in an appropriate unit. The scope of representation in "meet and confer" sessions defined in the statute is limited to wages, hours of employment, and other "terms and conditions of employment." Those terms and conditions include all of the matters covered in the contract I had worked out in 1970: leave, transfer, and reassignment policies, safety conditions, class size, and procedures to be used in evaluating teachers, among others.

The right to "consult," as distinguished from "negotiate," embraces the definition of educational objectives, determination of the contents of courses and curriculum, and selection of textbooks. EERA also authorizes the school employer and the exclusive representative to enter into a written agreement covering matters within the scope of representation, which specifies procedures for final and binding arbitration of disputes involving the interpretation and application of the agreement. Finally, although EERA does not authorize teacher strikes, it does not explicitly forbid them. Instead, it includes provisions for dealing with negotiation impasses, including mediation and fact-finding with recommendations, to resolve disputes peacefully. I think the history of the 1970 Los Angeles teachers' strike and its aftermath had a significant influence in shaping this statutory approach to teachers' strikes.

The decisive blow in California to the common law doctrine limiting the rights of public employees to organize and to bargain collectively and outlawing the right to strike, which had informed the judicial decisions in the Los Angeles teachers' strike, was delivered in 1985 by the California Supreme Court in *Los Angeles Sanitation District No. 2 v. Local 660, SEIU*.[4] The case involved the question of whether a striking union could be held liable in tort for compensatory damages. The trial court held that the strike was unlawful and in violation of the state's public policy. Its award of substantial damages to the sanitation district was sustained by the court of appeal and was then appealed by the union to the state's highest court. The latter, after noting that the California legislature had neither authorized nor forbidden the right to strike in the governing statute (the Meyers-Milias-Brown Act of 1968, applicable to employees of any political subdivision of the state) and declaring that legislative silence does not preclude judicial reevaluation of common law doctrine, adopted the following standard to guide the courts in the resolution of future disputes involving strikes by public employees not specifically governed by other statues:

> Strikes by public employees are not unlawful at common law unless or until it is
> clearly demonstrated that such a strike creates a substantial and imminent threat

---

[4] 38 Cal.3d.564 (1985).

to the health and safety of the public. This standard allows exceptions in certain essential areas of public employment (e.g., the prohibition against firefighters and law enforcement personnel) and also requires the courts to determine on a case-by-case basis whether the public interest overrides the basic right to strike.

Looking back, more than 30 years later, on my role as the mediator in the Los Angeles teachers' strike, I conclude that my efforts to resolve the dispute were not entirely in vain. I did achieve one of my principal goals: to bring an end to the walkout and the return to work by the striking teachers. I also secured for the teachers a bilateral contract with the board, only to have it nullified by the lower California courts. But I take comfort in the fact that those decisions were eventually discredited in part by the California Supreme Court and ultimately made irrelevant by the EERA. And one of the most interesting aspects of the 1970 teacher walkout was that in spite of the popular aversion to strikes by public employees, there was a surprising amount of support for the teachers in Los Angeles. As the article in *California Public Employee Relations* noted,

> Only one or two of the numerous mass meetings of parents and taxpayers held throughout the district could be said on the basis of press coverage to have overtones derogatory to the teachers' position. Several parental groups organized fund drives to help replace a part of the approximately $1,100 the average striking teacher lost in income. The *Los Angeles Times*…ran several editorials sympathetic to teachers and never once formally censured them for boycotting classes. Several community organizations…came out in support of the teachers' stance.

If the dispute proved anything, it was that strikes by public employees cannot be prevented merely by outlawing them; something else is needed. This truth was explicitly recognized by the California Supreme Court in the sanitation district case, and the EERA has introduced some flexibility into the process of dispute resolution by establishing impasse procedures designed to forestall strikes. However flawed they may be, they represent an important step in the right direction.

Finally, the brevity of my celebrity as a public figure was further proof, which I hardly needed, of the fleeting nature of fame. Like my adversary, Powell, I returned to my relatively anonymous status within days following the termination of the strike, but unlike him, I did reappear briefly on the public's radar screen on a number of subsequent occasions.

CHAPTER 8

THE LOS ANGELES COUNTY EMPLOYEE RELATIONS ORDINANCE, 1968-1972

In 1967 there had been increasing agitation by organizations representing various groups of Los Angeles County employees for an ordinance that would establish a framework for the governance of their relations with their employer. Several versions of a proposed ordinance drafted by the county's personnel director, Gordon T. Nesvig, were strongly opposed by both the AFL-CIO and the Los Angles County Employees Association, although for quite different reasons. In January 1968, the Los Angeles County Board of Supervisors appointed me to serve as chairman of a three-person consultants' committee to draft a proposed ordinance that would be acceptable to all the parties concerned. The two other members were Howard S. Block and Lloyd H. Bailer. Block, an old friend, was a lawyer and arbitrator whose relevant experience included service as city attorney for the city of Placentia, California, and as arbitrator in a number of labor disputes involving public employees. Bailer, an economist and arbitrator, had considerable experience both as an arbitrator in the public sector and as a member of presidential emergency boards under the Railway Labor Act. After obtaining and considering the views of a number of individuals and groups, including the county's chief administrative officer, its department of personnel, the Los Angeles County Civil Service Commission (CSC), various organizations representing county employees, and the Los Angeles Chamber of Commerce, Block, Bailer, and I submitted our report and recommendations, together with the text of our proposed ordinance, to the board of supervisors on 25 July 1968. The board took the matter under advisement and scheduled a formal hearing for 3 September 1968.

223

Our report and recommendations included a preliminary section designed to bring the board up to date on the changing situation in public employment. This was necessary because, as we suspected, all or most of the board members were prejudiced in varying degrees of intensity against giving county employees the right to share in the determination of their wages, hours, and working conditions. Like the public generally, they were chiefly worried about strikes. After briefly reviewing the rapid rise in public employment in the preceding decade and the corresponding increase in employee organizational activity, we noted that the right of public employees to organize, once denied in some jurisdictions, was now generally recognized, and that the contention that a concept of government sovereignty is incompatible with a system of collective negotiation between governmental bodies and public employee organizations had been widely repudiated.

We further indicated that the assumption that the public service functions of government agencies, together with the absence of a profit motive, were sufficient guarantees against unfair treatment of public employees had gradually been replaced by an awareness that the imposition of arbitrary and unreasonable employment conditions was not a phenomenon occurring only in the private sector. Many public employees, we explained, had legitimate grievances that could be effectively redressed only through some form of collective negotiation between their designated representatives and the public agencies.

Another popular assumption that had been modified in recent years, we continued, was that because wages, hours, and working conditions in public employment must be set by the appropriate legislative body, public employees had nothing to negotiate. According to this theory, the only legitimate way for employee organizations to make their complaints and desires known was to petition the legislative body exercising the ultimate power. But it was common knowledge, we pointed out, that many problems arising in the day-to-day administration of the affairs of any public agency were not specifically covered by legislation. Typically, these problems were generated by policies or regulations unilaterally promulgated by the managements of public agencies pursuant to their delegated powers. The most effective as well as the fairest method of dealing with these problems, we submitted, was by collective negotiation between a particular agency and the representatives of the employees directly affected. For example, in respect of wage and salary schedules specifically covered by legislation, experience had shown that prior negotiations between the parties could provide invaluable information and advice to the legislators empowered to make the ultimate decisions.

Finally, we addressed the issue probably uppermost in the minds of the board members: strikes by public employees. We noted that such strikes were prohibited, either expressly by statute or by judicial decision, in all 50 states and that some state statutes also imposed upon strikers and their leaders and organizations severe penalties for violation of the prohibition. Yet in defiance of these laws, teachers, transit workers, sanitation workers, social workers, and even police officers had struck, often successfully. It seemed apparent, we concluded, that achievement of the principal objective—maintenance of uninterrupted public services—was not to be attained simply by enacting draconian anti-strike measures; other, more imaginative, approaches were required.

At the same time, our report conceded that although the sharpness of some of the fundamental differences between private and public employment may have been blunted, those differences had by no means been obliterated. In this regard, we registered our agreement with the following excerpt from a 1967 report by the Illinois Governor's Advisory Commission on Labor-Management Policy for Public Employees:

> In private industry, decisions about...[the amount and quality of services provided] are generally influenced by market forces; in public agencies, these services are generally supplied "free of price" and are determined by political processes in which legislative bodies decide how much revenue can be raised and how it is to be allocated among many competing demands. These factors make the determination of employment conditions in public agencies different from the process followed in private industry.

Use of the term "collective bargaining," implying as it did some degree of equality of status between public agencies and the representatives of their employees, was like a red flag to a bull to most public agency managers. Because of the differences between private and public employment, and because collective bargaining in the private sector presupposed the relatively unrestricted right of employees to strike and employers to lock out workers—weapons generally considered unacceptable in the public sector—we finessed the semantic problem by substituting "collective negotiation" for "collective bargaining" in the recommended ordinance. Rejecting the urging of various organizations representing county employees to adopt the latter term on the grounds that it had a well-established meaning, we pointed out that this meaning derived exclusively from a 30-year accretion of federal and state statutes, court decisions, and administrative rulings relating to private employment. It was precisely for that reason that the term was inappropriate in the context of a public employee relations ordinance.

The text of the proposed ordinance reflected the input of all three of us, although I served as principal draftsman. The section on employee rights adopted in substance the language included in one of Nesvig's proposed drafts, which restated those rights and protections already guaranteed to public employees by sections of the California Government Code. There was no real dispute between the parties over the adequacy of this provision. Most of the employee organizations would have preferred to substitute the language used in corresponding provisions of the National Labor Relations Act, applicable only to the private sector, but for the reasons previously stated we rejected the suggestion.

In respect of employer rights, on the other hand, there was considerable disagreement between county management and the representatives of county employees over both the need for and the scope of a provision on that subject. The employee organizations argued that this was a proper subject for negotiation between themselves and county management and strongly objected to having employer rights spelled out in the ordinance. County officials countered that the failure clearly to enunciate those functions reserved to various agencies of county government would invite meaningless and unlawful attempts by employee organizations to widen the legally permissible scope of negotiation.

On this issue we sided with county management. Rejecting attempts to draw an analogy with the private sector as misguided and dangerous, we pointed out in our report that the extent to which employers in the private sector had agreed to share traditional managerial decisions with labor organizations had varied widely among industries and sometimes among enterprises in the same industry. Concessions on this subject were often merely pragmatic adjustments to special situations. Moreover, when parties in the private sector reached an impasse on this issue, they usually resorted to the strike and the lockout to settle the dispute. By contrast, we explained, managers of governmental agencies had to insure that the functions entrusted to them by law were carried out promptly and without interruption. Accordingly, the provision in our proposed ordinance on this point explicitly set forth those rights that county management could exercise unilaterally and without prior negotiation with employees or their organizations. These included determining the mission of constituent departments, standards of service to be offered the public, exercising control over operations, disciplining employees for proper cause, and determining the methods and personnel by which county operations would be conducted. To put a brake on unnecessary or arbitrary actions by management, we added the following proviso to the section on county rights: "provided, however, that the exercise of such rights does not preclude employees or their representatives from conferring or raising grievances about the practical consequences that decisions on those matters may have on wages, hours, or other terms and conditions of employment."

At the heart of the proposed ordinance was the provision establishing an employee relations commission (ERCOM), consisting of three members appointed by the board of supervisors. This provision substantially reduced the board's appointment power, however, by limiting the choice of the three ERCOM members to a list of seven nominees initially proposed by the consultants' committee and then submitted to the Los Angeles County Management Council and to a committee representing employee organizations currently recognized by the county. Each of these two bodies would be permitted to strike a maximum of two names from the initial list. By mutual agreement, they could substitute nominees to replace those whose names were stricken. If they were unable to agree on the names of substitute nominees, the consultants would supply them and submit the revised list to the board of supervisors. This arrangement subsequently proved to be the cause of considerable controversy.

The provision enumerated 13 duties and powers of ERCOM, including the following: determining in disputed cases or otherwise approving appropriate employee representation units; investigating charges of unfair employee relations practices or violations of the ordinance, and taking such action as it deemed necessary to effectuate the policies of the ordinance, including, but not limited to, issuing cease and desist orders; and conducting investigations, hearing testimony, and taking evidence under oath at hearings on any matter subject to its jurisdiction.

In our commentary on this provision, we emphasized that ERCOM should be absolutely independent and free, within the limits of the law, to establish policies and procedures that in its informed judgment would best effectuate the policies of the ordinance. This principle necessarily included allowing ERCOM broad latitude in developing its policies and regulations.

One of the crucial problems dealt with in the proposed ordinance was the determination of employee representation units. We recognized that a number of important and sometimes conflicting interests had to be given consideration and some protection. For example, the county had a legitimate interest in establishing representative units that would correspond as closely as possible to the functional responsibilities of its constituent departments and in avoiding fractionalized units determined merely by the extent of employee organizations. Employee organizations, on the other hand, understandably desired to be allowed, to the greatest extent possible, to organize their own negotiation units, based in part on their community of interest and on past practice. We also acknowledged the public's substantial interest in these matters, but noted that its concern was with the stability and efficiency of public services rather than with unit determinations and elections as such.

In our report, we stated our conviction that problems of unit determination could not be disposed of in advance by incorporating a detailed formula in the proposed ordinance, yet we felt it essential that ERCOM be provided with a framework within which it could take the necessary decisions on a case-by-case basis. Our solution was to enumerate in the ordinance the following five criteria, which represented in our judgment the best guides for unit determination in Los Angeles county: (1) assuring public employees the fullest freedom in the exercise of rights granted by the ordinance; (2) reflecting the community of interest of the employees; (3) taking into account the history of collective relations among other county employees and in similar public employment; (4) avoiding adverse impact on the efficient operation of the public services or on sound employee relations; and (5) providing county officials at the level of the designated unit with the power to agree to or to make effective recommendations to higher administrative authority or to the board of supervisors in respect of terms and conditions of employment subject to collective negotiation.

It was not our intention to foreclose consideration by ERCOM of other criteria not inconsistent with those enumerated in the provision that it might deem necessary in particular cases to effectuate the overall purposes of the ordinance. We did, however, recommend that ERCOM be prohibited from designating a unit solely on the basis of the extent of employee organization or a preference for, or antipathy against, any particular employee organization qualified as such under the terms of the ordinance.

A common objective of most employee organizations in both the private and the public sectors is to be certified as the exclusive representatives of all employees within an appropriate unit for purposes of negotiating or bargaining with the employer over wages, hours, and working conditions. In our report on this issue, we expressed our belief that exclusive representation tended not only to enhance administrative efficiency but also to increase the responsibility as well as the power of the exclusive representative. Thus, while the exclusive representative could speak for all employees in the appropriate unit, the organization granted that status would also be legally bound to represent each employee in the unit, regardless of whether the employee was a member of that organization.

Nevertheless, we did not provide for exclusive representation rights in our proposed ordinance, for two reasons. First, we took into account the possibility that initial determinations of appropriate employee representation might have to be changed in the light of subsequent experience. To grant any organization exclusive representation rights at the outset of collective relations under the ordinance would tend to deprive subsequent unit determinations of desirable flexibility and might give the exclusive representative an unfair advantage over others. Second, there were serious questions as to whether exclusive representation was even permissible under the California Government Code, which took precedence over a county ordinance when both covered the same subject. Relevant sections of the code provided that public employees had the right to represent themselves "individually" in their employment relations with a public agency, that employee organizations had the right to represent "their members" in such relations, and that the governing body of a public agency was obligated to "meet and confer" with representatives of an employee organization "on behalf of its members."

We therefore recommended only one type of formal recognition: that accorded to the organization representing a majority of the employees in the appropriate unit. Status as majority representative would entitle the organization to negotiate with the management of the unit and to insist that any agreement reached be embodied in a written instrument signed by both parties. We also recommended that other employee organizations not representing a majority of employees within an appropriate unit should have the right to "negotiate" in accordance to how that term was used in the proposed ordinance. Individual employees would retain whatever rights were guaranteed to them by the code.

In the section of our report dealing with the settlement of grievances, we explained that employee relations in the public sector comprise much more than periodic negotiation of the terms of written agreements; as in the private sector, the major part of the collective relationship consists of daily adjustments concerning a wide variety of problems, some of which may not even have been anticipated by the parties. We therefore recommended that a grievance procedure be included in any agreement between management and a certified majority representative of its employees. We also advised against devising a single grievance procedure for all county employees. Instead, we recommended that various procedures should be fashioned to deal with the peculiar problems of any given unit, pointing out by way of illustration that what worked well for a group of mechanics might be quite unsuitable for a group of social workers.

The definition of a grievance in the proposed ordinance confined it to any dispute over the interpretation or application of the ordinance, or of a written agreement between county management and a certified majority representative, or of any rules or regulations governing personnel practices or working conditions. Excluded from the definition were disputes over the terms of initial or renewed agreements.

Our report also recommended that any grievance procedure adopted should terminate in final and binding arbitration by neutral arbitrators, with the proceedings to be governed by relevant provisions of the California Code of Civil Procedure. Recognizing that under the Los Angeles Charter, CSC had jurisdiction over specific types of grievances, notably those involving promotions and disciplinary suspensions and discharges, we suggested that if an agreement contained an arbitration provision, an employee should be given an election to appeal a grievance either to CSC or to arbitration. We also argued against allowing an employee who chose one avenue of appeal subsequently to switch to the other. In the event insistence on finality of choice was declared to be illegal, we suggested that CSC refuse to grant a hearing de novo in any case in which the grievant initially elected arbitration, the arbitration proceedings were in all respects fair and regular, and the arbitration award did not violate any laws or regulations administered by CSC.

Finally, we strongly advised against making a distinction between individual grievances and those brought by the certified employee representative. Instead, we recommended that the certified employee representative be given the status of a principal party to a collective agreement, not simply the agent of its members, and be given the right to grieve either in its own behalf or on behalf of any employee whom it represented in the unit involved.

Another important provision in the proposed ordinance concerned unfair employee relations practices. Tracking corresponding language in the National Labor Relations Act, we recommended a provision declaring it to be an unfair practice for the county to interfere with, restrain, or coerce employees in the exercise of rights recognized or granted by the ordinance; to dominate or interfere with the formation of any employee organization or contribute financial support to it, subject to well-established exceptions relating to use of county facilities, check-off of dues, and payment for time spent in handling grievances; and to refuse to negotiate on negotiable matters with an organization certified as a majority representative. Similarly, we recommended that the provision denominate as unfair practices the interference with, restraint, or coercion by any employee organization of employees in the exercise of rights recognized or granted by the ordinance, and the refusal by a certified majority representative to negotiate on negotiable matters with the county.

With reference to ERCOM's power to take such actions as it deemed necessary to effectuate the policies of the proposed ordinances, including those to enforce the prohibition against unfair employee relations practices, we recommended that such actions should be remedial rather than punitive. Although expressing the hope that ERCOM's findings and orders in unfair practice cases would be respected by all parties involved, we nevertheless felt it necessary to comment briefly in our report on the remedies that would be available to the injured party in the event that the other party refused to abide by ERCOM's order. We first observed that because of the very nature of public employment, complete mutuality of remedy was not possible in such a situation. ERCOM would lack authority to compel the county to obey its orders, although it would presumably advise the board of supervisors of any refusal by a county agency to comply. Thus, ultimately, enforcement would depend on the willingness of the board of supervisors to support ERCOM. Refusal by the board to do so, we warned, would endanger the continued existence of ERCOM.

In the case of refusal by an employee organization to obey an order of ERCOM, the county would be free to take such action as it deemed necessary. We recommended, however, that ERCOM be empowered to review the county's action at the request of the employee organization involved, on the grounds that such action was immoderately punitive, or on application by an individual employee claiming to have been unjustly injured by the county's action.

The last major subject covered in the proposed ordinance was impasse procedures. In our report we began a discussion of this matter with the categorical statement that strikes by public employees were and should be unlawful, but we added that to say so was merely to add a dimension to the problem without contributing to its solution. The only effective way to deal with strikes in the public sector, we observed, was to devise dispute settlement procedures that the parties could be persuaded to substitute for economic combat.

Assuming that potential strike situations typically originate in disputes over proposed new wages, hours, and terms and conditions of employment, we recommended that when a negotiating impasse was reached in such situations, either party be permitted to invoke ERCOM's assistance. It would be up to ERCOM to decide in the first instance whether an impasse had in fact been reached. In that event, it would itself be free to attempt to mediate a settlement of the dispute. If it were unsuccessful in that effort, ERCOM could then ascertain if the parties were willing to submit the dispute to arbitration. In the absence of a mutual agreement to arbitrate, ERCOM would be empowered to call in one or more neutral outsiders to assist in finding a solution to the dispute. Depending upon the requests of the parties and its own estimate of the situation, ERCOM could ask the neutrals to undertake further mediation or fact-finding with or without recommendations. Failure of any party to cooperate fully with ERCOM or its agents at any stage of the impasse procedure would constitute an unfair employee relations practice. The costs of such proceeding would be borne equally by the parties to the dispute. Mediation reports would be filed with CSC and be kept confidential. Fact-finding reports would be filed with ERCOM and then transmitted by it to the parties. Public release of the fact-finding report and recommendations, if any, would be within CSC's discretion. Release of the fact-finding report would exhaust the legal authority and responsibility of ERCOM. This would not preclude either party, however, from urging the board of supervisors to summon the disputants to a hearing to show cause why the fact-finder's recommendations were not being accepted.

Despite our opposition to strikes by public employees, we rejected suggestions that the proposed ordinance include specific penalties against employee organizations and their officers and members who engaged in strikes, stoppages, or other illegal interruptions of county services. In our view, such measures would be self-defeating, for three reasons. First, if a group of county employees were sufficiently aroused over what it regarded as unfair treatment, the prescribed penalties for illegal conduct might be regarded as a challenge rather than a restraint. Second, specific penalties would deprive the county and judicial authorities of the flexibility so necessary in fashioning an appropriate remedy in a given situation. Third, experience in other jurisdictions had shown that in order to settle a strike the authorities had sometimes been forced to ignore or evade the express provisions of the law they had sworn to uphold.

In our report we argued that by specifying no penalties in the ordinance we would preserve the county's freedom to act in whatever way it deemed necessary to deal with a particular situation. Thus, it could take various administrative actions against the offending organization and employees, such as cancellation of check-off or dismissal, or seek an appropriate remedy in the courts, such as an injunction. It was our belief that uncertainty as to what the county might do would itself constitute a likely deterrent against strikes and stoppages. Finally, we reiterated our firm conviction that the solution to the problem of strikes by public employees is not to prescribe increasingly severe sanctions, but, rather, to continue unremitting efforts to resolve in a fair and orderly way the issues giving rise to strikes.

In a letter dated 30 August 1968 to the board of supervisors and in my written statement to the board on 3 September, when it held a formal hearing to consider adoption of the proposed ordinance, I summarized the relevant developments since the consultants' committee had submitted its initial recommendations on 25 July. These included meetings and discussions with the county department of personnel, the county counsel, and the chief administrative officer, as well as with representatives of the Los Angeles County Federation of Labor, concerning their suggested revisions in the proposed ordinance. I also provided detailed responses to the specific objections and suggested changes submitted by CSC, the California Nurses' Association, and the Los Angeles Chamber of Commerce, all of which, despite their reservations, endorsed the proposed ordinance.

The sole holdout was the Los Angeles County Employees Association (LACEA), which had consistently opposed the ordinance. Because LACEA never submitted a statement of the reasons for its opposition to the consultants' committee, we could only speculate on what they were. One of its criticisms previously made public was that the proposed ordinance was in violation of the California Government Code, a charge that we refuted. Its principal objection, we assumed, was to the idea of a certified majority representative for an appropriate employee representative unit, unless that unit were determined to be countywide. From its point of view, that position was understandable: LACEA claimed to represent approximately 34,000 of the county's 57,000 employees in the classified civil service; in a single, countywide unit LACEA would enjoy a decisive advantage over its rivals, whether or not it was officially recognized as a majority representative of the employees. Although we did not question the right of LACEA to adhere to this position, we did observe that the result so far of its refusal to concede the feasibility or legality of any other approach had been to prevent the development of orderly, constructive, and equitable relations between the county and its employees. We pointed out that the proposed ordinance did not discriminate against LACEA or any other employee organization, and we expressed the opinion that neither LACEA nor any other organization should be permitted to pursue its objective of institutional aggrandizement at the expense of the whole community.

At the conclusion of the public hearing before the board of supervisors on 3 September, a motion to approve the ordinance as submitted was adopted by a unanimous vote of the board. Counsel for LACEA heatedly argued against adoption, and after the vote he announced that his organization would seek legal recourse against the board. He was as good as his word: on 17 September LACEA filed suit in California Superior Court, alleging that the ordinance was unconstitutional and charging that the supervisors had illegally delegated their authority to the newly created Los Angeles County Employee Relations Commission. It also claimed that the board had illegally taken away CSC's powers and that the ordinance could lead to the creation of up to 400 separate bargaining units. I had already dismissed this latter charge as ridiculous and based on the false assumption that the commission would prefer to destroy the basic purpose of the ordinance by creating an unmanageable number of bargaining units. The Superior Court set a hearing on 2 October on the LACEA's request for a temporary injunction to block implementation of the ordinance pending a full hearing on a variety of its objections. Approximately three months later, in January 1969, Superior Court Judge Harold F. Collins dissolved a temporary injunction blocking the ordinance and ruled that it was valid, stating that LACEA had "not made out a case" for killing it.

At this point I assumed, erroneously as it turned out, that my participation in county employee relations had come to an end. Early in October 1968, the board of supervisors had appointed the first three members of the Los Angeles County Employment Relations Commission. Lloyd Bailer was designated chairman for a three-year term. The other two members were Neely D. Gardner, a USC professor of public administration, and Melvin Lennard, an attorney and arbitrator. Some supervisors were already complaining about the procedure by which candidates for membership were selected. Kenneth Hahn, in particular, was unhappy with this process. "I see a very dangerous trend here," he was quoted in the *Los Angeles Times* as saying. He complained that a veteran business manager for craft unions was not among the seven nominees from which the board was forced to designate the commission members, and although he had joined in the unanimous vote to approve the ordinance, he had moved immediately thereafter to amend it to give the board of supervisors "complete freedom" in selecting commission members. This motion had been defeated 4 to 1 by the board. Hahn was a caustic critic of the commission from the outset.

By November 1971, approximately three years after the employee relations ordinance had been adopted, a sufficient number of issues concerning its substantive provisions and the administrative practices of the commission had been raised by various groups to convince the board of supervisors that the time was ripe to consider amendments to the ordinance. Accordingly, on 9 November 1971, the board retained the original consultants' committee (Bailer having served out his term as chairman of the commission) to consult with all interested parties and then submit to the board recommended amendments to the ordinance that would be calculated to

1. Maintain an orderly and workable system or method to regulate the relations between county management and its employees.
2. Continue procedures for, methods of, and otherwise regulate the county's employer-employee relations in such a manner as to be fair to all parties concerned.
3. Recognize, represent, and adequately protect the public interest.

After giving all interested parties advance written notice, the consultants' committee held a public hearing on 4 February 1972, at which time it received oral and written presentations by the county's director of personnel, its management council and subcouncil, several SEIU) locals, the Los Angeles County Firefighters, the California Association of Professional Employees, and the Los Angeles County Employee Relations Commission. Subsequent to the public hearing, the consultant's committee met informally with the county's chief administrative officer, the director of personnel, the chairman of CSC, and the county counsel, as well as with representatives of organizations representing county employees.

We filed our report and recommendations with the board of supervisors on 7 June 1972, but we were unable to present them to the board at a public hearing until 24 August. In an introductory section, we briefly summarized what we characterized as the commission's "impressive record of accomplishments" since its establishment in 1968. We noted that the ordinance itself had been the subject of widespread and favorable comment and that the board of supervisors had been praised for enacting "progressive and path-breaking legislation in the field of government-employee relations at the local level." We reported that we had reduced the various proposals we had received from interested parties to amend, add, or delete provisions of the ordinance to 11 specific issues. Finally, we called the board's attention to "one significant fact: no group has asserted that the system of employer-employee relations initiated by the Ordinance is a failure; all proposals are designed to improve this system, not to abolish it or substitute an entirely different one." I shall not recapitulate here our discussion of all 11 issues, but will summarize our comments on a few of the most important ones.

The first of these concerned overlapping jurisdictions of ERCOM and CSC. Under authority granted by the Los Angeles County charter, CSC had promulgated comprehensive rules prohibiting, among other things, discharges or reductions in rank for insufficient reasons, unjustified suspensions, and arbitrary assignments, transfers, or reassignments. Under the ordinance, ERCOM had jurisdiction over unfair employee relations practices, including interference with, restraint, or coercion by the county of employees in the exercise of rights recognized or granted by the ordinance. In the face of this obvious overlapping of authority, CSC took the position that its jurisdiction supplanted ERCOM's because CSC's jurisdiction derived from the county charter, which was superior to the ordinance.

We recognized the potential seriousness of the jurisdictional overlap; indeed, we pointed to a third dimension of the problem, arising from the fact that some collective agreements between the county and organizations representing its employees provided for voluntary arbitration of grievances alleging discrimination based on union activity. Thus, it might be possible for an aggrieved employee to pursue the same complaint before CSC, ERCOM, or an arbitrator. To obviate this undesirable result, we proposed, in lieu of CSC's proposal, which we found unrealistic and unpersuasive, that CSC and ERCOM adopt corresponding regulations that would establish a policy of not hearing any part of a complaint that was within the jurisdiction and had been heard either by the other body or by an arbitrator. Prior to making this proposal to the board of supervisors, we had discussed with and gained the approval of county management, CSC, ERCOM, and county employee representatives. The specific language adopted, which made any amendment to the ordinance unnecessary, was drafted by county management.

Another issue concerned binding arbitration of grievances and of interest disputes—that is, those over specific new contract terms. In our 1968 report we had expressed the view that the most effective grievance procedures are those terminating in binding arbitration, and we strongly recommended that agreements between the county and organizations representing a majority of employees in appropriate units include such arbitration provisions. The pattern that developed, however, was one providing advisory, rather than binding, arbitration of grievances. Some labor organizations representing county employees proposed amending the ordinance to require that all agreements between the county and employee organizations include a provision for the binding arbitration of grievances. All parties conceded that the ordinance did not prohibit such provisions even though it did not require them. Our investigation disclosed that in not a single instance to date had the county failed to abide by an advisory arbitration award. Moreover, its representatives had publicly advised us that they had no objections in principle to final and binding arbitration, but simply preferred advisory arbitration until collective relations between the parties became better established and more mature.

While reasserting our preference for final and binding arbitration of grievances, we conceded the success so far of advisory arbitration in Los Angeles County. Moreover, we opposed in principle legislative requirements that specific provisions be incorporated in collective agreements. We therefore rejected the proposal to amend the ordinance to require the final and binding arbitration of grievances. We similarly rejected a proposal by the firefighters union, strongly opposed by the county, that all unresolved disputes over new contract terms for fire and police services be settled by binding arbitration. The substitution of binding arbitration for strikes by employees in essential services such as fire and police had often been proposed and had been adopted in some jurisdictions. Our review of the experience in those jurisdictions as well as the record of new contract negotiations in Los Angeles County since the ordinance was adopted, however, failed to persuade us that the present methods of impasse resolution under the ordinance had failed or that binding arbitration of new contract terms represented the only or best alternative.

The vital question of exclusive recognition by the county of the majority representative of employees in an appropriate unit also arose in our review of the ordinance. In our 1968 report, we had endorsed exclusive recognition in principle, but had declined to recommend it because of a lack of collective bargaining experience between the parties and also because of our doubts that exclusive recognition was permissible under the California Labor Code. By 1972, however, the factors causing our initial reluctance to recommend exclusive recognition were no longer present. Collective relations between the county and the labor organizations representing its employees were now on a firm footing, and the California Government Code had recently been amended to provide that a public agency could adopt provisions for exclusive recognition of majority representatives, subject to the continued right of an employee to represent himself or herself. Interpreting that condition as applicable only to grievances arising under existing collective agreements, not to negotiation of new terms and conditions governing employment, we strongly recommended that employee organizations presently certified as majority representatives be henceforth recognized as exclusive representatives, and that those which in the future might win representation elections by majority votes be similarly certified as exclusive representatives.

Union security was another issue we were asked to reconsider. The 1968 ordinance did not provide for it, and employee organizations now asked us to permit or require some form of union security modeled after either the Taft-Hartley union shop or the agency shop. The former was an arrangement under which employees in an appropriate bargaining unit must join the union certified or recognized as the exclusive bargaining representative within 30 days of their initial employment or the effective date of the union-shop agreement, whichever came later. The agency shop typically provided that employees need not become members of the majority union but must contribute their fair share of the costs of collective bargaining by remitting to the union an amount equivalent to the initiation fee and monthly dues paid by union members.

As I have previously indicated, there is no more contentious issue than union security in either private or public sector collective bargaining. In responding to the employee organizations' request, we first observed that in terms of entitlement to employment, there was no difference between the union shop or the agency shop: under neither could an employee be lawfully deprived of a job or otherwise discriminated against for refusing to join a union or be suspended from membership for any reason other than failure to pay the equivalent of an initiation fee and regular monthly dues. We then expressed the opinion that democracy at work is best served if employees are free to decide whether they wish to join a particular employee organization or, indeed, any organization. At the same time we stated our equally strong conviction that collective relations are weakened and unfairly hampered if some employees reap the benefits gained by the recognized bargaining agent without paying their fair share of the costs. We declared our lack of sympathy for "free riders" and professed to discern no interest that they asserted that was worthy of protection. Nevertheless, we concluded that the present law remained unclear as to whether public employees and employee organizations could legally negotiate binding union security agreements. We therefore declined to recommend any change in the ordinance until the law was clarified or changed to permit the voluntary adoption of such agreements—a development we strongly endorsed.

Adoption of a new provision in the ordinance granting ERCOM the right to retain independent legal counsel was strongly urged by the employee organizations. The only legal advice then available to ERCOM was from the office of the county counsel, which also advised county management in adversary proceedings before ERCOM. The employee organizations alleged, and the county conceded, that these situations involved the county counsel in possible conflicts of interest, although the county denied that ERCOM decisions had thereby been affected one way or the other. In our discussions with the Los Angeles county counsel, John D. Maharg, he had recognized the possibility that his office might on occasion be confronted by a conflict of interest when called upon to advise both the county and ERCOM in a proceeding before the latter. He did not oppose an arrangement permitting ERCOM to retain independent counsel in such circumstances, provided that a limit be imposed in advance on the amount of money available for such purposes.

In commenting on this issue we expressed the opinion that the county counsel inevitably became involved in conflicts of interest in seeking to advise county management and ERCOM and, also, that the instances in which ERCOM would require the advice of independent counsel were not likely to occur very often. In regard to the latter point, we noted that all three present ERCOM members, one of whom was an attorney and professor of law, were experts in the field of public employer-employee relations. We concluded, therefore, that in most situations ERCOM probably would not need any outside legal advice. At the same time, we expressed the view that it was entirely fitting and proper that ERCOM be empowered to hire outside counsel if and when it felt the need of independent legal advice. Moreover, we endorsed the idea that ERCOM should be given the right, if it so desired, to use the same outside counsel on a continuous basis, so that it would have the advice of an attorney familiar with its particular problems. We therefore recommended that the ordinance be amended to permit ERCOM to retain independent counsel on an as-needed basis and that a suitable appropriation be made by the board of supervisors for that purpose.

Finally, we had to deal with the most serious difference that had arisen between the county, the employees, and ERCOM: the enforcement of those ERCOM decisions that the county had declined to accept. Although the number of such decisions was small, the issue went to the heart of ERCOM's ability to function effectively, and it would continue to cause problems for some time to come.

The employee organizations objected to the lack of mutuality in the existing arrangement. If, for example, one of them defied ERCOM and refused to abide by one of its decisions, the county director of personnel was free to take appropriate action, subject to the right of the affected party to appeal to ERCOM. The director of personnel was also free to secure the assistance of the county counsel in obtaining judicial or other relief. If, on the other hand, the county unit involved rejected a decision by ERCOM, the latter was powerless to enforce its ruling and the employee organization involved would be forced either to drop the matter or expend its own funds in seeking a remedy from the courts.

The county's response was that ERCOM's final authority was limited to determining appropriate units and certifying employee organizations. In all other matters, the county contended, the authority of the board of supervisors was plenary and could not be delegated. Thus, in the county's view, ERCOM's decisions in those areas were advisory only and could be rejected by the county, so long as it did so in good faith. It conceded, however, that employee organizations did have the right to seek court enforcement of ERCOM decisions against the county.

ERCOM's position was that it could not perform the functions for which it was created unless it had the right to seek court enforcement of its decisions against any party that rejected them. Practically speaking, "any party" meant the county. ERCOM argued that its responsibilities under the ordinance included far more than determining appropriate units and certifying employee organizations. It pointed specifically to its duty to investigate charges of unfair employee relations practices or violations of the ordinance and to take "such actions as the Commission deems necessary to effectuate the policies of the Ordinance, including, but not limited to, the issuance of cease and desist orders." It warned that if the county were allowed to treat cease and desist orders and other ERCOM rulings as mere advice that it was free to reject, and if ERCOM continued to be denied the right to seek enforcement of those decisions in the courts, its effectiveness would be completely undermined.

Between November 1971 and June 1972, the consultants' committee had spent considerable time trying to reconcile the opposing views on this issue of the employee organizations, on the one hand, and county management and the county counsel, on the other. Our efforts were completely unsuccessful. The county counsel's position, in particular, was inflexible; he strongly denied that there was any merit in the position of the employee organizations and ERCOM. Given these circumstances, we decided that it was up to us to cut the Gordian knot. First, we declared that ERCOM decisions and orders were intended by the ordinance to be obeyed—they were more than mere advice or recommendations. Second, we emphasized that ERCOM was a public agency with the duty to protect public, not private, rights. We therefore rejected the view that it was up to the successful plaintiffs in an adversary proceeding before ERCOM to obtain enforcement of its orders at their own expense. Such a view, we said, was completely at odds with the board of supervisors' responsibility to protect the integrity of its own law and the instrumentality it created to enforce that law. To deny ERCOM the right independently to seek enforcement of its orders, while at the same time conceding that employee organizations had the right to do so, we concluded, was to elevate private interests above the public interest and to repudiate one of the principal objectives of the ordinance. Accordingly, we proposed what we knew would not be acceptable to all parties but what we were convinced was the only proper solution to the problem. Specifically, we recommended that the ordinance be amended to give ERCOM the authority and the budget that would allow it independently to seek enforcement of its orders by initiating appropriate legal action when necessary.

By the time we had our hearing before the board of supervisors on 24 August 1972, I was impatient to conclude the work of the consultants' committee. Since July, I had also been heavily involved as chairman of the California Assembly Advisory Council on Public Employee Relations, which was charged with, among other things, the responsibility for drafting a bill regulating relations between public jurisdictions and their employees. In addition, Eleanor and I were preparing to drive to Cambridge, Massachusetts; I had agreed to teach at the Harvard Law School and the Business School during the fall semester. Immediately thereafter, we were going to England, where I was scheduled to spend my sabbatical year as a visiting fellow at Clare Hall, Cambridge University. I was already busy preparing for both undertakings, and I couldn't wait to leave Los Angeles and the employee relations ordinance behind me. In my prepared statement to the board of supervisors, I expressed the hope that they had reviewed our report and recommendations, which they had had for over a month, and said I would simply summarize our recommendations on each of the 11 issues discussed at length in the report.

I had hardly begun my presentation when I was interrupted by Hahn, who had earlier publicly indicated his displeasure with some of the terms of the ordinance approved in 1968. He asked me some factual questions about one of the issues, and I committed a stupid and disastrous mistake. I suggested to Hahn that a complete answer to his question was to be found in our previously submitted report, if only he had taken the trouble to read it. The term "going postal" had not yet gained common currency, but it perfectly describes Hahn's reaction. Recognizing in me the perfect target on which to vent his rage ("conceited professor with no responsibility to the voters"), he proceeded to give me a thorough lambasting, in the course of which he questioned my competence, declared I was overpaid, and generally sought to cut me down to size. None of his colleagues came to my rescue, and I was left to defend myself as best I could. In the circumstances, all I could do was to contain my temper and try to reduce the damage caused by my initial blunder. I therefore remained silent during Hahn's lengthy tirade and made no effort to respond to his animadversions. When he stopped, I said that I thought it best to say nothing further and let our report and recommendations speak for themselves. Then, seething internally, I got up and left.

Ironically, I received a letter dated the next day from another county supervisor, Pete Schabarum, a former University of Southern California football star and probably the most reactionary member of the board, whose views on most social issues were the opposite of my own. In it he stated that he considered Hahn's "attitude and line of questioning to be totally out of order and not reflective of my vision," and that before the board acted on any of the suggested amendments to the ordinance, he hoped to have the opportunity to "personally discuss" some of the recommendations and findings. Fortunately, I was spared that meeting, which I'm sure would have been depressing from my point of view.

Getting a little of my own back, on 25 August I wrote to the chairman of the board of supervisors, Warren M. Dorn. I mentioned I had been advised that in the previous day's afternoon session, Hahn had raised a question whether the consultants' committee had fulfilled its contract with the county and whether I would return to make my statement the next time our report and recommendations were considered by the board. I then restated the terms of our engagement and reminded Dorn that we had filed our report well ahead of the 30 June 1972 deadline and had fulfilled each and every condition of the contract. Finally, I told Dorn that inasmuch as my leave of absence from UCLA took effect on 1 September and I was about to leave for Harvard, I did not intend to appear again before the board of supervisors and was not required by our contract to do so. I added that Block and Bailer would have to decide for themselves whether to appear. I enclosed five copies of the prepared statement that I had been unable to present. Dorn responded courteously on 2 October, wishing me well in my new assignment at Harvard and thanking me for "the efforts extended on behalf of Los Angeles County."

Thus was my connection with the Los Angeles County Employee Relations Ordinance finally terminated. I gladly put the experience behind me and did not inquire during my 18 months' absence from Los Angeles as to what action, if any, the board of supervisors had taken on our proposed amendments. As I subsequently learned, the board took no action whatsoever, thereby rejecting the product of our previous nine month's work and causing me to conclude once again that in a democracy, when there is a clash between the recommendations of "experts" and the personal political concerns of legislators, the latter will almost always prevail.

CHAPTER 9

THE CALIFORNIA ASSEMBLY ADVISORY COUNCIL ON PUBLIC EMPLOYEE RELATIONS, 1972–1973

On 22 June 1972, the California State Assembly passed House Resolution 51, which created an Advisory Council on Public Employee Relations as an advisory agency to the Assembly's General Research Committee to provide "expert advice pertaining to the policy questions relating to the resolution of disputes between public employees and their public employers." Specifically, the council was directed to review the effectiveness of the present California statutes pertaining to public employer–employee relations, to evaluate the statutory solutions adopted by other states in this subject area, to appraise the current trends in California pertaining to collective negotiations, and to hold public hearings and report to the Assembly by 30 December 1972 "specific proposals for establishing an appropriate framework within which disputes can be settled between public jurisdictions and their employees." The council was to consist of five members, with the chairman to be appointed by the chairman of the General Research Committee.

As noted in the resolution, the number of public employees had increased significantly in the preceding decade; disputes by those employees with their governmental employers over salaries, benefits, and working conditions had led in recent years to work disruptions involving teachers, firefighters, and police, county and municipal employees, and social workers in various parts of the state; and reports from other jurisdictions indicated the possibility of further disruptions "at an alarming rate." Ever since the mid-1940s, public sector employment had outpaced growth in the private sector, and despite their exclusion from coverage under the National Labor Relations Act (NLRA), government employees had played an increasingly vital role in the labor movement.

Indeed, union membership had grown much more rapidly among public employees than among workers in the private sector. Beginning in the late 1950s and throughout the 1960s, a number of states adopted statutes extending some bargaining rights to public employees, but many went no further than granting them the right to "meet and confer" with their employers, and all but a few forbade strikes or picketing. It was still the case, therefore, that unless public employers agreed to the demands of their employees, the latter were nearly powerless to force better terms.

In 1972, some large states had still not enacted collective bargaining statutes for public employees; others that had such laws for specialized groups, such as police or firefighters, were considering adopting more comprehensive laws covering most government workers. I had been a firm and vocal supporter of the idea that public employees were entitled to most of the basic rights conferred on workers in the private sector by the NLRA and other federal labor laws. Consequently, when I was asked by Bob Moretti, speaker of the California Assembly, if I would serve as chairman of the Advisory Council on Public Employee Relations, I looked on the invitation as an opportunity to make an impact on the debate over granting expanded rights to public employees not only in California but in other states as well. But I hesitated to accept his invitation because of two considerations. First, I knew that even in the unlikely event that the California legislature could be persuaded to adopt the kind of public employee collective bargaining law I favored, it was a 100 percent certainty that the governor, Ronald Reagan, would veto it. Second, I was worried about who else would be appointed to serve on the council. Aware of the penchant of politicians to select such persons for reasons unrelated to their relevant experience or competence, I feared that the effectiveness of the council might be fatally undermined by members totally unsuited for such an important task. For those reasons, I told Moretti that I would accept only on certain conditions. One was that I be delegated the sole authority to select the four other members of the council. I also explained why there was no possibility of securing enactment of a comprehensive collective bargaining law for public employees at this time and said that my only interest in serving on the council would be to draft a bill that could serve as a model to emulate in the future. I therefore asked him to promise that he would introduce the bill exactly in the form submitted, without regard to the possibility of its acceptance by the legislature or the governor. Insistence on these conditions must have seemed to him insufferably arrogant, but to my surprise, he accepted my terms.

Choosing my colleagues on the council was relatively easy. They were either close friends or men I had previously worked with from time to time and knew well. Donald H. Wollett, a longtime colleague, was an experienced labor law professor who had also represented some teachers' unions.[1] Some years earlier he and I had jointly edited a labor law casebook. Howard S. Block, as I've previously indicated, was an old friend and a widely respected labor arbitrator who had been jointly appointed by government employers and their unions in California and Nevada to decide important interest disputes. Morris L. Myers was a former general counsel of the Federal Mediation and Conciliation Service, and he also had considerable experience as an arbitrator in both the private and public sectors. Don Vial, with whom I had worked on a number of projects, was chairman of the Center for Labor Research and Education of the Institute of Industrial Relations at Berkeley. While differing in our views on some issues, we all shared the belief that collective bargaining was the best system for creating equitable relationships between employers and workers and that public employees should be given broader collective bargaining rights than they presently enjoyed.

As colleagues, we worked together easily and relatively harmoniously during the approximately nine months we spent on the project, several months of which, as previously mentioned, overlapped the work of the Consultants' Committee on the Los Angeles County Employee Relations ordinance. As chairman, I considered myself no more than first among equals. Every member of the council contributed substantially to the final product of our labors—a draft comprehensive statute and a

---

[1] Wollett waited until 2002 to tell me that it was he who had urged Moretti (then planning to run for governor) to make a proposed law granting collective bargaining rights to government employees a major plank in his campaign platform and to appoint me chairman of a panel of experts assigned the job of drafting such a law.

lengthy report in support of its provisions—although I served as principal draftsman and editor, more to insure a uniformity of style than for any other reason. I also undertook, as part of my duties as chairman, to outline a framework for our report, to propose a division of labor in its preparation, and to suggest a procedure by which we could most usefully exchange views.

Our staff consisted of two persons: Leah Cartabruno, who worked in the California Assembly Office of Research in Sacramento, and Philip Tamoush, a staff member of the UCLA Institute of Industrial Relations.

We began our work in the usual way by holding public hearings in July and August 1972 in Sacramento, San Francisco, and Los Angeles. The amount of interest in our undertaking can be judged by the number of persons who testified (53) and the number of individuals or organizations who submitted written statements (92). Problems of coordination and communication were exacerbated by my departure on 27 August for Harvard, where I was to spend the fall semester teaching in the law and business schools. On 18 August, I sent a memorandum to my fellow council members that outlined the first steps of a proposed procedure for carrying out the tasks assigned to us by House Resolution 51. After suggesting some immediate assignments for Cartabruno and Tamoush, I proposed that our report cover the following five general topics: (1) coverage of the model statute; (2) criteria and procedures for the establishment of appropriate bargaining units; (3) scope of negotiations; (4) impasse resolution and strikes; and (5) union security and the duty of fair representation. At the same time I conceded that those five topics probably did not include all the matters that would have to be covered in the proposed bill. In addition, on the basis of my experience working with five other colleagues from as many countries on an extended program of comparative labor law research (which I shall discuss at length in a later portion of these memoirs), I suggested that each council member write a narrative report on his assignment topic, describing it in detail, reviewing the options, and concluding with specific recommendations. Those separate reports would then be circulated among all council members and the staff, and each one of us would be free to prepare and circulate written criticisms, suggestions, alternative conclusions, and so on, in response. Finally, I offered my view that the report accompanying the draft bill was the most important document because it would be given wider circulation, would have greater influence, and would likely have a more enduring effect.

The next meeting of the council was on 13–14 November 1972, in Los Angeles; I returned from Harvard to attend. During this meeting we settled on the outline of our report, which was to consist of a summary of our principal recommendations and the following seven parts: (I) Nature and Scope of Proposed New Law; (II) Public Employment Relations Board; (III) Bargaining and Representation Rights; (IV) Bargaining Unit Determination; (V) The Scope of Bargaining; (VI) Resolution of Disputes that Reach Impasse; and (VII) Organizational Security. The group met again, without me (by that time I was in Cambridge, England, on a year's sabbatical) on 27–28 January 1973, in Sacramento. At that meeting, presided over by Wollett, a number of questions arose upon which my colleagues could not reach a unanimous agreement. Consequently, Cartabruno telephoned me in Cambridge to inquire if I would be willing to return to the United States for one last meeting of the council on 19–21 February 1973 to help resolve all remaining issues. I had just finished spending the first two weeks of my sabbatical year grading blue books from my labor law course at Harvard, and I was anxious to get started on my own research. Nevertheless, I did not see how I could refuse my colleagues' request, so I agreed to return. On 2 February, Wollett sent me a long letter summarizing some 20 questions that needed to be decided. By that time, I had in hand the drafts of the various sections of the report prepared by other council members, so I used the time on my flight to Los Angeles on 18 February to edit them. At the end of our three days of meetings, during which we reached unanimous agreement on all disputed points, I flew back to England. Just before doing so, however, I wrote to Moretti to let him know that the council had completed the substantial part of its work, and that our report, together with a draft of our proposed statute, would be submitted by the new deadline date of 15 March 1973. I also took note of a rumor that some assembly staff members had proposed to review and edit our report before its release. Commenting on this rumor, I wrote: "[I]t must be obvious to you that the one thing the Advisory Council cannot and will not tolerate is any editing, however miniscule, in the text of our Report and the proposed statute prior to their release. What happens afterward is obviously beyond our control, but we do feel that our product should be published exactly as it was prepared." Continuing my editing for the duration of the return flight and on the train trip from London to Cambridge, I completed the job just as the train pulled into the Cambridge station.

Thanks to the heroic efforts of my colleagues on the council and of our two staff members, our report and recommendations, after nine months of gestation, were produced and made public on 15 March 1973.[2] Press coverage throughout California was extensive, and at least one national specialized reporting service, the Bureau of National Affairs' *Government Employee Relations Reports*, published a detailed summary of the recommendations. Harry Bernstein, the highly respected labor writer for the *Los Angeles Times*, wrote a lengthy article in which he described the proposed law as "more complete, more innovative and more daring than any on the books in any other city or state in the nation."[3]

It is not feasible in this account even to summarize all of the discussion and specific recommendations contained in our 267-page report. Instead, I shall outline our general approach to the principal areas covered by our report and, in a few instances, comment briefly on our reasoning. The first major area was the coverage of the proposed statute. In place of existing statutes applicable to local government employees, state employees, school district employees, and firefighters, all of which we recommended be repealed, we proposed a single comprehensive, preemptive state law that would be applicable to all public employees except management and confidential employees, supervisory employees (unless the public agency elected to bargain with them), employees subject to transit district acts, and elected public officials. Under our

---

[2] *Final Report of the Assembly Advisory Council on Public Employee Relations*; hereafter *Final Report*.
[3] *Los Angeles Times*, 15 March 1973, 26–27.

proposal, local legislative bodies would be permitted to continue, or to enact, their own employer-employee relations policies, provided that the local law was in substantial compliance with the proposed statute and was administered by a board or commission of impartial persons, broadly representative of the public, with experience in the field of employer-employee relations. Finally, we recommended that negotiated agreements on matters within the scope of bargaining that were approved as provided in the proposed statute should prevail over any conflicting state or local statute, charter provision, ordinance, resolution, or regulation adopted by a public employer or its agent, such as a personnel board or civil service commission.

The foregoing recommendations on coverage were among the more important ones included in our report. They were based on our findings that the diverse provisions of existing laws applicable to California public employment had resulted in sharply conflicting policies among public employers in the state. Some employees were granted rights denied to others, interpretations of identical statutory language had varied considerably, and, all too often, necessary procedures for recognition, impasse resolution, and enforcement of administrative decisions were either inadequate or nonexistent. Our recommendations were also consistent with conclusions reached by the National Governors' Conference in 1967 and by the Advisory Commission on Intergovernmental Relations in 1969, both of which endorsed the single-law approach.

One particularly contentious coverage issue concerned academic personnel of state colleges and universities. The council had received a considerable amount of testimony on this subject; the views expressed revealed sharply conflicting perceptions of both the present situation and the need for change. Administrators speaking for management in all of the academic institutions involved concurred in the judgment that present arrangements were satisfactory on the whole and that any system of collective bargaining of the type contemplated for other state employees not only would be detrimental to the interest and welfare of colleges and universities and their faculties but also would present formidable, if not insuperable, administrative problems. A key point in this argument was that college and university faculties presently exercised a high degree of self-government, which could scarcely be enhanced, and might well be severely curtailed, under a system of collective bargaining.

Those views were sharply contradicted by spokesmen for virtually every faculty group that submitted testimony to the council. The general feeling expressed was one of dissatisfaction with existing arrangements and a desire to have at least the option to engage in collective bargaining as an alternative. At the same time, some organizations indicated an ambivalence toward traditional collective bargaining and a desire for special statutory procedures for college and university faculties in the selection of collective bargaining representatives. They proposed a two-step procedure in the employee election process to determine bargaining representatives for college and university teachers: first, to permit voters to express a choice between collective bargaining and the existing system of employer-faculty relations in the institution involved; and second, to vote for or against the organization seeking certification as the bargaining representative, but only if a majority had already voted in favor of collective bargaining.

In our report we expressed the conviction that there is nothing intrinsic in the teaching profession in institutions of higher learning that absolutely rules out collective bargaining as an alternative to other methods of faculty governance. Without expressing an opinion on the relative merits of conflicting theories, we concluded that faculties of state colleges and universities should have the same rights and protections granted to other public employees in the state: they should be allowed to decide for themselves whether they wished to organize and to engage in collective bargaining with their employers. We also declined to adopt the proposal for the two-step election procedures for academic employees described above. In our view, the suggested procedure would present serious administrative difficulties in the determination of appropriate units. Moreover, we pointed out that nothing would prevent academic employees from indicating their wishes regarding collective bargaining in a single election in which they could cast a ballot for or against the employee organization or organizations seeking to represent them.

The second major area was the administration of the proposed statute. We proposed that this should be the responsibility of a Public Employment Relations Board (PERB), composed of three persons broadly representative of the public and experienced in the field of employer-employee relations. In order to reconcile the usual political considerations with the need to assure the competence of PERB members, we recommended that they should be appointed by the governor, by and with the advice and consent of the California Senate, from a list of 12 names submitted by a panel composed of the chief justice of California, the director of the California State Conciliation Service, and the president of the American Arbitration Association. We also recommended that PERB members should serve full-time, should hold no other public or private office, and should receive no compensation from any source other than their salaries.

We also recommended that the extent of the PERB's authority to administer the proposed statute be commensurate with the breadth of its statutory responsibilities. Among our specific suggestions in this regard was that the PERB be vested with the following powers and duties: to arrange for and supervise the determination of certified employee representatives for appropriate bargaining units by means of secret-ballot elections and to certify the results; to decide contested matters involving recognition, certification, or decertification of employee organizations; to investigate unfair practice charges and to take whatever action it deemed necessary to effectuate the purposes of the statute; and to bring an action in a court of competent jurisdiction to enforce any of its orders, decisions, or rulings.

We further urged that the PERB should have exclusive jurisdiction over the initial determination of whether charges of unfair practices were justifiable and, if so, what remedy was necessary to effect the purposes of the statute. At the same time, we argued that the PERB should not have authority to enforce collective agreements or to issue a complaint on any charge based on an alleged violation of a collective agreement that would not also constitute an unfair practice under the statute.

In respect of the PERB's enforcement powers, we recommended that these should include the authority not only to issue decisions and orders directing offending parties to cease and desist from engaging in unfair practices but also to take such affirmative action, including but not limited to the reinstatement of employees, to effectuate the purposes of the statute, but excluding the authority to assess punitive damages against an offending party. We further recommended that any charging party, respondent, or intervener aggrieved by a PERB decision or order in an unfair practice case should have the right to seek review in a court of competent jurisdiction. In that event, the PERB's findings of fact, if supported by substantial evidence on the record considered as whole, would be conclusive.

Persons familiar with the NLRA will immediately note that the foregoing recommendations regarding the PERB's powers and duties track corresponding provisions of the NLRA in regard to the National Labor Relations Board (NLRB), even though the federal statute's coverage is limited to the private sector. Similarly, our proposals on employee rights, exclusive representation, bargaining units, and unfair practices under the proposed statute were modeled, with certain variations to deal with factors peculiar to public employment, on corresponding provisions of the NLRA. We adopted the federal statute as a model because our nearly 40 years of experience with it convinced us of the essential soundness of those provisions, whether applied to private or public employees.

The third major area covered in our report concerned resolution of disputes over "rights" (grievances alleging violation of rights created by collective agreements or public agency policies or practices that the employer and employee organization have agreed are subject to arbitration) and disputes over "interests" (impasses over the provisions of initial or renegotiated collective agreements). In respect of grievances, our principal proposal was that public employers and employee organizations should have the authority to include in their collective agreements procedures for binding arbitration. (As I noted in my account of the litigation arising out of the Los Angeles teachers' strike in 1970, the power of the school district to agree to binding arbitration was denied by the courts, although those decisions were subsequently rendered irrelevant by state statutes.) Our other recommendations were that agreements to submit grievances to arbitration, as well as arbitration awards made pursuant to such agreements, should be enforceable in the courts; that strikes and lockouts over arbitrable grievances should be prohibited; and that violators of that prohibition should be liable for compensatory damages and be subject to injunctions.

Inevitably, the council's report and recommendations with reference to the settlement of interest disputes was one of the principal subjects of legislative and public concern. We began our discussion with a brief history of the gradual acceptance and spread of collective bargaining in the public sector. We reported that although bargaining arrangements varied widely in respect of structure and coverage among the several states, a common denominator was apparent: a thrust toward formalized systems pursuant to which public employees, through designated organizational representatives, participated with their governmental employers in decisions affecting their working environment.

We turned next to the matter of preeminent popular concern: strike activity in the public sector. As in most states at that time, public employees in California, with the exception of those employed by certain transit authorities that had acquired private transportation facilities and inherited collective bargaining relationships permitting strikes in specified circumstances, did not have the right to strike. Nevertheless, the frequency and duration of public employee strikes and the number of man-days lost had increased steadily as collective bargaining had developed in the public sector. There were three principal reasons, we found, for the general intolerance of strikes by public employees. The first was based on the notion that the government is sovereign and that a strike by its civil servants is a form of insurrection. This we dismissed summarily as anachronistic and insupportable. The second and more substantial reason was based on the argument that governmental services are essential, that there are no alternatives readily available to consumers, and that therefore concerted interruptions of services could not be countenanced. We rejected this argument on the ground that it did not stand up under objective analysis. Many governmental services, we pointed out, either are not as essential to the community as those provided by private sources whose employees may legally strike, or their essentiality does not depend upon whether the employer is public or private. Few would argue, we observed, that the operation of a public golf course is as important to the community as the operation of a private hospital or medical clinic. Moreover, a strike by employees of a municipally owned utility would have no greater impact on public health or safety than a strike by employees of a privately owned utility. On the matter of availability of alternative arrangements in case of a strike by public employees, we noted that such arrangements could frequently be made by subcontracting the work involved (garbage collection, for example) to private companies.

The third objection to strikes by public employees was the most serious and troublesome. It was predicated on the notion that such strikes introduced an "alien force" in the political process, leading to distortions of decision making in regard to allocation of public moneys and interfering with orderly representative government in the determination of priorities by permitting the lion to take the lion's share at the expense of weaker employee groups and consumers who have an interest in the matters being decided, particularly if they involve a sacrifice of services in order to improve working conditions. We conceded the seriousness of the questions raised by this argument. Whether a strong employee group can, through strike action, gain a disproportionate share of available public funds at the expense of weak or docile groups of employees and consumers is an appropriate public concern. A related cause for alarm is the possibility that a contract settlement figure being pressed by an employee organization possessing a high degree of bargaining power will arouse unrealistic expectations among other equally powerful public employee groups and thus create a "domino effect." Nevertheless, we concluded that the degree of popular anxiety concerning the possible consequences of public employee strikes was to a considerable extent the result of a general misunderstanding of the effect of such activity. We noted, for example, that unlike the situation in the private sector, where strikes are usually economically harmful to both parties, in the public sector most strikes do not inflict economic injury on the employer. Indeed, more often than not, the employer will save money because it does not have to pay the strikers for the time they are on strike. In most cases, therefore, the economic loss will fall upon the strikers and their dependants, as well as, in some instances, the consumers who must make alternative arrangements for the services interrupted by the strike (such as working parents who must hire a babysitter during a teachers' strike). We conceded that there are certain public employee strikes, such as those involving firefighters, police, and teachers, for which the use of alternative services is not an available response and in which the strikers can hold out longer than the public. These essential services, we pointed out, were protected even in those few states that permitted some types of public employee strikes.

We then considered the principal methods relied upon by the federal government and other state governments and municipalities to make the bargaining process in the public sector work without resort to strike action: mediation, factfinding, and imposed settlements by voluntary or compulsory arbitration or by legislation. Our discussion of these methods is too long to summarize here.[4] After reviewing the relevant experience under federal and state laws, as well as the testimony presented to us at our public hearings, we offered our own conclusions and recommendations based on three main considerations. First, we favored a prescription that would encourage public employers and employee organizations to reach voluntary settlements or agreements on procedures that they themselves devised, preferably without third-party intervention. Second, we believed in the efficacy of a procedure that would introduce an uncertainty among the bargaining parties as to the consequences of not reaching an agreement, making it impossible for either one to predict with accuracy what might happen if the dispute persisted to the point of impasse and thus ensuring that negotiations would be conducted in a context of mutual anxiety. Third, we recognized the necessity of providing a mechanism for protecting public health or safety if either should be jeopardized. Our principal recommendations may be summarized as follows:

---

[4] See *Final Report*, 207–35.

1. Both parties should be required to bargain in good faith in an effort to reach agreement prior to the adoption by the public employer of its budget for the ensuing year or years.

2. If a public employer and the employee representative reach an impasse (that is, a point in negotiations at which their differences are so substantial or prolonged that further meetings would be futile), either or both sides should declare that an impasse has been reached and either ask the PERB for a list of mediators from which the parties may make a selection, or ask either the PERB or the California State Conciliation Service to designate a mediator. The PERB should have the right, on its own motion, to appoint a mediator if it is satisfied that an impasse exists and that the exigencies created by the failure of the parties to request or designate a mediator justify such intervention. The mediator's function should be to assist the parties to reach a voluntary resolution of their impasse.

3. If the impasse has not been resolved by mediation within 15 days, either or both parties should request that the dispute be submitted to a tripartite factfinding panel, led by a chairman selected by the panel's partisan members. If these factfinders cannot agree, the PERB should make the selection. The factfinders should identify the issues, review the parties' positions, resolve factual differences, and make recommendations for settlement of the dispute. In doing so they should be guided by criteria set forth in the statute (including the lawful authority of the employer; the stipulation of the parties; the interests and welfare of the public; the financial ability of the employer to provide wages, hours, working conditions, and fringe benefits comparable to those of other employees performing similar services in both public and private employment; and the average consumer prices for goods and services) and other factors normally or traditionally taken into consideration in similar cases. If the dispute is not settled within 30 days following the formation of the panel, the factfinders should issue recommendations privately to the parties for settlement of the dispute, and they should do so without publicity.

4. If the parties do not accept the recommendations of the factfinders as a basis for settlement of the dispute, they should resume negotiations and continue for a period of 10 calendar days, or longer if they agree. During this time the PERB should exercise continuing jurisdiction to facilitate settlement of the dispute. If at the end of the 10-day period, or such extended period as the parties may have agreed to, the dispute has not been settled, the findings and recommendations of the factfinders should be made public.

5. If at this point no settlement has been reached, the employee organization, as a condition precedent to striking, should call a meeting of its membership, at which those attending should vote by secret ballot on the following question: "Do you wish to accept the factfinders' recommendations?" Similarly, as a condition precedent to locking out the employees, the legislative body of the employer should vote on the same question.

6. If both parties answer the question in the affirmative, the dispute should be settled on the basis of those recommendations. If one party answers the question in the negative, the employees should be permitted to strike and the employer to lock out, but the decision to do so should be communicated to the other party in writing and announced to the public immediately, and the strike or lockout should not commence until five calendar days from the date of such notice.

7. Any party in interest, including an employee organization, a public employer, a citizen who would be affected by the interruption of services, or a taxpayer, should be permitted, either during the five-day period previously specified or after a strike or lockout has commenced, to initiate proceedings in superior court for injunctive relief to prevent or stop the strike or lockout.

8. The court in which such proceedings are brought should not issue any form of injunctive relief, including a temporary restraining order, except on the basis of findings of fact, supported by evidence elicited at a hearing, that the strike or lockout imminently threatens public health or safety. If the court finds that the evidence

establishes the existence of such a threat, and also that there is no feasible alternative method for protecting public health or safety, it should issue injunctive relief and direct the parties to accept the recommendations of the factfinders in settlement of their dispute.

9. If the court does not make these findings, injunctive relief should be denied and the strike or lockout permitted to commence or continue, with the court having the authority in its discretion to retain jurisdiction of the case until the dispute is resolved.

10. The merits of the factfinders' recommendations should play no part in the court's determination. If made binding by court decree, the factfinders' recommendations should be subject to judicial review in a separate proceeding, with review limited as specified in existing California statutes dealing with the vacation of arbitration awards.

11. The issuance or denial of injunctive relief should be subject to an expedited review before the appropriate court of appeal.

The fourth major area covered by our report dealt with organizational (union) security.[5] As I have previously observed, in the private sector this issue has always been steeped in controversy. The same is true in the public sector. Given the pervasive ignorance about the justification for various types of organizational security, we prefaced our recommendations with a good deal of descriptive and explanatory material. We began our discussion with the observation that the issue should be examined dispassionately and only in the light of two basic principles: majority rule, and its logical concomitant, majority representation. Those two principles, which are embodied in the NLRA, have undergirded the national labor policy since 1935 and are reflected in some state laws governing collective bargaining in the public sector. They have been qualified, however, by a number of Supreme Court decisions requiring any exclusive bargaining representative to represent all employees in

---

[5] We used the term *organizational security* rather than *union security* because of the antipathy to the use of the latter term in the public sector evinced by some elements of management, employee organizations, and the public.

a bargaining unit, whether or not they are union members, fairly and without discrimination.[6]

In this connection, we explained the basis of the "free rider" problem— that is, the refusal by some employees in a bargaining unit who enjoy all the benefits of the collective agreement to pay anything to defray the cost of securing and maintaining them. We noted that there are unavoidable financial costs associated with collective bargaining. Labor organizations, no less than employers, must maintain offices and a paid staff. Increasingly, economic research in connection with the negotiation of a collective agreement necessitates the expenditure of considerable time and money and the employment of skilled professionals such as lawyers, economists, accountants, and actuaries. For the typical labor organization, the chief, if not the sole, source of funds is the member-ship itself, with each member paying an initiation fee, monthly dues, and general assessments. Under the NLRA, it is an unfair labor practice for a union that has a legal union-shop agreement with an employer to charge an initiation fee in an amount deemed excessive or discriminatory by the NLRB. Few instances of excessive or discriminatory initiative fees have been reported, and studies of union dues schedules have shown that the great majority of dues are reasonable. Thus, it is understand-able why labor organizations in both the private and public sectors have such an antipathy toward "free riders," and why they seek to eliminate them by negotiating some form of organizational security arrangement that will require all employees covered by a collective agreement to pay their fair share of the costs of collective bargaining. I have previously described the principal forms of such arrangements that are legal under the NLRA (the union shop and maintenance of membership) and have been adopted in both the private and the public sectors. To these should be added the agency shop and the check-off. The agency shop differs from the union shop only in that it does not require membership in the union as a condition of employment. The relation between employee and union is purely financial: the employee pays a fee equal in amount to the

---

[6] The so-called duty of fair representation was first enunciated by the Supreme Court in *Steele v. Louisville & N.R. Co.*, 323 U.S. 192 (1944).

union initiation fee, periodic dues, and general assessments as the price of continued employment. The fee represents the pro-rata share of the union's collective bargaining costs. Any practical distinction between the union shop and the agency shop was eliminated by the Supreme Court in a 1963 decision,[7] in which it declared, on the basis of a 1954 decision,[8] that "'Membership' as a condition of employment is whittled down to its financial core." In the earlier decision, the Court had declared that "Congress recognized the validity of unions' concerns about 'free riders'... and gave the unions the power to contract to meet the problem while withholding from unions the power to cause the discharge of employees for any other reason." The check-off is an arrangement pursuant to which the employer deducts union initiation fees, dues, and general assessments from the pay of employees and remits them to the union. Under the Labor Management Relations Act of 1947, applicable to the private sector, the employer may check off these charges only for employees who have executed a written assignment, irrevocable for a fixed period, usually a year.

We next discussed the tension between organizational security and individual freedom. Accepting that any such arrangement contains an element of compulsion, we also conceded that the alleged justification for the fees, dues, and assessments levied by the union, based on an analogy to the taxes paid by citizens to the government, is not persuasive. The functions performed by the government and by unions are entirely different, and the latter would be the first to resist acceptance of the burden of many responsibilities that government must assume in respect of its citizens. In our view, the justification for organizational security had to be based on general principles of equity and on the need to balance the conflicting interest of unions and those of nonmember employees whom they are obliged to represent, to insure that the legitimate claim of a union for contribution to its costs by all beneficiaries of the collective agreement does not unduly restrict the freedom of those beneficiaries to speak and act independently of the union.

[7] *NLRB v. General Motors Corp.*, 373 U.S.734 (1963).
[8] *Radio Officers' Union v. NLRB*, 347 U.S. 17 (1954).

We also discussed the objection that organizational security devices permit unions to spend moneys contributed by employees in the form of initiation fees, dues, and assessments, not only for "legitimate" collective bargaining purposes but also to support political candidates or ideologies opposed by some employees. After describing the ways in which Great Britain and a number of states dealt with this problem, we explained that the Supreme Court had ruled that employees are entitled, upon making timely objections to the spending of any initiation fees and dues payments for political purposes, to a rebate of their payments in the same proportion that the union's political expenditures bear to its total expenditures.[9]

Our recommendations regarding organizational security were as follows:

1. That organizational security be a mandatory subject of bargaining between a public employer and an organization representing the majority of its employees in an appropriate bargaining unit.

2. That any form of organizational security, to become effective, must be agreed upon by both parties to the collective agreement.

3. That any form of organizational security permissible under the law and actually in effect may be rescinded by a majority vote of the employees in the bargaining unit covered by such arrangement, in accordance with rules promulgated by the PERB.

4. That the law expressly permit: a voluntary dues check-off; the agency shop; any other arrangement that permits an employee to choose whether to join the organization representing the majority of employees or, in the alternative, to pay to that organization a service fee not to exceed the standard initiation fee, periodic dues, and general assessments paid by members of the organization; and maintenance of membership.

5. That an exception be made for those employees who, because of religious conviction or belief, refuse either to join an employee organization or to make any monetary contribution to it; the exception would allow such persons to contribute a sum equivalent to the

---

[9] *Brotherhood of Ry. & S.S. Clerks v. Allen*, 373 U.S.113 (1963); *International Ass'n of Machinists v. Street*, 367 U.S.740 (1965).

service fee to a charitable organization qualified as such under the laws of the United States in accordance with rules prescribed by the PERB.

Despite some earlier deals with sponsors of rival bills, Moretti came through for us when it counted. On 12 April 1973, he introduced our proposed statute, without change, as Assembly Bill 1243 and actually succeeded in winning its approval in the lower house. It failed passage in the California Senate, but we knew that, in any case, it would have been vetoed by Governor Reagan, whose well-publicized opposition to collective bargaining rights for public employees remained implacable.

Of the various instances in which I worked with others to devise labor legislation, this was, for me, the most satisfactory. My colleagues and I resolved our initial disagreements on a few provisions of our proposed statute and eventually produced a draft and accompanying report in which we all took considerable pride. Although realizing from the outset that our model bill would never become law, we were gratified by the extensive publicity and general critical approval it received. Indeed, many of the ideas we put forward later surfaced in statutes adopted in California and in other states.

On the other hand, distance sometimes lends disenchantment. In February 1977, following some events I shall recount in subsequent chapters, I wrote to someone interested in the *Final Report* in part as follows:

> At the time [the *Final Report*] was written, there had been no transit strike and none appeared to be likely. That fact, plus the existence of a special statute for transit districts, led my colleagues and me to conclude that transit districts should be excluded from the coverage of our proposed comprehensive statute for the public sector. My thinking was changed by the transit strike [of 1974], however, and I now think transit districts should be included in any comprehensive legislation. I so provided in a bill I drafted for the state legislature a little over a year ago, but it was the first provision knocked out in committee.
>
> My views have also changed in respect of impasse resolution procedures in the public sector. The procedure incorporated in the Advisory Council's model bill is probably unworkable. Moreover, the people in this state are not yet ready, and may never be, for a law authorizing even a carefully circumscribed right to strike for public employees. Accordingly, I now favor, among a number of possible options, one modeled on the Michigan law applicable to police and firefighters.

The Michigan law to which I referred provided that, after an impasse had been reached, the parties would present their respective positions on each unresolved issue to a tripartite panel, which would explore each issue fully with the parties. The panel would have the authority to mediate during the factfinding process. At the conclusion of the hearing, the parties would be directed to resume their collective bargaining for a fixed number of days. If they were still at an impasse over any of the issues at the end of that period, each side would submit to the panel a final proposal on each unresolved issue. The panel would have authority to choose one or the other proposal on each issue; it could not modify any proposal or substitute a judgment of its own. The panel's decision would be final and binding on the parties, except that any decision involving the appropriation of funds would have to be approved by the appropriate legislative body before becoming effective.

CHAPTER 10

THE JOINT COMMITTEE ON PUBLIC EMPLOYER-EMPLOYEE RELATIONS, CALIFORNIA LEGISLATURE, 1974–1975

My final involvement in drafting California employment relations legislation for public employees was as a consultant to the California legislature's Joint Committee on Public Employer-Employee Relations. That committee was charged with preparing legislation that would replace all existing labor laws relative to public employees in California.[1]

The joint committee was chaired by Senator Ralph C. Dills; the vice-chair was Assemblyman Howard Berman, a former student of mine, who subsequently was elected to the U.S. House of Representatives and became one of its most influential members.

As set forth in my employment contract, my duties were as follows:

> To provide consulting services to State relating to preparation of a comprehensive public employee labor relations law. Such services shall include, but not be limited to the following:
>
> 1. Advice to the joint committee members and staff in the drafting of proposed legislation.
> 2. Assistance in drafting specific provisions of proposed legislation.
> 3. Mediation of the differences between the affected parties, and submission to the joint committee of reports on such activities.
> 4. Service as an expert witness in appropriate legislative and committee hearings.
> 5. Research relative to problem areas, as directed by the joint committee and submission to the joint committee of reports on such activities.
> 6. Meeting with parties which might be affected by the legislation.

---

[1] Unfortunately, the file containing all my working papers during the period of my employment was lost, so my account of my experiences is based solely on my memory. I know I have forgotten many details of the complex negotiations with the governor and his personal representative, various legislators, members of the joint committee staff, and representatives of public employees and employers in which I became involved. I also acknowledge that what I do remember may be factually inaccurate. For this reason, I shall avoid relating, except in a few instances, specific details of my experience and confine myself to a general description of the process and of its outcome.

The period of my employment was to be from 1 December 1974 to 30 June 1975.

I had been dimly aware of the Byzantine political maneuvering that is so much a part of lawmaking, but before my service as a consultant I had never before witnessed it at first hand. Each of the parties with a stake in the proposed legislation seemed to have a separate agenda, giving rise to proposals that were irreconcilable with those presented by one or more of the other parties. In retrospect, that does not seem so surprising, given the importance of the issues at stake, but at the time I was somewhat taken aback by all the infighting.

The first big surprise came during my initial meeting with Governor Jerry Brown at his office in Sacramento. Brown's successful gubernatorial campaign had been strongly supported by public employee unions, in part because he had endorsed a law that extended to them full collective bargaining rights. I had seen a copy of a letter he wrote to a union of firefighters, promising that securing the passage of such a law would be high on his legislative agenda. Yet I had no sooner been introduced to him when he asked, "Why do we need a collective bargaining law for public employees anyway? They're all underworked and overpaid as it is." Unprepared for this opening salvo, I could only fall back on the familiar arguments that collective bargaining was about more than wages and salaries, that among other things it gave employees a sense of democratic participation in the enterprise and a means of securing redress of their grievances, and so on. Brown replied that during his tenure as secretary of state the employees in his office had no grievances. I was saved from making an impolite rejoinder by one of the governor's aides, who said quietly, "Governor, we had grievances."

It did not take me long to realize that Brown enjoyed making similar kinds of statements just to shock and challenge me. It was difficult for me, however, to know when he was serious and when he was merely playing the devil's advocate.

Fortunately for me and everyone else concerned, Brown almost immediately decided to appoint a personal representative to carry on negotiations with the affected parties concerning the details of the proposed legislation. He chose wisely, selecting Raymond Fisher, a young attorney from his former law firm of Tuttle & Taylor. Fisher was person-able, bright, and resourceful. Knowing virtually nothing about collective bargaining in either the public or the private sector, he immediately embarked on a rigorous program of self-education, reading intensively about the subject. He visited a number of states that had adopted similar legislation to see how these laws were administered and to judge how well they were working. In his dealings with California's public employee unions, in particular, he dutifully and forcefully set forth the governor's positions. Although his first efforts were greeted by the union represen-tatives with irritation and disdain, he persevered. Gradually, they came to accept him as someone who had to be reckoned with. I, too, was at first inclined to dismiss Fisher as a lightweight, but I soon developed considerable respect for him and we became and remained good friends. He subsequently moved on to various responsible positions in and out of government and was eventually appointed to the Court of Appeals for the Ninth Circuit.

During my six months' service as a legislative consultant I met fairly often with Brown. I had voted for him and had looked forward to working with him on the proposed legislation, but my enthusiasm soon waned. Our relationship seemed more adversarial than coopera-tive, largely because he had made up his mind in advance on the most troublesome issues, about which, in my view, he had no more than a "smattering of ignorance." His briefcase was always full of paperback books on a wide variety of subjects, and it was his habit to pull out one that had caught his fancy and to quote out of context some phrase that he considered an effective counter to what I was proposing. My dissatis-faction was not based on his rejection of my ideas, for as governor he had the unquestioned right and responsibility to make the final decision on all disputed issues. Rather, it was caused by his summary rejection of any views contrary to his own. When compelled by political considerations to compromise, he did so, but without allowing for the possibility that his own opinion about the issues involved may have been questionable.

To me, perhaps the most repellant aspect of Brown's character was his treatment of subordinates and associates. His manner toward them was coldly reserved, humorless, and extremely demanding. He exhibited all of those characteristics in an incident that is indelibly etched in my memory. The governor had scheduled a meeting in Los Angeles with Fisher and me to discuss one of the more troublesome issues in the proposed legislation. The meeting was set to begin at 9:00 a.m. Brown, who was chronically late to all meetings, did not arrive until about 9:30. While we were waiting, I noticed that Fisher seemed distracted, and I asked him if anything was wrong. He replied that his mother had died the night before, and although her death had been anticipated, his father, a distinguished professor of Russian history at UCLA, was overcome with grief. When I asked in astonishment why Ray had shown up for our meeting, he replied that the governor needed him. He added, however, that as soon as the meeting was over, he would go home and spend a few hours with his father.

Brown was in good spirits when he arrived accompanied by several aides. He announced that he had spent much of the previous evening reading up on medical malpractice and was now confident that he knew exactly the kind of legislation needed to deal with the problem. We then began discussing the principal subject of our meeting, which was the definition of "supervisor" in the proposed legislation. After about half an hour, Brown's aides started to remind him of other meetings in Sacramento later that day and urged that he leave soon for the airport. Brown continued the discussion for a few more minutes, then rose abruptly and said he was leaving. Looking at Fisher, he said, "Coming Ray?" Fisher replied that he could not leave immediately, explaining that his mother had died the night before and that he wanted to spend a few hours with his father before returning to Sacramento. I was curious about how Brown would react to this information, and I watched him closely. He offered not one word of sympathy, nor did his face or his voice evince the slightest compassion. What he said was, "Well then, we'll expect you in Sacramento later this afternoon." Then he left.

Most of my duties involved interaction with others apart from the governor. They included meetings with members and staff of the joint committee and with representatives of the affected parties. In some instances I mediated between Fisher and (usually) the spokesmen for the various unions involved. I also did a certain amount of lobbying in support of the proposed legislation with various legislators—an exercise for which I had little talent and which I detested. Most were either skeptical or openly hostile, and I don't believe I was very successful in my efforts to win their support.

The issues at stake were similar or identical to those dealt with by the California Assembly Advisory Council a year earlier, on which I have reported in some detail in a previous chapter. My efforts to persuade the joint committee to recommend a single, comprehensive statute were unsuccessful. No final action was taken on the proposed legislation during the period of my service. Subsequently, however, the legislature enacted three statutes: the Educational Employment Relations Act (EERA), in 1975; the State Employer-Employee Relations Act (SEERA), in 1977; and the Higher Education Employer-Employee Relations Act (HEERA), in 1978. All three reflected some of the recommendations made in the final report of the California Assembly Advisory Council. Each was administered by the same agency—the Public Employment Relations Board. All provided for exclusive representation of employees in an appropriate unit by the employee organization representing a majority of them and for some form of organizational security. Although each statute substituted the phrase "meet and confer" for "collective bargaining," in most instances there was little to distinguish one from the other. In one important respect—the rights of supervisors—the state law, although adopting the same definition of "supervisor," was considerably more liberal than the federal Labor Management Relations Act (LMRA), which was applicable to the private sector. The LMRA provides, "Nothing herein shall prohibit any individual employed as a supervisor from becoming or remaining a member of a labor organization, but no employer subject to the Act shall be compelled to deem individuals defined herein as supervisors as employees for the purpose of any law, either national or local, relating to collective bargaining." By contrast, SEERA provides, "Supervisory employees shall have the right to form, join, and participate in the activities of employee organizations of their own choosing for the purpose of representation on all matters of supervisory employer-employee relations…[and employee organizations] shall have the right to represent their supervisory employee members in their employment relations, including grievances, with the employer."

My brief period as a legislative consultant was not very pleasant, although it was certainly instructive. It persuaded me that my temperament was ill suited for this kind of work, particularly that aspect requiring one to lobby individual legislators. On the other hand, it strengthened my conviction that the only hope of enacting legislation in the controversial area of labor-management relations is to obtain through mediation a consensus among the affected parties that they can then jointly propose to the legislature. Model statutes drafted by academics, such as that proposed by California Assembly Advisory Council, are almost certain to be modified during the legislative process, sometimes to the extent of frustrating the basic principles embodied in the original proposal. Willingness to compromise is an absolute necessity, and those engaged in the process must constantly keep in mind the adage that the best is the enemy of the better.

CHAPTER 11

THE LOS ANGELES MAYOR'S LABOR-MANAGEMENT ADVISORY COMMITTEE, 1974–1978

On 25 March 1974, the mayor of Los Angeles, Tom Bradley, appointed me chairman of his newly created Labor-Management Advisory Committee. I had agreed to serve because I admired Bradley and wanted to help him in any way I could. The advisory committee consisted of a 10-person executive committee and a general committee of more than 50 persons representing labor, business, and the public. My misgivings about the unwieldy size of both groups were offset by my expectation, which proved to be correct, that most of the members would be inactive.

The executive committee held its first meeting on 3 April 1974. At that meeting, and subsequently in a letter to me dated 12 April, Bradley noted that the Los Angeles City Employee Relations Ordinance, originally adopted in 1971 (not to be confused with the Los Angeles County Employee Relations Ordinance, adopted in 1968), had been in effect for over three years and that the time had come to assess the efficiency of the meet and confer process set forth in the ordinance and to determine what, if anything, needed to be done to make that process a "viable instrument of collective bargaining in the City."

In response to the mayor's request, a subcommittee of the executive committee met privately with representatives of the Employee Relations Board (ERB), which was established to administer the ordinance, the city administrative officer (CAO), managers of city departments, the personnel committee of the Council of the City of Los Angeles, and representatives of employee organizations. In addition, the executive committee solicited written comments from all interested parties. Although the executive committee's subsequent report was devoted largely to the meet and confer process, it also touched on closely related topics, including impasse procedures.

The executive committee's investigation revealed widespread dissatisfaction in varying degrees of intensity among all the parties involved in the meet and confer process. The full Labor-Management Advisory Committee's report included the following findings of fact and observations:

1. The meet and confer process was not working in the manner contemplated by the ordinance.

2. The causes of this failure could be traced to the action or inaction of all the interested parties. Specifically, the personnel committee, with the approval of the city council, had until recently effectively retained control of wages, salaries, and fringe benefits, and had encouraged or tolerated efforts by employee organizations to "run around" the meet and confer process and to come directly to the personnel committee for decisions. The city council had been unwilling to give up its traditional control of relations between the city and its employees and had not given full support to the meet and confer procedures contemplated by the ordinance. Some employee organizations had made no real effort to make the meet and confer process work, but had deliberately sought to make deals directly with the personnel committee. The CAO's office had made no determined effort to make the meet and confer process work; indeed, until quite recently it had shown little inclination to consider modification of existing policies and only minimal desire to reach final agreement on anything but its own proposals. The powerlessness of the ERB to enforce its own orders had discouraged employee organizations from filing charges of unfair employee relations practices, including charges of refusal to meet and confer in good faith. This discouragement, however, did not fully explain or justify the virtual boycott of the ERB by the parties except for elections and unit certifications. The ERB had contributed to this situation by its failure to take even the normal initiatives reasonably to be expected from an agency of its competence during the formative stages of employer-employee relationships created by the ordinance. The ERB had also discouraged resort to fact-finding by

employee organizations by refusing to order publication of fact-finders' reports and by directing at least one fact-finder to submit his report without recommendations.

3. The policy of requiring the city to pay its employees prevailing rates placed some limitation on management's negotiation flexibility under the present meet and confer system, but it did not constitute an obstacle of the magnitude suggested by the CAO and the ERB. Los Angeles County, for example, was bound by the same policy, yet it had experienced no difficulty in reaching full agreement on economic issues with its employee organizations.

4. Finally, the threat of strikes by city employees frustrated by their inability to negotiate memoranda of understanding was steadily increasing. In one instance, Department of Water and Power employees called a strike that caused severe hardship to some communities in which electric power was cut off for several days. Although illegal, this strike continued in open defiance of a temporary restraining order issued by the California Superior Court. It was settled only after the department agreed to pay a wage increase substantially higher than those granted by other city departments and also agreed not to prosecute any strikers or their leaders for contempt of the restraining order.

The advisory committee's recommendations were based largely on its investigation and findings of fact. Initially, the advisory committee expressed the view that the present meet and confer procedure provided for in the ordinance was not working well and had substantial defects that could and should be corrected. At the same time, it warned that concentrating exclusively on the needed improvements in the meet and confer process while ignoring procedures for resolving impasses in disputes over new terms and conditions of employment would be a serious mistake. Citing the recent strikes affecting city departments, the advisory committee declared that laws against strikes were ineffective in the absence of credible alternatives and that impasse procedures currently provided in the ordinance were inadequate and should be supplemented. Included in the recommendations were a number of specific proposals designed to improve the city's administrative structure for dealing with its unions and to eliminate certain practices deemed detrimental to an efficient meet and confer process.

On 12 September 1974, I submitted the advisory committee's report and recommendations to Bradley. Before submission, the report had been reviewed by the executive committee and modified in some respects. It was subsequently approved by the full advisory committee. With specific reference to the meet and confer process—the only section of the recommendations on which the advisory committee was not unanimous—my cover letter to Bradley read as follows:

> The majority felt that the meet and confer process, when and if amended in the manner set forth in this Report, would be a greatly improved and viable alternative to full collective bargaining. At the same time, the majority felt that the Advisory Committee would be derelict in its responsibility to you if it failed to express its belief in the inevitability of the adoption by statute of a policy guaranteeing full collective bargaining rights to government employees in the State of California. Furthermore... the majority adheres to the opinion that if the...Ordinance is not amended along the lines suggested in the Report, it is probable that it would not meet the minimum standards included in any new state or federal legislation in this area.

My letter concluded with the acknowledgement that the advisory committee's recommendations "were not drafted with an eye to their political acceptability," but simply constituted the best advice we were able to give.

The advisory committee's report, other than provoking angry or defensive responses from those it had criticized, resulted in no immediate substantive changes in the status quo of any real significance. Rather belatedly, on 14 November 1974, Bradley wrote me a personal letter, commending "the excellence of your evaluation and report." He also stated that he was forwarding a copy of the report and recommendations to the city council for action, adding that he felt certain "that members of the Labor Management Committee will be called upon to testify before the Council's Personnel Committee." But the mayor's expectations were not realized. The city council virtually ignored our report and recommendations, and so far as I am aware, no member of the advisory committee was ever called to testify before the personnel committee.

Among other things, this experience confirmed my distaste for working with so large a committee. Obviously, in establishing the advisory committee Bradley sought to touch all his political bases. But the investigation and preparation of the report and recommendations were actually the work of no more than six members of the executive committee, and the responsibility for drafting the report rested with me. The need to convene formal sessions of the full advisory committee, which were poorly attended and designed only to obtain approval of what had already been done, simply delayed the completion of our assigned task.

In my initial talks with Bradley about accepting the chairmanship of the Labor-Management Advisory Committee, I strongly urged him not to involve the advisory committee in specific disputes, and I pointed out the dangers of conflicts with other governmental bodies having statutory powers to deal with such matters. As he was to do throughout the period of our relationship, however, the mayor gave me a courteous hearing but kept his own counsel, and more often than not he rejected my advice. Of course, as mayor of a big city with a number of different constituencies upon whom he depended to support and sustain his administration, Bradley could not afford to ignore the political consequences of backing the advisory committee's recommendations or of accepting my advice on other issues. That seems apparent, in retrospect, but at the time I was inclined to resent it when he decided not to adopt our ideas.

The most important event that occurred during the life of the Labor-Management Advisory Committee was the strike in 1974 against the Southern California Rapid Transit District (RTD) by 700 mechanics represented by the Amalgamated Transit Union (ATU) and by 2,000 drivers represented by the United Transportation Union (UTU). Although the RTD was a governmental agency, its employees had the right to strike, which had been carried over from their collective bargaining agreements with their former, private employer. Under the prevailing law, both parties had to maintain the status quo for 60 days during fact-finding proceedings initiated by the governor and for 10 additional days following issuance of the fact-finders' recommendations for the settlement of the dispute. Those procedures were exhausted. RTD management accepted the fact-finders' recommendations, but both unions rejected them. The strike began on 12 August and lasted for 65 days, making it the largest transportation strike in Southern California history. The work stoppage deprived 685,000 persons in the Los Angeles metropolitan area of their customary means of transportation and caused extreme hardship, particularly among older people and minorities who had no other means of getting to work. Many were forced to walk long distances to get to their jobs or to rely on the uncertain tactic of thumbing a ride. The situation was exacerbated by the return to school in September of about 100,000 children. Surface streets, particularly in the downtown area, were heavily congested as former bus passengers with cars drove to work and others with the wherewithal took taxis. The more affluent majority of workers who regularly drove to work and used the freeways were largely unaffected by the strike.

In the face of this widespread hardship, the parties to the dispute maintained an incredible inflexibility almost to the very end. The RTD adopted the fact-finders' recommendations as its final offer. Both unions indignantly rejected that offer, terming it an "insult." Despite intensive efforts by state mediators, the disputants remained far apart. Bradley met repeatedly with the parties and urged them to settle the dispute by arbitration, but his suggestions, although accepted by the RTD, were uniformly rejected by the unions. A strong believer in collective bargaining, Bradley was reluctant to do anything that might circumvent that process. On 27 August he announced a meeting with the advisory committee to "discuss the bus strike and make recommendations for a possible solution." I have no notes of that meeting, but my recollection is that I and the few other members present argued strenuously against any involvement of the advisory committee in the negotiations. A few days later, Bradley called for around-the-clock bargaining talks, indicating an intention to participate himself, but he backed off almost immediately, declaring that the "complex situation" could be settled only by a "reasonable compromise." Advisory committee members could not understand why adherence to that principle precluded his active participation in the negotiations, which we had strongly recommended.

The issues were indeed complex, involving wages, split shifts, and cost-of-living adjustments, among others. As time went on, I became increasingly disgusted with both sides, whose "negotiating" tactics seemed to consist of making public statements accusing each other of selfishness, stubbornness, and bad faith. Competition among union leaders, heightened by upcoming elections of officers, tended to increase union militancy and to discourage serious consideration of compromise. The situation was thus one in which the public emergency caused by the work stoppage was obviously less of concern to the disputants than pursuing their respective objectives. Moreover, both the RTD and the two unions were in a position to hold out longer than the public. By law, the RTD received a daily subsidy of $136,000 derived from sales taxes. While the strike continued, with only a few hundred of its employees still working, the RTD was netting about $40,000 per week. Both unions were paying strike benefits, and although those were not enough to make up more than a fraction of the pay lost by their members, they were sufficient to prevent any substantial erosion in membership support of the union's demands.

Having become convinced that some drastic intervention was called for, I tried to persuade Bradley to threaten to authorize the use of jitneys as long as the strike remained unsettled. Such authorization would permit any car owner to pick up passengers desiring a ride and to charge them a fare not governed by an established tariff fixed by the legislative authority. In practice, this would mean that most jitney passengers would pay less than the bus fare for travel over the same distance. This action would thus present a serious threat to both sides in the dispute, because experience had shown that it was very difficult to get jitneys off the streets after normal bus service was restored. Moreover, following a transportation strike, passenger loads customarily dropped by about 15 percent. Taken together, those two factors would cause a substantial reduction of RTD post-strike revenues and indirectly, but adversely, affect its labor force. I argued that the disputants' fear that Bradley would carry out his threat would likely force them to settle the strike fairly quickly.

Bradley recoiled with horror from my suggestion. "What you are proposing," he said in shocked tones, "is nothing less than strike-breaking!" I readily agreed, but argued that this was a strike that urgently needed to be broken. The purpose of a strike, I told him, using a phrase of George W. Taylor's, was to provide the "motive power for agreement." In this instance, I pointed out, the strike was not providing any notice-able movement toward agreement, and although in most circumstances a strike should be allowed to play itself out until the disputants mutu-ally conclude that it its better to settle than to continue fighting, that approach was singularly inappropriate in this case because of the devas-tating impact of the stoppage on public welfare. My arguments proved unavailing, and the subject of jitneys was dropped. The strike continued to drag on. At the beginning of September, Bradley left for a two-week "working vacation" in Europe. During his absence, Governor Ronald Reagan asked the unions to let their members vote by secret ballot whether to accept the RTD's last offer. His request, which was regarded by most knowledgeable observers as a needless distraction, was rejected. Meanwhile, both the Los Angeles County Board of Supervisors and the city council interjected themselves into the negotiations but failed to bring about any significant change in the situation.

Earlier, Bradley had asked my opinion on whether a high-powered mediator should be engaged in an effort to break the deadlock. I told him that successful mediation was based on the willingness of the disputants to consider a compromise, and given the determination of the parties to adhere to their respective positions, no mediation, however skillful, was likely to succeed. When Bradley returned from Europe, he ran into a storm of criticism for leaving town while the strike was in progress and for not himself playing a much more active role in trying to settle it. He responded that he had been in touch with the situation while he was away, and that, in any case, no one person, not even the mayor, had the power to force the parties to agree. He declined to blame either side for the lack of progress in the negotiations. On 17 September, he announced that he had secured the agreement of the disputants to accept Adolph Koven, an experienced and highly regarded mediator and arbitrator from San Francisco, as his "personal representative." The city council appropriated $10,000 to pay for Koven's services. Koven worked intensively with the parties for 10 days, but was unable to bring about a settlement; then, as I had predicted, he admitted that he could do no more and backed out.

In the seventh week of the strike, Bradley finally yielded to the pressure to play a more active role in ending it, and on 26 September he issued an ultimatum to the disputants: if the strike were not settled in 72 hours, he would take specific but undisclosed action to end it. At the expiration of the time limit, he addressed mass meetings of union members and presented his plan to end the strike, which had been drafted by Koven just before he returned to San Francisco. His proposal, which contained few surprises, called for the strikers to return to work while the issues were submitted to binding arbitration by nationally known arbitrators, and it also included a wage increase retroactive to 1 July 1974. The proposal to submit the issues to binding arbitration, previously endorsed by the RTD, was overwhelmingly rejected by the strikers in a secret-ballot vote.

Having suffered this rebuff, Bradley went to Sacramento to appeal to the state legislature to pass a bill that would force the dispute into binding arbitration. Acting with unexpected speed, the senate moved to cut off the RTD's daily sales tax subsidy for the duration of the strike and the assembly began consideration of a bill to terminate the dispute by compulsory arbitration. But those efforts ended abruptly when an assembly measure to send the strikers back to work for a 75-day cooling off period was defeated, and the senate adjourned after finishing its special and general session business. On 4 October Reagan again proposed that the strikers return to work for 90 days to allow time for a new group of fact-finders to propose recommendations to settle the dispute. He also proposed that upon their return to work the strikers be paid the wage increases recommended by his earlier fact-finding commission. The reaction of the two unions was epitomized in the statement of the president of the ATU, who termed the governor's suggestion "lousy." The next day a long meeting between representatives of the disputants and Reagan, board of supervisors chairman Kenneth Hahn, and Bradley failed to produce any break in the deadlock, but it did seem finally to introduce a sense of urgency in the negotiations, which continued on an around-the-clock basis. On 8 October the RTD and the ATU, representing the mechanics, announced that they had reached a tentative agreement, which was promptly ratified by both parties. Negotiations continued between the RTD and the UTO, representing the bus drivers, and a tentative accord was reached on 13 October and ratified a few days later. The settlements with both unions provided for substantially greater wage increases than had been proposed by the fact-finding commission and adopted by the RTD as its "last" offer. But the RTD agreed only after the board of supervisors guaranteed that the RTD's annual subsidy of $32.5 million would be continued and that in the next year the county would also give the RTD $42.5 to $44.5 million to maintain the 25-cent fare and pay for increased costs resulting from the settlement.

On 15 October Bradley sent a letter to me that began: "The RTD bus strike is about over. All of us are happy about the results." It went on to thank me for my "generous support and assistance" and my "thoughtful suggestions." I understood, however, that his words were purely formulaic; after all, my "thoughtful suggestions" had been rejected, and I had not been very supportive of the actions he had taken until the very end of the dispute. The response of the mayor and other public authorities to the strike exemplified the weakness of public policy in dealing with a genuine community emergency. It seemed to me then, as it still does today, that any system that permits a strike causing untold hardship to hundreds of thousands of citizens to continue for over two months should not be tolerated. Of course, the fault lay primarily with the disputants, whose stubborn refusal to consider a compromise, regardless of the difficulties imposed by the strike on the public they were supposed to serve, defeated all efforts to resolve the impasse through fact-finding and mediation. My disappointment with Bradley was that his otherwise praiseworthy belief in the principle of collective bargaining had blinded him to the realization that in this atypical situation normal collective bargaining was not working. Only in the final days of the strike did he concede that fact and urge that the parties be forced to submit their dispute to binding arbitration. By then, much damage had been done.

Over the last forty years I have struggled with the problem and written a number of articles on how to deal with the limited number of genuine national and local emergency disputes, as distinguished from disputes that result only in some inconvenience to the public. As a strong believer in collective bargaining and an opponent of governmental interference in the process, I have been against legislation that forbids strikes in the public sector and requires all unresolved disputes to be settled by arbitration. Nevertheless, I have come to conclude that in situations such as that created by the RTD strike of 1974 the legislature should intervene if the parties fail to reach agreement within a reasonable period and should enact a law requiring binding arbitration for that case only. I am mindful of the difficulties involved in this course of action: among others, the inevitable delays and "politicking" by legislators with little knowledge of labor-management relations and with axes to grind, and the establishment of guidelines and limitations on the arbitrators in respect of wages and fringe benefits. The procedure is admittedly imperfect, but to my mind it is superior to any alternative that has yet been suggested.

About a year after the settlement of the RTD strike, Bradley again involved the advisory committee in a local labor dispute, this time one between the Yellow Cab Company and a local of the Teamsters' Union. Specifically, he asked me to convene a meeting of the advisory committee's executive committee to conduct preliminary inquiries into a proposed rollback in wages, with the aim of determining "an appropriate course of action." Reluctantly, a subcommittee of the mayor's Labor-Management Advisory Committee, consisting of Ralph Woolpert, a major figure in the Los Angeles retail drug and food industries; Joanne Bernstein, the wife of Los Angeles Times labor reporter; Barbara Schlei, a prominent Los Angeles attorney; and myself complied with Bradley's request. We subsequently reported that the parties had reached a tentative agreement on the issues between them, dependent upon the satisfaction of certain conditions, and had jointly asked our committee publicly to recommend approval of its terms, which involved actions by various public agencies. While expressing our belief in the sincerity and bona fides of both sides, we refused to comply with their request. Our explanation for not doing so included an implicit rebuke to the mayor for involving us in the first place:

> Clearly, we do not have all the relevant facts before us. Specifically, we have not heard the views of any consumer groups on the impact the proposed settlement may have on their interests. We also have not heard the views of other cab companies. We have not been presented with any other feasible plan to insure better service to the public, nor do we know whether any such alternative exists. In any case, we do not feel that this committee is the body to study this matter which now rests with the Mayor, the City Council, and other appropriate public agencies.

Accordingly, we submitted our factual report without any recommendation on the proposed agreement.

That constituted the last official action of the mayor's Labor-Management Advisory Committee. On 20 December 1978, I sent Bradley a letter of resignation. My immediate reason, I explained, was my imminent departure to begin a semester-long visiting professorship at the University of Michigan Law School. I then added a paragraph that reflected my disappointment about the way the advisory committee had been used:

> Beyond that [my departure], however, it is obvious that the committee, as such, no longer exists; almost all of the members have died, left the metropolitan area, or have become inactive. Moreover, I have always felt, and still do, that the committee was used improperly. I do not believe that it serves a useful purpose to inject the committee into an existing dispute. The committee's one worthwhile endeavor was its report on the operation of the City's meet and confer process, even though the report was largely ignored by the City Council.

In the circumstances, it is understandable that the mayor would not have acknowledged my letter; if, contrary to my recollection, he did, I have no copy of his reply in my files.

CHAPTER 12

THE LABOR LAW GROUP, 1947–1985

I have been exceptionally fortunate in my experience as a member of two group research projects, the first of which was the Labor Law Group. This organization was given its impetus by an article, one of the relatively few that may be accurately termed "seminal," by Willard Wirtz, then a law professor at Northwestern University. His article was originally delivered as a speech, titled "A New Prospectus for the Labor Law Course," to the Labor Law Round Table at a meeting of the Association of American Law Schools in 1946, and it then appeared in revised form in the *Illinois Law Review* of Northwestern University the following year. Analyzing three leading labor law casebooks, Wirtz noted:

> These three "texts" reveal a course centering…[on] the consideration of a collection of judicial and administrative opinions set out in virtually chronological outline order. The course is organized and the materials selected primarily on the basis of the historical development of the case-law in the field.…Those books reveal, in the main, very little of the pruning and grafting which has produced a variety of hybrids in some of the other fields.[1]

As currently constructed, Wirtz observed, the labor law course was primarily a record of cases involving the breakdown of labor relations: "conceptions of what a union is and why it is and of the basic principles which motivate normal and satisfactory labor relations must be pieced together by the student from the record of judges' reactions to what unions do when they are desperate and to the anachronistic tactics of atypical employers." If these cases constituted the corpus of labor law, he continued, "it is a sterile social instrument and its study in the law schools should probably be abandoned." What Wirtz suggested instead was that labor law students should be trained in the arts and techniques of collective bargaining, and that the texts used should emphasize the constructive role of lawyers as advisors and facilitators, rather than as hired guns when employer-union relations break down.

---

[1] W. Willard Wirtz, "On Teaching Labor Law," *Illinois Law Review* 42 (1947): 1.

Another innovative idea put forth by Wirtz in his path-breaking essay was that the development of labor law courses and materials could be accomplished most effectively by a group of scholars working together. This heretical proposal to depart from the long-established practice of individual research and publication did not fall on deaf ears. At the close of the 1946 Round Table session, those in attendance unanimously adopted a resolution declaring that "there exists in the Labor Law field today a new situation which necessitates the development of new teaching materials and techniques, and that this problem cannot be met satisfactorily through the isolated activities of the individual teachers in the various schools." The resolution also recommended that as soon as possible a conference of labor law teachers be convened, that representatives of various interests in this field be invited to participate, and that new teaching materials and techniques be developed along lines adopted by the conference.

Early in 1947, a new Round Table, chaired by Robert E. Mathews, a law professor at the Ohio State College of Law, issued its first call for a show of interest in the proposed conference, to be based on four assumptions:

1. That the materials and techniques heretofore used in teaching labor law had not proved adequate for the training of lawyers in their functions and responsibilities in the field of labor relations.
2. That an intensive *group* analysis, participated in by *all* interested teachers of labor law, was the most promising approach to determining the most effective materials and techniques.
3. That evidence provided by persons informed and experienced in the functions and responsibilities of lawyers in labor relations would facilitate group analysis.
4. That it was possible by means of a conference of this type for a group of teachers to prepare an adequate set of teaching materials in this field.

To finance the proposed conference, a grant of $25,000 was obtained from the Carnegie Corporation. The 10-day Conference on the Training of Law Students in Labor Relations was subsequently held in June 1947 at the University of Michigan. It was attended by representatives of 32 law schools and was addressed by outstanding figures representing the points of view of labor, management, and the public in the field of labor-management relations. A majority of the law teachers in attendance expressed a desire to make the fullest possible use of their experience by putting into trial form a collection of materials for classroom teaching. At later dates they were joined by others with similar interests. The funds remaining from the Carnegie Corporation grant ($6,500) were used to finance two week-long conferences of the working group of law teachers in 1949 and 1951, as well as several small committee conferences during various stages of their work. In 1953, the Labor Law Group, as it came to be known, established a trust to receive and hold all money and things of value accruing from the members' past or future activities. A unique feature of the trust was its provision that all royalties from members' publications be used for educational purposes and that none of those monies would ever be distributed to the benefit of individual members of the group. To most law school teachers who had traditionally relied on the royalties from the sale of their casebooks as a supplement to their income from teaching, this was indeed a novel, even subversive, idea. Russell A. Smith, a distinguished labor law professor at the University of Michigan, who declined to join the Labor Law Group but cooperated with it by sharing with its members preliminary drafts of his own case-book, jokingly referred to the group as "that socialist enterprise."

I cannot adequately describe how strongly I was influenced by my partic-ipation in the 1947 law teaching conference; in retrospect, I realize that it profoundly affected my teaching as well as my future research. I don't know who was responsible for my being invited to the conference; I suspect it was Wirtz. I had just joined the staff of the UCLA Institute of Industrial Relations, was teaching only one course in labor law to undergraduates, and had published nothing. Associating at the conference with a group of older and much more experienced labor law teachers was exhilarating but somewhat daunting. Fortunately, unlike many of the conferees, I knew most of the featured speakers from the War Labor Board days, and this familiarity somewhat counteracted my unease as an outsider. I also met Mathews, who was to become the first chairman of the Labor Law Group.

When I got to know him better, I came to realize what a truly remarkable person he was and how privileged I was to be his collaborator and friend.

The first product of the Labor Law Group's collective efforts was *Labor Relations and the Law (LRL)*, published in 1953 by Little, Brown and Company. Reflecting on this initial enterprise some 35 years later, Mathews wrote in a communication to members of the group:

> Our first volume was refreshingly novel, both in substance and in process of compilation. For instance, unlike any casebook, before or after, the book was permeated by one single long problem [conceived by Wirtz], or series of 14 problems, distributed over some 450 pages…[which] if put together, would have been the complete life story of employer-employee relation[s] from initial efforts for recognition, to the negotiation of a collective agreement and its interpretation through arbitration.

Another novel feature of the casebook was its inclusion of comparative labor law materials from a number of different countries. This effort, as Mathews conceded, had proved somewhat disappointing, but it pointed the way to more effective use of such information. The book's principal contribution in terms of content, in Mathews's view, was its emphasis on the importance of the bargaining process and the solution of subsequent differences and conflicts over interpretation, rather than on breakdowns and unfair labor practices.

The Labor Law Group's process of collective planning and realization in final decisions on policy was something of a landmark. By dividing our members into five or six committees, we profited from the contributions of each of the participants and came to imaginative decisions that were ultimately acted upon by all participants. Subcommittee membership was rotated, reports were submitted by each subcommittee on the work of other subcommittees, and experimental teaching materials were prepared for classroom trial and critical comment. The resulting comments and criticism were consolidated, and the revisions were resubmitted and used again in teaching, and finally discussed by the whole group before being processed in bound mimeographed form for re-use and ultimate submission for publication. Some years later Mathews was to recall with pride that

> every decision was acted upon by every member; no one viewpoint ever prevailed, every decision was group activated, group prepared and group achieved.…We were

all cooperating editors together; we all became close friends and we all enjoyed immensely our frequent sessions together. For me, and I hope for all of us, this became a permanently gratifying experience.

Mathews's nostalgic recollection glossed over some of the tensions caused by sharp disagreements over issues of content and presentation. Perhaps the most exacerbated conflict concerned the introduction of foreign law materials, almost all of which, unlike the rest of the casebook, were the product of only one participant, Arthur Lenhoff. Lenhoff was a naturalized citizen who had left his native Austria, where he had been a successful lawyer, university professor, and judge of the Constitutional Court, and had come to the United States at the age of 52, a refugee from Nazi persecution. Mastering our alien system of law with astonishing rapidity, he built a second distinguished career as a professor of law, scholar, and legal practitioner. In the field of labor law his writings were remarkable for the explanation of differences between American laws and those of continental European countries—differences of which most American labor scholars had previously been unaware. Some of these comparisons, composed solely by Lenhoff, were inserted in various parts of the casebook. But some participants questioned their utility and opposed their inclusion. Lenhoff, nurtured in the polemical style of debate, strongly, often violently opposed any suggestion that the length of some of his commentaries be curtailed in the interest of providing additional pages for more conventional topics. His manner was much the same as that of the philosopher, Karl Popper, described in a memoir by Bryan Maggee:

> He seemed unable to accept the continued existence of different points of view, but went on and on and *on* about them with a kind of unforgivingness until the dissenter, so to speak, put his signature on a confession that he was wrong and Popper was right.[2]

Dealing with Lenhoff, whose pride was easily hurt, was a delicate matter, handled mostly by Mathews, whose tact and sensibility were legendary. On occasion, however, because I had established a warm relationship with Lenhoff, Mathews asked me to assume the respon-

[2] Quoted in Adam Gopnik, "The Porcupine," *The New Yorker*, 1 April 2002, 88, 92.

sibility for editing the latter's written submissions. I approached this dicey task with some trepidation and great care, but had only mixed success. I recall in particular one occasion when our subcommittee met in the law library of Northwestern Law School to review a set of materials prepared by another subcommittee and also a few comparative law commentaries submitted by Lenhoff. In looking over what Lenhoff had written, I noticed that he had frequently used the word "voluntaryism," and I casually mentioned to him that in the United States the word "voluntarism" was preferred. Lenhoff bristled and said that his spelling was perfectly correct and that he objected to any change. I gently assured him that "voluntaryism" was simply not used in this country, whereupon he marched off in a huff. About an hour later he returned, carrying an English dictionary with which I was unfamiliar. He plunked it down on the table and triumphantly pointed out that included in the definition of "voluntarism" was the statement, "also voluntaryism." I commented that one obscure reference to his preferred word could not outweigh standard usage, but he remained unconvinced. At that point, I simply dropped the matter, but we substituted "voluntarism" for "voluntaryism" in the published version of the book.

Despite his lack of flexibility and his insistence on winning every argument, Lenhoff's contributions to the casebook were, in my opinion, invaluable. Most if not all of his American colleagues knew little of continental European labor law and, I suspect, had never really thought much about how or why it differed from American law. His answers to those questions were eye-openers, at least for me, and they put a halt, once and for all, to any solipsistic tendencies I may have had to view the American labor law and labor relations systems as representing the acknowledged standard for the rest of the world. He aroused in me an interest in comparative labor law that increased over the years and has never diminished. Prickly though Lenhoff may have been at times, he and I got along well together, and I shall always be grateful for his friendship and for what he taught me.

As may be imagined, many other tensions developed within the group during the approximately five years it took to complete the work on

LRL. That they were resolved with little or no damage to the generally friendly and cooperative relationship fostered by our joint enterprise was due largely to the efforts of Mathews. His sympathetic responses to the concerns of every single participant, his never-failing amiability and good humor, and, above all, his unwavering adherence to the principles that gave our project its reason for being inspired all of us with admiration and affection. He and Wirtz were the two most dominant personalities in our group, although each played down his own contributions.

On the whole, *LRL* was well received by the academic community and secured a respectable number of adoptions, although most were by law schools in which members of the group taught the labor law course. The reactions of two well-known labor law practitioners, both representing management and both conservative, were mixed. In a review in the *Harvard Law Review,* Gerard D. Reilly, a former member of the NLRB, took issue with the stated attempt in *LRL,* as explained in the foreword, "to shift the weight of discussion from the breakdown in labor relations to the constructive working program that today, happily, is vastly more characteristic of this relationship…and to develop in the student's mind a realistic sense of his functions as a lawyer in working with and playing his part in this long-established cooperative practice."[3] According to Reilly, the current dissatisfaction of the bar with the administration of labor law was that "many people who get into the arbitration or mediation field are inclined to subordinate the establishment of legal principle to the advantages of a temporary settlement." The underlying fallacy of the group's approach, he opined, seemed to be the implied notion, with which he sharply disagreed, "that it is…the duty of the lawyer to further 'cooperative practices' in the sense of advising his clients to invoke the assistance of mediators or arbitrators rather than invoking the law or, if the law permits them to do so, self-help." Although it is a lawyer's duty to remind his client of his legal obligations, Reilly concluded, "it is not his duty in any sense of the word to persuade his client to agree to

---

[3] *Harvard Law Review* 67 (1954): 532. Also included in this review was the second edition of Russell Smith's *Labor Law Cases and Materials.*

some proposed contract interpretation which might prove economically ruinous in the long run in order to avoid a strike."

In another review of *LRL* in the *Columbia Law Review*, Theodore R. Iserman reacted more favorably. He devoted most of his review to describing the contents of the casebook, concluding that to a large extent it justified the editors' claims that it made four contributions to the teaching of labor law: (1) a new approach to the process of compiling a casebook; (2) a major shift in emphasis; (3) an expansion in the use of problems as teaching devices; and (4) the introduction of comparative labor law materials. In respect of the comparative labor law materials, a feature totally ignored by Reilly, Iserman commented that, although interesting and provocative, "they seem to raise the level of discussion somewhat higher than is useful to students who have not yet determined to devote their careers to labor law." Iserman also criticized some of the material in the part on collective bargaining, saying that "many economists, and particularly more conservative ones, would disagree." Moreover,

> some of it, such as that dealing with the value of a competitive economy, compulsory unionism, secondary boycotts, organizing strikes, and acts of unions against their members, reflects the viewpoint of the union apologist rather than a balanced and penetrating appraisal of all points of view, including that of the consumer. In the extensive bibliography there is a notable paucity of references to writings critical of our labor movement and of collective bargaining as we practice it.[4]

Both reviews also criticized the casebook for its virtual disregard of laws affecting employment, such as wage and hour, workers' compensation, and social security laws.

Members of the Labor Law Group were well aware of the need for a casebook devoted to those aspects of the employment relation not regulated by collective bargaining. Preliminary work on this project began before *LRL* was published. Under the editorship of Mathews, two preliminary editions—*The Employment Relation and Protective Rights* (1950) and *The Employment Relation and Protective Labor Legislation* (1952)—were published in mimeographed form. As usual, a number of

---

[4]*Columbia Law Review* 54 (1984): 302.

members of the group participated actively in their preparation, this time assisted by two lawyers from the U.S. Department of Labor. In 1954 it was decided to re-examine these materials with a view to publication in final form. I agreed to serve as editor (the title page of *The Employment Relation and the Law* [ERL], published in 1957 by Little, Brown, noted that the book was compiled by the Labor Law Group "Under the immediate editorship of Benjamin Aaron and the general editorship of Robert E. Mathews"). In the foreword, written by Mathews, the contents of the volume was summarized as follows:

> The opening portion deals with…comparative statutory employment. While the obvious comparison with nonstatutory agency and master-servant relations is included by way of pedagogical transition, the chief emphasis is upon the varieties of legislative treatment of the [employment] relation. Statutes and cases from all principal segments of social legislation are here gathered together for comparative analysis of policy, of language, and of historical trend. Thus the student is introduced to the one basic condition precedent to each of the statutes whose other provisions he will study later….
>
> Broadly speaking, the arrangement of the book next progresses to the newly recognized right to equality of employment opportunity and then to protection relating first to physical and then to economic risks. Discussion of efforts to prevent physical risks…is followed by materials on compensation for such injuries as were not thus prevented. Here…is found employers' liability and workmen's compensation legislation. Devices to minimize economic insecurity follow, with treatment of minimum wage legislation, Social Security, including unemployment insurance and Old Age and Survivors Insurance, and private pension plans. The book ends with a brief discussion of protective legislation in other countries.

As co-editor, I contributed little of substance to *ERL*. Bob Mathews's overgenerous description of my role applied much more accurately to his own: "His patient and tireless efforts, his constructive and imaginative suggestions to the cooperating editors, his broad understanding and tolerance of diversity, and his faithful and conscientious care in detail have made this final edition possible."

Although *ERL* received thoughtful and generally favorable reviews—including those by Merton C. Bernstein, then special counsel for the Senate Committee on Labor and Public Welfare, in the *Yale Law Journal*; R.W. Fleming, the University of Illinois, in *Journal of Legal Education*; and Allan

H. McCoid, UCLA School of Law, in the *UCLA Law Review*—it was not a commercial success.[5] Courses in social legislation were seldom given in law schools, and professors of labor law preferred to concentrate on the more topical and more exciting subjects of collective bargaining, labor-management strife, and arbitration. After publishing a short supplement in 1962, the group allowed the book to lapse into a state of desuetude. Ironically, the 1960s marked the beginning of a flood of social legislation affecting employment relations, including the Equal Pay Act of 1963, Title VII of the Civil Rights Act of 1964, and the Age Discrimination in Employment Act of 1967. Had we postponed the publication of *ERL* (which would, of course, have been a considerably different book) until the late 1960s, it would have had a better reception.

In 1958, Mathews resigned as chairman of the Labor Law Group and was succeeded by Charles A. Reynard, a law professor at Louisiana State University. Reynard had edited another group volume, *Readings on Labor Law*, published in 1955, which was a collection of articles, reports, and excerpts from books for use as collateral reading in connection with the earlier volume. He had also made substantial contributions to *LRL* and *ERL*. Under his leadership, general plans for a new edition of *LRL* were blocked out, and various committees were appointed to work on the main section of the book. Reynard's sudden and untimely death in February 1959, at the age of 46, shortly after a meeting of committee chairmen at which detailed plans were agreed upon, cast a pall over our cooperative enterprise. A man possessed of warmth and wisdom, as well as unflagging courage and integrity, he was remembered by his colleagues with respect and affection. Donald H. Wollett, also a professor at the LSU Law School, and I were selected to serve as co-chairmen of the group and co-editors of the new volume, which was dedicated to Reynard's memory. In this effort, Wollett's contributions were much greater than my own.

As noted in the foreword of the second edition of *LRL* (*LRL* 2d), published in 1960 by Little, Brown, the book retained some features of *LRL*, such as extensive use of problems and inclusion of nonlegal

---

[5] *Yale Law Journal* 67 (1958): 955; *Journal of Legal Education* 12 (1959): 141; and *UCLA Law Review*. 5 (1958): 684.

materials that shed light on issues of concern to lawyers. Like *LRL*, it was a product of group effort. Also noted, however, was the fact that rather than being merely a second edition, *LRL* 2d was in a very real sense a new book using the same title as the 1953 volume. Indeed, it retained only about 10 percent of the original material.

There were compelling reasons for the radical changes. First, in the seven years since the publication of *LRL*, many important decisional and statutory developments had occurred, which necessitated either replacing or supplementing old material. Second, the 1953 book had placed relatively little emphasis on the "pathology" of labor relations—that is, strikes, lockouts, boycotts, and picketing. The passage of the Labor-Management Reporting and Disclosure Act of 1959, which produced a rash of litigation over the legality of various forms of union self-help, necessitated the strengthening of that emphasis. Third, many of the problems used in the 1953 book had become obsolete; these were either revised or replaced, and many new problems were added.

The original *LRL* contained over 1,000 pages, exclusive of a substantial statutory appendix and an index. *LRL* 2d had fewer than 1,000 pages, including a statutory appendix and index. This reduction was accomplished only by the removal of some admittedly valuable material and the abridgment of most of the comparative law notes that had been interspersed throughout the 1953 volume; these notes were now concentrated in part one, "The Individual Employee, the Union, the Employer, and the Government." Unfortunately, Lenhoff construed this decision as a repudiation of the value of his work. He wrote letters to various members of the group, arguing vehemently against the reduction of comparative law references, and he remained unreconciled to the group's decision. As I recall, his participation in the cooperative enterprise terminated with the publication of *LRL* 2d.

The impact of *LRL* 2d on teachers and practitioners in the labor field was no greater than that of a pebble dropped into a large lake. Of course it had a captive market: most of those teachers who had participated in its preparation adopted it for use in their labor law courses, but it received little attention from others. A search by the UCLA Law Library came up with only one review, which dealt with two labor law casebooks: Russell A. Smith and Leroy S. Merrifield's *Cases and Materials on Labor Relations Law* (1960) and *LRL* 2d. The reviewer, Walter H.E. Jaeger, professor at Georgetown University Law Center, began his appraisal with the somewhat puzzling statement that the Smith and Merrifield book "is essentially a student book, intended and devised for use in the classroom," whereas *LRL* 2d "is a compendium or anthology and represents a series of contributions of some thirty-one cooperating editors in the first edition, twenty-six in the second edition." After stating that he had used the Smith and Merrifield book "and found [it] to be an excellent medium for the development of a course on Labor Law," Jaeger proceeded to describe, fairly accurately but largely without comment, the contents of both books, and concluded with the following brief observation:

> In conclusion, it would appear that the recent publication by Professors Smith and Merrifield is more useful for teaching purposes than *Labor Relations and the Law*. This evaluation is based on a careful comparison of these volumes and experience in the field gained by more than 25 years of teaching labor law."[6]

Always interested in new ideas concerning the preparation of materials and the teaching of labor law, the group welcomed additions to its ranks. How successful we were can be judged by the fact that all but one of the chairmen who followed Wollett and me in succeeding years joined the group after 1960.

A third and final edition of *Labor Relations and the Law*, edited by Jerre S. Williams, then a law professor at the University of Texas, was published in 1965. It met approximately the same fate as *LRL* 2d.

The first major shift in the group's approach to the preparation of labor law materials came as a result of a week-long conference held in Boulder, Colorado, in the summer of 1969, which was attended by law teachers, academics from other disciplines, and management and labor representatives. Following this conference and a smaller meeting of group members in Chicago in September of that year, the decision was made to publish a series of smaller books under the general heading of Labor Relations and Social Problems. About this time we also switched publishers from

---

[6] *Notre Dame Lawyer* 35 (1960): 277.

Little, Brown to the Bureau of National Affairs. Between 1971 and 1977 we published several of these books.

Mathews, who had moved in the late 1950s from the Ohio State College of Law to the University of Texas Law School, was no longer an active participant in the preparation of any of theses books, but his interest in the group remained strong, and he attended the Colorado conference. Wirtz was one of the principal speakers at that gathering. In a letter to him immediately afterward (a copy of which he sent to me), Mathews praised Wirtz's speech, but also expressed a deep concern about the group's future.

> You reintroduced the spirit of 1946 and 1947, the spirit that has so long kept our Group going, but a spirit that has, I greatly fear, been losing its force as newcomers join us, men who have not previously sensed the devotion, the educational idealism and the heartwarming quality of cooperative group action [of former years].

Mathews noted that during a business session of group members that he had attended, "an ominous ring of personal ambition, of the introduction of issues that previously had never been thought important because of the high degree of confidence we have always had in each other." He wondered whether a "power struggle" would divide the group "after all these years of unselfish devotion." He importuned Wirtz to attend the next meeting in Chicago, stating that "no one is more dedicated than you to the retention of the idealism that has guided us these many rewarding years together. I believe...that you more than any one else among us, can reactivate that spirit; can save our project from a deterioration that several of us think may become an ominous danger."

Mathews was unable to attend the Chicago meeting in September 1969, but I was able to assure him in a letter written immediately thereafter "that the undercurrents that you detected and that caused you so much disquietude at the close of the last meeting were simply not present at this one," and that "Bill Wirtz made his usual insightful and stimulating comments, which had their customary exhilarating effect."

Between 1971 and 1977 the group published ten books, and subsequent editions of several of them. In 1976 the group reorganized the materials for future books (starting in 1978) and thereafter published six, including a substantial amount of nondoctrinal material, on the following subjects: collective bargaining in private employment, social legislation, discrimination in employment, collective bargaining in public employment, negotiation, and arbitration and conflict resolution. In the foreword to *Collective Bargaining in Private Employment* (1978), the group's editorial policy committee pointed out a number of features that distinguished this series from standard labor law casebooks:

1. The format of separate units (each dealing with a separable topic in the general field) in recognition of the fact that it is impossible to teach all of these subjects in one course.
2. For each subject a book which is shorter in length than a standard casebook, thus making it more practical to use in a typical course....
5. Coverage of matters not covered in standard casebooks, e.g., the art and techniques of negotiation and the myth of expertise.
6. Inclusion of material on professional responsibility and comparative law.
7. A blending of legal and nondoctrinal materials so that a greater appreciation of the "law" can be achieved....
10. Greater flexibility for the law teacher in putting together a course or courses of the teacher's own liking.

The foreword also noted that the 23 active group members included only three of the original Labor Law Group—Don Wollett, Ed Teple, and me. Although I had been very active in 1969, supporting the idea of preparing shorter books on specialized subjects that could be put together in packages to meet the specialized needs of individual law professors, I contributed very little to the preparation of those books. At a group meeting in 1982, at the request of the chairman, Robert Rabin, a law professor at Syracuse University, I gave a speech on the history of the group from 1947 to 1982, but I concentrated largely on the period between 1947 and 1953. My reasons for doing so, I explained, were as follows:

> First, I suspect that some, if not most, of our present membership have little or no knowledge of our origins and early development. Second, I want to communicate, as

best I can, some sense of the excitement, dedication, and sacrifice that characterized the early years of the Group—qualities that I think have, perhaps inevitably but also regrettably, diminished with the passage of time.

By way of conclusion, I read to those assembled a message for the group from Mathews, titled "Myths Have Their Cycles Too," which reviewed the origin and history of the group, paying tribute to Wirtz as the initiator of the project, as well as its frequent stimulator. Mathews reported that "even now, after nearly 35 years, I feel the old enthusiasm welling up in me again. How deeply I wish I had the capacity to communicate it to the many of you who have not gone through it all from the start."

Mathews concluded with an observation that seemed particularly apt: "All associations, even as nations and individuals—even as myths—have their life cycles. Perhaps we have reached that point now. It is for you at this conference either to consider the cycle as completed, or with your own new enthusiasm, to move into new and fascinating areas of exploration." The group decided to continue, and so it has done, into the twenty-first century, with a constantly changing membership and a shifting emphasis on the kinds of materials to publish.

The last of the major group-sponsored conferences that I attended was held in Park City, Utah, in the summer of 1984.[7] Wirtz gave the keynote address, in which he proposed "to inquire into the possibility of developing…a Labor Law I course that would cover in about equal measure and in substantially (though not entirely) integrated form the heart (but not the hands and feet) of both the law relating to union/management activities, especially collective bargaining and the law regarding individual employment relationships." Observing that the emphasis on union activities and collective bargaining in the traditional Labor Law I course "reflects the persuasion that the history and vitality of this branch of the law have special attraction and value to students," Wirtz argued that "the teaching and learning of these 'collective' developments can be enlarged if they are made part of a broader analysis of the

[7] See Labor Law Group Conference on Labor and Employment Law, *The Park City Papers* (Nashville: Labor Law Group, 1985).

law's pluralistic approach to the entire employment relationship" and that "this broader course provides a superior opportunity for toughening and testing students' intellectual interests and competitiveness." His argument, Wirtz continued, was "for a course that can give students special understanding of the law's potential and can carry their thinking beyond the craft of litigation to the art of efficient and constructive settlement of controversy."

As Wirtz conceived it, the suggested course would be developed from the recognition of the distinguishing and interrelated characteristics of labor law:

> The employment relationship is an extraordinary compound of economic, political, social and personal elements. The law that has developed to establish a balance among these elements is uniquely pluralistic; in no other area is there a comparable experience of reliance on common law, legislation, administrative agency regulation, privately bargained agreements, and privately developed adjudication. The employment relationship is so protean that despite this already established pluralistic character, there is particular need here today for both the revision of concepts and the development of alternative forms of dispute resolution.

After presenting a rough organizational outline of the kind of course he envisioned, Wirtz concluded by extolling labor law as a subject permitting the exploration of "questions of how a free society, wanting to stay that way, handles problems in which individual and system interests frequently conflict and human and economic values often compete." "Teaching Labor Law," he said, "affords a superior opportunity to inquire into how we can see to it that the future will continue to be a good idea."

I have dwelled at such length upon Wirtz's insightful and provocative address not only because his 1946 paper, "On Teaching Labor Law," led to the establishment of the Labor Law Group but also because during the next four decades he continued to play a key role in the development of new teaching materials and, finally, because his 1984 Park City proposal brought about a significant change in the group's approach to the subject.

The seed planted by Wirtz and others at Park City took a little time to germinate. Following the Park City conference, the group decided to devote principal attention to three new conventional-length course books, one devoted to employment discrimination, one to union-management relations, and one to the individual employment relationship. Meanwhile, various members of the group contributed ideas of how a book embodying the diverse but related elements described by Wirtz should be organized. Finally, three members, Robert Rabin, Eileen Silverstein, and George Schatzki, edited a new volume, *Labor Employment Law/ Problems, Cases and Materials in the Law of Work*, published in 1988 by West Publishing Co. In the foreword to the second, substantially revised edition that appeared in 1995, the first edition was described as having moved "well beyond the boundaries of the traditional labor law course. It shifted the unifying focus from collective organization of workers to the search for legal structures and principles that promote fairness, participation and protection in the employment relationship. It also adapted new narrative techniques for introducing legal principles and worklife problems."

In 1997, after a 10-year hiatus, I agreed to teach a labor law course for one semester at the UCLA School of Law. Because the decision to do so was made shortly before the course was to begin, I did not have time carefully to look through and compare the current leading labor law casebooks. Instead, out of loyalty to the Labor Law Group, I chose the second edition of the Rabin, Silverstein, Schatzki book. I confess to having been deeply disappointed with it, and my own reaction was duplicated by most of the students, who expressed their dislike of the book in much stronger terms. Although I certainly was in sympathy with what the editors, whom I greatly respect, were attempting to do, I was forced to conclude that their reach far exceeded their grasp. That said, I must also admit that an incomparably better set of unpublished materials, compiled by Wirtz and Donald T. Weckstein for a course on the law of work at the University of San Diego School of Law in 1996, presented pedagogical problems too difficult for one with my limited skill as a teacher to use effectively.

My own views about the kind of labor law course and casebook I preferred were briefly set forth in a letter I wrote in October 1969, in response to a request from Harry W. Arthurs, then dean of Osgoode Law School in Toronto and a preeminent labor law scholar, to review and comment on an "informal" edition of a volume put together by a Canadian labor relations casebook group. My first comment, a facetious one, referred to the book's formidable size:

> When I first started going through it, I held it in my lap; but this soon made both of my legs go to sleep, so I had to shift it to the desk. If one of your stronger students were able to throw it at another, and if he did so in anger, he could properly be charged with assault with a deadly weapon.

In respect of the book's content, my chief criticism was

> that it includes...too much material, including relatively unimportant technical details that I would just as soon see ignored in a law school course. As I view the [typical] course, it is primarily for those law students who will never specialize in the practice of labor law. Even those who do will pick up most of the knowledge they require on the job, after they graduate. A book of cases and materials, therefore, ought to concentrate on a few major policy issues, the kind that will confront the student in later life in his role as a general practitioner, as a business man, as a public servant, as a legislator, or as a citizen.

Summing up my rather random criticisms of the book, I wrote:

> I think it needs to be shortened considerably, and the way I would be inclined to do that is to concentrate on basic policy issues through the judicious use of non-case material consisting of problems, excerpts from published writings, and notes prepared specially for the book. I would keep a few "landmark" cases under each major policy heading and summarize other leading cases in narrative notes....I think I would expand the treatment of ethics, raising at least one ethical problem in each of the major sections.

In the ensuing years I have adhered pretty much to these opinions. In light of the increasing trend toward "globalization," and because I think the study of comparative labor law is assuming ever-growing importance, I would include in my ideal book a considerable amount of comparative material. But, as usual, the devil is in the details. No published book has yet measured up to the perhaps unachievable standards I have proposed. And even the best and most popular of the current labor law casebooks still adhere in many respects to the basic organization first criticized by Wirtz in 1946. Moreover, at least in my view, they are all too long for the typical one-semester course. To give but two examples—*Labor Law/Cases and Materials*, edited by Cox, Bok, Gorman, and Finkin (13th edition, 2001), and *Labor Relations Law/Cases and Materials*, edited by St. Antoine, Craver, and Crain (10th edition, 1999)—exceeds 1,000 pages.

Of far greater importance, however, is that efforts to produce labor law materials by the Labor Law Group and others continue. It is safe to predict that no one book will ever satisfy all teachers of labor law, but I venture to hope that because of the constant striving by the Labor Law Group and perhaps others toward the objective so eloquently outlined by Wirtz in 1984, the interests of both teachers and students will be increasingly well served.

Although I continued to be listed as a working member of the Labor Law Group for a few more years and maintained a lively interest in its activities, my effective participation had ended by 1985, and that is the point at which my chronicle of its history ceases. I look back on my long period of association with the Labor Law Group with pride and gratitude. And as I do so, like Mathews before me, "I feel the old enthusiasm welling up in me again" and wish I had the capacity to communicate it to the present members of the group. I think we did some valuable pioneering work and delivered more for our initial $25,000 grant, the only subsidy we ever received, than the grantor ever imagined or expected. Most of all, I cherish the lasting friendships I formed with other members of the group. My great regret is that in this account I have failed adequately to convey the enormous impact that Wirtz and Mathews had on all of those associated in our collaborative efforts. Wirtz best expressed what I feel. At the end of his 1984 Park City address he said, "I have said nothing of Bob Mathews. This is because I couldn't manage it. We wouldn't be here if he hadn't been. He was the most human being most of us have ever known." The same can be said of Bill Wirtz.

CHAPTER 13

THE COMPARATIVE LABOR LAW GROUP, 1966–1978

The second group research project in which I became deeply involved was the Comparative Labor Law Group. The idea for the project originated in a discussion I had with Otto Kahn-Freund, then professor of comparative law at Oxford University, at a colloquium on labor law that took place in December 1962 in London.[1] I had mentioned to him that I was thinking about doing an analytical comparison between the American system of grievance arbitration and the systems in some European countries for adjudicating such matters, commonly known as disputes over rights, in labor courts. Kahn-Freund was enthusiastic about the project and urged me to proceed.[2]

The countries I selected for comparative study were Britain, France, (then) West Germany, Italy, and Sweden. France, Germany, and Sweden had labor court systems. Italy, an interesting contrast, provided for the litigation of disputes over rights in the civil courts. Britain had been experimenting with industrial tribunals similar to labor courts in specialized cases. (At the time I drafted my study proposal, the Royal Commission on Trade Unions and Employers' Associations [the Donovan Commission] had just been appointed, and there appeared to be at least the possibility that the commission might recommend some form of labor court for Britain; its report, published in 1968, made no such recommendation.) Labor arbitration of disputes over rights also

---

[1] Kahn-Freund was the preeminent authority of his time on comparative labor law. He was also my mentor and friend. I shall discuss our relationship later in these memoirs.

[2] For those unfamiliar with the term "disputes over rights," it applies to disputes over the enforcement of rights created by statutes, individual contracts of employment, or collective bargaining agreements. In theory, at least, such disputes are not concerned with efforts to obtain rights not presently in being. Conflicts over the establishment of new rights (e.g., higher wage rates or improved contract terms) are commonly referred to as "disputes over interests."

existed in all five of these countries, but in none had it assumed anything like the importance it has in the United States.

The first task was to recruit the members of the group. In this effort I was singularly fortunate. Each person selected was a professor of labor law, well known in his own country; several had international reputations. I first enlisted the two men I knew personally: Gino Giugni, then at the University of Bari, Italy, and later at the University of Rome; and Folke Schmidt, University of Stockholm, Sweden. Next, I invited two men I had met but did not know well: Thilo Ramm, then at the University of Giessen, Germany; and K.W. (Bill) Wedderburn, London School of Economics. The task of choosing a French colleague was the most diffi-cult, not only because I had not met any of the possible choices but also because of the well-known aversion of French scholars to speak or write in another language, especially English. Acting on the recommendations of Kahn-Freund and Schmidt, I finally contacted Xavier Blanc-Jouvan, then at the University of Aix-en-Provence, and later at the University of Paris I. Blanc-Jouvan had studied and traveled in the United States and had a good command of English.

The project, as originally planned, envisaged reports by each of my European colleagues on procedures for the settlement of disputes over rights in his own country (thus following the current pattern of compar-ative law publications), to be published in a single volume edited by me, to which I would contribute an introduction. This was to be followed by a second volume, written solely by me, that would discuss the American system of grievance arbitration and compare it with the systems of the other five countries.

Another distinct feature of the project was the plan to bring all five European members of the group to UCLA for a quarter. They would teach as visiting professors in an academic department or school while participating in a more or less continuing colloquium on our project, which would also be open to interested faculty and graduate students. At the end of the quarter, by which time the manuscripts of the individual chapters of the first volume were to be completed, the project plan called for a conference of invited scholars from throughout the United States and Canada that would feature reports by the individual members of the group on their research findings. The expected time span of the study was from January 1966 until June 1968.

Financial support for our project consisted primarily of funds from two sources. In the early 1960s the Ford Foundation had given UCLA a multimillion-dollar grant for comparative and international studies. A committee established to administer the grant held an open, campus-wide competition for research proposals. Mine was one of those chosen, and I received a total of $28,955 for 1966-67 through 1968-69. This was supplemented by a smaller grant I obtained from the Walter E. Meyer Research Institute of Law at Columbia University. The UCLA Institute of Industrial Relations (IIR) provided me with research and secretarial assistance and editorial assistance for my European colleagues in the person of our publications director, Faye Hinman. The money from the two grants proved to be sufficient to finance the first three publications of the group.

As is the case with most schedules of this kind, our original plan was extensively modified as time went on. The first meeting of the group to organize the project was held in Stockholm in August 1966. To achieve a general uniformity in the structure of the national reports, I had prepared and circulated to my colleagues in advance a proposed outline to be followed in their preparation. After some modification, my outline was approved. This inaugural meeting also provided us the opportunity to get better acquainted and to deal with problems caused by differences in languages. Thus, in the course of our discussions we came to realize that the vocabulary of industrial relations and labor law has no universally understood terms. Commonly used terms such as "strike," "worker participation," "mediation," and "arbitration" meant different things in the several countries covered by our survey. It took considerable time to get these differences sorted out.

Following the meeting in Stockholm, I made a quick trip to Europe in January 1967 and spent several days conferring with each of my colleagues on his own ground about the progress of his work. Then, in July of that year, we spent a week together in a suburb of Rome, going over the outlines of each national report, as well as the partially completed chapter manuscripts.

In the fall of 1967 the five Europeans came to UCLA. During that quarter, Schmidt taught a course in the School of Law; Ramm and Blanc-Jouvan gave courses in the Department of Political Science; Wedderburn taught in the Graduate School of Management; and Giugni gave a series of lectures under the auspices of the IIR. The continuing colloquium was also held as planned, but most of our time was occupied in numerous private sessions between various members of our group.

During this period I learned a great deal more about the attitudes and habits of my colleagues. Schmidt, Wedderburn, and Blanc-Jouvan came alone, but Giugni was accompanied by his wife and two young children, and Ramm brought his wife, son, and an academic assistant who, in the German tradition, served as chauffeur (they drove across the country from New York to Los Angeles), child-minder, researcher, and general "gofer." On the whole, we all got along very well and frequently spent our leisure times together. I had some difficulty accustoming myself to the work habits of several of my colleagues, especially Giugni, who was habitually late for any meeting during the morning hours. A delightful person with a brilliant mind, he followed his own timetable and seemed unable fully to wake up before late afternoon. On one occasion he came to my office shortly before noon to discuss some aspect of American labor law that he did not understand. We sat side by side at my desk and he began to question me. Gradually, his speech became more hesitant, then it stopped; he had fallen asleep. I did not disturb him and continued with my own work. He slept for about 20 minutes and did not seem in the least embarrassed when he awoke, but simply continued his questions from where he had left off.

In November 1967, the group held a one-day conference to present reports by the five European members on their research findings. It was attended by over 100 invited scholars, who came at their own expense from throughout the United States and Canada. At this conference, which I chaired, each of my colleagues presented a summary of his own work in progress and responded to questions and comments from the audience. The five reports were published in 1969 by the IIR in a 90-page paperback titled *Dispute Settlement Procedures in Five Western European Countries*. I had first offered the reports to the *UCLA Law Review*, but, after a considerable delay, was informed that the student editors did not consider them to be suitable for publication in a law review. Asking for a further explanation, I was told that the presentations by my colleagues contained no footnotes and that the subject itself was of little or no interest to readers of the *Review*. Happily for the IIR, its own publication proved to be one of the best sellers on its list and was purchased by readers in countries throughout the world.

So far, our project had proceeded exactly according to the original plan. Following completion of the first phase, however, a major change occurred. Wedderburn had indicated from the outset that he would have difficulty in confining his national report for Britain to the approximately 75 printed pages allocated to each author. Before leaving the United States, he submitted instead a book-length manuscript, co-authored by a brilliant law student, Paul L. Davies, who served as his assistant at the London School of Economics. Davies subsequently became one of Britain's outstanding scholars in the field of labor law and industrial relations. Wedderburn's decision to depart from our original understanding came as a great surprise to his European colleagues, who initially expressed some resentment. We all realized, however, that the Wedderburn-Davies study was an outstanding one. Accordingly, albeit with some reluctance, we agreed that it should be published as a separate volume and that the other four national reports should be included in a second volume. This was done. Wedderburn and Davies, *Employment Grievances and Disputes Procedures in Britain*, to which I contributed a short foreword, was published by the University of California Press in 1969. *Labor Courts and Grievance Settlement in Western Europe*, containing the national reports for France, Italy, West Germany, and Sweden, followed in 1971. For this volume I provided a somewhat longer foreword.

On the whole, the two books were well received. Writing in *The Journal of Business*, Milton Derber, the distinguished American labor historian from the University of Wisconsin, praised the Wedderburn-Davies study for adding "significantly to our knowledge of British grievance handling and dispute settlement by combining a comprehensive survey of the empirical literature on the structure and functioning of negotiated procedures in major industries as well as of official arbitration bodies with an analysis of relevant statutes and legal decisions." In England, Arthur Marsh from the University of Oxford reviewed the Wedderburn-Davies survey in the *Industrial Relations Journal*. Marsh described the book as attempting "to bridge the legal-non-legal gap; it is stimulating in questioning legalism at a time when the tide is moving...towards greater legal regulation. Finally...it provides us with information, not previously available, on many aspects of procedures of voluntary arbitration in Britain. And all presented with a skill which even the severest critic of the legal approach among students of industrial relations could not but admire."

Labor Courts and Grievance Settlement in Western Europe also received generally favorable reviews. Perhaps the most thoughtful, appearing in *The American Journal of Comparative Law*, was written by Clyde Summers, then of the Yale Law School, the foremost comparative labor law scholar in the United States. Summers described the book as the "product of a genuine group effort in which those involved shared ideas, came to understand each other's institutional framework, and then developed a common approach which would focus on the similarities and differences in their various systems." He identified three qualities that gave the separate reports special interest and value: "First, each of the authors covers essentially the same basic element and problem areas, but at the same time presents his system in terms of its own theoretical structure and emphasizes those characteristics which he believes are central to his system." These "highly individualistic" emphases, Summers wrote, "carry us past formal characteristics and give us some sense of the subtle qualities special to each system, and particularly show us the way those within the system view its character," thus helping the reader in "that most difficult demand of comparative studies, getting inside the skin of another system."

The second valuable feature of these studies, Summers continued, was that they extended to the whole range of procedures public and private, used in each of the four countries to settle labor disputes.

The third special quality of these studies, in Summers's opinion, was that "they go beyond the formal legal provisions, structures and procedures, to give some glimpse of the actual work of the institutions involved....Our understanding and appreciation of each system as a set of living, working institutions is sharpened by the willingness of each author to subject his system to critical examination...in terms of the practical effectiveness in settling disputes and providing adequate remedies."

Yet, Summers concluded, "the book somehow fails to satisfy. Reading it seems unaccountably burdensome, retaining and integrating the material seems unduly difficult, and grasping its relevance remains a bit beyond our reach." He pointed to two possible reasons for this result. First, the four individual essays are parallel, not comparative, studies. The process of comparison is left to the reader, a process available only to one who has substantial knowledge and a "sense of the essence" of the systems being compared. Second, the essays do not present the dispute settlement procedures in each country in the context of the social institutions of which they are a part.

Once we had agreed to the publication of the Wedderburn-Davies national report as a separate volume, I decided to abandon the rest of my original plan, which was to write a book by myself on grievance arbitration in the United States with comparative references to the five European countries treated in our earlier publications. My decision was prompted by the conviction that it was more important to keep the group together for more comparative research. My colleagues were enthusiastically in favor of embarking on another study; all of us felt that the experience we had gained so far would make it possible to improve both our research techniques and the quality of our subsequent publications. Accordingly, we decided to write a book on industrial conflict in the same six countries. In fact, that decision was taken in 1969, prior to the publication of the first two volumes.

Once again, the group held an organizational meeting in Stockholm, in August 1969. At that time we decided upon a radical change in the organization of our research to make the results more truly comparative. We divided the subject of our study of industrial conflict into six parts, assigning one part to each member of the group. Each of us then had the responsibility of dealing with the laws and practices of all six countries relating to his assigned part. In September 1969, I set forth the decision taken at the Stockholm meeting in the following memorandum to my colleagues, which read in part:

The six subjects to be explored and the persons responsible for each of these subjects are as follows:

1. Objectives, types, and methods of industrial action (including mass pressures and political strikes) (Aaron).
2. Unions, employers' associations, and other coalitions: internal sanctions and rules (Schmidt).
3. External sanctions against unlawful industrial action and state prevention and settlement procedures (including damages and injunctions) (Ramm).
4. Industrial action against the government or the "public interest" (including incomes policies and political strikes; query whether industrial action by state employees will also be covered) (Wedderburn).
5. The peace obligation under collective agreements: no-strike clauses, expressed and implied, and tort liability (Giugni).
6. Industrial action and continuity of employment: its impact on wages and social security (including workers in other factories or establishments) (Blanc-Jouvan).

It was agreed that the six essays would be published in a single volume. This meant that none of the essays could exceed 25,000 words. This limitation on the length of the essays was expressly agreed to by each of us; no exceptions would be made. The agreed order of procedure was as follows:

1. Each author will prepare a short essay on his own topic as it relates to his own country. He will also add a list of specific questions directed to the situation affecting his topic in the five other countries. He will then send copies of the essay and questions to all other members of the Group. The deadline for completion of this phase of the work is 1 February 1970. Ramm, Giugni, and Aaron

have agreed to try to submit their essays and questions in advance of that deadline.

2. Each member of the Group will then prepare written replies to the questions submitted to him by all the other members.

3. The replies will doubtless stimulate further correspondence between the members of the Group; meanwhile individual research will continue. The deadline for completion of steps 2 and 3 is September 1970.

4. Immediately following conclusion of the International Congress of ISLLSL [International Society For Labor Law & Social Legislation] in Warsaw in September 1970, we shall meet for two days (probably 19-20 September) to discuss the progress of our work.

5. Following the meeting in September 1970, each of us will continue with his individual research and the writing of his paper. As soon as a complete draft of a paper is ready, it should be circulated among all members of the Group.

6. The final phase will be a meeting at UCLA for approximately one month preceding a two-day conference at which the six papers will be presented. During this month, we shall discuss the papers and make such corrections, amendments, etc. as seem necessary or desirable. It is absolutely indispensable that each member of the Group has a completed first draft before coming to the United States. The entire purpose of the month-long meeting preceding the conference will be frustrated if any member of the Group uses that time to complete, rather than to discuss, his first draft.

At this point the source of funds to finance the project was yet to be determined. I subsequently obtained an additional grant of $30,400 from the Ford Foundation.

At the time we adopted the foregoing procedures and arrangements, none of us had a clear idea of the amount of work they would entail. For the better part of the next three years we exchanged numerous questionnaires and prepared lengthy memoranda on various aspects of law and practice in our own countries for the benefit of our colleagues. In this phase of the work, I think I bore the heaviest burden because my European colleagues knew more about the situation in their respective countries than they knew about the relevant laws and practices in the United States. My files reveal that in 1970-71, for example, I sent letters and memoranda totaling almost 100 single-spaced pages to my colleagues in response to their detailed questionnaires or random requests for information about American law and practice relating to such diverse matters as strikes, lockouts, boycotts, picketing, remedies for unjust dismissals, no-strike clauses, political strikes, emergency disputes, economic controls, multi-employer bargaining, the use of troops or police to do the work of strikers, trade union ideology and the conduct of internal union affairs, and the effect of strikes and lockouts on the status of individual employees. Needless to say, the amount of time I spent accumulating this information and presenting it in a helpful way was considerable.

In September 1970, the group met for two days at the Salzburg Seminar's Schloss Leopoldskron in Salzburg, Austria, to discuss problems individual members had encountered in preparing their respective chapters. In January of that year, Wedderburn had sent a letter to me and another to the other members of our group, bitterly complaining about the delays in the publishing of the Wedderburn-Davies volume by the University of California Press and urging that no future work of ours be published by that organization. His letters, copies of which, unfortunately, are missing from my files, must have gotten under my skin: the tone of my reply reflected my irritation. Although I conceded and regretted that the press had mismanaged the publication of the Wedderburn-Davies volume, I also insisted that the final product measured up to its high standards. I also reminded him that our contract with the press provided that our second volume containing the national reports prepared by our four other members would be published by the press. At our meeting in Salzburg, my colleagues strongly supported Wedderburn's position and expressed dissatisfaction with the alleged inadequacy of the press's marketing efforts. I was particularly irritated by Schmidt's objection that the editing of the first two volumes employed "American English" and by his insistence that subsequent volumes be printed in "English English." Considering that his own grasp of the English language, whether "American" or "English," was tenuous at best, I considered his comments on this subject gratuitous and unhelpful. I mention this teapot tempest only as an example of the kinds of short-lived disagreements that frequently arose during the life of our joint enterprise. At the conclusion of our discussion of possible publishers, we unanimously agreed to authorize Wedderburn to explore publication of our volume on industrial conflict with a British publishing house.

From 30 August to 20 September 1971, the group met again at UCLA, but this time only for the purpose of putting our respective chapters in shape. We took that occasion, however, to discuss our next project, and agreed that it should be on discrimination in employment. Meanwhile, Wedderburn had been negotiating with Charles Clark of Penguin Books over the publication of our volume on industrial conflict. His efforts were successful, and in October 1970, Clark wrote to me, expressing his enthusiasm about the proposed book, but warning that it could not exceed 150,000 words. In January 1971, Clark sent me a formal publishing contract. Unfortunately, this contract was never executed.

Although we should perhaps have anticipated the troubles that lay ahead, I don't think any of us was prepared for the crisis that developed. The situation was summarized in the following letter, dated 15 October 1971, which Wedderburn sent to the rest of us. He gave vent to his frustration, his intense disappointment, and his misgivings about future group projects:

> It is today October 15th. I have received chapters for submission to the publisher only from Ben (with subsequent list of amendments)....
>
> It was a solemn compact made between us all in Los Angeles that the chapters would be here in London by October 15 at latest. Since on the basis of that agreement I promised to present the book this weekend, I am left in the greatest personal difficulty. Much more important, this has the appearance of a beginning of a process through which our work will not be published for a long time.
>
> I have reminded myself of our agreement in Stockholm two years ago. It was to circulate memoranda [by a date certain] and [to make sure that each of us] arrive in Los Angeles in 1971 *without fail* with a draft chapter. As a team we did not do so. Now, the latest agreement for October 15, made after the deepest consideration, has been broken.

I am sure there are good reasons for the failure. But surely they could have been foreseen when we made the agreement in Los Angeles. For my part, I feel that what has happened raises the question whether we are a sufficiently coherent team to work together on a third project.

As dismal as Wedderburn's appraisal of the situation was, it did not touch on another major problem. As previously indicated, we had unanimously agreed as a condition of publication by Penguin that our book would not exceed 150,000 words. As submitted, however, our proposed text amounted to an estimated 230,000 words, or 568 printed pages. That proved to be decisive as far as Charles Clark was concerned; in a letter to Wedderburn in November 1971, he reluctantly informed him that Penguin could not publish our book. At the same time, he generously promised to exert his best efforts to find another publisher. His willingness to do so provided cold comfort at best; our data were extremely time-sensitive and negotiations with another publisher would almost certainly delay publication and render at least some of our findings obsolete.

Faced with this prospect, we decided to undertake a massive reduction of our manuscript in order to make it more attractive to another publisher. Because my chapter was the longest of the six, my colleagues all agreed that it should be cut by about one-third. Complying with this decision, I reduced it by about 50 pages, or approximately 23,000 words. Schmidt followed suit, although his chapter, shorter than mine, required less drastic treatment. Ramm agreed to eliminate the first 73 pages of his chapter, but then concluded that, thus reduced, it would not be worth including in the book. Accordingly, he offered to withdraw it entirely, concluding, "For myself I am satisfied with the honour of having participated in the work." In response, I wrote to my colleagues that it was unthinkable that we should even consider omitting Ramm's contribution and declared: "In whatever form our book appears, it must represent the contribution of each member of the Group." That conclusion was tacitly accepted by the others.

Blanc-Jouvan also agreed in principle that his chapter needed shortening, but added that he would have great difficulty in reducing his manuscript by the recommended one-third, and that, in any event, it would require at least two weeks more work after a firm decision had been made. This was particularly bad news because we were still hoping to have our book published in 1972.

Despite all our difficulties, and thanks to the heroic efforts of Wedderburn, who found another British publisher, Longman, and was responsible for the final editing of our book, *Industrial Conflict / A Comparative Legal Survey*, edited by Wedderburn and myself, was published in late 1972. It came to 396 pages, including an index. Unfortunately, the price of $26.00 was astronomical for those days and resulted in very limited sales.

Whatever its flaws, *Industrial Conflict* was a more comparative work than either of our two preceding books. Each of its chapters, although written by one person, reflected the input of the entire group. Collectively, we endeavored to show how similar kinds of employer-employee and employer-union relationships in the six countries covered by our survey had been influenced by different historical and cultural factors, leading to the development of a rich variety of governmental and private mechanisms by which those relationships are governed.

Regrettably, the book was not reviewed by any of the major journals, and the few notices I saw failed to emphasize what my colleagues and I deemed its principal contribution: a new methodology for the conduct of comparative labor law research. We had to content ourselves with letters of appreciation from other colleagues in the field.

Although the misgivings about the group's ability to complete another project expressed in Wedderburn's letter of 15 October were shared to a considerable degree by all of us, we finally decided to go ahead with the new book on discrimination in employment we had agreed upon at our meeting at UCLA in September 1971. Once again, an organizational meeting was held in Stockholm in March 1972, at which time we divided the topic into six parts and tentatively assigned them as follows:

Chapter 1. Introduction. Origin of the ideas of equal opportunity and history of the idea of legal remedies against discrimination; legal sources, including international instruments and national constitutions; and the concept of discrimination (comparing equal opportunity with the idea of fairness) (Ramm).

Chapter 2. Discrimination on grounds relating to politics, religion, and private affairs (Giugni).

Chapter 3. Discrimination due to race, color, and ethnic or national origin (Aaron).

Chapter 4. Discrimination against foreign workers (Blanc-Jouvan).

Chapter 5. Discrimination based on sex (Schmidt).

Chapter 6. Discrimination based on participation or nonparticipation in trade union activities (Wedderburn).

We also reserved for consideration a possible seventh chapter to be written jointly, consisting of an evaluation of existing legal remedies against discrimination in employment, together with some indications of likely future developments in the law on that subject.

We proceeded with these plans without having first secured the necessary funding. In November 1971, I had submitted to the Ford Foundation a narrative account and financial details of its grants totaling $30,400 to the group together with a description of our proposed study on discrimination in employment. Although I had not specifically asked for a further grant to underwrite that project, such a request was implicit in my letter. In February 1972 I received a reply from the foundation wishing us well with our proposed new study and applauding our efforts to obtain support from sources other than those in the United States. I had expected this response but not the decision that "it would not be appropriate under the terms of the previous grant to approve use of the unexpended balance of $2,849.09 to help finance the new study. Regrettably, therefore, we request return of this amount." It seemed to me that the foundation was straining on a gnat after swallowing a camel, but of course I returned the money.

In the months following our March 1972 meeting in Stockholm, we tried unsuccessfully to obtain a grant from the German Marshall Plan, the Volkswagen Foundation, the National Science Foundation, and the U.S. Department of Labor, among others. Just as it looked as if our project would die for lack of financial support, Schmidt informed us that he had obtained a grant of about $38,000 from the Bank of Sweden Tercentenary Foundation. This amount, supplemented by the grant of $7,500 I obtained from the Manpower Research Center of the UCLA Institute of Industrial Relations, seemed sufficient to fund the study. Aside from covering expenses of our meetings, the money provided research assistance and a modest honorarium for the European members of our team. We held a three-day meeting in Cambridge, England, in September 1975; a three-week meeting in Bologna, in September 1975; and a final five-day meeting in Florence, in March 1977.

The last session in Florence was particularly important. In advance of the meeting, I sent a circular letter to the other members of the group outlining some of the arrangements previously agreed to. This letter read in part:

2. Before the…[Florence] meeting, the chapters of Thilo, Gino, Xavier, and Folke should be reviewed by a competent person and put into correct English. Faye Hinman has agreed to do this for Thilo. She will also help me with Xavier's chapter. Thereafter, Bill and I will review them again for final correction.

3. All information which any member of the Group has agreed to furnish to another member must be sent immediately.

4. Except in the case of some crucially significant development, nothing that occurs after 1 December 1976 will be included in the volume.

5. All chapters must be completed and sent by air mail…to all members of the Group no later than 15 February 1977. Because of its general character and application to all other chapters, however, Thilo's chapter should be circulated no later than 1 February 1977. Comments on his new draft should, if possible, be sent to him in advance of the meeting.…

7. Regarding plans for continuing our collective efforts [see paragraph 8], we have reached general agreement on a two-stage approach. The first stage will be devoted to national reports on the selected topic, preferably within a flexible framework consisting of key questions to be addressed by each writer. Each writer will be free, however,

to determine for himself the amount of attention given to each question, and also to discuss other questions of particular importance in his own country. Some time after the national reports have been completed and circulated, the Group will meet for about two weeks to discuss each national report in detail and to divide the general topic into six subdivisions. Thereafter, each member of the Group will prepare a chapter on his topic for all six countries, based primarily on the national reports, but supplemented by further specific information as agreed at the meeting. Upon the completion and circulation of the chapters, there will be a final meeting to review them.

8. Regarding the topic for our next study, Bill has suggested Managerial Prerogative and Joint Regulation of Policies in Enterprises and Public Activities in the Private and Public Sectors....Between now and our next meeting, he will submit a tentative outline of the scope of the topic; we shall review and discuss it at the Florence meeting. Meanwhile, I shall report to the German Marshall Fund that we are considering a topic of the nature suggested by Bill, and that we may possibly be able to submit a formal proposal following the Florence meeting. I shall report to the Group on the reaction, if any, of the Fund representatives to that information. At the same time, Bill will explore the possibility of obtaining funding for the project from the EEC, while Gino will apply to the appropriate Italian authorities for a contribution to support his research on the project....

Finally, I submit, with respect, that compliance with our agreement on procedure for preparation for our next meeting will be a true measure of our individual commitments to our joint enterprise.

Immediately following the meeting, I sent another circular letter summarizing the action taken on that occasion, most of which concerned our study of discrimination in employment. The deadline for the submission to Schmidt of our respective chapters in final form was set for 1 June 1977. Reporting the unanimous agreement on this point, I stated, "This date cannot and will not be changed." In respect of our proposed new project, a tentative outline, schedule, and budget prepared by Wedderburn and me was discussed but not finally agreed upon. Wedderburn and Giugni were to make some revisions and advise me of the changes, after which I would again contact the German Marshall Fund to ascertain whether it would be willing to finance the study.

From this point onward, our difficulties in completing work on the employment discrimination volume multiplied at a frightening rate. Some things could and should have been anticipated; others were completely fortuitous and unpreventable. Between March and August 1977, Schmidt, the senior member of our group, had suffered a stroke. He had also retired from his academic position at the University of Stockholm and had consequently lost his office and his secretary. Although, fortunately, Schmidt recovered rather quickly from the partial paralysis resulting from his stroke, he did not retain all of his former physical vigor, and the loss of his office and secretarial assistance made his editorial responsibilities increasingly burdensome. During the same period, Blanc-Jouvan's wife developed a life-threatening illness. Caring for her and their children consumed much of his time and inevitably delayed completion of his chapter.

More serious problems lay ahead. Among the earliest storm warnings was a letter sent to me in August 1977 by Wedderburn, complaining about the failure of some members of the group to complete their chapters on time and expressing grave concern about the possibility that much of our work would be outdated before the book was published. He also expressed doubt about the group's ability to complete a new project and reported that Giugni had said he thought the group had "come to the end of its possible life." In my response, I acknowledged that his fears were justified, but I also reminded him that Blanc-Jouvan's situation, now greatly improved by his wife's recovery, was a special one not likely to recur, and that under the procedure we proposed to follow in our new undertaking, we could probably count on him to finish his work on time.

Giugni seemed to me to present a more difficult case because of his apparent loss of interest in our research projects and his resentment of even mild criticism of his failure to meet time commitments. On the other hand, I noted, Schmidt seemed keen to pursue the new project, and I suggested that if Giugni was the only member of the group unwilling to commit to the proposed new study, perhaps we should recruit a replacement and then go ahead as previously planned. This, I speedily realized, was a bad idea, and I resolved not to press it. In September, Ramm wrote to voice his doubts about the new project based principally on the breadth of its scope, which he thought was beyond our capacity. He expressed willingness to participate, provided that the project was reduced in scope. Later that month, Wedderburn again wrote to me complaining that Giugni's and Blanc-Jouvan's chapters for our employment discrimination book were still not completed, a year after they were supposed to have been submitted. "I find myself," he said, "plunged into the deepest depression at the thought of starting another project which, whatever the changes of working method, would probably produce the same thing in the end." There were doubtless contributing causes for Wedderburn's depression. In a letter sent to all group members in late September, he revealed that he was seriously ill and suffering from an "anxiety-depression neurosis" for which he was being treated. He repeated his concern that because Blanc-Jouvan had still not completed his chapter, our book on employment discrimination was "on the edge of being ruined" and would be virtually obsolete by the time it was published, and he also expressed his intensified doubts about the feasibility of embarking on a new project. In connection with this latter point, he opposed as impracticable the idea of reconstructing the group.

In October, Blanc-Jouvan wrote to me urging that the group not be allowed to disband because of his tardiness in completing his chapter. If the group wished it, he said, "I will retire—with great despair, but without any bitterness," and he promised to find an adequate substitute. In reply, I told him that to bring a new member, no matter how well qualified, into our group at this stage would be counterproductive. Moreover, I pointed out, it would not solve our real problem, which was how to manage our multiple individual commitments in such a way as to meet the deadlines of our group projects. I concluded by saying that although I wished the work of our group could continue, I feared that was no longer possible. I sent to Schmidt and Wedderburn copies of my letter to Blanc-Jouvan. In his reply to me, Schmidt confessed his doubt that the group would be able to launch a new project. He referred for the first time to the fact that Ramm had not yet submitted his manuscript for the employment discrimination book (Blanc-Jouvan's chapter was also late, although Giugni's had finally arrived), and he admitted that "in my black hours I am almost as irritated as Bill." He also warned that although he was back at work in fairly good shape, he had to be considered a bad risk, since he was unlikely to be able to work efficiently for more than a couple of years.

With the book on employment discrimination still not completed and with increasing signs of tension among the members of our group, I reluctantly sent a circular letter in November 1977 that began, "The time has come...to say directly what I'm sure we have all been considering for some time, namely, that the Comparative Labor Law Group has reached the end of its useful existence and should be disbanded." My letter concluded in part:

> A group such as ours has its own life cycle. It seems to me that we have long since passed the point when each of us was willing to forego any opportunity, however attractive, that might conflict with his primary obligation to our current project. Once that sense of commitment is lost, our Group cannot survive.
>
> Rather than dwell upon the reasons for the Group's demise, I would remind you of our accomplishments, which I think are not inconsiderable. Our previous publications, whatever their shortcomings, have made solid contributions to the literature of comparative labor law. Of greater importance, at least in my view, have been the techniques we developed for group comparative research; this, I think, will be viewed in the long run as our most notable achievement. My only regret is that we shall not be able to see whether the revised procedures we had planned for our new project would have worked in the manner we foresaw.
>
> Best of all, we have maintained a close personal and professional relationship over the years that, so far as I am concerned, made the whole experience worthwhile. I cherish the memory of our times together, and for each of you I shall always have the greatest respect and the warmest personal feelings. Friendships, certainly, need not end with the disbanding of the Group.
>
> I am, of course, aware that the announcement of the dissolution of our Group represents a unilateral act on my part...[but] I am simply stating what all of you recognize must be. Moreover, my own assessment of our continuing ability to function effectively convinces me that I could not in good conscience ask the German Marshall Fund for the large grant of money necessary to finance a new project.

No member of the group dissented from this decision to disband.

We still had to deal with the unfinished business of completing our book on employment discrimination, and the final period of our collaborative efforts proved to be a very sad one. A principal complication arose from Ramm's inability to write intelligibly in English. It became my onerous duty to "translate" his manuscript, with the aid of Faye Hinman, who was fluent in German, into prose that the average reader could understand. An even bigger problem was created by the group itself. At our March 1977 meeting in Florence, we decided that Ramm's contribution should be divided into two parts. The first, titled simply "Introduction" (chapter 1), would deal in a general way with equal opportunity, legal remedies against discrimination, and international instruments and national constitutions relating to those topics. The second (chapter 7) would be devoted to international development and remarks on legal theory. Despite considerable difficulty and much delay in translating and clarifying chapter 1, Faye and I were ultimately successful in producing a manuscript that was satisfactory to Ramm and Schmidt, but chapter 7 proved to be the rock on which the entire volume almost foundered.

The original deadline for completion of the book was June 1977, a date we had all agreed at our Florence meeting "cannot and will not be changed." Unfortunately, as so often happens in the writing of books, especially those with multiple authors, our performance fell far short of our mutual commitments. Schmidt, Wedderburn, and I submitted our manuscripts on time, but Giugni, Blanc-Jouvan, and Ramm were months late. By December 1977, six months past our deadline, Schmidt had received the chapters of Giugni and Blanc-Jouvan; only Ramm's chapter 7 remained unfinished. There were a number of reasons for this delay: difficulties in translating his various drafts, misunderstandings over the organization of the chapter involving Schmidt, Ramm, and me, and strong objections by Schmidt to Ramm's "remarks on legal theory," which Schmidt felt were unrelated to the rest of the book and wrong from a theoretical point of view. Tensions and ill feeling between Schmidt and Ramm increased and led to mounting concern by other members of the group, especially Wedderburn, over the delayed publication of the book, which could result in rendering many of our findings out of date.

Things started to come to a head in December 1977, when in a circular letter to the group Schmidt reported that the manuscript of the book, minus chapter 7, had been delivered to the publisher. He suggested that this chapter should be included only if it could be completed "without considerable delay." In February 1978, Schmidt sent another circular letter to the group announcing that "the time limit is now exceeded and…the book will be printed without a chapter VII" and reviewing the events leading to his decision. His version of preceding events prompted further bitter correspondence between him and Ramm, full of mutual recriminations concerning who was responsible for the delay. In March, Schmidt advised the group that Ramm had refused to accept his decision to exclude chapter 7 from the book and had demanded that the chapter, now virtually complete, be sent to the publisher within 14 days. If this were not done, he threatened to sue in court to prevent publication of the entire volume.

Appalled by these developments, various members of the group urged both Schmidt and Ramm to compromise their differences. Otto Kahn-Freund was asked by Ramm and Schmidt to serve as referee. He declined, but offered the sensible suggestion that a statement be included in the book's preface that the views of each of the authors were strictly their own and did not reflect the endorsement or consensus of the group. My own efforts to resolve the impasse included a letter to all members of the group pointing out, among other things, that we had already fallen behind our target publication date by at least one year, so a few more months' delay would not make much difference. Schmidt had stated, however, that he did not have the strength to do the necessary bargaining for a further delay with the publisher, the printer, and the Tercentenary Fund. If his decision on that score remained unchanged, I thought, we must all accept it as final, but I offered to arrange separate publication of chapter 7 in a reputable journal in the Untied States—a proposal immediately rejected by Ramm. I concluded my letter with the following plea:

Despite the predictable gap between our reach and our grasp, we did important pioneering work together in comparative labor law. We have laid a sound foundation upon which others can build....Having surmounted so many problems during our life as a Group, we ought to be able...to overcome this last one, so that we can look back on our long collaboration with pride and pleasure, rather than with bitterness and anger.

Like those of my colleagues, my intervention had no effect; both Schmidt and Ramm refused to budge. In an effort to justify his decision not to include chapter 7 in our book, Schmidt gave a copy to Clyde Summers, the pre-eminent American authority on comparative labor law who was in Sweden at the time, and asked for his evaluation. Summers's detailed analysis was extremely unfavorable. In summary, he expressed the view that "inclusion of Chapter 7 in its present form would detract from the value and the credibility of the book as a whole." Predictably, Ramm dismissed Summers's memorandum as "unscholarly...very vague in its arguments but very strong in its conclusions...without any point which can be checked." He offered in rebuttal a commentary on his chapter, written in French, by Elaine Vogel-Polsky, a law professor and research director of the Institute of Sociology at the Free University of Brussels. Her lengthy analysis was the antithesis of Summers's and strongly supported publication. At the end of March, Ramm informed Schmidt that he had completely revised chapter 7 in light of the criticisms and comments of other members of the group. Meanwhile, I continued to urge Schmidt to reverse his decision and include chapter 7 in the book. Finally, in mid-April, Schmidt reluctantly agreed to do so.

Some bitterness remained. In June, Schmidt wrote me that having reread the portion of chapter 7 devoted to legal theory, he regretted having yielded to the pressure to publish it. He felt that reviews of the book would criticize chapter 7 for the reasons detailed by Summers and ignore the other chapters. Summing up, he said that the whole controversy had left him "badly scarred," and that he took no comfort in knowing that Ramm had "happy feelings of victory." I don't think he and Ramm ever became fully reconciled.

Like our previous volumes, *Discrimination in Employment* did not attract much public attention, although a favorable review by Alice H.

Cook of Cornell University was published in the prestigious *Industrial and Labor Relations Review*. She described the book's objective as "almost a daunting undertaking" but concluded that, on the whole, the six authors had met the challenge and "produced a nearly definitive and well-integrated study of their subjects." She found the volume to be "an extremely useful compendium of facts and practice":

> Differences in national law, definitions, and practice are…clearly explained. A vast number of useful parallels are drawn. The book does not try to evaluate national behavior in handling discrimination nor attempt to measure achievements on some scale of equity. It brings together a wealth of information with which the non-legal as well as the legal scholar in any of these fields will want to familiarize himself. In addition, it achieves an unusually high level of comparability of treatment of the many facets of its topics.[3]

I wish I could report that the Comparative Labor Law Group went out of existence with a triumphant flourish, but the truth is that we limped to the finish battered and bruised and with a sense of disappointment at our failure to accomplish what we had hoped to attain. Nevertheless, I found my experiences with the Comparative Labor Law Group, like those with the Labor Law Group Trust, among the most stimulating and intellectually rewarding of my professional life.

The strongest single conviction produced by my participation in the work of the Comparative Labor Law Group is that our various methods of conducting our research represent a unique and lasting contribution to comparative research. I knew at the start that no one person could learn within a reasonable time, if ever, as much about the system in any other country as was already known by a competent scholar from that country. Hence, we began with the national reports. But preparing a series of national reports is really not comparative research; it may sometimes be essential, but it is never sufficient. Accordingly, we moved to the next step: each member writing on one subject but comparing and contrasting the law and practice in all six countries. This was the real thing, but the time and effort it took—the preparation of dozens of memoranda amounting to hundreds of pages, the time lags between sending an inquiry and receiving

---

[3] *Industrial and Labor Relations Review* 34, no. 1 (1980): 40–41.

an answer (now greatly alleviated by the widespread use of the personal computer and the fax machine)—tended to become frustrating and to build up tensions, which the occasional group meetings did not entirely dispel. Finally, we evolved a method more likely to ensure the optimum results: extensive national reports providing almost all the information needed by the individual authors when they finally begin to write about law and practice in respect of their assigned topics for all of the countries included in the study. It is indeed a pity that our group never got the chance to see how this last method works.

Interruptions in the time available for research proved to be our greatest difficulty. Each one of us had many demands on his time, and many chances to take on interesting new assignments. In some instances this led to a lack of concentration on our project and the failure of individual members of the group to meet agreed-upon deadlines.

Our books tended to be more descriptive than analytical, but the descriptions reflected our perceptions of how the law actually works, as well as of customs and practices that coexist with and affect the operation of common and statutory law. We had hoped that our proposed new project, ultimately abandoned, would put relatively greater stress on analysis than previous studies had done, and would also present some conclusions relating to policy.

I think one reason we avoided making value judgments about the various systems we described was that our respective political and social philosophies were remarkably diverse. Group discussions of the political situation within any one country were always conducted cautiously, even delicately; even so, there were occasional flare-ups.

So far as I am aware, in the period since the Comparative Labor Law Group wound up its work there has been no similar undertaking by any other group of scholars. Smaller groups have worked on comparative labor law projects resulting in a book or symposium, but none has followed our research procedures or continued to work together for so many years. That we were able to do so in spite of our differences in temperament, political views, and work habits, among other things, was due to the remarkable dedication each of us brought to the pursuit of our common goal. Looking back, I wonder how we managed to stay together for 11 years; it was quite a run.

I initiated our project with few theories and even less factual information about the foreign countries included in the study. One working hypothesis with which I began was, as far as I am concerned, conclusively confirmed—namely, that institutional arrangements for the conduct of labor-management relations are products of the unique geographic, demographic, historical, political, economic and social factors within each country; they cannot be transplanted to alien soil.[4] A study of systems that have evolved in other countries, however, like the exploration of outer space, teaches us much about our own country (or world) because it gives us a perspective from which to view it. As a consequence, we ask questions about our own system that would otherwise not have occurred to us.

---

[4]For an elegant and definitive demonstration of this proposition, see Otto Kahn-Freund, "On Uses and Misuses of Comparative Law," Modern *Law Review* 1 (1974): 37.

CHAPTER 14

THE NATIONAL ACADEMY OF ARBITRATORS, 1947–2007

Service as an arbitrator, factfinder, and mediator in labor-management disputes has been an important but relatively small part of my career, but participation in the affairs of the National Academy of Arbitrators (NAA or Academy), of which I am a charter member, has been a major preoccupation of mine since the Academy was established.[1]

The Academy had its founding meeting in September 1947 in Chicago, following two preliminary meetings in Washington, D.C., convened a month earlier by Edgar L. Warren, then Director of the U.S. Conciliation Service.[2] I attended the first of these and was excited, if somewhat overawed, by this opportunity to meet and talk to other arbitrators, all of whom were older and more experienced than I. Although unable to attend the founding meeting in Chicago, I was among the 105 persons designated as charter members, few of whom are still alive.[3]

I was attracted to the Academy primarily because of the purposes set forth in its constitution and bylaws, including the following:

1. To establish and foster the highest standards of integrity, competence, honor and character among those engaged in the arbitration of industrial disputes on a professional basis.

---

[1] For a definitive history of the National Academy of Arbitrators, see Gladys W. Gruenberg, Joyce M. Najita, and Dennis Nolan, *The National Academy of Arbitrators: Fifty Years in the World of Work* (1990). In what follows, I have relied on *Fifty Years* for specific factual details missing from my own files.

[2] The Conciliation Service, an agency within the Department of Labor, was replaced under the Taft-Hartley Act by the Federal Mediation and Conciliation Service, an independent agency.

[3] The group included only one woman, Jean T. McKelvey, a professor at the Cornell University School of Industrial and Labor Relations. Jean was also the first woman elected president of the Academy (1970), and throughout her long life was not only a prominent member of that organization but an influential teacher whose former students, including many women, occupied important positions in unions, business organizations, government agencies, and academic institutions. As a result of her efforts, many women and minorities entered the arbitration field and became members of the Academy.

2. To adopt and encourage the acceptance of and adherence to canons of ethics to govern the conduct of arbitrators.
3. To promote the study and understanding of the arbitration of industrial disputes.

I strongly supported those purposes and have done my best ever since to insure that the Academy continued to uphold them. In my perception, however, and to my profound regret, the membership has lost sight of some of the organization's goals over the years, a matter that I shall discuss in greater detail later.

Although unable to attend the Academy's annual meetings for the first few years following its establishment, I took an active part in the formulation of developing policy issues by means of correspondence with some of my fellow members. One objective I vigorously promoted was to make the annual meetings more like those of academic associations such as the Industrial Relations Research Association, established in 1948. The earlier meetings were mainly social occasions for the small group of arbitrators who attended, although each featured at least one serious paper or address.[4] Along with other academics, I urged that the programs of annual meetings feature the presentation of papers by Academy members and others on topics of interest to those active in the arbitration of labor-management disputes and that these be published in annual proceedings. This transition was accomplished by 1955 with the publication of the proceedings of the eighth annual meeting. Proceedings of all annual meetings since then have been published by the Bureau of National Affairs, and in them may be found some of the best papers ever written on the subject of the arbitration of labor-management disputes. Collectively, the proceedings constitute one of the Academy's major accomplishments.

Another policy in which I took a keen interest concerned eligibility for Academy membership. Among the charter members there was a group favoring stringent admission standards that would have had the effect

---

[4] These are collected in one volume: National Academy of Arbitrators, *The Profession of Labor Arbitration*, ed. J. T. McKelvey (Washington, D.C.: Bureau of National Affairs, 1957), consisting of selected papers from annual meetings in 1948–1954.

of limiting membership to older, well-established white males who were mostly full-time arbitrators. The most vocal proponents of this approach seemed to me to be more interested in suppressing competition than in promoting the objectives of the Academy. A much larger group among the charter members was composed of teachers in a variety of disciplines, including law, economics, political science, and business administration, who were interested in labor arbitration as an avocation, not as a full-time occupation. As noted earlier, after a brief flirtation with the idea of becoming a full-time arbitrator, I had decided to pursue arbitration only on a part-time basis. My sympathies, therefore, were with the larger group favoring more relaxed rules of admission to the Academy, without regard to their race or gender, of arbitrators who did not arbitrate full-time but who met the standards of good character, general acceptability by labor and management, and sufficient experience to demonstrate those qualities.

Another eligibility issue concerned the status of part-time arbitrators who also represented or acted as consultants to labor or management organizations. This group included some well-known arbitrators who had been admitted to membership shortly after the Academy was founded. A majority of members felt that engaging in partisan activity on behalf of either labor or management was incompatible with membership in the Academy. This potentially divisive issue was ultimately resolved by adopting a 1976 constitutional amendment declaring it to be

> inconsistent with continued membership in the Academy (a) for any member... admitted to membership since April 21, 1976, to undertake thereafter to serve partisan interests as advocate or consultant for Labor or Management in labor-management relations or to become associated with or to become a member of a firm which performs such advocate or consultant work; (b) for any member to appear, from and after April 21, 1977, in any partisan role before another Academy member serving as a neutral in a labor-relations arbitration or fact-finding proceeding.

Still another eligibility issue of particular concern primarily to the academic members of the Academy related to some of our colleagues with limited experience as arbitrators who were, nevertheless, recognized as authorities in the field of labor-management relations as a result of their scholarly work. This matter was dealt with in a 1976 policy statement making eligible for membership applicants with limited but current experience in arbitration who have attained "general recognition through scholarly publication or other activities as an important authority on labor-management relations," and who are "of good moral character, as demonstrated by adherence to sound ethical standards in professional activities."

I became active in the administration of the Academy almost from the start, serving as a member of the board of governors from 1948 to 1950 and as vice-president in 1952 and 1953, and chairing the Ethics Committee in 1950 and 1951. In 1962, at the age of 47, I was elected the 14th president of the Academy—the youngest person to hold the position up to that time. Also in 1962, the Academy elected its first president-elect, Sylvester Garrett. During my incumbency, he and I worked closely and harmoniously together. Our job was made considerably easier by the dedicated efforts of David Miller, who served as the Academy's secretary from 1962 to 1967 and as its president in 1974.

Academy presidents had traditionally selected a specific theme for their terms of office. With the agreement of Syl Garrett, I chose a two-year objective: improving the profession by training arbitrators. Prompted by an initiative of the American Bar Association's Section of Labor Relations Law, the Academy, and the principal arbitrator appointing agencies—the American Arbitration Association (AAA) and the Federal Mediation and Conciliation Service (FMCS)—agreed to promote the development of qualified, experienced, and acceptable new arbitrators. It quickly became apparent, however, that I could scarcely have chosen a project less popular among my fellow Academy members, many of whom regarded arbitrator training as a threat to their livelihood. This attitude was reflected in a letter from my close friend, Peter Seitz, to Ralph Seward, the Academy's first president, reading in part:

> With respect to the development of qualified, experienced and acceptable new arbitrators, please record me as saying "nyet." My reasons…are:
>
> One. I distrust young persons….Show me a "new arbitrator" and I will show you a person with his hand in my pocket, claiming my sustenance as his own and robbing my grandchildren of their security.[5]

---

[5] Gruenberg et al., *Fifty Years*, 78.

Seitz's letter, which though humorous in tone had a serious intent, gave voice to the feelings of many Academy members, even if they kept their thoughts to themselves. During his presidency, Garrett continued to emphasize arbitrator training, but he, too, was unsuccessful. A 1964 report by a special committee on the training of new arbitrators found that only a few Academy members had helped increase the supply. Fortunately, by 1967 the special committee was able to report that the previous shortage of professional arbitrators no longer existed, thus ending the uneven struggle within the Academy between altruism and self-interest.

As the Academy thrived and its membership increased, standards of admission, particularly in respect to the minimum number of decisions required before a membership application would be considered, became more stringent. At the same time, the most successful members with large caseloads began to take on assistants and to monitor their progress until they were able to start off on their own, and eventually sponsored their admission. Nevertheless, the early rejection by the Academy of the programs initiated by Garrett and me seems to me, in retrospect, to have been one of the first intimations of the slow but ineluctable transition from an academy of professional arbitrators and scholars pledged to promote the institution of arbitration to an organization on the trade association model devoted principally to enhancing the welfare of its individual members.

In 1962, presidency of the Academy was not nearly so demanding a job as it has since become. During my year in office there were few urgent situations to deal with, but the memory of one, which caused a brief rift in my long friendship with Peter Seitz, remains with me still. The incident arose when President Kennedy nominated Arthur Goldberg to serve on the United States Supreme Court. Despite the Academy's policy of not making political endorsements, Seitz, a close friend and warm admirer of Goldberg, felt impelled to send a telegram to the Senate Judiciary Committee endorsing the nomination on behalf of the Academy. Unable to reach me, he nevertheless signed my name to the telegram. When Peter informed me what he had done, I was furious.

My anger that he had signed my name without my permission was not at all assuaged by Peter's excuse that he had consulted with Ralph Seward, a mutual friend and one of the Academy's most revered figures, before sending the telegram and that Ralph had told him to go ahead. I wrote Peter an uncharacteristically severe letter, saying in part that it was "highly questionable whether the Academy should take any position on matters of this kind... [and it is] improper for the president of the Academy or anyone else to send a supporting telegram without at least consulting the Executive Committee."[6] The Academy's policy against endorsement of political appointments or candidacies has remained, but in subsequent years it did, quite properly in my view, take official positions on proposed statutory regulation of arbitration, and it filed amicus curiae briefs on important issues affecting the practice of arbitration before the Supreme Court.

My presidential term came to an end in January 1963 at the Academy's 16th annual meeting in Chicago. My presidential address was, compared to those given by other presidents before and since, brief, inconsequential, and forgettable. Trying to recall why I passed up this opportunity to expound on some major issues affecting the arbitration process and the Academy's role in it, I think it was because of my feeling that a noon luncheon was not an appropriate time or place for a serious speech. In those days, many of the labor and management representatives attending our meetings, as well as some of our own members, frequently had a few drinks before lunch and were not in the mood for intellectual challenges after a full meal. Having concluded that it would be easier to make my audience laugh instead of think, I deliberately chose the former course, explaining to my listeners that I had "reluctantly rejected all of the current major issues in our common field of interest as being either too big to be dealt with adequately within the time limit available or so controversial that any discussion of them immediately after lunch is likely to 'angry up the blood,' as Satchel Paige would say, and produce a generally dyspeptic reaction." Instead, I described and commented on a few arbitration decisions, none of which involved an issue of great importance

---

[6] Gruenberg et al., *Fifty Years*, 99.

or was particularly memorable, but each of which was "sufficiently out of the ordinary to merit the passing tribute of a laugh." My speech was well received, probably more because of its brevity than because of its content, but at least everyone stayed awake.

My involvement in Academy affairs did not cease when my term as president ended; rather, it intensified. Over the years I have served as chairman or member of a number of standing or special committees, particularly the Ethics Committee and its successor, the Committee on Professional Responsibility and Grievances (CPRG). Before turning to that aspect of my Academy service, however, I want to describe my experience as chairman of the special Committee on Academy Governance (CAG) established by Howard Block during his presidency in 1990.

The CAG was established pursuant to a motion adopted by the NAA Board of Governors in response to many complaints by newer members that the Academy was being governed by a relatively small "elite" and that the views and desires of a majority of NAA members were being ignored. That sentiment was borne out by a questionnaire distributed to 315 newer members in the United States and Canada and reported on by Academy member Bruce Fraser.[7] On the issue of Academy governance, 60 percent of the responses agreed with the statement: "The NAA is under the influence of a small elite group of older members"; only 20 percent disagreed. Forty-five percent agreed with the statement: "The nomination of officers fails to reflect the entire NAA"; only 19 percent disagreed. One of the most outspoken of the disaffected members, writing in the *Chronicle*, the Academy's official news organ, declared that the Academy was an undemocratic institution run by an "Eastern Mafia." It is doubtful that more than a few supported this extreme view, but there was ample evidence of considerable dissatisfaction, not entirely limited to newer members, with the existing governance of the NAA.[8]

---

[7] National Academy of Arbitrators, *Arbitration 1990: New Perspectives on Old Issues: Proceedings of the 43rd Annual Meeting of the National Academy of Arbitrators*, ed. Gladys Gruenberg (Washington, D.C.: BNA, 1990), 285–90.

[8] See also the comments of member Mei L. Bickner, in the chapter titled "New Voices in the Academy," in National Academy of Arbitrators, *Arbitration 1990*, 256–63.

The CAG consisted of eleven members, all but three of whom were senior Academy members.[9] Of the three newer members, two, Jonathan Dworkin and David Petersen, were among the most vocal in expressing their dissatisfaction with the status quo. Only one committee member was a woman. Our first act as a committee was to sponsor an open forum on Academy governance in November 1990 at the NAA's Continuing Education Conference in Dearborn, Michigan. Only 30 members out of the 100 in attendance joined in the discussion, and subsequently only 38 (with some duplication) sent written comments to the committee. In the committee's final report, we expressed disappointment at the low participation level, which we said could be construed as an endorsement of the status quo, a tacit acceptance of the view that "if it ain't broke, don't fix it." But the CAG rejected that interpretation, saying

> Despite the...paucity of comments, a number of thoughtful criticisms and sugges-
> tions were received, indicating some defects in the Academy's system of governance
> and proposing various ways to correct them. We have found some of these criticisms
> to be valid and some suggestions worthy of adoption and have so recommended in
> our report.

Convinced from the start that the *process* of reviewing the governance of the NAA was as important as the substantive recommendations by the CAG, in December 1990 I wrote a letter on behalf of the CAG to all Academy members summarizing the discussion at the November meeting and inviting them to join in the sharing of ideas on the topics raised at that meeting, the principal ones being voting rights, nominations to Academy office and elections, and composition of the board of governors. The letter brought a number of responses, most of them mild in tone; but a few revealed deep resentments about the alleged arrogance and dominance of Academy policies and procedures by the "old guard." Some of the latter indicated a deep suspicion of the CAG itself. One angry letter began, "I am attempting to determine whether the activity you are engaged in is 'damage control' and 'stonewalling' or whether there

---

[9] In addition to me, those serving were John E. Dunsford, Jonathan Dworkin, David E. Feller, Claude H. Foisy, James M. Harkless, David A. Petersen, Lois A. Rappaport, James J. Sherman, James L. Stern, and J. Earl Williams.

is a sincere desire on the part of the hierarchy of the Academy to allow more participation from its members and thereby create a broader base of leadership from its members."

Following receipt of these communications, the CAG met for the first time in July 1991 to consider its recommendations. In anticipation of that meeting, I prepared a proposed discussion outline, emphasizing in my transmittal letter to members of the committee, that the outline was not intended to preclude discussion of other matters but only to insure that we did not overlook those issues raised by our respondents that seemed most important. I also prepared and distributed to CAG members a detailed summary of oral and written criticisms, suggestions, and comments on Academy governance, broken down by topic, and identifying by name and comment each Academy member who had participated in the discussion. All CAG members attended the July meeting and participated actively in the discussion. On 23 July, I sent a first draft of our report to my committee colleagues, conceding in the letter of transmittal that the report might not have truly reflected our consensus on each of the various issues discussed, and encouraging each member of the committee to make any corrections, deletions, or additions he or she deemed appropriate.

The responses to my draft from my fellow CAG members were unanimously favorable, but each one submitted various suggestions or objections. What emerged was a broad consensus on the proposed recommendations, with several members continuing to object to certain recommendations and to the rejection of others they favored. I then prepared a revised draft incorporating a number of language changes suggested by my colleagues, together with some second thoughts of my own, and sent it to the CAG members on 3 October. The final report was sent to the board of governors later that month.

There is no need to present a detailed summary of the discussion of each of the issues covered in the final report.[10] Our conclusions included the following:

---

[10] The full text of the report and recommendations is reprinted in National Academy of Arbitrators, *Arbitration 1992: Improving Arbitral and Advocacy Skills: Proceedings of the 45th Annual Meeting of the*

For those Academy members who favor wholesale and radical changes in our system of governance, this report will be a disappointment. After an extensive review of that system, the CAG concludes that it has, for the most part, served the Academy well. We acknowledge that there is a perception, especially among newer members, that the Academy is governed by an "elite" of older members....Our review, however, convinces us that the present quality of governance is approved by a majority of the membership....Nevertheless, we think that the quality of governance can be improved and the perception of the system can perhaps be altered by adoption of the modest affirmative recommendations we have made....

The nomination process has been the focus of considerable dissatisfaction. Our recommendations are designed to bring about modest changes: increasing the size of the Nominating Committee [from 5 to 7 persons] to make it more representative; limiting the terms of committee members to insure adequate turnover; and publishing criteria for eligibility for Academy office or membership on the Board of Governors, so that everyone will have the necessary information....

So far as we can discern, the sentiment of the Academy membership is rather strongly against contested elections for membership on the Board of Governors and the expansion of the Board to encompass one representative from each [of the 17] region[s]. Our consideration of those proposals has led us to conclude...that neither would improve the quality of Academy governance; rather, each would have a predominantly detrimental effect....To conclude, it is our opinion that the present system of Academy governance is basically sound and effective, and that minor adjustments rather than fundamental changes are what a substantial majority of Academy members desires.

The other major recommendation in the final report concerned appointments to committees—a subject on which a number of NAA members had expressed anger and frustration. In general, the report recommended that each incoming president "should strive, to the greatest extent feasible, to maximize the number of appointments of Academy members indicating a desire to serve." Specifically, the report made the following recommendations:

In exercising discretion the incoming President should adhere to the following policies except when it is clear to the President that the interests of the Academy would best be served otherwise:

(a) No Academy member should be appointed to more than one of [most of] the standing and special committees....

(b) Officers and governors should not be appointed to chair or serve on committees.

National Academy of Arbitrators, ed. Gladys Gruenberg (Washington, D.C.: BNA, 1992), 337–54.

(c) Membership on committees should continue to be limited to three one-year terms except with respect to the chairs of the Future Meeting Arrangements and Professional Responsibility and Grievances Committees [among whom] some reasonable turnover should take place to the extent feasible without suffering losses of accumulated expertise.

The Board of Governors approved the CAG report and directed the preparation of appropriate constitutional amendments, which were adopted by the membership in May 1992.

I received a great many letters complimenting me on my leadership of the CAG. None pleased me more than those from our two "militant" committee members. In response to the draft report, David Petersen wrote in part: "I commend you for having so successfully distilled the numerous issues and arguments to their essence and for having presented them and the Committee's conclusions in such a fair and reasonable manner. We are all in your debt for the fine work you have done on this project." In similar vein, Jonathan Dworkin wrote in part: "Your draft report is outstanding. It demonstrates the commitment and impartiality which have characterized your leadership of the CAG from its beginning....Not only you, but the entire Committee (even those who disagreed with me) were fair and open to dissenting views. Frankly, it made my own initial posture as a true believer a little embarrassing." And to my surprise and delight, Willard Wirtz wrote me to say that although not reading committee reports was "very high among the geriatric perks," he had read ours and was glad he had. It renewed, he said, "my faith that the old standard of both thoughtful, fair-minded deciding and lean, straight-forward expression is only endangered, not extinct."

The final word belonged to Block, whose astuteness in selecting the membership of the CAG contributed so much to its success. In a short note of thanks to members of the committee, he remarked on the favorable reception given our report by the 1992 membership meeting in Atlanta. "As I listened to the brief discussion," he wrote, "it was hard for me to believe those were the same issues that were so controversial at the 1991 San Diego meeting. You have performed an important and valuable service for the Academy and we are all indebted to you."

Heading the CAG was one of my most satisfactory experiences as an Academy member. Our discussion of the various complaints and proposals submitted by the membership, which is largely omitted from this account, proved to be generally persuasive; the process by which we conducted our investigation tuned out to be as important, if not more so, as the recommendations themselves. Moreover, I was extremely fortunate to have had such an outstanding committee to work with. Each member made important contributions to the report, and despite the wide variety in the views expressed we achieved an internal harmony that was particularly gratifying.

I had always been concerned with ethical problems confronting arbitrators, and in the years 1957–1958, when serving as a chairman of the Academy's Ethics Committee, I tended to take a rather hard line. In 1958, for example, the committee was asked to rule on the propriety of an arbitrator's "loquacious letterhead," which listed a variety of affiliations. Despite the advice of Academy secretary Bert Luskin that "the general consensus…was that the practice of listing one's affiliations on a letterhead was an exhibition of poor taste; it…should be 'frowned upon'; but I do not recall that anyone at any time held that it is a violation of the code of Ethics,"[11] my report to the board of governors, reflecting the judgment of the Ethics Committee, concluded that the letterhead in question was advertising in violation of Canon E, Part I, of the Code of Ethics and Procedural Standards for Labor-Management Arbitration approved in 1951 by the AAA, the Academy, and the FMCS. Also in 1958, I interpreted Canon 8 of the 1951 Code of Ethics as prohibiting an arbitrator from publishing an award without the parties' approval. My report to the board of governors recommended that "the [ethics] committee ought not to wait for questions or complaints to be referred to it but should on its own motion study and report on known or suspected problems." During my presidency, I appointed a special committee headed by Eli Rock to study code enforcement procedure. The charge to the committee set forth the problem as I saw it:

---

[11] Gruenberg et al., *Fifty Years*, 49.

Clearly the membership wants some kind of Grievance Committee established. Everyone is aware, however, that great care must be exercised in establishing machinery which will not only be effective but which will provide due process to all persons against whom grievances are lodged and will protect the Academy, its officers, and its individual members from liability arising out of the filing or disposition of grievances.[12]

The special committee's recommendation to create a new Ethics and Grievance Committee was adopted by the Academy in 1965.

Those earlier concerns with ethical problems continued after my presidency. There was a growing conviction among Academy members that the 1951 code needed substantial revision in order to deal with new problems facing arbitrators. Such a revision was formally proposed by President Gerald Barrett in 1972. He asked William E. Simkin, a founding member of the Academy, a past president, and the first chairman of the Ethics Committee, to lead the revision process. Simkin and the other members of his committee[13] prepared numerous drafts of a proposed new Code of Professional Responsibility for Arbitrators of Labor-Management Disputes. Debate over the document was the sole subject at the business session of the Academy's 1974 annual meeting. The meeting lasted all day and ended with a referral back to the committee. The draft under consideration consisted of two major parts: the first included the norms of the current code; the second, characterized by Simkin as an "Addendum," included detailed rules about arbitration practices such as the time of the hearing, amount of notice to be given, the taking of evidence, and the use of verbatim transcripts and briefs. The debate was vigorous, concentrating primarily on the addendum, thought by most members to be too intrusive in respect of the exercise by arbitrators of their judgment about the conduct of the hearing. Participating in this debate, I drew a distinction between practices which a majority of Academy members believed to be wrong and those concerning which there was a wide divergence of opinion. Matters of style or taste, I argued, need not necessarily

[12] Gruenberg et al., *Fifty Years*, 108.
[13] Frederick H. Bollen and Donald B. Straus, representing the American Arbitration Association; Lawrence B. Babcock Jr. and L. Lawrence Shultz, representing the Federal Mediation and Conciliation Service; and Sylvester Garrett and Ralph T. Seward, representing the Academy.

constitute violations of professional responsibility. My lengthy written comments submitted subsequently urged that there should be no effort to draw up a list of "shalt nots," but that arbitrators should be required to disclose to appointing agencies their per diem fees, charges for study time, postponements, cancellations, travel, and use of part-time assistants, so that parties would know what to expect. Taking heed of these and similar suggestions from other Academy members, Simkin agreed to drop the addendum and replace it with a disclosure section.

The new code, adopted by an overwhelming majority at the Academy's 1975 annual meeting, declared that the essential personal qualifications of an arbitrator "include honesty, integrity, impartiality and general competency in labor relations matters." It also specified a number of affirmative obligations, including one relating to disclosure of labor-management relationships at the time of appointment:

> [A]n arbitrator must disclose directly or through the administrative agency involved [e.g., the AAA or the FMCS] any current or past managerial, representational, or consultative relationship with any company or union involved....Disclosure must also be made of any pertinent pecuniary interest.

A key provision of the new code dealt with advertising and solicitation:

> An arbitrator must not advertise or solicit arbitration assignments.
> a. For purposes of this standard, advertising shall not include:
>   (1) providing accurate, objectively verifiable biographical information (including fees and expenses) for inclusion in administrative agency arbitration rosters, dispute resolution directories, and
>   (2) providing name, address, phone numbers and identification as an arbitrator in telephone directories, change of address and/or change of services offered announcements.
> b. Information provided under paragraph a. may not include editorial or adjectival comments concerning the arbitrator's qualifications.
> c. It is a matter of personal preference whether an arbitrator includes "Labor Arbitrator" or similar titles on professional letterheads, cards and announcements.
> d. Solicitation, as prohibited by this section, includes the making of requests for arbitration work through personal contacts with individual parties, orally or in writing.

To the best of my recollection, the debate preceding the adoption of this provision concentrated on paragraphs (a)(1) and (2) and (b). No serious objection was raised to the outright prohibition of advertising or solicitation.

From 1972 to 1991, I served as a member of CPRG (the successor to the Ethics and Grievance Committee). Throughout that period, issues concerning the interpretation and application of the code prohibitions against advertising and solicitation frequently arose. Among those made the subject of advisory opinions were the following:

Advisory Opinion No. 5 (1979) related to the unilateral interviewing of arbitrators by labor or management, and read in part:

> The Committee believes it is not consonant with "the dignity and integrity of the office" for an arbitrator to seek an interview with a potential client party, alone, particularly where the announced purpose of the interview is to be considered for selection in future cases.... The appropriate choice of conduct for an arbitrator invited to such an interview is to decline.

Advisory Opinion No. 14 (1986) condemned as a clear violation of the ban against solicitation an arbitrator's letter to labor and management representatives throughout the country stating:

> I am writing to introduce myself to you and to advise you that I am interested in expanding my labor arbitration practice in your area. My experience in this field now spans more than a decade, and I am anxious to communicate my availability to parties in diverse regions of America. Enclosed…is my biographical sketch.

Advisory Opinion No. 16 (1987) declared that an attorney-arbitrator who sent a printed announcement of the relocation of his law office to members of the local bar association, to attorneys practicing labor law in his state, and to unions throughout the state, not all of whom had used his professional services, and who included in the announcement, among other things, a statement of "availability" to accept disputes in many areas, using the "techniques of Arbitration, Expedited Arbitration, Mediation/Conciliation, Med/Arb. Fact Finding, Training Programs and Expert Witness," violated the ban against solicitation.

Advisory Opinion No. 19 (1989) involved an arbitrator who purchased a quantity of ballpoint pens imprinted with his name and new business address. During all subsequent hearings he handed a pen to each of the parties' representatives with instructions to deliver their briefs and other communications to him at the address indicated on the pen. He also gave pens to others at the hearing as souvenirs. The CPRG concluded that the arbitrator had violated the code's provision against advertising and solicitation. Although declaring there was nothing improper in an arbitrator's handing out business cards with his new address at a hearing, it pointed out that the ballpoint pens:

> also constitute a useful writing tool which, to the extent it was thereafter used, would serve as a continuing reminder of the arbitrator's availability. Those characteristics convert the pens into a form of advertising or solicitation prohibited by [the code].

Finally, Advisory Opinion No. 21 (1991) involved a hypothetical situation in which an arbitrator sent letters to the subsidiaries of a national corporation in several states and to the union with which they had bargaining relations, offering his services as a mediator in resolving negotiations or grievance impasses. His letterhead described him as a mediator, and the letters described the function of a mediator as not being that of an arbitrator. The letters also enclosed an extensive curriculum vitae briefly describing the arbitrator's mediation experience but also listing at much greater length his experience as an arbitrator. Among the numerous professional societies he listed were the Academy and the AAA. The CPRG ruled that on those hypothetical facts the letter would constitute a violation of the code. After noting that the code does not apply to mediation activities, the CPRG restated rulings made in previous advisory opinions that solicitation of arbitration assignments may violate the code even if it is not explicit. It concluded that, if a communication nominally seeking employment only as a mediator could reasonably be construed as an indirect suggestion of availability of the writer for arbitration assignments, there would be a violation of the code.

These advisory opinions emphasize that, at least until the early 1990s, the CPRG, reflecting the dominant feeling of the Academy membership, upheld a strict interpretation of the code provisions against advertising and solicitation. The mood of the membership, however, was gradually undergoing a profound change, due in substantial part to external factors referred to later.

The Achilles heel of the code ban of advertising and solicitation was the difficulty of enforcing it. Under the Academy's bylaws, a written charge by a member or "any affected person" that a member had violated any provision of the code was handled under a four-step and very time-consuming procedure designed to afford the charged member ("CM" in CPRG parlance) a panoply of due process rights. Briefly summarized, this procedure required an investigation by the CPRG chairman or his designee, "using an informal and conciliatory approach where appropriate," and then a written report by the chairman, after consultation with two other CPRG members, finding that probable cause for the charge had or had not been established.[14] Upon a finding of probable cause, the chairman was to appoint a hearing officer from among the members of the CPRG to continue the investigation of the charge based on written responses by the CM to the charge and, following an informal hearing to resolve disputed issues of fact, at which both the complainant and the charged member would appear, to file a written report stating his conclusions. The hearing officer's decision either to discipline the offending member or to dismiss the charge was final unless appealed. By an amendment to the bylaws adopted in May 1991, any appeal was to be heard by a tribunal consisting of three Academy members appointed by the Academy president with the consent of the board of governors. The tribunal was to review all material pertinent to the charge and decide whether to uphold the dismissal of the complaint or the discipline imposed based on the appellate record and not on a de novo proceeding. The hearing officer's findings of fact were to be deemed final if supported by substantial evidence. Determination of a code violation had to be supported by "clear and convincing evidence." The decision of the tribunal was final. The rules established by the Academy's board of governors provided that discipline for a code violation could be advice, censure, suspension, or expulsion. If no more than advice or censure was directed, only the CM and the complainant were so advised. Under an additional bylaw amendment of May 1992, if suspension or expulsion were found to be appropriate, notice of the action was to be given to the

---

[14]CPRG chairmen were among the oldest and most experienced members of the Academy. Despite the growing number of female Academy members, none has ever served as chairman of the CPRG.

offending member, the complainant, and the executive secretary-treasurer of the Academy, who was to inform the NAA membership of the name of the offending member, the nature of the offense committed, and the discipline imposed.

Both the complainant and the CM were entitled to be represented by a person of their choice at all stages of the procedure, and the CM could terminate the procedure at any time by resigning from Academy membership. If the case proceeded through all stages of the procedure, the minimum time consumed would be at least 165 days.

These elaborate procedures were seldom, if ever, tested to the full. To begin with, although members of the CPRG increasingly received informal reports of conduct which, if proved, clearly violated the code, the requisite formal written charges were rarely filed. Those that were commonly involved excessive and inexcusable delays by arbitrators in delivering their awards to the parties—in some instances, not until years after the case had been heard. In most of those, the offending arbitrators, including some eminent members of the Academy and at least one past president, admitted culpability and apologized to the parties, after which the charges were dropped. In others, the arbitrator, unable to cope with personal problems (sometimes involving alcoholism, an occupational hazard for arbitrators spending large amounts of time alone and away from home), simply resigned. What particularly disturbed at least some members of the CPRG were reports of dishonest conduct by a few Academy members, such as hearing two cases involving different parties in one day and charging each set of parties for a full day of hearing, or openly soliciting cases.

For some time I had urged a change in the Academy's bylaws to permit the CPRG to investigate reports of arbitral conduct in violation of the code even in the absence of a formal charge. In one case that arose after my term as a member of the CPRG had expired, I was so angered by the behavior of the arbitrator reported in the *New York Times*, that I wrote to the then chairman of the committee calling his attention to the case and volunteering to file a charge against the offending Academy member. In the end, this proved unnecessary because the arbitrator announced his retirement and subsequently resigned from the Academy. In any case, my view did not prevail, and the requirement of a written charge of a code violation by an NAA member or any "affected person" remained unchanged.

Prior to 1988, not a single member of the Academy had been suspended or expelled for violations of the code, although some admittedly guilty of such offenses had resigned and charges against others had been withdrawn by the complainants upon receipt of apologies by the offending arbitrators. It fell to my unhappy lot to be designated as a CPRG hearing officer in the first case resulting in suspension of the CM.

The case came to the CPRG's attention in mid-March 1987, when an employer and union jointly notified the Academy and several other organizations that the CM had not rendered a decision in a case he had heard in July 1985 and in which briefs had been filed in November 1985, and that he had not acknowledged their repeated calls and letters concerning the status of the case. On 5 April 1987, the CM submitted his award to the parties but without an explanatory opinion, which he promised to send within two weeks. He failed to do so. In early June, Arthur Stark, the long-serving and greatly respected chairman of the CPRG, asked the CM for an explanation of the 17-month delay in rendering his decision. In July, the CM wrote to Stark describing a series of serious family problems but conceding that they did not excuse the delay. He concluded his letter by saying, "I am prepared to accept whatever action the Academy may wish to take in this matter." By January 1988, the CM had still not submitted the promised opinion explaining his award to the parties, who deemed it essential to an understanding of the employer's obligation to recall certain employees from layoff. The CM had also failed to respond to the parties' calls in June and July 1987. Stark then consulted with two CPRG members, who concurred that a hearing officer should be appointed.

On 18 January 1988, after inquiring of me whether there was any possible reason why I should reject the appointment (I could think of none), Stark appointed me hearing officer. He also advised the CM that he had found probable cause to proceed further with the charge of code violations and that he had appointed a hearing officer. I approached my assignment gingerly, hoping to work out some accommodation between the CM and the charging parties. Unable to reach the CM by telephone, I wrote to him in February 1988 suggesting that we get together for an informal chat. A week later the CM replied, again admitting the facts asserted in the charge and stating that he had no intention of contesting or appealing against any punishment the Academy felt appropriate, including his resignation. In addition, he waived "any and all" rights to which he was entitled under the constitution and bylaws of the Academy in connection with this matter.

With the case in this posture, I had no alternative but to prepare and submit my report. After setting forth the relevant facts, all of which had been confirmed by the CM, I cited the applicable code provision (Part 2 J 3):

> Once the case record has been closed, an arbitrator must adhere to the time limits for an award, as stipulated in the labor agreement or as provided by regulation of an administrative agency or as otherwise agreed.
>
> a. If an appropriate award cannot be rendered within the required time, it is incumbent on the arbitrator to seek an extension of time from the parties.

Noting that there were extenuating circumstances in this case, I pointed out that had the CM explained his predicament to the complaining parties in a timely fashion, some accommodation might have been arranged. The vice of the CM's behavior, in my view, was his failure to acknowledge or reply to the calls and letters he received during the approximately 16 months that elapsed between the submission of briefs and the issuance of his award. Moreover, the CM's letter of apology accompanying the award dated 25 March 1987 came much too late, and although he promised an opinion within two weeks, the CM not only did not deliver it but once again failed to respond to calls and letters from the complaining parties. He also admitted handling other cases during this period. On the basis of these facts I concluded:

> The [CM's] Code violation is a serious one. The complaining parties have been put to great inconvenience, and relations between them have suffered because of his neglect of duty. Although sympathizing with the [CM's] personal problems, the undersigned cannot condone his failure to meet his elementary responsibilities in this matter. A penalty of greater severity than advice or censure is clearly required if more than lip service is to be given to the Code.

As required by the procedure outlined in the bylaws, I had consulted with two past presidents of the Academy before arriving at my decision. Both of them concurred in my decision, which was to suspend the CM for one calendar year, provided that if the promised opinion was not delivered to the parties within 30 days, the suspension would automatically be converted to expulsion.

In late February 1988, Stark submitted a copy of my report to the CM. On 1 April, the CM wrote to Stark advising that he had that day sent his opinion to the charging parties with an apology, and acknowledging receipt of my report. He reiterated that he had no intention of appealing from my decision and again expressed his thanks to Stark and me for our "compassion" and "courtesy."

The Academy's bylaws did not specify what a suspension entailed. Asked by Stark for my opinion, I suggested in a letter dated 15 April the following:

1. Removal of the member's name from the Academy directory and mailing list.
2. No use by the member of the Academy's name for purposes of identification.
3. No attendance by the member at national or regional Academy meetings for members only.
4. No service by the member on Academy committees.
5. Notification to appointing agencies that the member has been suspended, with the request that reference to Academy membership be omitted from his biography for the period of the suspension.

In early May, Stark informed Academy president Arvid Anderson of the situation and suggested that the CM be given another 30 days to appeal from his suspension, as recommended by the hearing officer, if he so desired. Permission to do so was granted and the CM was duly notified. Later in May he informed Stark that he accepted the ruling regarding the suspension. He was also informed that the AAA and the FMCS would be notified of the suspension.

The Academy's bylaws provided that once a decision had been rendered to suspend or expel an offending member, "notice of the action shall be given to the offending member, to the complainant or complainants, to the membership of the Academy, and to such others and in such form as will best serve the interests of the Academy." As to this provision, I commented: "The purpose of advising the membership is educational; it is not to punish or humiliate the offending member, for whom the suspension is sufficient punishment. Therefore, I favor not revealing the name of the member. On the other hand, I think the offense should be described in sufficient detail to explain why the suspension has been imposed."[15]

In June 1988, the Academy's secretary-treasurer, Dallas Jones, informed all Academy members of the suspension of the CM, without revealing his name. His memorandum summarized and quoted from my report, and explained that the suspension involved the five conditions outlined in my earlier letter to Stark. The announcement provoked very little response from the membership, but one member did raise a number of procedural objections. He challenged, among other things, the revelation of the suspended member's name to the AAA and the FMCS, which he correctly asserted was not specifically authorized by the Academy's bylaws; the failure of the CPRG to appoint a hearing officer from outside the CM's region; and the refusal of the hearing officer to disqualify himself because he was acquainted with the CM.

At the May 1990 meeting of the board of governors, Stark submitted a report responding to these and related criticisms. In respect of the charge that the bylaws did not authorize an appeal extension of any kind and did not allow for the involvement of CPRG or the board of governors in the disciplinary process following the appointment of a hearing officer, he conceded that the criticism was "technically accurate," but he asked,

> was justice and due process served or denied? The omission of a definition of suspension would clearly have rendered the decision meaningless in this first NAA suspension case. That omission was quickly discovered and bases were touched in order to insure that the CM's due process rights were protected.

---

[15] In 1992, the bylaw provision in question was amended to read: "the Executive Secretary-Treasurer...will advise the membership...of the name of the member disciplined, the nature of the offense committed, and the discipline imposed."

Regarding the proposal that no hearing officer should be from the same region as the CM or be personally acquainted with him or her, Stark reported that the CPRG agreed that in some cases this might be desirable, but that it should not be converted into an inflexible rule. For example, "a regional member may be more sensitive to the nuances of local practices and expectations of both arbitrators and parties. This might be of particular importance in fashioning an appropriate disciplinary penalty." In the CPRG's view, disqualification of a hearing officer "should depend upon the nature and depth of the acquaintanceship [with the CM], the mature judgment of the prospective hearing officer as to his or her capacity to be fair, as well as the positions, if any, of the [CM] and the charging parties as to that capacity."

Stark's report then turned to the claim that the bylaws did not authorize the hearing officer to define "suspension" to include notification of the suspension to the AAA, FMCS, or any government agency having jurisdiction to appoint arbitrators. This argument was based on the fact that although a provision in a previous bylaw had authorized such action only in expulsion cases, the present bylaw failed to specify such notification even in expulsion cases. The CPRG, on the other hand, had decided that a definition of "suspension" should not be included in the bylaws but should be defined by the hearing officer on a case by case basis, with a review by the tribunal when such was requested. The omission of agency notification, therefore, was deliberate and not intended to eliminate that factor. The board of governors accepted the CPRG's report, thereby bringing this case to a close.

Far more serious problems than the Academy's disciplinary procedures emerged in the 1990s and continued into the 21st century. They were given impetus by several fundamental changes in the employment environment in this country; I shall mention only two.

The first of these was the continuing decline, dating back to the 1970s, of labor union membership. By the year 2000, the number of unionized wage and salary workers had been reduced to less than 10 percent of the labor force. Today, most of the unorganized workers in the private sector are employed under individual contracts at will, pursuant to which they may be dismissed by their employers at any time for any reason or no reason. Despite the advantages employers enjoy in dealing with their unorganized employees, many have come to recognize a need to provide employees protection against arbitrary treatment, especially discipline and dismissal. This recognition is not purely altruistic; rather, it reflects a prudential policy to avoid large damage verdicts in successful court cases brought by employees alleging violation of one or another of numerous federal and state statutes establishing protection against various forms of employment discrimination.

The second major change was the rapid growth of grievance and arbitration procedures unilaterally initiated by employers to deal with labor disputes.[16] The early employer-promulgated arbitration plans tended to include certain common characteristics. Employees were not consulted prior to institution of the plan, nor were they given any voice in the selection of the arbitrator. Grievants were not permitted to select representatives of their own choosing in arbitration proceedings but were limited in their choice to fellow employees or members of management. Grievants were also denied access to relevant information in the possession of the employer. Limitations were placed on the remedial powers of the arbitrator. Finally, the arbitrator's fee and expenses were commonly paid solely by the employer, thus creating a suspicion, whether well-founded or not, that the arbitrator would be favorably disposed to the employer's view of the case. Because of the obvious unfairness of such arbitration procedures, most reputable arbitrators refused to participate.

Employers were not slow to react. A new generation of unilaterally promulgated arbitration plans reveals a greater sophistication and an effort to eliminate the more egregious features in earlier plans that provoked the most criticism. Thus, many of the new procedures permit the individual grievant to participate in the selection of the arbitrator, although the pool from which such selection may be made still frequently remains in the exclusive control of the employer. Also, some employers now permit the

---

[16] The term "employment arbitration" is applied to employers' unilaterally imposed procedures applicable to their unorganized employees to distinguish it from labor-management arbitration between employers and unions representing their employees.

354 NATIONAL ACADEMY OF ARBITRATORS

grievant to be represented by anyone of his or her own choosing, including an outside attorney. On the other hand, employer plans increasingly stipulate, as a condition of employment, that employees agree that any employment dispute, including one based on alleged violations of statutory rights, be resolved exclusively by private arbitration. Such contracts were held to be enforceable by the United States Supreme Court in a landmark decision handed down in 1991.[17] The result was an immediate increase in such mandatory agreements and a greater willingness by many arbitrators to serve under them. At the same time, the exact language of such agreements, as well as of the conditions under which they were executed, came under more intense scrutiny. Efforts have been made to develop a consensus among all parties involved about what minimal requirements are necessary to protect the legitimate interests of individual employees. In 1995, a group of public and private organizations, including the NAA, announced agreement on a "due process protocol," which sets forth standards covering such matters as the employee's rights of representation and discovery, the training, selection, and compensation of arbitrators and mediators, the nature of the arbitrator's authority, and the scope of judicial review. Adherence to the protocol, however, is purely voluntary.

The due process protocol is unquestionably an important step in protecting the legitimate interests of unorganized employees in the employment arbitration process, but it has serious weaknesses. For one thing, it is voluntary and is applicable only to the relatively small number of employers who have so far agreed to adhere to its terms. If an employer accepts the protocol and subsequently violates its terms, his employees' ability to obtain specific performance or damages is very unlikely. Moreover, the organizations that drew up and subscribed to the protocol could not agree on whether the agreement to arbitrate should apply to all disputes in advance, or should not be effectuated until a specific dispute arises.[18] I am unaware of any employer who has accepted the latter alter-

---

[17] *Gilmer v. Interstate/Johnson Lane*, 500 U.S. 20 (1991).

[18] The National Academy of Arbitrators, the Labor and Employment Section of the American Bar Association, the Society of Professionals in Dispute Resolution, the American Bar Association, the Federal Mediation and Conciliation Service, the American Civil Liberties Union's Workplace Rights Project, and a lawyers' group representing plaintiffs.

native. Indeed, most employers who have unilaterally established an arbitration procedure for their unorganized employees insist that each employee accept, as a condition of employment, that every unresolved grievance, whatever the basis for it, be submitted to arbitration and that the right to seek redress in court for violation even of statutory rights be specifically waived. This requirement, although usually enforced by the courts, seems to me to be outrageous, in that it substitutes a contract of adhesion for a voluntary choice.

The Code of Professional Responsibility for Arbitrators of Labor-Management Disputes, which is binding on all members of the Academy, is by its terms not applicable to arbitrators engaged in the practice of employment arbitration. For most of its existence, the Academy's membership consisted exclusively of labor-management arbitrators, but in recent years, a growing number of its members have engaged in employment arbitration as well. This has put them in competition with nonmembers of the Academy whose practice is entirely devoted to employment arbitration. Arbitrators not bound by the code engage, often extensively, in advertising their services, and some openly solicit business. As a result, NAA employment arbitrators brought increasing pressure on the Academy to amend the code's outright ban against advertising and solicitation. Their efforts ultimately proved successful. Advisory Opinion No. 18 (1988) declared that purchased listings in publications such as Yellow Pages and sending change of address announcements to persons other than those with whom the arbitrator has worked, were held to be violations of the advertising-soliciting ban; that prohibition was abandoned in 1996. Also in 1996, the Academy membership approved the so-called website amendment to the code. This amendment permits an arbitrator to include on his or her website (1) references to or the texts of arbitration awards that are publishable; and (2) references to the texts of published writings, including the means of accessing them through site links; references to panel memberships; and the names of employers and unions who have used the arbitrator's services.[19] Finally, in 2001, after

---

[19] Another code provision declares it to be a violation of professional responsibility for an arbitrator to publish an award without the consent of the parties involved.

protracted debate, the Academy membership adopted an amendment to the code providing: "An arbitrator shall not engage in false or misleading advertising." The use of the qualifying words, "False or misleading," thus removed the ban against "advertising," *per se.* The amendment was subsequently approved by the AAA and FMCS.

Academy membership and active participation in its affairs had always been a source of deep satisfaction for me. The papers delivered and the discussion of their topics, particularly in the early years, were intellectually exciting. In later years, amicus curiae briefs filed by the Academy in important Supreme Court cases influenced the development of labor law in ways beneficial to a wide segment of the public. And individual Academy members, through their speeches and journal articles, not only contributed to the developing labor law but also enhanced the reputation of our organization. Equally important were the friendships established with many of my fellow members. In recent years, however, I had become increasingly disturbed by changes in the internal culture of the Academy. Some of those changes were the natural result of the growing number of members who engaged in full-time arbitration and, of necessity, had a greater concern about obtaining and keeping new clients than did the dwindling number of part-time arbitrators. Some of the newer members seemed chiefly interested in being admitted to the Academy; once that was accomplished, they showed little interest in its activities, and rarely, if ever, attended its national or regional meetings. When they did show up, it was to urge that the Academy devote greater efforts to promote the financial welfare of its members. Discussions over the Academy's e-mail network tended increasingly to concentrate on complaints about the way the AAA and the FMCS composed the panels of arbitrators requested by employers and unions, fee practices, and various aspects of office management. It seemed to me and to some of my colleagues that what a growing number of members wanted was an efficient trade association, rather than an organization formed in part, in the words of the Academy's constitution, "to establish and foster the highest standards of integrity, competence, honor, and character among those engaged in the arbitration of labor-management disputes on a professional basis." As far as I was concerned, the drive to remove the outright ban on advertising, if successful, would constitute a betrayal of the founding principles of the Academy. Accordingly, I joined my close friends Howard Block, Richard Mittenthal, and Rolf Valtin, all former presidents of the Academy, in a last-ditch campaign to defeat the proposed code amendment.

We knew that the odds were overwhelmingly against us. The momentum was all with those favoring the proposed amendment. Moreover, serious questions had been raised about the existing ban on the grounds, among others, that it violated constitutional rights of free speech and the antitrust laws. Although we considered those possibilities, we ended up dismissing them as ill founded and unrealistic. After much discussion among ourselves and with a number of other like-minded Academy members, we prepared and circulated among the entire membership a lengthy statement in opposition to the proposed amendment, from which I quote only the concluding paragraph:

> In summary, we are against the proposed amendment because we believe that the present ban on advertising is an affirmation of the most cherished values of the Academy; that the ban does not violate constitutional or statutory rights; that comparisons between our members and other professionals who advertise are inappropriate and inapposite; and that any further retreat from our policy against advertising would be a betrayal of the principles on which the Academy was founded and would lead ineluctably to a diminution in the dignity of our calling and in the high regard with which members are presently held by the parties who employ them. Finally, given the long history of the advertising prohibition and the ability of individuals with a wide variety of backgrounds to gain acceptability as arbitrators of labor-management disputes, the burden of demonstrating how the present ban has been harmful rests with the advocates of the proposed change. So far, they have failed to meet it.

Our statement was endorsed by only 39 other members of the Academy.

The problem raised by the presence in the Academy of members who handled both labor-management and employment arbitration cases was an extremely painful one. That group included some of our older members, good friends who had also participated actively in Academy affairs. If the amendment were defeated, how could we reconcile their practice of advertising their availability for employment-arbitration cases with the ban applicable to their fellow-members who engaged exclusively in labor-management arbitration? My personal conclusion was that the only solution was to compel members who engaged in employment arbitration to make a difficult choice: either refrain from any advertising or solicitation or resign from the Academy.

When the matter finally came to a vote at the 54th annual meeting of the Academy in Atlanta in 2001, it was apparent that the repeal of the advertising ban would pass by a substantial vote. A number of good friends whose views I respected spoke in favor of the amendment, but the principal impetus for the drive to repeal the advertising ban seemed to come from a large group of Academy members who had begun to arbitrate employment disputes. Typically, most of them did not participate in the debate on the question, other than to demand an immediate vote on the issue. Still, my colleagues and I spoke out against the amendment, concentrating on the undesirable self-promotional activities that would almost certainly come into play once the ban was lifted. Among other things, we stressed that the language of the proposed amendment—"An arbitrator shall not engage in false or misleading advertising"—opened the way for out-and-out solicitation. Reporting on our inevitable defeat in an e-mail message to one of our supporters who had been unable to attend the meeting, I gave the following brief summary of the floor debate:

> I regret to report that the proposed advertising amendment was adopted by a large margin. The issue was fully debated and everyone who wanted to speak was allowed to do so. The chief argument relied upon by the proponents was that the present ban is unenforceable, largely because even those reporting violations are unwilling to file formal written complaints with the CPRG, without which the CPRG is powerless to investigate. A number of the proponents (mostly arbitrators of employment disputes) simply said that everyone else doing that kind of work is advertising and that they are compelled to do the same in order successfully to compete for cases. Others simply wanted to get rid of the issue and, knowing that they had the votes, kept insisting that we approve the proposed amendment and be done with it. Some of the opponents argued that the proposed "false or misleading" limitation on advertising is too vague and needs elaboration. A motion...to send back the proposed amendment to the CPRG with instructions to prepare a set of guidelines or what constitutes false and misleading advertising and solicitation was defeated. Howard, Dick, Rolf, and I all spoke against the proposed amendment...and so did a number of the older

members, including other past presidents. Indeed, the vote seemed to split along generational lines, with most of the newer members voting for the proposed amendment. Of course I'm disappointed, although not surprised, by the outcome, but none of us who led the fight against removing the ban on advertising regrets the time and effort we spent in doing so. Now all of us who opposed advertising must band together to see that the limitations that remain, inadequate though they may be, are strictly enforced.

A few months later, Alex Elson, the oldest member of the Academy, a charter member, and an arbitrator revered for his rectitude and integrity, wrote to the chairman of the CPRG (a post he had once held) expressing his reactions to the decision taken at the Atlanta meeting. He sent me a copy, which read in part:

> I came away from the Atlanta meeting with a sense of unease about the action taken, partly because there was such a sharp division, with approximately one-third of the members, including most of the past-presidents, and others with a history of distinguished services and leadership in the Academy unhappy with the results, and partly because of a growing conviction that the Academy, acting for the AAA and the FMCS, and therefore as a practical matter for most of the arbitration profession, fell short of its reputation for excellence in standard setting for the profession.

As early as 1994, Alex had called for lifting the ban on advertising "because it served as an entry barrier to aspiring new arbitrators." He believed that the rule should be revised, but should be "narrowly tailored to allow a free flow of information about arbitrators to the parties, subject to clearly enunciated restrictions on untruthful or misleading communications, subjective judgments by the arbitrator or others about the arbitrator's abilities or how he is likely to rule, and communications addressed only to one of the parties." He also favored as part of the revised rule "an unequivocal aspirational standard, a goal for all arbitrators—the avoidance of self-promotional or glorification material."

Elson's objection to the new rule banning only false or misleading advertising was that it overlooked conduct that might "seriously reflect adversely on the arbitration profession." With the lifting of the advertising ban, he reasoned, the CPRG could now take the time to fashion standards permitting advertising but with safeguards tailored to the needs and character of labor arbitration. He stressed the need to protect "the most important aspect of arbitration—maintenance of impartiality, an issue not addressed by the present rule." Alex also cautioned against permitting self-promotion reflecting adversely on the arbitrator's role as impartial judge, such as buying advertising in a union newspaper or an employer's trade journal—now permissible under the new rule. He included in the same category advertising implying how an arbitrator may rule or which makes known that the arbitrator will allow punitive damages or other special remedies. Expressing confidence that Academy members would not likely engage in such practices (a confidence which I, unhappily, did not share), he pointed out that the code is intended to govern all labor-management arbitrators, not just Academy members.

Finally, Elson declared himself "appalled by the excesses in advertising by lawyers." He conceded that the Academy could not bar self-glorifica-tion material so long as it is not false or misleading, but he thought that "we can say affirmatively that, in the interest of protecting the public face of the profession, arbitrators who advertise should do so in a dignified manner consistent with their quasi-judicial status and should exercise self-restraint and avoid excessive self-promotion."

Much as I admired Elson, I could not agree with his basic premise that the advertising ban should be lifted "because it served as an entry barrier to aspiring new arbitrators." The entry barrier, if such it was, was not to the practice of arbitration, but only to admission to the NAA. I saw no reason why the Academy, a private association, could not insist that those wishing to join comply with all provisions of the code. I did share his misgivings about the failure of the revised ban to indicate the types of advertising which, if approved by implication, demean the practice of arbitration and compromise the reputation of arbitrators for fairness and impartiality. But I could not accept his assumption that Academy members were unlikely to engage in just such conduct; indeed, there was some solid evidence to the contrary.

The problem was that the Academy had consistently failed to enforce its rules. It had, to be sure, suspended a few members for such offenses as failing, without a satisfactory excuse, to render an award within a reason-able time. But this discipline had been imposed only when one or both parties to the dispute had filed a formal complaint with the CPRG. Unless and until the CPRG was given authority to investigate instances of alleged misconduct by arbitrators and to initiate formal complaints on its own motion, there was really no chance of developing an effective enforcement program. Even more unlikely was the prospect of gaining membership support for the kinds of glosses on the new rule suggested by Elson.

The 2001 revision of the code provision against advertising left opponents of the revision with the cold comfort that at least the ban on solicitation of arbitration assignments ("Solicitation, as prohibited by this section, includes the making of requests for arbitration work through personal contacts with individual parties, orally or in writing") remained intact. But even this small consolation was soon to be destroyed. In 2001, the Federal Trade Commission initiated an investigation of the Academy. The reason it decided to do so remains a mystery. The Academy is a relatively small organization of about 600 members. Why it became the object of the FTC's interest during a period when possible restraints of trade were being engaged in by a number of giant corporations is hard to imagine. Perhaps it acted on the complaints of individual arbitrators, some of whom may even have been Academy members, or perhaps FTC lawyers were looking for an easy conquest; we shall never know. What we do know, officially, is that in May 2002, the FTC notified the Academy that it was preparing to bring an action against it for enforcing the code's existing ban on solicitation. In its letter of 16 May 2002, the FTC said in part:

> NAA's flat ban on solicitation in its Code of Professional Responsibility raises serious questions under the anti-trust laws since it and certain related advisory opinions or parts thereof appear to be broader than necessary to deal with the asserted rationale for them: that solicitation can compromise or appear to compromise the impartiality of neutral arbitrators.

The FTC's formal complaint alleged, among other things, that the Academy engages in "substantial economic activities for the benefit of its members…and has been organized in part for the profit of its members"; that "[e]xcept to the extent that competition has been restrained as herein alleged, many of the NAA's members have been and are now in competition among themselves and with other Arbitrators of labor-management disputes"; that the NAA, "acting as a combination of its members, and in agreement with at least some of its members, has acted to restrain competition by restricting advertising and solicitation by its members"; that these acts and practices "restrain competition unreasonably and injure consumers by depriving consumers of Arbitrators' services for labor-management disputes of truthful, non-deceptive information and of the benefits of free and open competition among Arbitrators"; and that the alleged "combination, agreement, acts and practices...constitute unfair methods of competition and unfair acts and practices in violation of...the Federal Trade Commission Act."

The references in the complaint to advertising were obviously superfluous; the Academy had already adopted the code amendment permitting everything except false or misleading advertising before the complaint was filed. The allegations that the Academy's practices unreasonably restrained and injured consumers of arbitrators' services by depriving them of truthful, nondeceptive information and the benefits of competition among arbitrators was groundless on its face. Under rules in effect when the complaint was filed, Academy members were free to advertise for the benefit of potential users of their services what fees they charged, truthful details of their experience, lists of decisions (including full texts), names of parties who had previously employed them, and other details. The charge that the Academy was restricting competition among its members was also without merit. Individual members of the Academy are, and always have been, free to set their own schedules of fees and charges.

Nevertheless, the FTC proposed discussions designed to lead to a consent order pursuant to which the Academy would, among other things, revise the rule against solicitation to be more in accordance with what the agency saw as "the positive change that NAA has made with respect to advertising." When he assumed the presidency of the Academy in 2002, Richard Bloch, who had opposed removal of the flat ban on advertising, and had strongly supported the non-solicitation rule, was determined to avoid signing any consent decree. However, after retaining a distinguished Washington law firm and participating in preliminary negotiations with the FTC, he reluctantly concluded that the Academy lacked the financial resources to litigate the issue in court, that many Academy members probably wanted to begin or continue to solicit, and that, in any event, the chances of prevailing were problematical at best. Accordingly, with the unanimous support of the board of governors and indications that the AAA and the FMCS also approved, he signed off on the FTC consent order on 19 September 2002. The code revision ("An arbitrator shall not make false or deceptive representations in the advertising and/or solicitization of arbitration work") was scheduled for presentation to the membership at the Academy's 2003 annual meeting.

Under the terms of the FTC's decision and order, the Academy was ordered to cease and desist from "Regulating, restricting, impeding, declaring unethical, interfering with, or advising against the advertising or publishing by any person of the prices, terms or conditions of sale of Arbitrators' services, or of information about Arbitrators' services that are offered for sale or made available by Arbitrators or by any organization with which Arbitrators are affiliated"; or from taking similar objections against "solicitation of arbitration work, through advertising or other means, by any Arbitrator or by any organization with which Arbitrators are affiliated." The order was to remain in effect for 20 years. Some amelioration was afforded by two provisos to the order. The first provided that the Academy was not prohibited from "formulating, adopting, disseminating to its members, and enforcing reasonable ethics guidelines governing the conduct of its members with respect to representations that [it] reasonably believes would be false or deceptive within the meaning of…the Federal Trade Commission Act." The second permitted the Academy to adopt and enforce "reasonable ethics guidelines governing conduct that [it] reasonably believes would compromise or appear to compromise the impartiality of Arbitrators." It also provided that if the Academy determines that the dissemination or transmission of material by arbitrators "may create an appearance of partiality, the NAA may promulgate reasonable guidelines that require, in a manner that is not unduly burdensome, that such material and information be… [given] in good faith to representatives of both management and labor."

In a memorandum to the Academy membership dated 26 September 2002, Bloch stated that although he believed that the non-solicitation rule was "a valid and prudent provision aimed at protecting the parties, not constraining them," he had no real quarrel with the substantive terms of the FTC order as it related to solicitation, "particularly with the provisos, and considering…that we have already removed our ban on advertising." He stressed that the order specified there was no finding of wrongdoing by the Academy, and gave it "substantial leeway to uphold our interests in ensuring prudent practices by our members." In a letter to me dated 26 December 2002, he expressed the belief that "to the extent we, as an organization, are *willing* to be serious about decrying unethical conduct (I grant you—there's the rub) nothing the FTC has done will deter us." He added:

> On that specific point…we need some organized discussion of Ethics. New members should be routinely exposed to questions of propriety as seen by the Academy. Existing members ought to conduct and attend workshops at regional and annual meetings. And, our CPRG has to be willing to take an active stance in order to protect the [Academy's] founding principles.…A good deal of this…can be initiated through the re-writing of the Ethics opinions, a project that is the next step in complying with our FTC commitments.

The dilemma faced by Bloch, whether to accept or reject the FTC decision and order, was indeed a serious one. But, unlike him, I did have a real quarrel with the substantive terms of the order as it related to solicitation. My objections, in addition to those already mentioned, were essentially the same as those I advanced during the debate on advertising, namely, that there was a major distinction, which the FTC failed to grasp, between arbitrators and lawyers, doctors, or other professionals. Labor-management arbitration developed as an integral part of a system of collective bargaining, a cooperative venture by employers and unions to substitute the peaceful settlement of grievances (as opposed to issues involving new terms and conditions of employment) for strikes and lockouts. The role of the arbitrator in this system was that of an unbiased neutral, and the powers of the office were quasi-judicial in nature. The founding principles of the NAA were designed to promote and encourage the acceptance of an industrial rule of law embodying those objectives. To the founding members, the thought that arbitrators should be free to advertise their services or to solicit one or both parties for cases was utterly repugnant, and their views on that subject were expressly set forth in the original Code of Ethics and Procedural Standards and in its successor, the Code of Professional Responsibility. Advertising and solicitation were deemed unethical and unseemly; the relatively few arbitrators engaging in those practices were rightly viewed as undermining the confidence and respect that employers and unions had regarding the profession as a whole. Moreover, whereas admission to a bar or medical association is a virtual necessity for practicing lawyers and doctors, membership in the Academy has not been a requirement for the practice of arbitration. At no time in its history has the Academy represented more than a minority of arbitrators. No advanced degree, prescribed course of study, or license or certificate is a prerequisite to become an arbitrator; one need only announce his or her availability to serve in that capacity. To be sure, members of the Academy comprise an elite group. Many collective bargaining agreements specify that any arbitrator selected to decide a grievance must be an Academy member. But the Academy has constantly sought to expand its membership, not to restrict it. There seemed to me to be no justification for denying it the right to impose its ethical standards on those who voluntarily sought membership in the organization and were accepted.

The Academy has never served as an appointment agency for arbitration. Parties wishing to obtain a list of names of arbitrators from which to select one for a particular case or series of cases usually apply for the list to either the AAA or the FMCS. By becoming signatories to the code, those agencies presumably insist on the observance of code provisions by all arbitrators listed on their panels, but that is their decision. The Academy has never attempted to impose its ethical standards on nonmembers. The FTC order deprived the Academy of its right to protect its reputation for impartiality and integrity while providing employers and unions with no relevant information about individual arbitrators not already readily available to them.

The fundamental error of the FTC complaint, it seemed to me, was that it completely overlooked or disregarded the basic principles that gave the Academy its reason for being. It is true that in 1965 the Academy amended its constitution to reconstitute itself as a "non-profit corporation." But nothing in its original statement of purposes, its bylaws, or its activities, supports the assertion in the FTC complaint that the "NAA engages, among its various activities, in substantial economic activities for the benefit of its members." In fact, the Academy, as an organization, does not engage in "economic activities" of any kind. The NAA is inherently different from the corporations over which the FTC exercises its jurisdiction.

Although I had understood from Bloch's communications to the Academy membership and to me personally that the NAA's acceptance of the consent order was a "done deal," it came up for formal ratification at the 2003 annual meeting in San Juan, Puerto Rico. Specifically, a vote among the Academy members attending was held on the CPRG's following proposed amendment of the section of the code dealing with responsibilities of the profession:

> 3. An arbitrator shall not engage in conduct that would compromise or appear to compromise the arbitrator's impartiality.
> a. Arbitrators may disseminate or transmit truthful information about themselves through brochures or letters, among other means, provided that such material and information is disclosed, disseminated or transmitted in good faith to representatives of both management and labor.

The CPRG also disclosed that it had unanimously agreed, in order to comply with the FTC consent orders, to rescind eight advisory opinions previously issued, including those I referred to earlier.

This news served to resurrect the small coalition of Howard, Dick, Rolf, and me that had waged a vigorous but unsuccessful campaign against the repeal of the ban in the code against all advertising. Although we were united in our opposition to the consent order and the proposed code amendment to comply with it, we were not in agreement on just how we should resist it. Rolf and Dick felt very strongly that the Academy should refuse to comply and should challenge the Order in a lawsuit. I felt that such a course would never be approved by the membership and that, even if it were, fighting the FTC in court would be inadvisable for the reasons cited earlier by Bloch. My preferred approach was to switch attention to our enforcement of the code as modified and to persuade the membership finally to acknowledge our collective responsibility to take action against those who violated its provisions. In this connection, I again urged that our bylaws be amended to permit the CPRG to initiate enforcement procedures against suspected violators on its own motion, and to repeal the existing requirement that the CPRG could act only upon a written charge filed by an Academy member or any affected person.

In the months immediately preceding the San Juan meeting, Rolf set forth his views in a passionate letter published in the *Chronicle*, our house newspaper. Both he and Dick contacted many members of the Academy to urge them to join in defying the FTC and opposing the proposed code amendment relating to solicitation. Howard originally took a position similar to mine, but was eventually swayed by the oral presentations made by Rolf and Dick at the Academy meeting and ended up joining them.

All four of us took part in the lively debate on the issue at our annual meeting. In my own remarks I attacked the FTC order primarily on the ground that it revealed an utter lack of appreciation of the fact that *any* solicitation of arbitration work is unethical and degrading, casts doubt on the soliciting arbitrator's impartiality and integrity, and if permitted to flourish, would reflect adversely on all arbitrators. Nor could I accept the proposed code amendment permitting by implication the solicitation of arbitration work by disseminating truthful information about the arbitrator so long as it was transmitted to both parties; the very act of solicitation itself was objectionable and, in my view, was not cured by directing it to both parties.

Despite the eloquent statements at the meeting by Rolf, Dick, and Howard, which persuaded a few members who had either favored accepting the consent order and the proposed code amendment, or had been on the fence, to oppose both, our side was again outvoted by about three to one. Reflecting on the outcome, I attributed it primarily to two factors. The first was that by the earlier vote abolishing the ban in the code against all advertising, which by definition applied also to solicitation, and substituting a provision that permits all advertising except that which is "false or misleading," the Academy had voluntarily abandoned one of its fundamental principles. Subsequently to oppose an explicit removal of a similar ban on solicitation could rightly be considered to be straining at a gnat after swallowing a camel. The second factor was the likelihood that some of our members either were already engaged in the solicitation of arbitration work or were on the verge of doing so. I emphasize my belief that all but a few of them will avoid making false or misleading statements to the parties, but that in no way diminishes, in my view, the essential impropriety of any solicitation, truthful or otherwise.

The outcome of the debate at the 2003 annual meeting convinced me that the organization I helped establish in 1947 no longer exists. The lofty purposes for which it once stood have gradually been abandoned and have been replaced by those designed to promote the economic interests of its members. Ironically, the FTC consent order, based in part on the false assertion that the Academy "engages…in substantial economic activities for the benefit of its members," will go a long way toward making that claim a reality.

At the end of the meeting, I seriously considered resigning from the Academy, but I ultimately decided to remain a member, not only because my resignation would change nothing, but also because I felt there was still a chance that the CPRG, supported by the membership, might finally resolve to take decisive disciplinary action against any members found to have violated even the greatly weakened restrictions against advertising and solicitation. What kept this dim hope alive was the assurance given to me publicly at the end of the 2003 annual meeting that the CPRG would immediately take under consideration my proposal to amend the bylaws to give it the authority to act on its own motion against suspected violators. Finally, despite my profound disappointment at what the Academy has become, I am tied to it by the relations, some of them very close, I have developed over the years with a number of my fellow members. Those relations in the time I have left are far more important to me than the Academy itself, and the annual NAA meetings provide the best, and sometimes the only, opportunities I have to renew and enjoy them.

At the end of 2006, at the age of 91 and after 60 years of active practice as an arbitrator, I decided to terminate my arbitration practice and to concentrate on carrying out my responsibilities as a member of the UAW Public Review Board and writing the history of my professional career. In May 2007, the NAA, at its annual meeting, conferred on me an honorary life membership. I took that occasion to comment on a current and rather heated debate within the NAA over whether to admit to membership arbitrators concentrating primarily on disputes between employers and unorganized employees, saying in part:

> Some of our members have repeatedly argued that the Academy must either increase its membership (and thereby enhance its influence on the practice of arbitration) or gradually fall into a state of innocuous desuetude. I suggest a third possibility. Every organization has a life cycle, and there may come a time when the pressures of expansion threaten to cause the abandonment of some of the principles upon which the Academy was founded. At present, that prospect seems distant, but when that time comes, as I believe it will, I hope that the Academy's members will accept that the cycle has come to an end rather than keep the body of our beloved organization alive at the cost of losing its soul.

CHAPTER 15

THE INTERNATIONAL SOCIETY FOR LABOUR AND SOCIAL SECURITY LAW, 1963-2007

I became involved in the activities of the International Society for Labour and Social Security Law (ISLSSL) shortly before 1963 at the urging of Bob Mathews, the first chairman of the U.S. national committee. Since then I have maintained an active interest in its affairs.

The ISLSSL, originally titled the International Society for Labour Law and Social Legislation, and renamed in 2003 the International Society for Labour and Social Security Law, was founded in Brussels in June 1958. It was the result of a merger of the International Society for Social Law and the International Congress of Labour Law. Its purpose, as set forth in its first constitution, was to study, for scientific purposes, labor law and social security law on a national as well as an international level, and to exchange ideas and information among students, scholars, jurists, and practitioners throughout the world. The constitution specified that membership was open to all who were interested in the purposes of the society and who had demonstrated this in terms of scholarly or professional activities. The society was to be entirely independent of "political, philosophic or religious considerations." National associations, sometimes referred to as branches, were established in countries belonging to the International Labour Organization (ILO). The U.S. national association rapidly became one of the largest of the national units, thanks to the energy and persuasive ability of Mathews, ably supported by Harold Katz, a Chicago labor lawyer who succeeded him as chairman.

The principal organs of the ISLSSL consist of a general assembly composed largely of members of national associations and an international executive committee (IEC) made up of the president, honorary presidents (without the right to vote), regional vice-presidents, the secretary-general, the treasurer, and one representative of each national association. The IEC usually holds two regular meetings in the period between world congresses. The general assembly meets on the occasion of each world congress and consists of those members who attend that gathering. Each member has one vote, subject to limitations relating to the number of dues contributions paid by a member's national association to the ISLSSL during the preceding three years. In practice, the general assembly endorses without debate decisions taken by the IEC in the interval between world congresses.

At the 1958 Brussels congress, Paul Durand, an internationally renowned professor of law at the University of Paris, was named the ISLSSL's first president. Alexandre Berenstein, then dean of the University of Geneva Law Faculty, became the first secretary-general. Less than two years later, Durand was killed in an earthquake in Morocco. He was succeeded by the equally eminent Otto Kahn-Freund, then about to leave his post as chairman of the law department of the London School of Economics to become professor of comparative labor law at Oxford.

The next ISLSSL world congress was held in 1963, in Lyon. The structure of this and subsequent world and regional congresses was as follows: the program was based on three or four topics, or "themes," one of which related to some aspect of social security; all the others involved issues in labor law. The discussion of each topic began with the presentation of a general report. The writer of this report prepared an outline of the subject, which he or she sent to all national reporters designated by the national associations. The general report was based on the national reports, supplemented by the observations and conclusions of the general reporter. The first topic at the Lyon congress was internal relations between unions and their members. The general report was prepared by Clyde Summers, the leading authority in the United States on comparative labor law. At the request of Katz, I agreed to prepare the national report for the United States. At the time, I was preoccupied with my teaching at the UCLA School of Law and with my duties as director of the UCLA Institute of Industrial Relations, and as the deadline approached for the submission of my national report, I become increasingly worried; my manuscript was too long and was generally unsatisfactory. In desperation, I sent a copy to Derek Bok asking for his editorial assistance. Shortly thereafter, Bok telephoned me from his home one evening to discuss the paper. The call lasted for over an hour, in the course of which he made detailed editorial suggestions that dealt effectively with all of the problems I had encountered. His was an act of friendship for which I shall be forever grateful.

In the event, as previously recounted in my discussion of the 1963 railroad work rules dispute, I never got to the Lyon congress, the proceedings of which, including my national report, were published in 1964.[1]

I did attend the next ISLSSL world congress, which took place in 1966 in Stockholm, and I was introduced for the first time to the utterly dreary protocol of the proceedings. Each of the three topics was presented at a plenary session; there was no provision for small-group discussions. First, the general reporter presented his report. This was followed by an endless number of "interventions"—that is, statements by representatives from various countries, who usually spoke only about the relevant law in their own countries and made no reference to the observations and conclusions of the general reporter. Moreover, most speakers ignored the time limits announced at the outset by the chairman of the session. I recall that at the first session of this meeting the chairman announced after some three hours of discussion that the remaining persons wishing to speak would be allowed only five minutes each. When a distinguished French professor arose to speak, the chairman reminded him of the time limitation. The professor turned to the audience and said in a voice that combined outrage and contempt, "Cinq minutes!" He then proceeded to speak for 30 minutes, during which the chairman, thoroughly cowed, made no effort to stop him.

Finally, there was the matter of languages. The ISLSSL has always had four official languages: English, French, German, and Spanish. All speeches at the plenary sessions of world congresses are simultaneously translated in the four languages. Many speakers, although fluent in English, which has replaced French as the leading international language, insist upon speaking in their own national languages. Not only is the cost

---

[1] *Rutgers Law Review* 18, no. 2 (1964).

of simultaneous translations very heavy, but in many instances the quality has proved to be mediocre and, in a few cases, simply inadequate.

As a result of this experience, I began a campaign to change the format of ISLSSL congresses to include designated commentators, who would be expected to discuss the general reporters' overall assessments and conclusions. This proposal was eventually tried once or twice but never caught on. Another of my proposals—to provide for "break-out," small-group sessions to permit informal discussions of the general reports—met with greater success and has finally become a part of the structure of ISLSSL congresses.

Despite the sterile and rather boring quality of the early congresses, the conversations with labor law scholars from many countries that took place outside the formal sessions were richly rewarding. Not only did I learn much from this interaction, I also developed a number of enduring friendships with my foreign colleagues.

Although the ISLSSL constitution specifically declared that the society was to be "entirely independent" of political considerations, I soon learned that politics, both internal and external, had an important effect on ISLSSL affairs. Internally, there was a constant tension between the industrial democracies of the west and the so-called socialist countries of the east: the USSR, Poland, East Germany, Hungary, and Yugoslavia. Externally, the war in Vietnam aroused widespread hostility against the United States by ISLSSL members from other countries. I experienced this hostility first-hand at the 1970 ISLSSL world congress in Warsaw. The U.S. national committee, which as its newly elected chairman I headed and represented on the IEC, had a very large delegation. During the congress, Kahn-Freund and Folke Schmidt, who had succeeded him as president of the ISLSSL, put considerable pressure on me to propose that the next world congress be held in the United States. I convened our delegation, consisting of virtually all of the active members of our national committee, to consider the proposal. After a long and not entirely amicable discussion, I finally managed to get a rather lukewarm endorsement of an invitation to the ISLSSL to hold a world congress in the United States in 1973 or 1974.

The following day, I formally presented the invitation at a plenary session of the congress, having been assured by Kahn-Freund and Schmidt that no competing invitations would be forthcoming from any other country. To the consternation of the U.S. members, Bill Wedderburn of Britain, Gerard Lyon-Caen of France, and several others opposed acceptance of the invitation and, in the course of their remarks, made some highly uncomplimentary comments about the United States, mainly inspired by its involvement in the war in Vietnam. The congress then voted to hold its next meeting in Italy, which had not even submitted a formal invitation. The U.S. delegation was left with the distinct impression that insofar as the ISLSSL was concerned, the next world congress could be held anywhere but in the United States.

Another extremely unpleasant issue that arose was the treatment of the members from Israel when they arrived at the Warsaw airport. Unlike the members from all of the other countries, who received a cordial welcome, the Israelis were treated brutally, subjected to strip searches, and generally humiliated. When these facts were brought to my attention, I again convened my American colleagues to apprise them of the situation. We unanimously resolved to demand a public apology from our Polish hosts, as well as assurances that the ill treatment of the Israelis would not be repeated when they left the country. Accordingly, I asked for and was granted a private interview with Waclav Szubert, the head of the Polish national association and the man nominally in charge of the congress arrangements. Professor Szubert, a sweet and gentle man and a fine scholar whom I greatly admired, was deeply embarrassed by the situation, but was essentially under the thumb of the Polish Communist authorities. He expressed his sincere regret for what had happened but was unable to agree to a public apology. Reluctantly, I advised him that the U.S. members would raise the issue at a plenary session of the congress. The situation remained in this posture until Lyon-Caen, acting as mediator, persuaded all interested parties to accept a settlement providing for a private meeting between Szubert and the Israelis at which he would apologize for the treatment they had received and would assure them that it would not be repeated when they left the country. Considering the circumstances, this was an acceptable if not entirely satisfactory formula for disposing of this regrettable incident, but it left a very bad taste in the mouths of the Israelis and their supporters.

The remaining incident I recall from the Warsaw congress was an example of some of the hidebound and, in my view, ridiculous procedures strictly observed by the ISLSSL. I had been asked to serve as chairman of one of the plenary sessions discussing a general report, my duties being simply to call upon various intervenors in the order in which they had registered with the secretary-general, and to try to hold each of them to the allowable time—a virtually impossible task. The opportunity to make an intervention was important for most of those asking to do so because it meant that their remarks would be included in the published proceedings and would demonstrate to the officials in their respective countries who had authorized their paid attendance at the congress that they had indeed made their contributions to the discussion. I did my best to insure the maximum number of interventions until about five o'clock in the afternoon. By that time, there were only about 10 persons in the audience, each of whom was waiting to be called upon. Deciding that enough was enough, I observed that we had been sitting for many hours, and that in my experience the mind could absorb only what the seat could endure. I declared the session terminated after first assuring those not given the opportunity to speak that if they submitted their remarks in writing to the secretary-general, the texts would be included in the published proceedings.

At this point Berenstein rushed up and whispered to me in great agitation that what I was doing had never been done before and could not be tolerated. He insisted that the session could not end until the last person asking to speak had been heard. Rather than provoking him, I acceded to his demand, and so he and I sat there for another hour while each of the remaining speakers said his piece and then departed. In the end, the only persons remaining in the large hall were the last speaker, Berenstein, and I.

The next world congress was held in 1974, a year late due to the inability of the Italians to organize it on time. The venue was a tiny town, Selva di Fasano, in southern Italy. Judged by the standard set by previous congresses, this one was a disaster. Prospective attendees from other countries received no notice of the location of the meeting, previously announced to be in Turin, or the necessary information about registration, hotel reservations, transportation, and so on, until it was almost too late to make arrangements to attend. Those who did go received no confirmation of their registration fees and hotel reservations, and they arrived without any assurance that they would be accommodated. The headquarters hotel was comfortable, but at least half of the ISLSSL members who made it to the meeting were housed in another town, over 20 miles away, and had to travel by bus to and from the conference hall at least twice a day. The administrative arrangements were in a continuous state of disarray: the general reports, usually available at the beginning of a congress, were not ready until the end. The rather ambitious social events were overwhelmed by the local populace, who swept through the buffets like a horde of locusts. All these inconveniences and irritations were largely offset, however, by the politeness and light-hearted charm of our Italian hosts.

The political issue that rocked the ISLSSL on this occasion was the selection of a successor to Schmidt, who had announced his intention to resign the presidency after one term. The procedure for electing a new president was, at this time, undemocratic and semi-secret. I remember sitting with Kahn-Freund and Schmidt at the Warsaw congress and discussing who should succeed Schmidt at the end of his term. We agreed that it should be Roger Blanpain, professor of law and director of the Institute of Industrial Relations at the University of Louvain, Belgium. Blanpain was a frequent visitor to the United States, a highly esteemed participant in many of our conferences, and a corresponding member of the NAA. He had published numerous papers on European labor law that, while not of the highest scholarly standard, were of great value to European and American lawyers and labor law teachers. In addition, Blanpain had a fluent command of English, French, German, and Spanish. Doubtless, other members of the IEC were informally consulted by Schmidt, but the process was anything but transparent. Blanpain was assured informally that he would be nominated by the IEC to succeed Schmidt at the congress in Selva di Fasano. He arrived there with a fairly large delegation of friends and associates from his hometown of Leuven to help him celebrate, with no inkling of what was about to occur. When Schmidt, supported by a majority of the IEC, formally proposed Blanpain's name, a political battle, characterized by Byzantine parliamentary maneuvers, developed. The eastern bloc rejected Blanpain on the (unstated) ground that he was too close to the Americans. The French evinced a strong antipathy to him based on their dismissive view of his scholarship and what they regarded as his undignified persona. Because of the ISLSSL's unwritten rule that the nomination of the president must be unanimous, Blanpain's candidacy was doomed. The plot thickened when Berenstein, who had previously announced that he was resigning as secretary-general of ISLSSL, declared that he was "available" to succeed Schmidt. It was clear that he would be satisfactory to the eastern bloc. At this point I informed Schmidt privately that I could not vote in favor of Berenstein. I acknowledged that Berenstein was a distinguished scholar and jurist and that as the first secretary-general he had played a leading role in the organization of the ISLSSL. But our personal relations had never been satisfactory. Although he had developed a close personal relationship with Edwin Teple, an American labor law professor and arbitrator who served as the international society's treasurer, this was not replicated with other Americans. Typical of his attitude was his practice of writing his periodic news bulletins to the members of the IEC only in French. At IEC meetings, also, he spoke only in French, although he was able to converse in English, and his manner toward me was distinctly chilly.

Following my conversation with Schmidt, he reluctantly announced that in the interest of unanimity, he would stand for reelection. But Berenstein refused to withdraw, and the IEC was deadlocked. After some earnest caucusing, a compromise was reached: Schmidt and Berenstein simultaneously withdrew from the contest and jointly nominated Jean-Maurice Verdier of France. The IEC unanimously accepted this compromise and also nominated both Schmidt and Berenstein to be honorary presidents. All nominations were then approved pro forma by the general assembly. Blanpain's consolation prize was membership on the IEC, but it hardly compensated for the humiliation he had suffered. Verdier spoke almost no English, but he promptly announced that he would do his best to learn. Unfortunately, his efforts, if he made any, were unsuccessful. At several congresses I attended during his presidency, he spoke at length in French, with no adequate simultaneous translations, to uncomprehending audiences composed predominantly of English speakers.

As far as I was concerned, by far the most important event that occurred at the Selva di Fasano congress was the election of Johannes Schregle to be the new secretary-general. At the time, Schregle was director of the ILO's Industrial Relations and Labour Administration Department in Geneva. A man of outstanding ability and great charm, Schregle was fluent in all the official languages of the ISLSSL, had an encyclopedic knowledge of labor law and industrial relations throughout the world, and was an able administrator. Almost immediately he became the single most important figure in the society. He and I got along well from the start, and in the succeeding years our professional association developed into a warm and lasting friendship.

At the Munich world congress in 1978, I presented the general report, titled "Arbitration and the Role of the Courts: The Administration of Justice in Labor Law." It was based on national reports from 23 countries in North and South America, Eastern and Western Europe, and Asia. The report covered the settlement of disputes over rights and dealt specifically with the structure and composition, jurisdictions, and procedures of various disputes-settlement bodies. In my brief conclusion, I emphasized a view repeated in my later writings on comparative labor law: that the legal system within any country is a product of a variety of historical, geographic, economic, and political forces, and that although comparisons of different legal system are always useful and informative because they stimulate ideas about one's own country's system, an evaluation of any nation's legal or social institutions must be made with regard to the total context created by those forces.[2]

---

[2] I do not mean to suggest that this approach was original; rather, it reflected what I had absorbed from my long association with Kahn-Freund and my experience with the Comparative Labor Law Group.

Referring to assertions that labor courts introduce a uniformity and precedent into the law governing the settlement of disputes over rights, whereas arbitration introduces diversity and inconsistency and makes impossible the establishment of binding precedents, I observed that those statements could hardly be denied, but that they merely posed a question without answering it. Indeed, I argued, there could obviously be no single answer, for the choice between those alternatives depended upon a complex of circumstances that vary from country to country.

Finally, I noted that elements of diversity existed even in some of those countries in which a conscious effort seemed to have been made to build a uniform system of labor law affecting the settlement of disputes, and I concluded by expressing my preference for any innovations that would lead to more realistic and effective problem-solving mechanisms than presently exist, even at the cost of uniformity and predictability.

As with all general reports, mine rapidly grew out of date as important changes took place in the laws and practices of disputes settlement in many of the countries covered by my survey. Still, preparation for the report was a valuable exercise for me, and the response to it at the Munich congress was generally favorable.

In terms of overall management and program content, the Munich congress set a very high standard. An important and welcome departure from the usual format was the inclusion of a report of a round table on the role of labor law in developing countries, organized by the ILO. The congress was well funded and superbly organized, due largely to the efforts of Franz Gamillscheg, an internationally recognized authority on labor law and director of the Institute for Labor Law at the University of Göttingen. Nevertheless, the Munich congress did not free itself from the smothering format of previous congresses. A memorandum I received shortly thereafter from Merton C. Bernstein, an American colleague, expressed feelings about that event and suggestions for a quite different format for the next world congress, to be held in the United States, that were in line with my own thinking. Under the heading, "Don't Play it Again, Sam," he wrote in part:

Without doubt the Munich conference was a masterpiece of planning and efficiency....

But the plenary sessions were deadly.... The presentation of mostly factual information—to which the present format limits the general reporters—does not warrant the enormous outpouring of resources that a Congress requires. The interventions, while occasionally interesting, do not represent the exchange of views that such an assembly of talent might achieve. The plenary sessions simply are too ponderous....

I suggest that for the 1982 meeting we attempt to organize small sessions in which segments of each agenda item constitute the subject of discussion. If we could arrange for the distribution of the rapporteurs' reports (and possibly the national reports) prior to the meeting, the "small sessions" could be led, not by additional rapporteurs, but individuals with some experience and ability in stimulating and guiding discussions, aided by strict rules on the length of individual observations.

In May 1977, prior to the Munich congress, I had received a letter from Schregle, on behalf of Verdier, Berenstein, Antonio F. Cesarino Jr. (Verdier's successor), Jean de Givry of the ILO, and Gamillscheg, asking if the U.S. national association would consent to be the host of the next world congress. In a letter to Schregle dated 11 July 1977, I reminded him of the fiasco at the 1970 Warsaw congress, when our proposal to hold the next world congress in the United States was summarily and rudely rejected. Nevertheless, I promised to submit the latest request to the new executive board of the U.S. national association. Subsequently, the executive board agreed to the proposal, and our formal offer to hold the 10th World Congress in Washington, D.C., in 1982 was enthusiastically accepted by the IEC and the general assembly.

During the years immediately preceding and following the Munich congress, I was heavily involved in ISLSSL affairs, especially those of the U.S. national association. As chairman of that group, I was active in reorganizing the structure of our organization and revising our articles of association pertaining to the make-up of the national executive board (NEB), which consisted of the chairman, secretary-treasurer, elected members, and representative members. In this effort I was dependent on the advice and assistance of our secretary-treasurer Alfred A. Giardino, a New York lawyer of tremendous vitality, ability, and charm.

Another preoccupation was a new journal, *Comparative Labor Law* (*CLL*), sponsored by the U.S. national association. *CLL* was the creation of David Ziskind, one of the most remarkable men I have ever met. Ziskind was by nature retiring and modest, but he was an independent-minded and dedicated scholar, a tireless investigator with insatiable curiosity, and a gadfly who did not hesitate to badger and cajole others to join with him in pushing back the frontiers of knowledge. Ziskind was a practicing lawyer and arbitrator, but his real interest was in public service, broadly defined. While employed in the solicitor's office of the U.S. Department of Labor, he wrote a monograph, *One Thousand Strikes of Government Employees*, initially published in 1940, which proved to be of such enduring value that it was reprinted in 1971. He had an early and continuing interest in labor law and the ILO, and he was one of the first Americans to become a member of the ISLSSL and the U.S. national association.

Beginning in 1967, Ziskind began publishing a mimeographed ISLSSL *Newsletter*, a brief composite of news items and editorials written by him. Four years later the *Newsletter* was replaced by a longer and more ambitious *United States National Committee Bulletin*, which included contributions by outsiders but again featured research notes, book reviews, and editorials by Ziskind. Ziskind did all of this on his own time and paid for all production costs out of his own pocket. Still not satisfied, he persuaded me to arrange for the publication of a quarterly journal, *Comparative Labor Law*, at the UCLA School of Law. I obtained the necessary permission from the law school, and the first issue appeared in Spring 1976. To finance this publication, Ziskind and I persuaded the U.S. national association to assess each member of the association a $10 fee, in return for which each would be given a subscription to the journal.

Ziskind served as editor of *CLL*. In a brief introduction to the first issue, which dealt with the crisis brought about by the U.S. withdrawal from the ILO, the new Swedish Labor Act, and the repeal of the British Industrial Relations Act of 1971, Ziskind wrote:

> Our goals are several. Broadly we seek a fuller knowledge of legal phenomena in the realm of labor relations. We will compare foreign with domestic labor law. Some contributors may probe theoretical implications to discover the essential features of

labor problems and legal institutions. Others may be content to compile information that will primarily assist lawyers to represent clients abroad. Hopefully the contents may lead to an enrichment of thought among those who shape and apply our labor laws.

The masks of men make their faces more interesting. To look upon labor laws everywhere and to peer behind the laws can be a fascinating way to study the nature and well-being of man.

As editor, Ziskind contributed to all four issues of the first volume of *CLL*. At the end of the year, however, he expressed a desire to pass on the editorship to someone else. Arrangements were made to transfer the journal to another law school in Southern California and the editorship to a member of its faculty. Ziskind agreed to continue to serve as associate editor. This arrangement proved to be unsatisfactory; serious differences of opinion developed between Ziskind and the new editor over the proposed content of this next issue of *CLL*. In the end I was compelled, in my capacity of chairman of the national association, and with the approval of the NEB, to terminate our relationship with the other law school. After a year's delay, during which no issue of the journal was published, *CLL* returned to UCLA and continued publishing under my editorship. My task was eased by the help from two associate directors—Ziskind and Frederic Meyers, a labor economist in the UCLA Graduate School of Management. After a year, Daniel J.B. Mitchell, also at the UCLA Graduate School of Management, replaced Meyers. Ziskind continued to serve as an associate editor, making frequent contributions to the journal until Fall 1982. At that time, I could no longer continue my duties as editor owing to the press of other obligations, so the *CLL* was transferred to the University of Pennsylvania, where it continued to be published under the joint editorship of Clyde Summers and Janice Bellace of the Wharton School. The name changed to *Comparative Labor Law Journal*. In 1998, it was transferred to the University of Illinois College of Law and retitled *Comparative Labor Law & Policy Journal*. Matthew W. Finkin of that institution and Sanford M. Jacoby, professor of history, management and policy studies at UCLA, took over as general editors. Each of the successors to *CLL* greatly improved its format and content, but I am proud of my modest contributions to the establishment and continuation of the journal, which remains as a monument to the inspiration and dedication of Ziskind.

The period between the Munich world congress in September 1978 and the Washington, D.C., world congress in September 1982 was one of the most hectic I have ever experienced. Preparations for the latter congress consumed much of my time, but they had to compete with my other obligations, including: teaching; two years' service, ending in the spring of 1982, as vice-chairman and chairman of the University of California's statewide academic council, an extremely time-consuming job; service as a member of the United Automobile Workers public review board and of the arbitration services advisory committee of the FMCS; and as arbitrator in a number of labor-management disputes.

By far the most onerous and worrisome of the preparations for the Washington congress was raising money to finance it. Alone among the countries that have provided the venues for world congresses, the United States government refused to give any financial support whatsoever. Appeals to the U.S. State, Labor, and Commerce Departments were rejected. This meant that we had to rely upon the registration fees paid by those attending the congress and donations from individuals, corporations, unions, and foundations to finance the entire operation. The most expensive items were for simultaneous translations in four languages at all of our plenary sessions, publication of general and national reports, and entertainment costs for receptions, dinners, and excursions.

After consulting with the NEB of our national association, I appointed a committee composed of members residing in the Washington area, headed by an old and trusted friend, Rolf Valtin, to find a suitable headquarters hotel for our congress and to arrange a social program for our guests. Negotiation of the complicated contract with the hotel was left to another old friend, Tom Roberts, who spent six months in hard bargaining before producing a contract very favorable to the national association. Rolf and his associates, Richard Block and Lawrence Seibel, did an outstanding job, not the least important aspect of which was engaging the services of Harriet Schwartz, of Washington Whirl-Around, to arrange for most of the social program. The NEB also approved the selection of the Bureau of National

Affairs (BNA), a publisher of various reports and hardcover books dealing with, among other things, labor-management issues, to print and distribute all the forms and announcements in connection with the congress, as well as all of the general and national reports dealing with the three themes: "Worker Participation in Decisions Within Undertakings," "Termination of Employment on the Initiative of the Employer and Income Security of the Worker Concerned," and "The Position of Women in Labor Law and Social Security." Donald F. Farwell, a consultant to BNA Conferences, was responsible for all of these functions and also for the critical assignment of recruiting a team of interpreters from the United Nations to provide simultaneous translations at all plenary sessions. He carried out his diffi-cult assignments with exemplary efficiency. The job of coordinating all the various activities and, in particular, handling the registrations of some 500 persons from 47 countries was undertaken by our indispensable secre-tary-treasurer, Al Giardino. Giardino's multilingual skills were especially valuable, as were his tact and skill in dealing with numerous questions and complaints.

The overall responsibility for the planning and conduct of the congress was of course mine. Moreover, I had to assume the unenvi-able task of raising the money to finance much of the enterprise. In this effort I received very little practical help from the other members of the NEB, and I found writing the endless numbers of begging letters and making countless telephone calls and solicitations frustrating and humil-iating—so much so that I made a vow, and kept it, never again to become involved in fund-raising for any cause, no matter how worthy. One huge disappointment was the decision of the AFL-CIO not to lend financial support or to participate in the congress. Earlier on, I had received many unsolicited offers of financial contributions from unions for which I arbi-trated. But the word must have gone out from AFL-CIO headquarters to have nothing to do with the congress, because the promised donations were never forthcoming. My own attempts to get in touch by letter and telephone with friends at the federation's office in Washington were futile: my letters went unanswered and my calls were not returned. The reason, conveyed to me indirectly, was that the ISLSSL admitted to membership

Eastern European countries and that a USSR representative, Semion A. Ivanov, who was also a member of the ILO's committee of experts on the application of conventions and recommendations, had been selected as the general reporters for one of the themes discussed at the congress. Whatever the reason, the implacable hostility by the AFL-CIO hierarchy against the USSR and its satellites resulted in a virtual boycott of the congress by American unions. Only three unions sent contributions: the United Automobile Workers; the United Steelworkers, which asked that its donation not be acknowledged publicly; and the International Brotherhood of Teamsters, which at the time was not affiliated with the AFL-CIO. A handful of corporations and business associations gave us substantial contributions; lesser amounts were provided by a number of individuals and by smaller firms and companies. My fund-raising activities over a three-year period produced only about $54,000.

By way of comparison, the amount of money raised for the Munich congress was $200,000. But Gamillscheg, the person in charge of arrangements, had no problem obtaining the necessary funding; he simply applied to Gerhard Müller, president of the tripartite Federal Labor Court (*Bundesarbeitsgericht*), for assistance. Müller obliged by writing to the employers' associations and unions regularly appearing before that court inviting contributions to pay for the congress. Not surprisingly, the contributions were immediately forthcoming.

The program of the congress departed from the usual format. Members of our national association's NEB and I had agreed that we wanted to provide informal sessions at which smaller groups could discuss the general reports. We also wanted to designate specially qualified commentators to discuss the general reports in the plenary sessions before the interventions began. In September 1981, the IEC met in Wiesbaden, Germany. The principal item on its agenda was the Washington congress, and I attended in order to brief my colleagues on our plans. The IEC approved our proposed changes in the organization of the congress, including the division of the participants into two groups that would meet concurrently following the plenary sessions to discuss the general reports. This approval was granted despite my express

warning that we could not afford to provide for simultaneous translations in four languages at the meetings of the smaller groups. After
considerable discussion, it was agreed that for those small-group sessions,
simultaneous translations in two languages would be sufficient. And
because the two most numerous language groups at the congress would
be English and Spanish, those were the languages for which simultaneous translations would be provided. All of this was fully understood
and unanimously agreed to by the IEC.

Nevertheless, when we held the small-group sessions at the congress,
a few members of the rather small French contingent raised violent
objections to the absence of a simultaneous translation in their language,
carrying their protest all the way to the U.S. Department of State.
Although their appeals were in vain, they created such a disturbance
during the congress that I felt obliged to respond in my closing remarks
at the final plenary session of the congress. After explaining the background of our discussion to confine simultaneous translations to English
and Spanish in the small-group sessions, I concluded:

> Fortunately, the situation turned out to be not nearly so bad as some people had
> anticipated. As it turned out, thanks to their wonderful cooperation, our translators
> picked up the slack, even though they were not supposed to do so; and in two of
> the sessions, I think we managed at least part way through to have a translation in
> three languages, although only two had originally been planned. But it is quite clear
> that the arrangement remains unsatisfactory and that this is a problem to which the
> [ISLSSL's] Executive Committee must address itself in future Congresses.[3]

And, indeed, the matter of simultaneous translations in all four of the
ISLSSL's official languages other than in plenary sessions remains a troublesome problem to this day.

Because this was the first ISLSSL world congress in North America,
and because so many of the participants had never before visited the
United States, we were determined to make the experience a particularly
enjoyable one. The process began with registration. This task was handled
by a team of amateurs: Giardino, Rolf and Nancy Valtin, Howard Bloch,

---

and my wife, Eleanor. They all worked long hours at the registration desk and performed their duties with such efficiency and good humor that a great many of the participants expressed their appreciation publicly during the final session or privately in letters of thanks written after they had returned to their respective countries.

Highlighting the events, which included the usual receptions, dinners, and tours, was an elaborate country picnic at an historic site in Virginia, featuring a band and square dance music with a caller. This event was a spectacular success, with just about everyone joining in the square dancing. I have a vivid recollection of Ivanov, the sole participant from the USSR, who had been given a hard time by the U. S. State Department before it finally gave him an entry visa, dancing dreamily by himself while clutching a bottle of champagne. When the party finally broke up that evening, I knew that our congress would be happily remembered for years to come by those who attended.

The closing session of the congress included announcements by Schregle of recent decisions by the IEC, including the appointment of four regional vice-presidents. I was designated vice-president for North America. Several other international officers made brief speeches, of which certainly the funniest and most fulsome was that of the incoming president, Cesarino.

> Dear friends of our Society, God created the world, as Benjamin Aaron created this Congress. He was also the alma mater of this Congress.…I want to say, again, that we have great admiration for all aspects of this Congress. We have had many Congresses, but this one is perfect.

I considered this extravagant praise as a fitting retribution to our obstreperous French colleagues and half-expected them to demand equal time to submit a dissenting opinion.

In the months immediately following the congress, we were absorbed primarily in getting the proceedings ready for publication—an immensely complicated job requiring extraordinary patience in dealing not only with the general and national reporters but also with those who had made "interventions" and wanted their remarks included in the proceedings. Despite the sometimes angry protests of some of the participants, we firmly rejected all requests (and there were a great many) to revise and extend written or oral contributions. Of course, the deadlines we set were almost universally ignored. Nevertheless, thanks largely to the efforts of Farwell, the job was eventually completed in 1984. At my urging, the proceedings, jointly edited by Farwell and me, were dedicated "with gratitude and affection to the memory of the late Professor Robert E. Mathews, founder and first Chairman of the United States National Branch, who inspired by precept and example a generation of labor law scholars, teachers, and practitioners in the United States."[4]

In November 1982, I sent to all members of the U.S. national association a report on the Washington congress and a number of other matters. In respect of the congress, which I described as a success "in most respects," I added a paragraph expressing my disappointment, greatly toned-down, with certain aspects of the congress:

> First, the enormous amount of work required to make all of the arrangements and to raise the funds essential to its success was shouldered by a disproportionately small group. Many who, by virtue of their positions [i.e., membership on the IEC] and past expressions of interest, could and should have helped us, did not do so. Second, the participation by members of our Branch in the Congress itself was meager. Only 60 registered, and of...[them]...a number did not actually attend. Some foreign visitors commented that they had come hoping to meet and talk to Americans with common interests, but had been unable to find any. In this respect, therefore, we missed the opportunity to further one of the principal aims of the ISLSSL.

I also announced my resignation, after 12 years of service, as chairman of the U.S. national association and my appointment of a nominating committee to receive nominations for new officers and members of the NEB. The election was completed in April 1983, and my good friend Leroy Merrifield, professor of law at George Washington Law School, was chosen as the new chairman of our national association.

Although remaining a member ex officio of the NEB, by virtue of my new position of regional vice-president, I now became more heavily involved in the international operations of the society. For example, along with other ISLSSL officers, I was asked to comment on a 1983 proposal by Cesarino that the society should support an "Appeal to all Scientists of the World" by the USSR Academy of Sciences, as well as

---

[4]Bob had died in 1983.

its "Declaration on Prevention of Nuclear War." In response, I wrote to Cesarino that despite my wholehearted opposition to nuclear war, I thought it

> inappropriate for our Society to endorse any initiatives not closely identified with the aims of the Society, which, as stated in Article I of our Statutes, "are of a purely scientific character, independent of all considerations of a political, philosophic or religious nature."
>
> Although I imagine that most, if not all, of our members are strongly in favor of preventing nuclear war, I also feel sure that there is a considerable variation of opinion within our ranks as to how that objective can best be achieved. I fear that the Society's official endorsement of any one proposal or set of proposals would prove divisive and counterproductive.

Apparently, the other officers felt the same way; Cesarino's proposal was never formally considered by the IEC.

The first European regional congress was held in Szeged, Hungary, in September 1984. It was preceded and followed by a meeting of the IEC, whose agenda included the nomination of a president to succeed Cesarino. Once again the process was dominated by purely political considerations. Prior to that congress, Cesarino had proposed in a letter to Schregle that Berenstein be nominated for president and that Szubert, Gamillscheg, and I be nominated for honorary president. Schregle then transmitted to the ISLSSL officers the text of Cesarino's proposal and explanation, which read as follows:

> The reasons for these proposals are: (a) Prof. Berenstein is one of the founders of the ISLSSL (1958) and as Secretary-General, from 1958 to 1974, he really has built our Society. Otherwise he deserves also the proposal nomination, because in 1974 this nomination, already proposed by me then was not accepted... ; (b) it is a habit of our Society to elect Honorary Presidents those colleagues who have organized our world-wide Congress in their country and this was not observed concerning the three now proposed.

In a separate letter to me, Schregle reported that he had chanced to meet Cesarino while on an ILO mission to Argentina and had discussed the latter's proposal with him. At that time Schregle had explained to Cesarino the reasons why he thought that I ought to be the next ISLSSL president. He quoted Cesarino as saying that although he had the highest esteem and personal friendship for me, because of what had happened at Selva di Fasano he thought Berenstein should be our next president. Shortly thereafter, Schregle wrote me again to say that Berenstein had asked him to inform me that he was not a candidate for the next presidency of ISLSSL.

I did not comment on Cesarino's proposal. Gamillscheg wrote me that he intended to inform Cesarino that, although "highly appreciating the merits of Berenstein," he would propose to elect me as the next president. He also indicated his opposition to the automatic election to the office of honorary president of every person who organized a congress, on the ground that "the title of honorary president ought to be restricted to distinguished older colleagues to be honored for their continuous and long-lasting services for the Society." I certainly agreed with Gamillscheg on this issue; it seemed to me ridiculous that I should be made an honorary president simply because the Washington congress had been generally regarded as a great success. Nevertheless, in succeeding years, the tendency has been to reward the organizer of a world congress with an honorary presidency.

By the time Eleanor and I arrived in Szeged, it seemed apparent that I would be nominated by the IEC as president-elect of the ISLSSL, succeeding Cesarino. Soon after our arrival, a number of IEC members representing countries in Europe, North and South America, and Asia indicated to me that they would support my nomination. It should not have been a surprise to me, although it was, to learn from Schregle that the Eastern bloc was opposed to my candidacy. I was assured that their opposition had nothing to do with me personally; it was simply the result of Cold War politics. But having become completely fed up with these political games, so irrelevant to the business of the ISLSSL, I told Schregle that, in my view, the time had come to abandon the unwritten policy of choosing our presidents only by unanimous agreement, and that I would press for a secret-ballot vote and the selection of the candidate receiving a majority of the votes cast. But Schregle refused to give up. Employing his extraordinary talents as a mediator, and ably abetted by Gamillscheg, he was able in an all-night session involving most of the principal persons involved other than me, to work out an acceptable compromise: opposition to my candidacy would be withdrawn, with the understanding that Laszlo Nagy, the person in charge of the Szeged congress, would be nominated to succeed me for the period 1988–1991. On the basis of this arrangement, I was unanimously nominated by the IEC to serve as president for the period 1985–1988.

My formal election as president of the ISLSSL took place at the conclusion of the 11th world congress, in Caracas, Venezuela, in September 1985. In preparing my brief remarks for this occasion, I sought to reduce national rivalries in the conduct of our affairs by using all four of our official languages. The speech I wrote with the help of staff members at the UCLA Institute of Industrial Relations and the Law School who were fluent in French, German, and Spanish was grammatically correct, but my delivery provoked amusement in the audience. Nevertheless, they applauded the effort and appreciated the fact that I had made it.

A special feature of the Caracas congress was a symposium on teaching and research in comparative labor law. Along with a few others, I was asked to contribute my comments. Conceding that my remarks merely reflected conventional wisdom, I observed that some pieces of conventional wisdom should be constantly reiterated, lest they be ignored or forgotten. My remarks included the following:

> A study of comparative labor law, or any other form of comparative law for that matter, should be undertaken with humility; for there is no country, no culture in our shrinking and cosmically insignificant world community that does not have something to learn from and something to teach other countries and cultures. An informed and sophisticated typology can impose some kind of pattern upon the types of problems affecting various forms of work, the employment relationship, and the relations between and within organizations of those who provide the work and organizations of those who perform it; but the ways in which these problems are approached are not so easily cabined within a theoretical framework. They require detailed, patient and tolerant study according to flexible and changing protocols.
>
> No form of research seems to me to demand more imperatively than does comparative labor law the free trade of ideas across cultural and geographical boundaries. Let us, by all means, establish informal work groups to facilitate our comparative law studies; let us support...journals which publish and disseminate the research; but

let us eschew any...efforts to establish larger and more inflexible formal structures for the study of comparative labor law. And finally, let us, while keeping an open mind to all published research in this field, be ever suspicious of any proclaimed "universal truths."

The following three years of my presidency were, on the whole, the most interesting and satisfactory of the many in my long association with the ISLSSL. The president is expected to attend as many world and regional congresses as possible. In that capacity I took part in the third and fourth Asian regional congresses in Bangkok in 1985 and in Singapore in 1987; the second European regional congress in Jesolo, Italy, in 1986; the first American regional congress in Buenos Aires in 1987; and the 12th world congress in Madrid in 1988. In addition, I was appointed in 1985 by the general assembly of the ILO to membership on the Committee of Experts (COE) on the Application of Conventions and Recommendations, which meets annually in Geneva for several weeks. (My experience on the COE is discussed in a later chapter.)

In February 1985, Schregle officially informed the officers of the ISLSSL that his third conservative three-year term as secretary-general would expire in 1988 and that his successor would have to be elected at the next world congress, which would be in Madrid. The automatic reaction of the officers was to urge him to reconsider and to agree to serve for another three-year term, but he declared that his decision to resign was final. He did, however, suggest four qualifications to look for in his successor, all of which he possessed in abundance. His decision was, as I wrote in response to his announcement, "a melancholy reminder that all good things must come to an end." Agreeing that he had correctly identified the necessary attributes that his successor should possess (familiarity with the labor law in his own country and some experience in comparative labor law; fluency in at least English and French; acceptability to executive committee members coming from different economic, social, and political systems; and access to a secretariat able to handle multilingual correspondence, circular letters, and so on.), I told Schregle that he had omitted other talents he possessed: skill in mediation and conciliation, tact and charm, and the ability to resolve intractable disagreements by means of creative and principled compromise. It was my good fortune that Schregle would continue as our secretary-general for the duration of my presidency, but one of my duties was to organize a search for his predecessor. Eventually, the IEC agreed on another person with ILO connections: Jean-Michel Servais, then assistant to the chief of ILO's International Labor Standards Department. A Belgian who had risen steadily in the ranks of ILO officials, Servais possessed in some measure all of the qualifications recommended by Schregle, and he proved to be an excellent secretary-general.

My involvement in preparations for regional and world congresses was minimal, consisting largely of reviewing and approving decisions taken by Schregle, who meticulously consulted me before taking final action on a variety of issues. Although I occasionally made suggestions of my own, the two of us were so closely attuned to each other's thinking that we never had substantial differences of opinion on any issue. Most of my duties were ceremonial: making welcoming and concluding speeches at our congresses and conducting a voluminous correspondence with members of the IEC, answering questions from outsiders about the ISLSSL, and presiding at meetings of the IEC.

The ISLSSL's congresses are quite work-intensive, but all provide entertainment in the evening and opportunities for tourism before or after the main event. Eleanor accompanied me to most congresses during my presidency and we enjoyed the visits to new places. Best of all, we met people from other countries and made new friends, with some of whom we developed closer relationships over the years.

The IEC customarily convened one year before a world congress to review arrangements for that meeting and to take up other issues of importance. In September 1987 the IEC accepted the invitation of the Turkish national association to hold its meeting in the small seaside town of Cesme, near the larger city of Izmir. One of the most important questions considered was whether the IEC should continue the practice, initiated at the Szeged congress in 1984, of agreeing on a president-elect three years before his election by the general assembly. Opinions on that issue among members of the IEC differed, so a working party was appointed to examine all aspects of the procedure to be followed and to submit its recommendations for consideration at the IEC meeting in Madrid the following year. The working party, chaired by M.G. Rood of the University of Leiden, submitted recommendations for distribution to members of the IEC in April 1988. I thought the recommendations unsatisfactory for several reasons. They omitted any reference to the question of whether the ISLSSL, like most similar organizations, should establish the position of president-elect, and simply provided that nominations of ISLSSL officers should be considered by the IEC "preferably" a year before the general assembly voted on the nominations. They also provided that the IEC decisions on the nominations be determined by a vote of two-thirds of the members present, omitting what seemed to me to be the necessary requirement that such votes be by secret ballot. Nevertheless, the recommendations were adopted by the IEC without amendment at its meeting in Madrid.[5]

The Madrid congress, at which my term of office as president concluded, was for me the high point of my tenure. The participants were welcomed by King Juan Carlos, who then introduced me. Before the opening ceremonies began, I spent about 15 minutes with the king, who had an easy and affable manner. I found it interesting that one of his first questions to me was whether I knew George Meany, the former president of the AFL-CIO. Another unusual feature of the Madrid congress was that the American delegates were given a reception, honoring Eleanor and me, at our embassy. At every congress, the embassies of most of the countries represented give receptions for their nationals, but so far as I am aware, the United States had never done so prior or subsequent to the Madrid congress. This one exception was due to the efforts of my long-time friend and colleague Alvin Goldman, who was a friend of our ambassador. During the reception, Goldman, who was also chairman of the National Academy of Arbitrators' International Studies Committee, announced that two of the committee's recent comparative studies of the role of neutrals in the resolution of

---

[5] It was not until the 2002 European Regional Congress in Stockholm that the bylaws of the ISLSSL were amended to provide for the appointment by the IEC of a president-elect at its meeting one year prior to the next World Congress

shop floor disputes[6] and interest disputes[7] were dedicated to me. The latter study contained a "Tribute" by Alvin which read in part:

> In the course of designing and coordinating these projects, it soon became obvious that a single scholar and personality, Benjamin Aaron, has had a pervasive influence on the individual participants in this project, on the National Academy and on the research methods that were used.

The authors of these two studies, most of them friends of mine, were all internationally recognized scholars, and this tribute touched me deeply and is one I shall always cherish.[8]

At the IEC meeting in Madrid, no action was taken on the nomination of a successor to Nagy. My choice for president, and that of a number of other ICE members, was Schregle, who seemed to us to be by far the best qualified and also, because of his long outstanding service to the ISLSSL, the most deserving of the possible candidates. Servais and I worked hard to achieve that result, but lacking his extraordinary negotiating skills, we failed. His nomination was rejected for reasons having nothing to do with his qualifications. This was, for me, the most disappointing failure in all my years as a member of the society, and I have never ceased to blame myself for the inept way in which his nomination was handled.

At the Madrid meeting, Schregle and I were made honorary presidents, but because of the rejection of his candidacy for president, neither of us took much pleasure in this distinction.

The nomination of Nagy's successor was deferred to the next meeting of the IEC in September 1996 in Vienna. The two candidates were Gamillscheg and Gino Giugni. Both were highly qualified. Each was an internationally recognized scholar; each had organized a very successful ISLSSL congress. In April 1990, I received a letter from Giugni asking

---

[6] *Comparative Labor Law Journal* 9, no. 1 (1987).

[7] *Comparative Labor Law Journal* 16, no. 3 (1989).

[8] J.E. Isaac and R.C. McCallum (Australia), Theodor Tomandl (Austria), Martin Vranken and Roger Blanpain (Belgium), Antti Suviranta (Finland), Jacques Rojot (France), Manfred Weiss (Germany), Ruth Ben Israel and Mordehai Mironi (Israel), Tiziano Treu (Italy), Kazuo Sugeno and Kazutoshi (Japan), Reinhold Fahlbeck (Sweden), and Sir John Wood, B.A. Hepple, and T.C. Johnston (United Kingdom).

for my support, pointing out that "Italy has reached an outstanding position in labor law, both in theory and legislation. Reasonably, therefore, our Association, which has an excellent record—and [of which] I am now honorary president...would be flattered by an international acknowledgement such as the election of an Italian President." In my response, I agreed with Giugni that he would make an excellent president, but said that I favored Gamillscheg because of his long record or attending and participation in ISLSSL congresses. My letter read in part:

> I think that the President of the Society should satisfy two principal criteria. First, he should be a scholar of international standing. Inasmuch as the Society has no commitment to any particular ideology, it should make no difference whether the President is "liberal" or "conservative" (whatever those labels mean); his political views should be considered irrelevant. [This was a reference to the general perception of Giugni as "liberal" and of Gamillscheg as "conservative."] It should be sufficient that he has acquired the reputation for doing objective labor law research of a high quality.
>
> Second, the President must have demonstrated his interest in and devotion to the perpetuation of the Society as an institution, by sponsoring, attending, and participating in Regional and World Congresses, meetings of the executive committee, etc.

One unhappy consequence of this frank expression of my views was a distinct cooling in my long friendship with Giugni, a man for whom I still have great respect and affection.

The September 1990 IEC meeting in Vienna, which I was unable to attend because of a heart attack suffered in August, also failed to result in a nomination for the presidency. A vote was taken, and it favored Gamillscheg, but his margin over Giugni was so narrow that it was decided to consider the matter again at the World congress in Athens in 1991. On that occasion Gamillscheg was unanimously elected president.

My involvement in the affairs of the ISLSSL was reduced following the expiration of my presidential term, but my new status of honorary president included membership on the IEC. I continued to attend ISLSSL congresses and meetings of the IEC whenever possible and to participate in discussions about various policies of the ISLSSL. At the 1996 European Congress of the ISLSSL in Leiden, the Netherlands, I was presented with a volume of essays in my honor, to which 17 of my ISLSSL colleagues had contributed.[9] The overly generous foreword described me as "one of the foremost labor law and industrial relations scholars in the United States in this country." Needless to say, this tribute from my peers moved me deeply.

Shortly thereafter, I became actively involved in discussion about criteria for the election of future presidents of the ISLSSL. At the European regional congress in Warsaw in 1999, the IEC considered the presidential candidacy of Blanpain, who was the only nominee. The nominating procedures recommended by the Rood committee had been scrupulously followed, so I assumed that Blanpain's election was a foregone conclusion. But once again this expectation was not realized. The French member of the IEC, Antoine Lyon-Caen, attending his first meeting and admittedly ignorant of our past practices, demanded that before we voted on the presidency we deal with his proposal, presented without previous notice, that the office be rotated among the geographical regions of the ISLSSL. He asserted that some regions had been consistently slighted in this regard, naming in particular North America and "Southern Europe" (not heretofore recognized by the ISLSSL as a "region.") Some of us argued that whatever the merits of this proposal, it should not prevent immediate action on Blanpain's candidacy, but Lyon-Caen refused to back down. The president of the ISLSSL, Americo Pla Rodriguez, from Uruguay, called for a recess, during which he and Servais sought to work out a compromise. Lyon-Caen not only refused to consider it, but threatened France's withdrawal from membership in the society if we proceeded with a vote on Blanpain's candidacy. Pla Rodriguez, despite what appeared to be a substantial consensus for Blanpain, announced that no such consensus existed and postponed the decision until the world congress in 2000. A new working

[9] J. R. Bellace and M. G. Rood, eds., *Labour Law at the Crossroads: Changing Employment Relationships* (Boston: Kluwer, 1997). The contributors were Manueal Alonzo Olea (Spain), Janice R. Bellace (United States), Ruth Ben-Israel (Israel), Roger Blanpain (Belgium), Juan Carlos Fernadez Madrid (Argentina), Franz Gamillscheg (Germany), Chi-Sun Kim (South Korea), Berndt von Maydell (Germany), Laszlo Nagy (Hungary) Americo Pla Rodriguez (Uruguay), Max G. Rood (The Netherlands), Johannes Schregle (Switzerland), Jean-Michel Servais (Switzerland), Michel Sewerynski (Poland), Tore Sigeman (Sweden), Jean-Maurice Verdier (France), and Pierre Verge (Canada).

group composed of the officers, honorary president, and regional vice-presidents of the ISLSSL was directed to make recommendations on how to proceed with the nomination of the next president.

In February 2000, Pla Rodriguez sent a letter to members of the working group that proposed four criteria to be used for the election of future presidents. The first two, dealing with qualifications, were unobjectionable. The third and fourth criteria read as follows:

3. Where possible, a geographical balance should be respected, to ensure all juridical cultures are represented at the Directorate level of the Society. However, this rotation should not become an acquired right, but rather applied in an appropriate manner.

4. The proposed candidate should have a large consensus. Unanimity, however desirable, cannot be guaranteed.

My immediate response to these proposals raised an objection to the phrase "applied in an appropriate manner" in the third criterion, which I suggested was too vague and prone to inconsistent applications. My counter-proposal was to adopt a specific policy that when two or more candidates are equally qualified, the one coming from a region least often represented among the offices of the ISLSSL should be chosen. In respect of the fourth criterion, I wondered how large a consensus a candidate must have: a bare majority, two-thirds, three-fourths? Also, how were we to determine the degree of consensus: straw vote, or informal consultations? The latter was unreliable in my view because it could be influenced by those making the inquiries and by those being asked. In April, I wrote to Servais expressing my view that last-minute candidacies, which require the IEC to vote without sufficient time for reflection and evaluation, should not be allowed. My recommendation was that all national associations be advised as soon as possible that no candidacy submitted after 30 June 2000 would be eligible for consideration at the IEC meeting in Jerusalem in September 2000. Other IEC members expressed the same view.

In the event, at the Jerusalem congress Blanpain was finally elected president by a very close vote (the other candidate being Manuel Alonso Olea of Spain, a distinguished professor of labor law). Lyon-Caen worked hard to the very end to defeat him, even threatening to withdraw French sponsorship of the next world congress, scheduled to be held in Paris in 2003, if Blanpain were elected. I was unable to attend the Jerusalem congress, but I received a full report from Alvin Goldman, who was elected regional vice-president. In his acceptance speech Blanpain announced that Olea had been made an honorary president in recognition of his many contributions. He also proposed a series of steps to revitalize the ISLSSL, which were submitted to the national associations for consideration.

The French members seemed unable to accept the result. In October 2000, Lyon-Caen, in his capacity of president of the French Association of Labor Law and Social Security (AFTD), wrote a letter to Blanpain in which he referred to "the reservations which you have created among the labour lawyers" of the AFTD, and told him that his role at the Paris congress would be limited to making an opening and a closing speech and would not include any participation in the planning of the congress. ISLSSL presidents have always played an active and decisive part in the preparation and conduct of all congresses, and Blanpain was understandably outraged by both the tone and the substance of Lyon-Caen's letter. His first reaction was to confront Lyon-Caen with a threat to move the 2003 world congress to another county and to force a showdown on the issue of his authority, but he wisely decided to do nothing until he had consulted several friends, including me. My advice to him read in part:

> I agree that Lyon-Caen's letter to you is mean-spirited and insulting, and that neither he nor the French Association has the power to limit your participation in the World Congress of 2003 in the manner they propose. Nevertheless, my advice is not to reply to that letter or to communicate with him further for the time being....What is needed now is mediation by someone who has the confidence of both sides.... Clearly, nothing anyone does is likely to persuade Lyon-Caen to give up his irrational dislike of you, but it may still be possible to convince the French Association that its present position is untenable and must be modified, so that the Society and its President can perform their constitutional functions in respect of the planning and conduct of international congresses....In any case, pending receipt of the counsel you have solicited from others, I urge you not to reply to Lyon-Caen. A short cooling-off period can do no harm and may ease the situation.

The crisis was in fact resolved by a compromise: the venues and dates of the 17th and 18th world congresses were exchanged; the former would to be held in Montevideo, Uruguay, in 2003, and the latter in Paris in 2006 (when Blanpain would no longer be president). Meanwhile, Blanpain's highly successful term in office resulted in a number of important changes, of which the most important was extensive revision of the statutes of the ISLSSL, which was approved by the IEC at the Stockholm regional congress in 2002. At that meeting, which I attended, the IEC unanimously nominated Clyde Summers to be president in 2003–2006, succeeding Blanpain. Summers thus became the second American to hold that position.

Despite my continuing interest and involvement in the affairs of the ISLSSL, my account ends at this point. The political and personal rivalries that have wracked the society almost from the outset may seem to outsiders to be no more than teapot tempests, not worth writing about; such problems arise to a greater or lesser extent in all professional associations. My purpose in reporting them in such detail in these memoirs is to demonstrate the added difficulties when the organization is international in character, in which case the divisive tendency brought about by the vice of nationalism is unfortunately always present. My detailed accounts of national rivalries within the ISLSSL may have obscured its accomplishments.

Even though the format of so many of the congresses has seemed to me to be unnecessarily rigid, the substantive content of the programs has, on the whole, been of a high quality, as anyone who looks into the published proceedings will discover. But for me, and I suspect for most ISLSSL members who have attended these congresses, by far the greatest benefit has been the opportunity to meet and to establish professional and personal relationships with scholars from so many different countries. In many instances this has resulted in fruitful exchanges on subjects of mutual interest, and sometimes in close personal attachments. In my case, my friendship with Schregle has been one of the most significant events of my life. Over the years, he and I, and our two families, have grown increasingly close to each other, and gradually our social interaction has become more important to us than the purely professional interests that he and I have in common. This relationship is itself a more than sufficient reward for my many years of involvement in the ISLSSL.

CHAPTER 16

THE INTERNATIONAL LABOUR ORGANIZATION AND ITS COMMITTEE OF EXPERTS, 1985–1994

The International Labour Organization (ILO) is one of the oldest and most important agencies of the United Nations.[1] Created by the Peace Treaty of Versailles in 1919, its purpose is to bring governments, employers, and trade unions together for united action in the cause of social justice. These three groups have always met on equal terms, with labor and management representatives having an equal voice in the ILO.

The international focus of the ILO is an outgrowth of the social thought of the nineteenth century. Social reformers believed that any country introducing measures to improve working conditions would raise the cost of labor, thus putting it at an economic disadvantage compared to other countries. These reformers endeavored, therefore, to make better wages, hours, and working conditions the subject of international agreements, rather than just national policies. A broad concern for human life and dignity also nurtured the impulse to improve working conditions everywhere. Thus, the preamble to the ILO's constitution states

---

[1] Although this chapter focuses on the ILO Committee of Experts on the Application of Conventions and Recommendations, it also encompasses a description of and commentary on the ILO itself. I have relied upon the following sources, in addition to the contents of my own files: Bob Hepple, *Labour Laws and Global Trade* (Oxford: Hart, 2005); Héctor G. Bartolomei de la Cruz, Geraldo von Potobsky, and Lee Swepston, *The International Labor Organization: The International Standards System and Basic Human Rights* (Boulder: Westview Press, 1996); Edward E. Potter, *Freedom of Association, the Right to Organize and Collective Bargaining: The Impact on U.S. Law and Practice of Ratification of ILO Conventions No. 87 and No. 98* (Washington, D.C.: Labor Policy Association: 1984); Nicolas Valticos, *International Labor Law* (Deventer: Kluwer, 1979); Ernest A. Landy, *The Effectiveness of International Supervision* (London: Stevens & Sons, 1966); and Efrén Córdova, "Some Reflections on the Overproduction of International Labor Standards," *Comparative Labor Law* 14 (1992-93): 138–62.

in part that "universal and lasting peace can be established only if it is based upon social justice" (a term that, unfortunately, cannot be precisely defined), and also that "the failure of any nation to adopt humane conditions of labor is an obstacle in the way of other nations which desire to improve the conditions of their own countries."

Given the obvious importance of the ILO to the world community, it is sad that the origin, structure, and functions, even the name, of that body are unknown to most Americans.

My account in this chapter will focus less on the ILO itself than on one of its supervisory agencies, the Committee of Experts on the Application of Conventions and Recommendations (COE), established in 1926. To explain how the work of the CEO fits into the broader ILO agenda, it is necessary to start with a description of the ILO's structure.

The ILO is composed of a yearly general assembly (the International Labour Conference), an executive council (the Governing Body), and a permanent staff (the International Labour Office). The ILO also works through a variety of subsidiary bodies, such as regional conferences, industrial committees, and meetings of experts. It is headed by a director-general, appointed by the Governing Body, normally for a term of five years.

The International Labour Conference meets each June in Geneva. Every member state (at this writing, in 2005, there are over 158) sends a delegation to the conference to establish international labor standards, elect the Governing Body, adopt the ILO budget, and discuss social and labor problems. Each national delegation is composed of two government delegates, one employers' delegate, and one workers' delegate and is accompanied by technical advisers.

The Governing Body meets three times a year to debate questions of policy and working methods. The states of chief industrial importance, including the United States, have permanent representation on the Governing Body.

The International Labour Office is located in Geneva and is under the supervision of the director-general. It is charged with the ILO's operational and informational duties: preparing documents, recruiting and guiding the ILO's technical cooperation experts throughout the world, issuing a vast range of publications and technical reports, and working closely with the tripartite community.

Setting international standards and supervising their observance are two of the chief functions of the ILO. Standards emerge from the International Labour Conference in the form of conventions and recommendations. The former are similar to international treaties and are subject to ratification. When a member state ratifies a convention, it pledges to bring national legislation into conformity with its terms and provisions. Recommendations do not require ratification; they are intended to serve only as guidelines for national policy in given fields. Together, the ILO's conventions and recommendations make up the International Labour Code, which serves as a model and a stimulus for national legislation and practice in member countries, especially new and developing countries.

Since its inception, the ILO has adopted, as of 2004, 185 conventions and 195 recommendations. Over 7,000 ratifications of conventions have been registered. These instruments deal with such fundamental labor and social issues as hours of work, freedom of association, minimum age and wage, forced labor, occupational safety and health, employment discrimination, working environment, social security, equal pay, and labor relations.

Although the ILO cannot dictate actions by member countries, it can and does keep a watchful eye on the way governments carry out their obligations under ratified conventions. Two ILO bodies share responsibility for this supervision. The first is the COE, an independent body consisting, during my tenure, of 20 members theoretically appointed in their individual capacities. Actually, many are appointed in their representational capacities: thus, certain countries, including the United States, are tacitly considered to be entitled to membership on the COE. Terms of appointment are for three years and are renewable. The COE meets every winter in Geneva for a little more than two weeks.

The second supervisory body is the Tripartite Committee on the Application of Conventions and Recommendations of the International

Labour Conference. The conference committee meets annually in Geneva. From time to time, there has been considerable tension between the two committees, each on the alert against any real or fancied efforts to curtail its independence and supervisory powers.

The United States joined the ILO in 1934 but withdrew in 1937, alleging that ILO principles were being undermined by members of the Eastern Bloc, whose principal members were the USSR, Poland, Eastern Germany, and Czechoslovakia. This action was strongly supported by the AFL-CIO, whose president, George Meany, was an uncompromising foe of the communist government of the Soviet Union. But the withdrawal of the United States, the largest contributor to the ILO budget, proved to be largely counterproductive: it sharply reduced the ability of the organization to maintain and expand its global activities, and it deprived the United States of vital contacts with ILO delegates from other countries on matters of national concern. It turned out to be an unwise move in the Cold War maneuvers against the USSR, although the United States claimed that it had put a stop to developments within the ILO that had prompted the withdrawal. In the event, the United States rejoined the ILO in 1980.

Prior to my appointment to the COE in 1985, I had had relatively little contact with the ILO. My impressions were that its structure was excessively bureaucratic and that its staff, although generally competent, contained a lot of deadwood. About the COE I knew next to nothing.

In September 1985, I received a letter from Th. Sidibé, chief of the ILO's International Labour Standards Department, advising me of Frank McCulloch's resignation from the COE and of the director-general's desire that he be replaced by "another expert from the United States whose qualifications, experience and standing will enable him to make a substantial technical contribution to its work and also to maintain the committee's tradition of independent and impartial evaluation of compliance with obligations assumed by States in respect of ILO standards." Sidibé stated that the director-general would like to propose my appointment to the COE and wondered if I would accept it. I replied in the affirmative, and in November 1985, I received a letter from Director-

General Francis Blanchard officially confirming that my appointment had been approved by the Governing Body for a period of three years.

Prior to assuming my duties as a COE member, at the suggestion of McCulloch, who continued to give me helpful advice throughout my tenure on the COE, I was briefed in the United States by Ernest Landy, a former ILO official who had retired a few years earlier. Throughout my tenure he provided helpful advice on a number of matters. McCulloch also suggested that I seek an interview in Geneva with Nicolas Valticos, another retired ILO official who continued to maintain close ties with the organization and to carry out important special assignments for it. I met with Valticos soon after my arrival in Geneva. He was an urbane and worldly man—learned, wise, and charming. He gave me a splendid lunch at his favorite restaurant and sketched out for me, in a neutral way, the principal problems faced by the ILO and by the COE in particular. His death some years later was a great loss to the ILO and to the field of comparative labor law.

Another friend of McCulloch's whom I sought out was Klaus Samson, a high-ranking ILO official on the verge of compulsory retirement (age 60). Samson was a tireless advocate of civil rights and liberties, both within and outside the ILO, and he was deeply disturbed by the forces arrayed against them throughout the world. The major problem then confronting the ILO, he thought, was the continuing assault by the Soviet Union and its satellites on the supervisory policies and procedures of the COE.

Finally, on this visit to Geneva, the first in my capacity as a member of the COE, I met a remarkable woman, Felice Morgenstern, the second coordinating editor of *International Labour Law Reports* (*ILLR*), which had commenced publication in 1978.[2] The brainchild of Zvi H. Bar-Niv, president of the National Labour Court of Israel, *ILLR* is an annual volume of labor law judgments by the highest courts in, originally, 10 jurisdictions: the Court of Justice of the European Communities, Federal Republic of Germany, France, Great Britain, Israel, Italy, Japan, the Netherlands, Sweden, and the United States. By 2004, the list

---

[2] Volume 1 was published in 1978 and contains judgments dating back to 1974.

of jurisdictions covered had expanded to include Australia, Austria, Belgium, Canada, the Czech Republic, Finland, Hungary, India, Ireland, Poland, South Africa, Spain, and Switzerland.

The original members of *ILLR*'s editorial board were Bar-Niv, chairman; Thilo Ramm, University of Giessen; Folke Schmidt, University of Stockholm; Jean-Maurice Verdier, University of Paris, Nanterre; K.W. Wedderburn, London School of Economics and Political Science, University of London; and myself. The first coordinating editor was Peter Elman, a London barrister. Members of the editorial board also served as national reporters for their respective countries. Reporters were responsible for the selection and editing of judgments and the preparation of annotations of each judgment. These annotations were to be descriptive and analytical rather than critical; the editors aimed at providing the reader with factual information not colored by the personal views of the annotators.

In their introductory statement to volume 1 of *ILLR*, the editors explained that the jurisdictions originally selected for coverage were chosen "in order to provide the reader with judgments reflecting different legal systems and approaches to labor problems arising in industrialized countries, having as a common denominator a free collective bargaining system":

> *ILLR* is intended primarily for the use of judges, labor law practitioners, industrial relations specialists, scholars and students who need or desire ready access to authoritative information of a comparative nature on problems arising in the field of labor law and industrial relations. We define that field broadly: it includes basic human rights pertaining to labor, issues of manpower allocation and regulation and various aspects of individual and collective labor law.

Finally, the editors noted,

> because of their common belief, born of many years of experience as scholars, teachers, judges and practitioners, that the comparative study of problems of labor law will provide more acute insights and deeper understanding of the causes and ways of dealing with such problems than will studies limited to only one country. Generally, a study of laws and practices relating to common problems in countries with widely different historical backgrounds, economies and social organizations is

useful primarily because it influences judges, scholars, and practitioners to ask new questions about their own system which may eventually lead to different solutions.[3]

From the start *ILLR* was published in English. The first three volumes also contained brief summaries in French, but this practice was soon abandoned, a majority of the editors having concluded that it was neither practical nor necessary.

At the conclusion of a distinguished career as a specialist in industrial labor law with the ILO, Morgenstern replaced Elman as coordinating editor a few years after it was established, and she continued in that position for the next 17 years. For her, the job was quite literally a labor of love for which she neither sought nor received any compensation. Her wide-ranging responsibilities included reminding, cajoling, and importuning the many contributors to *ILLR* to submit their material approximately on schedule, and providing English translations of texts submitted in a variety of languages. She did all this and more with patience, tact, and good humor, and without any editorial or clerical assistance, even when she was seriously ill. Without her singular contribution, the *ILLR* could not have survived.

Morgenstern and I got along well from the start, and in the succeeding years, she, Eleanor (who accompanied me on each of my trips to Geneva except the first), and I would meet for lunch or dinner. In between these times, Morgenstern and I maintained a steady correspondence about the *ILLR* in which she asked for information about prospective national reporters and aired her frustrations in dealing with some current ones or with the staff of our publisher. Her death in 2000 brought to an end a career of unsurpassed dedication and deeply saddened those who had been fortunate enough to have known and worked with her.

The COE met in an elegant room dominated by a large round table with seats for its 20 members. In addition, there was a glass-enclosed space for the simultaneous translators, a small group of gifted people able to translate instantaneously any language used by the committee members. The two principal working languages were English and French,

---

[3] *International Labour Law Reports* 1 (1978): vii–viii.

but individual members sometimes also resorted to Spanish, Italian, or German during our discussions.

My colleagues were an interesting and impressive lot. The chairman, serving his final year, was Adetokunbo Ademola, former chief justice of Nigeria, who impressed me by his urbanity and firm control of the proceedings. Three members—Roberto Ago, a former professor of international law at the University of Rome; Kéba Mbaye, the first honorary president of the supreme court of Senegal; and José Ruda, professor of public international law at the University of Buenos Airés—were also judges of the International Court of Justice at the Hague. Four members—Prafullachandra Bhagwati, chief justice of India; William Douglas, chief justice of Barbados; Antti Suviranta, president of the Supreme Administrative Court of Finland; and Fernando Uribe Restrepo, president of the Supreme Court of Columbia—were sitting judges in their own countries. The remaining members—Badria Al-Awadhi, Kuwait, the only woman on the COE; Arnold Gubinski, Poland; Semion Ivanov, USSR; Benjamin Nwabueze, Nigeria; Bernd Baron von Maydall, Federal Republic of Germany; E. Razafindralambo, Madagascar; Akira Shigemitsu, Japan; Verdier, France; Budislav Vukas, Yugoslavia; and John Wood, United Kingdom—were academics or diplomats.

One of the first of these whom I met socially was Ago. At a dinner party he inquired if I knew any of a list of eminent American international scholars and jurists, none of whom I had even met. The list exhausted, Ago abruptly terminated our conversation; to the best of my recollection, he ignored me for the nine years of my membership on the COE, except for a nod and a chilly smile at the beginning of each new session.

A much warmer greeting was provided by Douglas and Wood, perhaps because of their great affection for my immediate predecessor, McCulloch. Whatever the reason, they treated me with great kindness and, among other things, explained to me informally not only the procedures to follow in carrying out my responsibilities but also the nature of some of the COE's internal conflicts. Douglas was a gentle man of unfailing courtesy. Wood had a keen and penetrating intelligence and a manner that at times could be sharp and acerbic. He had a habit of "joking" about the United States and American nationals that was characterized by ill-concealed barbs of criticism. It took me a while to get used to this, but I never revealed my annoyance, and in time we became friends.

Following Ademola's resignation, the members of the COE chose Ruda to be their new chairman. They could not have made a better choice. Ruda was a distinguished jurist and diplomat who presided over our deliberations calmly but firmly. His dignified manner was leavened by a lively sense of humor. Outside of our formal sessions, he was friendly and genial.

At my initial COE meeting in March 1986, I witnessed for the first time a recurring controversy over the committee's supervisory powers and procedures, which were being challenged by two of its members: Gubinski and Ivanov. The principal responsibility of the COE is to determine whether the requirements of a given convention are being met by the member states that have ratified it. Subject only to any derogations expressly permitted by the convention itself, those requirements remain constant and uniform for all countries, regardless of variations in their economic and social conditions:

> In carrying out this work the Committee is guided by the standards laid down in the Convention alone, mindful, however, of the fact that the modes of their implementation may be different in different countries. These are international standards, and the manner in which their implementation is evaluated must be uniform and must not be affected by concepts derived from any particular social or economic system.[4]

Each member of the committee has initial responsibility for a given group of conventions or subjects. After examining the reports from governments and other information available, including legal texts, collective agreements, court decisions, reports of specialized agencies of the United Nations, ILO technical cooperation reports, conclusions of ILO commissions of inquiry and of the ILO Committee on Freedom of

---

[4]"Report of the Committee of Experts on the Application of Conventions and Recommendations," in *Annual Report to the International Labour Conference* (Geneva: International Labour Office: 1977), para. 31.

Association, and observations by employers' and workers' organizations, he or she submits conclusions or comments in the form of draft "observations" or "direct requests" for discussion and approval by the committee. Observations are used for the most serious or persistent cases of noncompliance, and are published in the committee's annual report. The committee may add a footnote inviting the government concerned to "supply full particulars to the conference" at its next session, or to send a detailed report before it would otherwise be due, or both. Direct requests are used to obtain information, to clarify, or to deal with technical points on questions of minor importance. They are not published but are sent directly to the governments concerned. The annual report is submitted to the International Labour Conference.

Criticisms of this supervisory process were voiced strongly and at considerable length within the COE by Gubinski and Ivanov. The former was a dour, highly intelligent but completely humorless ideologue, well versed in the techniques of polemical debate. His Russian colleague, who was charming and good-humored, endeavored to persuade rather than to confront; nonetheless, he pursued the same goals that Gubinski did, and with the same persistence.

The position taken by these two dissenters can be summed up as follows:[5] The composition of the COE should reflect the different regions and systems fairly.[6] Its members should not only be legal experts, but also experts in economics, political science, and international trade unionism. They should be appointed by the conference and not by the Governing Body on the recommendation of the director-general (the established practice). Of greater importance, the committee should take account of different social and economic systems in examining the application of conventions. However, in evaluating the degree to which the basic human rights conventions are applied, it is necessary to constitute working groups that include members representing different points of view and different

[5] The following summary is based on Bartolomei de la Cruz et al., *International Labor Organization*, 114–17.

[6] During my tenure on the committee (1985–1994), the regional representatives were from Africa, Asia, the Arab Peninsula, Western and Eastern Europe, South America, the West Indies, and North America.

social and economic systems, who should each be able to present individual opinions.[7] Because the COE was created as a technical body, it cannot assume the function of interpreting conventions and recommendations, powers reserved in Article 37 of the ILO Constitution to the International Court of Justice. Neither the COE nor the conference committee may act as a supranational judicial body, as they increasingly have a tendency to do. Mentioning certain countries in the report of the conference committee in a special paragraph or in a special list is equivalent to a sanction having no constitutional basis, dissuades countries from ratifying conventions, and is prompted by political motives. The supervisory system should not be a pretext for confrontation, but rather a forum for dialogue, the exchange of experiences, and cooperation.

One specific objection concerned the committee's general observation in respect of Convention No. 87: Freedom of Association and Protection of the Right to Organize. The committee noted that in some countries persons who had been convicted of almost any type of criminal offense, or of certain specific crimes that were considered to indicate a lack of trustworthiness, could not, by law, hold a trade union office. In some countries a criminal record could result in the loss of civil or political rights, including eligibility for trade union office. In the committee's view, conviction for acts that did not call into question the integrity of the person concerned and were not prejudicial to the exercise of trade union functions should not constitute grounds for disqualification, and legislation providing for disqualification on the basis of any offense constituted an undue restriction on the right of workers to elect their representatives and was, accordingly, incompatible with the convention.

Gubinski stated that the committee's interpretation could not be applied to the German Democratic Republic, Poland, the USSR, or a number of other "socialist countries" because, in his opinion, account should be taken of the realities of the economic and social regimes existing in these countries. Equality of treatment, he continued, required that account be taken of the different situations and conditions that

---

[7] For example, opinions on freedom of association, forced labor, and equality of opportunity and treatment.

had been determined by the history of individual countries. To judge all countries according to criteria that are relevant to only one socio-economic system, he concluded, necessarily involved a risk of making inaccurate evaluations and consequently of favoring one group of countries and discriminating against others.

Associating himself with Gubinski's views, Ivanov observed that, given differing social, economic, political, and legal systems, the standards of universal international conventions, which were generally democratic in their nature, might in the course of their implementation engender norms of internal legal systems that could be socialist or capitalist. This meant, he said, that the social realities that exist or are produced as a result of the implementation of international labor conventions might be different in capitalist and socialist countries, although in both cases these realities might be in conformity with the conventions. This was especially true, he continued, of those conventions touching on fundamental principles and structures of existing social systems, such as Convention No. 87. In these circumstances, he stated, members tended to think that implementation methods and their results were in conformity with the conventions only in capitalist countries. Such an approach, he concluded, was incompatible with the very foundation of international law, which was peaceful coexistence, and had led to an erroneous evaluation of USSR legislation.

To remedy this alleged bias in the COE's supervisory policy procedures, Gubinski and Ivanov proposed that the committee abandon its established practice of designating each of its members to review the reports of individual member states on specific conventions. They urged, instead, that the more important conventions be reviewed by a subcommittee of the COE consisting of one representative of a capitalist country, one of a socialist country, and one of a developing (and presumably non-aligned) country, referred to informally as a "troika." Their proposal never found favor, however, either in the COE or the Tripartite Conference Committee on the Application of Conventions and Recommendations. Nevertheless, they persisted in their disruptive tactics until the collapse of the Soviet Union, which brought an instantaneous cessation of their efforts.

The COE has a policy, for which I was grateful, of exempting a new member from specific tasks of preliminary examination of designated conventions for the first year, so that he or she has the opportunity to become familiar with the committee's methods of work. In 1987 I was assigned the responsibility of reviewing a number of conventions, of which only one—No. 100, Remuneration for Men and Women Workers for Work of Equal Value, which came into force in 1953—was particularly interesting to me. The language of the convention was, unfortunately, interpreted in different ways by the ratifying member states. Article 1, for example, says in part that for the purpose of the convention, "the term 'equal remuneration for men and women workers for work of equal value' refers to rates of remuneration established without discrimination based on sex." A number of states ignored the phrase "work of equal value" and considered that they had complied with the convention by enacting legislation requiring that men and women be paid equal remuneration for doing the same work. Similarly, Article 3 provides: "Where such action will assist in giving effect to the provision of this Convention, measures shall be taken to promote objective appraisal of jobs on the basis of work to be performed," and, "The methods to be followed in this appraisal may be decided upon by the authorities responsible for the determination of rates of remuneration, or, when such rates are determined by collective agreements, by the parties thereto." Finally, Article 3 provides: "Differential rates between workers which correspond, without regard to sex, to differences as determined by such objective appraisal, in the work to be performed, shall not be considered as being contrary to the principle of equal remuneration for men and women workers for work of equal value." Most of the ratifying member states chose to disregard or misinterpret the phrase "work of equal value" in Articles 1 and 3 of the convention. This was hardly surprising when one considers that true compliance would require objective evaluation of myriads of job requirements, including many whose remuneration was based on factors other than sex. An example of the problem was presented by a case arising in the United States involving a claim by nurses in San Jose, California, that the work they performed was of equal value to that of highway engineers.

Of the hundreds of reports on Convention No. 100 that I reviewed in my nine years of service on the COE, I cannot recall a single instance in which a reporting member state called attention to a similar problem and disclosed how it had been handled.

In 1990, I proposed the following introductory comments to my review of the reports received that year from the ratifying member states on Convention No. 100:

> Convention No. 100 was adopted in 1951. Since then, some 110 countries have rati-fied it, but, paradoxically, relatively few have come close to abiding by its provisions.
>
> Some of the reports received exhibit a certain naiveté, or perhaps disingenuous-ness, in claiming compliance with the terms of the Convention. For example, some simply state that they are in compliance because their constitutions establish equality between men's and women's remuneration. Indeed, there seems to be a general tendency to confuse equal pay to men and women performing different work of equal value. Some countries report compliance with the Convention on the basis of a uniform minimum wage, applicable equally to male and female workers, but having nothing to say about differences in male and female wages above the minimum.
>
> It is obvious that the concept of paying equal pay for work of equal value is a diffi-cult one to grasp and was not fully understood by many, perhaps most, countries at the time that they ratified Convention No. 100. Full compliance with the Convention by even a majority of countries is not likely to be achieved for many years, and will require greater efforts on the part of not only governments, but of the social partners as well, to realize the full implications of the principle of equal pay for work of equal value. The ILO will also be required to provide additional educational and technical assistance.

My comments were intended for internal use only. They were briefly reflected in the general observation on Convention No. 100 contained in the COE's report to the International Labour Conference, which was couched in the bureaucratese characteristic of all ILO documents:

> From its review of governments' reports, the Committee concludes that most rati-fying countries have serious difficulties in applying the main requirement of the Convention, i.e. to "promote or ensure the application to all workers of the principle of equal remuneration for men and women workers for work of equal value."
>
> The difficulties encountered by governments which have ratified this Convention appear to be due to a number of factors, including: lack of knowledge of the true situation due to the unavailability or inadequacy of data and research; lack of under-standing of the concept of equal value as it is used in the Convention; ignorance of

the principles of job evaluation, without the application of which it is difficult to determine the relative value of jobs; and lack of the financial resources necessary to collect and analyze data, and to institute systems of job evaluation.

The Committee hopes that the governments of those countries whose legislation still does not embody the principle of equal pay for work of equal value will take the necessary steps to amend their legislation accordingly....

In addition, the Committee hopes that in all cases where it is not yet done, governments and employers' and workers' organizations will endeavor to collect and analyze data on earnings and related factors, in order to document fully the nature and extent of existing inequalities, and to devise measures to remedy them....

In taking the above measures, governments may wish to have recourse to the advice and technical co-operation of the ILO.

Although I became familiar fairly quickly with the major issues confronting the COE, it took considerably longer to learn about the inner workings and bureaucratic rivalries of the ILO and to become acquainted with members of the outstanding staff of the Labour Standards Division. My files contain the minutes of a meeting in Washington in April 1989 of the U.S. Consultative Group to the ILO, at which I was the invited speaker. After making a brief presentation, I answered a number of questions pertaining to the operations of the COE. I have no independent recollection of that meeting, but the minutes quote me as saying that I still considered myself very much of a newcomer to the COE, that I was frustrated by the amount of paperwork required of the committee members in our two-week sessions in Geneva, and that a great deal of committee time was spent making sure that English and French translations were precise. I also expressed warm praise of the ILO staff assisting the COE. In my opinion, the staff had no undue influence on the outcome of the COE's conclusions on politically sensitive cases. Acknowledging that the staff sometimes tried to steer the committee's conclusions, I declared that the committee members, aware that the staff tended to push certain ideas, pushed right back.

On another matter, I reported that even though I served on the committee as an independent expert, I was nonetheless regarded primarily as a representative of the United States and therefore felt somewhat restrained from playing an active role in the discussion of ILO human rights conventions that the United States had not ratified.

Indeed, this was a circumstance that limited my usefulness throughout my tenure on the COE. Thus, at a June 1986 session of the International Labour Conference, a government advisor to the USSR, in a thinly veiled criticism of the United States, said in part:

> The report of the Committee of Experts for 1986...informs us of the appointment of two experts, one of which is from a State that has ratified a grand total of seven ILO Conventions, not one of which is among the ILO's most important Conventions, and not one of which concerns human rights.
>
> We are told that the Governing Body selects objective experts, but was it really not possible to find a single expert from amongst the several dozen countries that have ratified the ILO's basic Conventions?[8]

Finally, I described the atmosphere of that year's COE as palpably post-Glasnost and confirmed that the Soviet and Polish experts had adopted a much softer line, ceasing to make their usual objections in committee meetings and merely submitting their dissents in writing to the ILO secretariat. I expressed the view that further attacks on the COE's supervisory policies and procedures were unlikely and that the "troika" proposal referred to earlier in this chapter was now dead.

The failure of the United States to ratify most of the human rights conventions was a source of continuing concern for Americans participating in any of the governing functions of the ILO.[9] The situation was aggravated by the strong stands taken by the United States against alleged violations of human rights conventions by other member states, notably the USSR and its ideological allies. The U.S. Council for International Business, which represents American employers in the ILO, has been the chief obstacle to ratification of ILO conventions by the U.S. Senate. Its legal counsel, Edward E. Potter, is the author of a monograph *Freedom of Association, the Right to Organize and Collective Bargaining: The Impact of U.S. Law and Practice of Ratification of ILO Conventions No. 87 & No. 98* (1984), which has been adopted by the council as its policy guide.

---

[8] International Labour Conference Provisional Record 38/19 (23 June 1986).

[9] From 1938 to 2001, the United States ratified only 14 conventions, six of which relate to maritime affairs. Of the remaining eight, only two—No. 105, Abolition of Forced Labor (ratified in 1991), and No. 182, Worst Forms of Child Labor (ratified in 1999)—relate to human rights. The United States has failed to ratify No. 87, Freedom of Association and Protection of the Right to Organize, and No. 98, Right to Organize and Collective Bargaining.

Potter alleged, in general, that the ratification by the United States of Convention No. 87 would violate the letter and the spirit of specific provisions of the Labor Management Relations (Taft-Hartley) Act of 1947 (LMRA) and the Labor-Management Reporting and Disclosure Act of 1959 (LMRDA). Those allegations, and other similar claims about ratification of Convention No. 98, were based on a worst-case scenario derived not only from the specific language of Convention No. 87 but also from prior observations by the COE and the ILO Committee on Freedom of Association (CFA). Potter argued that, at the very least, ratification of those conventions might create an obligation for the United States to change its laws on those matters. It seemed to me that whether his specific fears were justified was debatable. Indeed, in 1980 the U.S. Department of Labor prepared a briefing paper on Convention No. 87, to which it attached a memorandum of law prepared in 1976 by the Office of the Solicitor of Labor. The "executive summary" of the briefing paper stated that when President Truman submitted this convention to the U.S. Senate for advice and ratification in 1949, the "coordinated view of the Executive Branch was that ratification would not entail the obligation to enact new legislation nor to revise existing law since the United States was in full compliance with the terms of the Convention." The summary recognized, however, that some parties might still anticipate that ratification would unwittingly nullify domestic legislation through "creative judicial construction." Accordingly, it noted two possible approaches that, if employed, "would absolutely preclude such a result":

> First, the Convention could be ratified with a declaration that it is non self-executing. Second, the Convention could be ratified with an understanding that "all necessary and appropriate measures" as provided by article II [(of Convention No. 87][10] means, in the context of the United States, that the obligations contained in the Conventions have been acceded to only to the extent of the Commerce Power [as set forth in the U.S. Constitution]."

The attached memorandum of law was addressed, in particular, to questions raised by the U.S. Chamber of Commerce as to possible

---

[10] Article II provides: "Each member of the...[ILO] for which this Convention is in force undertakes to take all necessary and appropriate measures to ensure that workers and employers may exercise freely the right to organize."

inconsistencies with the LMRDA and the LMRA. The memorandum concluded that "provisions of the LMRDA are not regulations which impair the guarantees granted by the Convention." In respect of the LMRA, the memorandum explained that "[f]ederal legislation specifically protecting the right to organize against private interference is restricted to the scope of the Commerce Clause" of the Taft-Hartley Act, but that inasmuch as this was the only "appropriate" measure the federal government could take to protect those rights under our system of government, "it appears the obligations imposed by Article II are met."

Those arguments were unpersuasive, however, and the Senate refused to give its consent to ratification of Conventions No. 87 and 98.

The policy debate over ratification resumed in September 1985, when the Senate Committee on Labor and Human Resources, chaired by Senator Orrin C. Hatch of Utah, held a hearing on the United States and the ILO.[11] In the words of the committee chairman, the two main questions posed were, "First, what is the feasibility of U.S. ratification of ILO labor conventions without creating a detrimental effect on U.S. labor law? Second, is there any linkage between the U.S. ratification history... and our country's influence within the ILO?" The principal witnesses were Secretary of State George P. Shultz, Secretary of Labor William E. Brock, Lane Kirkland, president of the AFL-CIO, and Abraham Katz, president of the U.S. Council for International Business.

Shultz declared that the failure of the United States to ratify any but the maritime ILO conventions "conflicts with the obligations we assumed when we joined the ILO." Noting that the ILO's purpose is to "raise labor standards around the globe through the process of adoption and ratification of conventions," he pointed out that "[e]very member state has a moral obligation to make a good faith effort to determine whether it can ratify conventions." But, he observed, "our behavior sends a message that ILO procedures do not apply to us." Shultz also pointed out the "inconsistency between our failure to consider ratification of ILO conventions and the growing tendency in the Congress to refer to internationally

---

[11] The United States and the International Labor Organization, "Hearing before the Senate Committee on Labor and Human Resources," 99th Cong., 1st Sess. (1985).

recognized worker rights standards regarding freedom of association and forced labor in United States trade and legislation." He concluded that the United States should correct its approach

> by reopening the ledger on possible ratification, making a good-faith effort to review more systematically and vigorously those conventions which we can ratify without contravening U.S. labor laws. We should be more flexible and consider individual conventions on their own merits, rather than to contrive to make a priori judgments that only maritime conventions are suitable for the United States to ratify.

Brock defended the low number of U.S. ratifications of ILO conventions by attributing it mainly to our federal system of government. "Most conventions," he explained, "would require legislative action by the constituent states as well as, or instead of, by the Federal Government, and the United States cannot assume a treaty obligation under a convention which might fall wholly or in part within state jurisdiction." This was one of the arguments advanced by Potter in his monograph. Brock did report, however, that in 1980 the President's Committee on the ILO established a subgroup to study the legal implications of specific ILO conventions. This subgroup, the Tripartite Advisory Panel on International Labor Standards (TAPILS), is composed of legal experts from the Departments of Labor, State, and Commerce, the AFL-CIO, and the U.S. Council for International Business, as well as other U.S. agencies, depending upon the particular convention under discussion. Brock advised that in 1983, after two years of intermittent review and deliberation, TAPILS had unanimously determined that there were no objections of a legal nature to ratification of two ILO conventions: No. 144, Tripartite Consultations to Promote the Implementation of International Labour Standards, and No. 147, Minimum Standards in Merchant Ships.[12]

Kirkland termed the U.S. ratification record "deplorable," noting that of the countries with comparable years of ILO membership, only one—El Salvador—had fewer ratifications than the United States, whereas the members of the (then) European Economic Community averaged 70 convention ratifications each, and some had more than 100.

---

[12] Both were eventually ratified in 1988.

Of more critical importance, he continued, was "the fact that a nation that prides and proclaims itself...as a champion of human rights has ratified none of the basic human rights conventions."[13] Taking issue with Brock, Kirkland insisted that federal structure was not the reason for our nonratification record:

> Rather it stems from the resistance in the past by employer organizations because ratification would involve a supervisory scrutiny of our democratic laws and practices and involves some of our domestic labor standards. Their position on tripartite consultation is a classic example. This convention poses no Federal-State conflict of jurisdiction whatsoever. Their real argument has been that it would open the door for other ratifications.

In his testimony, Katz seemed to confirm Kirkland's explanation of the reasons for U.S. resistance to the ratification of ILO conventions. His first point was that modification of U.S. labor law through ratification of ILO conventions differing from U.S. law "would amount to a complete divestiture by Congress to the ILO of its delegated power to establish labor policy." His second point had more sweeping implications:

> On broader policy grounds, the business community remains opposed to ratification of ILO conventions because we are concerned that any ratification will be perceived by the ILO community as ending the longstanding U.S. policy of not ratifying nonmaritime ILO conventions.

Ratification of conventions with which our law is at variance, Katz continued, would "present an opportunity that does not now exist for our critics to criticize the United States." He went on to point out that the policy of not ratifying nonmaritime conventions had provided a ready response to "Soviet-bloc attitudes on our failure to ratify fundamental ILO conventions."

In a chapter of *Blessings of Liberty: The Constitution and the Practice of Law* (1988), a publication of the American Law Institute and the American Bar Association Committee on Continuing Professional Education, I reviewed the foregoing history of the U.S. policy of

---

[13] As previously noted, the United States subsequently ratified No. 105, Abolition of Forced Labor, and No. 182, Worst Forms of Child Labor, in 1991 and 1999, respectively.

nonratification of most ILO conventions.[14] Offering the opinion that the strategy and tactics of our policy toward the ILO seemed to be the product of our competition with the Soviet Union and its allies, I expressed the fear that the U.S. record of nonratification of nonmaritime conventions, especially those addressing human rights, would seriously weaken our influence and support among developing countries, which would prove to be of greater importance in the long run.

Summing up my personal views, I declared that, at bottom, the U.S. reluctance to ratify nonmaritime conventions rests upon a refusal to consider any external limitation upon our sovereign powers in the area of labor standards and labor relations. To me, the fears expressed by Potter and Katz were grossly exaggerated. In any case, if, following our ratification of a nonmaritime convention, exception should be taken by the COE or the Tripartite Committee of the International Labour Conference to some nonconforming aspect of our domestic labor law, I said that Congress should examine the exception on its merits and decide whether it warrants a legislative change. In conclusion, I stated:

> For too long in this country we have maintained a solipsistic attitude about our labor laws, rejecting out of hand the notion that we can ever improve them by adhering to selected international labor standards. A suspension of that attitude, pending a careful, tripartite review of the ILO Conventions we have not ratified, is...long overdue. As long as we refrain from doing so, and from acting promptly to ratify at least those Conventions compatible with democratic labor laws, we shall continue to neglect the opportunity to increase our influence in the ILO and to further its laudable efforts to revise labor standards—especially those fostering human freedom and social justice—throughout the world.

Regrettably, the establishment of TAPILS in 1980 and the more flexible attitude toward ratification of ILO conventions taken by the Reagan administration did not accomplish what many ILO supporters had hoped. Nonetheless, they did improve the U.S. ratification record: in the period from 1980 to 2005, the U.S. ratified eight conventions, only one of which dealt with maritime affairs.

---

[14]American Law Institute–American Bar Association Committee on Continuing Professional Education, *The United States and the ILO: Neglected Opportunities.*

In November 1988 I was informed by Blanchard that the Governing Body had renewed my appointment as a member of the COE. Blanchard's term ended in February 1989. He was succeeded by Michel Hansenne, a Belgian, who was dedicated to expanding the ILO's activities and enhancing its influence throughout the world. Unlike his predecessor, however, he lacked charm, smoothness, and an ability to overcome or moderate opposition through persuasion. Nor could it be said that his administration was noted for its transparency; he made a number of decisions without first consulting those directly affected by them. One of the most important of these related to membership on the COE, and in the ensuing uproar, I found myself an unexpected protagonist for the committee.

Members of the COE, unlike members of the ILO staff, are not subject to the U.N. Common System age limit of 60. Nevertheless, in November 1990, Hansenne let it be known that he believed the COE needed "rejuvenation." Accordingly, without providing the Governing Body with an opportunity to express its views, Hansenne initiated a de facto policy of "70 and out" for COE members, to go into effect beginning with the next annual meeting in 1991. Two committee members were immediately affected: Razafindralambo of Madagascar, the regularly elected reporter of the COE, who was responsible for drafting the committee's annual General Reports to the Governing Body, and me. The new rule was not consistently applied, however—Ago, eight years my senior, was reappointed. Although I received no formal notice that my service as a COE member was about to be terminated, my committee colleagues and the ILO staff assumed that our 1991 session would be my last. Various members of both groups personally expressed to me their regret that my service on the COE was to be cut short by the new age limitation.

Meanwhile, the U.S. Consultative Group prepared background information and talking points on the tripartite U.S. position on the new policy for U.S. Ambassador Morris B. Abram for his pre-conference meeting with Hansenne. Despite Abram's efforts, Hansenne was unmoved. The consultative committee took its views to the Governing Body in its 1991 post-conference meeting. That committee reported that although many governments in the general body shared its concerns, others were accustomed to mandating age limits and were not persuaded of the merits of the U.S. arguments, which were, in part, as follows:

> The U.S. Government is dismayed that the Director-General did not provide the Governing Body with an opportunity to express its views on this new policy before its implementation. We—and our social partners, the AFL-CIO and the U.S. Council for International Business—strongly believe that it should be overturned at the November 1991 session of the Governing Body, before long-term damage to the Committee is done.
>
> We believe that placing an age limit of 70 on members of the Committee of Experts is a misguided and destructive policy, for both intrinsic and extrinsic reasons.
>
> First, it is well established that, unlike mathematicians and scientists, for example, jurists come into their own only as they grow older, when they acquire the breadth of legal judgment that experience alone yields. Thus, *this new policy of 70-and-out will not only force out the most experienced and able current members of the Committee on the ground of age alone, it will also preclude the selection of most eminent jurists as new members of the Committee.* [emphasis in original]
>
> We believe that, with this new arbitrary age requirement, the ILO will not find it easy to recruit jurists who possess the experience, judgment, and stature required of this committee. (We also wonder how many eminent jurists will have the time, in the midst of their legal careers, to take on the considerable workload placed on this Committee.) ...
>
> A 70-and-out policy will also tend strongly to prevent members of this core body of the ILO supervisory machinery from becoming experienced participants in its work. If this age limit is not lifted, future as well as current members of the Committee will be forced to retire just when—or even before—they have acquired substantial experience in the specific work of the Committee itself.
>
> *We believe that the D-G's policy is also misguided because of the profound effect it will soon have on the composition of this Committee: it will require the D-G to replace more than half of its 20 members in the next three years....* [emphasis in original]
>
> We are not asking the Director-General to make a special exception for the American member of the Committee. Instead, we are seeking a change in the policy itself. Nevertheless, the U.S. member of this Committee is a good example of why this de facto policy is misguided. When he was initially appointed to the Committee of Experts, in November 1985, at the age of 70, he brought to it a broad as well as deep legal and industrial relations experience, both national and international. But he had little knowledge of the ILO and no experience in the highly technical and specialized work of its Committee of Experts. We do not believe it is in the interests of the Committee, or the ILO, to lose a seasoned, experienced participant in its work, on the ground of age alone....

Decisions to reappoint current members of the Committee of Experts should be handled on a case-by-case basis, taking into consideration the competence and willingness of each individual expert. Age should not *per se* preclude the reappointment of current members of this quasi-judicial body of the ILO's supervisory machinery, nor should it preclude the selection of new members.

The incident had its comic aspects. At the end of the COE's 1990 session, most of my colleagues, as well as a member of our staff, expressed to me their regret over my anticipated termination. I thanked them but pointed out that, so far, I had received no formal notice of my removal. In fact, that notice never came. Instead, in a letter dated 22 November 1991, Hansenne informed me that the Governing Body had decided to renew my appointment as a member of the COE for a period of three years. His letter concluded, "I would like to take this opportunity to convey to you my gratitude for your valuable contributions to the work of the Organization."

Upon my return to the next session of the COE, I was treated as if I were a Lazarus raised from the dead.

From time to time the COE prepares a general survey in respect of one or more conventions for presentation to the ILO Conference Committee on the Application of Standards. The general surveys are prepared by ILO staff under the supervision of designated COE members. Few conventions have aroused as much interest and provoked as much controversy as No. 87, Freedom of Association and Protection of the Right to Organize and No. 98, Right to Organize and Collective Bargaining.

The 1994 general survey of the same two conventions was the sixth of its kind. Previous surveys on freedom of association and collective bargaining were carried out in 1956, 1957, 1959, 1973, and 1983. It was my good fortune to be appointed a member of the working party responsible for preparing the 1994 general survey, in which the COE endeavored in particular to respond to questions and concerns expressed in the Conference Committee on the Application of Standards as to the scope of the two conventions.[15] These questions and concerns related principally to the right of workers to strike, which is not specifically

---

[15] The other members of the working party were Ruda, Wood, Verdier, and Mbaye.

referred to in either convention. In its 1983 general survey, the COE made a number of observations about the right to strike:

> The Committee considers that the right to strike is one of the essential means available to workers and their organizations for the promotion and protection of their economic and social interests.

> In international law, the right to strike is explicitly recognized in Article 8 of the International Covenant on Economic, Social and Cultural Rights. At the regional level, the European Social Charter was the first international text to recognize explicitly the right to strike in the case of a conflict of interests, subject to any commitments under collective agreements in force.

> A general ban on strikes seriously limits the means at the disposal of trade unions to further and defend the interests of their members...and their right to organize their activities...and is, therefore, not compatible with the principles of freedom of association.

> [I]nasmuch as the prohibition or general suppression of strikes constitutes a major restriction of one of the essential means available to workers and their organizations for furthering and defending their interests, such measures cannot be justified except in situations of acute national crisis, and then only for a limited period.

> In the opinion of the Committee, the principle whereby the right to strike may be limited or prohibited in the public service or in essential services, whether public, semi-public, or private, would become meaningless if the legislation defined the public service or essential services too broadly....[T]he prohibition should be confined to public servants, acting in their capacity as agents of the public authority or to services whose interruption would endanger the life, personal safety or health of the whole or part of the population....Restrictions should be offset by adequate impartial and speedy consideration and arbitration procedures, in which the parties concerned can take part at every stage and in which the awards should in all cases be binding on both parties. Such awards, once rendered, should be rapidly and fully implemented.

As might be expected, statements such as these aroused strong opposition, particularly from employer representatives in the International Labour Conference. Delegates from the United States played a major role in organizing the attack on the COE's position which, it was alleged, disregarded the plain language of the two conventions and substituted its own interpretation in an act of administrative legislation. Thus, the debate over the right to strike also involved the broader question of the extent of the COE's supervisory authority to decide disputed interpretations of conventions.

In respect of the COE's right to interpret provisions of ILO conventions, the COE had long recognized that Article 37 of the ILO constitution gives exclusive jurisdiction to decide "[a]ny question or dispute relating to the interpretation of this Constitution or any subsequent Convention concluded by the Members in pursuance of the provisions of this Constitution" to the International Court of Justice. In 1987, however, the COE declared that in order to carry out its function of evaluating the implementation of conventions, it had to consider and express its views on the meaning of certain provisions of conventions. Following challenges to its right to interpret Convention No. 87, in particular, as including the right to strike, the COE responded in 1990 by stating that as long as the International Court of Justice did not contradict it, the COE's interpretations might be regarded as valid and commonly accepted.

In preparing its 1994 general survey of Convention Nos. 87 and 98, the COE's working party carefully, and I think objectively, considered both sides of this debate, but its conclusions reiterated those in the 1983 survey. For me, the principal argument supporting those conclusions is that the right to organize and to protect the exercise of the rights specifically mentioned in Convention No. 87 necessarily implies the right to strike, subject to reasonable restrictions. The debate continued, but in my view the judgment of the authors of a respected book published in 1996, focusing on the ILO's international standards system and basic human rights, correctly states the situation:

> It is significant that in spite of the many questions raised about how the ILO adopts and supervises its international labor standards, the basis of the system has not been seriously questioned by anyone. There have been changes made, or points are being examined, at the margins of the system, but no change is proposed to the core. Even those parts of the ILO's constituency which have challenged various aspects of the system, have done so while reaffirming their faith in the integrity of the system as a whole....
>
> There appears little room for doubt...that the ILO's supervisory function has again been reaffirmed by the discussions which have taken place since its 75th Anniversary in 1994, and that it is set to last for many years into the future.[16]

---

[16] Bartolomei de la Cruz et al., *International Labor Organization*, 124.

My last three-year term on the COE ended in 1994. By that time Eleanor and I had exhausted what Geneva had to offer in the way of physical and cultural attractions. Except for occasional dinners with Douglas and Woods and several of our COE colleagues who were also active in the International Society for Labour and Social Security Law, we spent most of our free time alone. The social highlight of our annual visits to Geneva was a party given each year by our dear friends Johannes and Inge Schregle—an event that gave us the greatest pleasure. The shift in the timing of the COE sessions from December to March also tended to create conflicts with some of my other commitments in the United States. In light of all the circumstances, Eleanor and I agreed that the time had come for me to submit my resignation. Hansenne acknowledged my letter of resignation with a very gracious reply. I also unexpectedly received a letter from the Deputy Under Secretary of the U.S. Department of Labor, Joaquin F. Otero, thanking me for my contributions to the work of the ILO in general and to the COE in particular and soliciting my views on where the ILO should be going with its standards, what should be the relationship between the COE and the Conference Committee, what role the ILO should play in the development and implementation of international trade policies, what is the link between trade and standards, and what role the ILO, in general, should play in world affairs of the year 2000 and beyond. For reasons I can no longer recall, I did not send him a detailed response to each of his questions.

The climax of my final session of the COE was the annual cocktail party given by the ILO staff in honor of the COE. To my complete surprise, Ruda interrupted the proceedings by announcing my forthcoming retirement, saying some very complimentary things about my contributions to the work of the COE and presenting me with a wristwatch bearing the ILO logo. I chose that occasion to thank the staff for the high level of competence demonstrated by all of them helping the committee with its work.

More than 10 years after my departure from the COE, I have again been considering the probing questions put to me by Otero in March

1994. By far the most important of these was "where the ILO should be going with its standards." My views on that issue have been largely shaped by an article written by Efrén Córdova, a former chief of the ILO's labor law and labor relations branch. The gist of Córdova's argument is

> that the rate of adoption of international labor standards by the International Labour Organization (ILO) is reaching critical proportions and may soon bring about detrimental effects to the ILO and its Member States…[and] that such excessive proliferation of standards may lead to serious imbalances in the world socioeconomic order, thus defeating the very purpose that originally inspired the adoption of labor standards. While, admittedly…the standard setting function is one of the hallmarks of the ILO and has greatly contributed to social progress in many countries, the ILO has most likely exceeded its normal and expected bounds, both in terms of the quantity and quality of its standards. Should the present trend continue, application of such a voluminous set of standards might become unmanageable, and striking differences would appear among the Member States with respect to their compliance with international obligations and the degree of social development.[17]

These warnings have proved to be well founded and were confirmed by my own experience as a member of the COE. By the end of 1995, 176 conventions and 183 recommendations had been adopted by the ILO. In the ensuing decade, those numbers had increased to 185 and 195, respectively. During my tenure on the COE, ending in 1994, the number of periodic reports from the member states on the application of ratified conventions, as well as the quality of those reports, declined. Moreover, many of the reports were received too late to be included in the COE's annual report to the International Labour Conference on compliance with ratified conventions by member states. Particularly in the case of developing countries, it became quite clear in many instances that the reporting country lacked the human resources, economic support, and technical knowledge necessary to complete the required reports and to answer specific questions directed to them by the COE.

The preamble of the ILO constitution adopted in 1919 declares that universal and lasting peace can be established only if it is based on social justice, noting that "conditions of labor exist involving such injustice,

---

[17] Córdova, "Some Reflections," 138.

hardship and privation to large numbers of people as to produce unrest so great that the peace and harmony of the world are imperiled." It asserts further that "an improvement of these conditions is urgently required" and cites as examples

> the regulation of the hours of work, including the establishment of a maximum working day and week, the regulation of the labor supply, the prevention of unemployment, the provision of an adequate living wage, the protection of the worker against sickness, disease and injury arising out of his employment, the protection of children, young persons and women, provision for old age and injury, protection of the interests of workers when employed in countries other than their own, promulgation of the principle of freedom of association, the organization of vocational and technical education and other measures.

Achievement of these goals would seem to have been a sufficient challenge, but in its 1944 Declaration of Philadelphia, which was subsequently incorporated in its constitution, the ILO significantly expanded its aims and purposes, as Córdova noted in his article:

> The original mandate was rephrased in more comprehensive terms and the scope of specific subjects was broadened. The notion of social security replaced the protection of the worker against sickness, disease and injury arising out of employment; collective bargaining was added to the right of association; a program of full employment was to be developed instead of assistance to the unemployed; and several other matters, such as training, transfer of labor, maternity protection, safety and health, and the collaboration of employers and workers, were also included among the purposes of the ILO.

All of the issues listed in the preamble to its constitution fall within the ILO's general competence regarding labor, but the Declaration of Philadelphia sought to push the ILO toward areas alien to its original mandate, such as international economic and financial practices and measures, international trends, expansion of production and development, child welfare, nutrition, housing, equality of educational and vocational opportunity, health, and facilities for recreation and culture. As Córdova observed, "The authors of the Declaration of Philadelphia apparently visualized the ILO as an all-purpose organization capable of dealing with a diversity of subjects and more attuned to social and economic policy than to the sphere of labor."

To refer to but one example, the Employment Policy Convention No. 122 (1964), one of the so-called promotional conventions, provides in Article 1:

1. With a view to stimulating economic growth and development, raising levels of living, meeting manpower requirements and overcoming unemployment and underemployment, each Member shall declare and pursue, as a major goal, an active policy designed to promote full, productive and freely chosen employment.
2. The said policy shall aim at ensuring that—
   (a) there is work for all who are available for and seeking work;
   (b) such work is as productive as possible;
   (c) there is freedom of choice of employment and the fullest possible opportunity for each worker to qualify for, and to use his skills and endowments in a job for which he is well suited, irrespective of race, color, sex, religion, political opinion, national extraction or social origin.
3. The said policy shall take due account of the stage and level of economic development and the mutual relationships between employment objectives and other economic and social objectives, and shall be pursued by methods that are appropriate to national conditions and practices.[18]

To be sure, in time most of the non-labor questions detailed in the Declaration of Philadelphia were entrusted to other U.N. agencies, such as the Economic and Social Council and the Bretton Woods institutions, the U.N. International Children's Emergency Fund (UNICEF), the Food and Agricultural Organization (FAO), the U.N. Educational, Scientific, and Cultural Organization (UNESCO), the World Health Organization (WHO), the U.N. Industrial Development Organization (UNIDO), and the U.N. Conference on Trade and Development (UNCTAD). But these delegations have been offset to a considerable degree by the new conventions and recommendations, which themselves have become more detailed and technical (e.g., Convention No. 136, concerning protection against hazards of poisoning arising from benzine). New conventions have dealt with such questions as management training, vocational rehabilitation, human resource development, workers' education, welfare facilities, housing, protection of the environment, rural development,

---

[18] Promotional conventions, rather than laying down precise standards that a member state pledges to achieve once the convention is ratified, set objectives to be attained by means of a continuing program of action.

cooperatives, land holding (tenants and sharecroppers), and tripartite consultation. Although many of these topics had been the subject of research and technical cooperation, members of the ILO staff and employers' delegates expressed doubt about their suitability for international standards. Similar reservations regarding conventions dealing with the establishment of systems and services had been expanded inside and outside the International Labour Office. Broad subjects of employment and social policies, including their special aims and standards, found their place in the International Labour Code along such minute questions as the certification of ships' cooks, paid educational leave, crew accommodations, and anthrax prevention. The constitutional reference to a labor inspection system grew to the point of including 10 instruments (i.e., conventions and recommendations) on labor administration despite the striking differences among national labor departments, both in their structure and their functions.

Another cause for concern has been the growth of so-called sectoral instruments dealing with particular occupational sectors and with special segments of the labor force. After 1945, the ILO produced a veritable cascade of instruments dealing with public employees, dockworkers, fishermen, boatmen, road transport workers, plantation workers, tenants and sharecroppers, nursing personnel, and hotel and restaurant workers. Consequently, other groups of workers have demanded similar special treatment, notwithstanding the fact that since 1994 the ILO has created special machinery for that purpose, namely, permanent tripartite industrial committees looking more closely into the problems of each major industry of international importance and providing guidance for member states.

Moreover, changes relating to the nature of labor standards were coupled with alterations in the procedures governing the submission of proposals for new conference items to the Governing Body. Article 14 of the ILO constitution states that the agenda of the conference will be settled by the Governing Body, which shall consider any suggestions as to the agenda that may be made by the government of any of the member states, by any representative organization, or by any public international organization. However, Article 14 does not assign to the

International Labour Office the function of proposing new labor standards. Nevertheless, in practice, the International Labour Office has been the principal source of proposals to be considered by the Governing Body. Indeed, in the decade ending in 1994, the International Labour Office, on average, submitted seven proposals each year for the adoption of new standards. It also is in charge of sifting through the various standard-related ideas and selecting the ones it considers most appropriate for standard setting. Since 1984, it has considered the following criteria: (1) the number of workers concerned by the proposed subject; (2) the significance of the subject in all regions of the world; (3) the importance of the topic for the most disadvantaged workers; (4) the time elapsed since other instruments on the same subject were adopted; (5) the seriousness of the problem; and (6) the extent to which the adoption of the instrument would advance fundamental rights of workers.

Córdova believes that these criteria should be stricter:

> The impact of international labor standards, the diversity of the situations to which they are going to be applied, their possible use in connection with trade sanctions, and preferential trade treatment call for a cautious approach which may demand the application of stringent criteria.

Accordingly, he suggests that subject matters proposed for international normative action should also be: (1) suitable for the elaboration of precise minimum standards; (2) simple in their foundations; (3) dealing with matters where some compatibility can be found at the level of national laws and practices; and (4) timely.

The inevitable outcome of the changes mentioned above has been an extensive proliferation of international labor instruments. As of 2004, the ILO had adopted 185 conventions and 195 recommendations. Although the number of new instruments adopted each year has slowed in recent years—five conventions and eight recommendations since 1996—Córdova observes that "[c]onsideration of possible new instruments should…have been accompanied by greater emphasis on discussions about consolidation, revision, and simplification of existing texts."

The foregoing developments have resulted in serious consequences for the ILO's workload. In 1927, the newly established COE was called upon to examine annually only 150 reports from member states on the measures they had taken to give effect to the provisions of conventions to which they were a party. By 1959, however, the ILO had adopted 111 conventions with regard to which 2,000 ratifications had been registered. In the face of this burgeoning workload, the Governing Body, in 1959, changed the constitutional requirement of annual reports to biannual reports. In 1977, by which time the number of conventions had risen to 140 and the total number of member states to over 130, while the total number of ratifications had increased to 2000, the periodicity of required reports was changed again. After 1997, government reports dealing with certain particularly important conventions, such as those regarding basic human rights, were requested every two years; other convention reports were requested only at four-year intervals. As Córdova reported in his article, in the years 1989–1992 the COE had to examine between 36 and 44 conventions annually, less than a quarter of existing conventions. This limited examination, he observed, is bound to reduce the effective application of standards.

The growing number of new conventions has created additional problems for the member states, particularly in respect of the increased administrative duties involved. Governments are called upon to perform a lengthy list of tasks, including consultations with employers' and workers' organizations, preparation of reports, replies to questionnaires, study of the observations or requests for information made by the COE, submission of new texts to the competent national authorities, proposals for ratification, analysis of the measures that should be taken to give effect to the provisions of a convention, drafts of relevant pieces of legislation, and participation in the Conference Committee on the Application of Conventions and Recommendations.

Córdova has pointed to troubles of a different character arising when some governments felt the urge to ratify as many instruments as possible to avoid the risk of being regarded as socially backward. Governments are pressured especially by the ILO and the labor movement to measure up to other countries in respect of the number of conventions ratified. As the number of ratifications came to be considered in some circles as a yardstick for social progress, and as the number of instruments was constantly growing, some hasty and spurious forms of ratification began to appear.[19] Two glaring examples of bogus ratification were the ratification by landlocked Luxembourg of a number of maritime conventions and by Cuba of a convention on indigenous and tribal populations, which are nonexistent in that country. The former USSR adopted a number of conventions dealing with basic human rights, but those ratifications could be considered to be either "empty" or, at best, "in principle," because they were never really effectuated. The reason given was the usual one: the COE had misunderstood the principles of Soviet law and had not taken account of the economic and social systems existing in "socialist" countries.

Concerning the discrepancy between formal ratification and real compliance, it was formerly considered to be due to administrative deficiencies; indeed, that explanation is still partially true, but it is not the only one. Córdova observed that

> developing countries have the opportunity to avail themselves of the advisory services and the direct contact procedures of the ILO, whereby the Office puts at the disposal of Member States the expertise necessary to reconcile national legislation within international labor standards. Is it not fair to expect, under the circumstances, that a certain laxity prompted by the magnitude of the obligations assumed is also at work?

The net result of all this is that serious imbalances are being created between countries with few ratifications or a poor record of real compliance or both, and countries that have ratified and are complying with a reasonably high number of conventions. This means, Córdova declared, that situations close to the "'social dumping' that the founders of the ILO tried to eliminate are reappearing under a different guise in certain regions of the world."

Finally, a new and critically important issue has emerged in recent years: the compatibility of labor standards with economic development. The ILO has always been concerned about the application of a uniform set of standards to countries at different stages of economic development;

---

[19] See Landry, *Effectiveness of International Supervision*, 84–86.

accordingly, it attempted to solve this problem by introducing a measure of flexibility in the range, nature, and level of protection provided in international instruments. But as early as 1989, the COE noted that such devices, in general, are seldom used.

In general, international labor standards are probably less likely than national labor legislation to hamper economic development because the former has less impact on production costs. But some standards, such as those dealing with safety and health, are likely to affect international competitiveness. Thus, there is reason to believe that failure to ratify or respect those standards may entail some competitive advantages. Similarly, failure to ratify or to comply with standards relating to the employment of child labor is defended by some developing countries as the only means of retaining some competitive advantage in the global market.

Córdova concludes his analysis of the reasons for what he considers an overproduction of international labor standards with the following observation:

> Few people pondered whether the ILO...[had by the year 1992] already met the most pressing needs and could check the pace of standard setting. Whoever raised the question of changing the tempo of congress meetings was sure to meet with stiff resistance. However, those advocates of moderation were not proposing a halt in the production of standards, something that would run counter to the many obligations and praiseworthy commitment of the ILO as well as to a balanced socioeconomic development. They were simply suggesting that perhaps the time has come to slow down the creation of new instruments and to give priority to the consideration, revision, and better implementation of existing standards.

I have relied heavily on Córdova's article because much of it has been confirmed by my own observations and experiences as a member of the COE. Moreover, in the last decade or so, there has been increasing pressure, particularly by the employer members of the International Labour Conference, to reduce the number of new labor standards on the grounds that many of them are counterproductive. During the period of my incumbency and since, the number of ratifications has declined, the number of cases of noncompliance with ratified conventions has grown, and the sheer inability of some member states to file the required periodic reports in a timely manner has risen.

My conclusion, enforced by my experience as a member of the COE, is that the ILO, although motivated by understandable reasons, has bitten off more than it can chew. The collection of conventions and recommendations that make up the International Labour Code has imposed so many onerous duties on national governments that the burdens in some instances have outweighed the benefits sought. The long and ever-growing list of conventions and recommendations suggests that the goal of the ILO is an all-encompassing socioeconomic system of rules of conduct based on social justice. But if one compares the objectives specified in the preamble to the ILO constitution with the list of conventions and recommendations adopted since 1919, and particularly since 1945, one can only conclude that the ILO has broadened its mandate beyond what was originally intended without demonstrating the pressing necessity for doing so.

As for the COE, I believe it has consistently carried out its supervisory responsibilities in exemplary fashion. It is hampered, however, by the lateness and incompleteness of reports from member states and by the necessity of providing copies of its own reports in both English and French. During my tenure on the COE, an excessive amount of time was required to reconcile the texts in these languages. Of greater importance, the workloads of individual COE members are excessive because each member must review some conventions of minor importance. One way of dealing with this problem would be to assign the initial review of less important conventions to staff members of the standards division, subject to the approval of a COE member and, ultimately, of the whole committee.

I had originally intended to end the chapter at this point, but recent scholarship, especially the outstanding book by Bob Hepple, has caused me to rethink my earlier appraisal of the ILO and the COE, which now seems to me too narrow.[20] Hepple evaluates the work of the ILO and its specialized bodies such as the COE in the light of its role in an era of globalization. What follows is a partial summary of his perceptive analysis and recommendations, to which I subscribe, although with some qualifications.

---

[20] Hepple, *Labor Laws and Global Trade.*

Ratification alone, according to Hepple, is not a satisfactory measure of whether international labor standards are hitting their mark. Referring to Ernest Landry's pathbreaking study, previously cited, and his observations about the pressures on countries to engage in premature ratification of conventions, Hepple notes that these pressures have increased over recent decades as governments have been required to adopt ILO-compliant labor codes in order to ensure assistance from the World Bank and the International Monetary Fund. It is therefore necessary, he says, to consider both the number of ratifications and the number of observations made by the COE for noncompliance with ratified conventions.[21] In this connection he notes that countries with a high number of convention ratifications may not be complying with those conventions, while countries with a high number of observations in respect of certain conventions may be adequately fulfilling their obligations under many other ratified instruments. Therefore, Hepple concludes,

> [t]he real question posed by globalization…is not whether there are too many international standards, but whether or not the standards set are the ones that are needed to counteract the effects of globalization on the majority of the world's workers, and whether these standards are being effectively implemented. The issue is qualitative not quantitative. One indication that there is something seriously wrong is the failure of most developing countries to ratify ILO conventions, and to implement them. From this the inference may be drawn that the standards are not appropriate to the real needs of those countries.

The ILO's response to the various challenges it faces has been threefold: (1) promoting a Declaration of Fundamental Principles and Rights at Work adopted by the International Labour Conference in June 1998; (2) revitalizing international labor standards by making them more coherent and integrated; and (3) undergoing a campaign for "decent work."

In 1994 and again in 1997, the director-generals' reports outlined the ILO's new vision for reconciling the liberalization of trade with adherence to labor standards. This was to be achieved by universal respect for fundamental human rights in the workplace as defined in seven "core" conventions—namely, freedom of association and collective bargaining

---

[21] In the language of the ILO, an "observation" refers to a serious or long-standing violation of a ratified Convention.

(Nos. 87 and 98), forced labor (Nos. 29 and 105), non-discrimination (Nos. 100 and 111), and minimum age in employment (No. 138). An eighth core convention on the prohibition and immediate action for the elimination of the worst forms of child labor (No. 182) was added in 1999. In 1996, the World Trade Organization (WTO) Ministerial Conference also expressed a commitment to core labor standards, but resolved that the ILO, rather than the WTO, was the competent body to deal with those standards. These developments culminated in June 1998 with the adoption by the International Labour Conference of the ILO Declaration on Fundamental Principles and Rights of Work. A key provision of the declaration specifies that all members, even if they have not ratified the core conventions, have an obligation, arising from the very fact of membership in the ILO, "to respect, to promote and to realise, in good faith and in accordance with the constitution," the principles concerning the fundamental rights embodied in the core conventions.

The Decent Work Agenda was launched by ILO Director-General Juan Somavia in 1999. He proposed that the ILO's primary goal should be "to promote opportunities for women and men to obtain decent and productive work, in conditions of freedom, equity, security and human dignity." This goal is based on the idea that social justice is "about a set of regulations, institutions and policies that ensures a fair treatment to all members of society, and a relatively equal distribution of opportunities and income." The four strategic objectives are to: (1) promote and realize standards and fundamental principles and rights at work; (2) create greater opportunities for women and men to secure decent employment and income; (3) enhance the coverage and effectiveness of social protection for all; and (4) strengthen tripartisan and social dialogue. These strategic objectives have been subdivided into operational objectives with indicators and targets that make it possible to measure the progress achieved.

After reviewing these ILO initiatives, Hepple reaches three conclusions.

First is that the "ILO's founding principles remain enormously relevant in the new global economy, but its methods of action have become out-dated. It is no longer possible for a small number of relatively wealthy developed countries to dictate labour standards for the whole world, reflecting the models adopted in the North. The 1998 Declaration was a worthy attempt by the ILO to re-establish the universal legitimacy of the fundamental principles on which the Organization is based." But these principles have to be integrated sensitively, so as to take account of the level of socioeconomic development in each country. For example, a simple ban on child labor without corresponding steps to provide education and family support would be counterproductive. The concept of decent work places greater emphasis on the quality of life of all those engaged in productive labor.

Second is that "beyond the core and priority conventions, the present subjects of international regulation do not serve the real needs of developing countries. The concept of Decent Work provides an opportunity to move away from the model of paid employment in the formal sector, towards international regulation of productive work, whatever its legal form, on the basis of minimal socio-economic rights." There must also be a change in the traditional division between conventions and recommendations, replacing these with "promotional or framework conventions which set principles and codes of practice directed at specific groups of countries at similar stages of development." The understandable reluctance of countries to adopt standards that their competitors require could be overcome by regional dialogue based on the implementation of principles that are supplemented by flexible standards. The implementation of such promotional standards requires methods that are different from the traditional juristic technique of finding whether laws and practice conform to an abstract standard, a technique that is well-suited to core conventions, which specify fundamental human rights in the workplace. Hepple notes that a "rights-based approach is necessary and appropriate to the implementation of the 'core' standards, and that core should be regarded as progressive not static, taking in a wider range of fundamental human rights. Adversarial procedures should be improved for this purpose, including a complaints-mechanism for a wider range of human rights issues than freedom of association."

Finally, Hepple states that "outside this expanding core other frame-work conventions would set only general principles or common goals, which are to be progressively achieved. There has to be periodic evaluation of the outcomes, based on agreed indications or criteria (benchmarking). The evaluation is not simply a technical process, but also a political one that requires active social dialogue."

The foregoing proposals, I fear, despite their appeal to our better natures, are not likely to produce change in the immediate future. They are predicated upon extending the reach of the ILO so that it may exceed its grasp, but even a failed result cannot discredit so worthy an effort.

CHAPTER 17

THE UNITED AUTO WORKERS PUBLIC REVIEW BOARD, 1975–2007

The United Auto Workers Public Review Board (PRB) is one of the most significant instruments yet devised for the promotion and preservation of internal union democracy, yet its very existence is unknown to the vast majority of American citizens. Not much has been written about the PRB; nonetheless, I feel a responsibility to put this remarkable institution in its historical context and to offer some impressions of its successes and failures during my more than 30 years as a member.[1]

Concern about internal union democracy, or, rather, the lack of it, developed with the phenomenal growth in size and power of organized labor in the United States between the 1930s and 1950s. Public awareness of the role of labor unions as quasi-public institutions exercising considerable control over the lives of millions of people led to the realization that unions are fundamentally different from other private voluntary associations such as church groups and fraternal organizations, although no distinctions were made between them at common law.[2] A consensus emerged among scholars who had studied the constitutions and administrative policies and practices of labor unions that a majority of unions adhered, at least formally, to democratic policies and procedures, that a significant minority did not, and that the most desirable method of eliminating undemocratic practices was through voluntary action by offending unions. One observer noted that "the emergence and spread

---

[1] Among the best commentaries are David Y. Klein, "UAW Public Review Board Report," reprinted in *Rutgers Law Review* 18 (1964): 304; Jerome H. Brooks, "Impartial Public Review of Internal Union Disputes: Experiment in Democratic Self-Discipline," *Ohio State Law Journal* 22 (1961): 64; Walter E. Oberer, "Voluntary Impartial Review of Labor: Some Reflections," *Michigan Law Review* 58 (1959): 56; and Jack Stieber, Walter E. Oberer, and Michael Harrington, *Democracy and Public Review: An Analysis of the UAW Public Review Board* (Santa Barbara: Center for the Study of Democratic Institutions, 1960).

[2] See generally, Zechariah Chafee, "The Internal Affairs of Associations Not for Profit," *Harvard Law Review* 43 (1930): 993.

of bureaucracy and the decay of democracy in trade unions are not abnormal excesses but are rooted in the very nature of trade union organization, and of organization in general." He concluded that although the various institutional reforms suggested "must be within the trade-union movement itself...it is futile to talk of any reform of trade-union regimes without some effective guarantee of the elementary civic rights of members."[3]

By the mid-1950s, public attention had begun to focus on alleged corrupt and undemocratic practices in labor unions. In 1957, the U.S. Senate created a Select Committee on Improper Practices in the Labor and Management Field, popularly known as the McClellan Committee for its chairman, Senator John McClellan of Arkansas. The investigations of this committee, which were fully dramatized in the press and on radio and television, revealed extreme corruption and racketeering in a relatively small number of AFL-CIO unions, most of which were subsequently expelled from the federation. Unfortunately, expulsion proved to be an ineffective impetus to reform in most cases. For example, it brought about no change in the powerful Teamsters Union, which prospered and grew even stronger after being expelled. Similarly, ethical codes codified by the AFL-CIO for its affiliated unions were never successfully enforced and ultimately lapsed into a state of innocuous desuetude.

Largely in response to disclosures by the McClellan Committee, Congress enacted the Labor-Management Reporting and Disclosure Act of 1959 (LMRDA). In its declaration of findings, purposes, and policy, the act stated, "in order to accomplish the objective of a free flow of commerce it is essential that labor organizations, employers, and their officials adhere to the highest standard of responsibility and ethical conduct in administering the affairs of their organizations, particularly as they affect labor-management relations." Archibald Cox, one of the principal draftsmen of the LMRDA, explained:

> To the extent that this statement applies to unions, it reflects an awareness of their multiple functions; unions substitute group for individual bargaining power, secure

---

[3] Will Herberg, "Bureaucracy and Democracy in Labor Unions," *Antioch Review* 3 (1943): 405, 413, 414–15.

a measure of job security for their members, extend the rule of law to working establishments, and provide a means for workers to engage with management in the processes of industrial self-government.[4]

Title I of the new law, Bill of Rights of Members of Labor Organizations, dealt with, among other things, equal rights; freedom of speech and assembly; dues, initiation fees, and assessments; protection of the right to sue; and safeguards against improper disciplinary action. Reviewing the effects of Title I two years later, I expressed disappointment with what I regarded as the unnecessarily narrow interpretations of the statutory language by some courts, but nonetheless concluded:

> Finally, the reported judicial decisions do not and cannot reflect what is perhaps the most important, and certainly the most reassuring, consequence of the enactment of the LMRDA: the reforms of internal procedures voluntarily undertaken by many unions. It is that development, more than any other, which makes me guardedly optimistic about the long-range effectiveness of the new law. Whether these reforms are being undertaken willingly and with the conviction of their necessity, or represent merely a grudging and insincere concession to public pressure, is really unimportant. Union members who have learned to exercise their democratic rights will not readily give them up. The Bill of Rights and the LMRDA as a whole will never become truly effective, however, unless those whom the statute was intended to benefit insist upon the rights and carry out the obligations of union citizenship.[5]

The only successful result of a union's voluntary establishment of an instrument for the public oversight of internal union affairs was the PRB, which was established in 1957 at the constitutional convention of the United Auto workers (UAW). As explained in *A More Perfect Union*, an undated UAW publication, the idea of a public review board was not inspired by the McClellan Committee. Rather, UAW President Walter Reuther told the convention attendees that discussion of the plan had begun among the UAW's officers two years earlier. At that time, he explained, it was conceived of "primarily as part of the appeal procedure in our internal trial machinery. More recently, however, we thought it should be expanded to cover the broad area of moral and ethical

---

[4] Archibald Cox, "The Rule of Law in Preserving Union Democracy," *Harvard Law Review* 72 (1959): 610.

[5] Benjamin Aaron, "The Union Members 'Bill of Rights': First Two Years," *Industrial Relations* 1, no. 2 (1962): 71.

standards." The first public mention of the plan came in March 1957, in Reuther's report to the forthcoming UAW convention. Without doubt, he was the driving force behind the creation of the PRB. In speaking to the convention delegates about the proposed review board, Reuther cautioned them that "this is not window dressing. There are no constitutional loopholes.... These people are going to an essential part of our Constitution and they will have broad powers and responsibilities. They will make decisions as they relate to the decisions you make at the local level and that we make at the international level." The reason for establishing the board, Reuther explained, was the belief "that the kind of clean, democratic Union that we have and we hope to keep is the kind of Union that can have its decisions tested by a Public Review Board in keeping with accepted standards of morality of a free society."[6]

It is interesting that the UAW, then one of the biggest unions in the United States, with a membership of about 1.5 million, and generally regarded as the most democratically run union and the most free of corruption, should have been the only one to establish and maintain a public review board with real power.[7] One long-time UAW member, who had been promoted to a staff position, offered the following explanation:

> In the old days, we didn't need a Public Review Board. The membership was smaller, and the leaders were closer to the rank and file. And then, there used to be factions in every local. When a man had a grievance, one side or the other would jump at the chance to take up his defense. Now the factions don't exist in a lot of locals, the union is bigger, the leaders are more distant. That's why we have to have a Review Board.[8]

In its original form, the PRB's jurisdictional authority, as set forth in the UAW constitution, included, first, "matters related to alleged viola-

---

[6] United Auto Workers, *Proceedings, UAW 16th Constitutional Convention* (Detroit: UAW, 1957): 103–04.

[7] The first union to adopt an impartial public review system was the Upholsterers International Union, in 1953, but the scheme proved to be merely a public relations ploy. The board was chaired by Archibald Cox, and I was a member. Only several cases were submitted to us, and the first time we decided one in favor of a complaining member, the union refused to comply, whereupon the entire board resigned. So far as I am aware, a new board was never appointed.

[8] Michael Harrington, "What Union Members Think of Public Review," in Jack Stieber, Walter E. Oberer, and Michael Harrington, *Democracy and Public Review: An Analysis of the UAW Public Review Board* (Santa Barbara: Center for the Study of Democratic Institutions, 1960), 51.

tion of any AFL-CIO ethical practices codes and any additional ethical practices codes that may be adopted by the International Union," and second, of greater importance, "appeals arising under designated procedures set forth in the Union's Constitution." Two general limitations were placed on the scope of its review power: in appeals relating to the processing of shop grievances, the PRB had no jurisdiction unless the appellant alleged before the UAW's International Executive Board (IEB) that the grievance had been improperly handled because of fraud, discrimination, or collusion with management; also, it was prohibited from reviewing the official bargaining policy of the UAW. In 1980, a fourth ground for PRB jurisdiction was added: "that the disposition or handling of the matter was devoid of any rational basis." Over the years, this asserted reason for the PRB's jurisdiction has been relied upon by appellants more frequently than the other three.

The PRB is composed of seven "impartial persons of good public repute not working under the jurisdiction of the UAW or employed by the International Union or any of its subordinate bodies," who are initially appointed and periodically reappointed at the UAW's constitutional conventions. By common practice, board members who either arbitrate disputes between the UAW and various employers, or who represent clients who deal with the UAW, terminate all such relationships. Also by common practice, vacancies on the PRB are filled by the UAW from a list of candidates submitted by the remaining members, thus giving the board a considerable influence in determining its own composition. In recent years, the UAW leadership has informally suggested that the PRB consider some clergymen to fill vacancies in the board, but so far it has not done so.[9]

The operation of the PRB is financed by the UAW from its general operating fund. To provide financial independence that would be as complete as possible, the board and the union agreed upon a system whereby funds would be transferred from the union to the board, the

---

[9] The original board included a representative of the three principal religions in North America: Catholic, Protestant, and Jewish. This practice continued for several years with the replacement of Morris Adler by Jacob Weinstein and Bromley Oxnam by Henry Hitt Crane. There was also a custom of reserving a place for a Canadian until the Canadian Autoworkers withdrew from the UAW.

money being placed in bank accounts controlled solely by the PRB. Four times a year, the board's funds are replenished by the union in the amount necessary to bring the balance back to the agreed amount. Originally set at $30,000, that amount has increased more than tenfold over the years. Further, to ensure the PRB's independence, the UAW constitution provides that the board shall maintain its own offices separate and apart from any UAW buildings. The PRB is also responsible for the selection of its own professional and clerical staff, which has remained small, despite the considerable increase in the board's workload.[10]

Over the years, as was to be expected, the PRB has experienced considerable turnover of its membership. From 1957 to 2004, 26 persons have served for varying periods of time.[11] The seven original members were Rabbi Morris Adler, the first chairman, Msgr. George Higgins, Bishop G. Bromley Oxnam, J. Arthur Hanrahan, Clark Kerr, Wade McCree, and Edwin Witte. The longest-serving chairman was Higgins, who held that position for 28 years. Despite the amount of turnover, the PRB has maintained a continuity of membership and policy. As a member of the original board, Higgins provided its institutional memory, aided by other long-serving members including, Jean McKelvey, Jim Jones, Ted St. Antoine, and especially David Klein, our third executive director, who was the board's most visible public representative for 44 years.

I followed the PRB's work from the date of its establishment and had secretly hoped some day to become a member. My wish was granted in 1975, and my service as a member since then has been one of the most rewarding experiences of my professional life. Not only have the cases

---

[10] From 1957 to 2005, the board has had only four executive directors: Walter E. Oberer (1957–59), Jerome H. Brooks (1959–60), David Y. Klein (1960–2004), and Barbara A. Klein (2003–).

[11] In alphabetical order, they are: Benjamin Aaron (1975–), George W. Adams (1977–79), Rabbi Morris Adler (1957–66), Harry W. Arthurs (1967–76), Janice R. Bellace (1993–), Judge George E. Bowles (1961–62), James J. Brudney (2000–), Henry Steele Commager (1961–65), Henry H. Crane (1962–70), Robben W. Fleming (1966–72), Magistrate J. Arthur Hanrahan (1957–66), Msgr. George G. Higgins (1957–2000), James E. Jones Jr. (1970–), Clark Kerr (1957–59), George N. Leighton (1962–70), Frank W. McCulloch (1970–80), Judge Wade H. McCree Jr. (1957–61), Jean T. McKelvey (1960–98), Eleanor Holmes Norton (1989–91), Maria L. Ontiveros (2004–) Bishop G. Bromley Oxnam (1957–62), Theodore J. St. Antoine (1973–), Paul C. Weiler (1980–), Rabbi Jacob J. Weinstein (1966–75), Willard Wirtz (1960–61), Edwin E. Witte (1957–60), and Marilyn V. Yarbrough (1998–2004).

coming before us been challenging, but the opportunity to work closely with such a distinguished and remarkably able group of colleagues has proved to be exceptionally enjoyable.

The PRB functions exclusively as an appellate body. In a typical case, an aggrieved union member initially brings the complaint to the local union membership at its regular monthly meeting. If the membership denies the requested redress, the member may appeal the matter to the IEB. Originally, the UAW constitution required the IEB to appoint a three-man committee, composed of members of the IEB, that would hear appeals and make recommendations. The international union almost immediately adopted a rule that a two-man committee would constitute a quorum at any hearing. That ruling was challenged in the case of *Appeal of Smith, et al.* The PRB upheld the right of appellants to the three-man appeals committee directed by the constitution, saying in part:

> In the case of a union as large as the UAW, it would obviously overburden the Executive Board, charged as it is with multiple functions and duties, to sit in its entirety as a hearing board for every appeal presented to it. To meet this situation the Constitution wisely permits the Executive Board to set up a committee of three of its members to conduct a hearing and to report back to the Board. The committee is thus an arm of the Executive Board, preparing the way for the entire Board to discharge its duty on the matter of an appeal. Having heard the testimony, met the litigants, and fulfilled the indispensable requirement of studying the facts in the appeal at first hand, the members of the committee can transmit something of the immediacy and vitality of their direct encounters with the case. The decision rendered by the Executive Board is thus aided and fortified by the recommendations of part of the Board that has actually "heard" the case.[12]

The PRB concluded, therefore, that the denial of a three-man appeals committee violated the appellant's rights. Subsequently, the UAW constitution was amended in several ways, including the following: First, to permit the IEB to appoint a two-member appeals committee, composed of members of the IEB, to consider an appeal and make recommendations to the IEB, or, if the appeals committee concludes that no useful purpose would be served by a hearing, it may in its discretion make recommendations on the appeal without a hearing. Second,

---

[12] 1 PRB 44 (1958).

to authorize the international president, in his discretion, to decide an appeal rather than submitting it to an appeals committee. In such case, he may designate a representative to conduct any investigation or hearing deemed necessary.

In recent years, the union has moved ever further away from voluntarily providing hearings before an appeals committee (whose members are rarely members of the IEB). Such hearings are now the exception rather than the rule; almost all decisions are now made by the president, who delegates his authority in this respect to his staff. In virtually every case, the IEB approves the decision. From its decision the union member may appeal either to the PRB or to the constitutional convention. The second option is seldom pursued.

Hearings before the PRB are governed by procedural rules, promulgated by the board, that set time limits for submission of documents, request for extension of deadlines, and related matters. The international union is required to file a written statement of its position regarding the issues raised in the statement of appeal or, alternatively, to file a special answer challenging the board's jurisdiction over the appeal. The international union is also required to forward to the PRB the entire documentary record in the appeal, as presented to the IEB or the UAW president's office by any party, including exhibits or transcripts, if any, of local or international union hearings at the time of submission of its written statement of position. Copies of this documentary record must be reproduced and furnished to each party. One of the more important rules is that of limiting oral arguments before the board to material already included in the record; except in special cases, the PRB will not consider new evidence offered at the hearing. This requirement stems from the board's belief that because internal union disputes should be resolved whenever possible within the union itself, evidence that the union did not have before it at the time of its consideration of the appeal should not be accepted.

Each appeal to the PRB is considered first in an executive session, then, if necessary, at a subsequent formal hearing. A request by the complaining member to present oral arguments at the board hearing is usually granted, but many appeals are rejected and so not heard. Whether or not it hears the case, the board will usually issue a written decision setting forth the essential facts of the case, the arguments of the parties, and the reasons for its decision.

In the early years of the board's existence, the appeals were frequently heard by panels of three or four board members. Before long, however, that practice was abandoned, although still permitted by the UAW constitution, and all hearings are now made before the full board unless one or more members are unavoidably absent. A board member who is not present at a hearing may not participate in the decision in that case.

From the outset the board declined to endorse UAW policies or to issue advisory opinions; it confined itself to deciding actual controversies within the union over which it had specified jurisdiction. But the board's authority derives from the UAW international constitution. In some instances, the issue raised in an appeal to the PRB either is not dealt with specifically in the constitution or is dealt with ambiguously. On occasion this has given rise to sharp disagreements between board members. One view is that the PRB should never seek to expand its jurisdiction beyond what is specifically and unequivocally granted by the UAW constitution. A different and less categorical position is that in arguably ambiguous constitutional provisions, a proper interpretation should give weight to the intent of the framers as well as the literal text of the document to take account, for example, of "accepted standards of morality of a free society." A related problem arises in a situation that is referred to specifically in the constitution, for example:

> For an interpretation of a collective bargaining agreement by a National Department or Regional Director, *where the interpretation is so obviously correct that no purpose will be served by an appeal* [italics supplied], and where it is consistent with other provisions of this Constitution and International Union policy, the appeal shall be directly to the International Union President. There shall be no further appeal from that decision. [Art. 33, § 2 (b)]

This language was proposed by a UAW official as a device to filter out frivolous appeals.

Obviously, opinions could differ as to whether an interpretation is "so obviously correct" that no purpose would be served by an appeal. Whether the PRB is required to defer completely to the decision of the international president in such circumstances is an issue on which PRB members are not in complete agreement, probably because it seems to have been used primarily to deprive the PRB of jurisdiction.

Most of the appeals presented to the board involve grievance processing by the union. Cases in this category have increased significantly since the PRB's jurisdiction was expanded by constitutional amendment to include those in which "the disposition or handling of the matter was devoid of any rational basis." Other appeals present such issues as alleged irregularities in union elections, removals of officers or appointees, violations of the UAW Ethical Practices Codes, and many others.

On relatively few occasions, valid complaints against local union officers alleging minor instances of fraud or corruption have been appealed to the PRB, but in the entire period of my membership on the board only one involved an entire region of the UAW and was on a scale causing the highest concern to the international union and to the PRB. This case precipitated a major crisis, not only within the union itself but also between the union and the board.

On 24 August 1983, the IEB adopted and submitted a resolution to the PRB stating, preliminarily, that "information has come to light suggesting that great financial and other improprieties may have occurred in the administration of Region 4," which encompassed Illinois, Iowa, and Nebraska. The resolution was predicated on a provision of the UAW constitution relating to the handling of complaints about violations of any UAW Ethical Practices Codes. Specifically, the resolution referred the alleged irregularities to the PRB for "investigation, disposition, and, if necessary, remedy." It further directed all UAW members and employees "to cooperate fully with the Public Review Board in carrying out its duty." Relying upon the same constitutional provision invoked by the union, the board concluded that it should accept jurisdiction of the ethical practices complaint, which was designated as Case 640, representing its sequential filing with the PRB.

The board recognized at once that it lacked the staff to conduct the kind of investigation that would be necessary in Case 640. Accordingly, it established the office of special counsel to the PRB, with authority to investigate claims arising under the democratic practices, financial practices, health, welfare and retirement funds, and business and financial activities of union officials covered by the UAW Ethical Practices Codes. It appointed as special counsel Jerome H. Brooks, who was the second executive director of the PRB and the former regional director of the seventh regional office of the National Labor Relations Board (NLRB). This was a necessary step, because the complaint submitted by the IEB put the PRB in the difficult position of having not only to investigate and dispose of the complaint but also to fashion a remedy, if necessary. By creating the office of special counsel, the PRB isolated the investigation process from the judgment function: Brooks was charged with the responsibility to discover the underlying factual information and to make initial findings, conclusions, and recommendations to the PRB. Brooks promptly hired a staff and, in late November 1983, opened a temporary office in Chicago, where the regional office of UAW Region 4 was also located.

With the intent to afford maximum due process to anyone accused of wrongdoing, the board provided that in the event Brooks's findings and conclusions were contested by any individual or institution, there should be a hearing before an impartial third party, who would be selected by agreement between Brooks and the contesting party. Either side could appeal the decision of the third party to the PRB, whose decision would be final. These procedures were implemented through a special set of Rules of Procedures for Ethical Practices Complaints, which were adopted in proposed form and submitted for comment to more than 900 members and former members of Region 4 who were potentially affected by the investigation. When finally approved, the rules invested the office of special counsel with "full authority to investigate fully all matters submitted to it by order of the PRB, to interrogate witnesses, and to secure production of relevant documents."

Although they scrupulously provided full due process to all persons included in their investigations, Brooks and his staff were rigorous and thorough in the pursuit of their inquiries. Indubitably, this aroused some uneasiness on the part of the international union's officers and staff and led, in some instances, to considerable foot-dragging and even to open opposition. These tactics, in turn, led to protests by Brooks and to questioning by some board members of the UAW's sincerity to hold a responsible investigation and to punish any of its officers or members whose culpability was proven. On occasion, considerable tension developed, but with the assistance of our chairman, Higgins, whose tact, reasonableness, and persuasiveness were legendary, all differences were reconciled or compromised.

Brooks's investigation covered a ten-year span up to and including 31 December 1983. All Region 4 funds in operation during this period were examined.[13] Out-of-town expense statements submitted by Region 4 officers and international representatives were also examined. This examination was necessarily more thorough than a typical internal audit because transactions were examined in light of the proscriptions found in the Ethical Practice Codes. Brooks and his staff interviewed more than 100 persons, including UAW officers, members, and employees, and persons outside the union who had useful information. The latter included hotel and bank personnel, attorneys and other suppliers of goods and services, and state and local government officials.

The investigation was not without difficulties. Almost every decision concerning the spending of Region 4 funds involved the regional director, but neither person serving in that capacity during the period examined was accessible for interview by Brooks. The first served from 1956 until a few months before his death in October 1980. His surviving family members refused to cooperate in any way with the investigation. His successor suffered a stroke in January 1984, and he resigned in July 1984, during the middle of the investigation, citing ill health resulting from the stroke.

---

[13] Separate bank accounts and separate sets of books were maintained for each fund. Those funds were titled: Community Action Program Councils (CAPs), Education, Greater Chicago Fair Practices Council, John F. Kennedy Union Center, Retired Workers, Rotating, Sales Tax Override Proposition (STOP), Special Projects, Strike Assistance, Testimonials, and Women's Committee. The investigation also included "private" or "voluntary" funds. These included the Region 4 Club (or "Flower Fund"), election funds of leading candidates for regional director in 1980 and 1983, and several Testimonial Funds for union officers.

His attorney advised Brooks that, in his opinion, his client was physically and mentally unable to participate in his own defense. Much of the record keeping for Region 4 funds was inadequate or otherwise deficient. And there were delays caused, for example, by the fact that the many documents that the U.S. Department of Labor had subpoenaed for a parallel probe of Region 4 did not become accessible to Brooks until June 1984.

In those instances in which the Office of Special Counsel concluded that living persons had violated the codes and that remedial action was required, charges were issued, the violations specified, and the remedial actions proposed. The steps to be taken against charged ethical code violators that Brooks and the PRB proposed, and the international union endorsed, were more remedial than punitive. The following examples are illuminative of their approach. Based on the detailed investigation conducted by his staff, Brooks concluded that one former Region 4 director and two Region 4 staff representatives, all deceased, had violated the codes. The PRB Rules of Procedure were not applicable to deceased individuals, but Brooks's findings and conclusions in respect of those violations were set forth in his reports. He requested the IEB to take the action necessary to recover all money lost as a result of financial misconduct from the company that bonded the union against such losses.

In addition, Brooks concluded that six living union members or former members had violated its Ethical Practices Codes. An international representative was charged with offering a bribe to a local union president for the purposes of affecting the outcome of an election for Region 4 director. The case was settled by imposing a six-month disciplinary layoff without pay.

A former local union president, international representative, and retired Region 4 director was charged with receiving reimbursement for personal expenses not associated with union business. The case was settled by his repayment to the union of all the unauthorized reimbursements.

A member and employee of a local union, who was also a lobbyist for and recording secretary of a state CAP, was charged with receiving reimbursements for personal expenses not related to any legitimate CAP business. He, too, repaid the full amount of these illegal reimbursements.

A former manager of the JFK Union Center was similarly charged and agreed to resign his membership from, and office held in, the international union and any of its subordinate local unions, CAP councils, and retiree councils for a period of five years. In addition, he repaid an agreed sum of money to the JFK Union Center.

A former local union officer was charged with failing to account for a large sum of money that he had received in cash from the JFK Union Center. He settled the case by repaying the amount for which he could not account.

A former assistant director and director of Region 4 was charged with improperly authorizing or receiving a very large sum from various Region 4 funds. Because he was too incapacitated by illness to stand trial, the charges against him were not pursued, but the international union did agree to submit a claim to its bonding agent for recoupment of the monies he owed to the union.

In each instance it was agreed that the settlements did not constitute an admission by the charged party that he had violated the UAW Ethical Practices Codes in any respect.

The investigation, which was too lengthy and detailed to be summarized here, seems to me to have been a model of its kind. Brooks and his staff were indefatigable in pursuing every lead and in pinpointing every code violation disclosed by available evidence, sometimes in the face of hostility and noncooperation on the part of the person being investigated. They adhered steadfastly to the standards of objectivity and fairness outlined in the PRB Rules of Procedure. One fortuitous, and critical, circumstance—namely, that the most egregious code violator was no longer living—made it easier for the union to accept the results of the investigation and to agree to adopt the detailed recommendations of the Office of Special Counsel, as approved by the PRB.

The heart of Brooks's report consisted of some 20 remedial recommendations and the specific responses of the UAW to each of them. To illuminate the breadth of the remedies proposed and accepted, the most important are summarized below.

The Brooks report recommended that the international union should analyze the adequacy of the accounting systems employed at Region 4. The UAW's response was, first, that a further study of the accounting system at Region 4 was unnecessary; second, that the better course was to go directly to solving the problems disclosed in the report without further delay or expense; and third, that the resolutions must be enforced. To this end, the international union made the following pledge:

> We will produce an Accounting Standard which will specify *in detail* what is required of Region 4 at the International, Regional and Local levels. It will list the accounts that may be maintained. It will set the standards under which they must be operated, controlled, and audited. The control will exceed any presently suggested or required by the AFL-CIO, or historical UAW practice.

In addition, the UAW instituted eight specific accounting practices and measures to ensure that these standards would be followed.

A related recommendation was that the international union should take appropriate steps to ensure that audits of Region 4 funds be thorough and of value. To this the UAW responded in part:

> We have agreed that the staff auditors from other Regions will do the initial auditing of Region 4 accounts....
>
> The [UAW] Secretary-Treasurer will examine and revise the training provided for UAW staff auditors, focusing on prevention of the particular abuses found in Region 4.
>
> Drastic changes have *already* been made which will greatly simplify and tighten the audit process. The Regional Activities Fund exists, and is accounted for in Detroit. Other "off the chart" accounts have been eliminated. Publication of the Accounting Standards...will promulgate the detailed rules, and guide the auditor's inquiry. But we will, in addition, review and revise our internal audit standards, so as to require an auditor *both* to ask the central questions *and* to record the answers.

Several recommendations dealt with the regulation of various Region 4 funds. Typical of these was one proposing that the IEB adopt appropriate guidelines concerning the use of such funds to defray the cost of social affairs honoring UAW officials and other members, gifts to them, and memorials on behalf of them and their family members.

The UAW's response included a defense of retirement parties for staff, leadership, and members as an important part of the union and its history, as well as a recognition by the membership and others that there are people who devote their lives to helping others. It declared, therefore, that local unions and the international union would be allowed to continue the practice of holding retirement parties. At the same time, it promised to issue more detailed guidelines to assure that the practice would not be abused.

A matter of continuing concern in the past had been fund-raising by individuals seeking election to the position of Region 4 director. Brooks's report urged the UAW to adopt appropriate regulations covering this problem. The UAW responded that this is "a difficult and delicate area," explaining: "Since caucuses within our membership are *private* political groups, it is a delicate matter for the UAW, as an institution, to regulate their activities and bank accounts." Nevertheless, it agreed that regulation was required in some major areas. Accordingly, it volunteered to adopt regulations governing fund-raising for persons seeking election to the position of Region 4 director that are "consistent with the Constitution, Ethical Practices Codes, and applicable law. Once these regulations are promulgated we will work out a system for policing them."

Other recommendations dealt with such matters as the solicitation and acceptance of contributions to Region 4 from suppliers of goods and services to the UAW; operation of strike assistance funds; operation of the Region 4 Club (a private caucus account); employment of Region 4's officers' and representatives' families; and payment of Christmas and other bonuses to Region 4 clerical and maintenance employees.

To each of these the international union responded affirmatively, but with some reservations. Although defending the right of Region 4 to raise additional monies to assist striking members, the UAW promised that no bank accounts would be opened at either the local or regional levels for this purpose; rather, the funds, as collected and receipted under standard UAW accounting rules, would be deposited in the treasury of the international union. From there they would either be transferred directly to the embattled local or would be spent by the international to meet the needs of the strike. Concerning the operation of the Region 4 Club, the UAW pledged that there would be no subsidization through the regular use of UAW personnel, supplies, materials, or facilities. It explained that as a private repository of voluntary contributions of private funds, the monies in the fund were the property of the head of the caucus and presumably would be used at his or her discretion. Nevertheless, the UAW agreed that it was absolutely necessary to ensure that such accounts must not include UAW funds and that necessary steps would be taken to see to it that there be no commingling of UAW and private funds in the union's account. Concerning the employment of family members of Region 4's officers and representatives, the international union observed that such an act is not, as such, improper under the UAW constitution and the Ethical Practices Codes, but it agreed to underscore that hired family member must be qualified for the work required, be assigned to a job that must be performed, and receive compensation comparable to that paid to other employees for the same work. Finally, in respect of payment of Christmas and other bonuses to Region 4 clerical and maintenance workers, the UAW declared: "Since the wages and benefits paid by the UAW are fair and equitable, no bonuses will be paid to clerical and maintenance employees of Region 4 from union funds."

The PRB delivered its report to the UAW officers and membership in December 1985. It noted that it was the product of "the most difficult task ever assigned to and undertaken by the Public Review Board," and acknowledged that the findings it recognized and the conclusions and recommendations it incorporated largely reflected the efforts of Brooks and his staff.

The report's conclusion set forth the board's own appraisal of the value of the report while paying tribute to the international union for responding "positively and decisively to a situation which, if left unchecked, could undermine the high moral standards which have historically governed its conduct." In the final analysis, the PRB declared,

> it is not the recovery of monies nor the identification of those individuals who have committed the improper acts described in this report which constitute the principal contribution of the investigation. There will always be individuals who attempt to

abuse any system; that is simply an unfortunate aspect of human nature. Rather, it is the reforms which the union has promised to take in response to the findings, conclusions, and recommendations of Special Counsel which will, in our opinion, prove to be of lasting benefit to the union by making it substantially more difficult for abuses described herein to be repeated.

It is difficult, so many years later, to convey to those not actively involved in the background investigation and preparation of the final report of PRB Case 640, a process that took three years, the sense of strain it created between the UAW and the board. There were times when the union appeared to think that the PRB and its special counsel were exceeding their authority and seeking to expand it beyond the limits intended under the UAW constitution, and at least some board members and staff questioned the sincerity of some UAW officers who professed their desire to get to the bottom of the existing corruption in Region 4 and to punish those responsible. At the end of the day, however, most of the doubters were satisfied that the problems uncovered by the investigation had been honestly and reasonably dealt with. Indeed, speaking for the union in his introduction to the 28th Annual Report of the PRB, UAW President Owen Bieber said in part: "The seriousness and vigor that this Board lent to the investigation and the new safeguards adopted at the Board's recommendation have made our union stronger." No case raising issues of major internal corruption has arisen since then.

At the turn of the century the automotive industry began to experience a decline brought about by global competition and the constantly increasing burden of pension and health benefits for its employees. The American public clearly favored automobiles that were smaller and more efficient than those produced by American manufacturers, which continued to rely heavily on expensive sports utility vehicles (SUVs) and light trucks, which they were unable to sell without giving substantial discounts. General Motors, the largest automobile manufacturer in the world, has a multimillion-dollar unfunded pension debt and a growing number of retirees who are entitled under existing contracts to generous pension and health benefits. Ford and Chrysler are also experiencing heavy losses. The financial problems of the Big Three have also affected the UAW, whose members have lost their jobs as a result of plant closures and who have had to forego the steady increases in wages and benefits to which they were accustomed in the past. Forced to economize, the UAW has had to tighten its belt and to streamline its staff at its international headquarters. In 2002, Ron Gettelfinger succeeded to the presidency of the UAW and brought about some changes in the presidential staff.

All of these events resulted in a relationship with the PRB that was different—and more strained. Some of Gettelfinger's closest associates were increasingly outspoken in their criticisms of the PRB, challenging its jurisdiction in some cases and even suggesting that they might refuse to abide by some board decisions with which they disagreed. Indeed, in one 2005 case, a UAW vice-president refused to take the remedial action described by the PRB in a decision reversing his dismissal of one of his appointees. The resulting situation created a crisis without precedent in the history of the PRB. After some tense back-channel discussions between board chairman St. Antoine and the UAW general counsel, the crisis was resolved to the satisfaction of the PRB and the UAW, although the UAW vice-president involved remained unappeased.

Tension between the board and the union has become further exacerbated by the lack of experience and the intense competition between members of the UAW's headquarters staff. Previously, cases heard by the PRB were presented by just one person, who was totally familiar with the often complicated facts as well as the applicable board precedents, and who was able to present the union's arguments clearly and skillfully. Spokesmen such as these have been replaced by persons of lesser ability who have failed to win the respect and trust of the board.

As I mentioned earlier, one of the most stimulating and enjoyable aspects of many years of service on the PRB has been the association with my fellow board members, each of whom has made substantial contributions to the board's work.

Among the many former members who have served for varying periods, a few have had a considerable influence on me. First among them is George Higgins, whose tenure on the board lasted from 1957, the year it was established, until his retirement for reasons of health in 2000. For most of this time he served as chairman, a position for which he was particularly suited. His death, following a long and painful illness, was widely mourned and prompted an outpouring of warm and admiring recollections from persons in all walks of life. I am concerned here, however, primarily with his contributions to the PRB, on whose development he had such a profound influence. My views are undoubtedly influenced by our warm friendship, which enriched my life. We corresponded frequently, discussing a wide variety of subjects, and he often sent me copies of articles and, sometimes, books that he had read and thought I would enjoy. He was an ideal chairman, presiding at our hearings informally but firmly, always ensuring that all participants be permitted to have their say, and ever ready to ease a tense situation with a humorous comment. If ever a man could be said to have "the common touch," it was he. Higgins was one of the authentically great men I have been privileged to know.

Although he was widely known as "the labor priest," that description, while apt, did not encompass the whole man. Higgins fought for social justice for everyone; he championed not only the cause of organized labor but also social rights and religious tolerance. The many honors, so richly deserved, that came his way were almost certainly less important to him than the personal satisfaction he derived from serving the society in which he lived and which he improved by his efforts.

Higgins was less concerned about the letter of the UAW constitution than about its spirit. When his fellow board members, most of whom were lawyers or law professors, argued over technical questions of interpretation, he seldom participated in the debate, but on broader questions involving the fairness of constitutional applications to the actions of workers in the shop he was an active and influential contributor. Whether the board's decision ultimately upheld or denied appeal from the actions of the international union or one of its locals, the fact that Higgins supported it (he rarely dissented) did much to ensure its acceptance by the losing party.

That Higgins was a man of the cloth undoubtedly enhanced his moral authority, but he never made a point of it. He was addressed as "Monsignor" far less often than "Father," the choice of taxi drivers, bellmen, waiters, and workers generally. He had a relaxed, friendly manner that put everyone at ease. In presiding at board hearings, he was patient and almost never showed any irritation. In our executive sessions, which at times were quite heated, he made sure that each of us had his or her say, and when the debate threatened to get out of hand, he would restore order by calmly and often humorously reducing the tension. He was a "good" man in every sense of the word, and my respect for him was matched by my deep affection.

Frank W. McCulloch came to the PRB after a distinguished career in public service, most notably as chairman of the NLRB during a particularly difficult period in its history (1961–1970), when a hostile administration and a number of influential employers waged a relentless campaign against not only the NLRB but the National Labor Relations Act itself. Frank was the focus of their attacks and bore these with patience and dignity, often reacting with a wry humor reminiscent of Adlai Stevenson. He served on our board for an 18-year period (1970–1988), retiring when failing eyesight and other physical ailments made it too difficult for him to continue.

McCulloch's influence on his PRB colleagues was substantial. During hearings he confined himself to a few penetrating questions, politely persisting when he was dissatisfied with the initial responses. In executive sessions he usually remained silent until all his colleagues had exhausted their arguments, then he would offer his own views, often in the form of questions he felt had not been explored sufficiently. His analyses often persuaded me to adopt his point of view, even when I had tentatively decided in favor of another.

Like Higgins, McCulloch was passionately committed to the protection and enhancement of the rights of labor generally, as distinguished from labor unions, although he also strongly supported collective bargaining and the laws designed to strengthen it. His interests encompassed efforts to establish labor standards and to secure observance of basic human rights throughout the world. He was keenly interested in the work of the International Labor Organization (ILO), an agency of the United Nations created by the Treaty of Versailles at the end of World War I. For a number of years he served as a member of the ILO Committee of Experts on the Application of Conventions and Recommendations and was instrumental in securing my appointment to replace him when he retired from that position. Thereafter, he kept up a constant stream of correspondence with me, calling attention to issues before the committee that he considered most important, sending me relevant articles and bibliographic references, arranging meetings for me with persons in Geneva he thought could be most helpful, and in many other ways trying to smooth my path at the ILO and to make my service there more effective.

McCulloch was a moral gadfly who never ceased agitating until his objectives had been achieved. But everything he did was characterized by such sweetness of manner and delightful humor that even those whom he could not persuade to agree with him were captivated by his charm. He was a wonderful man, greatly loved and admired by his friends and colleagues.

Jean T. McKelvey, a very old friend, was appointed a member of the PRB in 1960, only three years after its establishment. It says something about the board's lack of consideration of female candidates that she was the sole woman member until she was joined briefly by Eleanor Holmes Norton in 1989. McKelvey remained on the board for 38 years, a record surpassed only by Higgins. Probably the most influential industrial relations teacher of her generation, McKelvey inspired countless students to pursue careers in that discipline in teaching, government service, business, and labor. In particular, she served as a role model for women, encouraging them by her example as a prominent teacher, scholar, arbitrator, and public servant, and opening doors for them into activities from which they had previously been excluded.

McKelvey's work on the PRB was equally outstanding. As her colleagues noted in a resolution commemorating her 75th birthday, she brought to this task "devotion, discipline, intelligence, and insight." In her later years she suffered the common physical indignities of old age, but she refused to let them slow her down. She showed up at each meeting after having traveled alone from her home in Rochester, N.Y., by air, economy class. She was invariably well prepared, and her close familiarity with the voluminous records was extraordinary. Her position on each of the cases before us was invariably well considered and firm, but she was flexible enough to change her mind when persuaded by the contrary opinions of her colleagues.

McKelvey was all business all the time. She had no gift or liking for small talk, even on social occasions. She did make one exception, however, enjoying gossip about her professional colleagues, to which she was a well-informed and enthusiastic contributor. Her mind remained sharp and clear until the end of her life, which came in her 89th year.

By singling out for praise only several former PRB members who are now dead, I do not wish it to be supposed that I hold any of my current colleagues in less regard. While I remain a member of the board, however, I prefer to emphasize one very important virtue that all of them possess: the willingness to strive for consensus even in those cases raising the most contentious issues and to refrain in most instances from writing dissenting opinions. Despite deep divisions over some issues, they have managed in almost all cases either to compromise their differences or to avoid the public airing of their dissenting views in the interest of presenting a common front to the board's constituents. Much of the credit for this suppression of individual egos must go to our current chairman, St. Antoine, whose tact and persuasiveness rival those of his immediate predecessor, Higgins. Two other members—James E. Jones Jr., the most senior in terms of years of service on the PRB, and James J. Brudney, one of the more recent appointees to the board—have exercised considerable influence on the way the PRB deals with the issues presented to it.

Jones, a professor of law emeritus at the University of Wisconsin, has unmatched experience as an African American working in a variety of occupations. He has a detailed knowledge of political rivalry within unions and an encyclopedic knowledge of shop practices that have been of invaluable aid to his colleagues on the board. In addition, although he is a fiercely loyal defender of the board, he has a well-articulated philosophy in respect of the limits of PRB power under the UAW constitution.

In case after case he has warned his colleagues of the evils of micromanaging the international union's conduct of its internal affairs. Brudney, a professor at the Ohio State College of Law, brings to the discussion of complex issues a skilled lawyer's power of analysis and an insistence upon examining a problem from a variety of viewpoints. He also has an imperturbable manner, never losing his temper and never straying from a matter of contention until it is resolved, often by a constructive compromise. Although these two men are often principal protagonists for opposing arguments, their mutual respect has made it easier to reach a consensus in even the most difficult cases.

Writing just four years after the establishment of the PRB, Brooks, the second executive director, said of the UAW: "It is doubtful that any other private association of individuals of comparable size and power had ever voluntarily relinquished power of this magnitude to another group." He was, of course, referring to the union's constitutional amendment that makes impartial public review available to its membership in a wide range of member grievances. The initial press reaction, he noted, was varied: "[T]o some it was a panacea; to others, a palliative or, worse yet, mere window dressing; most maintained a wait-and-see attitude."[14] Almost 50 years later, it is clear that the PRB is much more than mere window dressing, but although more than a palliative, it is not a panacea for all the problems of democratic governance in a large bureaucratic union such as the UAW.

Most of the more thoughtful reviews of the board's performance came early in its existence. One of the best of these was published in a brief report to the Center for the Study of Democratic Institutions that was authored by three highly qualified and respected observers: Jack Stieber, director of the Labor and Industrial Relations Center at Michigan State University; Walter E. Oberer, professor of law at University of Texas and the first executive director of the PRB; and Michael Harrington, a prominent social critic.[15] Harrington's essay is particularly helpful because it is based on his interviews of union members and officers across the

---

[14] Brooks, "Impartial Public Review," 64.
[15] Stieber et al., *Democracy and Public Review.*

country in the course of assessing the impact of the board on the local level. On the basis of his interviews, Harrington reached the following conclusion, among others:

> The existence of public review has not created democracy in the union. Where the membership is apathetic, the reform has meant little. But where there is participation and conflict...the Review Board has been significant. And finally, even in those areas where public review has not yet become a part of union life, it has a potential which is clearly recognized by the minority of union activists who may some day become leaders of revitalized locals.
>
> Seen from the vantage point of the local, public review has not been a miraculous solution for all the problems of union democracy, but it has been a spur and a complement to those democratic tendencies that do exist. In this sense, it can be characterized as a success.

Harrington went on to discuss the reactions of his interviewees to the new institution under five general headings: Review Consciousness, Acceptance of Public Review, Review Consensus, Informal Impact of Review, and Power and Public Review. By "review consciousness" he meant awareness by union members of their new rights. He reported the "striking unanimity" of union members at all levels that the majority of members were, at best, only dimly aware of the existence of the PRB. The minority conscious of the review mechanism were the active membership: "the local officials, the opposition where there is one, the rank and filers who regularly participate in the affairs of the local." He posited a theory that "as the Board establishes a history, as it develops cases in various areas, it educates the membership on its functions."

In the ensuing years, as Harrington predicted, the growing number of cases heard by the board has stimulated greater awareness among the UAW membership of its existence, as well as wider and more frequent resort to its processes. But certain questions remain. At the time that Harrington conducted his survey, the West Coast had yet to produce a single public review case. The reason, he suggested, was because most conflicts had been settled within the region, and he predicted that when a case involving an appeal to the PRB did develop on the West Coast, a much greater percentage of membership would be aware of their rights. Nevertheless, despite the fact that the entire union membership has access to the annual reports of the PRB summarizing its activities and that West Coast locals are bound to have encountered certain problems common to their counterparts throughout the country, only a handful of cases from that region have been appealed to the board. Lack of "review consciousness" seems an inadequate explanation for this phenomenon.

Harrington also warned of a reverse problem: the tendency of union areas—for example, Detroit, where a general awareness of the PRB and its processes exists—to attempt to short-circuit the well thought out preliminary screening procedures for the hearing of complaints before formally submitting them to the board. Frequently, the board's executive director has had to advise an individual member of his options under the UAW constitution; Harrington thought this function would lead to the board's becoming a "sort of union Legal Aid Society" and tend to promote an increase in intra-union litigation. That hasn't happened, but sure enough, the executive director has on occasion been criticized by some international union officers as being too free with his or her advice.

In discussing the acceptance of public review, Harrington again reported "striking unanimity" among the UAW membership in the value of a public review board. He could not find anyone in the union favoring abolition of the PRB. That feeling has only strengthened over the years. UAW presidents have regularly assured board members that the membership would never permit abolition of the PRB. At one time in the late 1990s, the UAW, the Machinists, and the Steelworkers entered into serious merger talks, which were quite advanced before they finally collapsed. The major deal breaker, we were informed, was the insistence by the Machinists and the Steelworkers that the merged organization not provide for a public review board, a proposal totally unacceptable to the UAW. Although this incident was further proof of the UAW's unshakable allegiance to the principle of public review, it also demonstrated that this ideal has never achieved the broader acceptance within the union movement hoped for by its supporters.

Harrington expressed surprise at the unanimity with regard to public review he found within the UAW. "Why is it," he wondered, that "winners and losers join together in supporting the principle of review despite their contrasting experiences in a given case?" One factor involved in this consciousness, he found, was the union's pride in its tradition of pioneering on trade union issues such as pensions and the guaranteed annual wage. Asked if they saw no paradox in the fact that their union needed public review the least, yet was the first to institute it on a wide basis, the persons he spoke to all gave the same answer: that it was further proof of the creativity of the UAW and that it demonstrated to labor's enemies in Congress and elsewhere that an honest union need not fear its membership.

These same attitudes may be said to have become institutionalized in succeeding years, despite the fact that individual decisions by the PRB have been bitterly criticized by disappointed appellants, as well as by the UAW's International Executive Board, and have prompted strong opposition by some of its members against the PRB itself. The most frequent charges have alleged that the PRB has exceeded its constitutional authority. Yet, in all cases thus far, the two bodies have thrashed out their differences, and the PRB has emerged from these encounters with its authority intact. It would, of course, be an exaggeration to say that the board has achieved the status of a sacred cow, but its position as a revered institution seems to be very nearly impregnable. In view of the current (2005) crisis in the automotive industry and its effects on the relationship between the UAW and the PRB, previously referred to, this last sentence may need to be revised.

In respect of the informal impact of review, Harrington pointed to another dimension observable on the local level as well as in the higher echelons of union governance: the encouragement of all officers and staff members to pay scrupulous attention to procedural requirements. He seems to have based this observation largely on an early case arising in Ford Local 897, in Buffalo, New York, which became something of a *cause célèbre*.[16] I have no reason to question his statement that one of the results of the decision in that case, which was against the international union, was an increased attention by union officials to procedural requirements, but our cases since then have provided many instances in

---

[16] Szymczak and Dewyea, "PRB Case No. 14 (30 April 1958)," *Annual Report of the Public Review Board 1* (Detroit: PRB, 1958): 35.

which both local and international officers have failed to observe procedures set forth in the UAW constitution or in local union bylaws. Of particular concern is the increasing reliance by the international president's staff on the formulaic excuse: "Based on the information provided by the Appellant and the Regional Office, a hearing regarding this matter was determined to be unnecessary," thus circumventing a vital step in the appeals procedure, as provided in Article 33, Section (3) (d) of the international constitution, which, however, as previously mentioned, has been amended to permit dispositions of appeals by members of the UAW staff without a formal hearing.

There is another aspect of the informal review mentioned by Harrington. On the basis of very few cases in which an administration defeat was followed by a more cautious approach by the international executive in its handling of certain disputes, Harrington suggested the possibility that intervention by the PRB promotes compromises, and that in fact its very existence will be a dominant factor in protecting and strengthening democracy in the union. He concluded:

> Public review works, particularly in areas where there is experience with it, to promote more responsible functioning by the holders of power, on both the staff and local levels. It may well work to strengthen the judicial process in the regions, and even as a force for the compromise of factional disputes. If the Board were to hear fewer and fewer cases as time goes on, this would not necessarily mean that it is ineffective or without importance. It would demonstrate the exact opposite—that it is so significant as to have strengthened the rule of democratic law throughout the union.

But the developing record has been quite different from that imagined by Harrington. The international has not been a significant factor in reconciling, through compromise, the different visions of the union's purposes held by competing factions. Instead, it has supported the groups in power against any serious rival for leadership within the union, such as the so-called New Directions movement. This no-holds-barred rivalry has been based on a winner-take-all philosophy embraced by both sides. Nor has the international been eager to intervene as a mediator between warring factions at the local union level; rather, it has tended to support the one allied with the caucus of the dominant group at the international level.

This is not to say, however, that the PRB has become less effective and of waning importance; to the contrary, it continues to be regarded as a powerful and respected body by both the top officials and the rank and file within the union. Its decisions are respected and deferred to by the federal and state courts, which have accepted the primary jurisdiction of the board over internal disputes within the union and have refused to hear such cases unless the appellants have first exhausted their internal union remedies.

Harrington's discussion of power and public review focused on the degree to which an individual UAW member can successfully pursue a claim against a local or the international without belonging to a power group in the union. He cautiously suggested this *possibility* (italicizing the word to emphasize its uncertainty), although he seemed to suggest the unlikelihood of such a result. But our own cases in the intervening years have turned up some outstanding examples of just such success, although they remain the exception to the rule.

It should also be pointed out that just as the changing economy and a political climate of indifference, if not open hostility, to the objectives of the union movement have taken their toll on the nation's unions, so the PRB has experienced new and more serious challenges to its former almost universal acceptance within the union and its open or tacit support among employers with whom the union bargains collectively.[17] Nonetheless, the board's status cannot yet be pronounced to be in serious danger. It is more likely to be imperiled by a breakdown of democracy within the UAW than by attacks prompted by dissatisfaction with some of its decisions or operating procedures.

Summing up, Harrington concluded:

> All of the evidence indicates that review works best where there is conflict within a democratic local framework. Under such conditions, the awareness of the rights guaranteed by the Board reaches a larger section of the rank and file; the individual who has a grievance always has a main political [sic] to whom he can turn for advice

---

[17] For example, the union's contracts with almost all of the employers with whom it deals provide that if the PRB finds that the union has wrongfully refused to process an employee's grievance, it may order that the grievance be put back into the grievance procedure, and that the employer not invoke the contractual time limits for the processing of grievances in such cases.

and help in prosecuting his appeal; and any financial question that might inhibit access to the review mechanism can be solved on a group basis. In such a situation, review acts to strengthen democratic tendencies that already exist and to establish a rule of law for any struggle that will take place within the local.

My personal concerns about the board's future relate to certain relatively new trends in the UAW itself. First among these is further evidence that the "iron law of oligarchy" has not been repealed. The combination of globalization, worsening domestic economy, increased employer hostility, and unfriendly legislative bodies has brought about a sharp decline in union membership, as well as a substantive reduction in its financial strength and political power. Perhaps in response, the diminished cadre of union representatives and staff has shown an increasing tendency to cut procedural corners and to arrogate powers not granted to them by the UAW constitution, thus diminishing rights granted by that document to individual union members. Moreover, the steps taken by the dominant caucus within the union to assure its continued power sometimes rival the most extreme "hard ball" tactics resorted to by the major political parties.

It may seem foolish and unfair to criticize the UAW for failing to adhere to standards of ethical behavior so much higher than those observed in the broader polity, but one is justified, I think, in reminding the union that it voluntarily embodied such standards in its own constitution and ethical codes and is properly subject to criticism when it fails to adhere to them.

As previously noted, appeals by union members from decisions of local bodies to the IEB are seldom heard any more by two-member appeals committees appointed by the IEB. Reference has already been made to the growing tendency of the IEB to dispense with a hearing before an appeals committee on the ground that the president's staff believes that no such hearing is necessary. But the problem does not stop there. An increasing cause of concern is the quality of most committees' reports, which are poorly written and typically contain little or no analysis of the record evidence that explains the reasons for the committees' conclusions submitted to the IEB. The seriousness of this deficiency is emphasized by the tendency of the IEB to adopt the appeals committees' recommendations as its own. The repeated efforts of the PRB executive director to improve the quality of appeals committee reports, including training sessions and other means, have so far been unsuccessful, so that the existing situation poses a substantial threat to the integrity of the union's internal appeals process and therefore to the adjudication system that controls cases coming before the PRB.

Finally, I have concerns about the ways some union members use the PRB processes. Not only have increasing numbers of members become familiar with these processes, but some have attempted to abuse them by repeatedly bringing meritless complaints supported by numerous petitions and motions, and reams of "evidence," most of which are either without verification or irrelevant. These efforts to "game" the system are a considerable drain on the time of the board's staff, as well as a waste of its limited financial resources. A related problem involves the excessive and incorrect efforts by union members who have lost cases before the PRB to obtain reconsideration of their claims. In a small number of cases the board has agreed to reconsider its decision when, for example, it is shown to have made a factual error that affected the outcome. In most cases, however, motions for reconsideration simply repeat the allegations that were thoroughly considered and rejected by the board. The PRB has to do a better job of educating the union membership not to abuse its processes in ways that are wasteful and counter-productive.

Summing up my experience to date as a member of the PRB, I have come to the hardly surprising conclusion that the fate of the board is inextricably related to that of the UAW. So far, the union has demonstrated an unshakable faith in this unique institution, even if on occasion it urges a change in some of its policies. The UAW, although battered by the hostile forces mentioned before, remains a model of institutional integrity within the American labor movement. Working with it for over 30 years, despite occasional aggravations, has been a privilege and a most satisfactory experience for which I am deeply grateful.

CHAPTER 18

ARBITRATION PRACTICE, 1946-2007

My career as an arbitrator, mediator, and factfinder is notable mostly for its duration (60 years) and for its variety, including arbitration experience in just about all of the major industries in the United States. I have served in a few instances as an umpire—that is, deciding all grievances going to arbitration under a collective bargaining agreement—but more often as a member of a panel of arbitrators chosen in turn to decide cases, and more often still as an ad hoc arbitrator—that is, one selected either directly by the parties or from a list of nominees submitted by either the American Arbitration Association (AAA), the Federal Mediation and Conciliation Service (FMCS), the National Mediation Board (NMB), or similar state agencies. In my early years of practice, I handled between 75 and 125 cases a year, but that volume declined substantially as other responsibilities—teaching, research, public service—became more demanding. Compared to my colleagues engaged in the full-time practice of arbitration, the total number of cases I have decided during my career is necessarily smaller than theirs.

The reader should be assured in advanced that I do not intend to describe in boring detail the nature and outcome of many disputes I have decided; instead, I shall concentrate on a few key cases.

At the end of World War II, perhaps the only element of the War Labor Board's dispute-resolution procedures that was enthusiastically accepted by employers and unions was the compulsory inclusion in all collective bargaining agreements of a grievance procedure culminating in "final and binding" arbitration. That acceptance was formalized in a national labor-management conference in 1946 and created a greatly increased demand for arbitrators. Because arbitration is not a licensed profession and requires no prescribed course of study or approval by a governmental board as a prerequisite to practice, the new class of arbitrators included lawyers, economists, political scientists, members of the clergy, and others. The only test that mattered was the acceptance of the would-be arbitrator by the employers and unions making use of his services. (I use only the masculine pronoun in this context because in the early post-war period, female arbitrators were a rarity.) The greatest demand was for ad hoc arbitrators to hear only one grievance, or at most a few. In a few industries—notably, auto, rubber, and steel—the employers and unions employed full-time umpires, but at no time has that system accounted for more than a small fraction of the nation's arbitrators.

The AAA antedated the establishment of the arbitration services division of the FMCS by a number of years. The formation of panels of labor arbitrators, from which the AAA selected names to submit to parties seeking an arbitrator, was an offshoot of its main activities, which focused on commercial and international arbitration. Moreover, the AAA initially regarded its arbitral functions as a form of pro bono work: persons chosen as a sole arbitrator or neutral chairman of a board of arbitration were supposed to perform their work without any monetary recompense. In 1946, when I launched my career as an arbitrator, I quickly learned the disadvantages of this policy. Having been made a member of the AAA's labor arbitration panel in Los Angeles on the recommendations of a few management and union friends, I was appointed to serve in several cases involving Douglas Aircraft Company and the International Association of Machinists (IAM), neither of which could reasonably plead inability to pay its share of a modest fee. Nevertheless, by securing my appointment through the AAA, they obtained my services for nothing. After dealing with a few assigned cases, each of which involved a hearing of one or more days and an equal amount of time to prepare my decision and opinion, I decided not to accept any more cases on a pro bono basis. Douglas and the IAM must have anticipated my decision, because they approached me directly, instead of going through the AAA, and offered to pay me $50.00 for each case I agreed to hear. The next one took the usual four days to decide. I submitted my bill and Douglas sent a check for its share of the cost—$25.00—by special messenger, who required me to sign a receipt for it. That was enough for me; I told the parties that my minimum charge henceforth would be $50.00 per day, not per case. They both considered that amount entirely too much, whereupon I foolishly reminded them that they still could get free arbitration through the AAA. A week later I was informed by the AAA that the same parties had chosen me to arbitrate a new case. I respectfully declined to accept the appointment. Apparently, other arbitrators on the AAA's labor panels began to reject cases on a pro bono basis, and shortly thereafter the AAA changed its policy to permit arbitrators to charge reasonable fees for their services.

During the eight months in 1941 that I spent in Washington D.C. looking for a job, I had devoted a lot of time to reading up on various labor-management relations systems of grievance settlement and arbitration. One result was that I acquired a rather starry-eyed view of both the process and the role of the arbitrator not only as an adjudicator of disputes but also as a key component in developing better labor-management relations.

In the late 1940s I become involved in my first big case, which involved factfinding with recommendations rather than arbitration. My file on the case, which involved a dispute between Kennecott Copper Corporation and a small local of the Brotherhood of Locomotive Engineers (BLE), has long since been lost, and I have been unsuccessful in finding any reference to the dispute in any contemporary publication reporting such events. The dispute had shut down Kennecott's large open-pit copper mine in Bingham Canyon, Utah, and it was finally submitted to a three-man factfinding board that was authorized to set forth the issues in dispute and the respective positions of the parties and to submit recommendations for a settlement. The chairman of the board, whose name I no longer recall, was a professor in the business school of the University of Chicago who had written a book about the Railway Labor Act (RLA) and who also served as a neutral referee for the National Railroad Adjustment Board (NRAB), an agency created by the RLA to adjudicate grievances in the railroad industry. He was a reserved and taciturn man who refrained from socializing with his two younger colleagues, Peter Kelliher, a well-known labor arbitrator from Chicago and a future president of the National Academy of Arbitrators (NAA), and me, the youngest and least experienced of the three.

The case was a very complicated one involving Kennecott's efforts to compel the BLE to accept a job classification system applicable to all of the other unions representing different groups of workers at the mine. My recollection is that the hearings lasted for about two weeks, during which a number of witnesses testified, dozens of exhibits were submitted, and a verbatim transcript of about a thousand pages was taken. At the close of the hearing the members of the factfinding board held a brief executive session at which we decided what our recommendations would be. I assumed that the chairman would prepare the initial draft of our report and recommendations, but as the very junior member of the board, I asked him if he would like me to prepare an outline and summary of the record for whatever use he would care to make of it. To my astonishment he replied, "Oh, I thought I'd ask you to prepare the initial draft." Kelliher immediately seconded the suggestion, and I was stuck with the job.

And what a job it was. I was already teaching at UCLA, and I could work on the report only at night. I first made a detailed outline of the transcript and an analysis of each of the many exhibits, and then I began to write the report, working past midnight almost every night for about three weeks. Throughout this period I kept saying to Eleanor, "They'll never believe I spent this much time." At length the job was done, and I sent copies of the report and recommendations to my two colleagues, together with abject apologies for taking so much time and accepting in advance the many changes I anticipated they would want to make. We had previously agreed to meet at Kelliher's house in Chicago to go over my draft and make the necessary changes before sending the final version to the parties.

When we got together, it became clear to me that my two colleagues had either not read my draft or, at most, had given it no more than a cursory scan. Kelliher pronounced the draft a masterpiece and declared that he would not change a line; the chairman agreed. Then they got down to what they evidently regarded as the real purpose of our meeting: determining how much to charge the parties, who had mutually agreed to compensate us at the rate of $200 per day spent in hearing the case and preparing the factfinding report and recommendations (an astronomical sum as far as I was concerned). To my great surprise, my two colleagues agreed that we should each charge the same amount; then they asked me how much time I had spent on the case. I said 18 days, and waited for their expressions of shock and disbelief. But Kelliher evidenced no disapproval; instead, he declared that he had spent 22 days. The chairman topped that whopper by claiming 23 days, explaining: "Referees for the NRAB, who are paid only $50.00 a day, have a custom of charging for each day they do no more than look at the file of a case. Each day since the close of this case, I have looked at the file." Then he and Kelliher agreed that they could not charge for more days than I had counted, but solved that problem to their own satisfaction by telling me to increase my listed days by about three. By this time I was so disillusioned and disgruntled that I flatly refused, so they each reluctantly reduced the number of days charged to equal mine. Our fee was paid promptly and without comment, but Kennecott summarily rejected our recommendations, and the parties eventually agreed on a different solution, thus putting an end to what was for me a devastating experience. I had never cared much for the chairman, but I really liked Kelliher, a genial colleague and a first-rate arbitrator. Still, I could not forgive him for his part in the Kennecott fiasco, which not only exploited my efforts but also effectively put an end to my innocence about how fees for services rendered were determined.

Although most of my arbitrations were of the ad hoc variety, I did hold a few umpireships during the active phase of my career as an arbitrator.

In 1946, shortly after joining the staff of the UCLA Institute of Industrial Relations, I was appointed the first umpire under the collective bargaining agreement between North American Aviation and a local of the United Auto Workers. The director of industrial relations for North America was Gene Starkweather. The procession of local union presidents was supervised by Ed Hall, the former CIO representative on the National Airframe Panel and now an international representative of the UAW.

North American's labor relations policy toward the union was one of containment rather than outright opposition; it consistently kept the union at arm's length and resisted any effort to make its relationship closer and more cooperative. It was initially represented in arbitration cases by Forrest Cool, a former law professor at the University of Southern California. Cool, who had almost no knowledge of industrial relations and collective bargaining, showed up at each hearing with an armful of volumes of published decisions by the California courts that were largely irrelevant to the issues at hand. Despite my efforts to keep the proceedings as informal as possible, Cool made constant objections on technical legal grounds. On one occasion, after the union had made a particularly inept presentation of its case, Cool asked me to give a "directed verdict" in the company's favor. Although it seemed clear to me that the union's arguments lacked merit, I denied Cool's motion and directed him to put on the company's case. With ill-concealed anger, he complied. After the hearing, Cool approached me and asked why I had denied his motion. I replied that one aspect of an arbitration hearing is to give union members, regardless of the merits of their grievances, the opportunity to see their employer being compelled to explain why they grievances had been denied. I also told him that in my experience, after a union had presented an apparently meritless case, an employer sometimes made inadvertent disclosures of facts previously unknown to the union that completely changed the situation and led to a decision in the union's favor. At this, Cool, a man of choleric temperament, turned deep red and then blue, and began to sputter. I was sure he was going to have a heart attack or a stroke, but he eventually grabbed his law books and stomped out. He never returned and was replaced by an experienced labor lawyer.

The union was in far worse shape than the company. It had no experienced and responsible leadership and was riven by factions; grievances without merit were routinely taken to arbitration because of internal political pressures. To make matters worse, grievances were presented by whoever happened to be president of the union and were usually mishandled. The result was that I decided the great majority of them in the company's favor.

After about a year, Hall took me aside one day and told me that the union was becoming increasingly upset because, in his words, it was not "winning its share of the cases." I explained that in my view neither party was automatically entitled to a "share" of favorable decisions, and that I would continue to decide the cases brought to me strictly on the merits. He nodded, and said he understood my point of view but simply wanted to warn me of its probable consequences. Sure enough, after I had decided two more grievances utterly devoid of merit in the company's favor, I received a special delivery letter from the union firing me as umpire.

My reaction was one of relief to be rid of an increasingly distasteful obligation and of gratitude to George Taylor for his prescient warning a few years earlier not to rely on arbitration as the sole source of my livelihood.[1] Although I was now teaching, I continued to accept ad hoc arbitration cases principally because they offered such a good opportunity to study different forms of labor-management relationships at first hand and to use the information thus obtained in my teaching.

In 1951 I was appointed umpire under the collective bargaining agreement between the B.F. Goodrich Rubber Company and the United Rubber Workers, succeeding G. Allan Dash Jr., a fellow member of the NAA. The company's headquarters and main plant were in Akron, Ohio, but the collective agreement also covered eight other plants around the country. As umpire, I served as chairman of an arbitration board; the other members consisted of two representatives each from the company and the union.

During the summer of that year I visited Akron for about a week in order to view the plant, a large multi-storied building older than I was, and to learn the company's complicated wage payment system. Just about every job in the plant was automated and classified according to a job-evaluation plan based on a wide range of factors (some of them highly subjective). All jobs were time-studied and given a rating of a certain numbers of "Bs" (representing the basic measuring unit derived from a

---

[1] See chapter 1.

piecework system invented by Charles Bedaux). The standard for a given job was supposed to reflect the output per hour of an employee working with due diligence at average speed, which was determined to be 60 Bs. The hourly rate for each job was set by collective bargaining. Any units produced over 60 Bs would be rewarded by an incentive bonus, which was also set by collective bargaining; any employee falling consistently below that standard of output would be subject to discipline. All time studies were jointly conducted by the company and the union, each with its own expert. If the two experts disagreed, a common occurrence, their principals would seek to reconcile the differences. If they were unsuccessful, the issue was submitted to arbitration.

If this system sounds complicated, that's because it was, and even after a year's experience, I found it extremely difficult to determine whether the rate of pay given to a worker was correct. The workforce consisted almost entirely of white males, a disproportionate number of whom came from West Virginia. A great number of them were functional illiterates, yet their mastery of the pay system was complete; any one of them could tell you in a second just what his pay should be, to a fraction of a cent.

Although almost every job in the plant was automated, there were a few conspicuous exceptions. In my first tour of the plant, accompanied by two representatives from each side, we started on the top floor and worked our way down to the basement. On the way, the representatives explained each phase of the operation, which consisted mainly of producing tires. As we approached the first floor, the union representatives began needling their counterparts, asking when they were going to take me to the basement. Obviously embarrassed, the company men first said there was nothing down there of interest to me, but eventually they yielded to the union's insistence. The temperature in the plant was about 90° F, but it was over 100° in the basement. The scene I beheld was so shocking that I could not suppress a cry of amazement, much to the delight of the union men accompanying me. In the middle of the room was a pool of molten lead, about 20 to 30 feet in diameter, which emitted an unpleasant smell as well as a constant shower of sparks. A large beam was attached to a pole in the center of the pool. Pushing the beam slowly around the circumference of the pool, stirring the molten liquid, was a giant of a man, at least six feet, four inches tall, bare to the waist, and with his head in a kind of harness. The skin of his upper torso and his arms bore multiple scars from burns caused by the sparks. The scene brought to mind an image of the blind Samson grinding corn.

How, I asked in bewilderment, in a plant in which almost every job was automated, could the continuance of this degrading operation be tolerated? The company representatives responded, first, that the work was paid for at a premium rate, and second, that their engineering experts had been unable to automate the job in a way that would produce a result equal to that achieved by human labor. Fortunately, during my brief tenure as umpire, I never was called upon to decide a grievance filed by the man pushing the beam; it would have been difficult, if not impossible, to disregard my personal revulsion to the nature of the job.

The most powerful member of the union and, indeed, the dominant personality among those on either side with whom I dealt on a regular basis, was its president, George Bass. Bass had from an early age worked in the Akron plant. He had also served for a time as a CIO organizer in the South, and he had been beaten up and almost lynched on several occasions. By the time I first encountered him he was, I judged, in his mid-fifties. He was burly, tough as nails, rude, and foul-mouthed, a dictator to his underlings in the union, and able also to intimidate most of the company representatives with whom he customarily dealt.

At the very first case I heard in Akron, I announced at noon, after several hours of hearings, that we would break for lunch. Bass immediately flung down the gauntlet; he responded that the timing of lunch breaks at this plant was determined not by the umpire but by the parties and that he was not ready to go to lunch. It seemed to me that I had no alternative but to accept the challenge, so I told Bass that regardless of past practice I would determine when we broke for lunch or other recesses and that he could eat or not, as he pleased, but that the hearing would recess for lunch for one hour. Bass gave me a cold stare, but then he and the other union men present left the room without further comment. Thereafter, despite periodic differences of opinion producing some sharp interchanges, Bass and I got along very well, and my feelings toward him progressed from dislike to appreciation of his obvious abilities.

The system of presentation of arbitration cases to the board wasted time and was frequently inadequate, but it was set in stone, and every suggestion on my part to improve it was summarily rejected or ignored by both parties. Every hearing began with the reading aloud by each side of its prehearing brief. The company's brief was invariably longer than the union's, but it consisted mostly of assertions accompanied by few supporting arguments. Much to my amusement, it always ended with the words "Respectively submitted." The union's brief typically consisted of only a few pages denouncing the company's decision on the merits of the grievance that the company had denied. The briefs having been read, Bass would begin the presentation of the union's case. He made no reference to the union brief, but limited his remarks to a withering analysis of the company's brief that was usually very effective and often positively brilliant. The most troubling feature of the hearing was that the arbitration board never got to see or to hear from the grievant(s) or any other witnesses; instead, any issues of fact, and there were many, were debated by union committeemen from the division or department in which the grievant(s) worked and by management representatives, most of them white-collar employees, who would rely only on what they were told by foremen.

It was customary for the board to hear two to four cases a day. We then adjourned, and I returned to California to review my notes and to study the applicable provisions of the collective bargaining agreement. When I was ready, I prepared a draft of a proposed decision and opinion in each case and scheduled a meeting of the arbitration board, usually in Chicago or some other place where the partisan members could not be pressured by their constituents during our deliberations. It was during these sessions that I came to appreciate the value of a tripartite board. Because of the technical nature of many of the issues, especially those involving the application of the company's complicated wage system, I sometimes made mistakes that were corrected by my colleagues. From them I also learned important facts, never referred to by the parties during the hearings, which were extremely helpful in arriving at workable solutions to problems raised by the grievances. This reliance on information supplied by someone who had never testified at the hearing or been subjected to cross-examination would have been decried by parties and arbitrators in the typical ad hoc arbitration case, but it was accepted by the partisan board members at Goodrich, whose chief aim was to produce a result satisfactory to both sides. One example will suffice to explain how the system worked. When a grievance involved the setting of wage rates, one of the company's regular representatives on the arbitration board was replaced by an industrial engineer, an exceptionally able man. Following the discussion by the board members, he usually made a statement in which he analyzed the arguments of both sides and expressed his candid view as to their respective merits. He would conclude by saying something like this: "I realize that this is probably improper, but I have studied the job in question and discussed it with the workers and supervisors involved, and I think I know what rate would be acceptable to both sides." The rate he proposed would invariably be adopted by the board. I once asked the union's secretary and chief representative on the board, who was in the habit of automatically dissenting from any decision upholding the company's action, why he was willing to accept the recommendation of a company representative. His answer was: "Because he has always been right; but if he ever persuades us to set a rate that our members object to, we'll never trust the son of a bitch again."

As the year progressed, Bass and I developed a good working relationship, and he was generally well behaved during our arbitration hearings. There was, however, one major exception. From time to time we would hear a grievance involving an alleged improper procedure by personnel in the plant medical office. On those occasions, Bass's manner became absolutely savage: he would berate the unfortunate person against whom the accusation had been made with a vehemence and bitterness that seemed to me completely out of proportion to the alleged offense. Seeking some explanation, I invited him to lunch one day and asked what it was about these cases that so aroused him. Bass held up his right hand; one of his fingers was a mere stump. He then told me this story:

> When I was a cocky kid about 18 years old, I was working on a lathe and cut through
> this finger. (There were no guards on machines in those days.) The finger was hanging
> by the skin, but I thought I was a tough guy and I walked over to the medical office to
> show them what I had done. The doctor on duty cursed me out for being so careless
> and then started pulling on the skin, trying unsuccessfully to cover the knuckle of the
> injured finger. Finally, he said to me, "you son of a bitch, we're going to have to ampu-
> tate that finger above the knuckle, which means the company's workers' compensation
> bill will be higher." Then he amputated the finger, leaving only this stump, and I went
> back to work. Ever since I have hated those bastards in the medical department.

So far as I could observe, either the machines in the plant still lacked sufficient guards or the machine operators were incredibly careless. The majority of the workers I saw had at least one finger missing.

It was during my term as umpire at Goodrich that I encountered a problem common to manufacturing companies using a piecework system of remuneration: the phenomenon of the "rate-buster." As previously explained, the standard production per hour for a particular job was established by time-studying an employee working with due diligence at an average speed. At Goodrich, this standard was 60 Bs, and employees exceeding 60 Bs were paid a bonus based on the amount of over-production. It was recognized that most machine operators will always find ways to perform a given job more rapidly than the standard permits, but if too many of them do so, management will call for a new time study, the likely result of which will be a tighter standard. Normally, the company would not seek a new time study if some operators produced at a rate as high as 90 Bs per hour, but if a majority of them did so, management would conclude that the standard was too loose. Thus, union members in the plant had a tacit understanding that no one would produce at a higher rate than 90 Bs in order not to "kill" the standard and to prompt management to replace it with a tighter one.

The rate-busters, who were a small minority in the plant, refused to abide by this understanding. Typically, they were highly skilled workers, who, although members of the bargaining unit, refused to join the union. They were interested only in increasing their own remuneration. It was not uncommon for them to produce at a rate of 100 or more Bs per hour. The union responded by filing a grievance accusing the offending worker(s) of achieving this amount of production either by (1) cheating; (2) working unsafely; or (3) slighting the quality of the item produced. The company usually denied the grievance, and the arbitration board, by a vote of three to two, generally upheld the company's action because nothing in the collective agreement specifically prohibited what the rate-busters were doing. In my opinions for the arbitration board on this issue, I warned of the dangers of unrestrained production over standard, thus following the dictum of William Leiserson, a legendary figure in American industrial relations and a pioneer umpire in the garment industry, that the arbitrator's decision in favor of one party ought to be ameliorated by language favorable to the opposing party's position, thereby encouraging a "consent to lose."

During my time as an umpire, I had occasion to visit all of the other eight Goodrich plants except the one nearest at hand, in Los Angeles. On 24 December 1951, I received a telephone call from a company and a union representative asking if they could come to my office at UCLA to discuss an urgent matter. I told them to come right away. When they arrived, I asked what the problem was. "We have no problem," they replied, "but because you have never been to our plant, we thought we'd bring you this. Merry Christmas." Whereupon they presented me with a bottle of very good bourbon whiskey, which we sampled on the spot.

On one visit to the plant in Clarksville, Tennessee, I learned an extremely valuable lesson that I have never forgotten. The workforce at the plant was employed in a number of divisions. One of these was manned entirely by Negroes; all of the others were lilywhite. The collective bargaining agreement provided that a worker laid off from a particular division could be recalled only to that division, even if there were job vacancies in other divisions that the worker was qualified to perform. The grievance was filed by two white workers who had been laid off from one division and whose bid for available jobs in another division had been rejected. After the union president had presented these facts, the company responded by quoting the applicable provision of the agreement. At this point the union president said: "You know damn well that that provision was intended for one reason only: to prevent blacks from transferring into any of the white divisions. It has never been applied in cases like this."

Full of righteous indignation, I declared that I did not want to hear anything more, and that the union's grievance was denied. I also said that I could never be party to such an outrageous case of racial discrimination. After the hearing, I was approached by the union president, who said, more in sorrow than in anger, "You know, Mr. Aaron, I expected to lose this grievance, as we should. But you don't understand the situation in this plant. I'm fighting racial discrimination any way I can a little at a time. It was a major victory when we ended segregation of the drinking fountains. But you humiliated me in front of my members and undermined my authority; now, it's going to be harder than ever to desegregate this plant." He made me feel ashamed and I apologized. Never again did I give vent to my personal feelings on the merits of an issue in an arbitration case.

My tenure as umpire at Goodrich ended after one year, when President Harry Truman appointed me a public member of the National Wage Stabilization Board. Before going to Washington D.C., I resigned my umpireship and severed ties with all other companies and unions for which I had arbitrated. As previously noted, this did not prevent members of Congress from subsequently accusing me and my fellow public members on the board of being "beholden" to labor leaders.[2]

Another of my umpireships was also in the rubber industry, under a collective bargaining agreement between the Los Angeles plant of Firestone Tire and Rubber Company and a local of the Rubber Workers Union. My files of the cases I heard under this agreement were unfortunately destroyed, but my tenure lasted for about 10 years, beginning in the 1960s and ending in the early 1970s.

As umpire, I chaired a tripartite panel. The union's cases were sometimes presented by a local attorney, an able and likeable fellow whose practice consisted mostly of criminal cases. He argued the union's positions as if he were in court and showed little inclination to explore possible settlements in lieu of arbitral decisions. The company's cases

---

[2] See chapter 3.

were presented by a member of its industrial relations department who had a better grasp than his opposite number did of plant practices and customs, as well as a greater flexibility in the arbitration of cases.

After hearing a case, the arbitration panel recessed until we had received copies of the transcript and post-hearing briefs from the parties. I then wrote a proposed decision and opinion and submitted it to my panel colleagues. If I was in town, we usually met at the plant to review my draft before signing it. The union members seemed to be interested only in the decision; when it went against them, they sometimes renewed their previous arguments, but they rarely took issue with the language of my opinion. The company members were more apt to question language in the opinion on the ground that it was inaccurate in some respect or that it was too broad and prejudged the company's position in future cases that might arise or were already in the pipeline of the grievance procedure. Voting either to accept or reject my proposed decision was pro forma; I can't recall a single instance in which it was rejected or that a partisan arbitrator failed to dissent when the result was against his principal.

In a number of instances, I was out of town when I finished my work on a case. It was my practice in these situations to mail in my proposed decision and opinion, which I signed in order to save time. The partisan arbitrators immediately made copies for their principals. In the cover letter to my panel colleagues, however, I always added a paragraph reserving my right to change my decision at the request of either party "for good cause shown." On one such occasion, I received a letter from the company, shortly after I had sent the proposed decision and opinion in the union's favor to the other panel members, pointing out that I had overlooked a provision of the collective bargaining agreement that would have required a reversal of the result. I immediately informed the other panel members that I was changing my decision for that reason. The union members of the panel protested violently, claiming that once I had signed an award, I could not change my mind. I reminded them of my customary reservation of the right to change my mind for just cause shown and rejected their argument that by signing the decision and opinion, I had forfeited the right to do so.

Shortly thereafter, the union informed me that, on advice of counsel, it was seeking to have my decision vacated by a state court. (Its effort was subsequently rejected by the court.) The union's attorney then proposed that the arbitration procedure set forth in the collective bargaining agreement be changed to provide that an attorney or other special representative for each side be authorized to participate in the panel's post-hearing process, including a discussion of the merits of the case. Whether that proposal was formally submitted to the company I do not know, but I had already decided to resign my umpireship. Accordingly, I wrote a letter to both parties, explaining, in essence, my view that the union's appeal to the court to vacate my decision constituted a vote of no confidence in my judgment and fairness and that I had concluded that it would be better if the parties replaced me with someone in whom they had greater trust. The union's attorney urged me to reconsider my decision, but the company neither acknowledged nor replied to my letter. This was the only instance in which the termination of a long-standing relationship with the parties left me with a sense of deep regret and considerable bitterness.

Prior to assuming the umpireship at the Fort Worth plant of General Dynamics under its collective bargaining agreement with the International Association of Machinists, I had previously served as an ad hoc arbitrator in a number of cases at the company's San Diego plant. Moreover, my extensive experience as chairman of the National War Labor Board's National Airframe Panel during World War II had provided me with a valuable background in the airframe manufacturing industry.[3]

My preparation notwithstanding, I did not enjoy my tenure as umpire at General Dynamics. I used to fly to Fort Worth from Los Angeles once or twice a month and remain there until I heard all the grievances on the arbitration docket. The relationship between the parties, like that at North American, was strictly at arm's length. Moreover, neither side had much respect for the other, although they generally managed to maintain a minimal level of civility. Both parties made one thing perfectly clear: they didn't trust the umpire much more than they trusted each other.

---

[3] See chapter 1.

The grievance-arbitration procedure was pretty much under the control of the union's president, a man of limited competence, and its district committeemen, each of whom was the unchallenged boss of the employees in his district insofar as the processing of grievances was concerned. The level of their abilities to carry out this important responsibility was relatively low, and their counterparts on the management side were similarly unimpressive. In many of the grievances submitted to me the chief difficulty was to sort out the facts in some coherent order. There always seemed to be a huge backlog of unsettled grievances, and from time to time the parties would go on a kind of retreat to another city, such as El Paso, with no grievants present, at which time they would try to settle as many cases as they could. The umpire accompanied them and was asked to decide any grievances the parties were unable to settle. The procedure adopted was rather bizarre and of dubious fairness.

I was left in my room and told to occupy myself however I wished but not to leave. The parties' representatives then sat down around a table somewhere else, discussed large numbers of grievances for a few minutes each, and disposed of them. Obviously, this was simply a trade-off process, without much regard to the merits of the grievances involved. My close friend, Arthur Ross, a labor economist at UC Berkeley and my predecessor as umpire at General Dynamics, famously termed these sessions "fire sales." On the rare instances in which the parties could not agree on a settlement, they would march into my room, lay the files before me, and ask for an immediate judgment, backed up by a short written memorandum. Despite my misgivings about the fairness of this process, which by then had existed for some years, I agreed to go along, with one exception: I flatly refused to uphold the discharge or serious discipline of an employee without first holding a full-dress hearing that might result in a contrary result.

In the evenings, the local union president would lead the entire crowd on a tour of some of the lowest dives I have ever seen—an exercise that left me particularly uncomfortable. It was an actual relief to be fired by the union after a year or two, although no particular reason was provided. I assumed that I had decided more cases against it than its leaders thought was "fair."

My final dealings with the parties had all the qualities of a comic opera. The local union president was finally deposed and his place was taken by a man I shall call Smith, although that was not his real name. Whereas his predecessor had been garrulous and not very bright, Smith was close-mouthed, saturnine of manner, and very intelligent. He immediately began not only giving management fits but also challenging directives from the national union. One day I received a call from Robert Biron, a corporate vice-president of General Dynamics in charge of industrial relations and an old friend. Biron began by asking me if I knew Smith, and upon learning that I did, he told me the following story. It seems that Smith and his wife had split up and were in the process of getting a divorce. Recently, she had come to the office of the plant manager at Fort Worth and asked him whether he knew that her husband had once been convicted of armed robbery and served a sentence in a federal penitentiary in Pennsylvania. This was unbelievably good news to the plant manager because, when filling out an employment application at the plant some years earlier, Smith had answered "No" to a question about whether he had ever been convicted of a crime. The manager immediately informed his superiors, and steps were taken to fire Smith for falsifying his employment application. Before taking final action, however, Biron decided to check out the situation with me. He posed a hypothetical question: if Smith were discharged for falsifying his employment application and protested that action by filing a grievance, how would I decide the issue?

Before giving my answer, I ascertained from Biron that Smith had been employed at the Fort Worth plant for over five years, had a disciplinary-free record, and was a first-rate mechanic. Under those circumstances, I told Biron, I would not be inclined to sustain the discharge, adding that this was a case in which something akin to a statute of limitations against punishment for the falsification of his employment application should be deemed to have run. I concluded by saying that having given my opinion on the proposed disposition of this case, I would of course have to disqualify myself from hearing it. To this Biron replied: "I know that. Having anticipated your response to my questions, I deliberately set out to disqualify you." We had a good laugh and then he rang off.

No more than 15 minutes later, I received a call from Ernie White, a vice-president of the International Association of Mechanics (IAM) and also an old friend. White started to discuss, very delicately, the case of Smith. I interrupted him to explain that I had already reviewed the facts with Biron and had disqualified myself from hearing a grievance arising out of Smith's discharge. Much relieved, White thanked me and said that the way was now open for the parties jointly to request the Federal Mediation & Conciliation Service (FMCS) to appoint an arbitrator. No more than an hour later, I received a telegram from the FMCS appointing me the ad hoc arbitrator to hear this dispute! Accordingly, I had to telegraph back that I could not accept the appointment and to explain the reasons why.

The story has a rather sad ending. The FMCS then appointed Nate Feinsinger, a nationally revered arbitrator and mediator and a dear friend of mine. Feinsinger must have known that Smith's discharge was a classic example of a "rigged case"—that is, one in which the parties secretly agree to get rid of an employee, and so advise the arbitrator in advance of the hearing, but go through all the usual procedures of an arbitration case, leaving it to the arbitrator to sustain the discharge supposedly on the basis of the evidence presented. It hurt me to hear that Feinsinger had voluntarily and knowingly entered into such a disreputable scheme. Indeed, I was subsequently told that he played his role overenthusiastically and made a number of procedural rulings during the hearing that outraged members of the local union, who were unaware of the secret deal between General Dynamics and the IAM.

It is possible that Feinsinger believed, along with a minority of arbitrators, that it was all right to go along with the secret arrangements between the company and the union so long as they produced credible evidence supporting the discharge of the grievant. In my view, however, such a justification is wholly unacceptable because the conspiring parties are exclusively in charge of presenting the evidence and there can be no possibility of a fair hearing.

The knowing and voluntary participation in a rigged case is one of the unforgivable sins an arbitrator can commit; I would equate it with the acceptance of a bribe. Nevertheless the practice is an old one and, unfortunately, still goes on today, although one hopes it occurs less frequently. That it still exists is explained by the continued willingness of some employers and unions to ignore their responsibilities for the sake of obtaining a result they both desire but fear they cannot achieve without depriving the object of their conspiracy of even a vestige of due process. A second explanation is that the NAA and the appointing agencies such as the AAA and the FMCS will not act against the perpetrators of such a scheme unless one of the collective bargaining parties files a formal complaint. Even if such a complaint is made, however, the current (1996) Code of Professional Responsibility for Arbitrators of Labor-Management Disputes refers to "Consent Awards" in section 2.I.1, but only in a limited way that fails to discuss employee dismissal by secret agreement of the employer and the union: "Prior to issuance of an award, the parties may jointly request the arbitrator to include in the award certain agreements between them, concerning some or all of the issues. *If the arbitrator believes that a suggested award is proper, fair, sound and lawful, it is consistent with professional responsibility to adopt it*" (italics supplied).

Having said all this, I must admit that on a few occasions I agreed to serve as arbitrator in an interest dispute over wages in which the parties compromised on a settlement that they agreed was fair, but that each felt would be rejected by their principals unless it was presented as a decision by the arbitrator. At the hearing, each party vigorously argued in favor of its initial proposal. I carefully reviewed and analyzed the extensive economic data in the record, concluded that the compromise was fair and sensible, and adopted it as my award.

This was undoubtedly a form of "rigged case," but it seemed to me quite different from one in which the parties secretly agree to the discharge of an employee, so inform the arbitrator, and then hold a sham hearing. In the interest arbitration cases, the parties bargained collectively in good faith and reached a compromise that was fully justified by the facts. It was true that the union's membership and the employer's board of directors remained ignorant of the agreement reached by their negotiators, but in my judgment neither side was prejudiced by the arbitration award.

This issue deserves more discussion than is feasible in this chapter. The interested reader is referred to an in-depth and more nuanced analysis by speakers Willard Wirtz and Abram H. Stockman, on due process of arbitration at an annual meeting of the NAA.[4]

One of the umpireships I enjoyed the most was under the collective bargaining agreement between Kennecott Copper Corporation and the independent Mine, Mill & Smelter Workers (MM&SW), whose members were mostly Mexicans and Native Americans, in whom the AFL-CIO unions like the Steelworkers and the Machinists had traditionally taken relatively little interest. The MM&SW had been affiliated with the CIO but had been expelled because of its alleged dominance by the Communist Party. Some of its top national officers were either Communists or followed the party line, but their representation of the rank-and-file was devoted, intelligent, and, as far as I observed, beyond reproach. The applicable collective bargaining agreement covered Kennecott-operated copper mines in Utah, Nevada, Arizona, and New Mexico. The company's headquarters were in Salt Lake City, and its open-pit mine in Bingham Canyon, just outside Salt Lake, was then by far the biggest in the United States, if not the world. It also operated smaller mines in company towns in Ely, Nevada, and Ray, Arizona, and in Silver City, Ajo, and Morenci, New Mexico. Although most of the cases I heard arose in Salt Lake, I did visit the mines in the other states from time to time.

Going into these mining communities was like stepping back into an earlier era. Kennecott owned and administered everything: houses, schools, local government, police and fire departments, public utilities, recreational facilities, and so on. Race and class lines were strictly observed. Members of the all-white management lived in fairly good houses in the most attractive part of what was, at best, a rather dreary town; the much larger group of Mexicans and Native Americans were housed in simple huts in less

---

[4] *The Arbitrator and the Parties: Proceedings of the 11th Annual Meeting of the National Academy of Arbitrators*, ed. J. T. McKelvey (Washington, D.C.: BNA, 1958), 26–36, 37–46.

desirable locations. Nevertheless, so far as I could observe on my brief visits, a rather easy relationship existed between management and workers. Thus, for example, the former had the good sense not to interfere with the miners' custom, observed throughout the southwest, to take time off from regularly scheduled work to go javalina (wild pig) hunting. All that was required was for the worker to obtain a substitute to work his shift during his absence and to inform his foreman of the arrangement.

On the other hand, the treatment of workers injured on the job was generally unfeeling and counterproductive. The first case I heard at the Silver City mine involved an employee who had been discharged for no longer being able to do his assigned job. He had suffered a severe back injury while working and had undergone major back surgery to repair it. The company provided and paid for skilled surgical care and attendant hospitalization through the recovery period, after which both parties virtually ignored him. He brought suit in the New Mexico courts for workers' compensation and received a substantial award. Thereafter, he sought to return to work on a medically restricted basis. The company provided a light-work assignment on a temporary basis, but the worker kept complaining that it was too difficult and became increasingly disaffected. Eventually, the company fired him.

I arrived in Silver City by bus from El Paso, Texas, on the day before the hearing. The bus ride reminded me of a story by John Steinbeck. The bus itself was a ramshackle vehicle that seemed to lack any working shock absorbers. It was so crowded that the driver had to place removable seats in the aisle to accommodate the passengers. At each of the frequent stops en route to Silver City, these seats had to be temporarily removed to permit passengers on board to depart and new ones to board. The passengers brought considerable baggage, consisting of everything from bulging suitcases to wooden crates containing chickens. Everyone was agreeable, but the press of bodies over such a long haul gradually became very uncomfortable. When we arrived in Silver City, I was so eager to get off the bus that I failed to notice that the distance between the running board and the street was almost three feet. As I stepped down, I felt something give in my back, followed by a sharp pain.

The pain increased substantially throughout a sleepless night, which I spent on the floor of my room. Early the next morning, I called the local union office and explained that I needed some medical attention. The union sent over someone who took me to a very modern, well-equipped clinic maintained by the MM&SW. The resident doctor filled me full of drugs until I was thoroughly stoned and then put me on a table and maneuvered my leg until the worst of the pain disappeared. He explained that I had popped a disc in my back and would require follow-up treatment. After a brief nap, I convened the hearing.

The hearing lasted all day and was very hard for me because I had to sit on a card table chair with no back support. A number of witnesses testified, but the decisive piece of evidence, provided by the union, was a copy of a memorandum from the plant manager to all management personnel stating that any employee who obtained a workers' compensation award against the company should be fired forthwith. In my decision I reinstated the discharged worker, but I took the occasion to criticize both parties for neglecting him during the critical phase of his recovery and thereby contributing to his subsequent disaffection. This was but one of many instances I observed over the years in which both employers and unions overlooked the rehabilitation of injured workers and concentrated exclusively on the amount of money awarded to them.

Both Kennecott and the MM&SW subsequently referred to this decision jokingly, saying that when I showed up for the hearing suffering from a sore back, they knew the union was bound to win. Although the plant manager did withdraw his memorandum and the company formally repudiated the policy he had initiated, I never saw any evidence that the parties subsequently placed a stronger emphasis on the rehabilitation of injured workers.

In contrast to the relatively long duration of my Kennecott-MM&SW umpireship, my tenure as umpire under the Phelps Dodge-MM&SW collective agreement was rather short and not very enjoyable. Phelps Dodge was a tough, essentially anti-union organization with considerable political and economic power. Compromise and accommodation were tactics undreamt of in its philosophy. Its industrial relations staff, reflecting the corporate outlook, regarded any arbitration decision against the company as a form of lèse-majesté. It was represented in labor matters by a large and powerful regional law firm in the person of John Boland, a good lawyer and also a decent and amiable person who didn't fit the corporate pattern.

Boland's opposite number, Sylvain Schnaittacher, was a member of the MM&SW who, although not legally trained, represented his clients brilliantly and often successfully. The scion of a wealthy Jewish family in San Francisco, Schnaittacher was a free soul whose principal hobby was exploring small towns in the mountains of Mexico for traces of Jewish families who had migrated from Spain during the Spanish Inquisition. He lived a bachelor existence, his sole companion a large Great Dane that he allowed to roam through the neighborhood searching for food. A peaceful animal, the Dane had one unfortunate anti-social trait: he had an incurable animosity against postmen and a habit of biting them. Schnaittacher paid the fines but, with the exception of posting "Beware of Dog" signs on his property, took no other action.

Schnaittacher had an easy rapport with the miners he represented and enjoyed their complete confidence. He had a great sense of humor and was a fascinating raconteur of his exploring adventures. I developed quite a fondness for him.

As previously mentioned, a number of the top officers of the MM&SW were either Communists or Communist Party sympathizers. Their political sympathies were shared by some of the rank-and-file. Among these was a charismatic local union chairman named Juan Chacon, who enjoyed a brief period of celebrity as the protagonist in a film, *Salt of the Earth*, made by the MM&SW, in which the key roles were played by members of the union. Chacon had appeared before me in an arbitration case, and he impressed me as a dedicated and capable representative of the union and its members. The film, which dealt with the hardships endured by copper miners, was strongly and relentlessly opposed as a piece of Communist propaganda by the Catholic Church and other anti-communist organizations. They were so successful in mass-picketing the theaters that had dared to screen it that I was never able to see it. Today, it would probably suffer a similar fate—not because of violent opposition but, rather, because of public indifference.

My service as the Phelps Dodge-MM&SW umpire came to an abrupt end when I was summarily fired by the company following my reinstatement of two discharged miners for refusal to obey a direct order by their foreman. The dischargees had refused to obey the order to free a clogged overhead chute while standing directly underneath it, on the ground that it was patently unsafe and necessitated a procedure that the company's own rules forbade. The foreman was a "bull-of-the-woods" type who ended up doing the job himself. The company argued that the dischargees could and should have obeyed the foreman's order. The union introduced evidence that one of the miners involved had been seriously injured doing the same job on an earlier occasion, when he was buried neck-deep in a mass of debris released from the chute that left his entire body badly bruised and might well have killed him. When the foreman performed the job, he narrowly avoided the same fate. I reinstated the two grievants, finding that their reason for refusing the foreman's order was reasonable and that the foreman had violated the company's established safety procedures by insisting that they carry out the assignment.

My consequent discharge came as no surprise; I had been given to understand on several occasions that the company would not tolerate an arbitrator's reversal of any major disciplinary action it took against any of its employees. I was taken aback, however, when several weeks after I had received my walking papers the company's director of industrial relations telephoned to ask my opinion of a candidate to succeed me as umpire. The man in question was L. Dale Coffman, a former dean of the UCLA School of Law, who had been ousted at the insistence of the great majority of the law faculty. Coffman was a right-wing Republican, a member of the John Birch Society, and an avowed and virulent anti-Semite. As dean, he had acted characteristically in a dictatorial and bullying manner. In responding to the request for my assessment of Coffman, I decided to avoid any reference to his attributes but to emphasize his lack of experience as an arbitrator. The company sent someone to interview him; in the event, he did not get the job.

By far the happiest experience I have enjoyed as a neutral was my long association with United Air Lines (UAL) and the Air Line Pilots Association (ALPA), which began early in the 1970s and continued into the 1990s. My role was not that of umpire; the parties preferred the dispute-settlement structure and terminology of the Railway Labor Act—that is, a tripartite adjustment board, aided as necessary by a neutral referee. The UAL-ALPA adjustment board consisted of two management and two union representatives. Unlike most similar bodies, it was able to settle a number of disputes submitted to it, but in the event of a deadlock, it brought in a referee to resolve the dispute. It maintained a large panel of referees, all well-known arbitrators, and for most of the period concerned I was called in first when the board of adjustment deadlocked.

The personnel of the four-member adjustment board varied, but during my tenure as referee the principal employer and union representative remained the same. The company representative was Stuart Bernstein, an attorney with a prominent Chicago law firm. Bernstein was, and is, a bundle of energy. He is very smart, non-confrontational but extremely persuasive, funny, and unpretentious. His counterpart on the union side was Ed Flynn, a senior pilot, who possessed the same qualities, with one exception: whereas Bernstein was ceaselessly energetic, Flynn was laid back and easy going. Both men were interested in solving problems, not winning arguments. Bernstein was short and Flynn was about 6'4"; physically, they reminded one of the comic strip characters Mutt and Jeff. The two men were good friends, but this did not prevent them from sometimes going at it hammer and tongs when arguing the merits of their respective positions in executive sessions of the adjustment board. I had a very easy relationship with both men and admired and respected them.

My services as referee were terminated in 1973, following a decision of the full adjustment board, by a vote of three to two, to uphold the discharge of a pilot named Ramey for negligence and disregard of company policy.

Ramey was captain of a Boeing 727 aircraft with a full passenger load on a flight from Boston to Denver. The plane experienced technical problems that made it extremely difficult to maintain level flight. Calling ahead to inquire about weather conditions in Denver, Ramey was advised that it was raining hard and that the runways were covered with water. Nevertheless, he elected to land the aircraft and so informed the tower at Denver. He did not ask that emergency crews be standing by. He made this decision, ignoring the advice of his first and second officers, both of whom favored circling the airport until they could talk to the Boeing people about such matters as whether the plane's antiskid mechanism would work in this situation. In so doing, he ignored the company's "crew concept," which encouraged discussion among members of the flight crew before making a decision involving a critical safety issue. As I recall, Ramey's explanation for his decision to ignore the views of the two other members of his flight crew was that they would only confuse him. Ramey landed the plane at a speed far greater than the maximum permitted by the flight manual and further down the runway than was normally permitted. The aircraft "hydroplaned" and overran the remaining section of the runway, tearing off its landing gear in the process. Fortunately, no passengers were seriously injured.

The hearings in the case lasted throughout 1972; in all, we met 13 times to hear all the evidence, most of which was highly technical and concentrated on the probable performance of the B-727 aircraft under the conditions previously described. The record in the case was extensive, and I did not have time to digest it all before leaving, at the first of 1973, for a sabbatical year as a visiting fellow at Clare Hall, Cambridge. In February 1973, I invited my colleagues on the system board to join me there for an executive session on the Ramey case. They enthusiastically agreed.

The executive session lasted for several days and was unusually heated and tense. The union's arguments challenging the fairness of the company's decision to fire Ramey (a relatively rare practice in the airline industry) were presented by the second member of the union team. Flynn was unusually quiet, leading me to suspect that he did not oppose the company's dismissal of Ramey. When the time came to vote, I sided with the company, knowing that ALPA, for internal political reasons, had to dismiss me in reprisal. I also understood why, also for political reasons, Flynn had to join his union

colleague in dissent, but I sensed that his heart was not in it. I never asked
him and he never volunteered an explanation. We remained good friends
until his death a few years later.

Although our session in Cambridge was not a particularly happy one,
there was one bright spot that I shall never forget. The other members
of the board were staying at a hotel in Cambridge, and we all spent
our evenings there after the day's work was done. I still remember the
occasion very late one evening when Flynn got behind the bar and
demonstrated to an enthralled group of locals how to make a martini.
He invested each step of the process with such drama, with particular
emphasis on the limited role of dry vermouth (he waived the cork of the
vermouth bottle gently over the several ounces of gin), as well as on the
importance of icing the cocktail (like James Bond he preferred shaking to
mixing and stirring), that when he concluded by tasting his concoction
with blissful appreciation, his audience applauded.

In due course, I received a formal notice from ALPA that my services
as a referee would no longer be required. I accepted this news with equanimity and without rancor or bitterness. A number of persons connected
with the union as well as with the company wrote to me expressing their
indignation at my dismissal. For example, a UAL captain and an alternate
to the system board sent me a copy of his letter to the acting chairman
of the ALPA local union involved in the Ramey case, which expressed
his strong displeasure with the "ill-timed and ill-considered action on
the part of the MEC [Master Executive Council]." He went on to say
that "to hire and fire a referee on the basis of win/lose obviates the whole
principle of having a neutral referee, and especially when we consider
that Mr. Aaron and the rest of the [neutral] panel are considered to be
of the highest caliber, not only in our industry, but throughout the whole
field of arbitration."

I quote at length from my reply because it expresses the philosophy
that has guided me throughout my career as an arbitrator:

> It was very good of you to come to my defense, and I deeply appreciate the sentiments
> that prompted you to do so. At the risk of appearing to be ungrateful, however, I think
> you may have been a little hard on your colleagues. One of the great strengths of the

institution of voluntary labor arbitration in this country is that it permits the parties to get rid of arbitrators in whom they have lost confidence, or whose continuing service has been politically embarrassing. Arbitrators generally understand the need for these changes, even though they may personally feel that they were not justified on an objective basis. It really doesn't matter whether the UAL-MEC was justified or unjustified, wise or foolish in removing me as chairman of the UAL-ALPA System Board. Whatever their reasons, I am quite content to accept them.

Several years later, a well-known arbitrator who had held a position as referee under an agreement between United and the IAM was summarily dismissed after rendering a decision that offended one of the parties. He called me in great distress, asking what he could do to retain his position. In keeping with my philosophy, I told him that he had no alternative but to accept his dismissal, that with the lapse of time he might be reappointed, and that, in any case, his career as an arbitrator was unlikely to be seriously affected.

My dismissal as referee under the United-ALPA collective bargaining agreement did not end my association with those parties. In 1976, somewhat to my surprise, I was invited by both sides to serve as moderator of their upcoming negotiations over the terms of a new agreement. Contract negotiations in the past had never gone smoothly. New agreements had not been reached until months after the expiration of the previous ones, a circumstance that exacerbated the already strained relations between the two sides.

This time, however, several propitious factors gave promise of a different result. The accession of a new president of United introduced a new era of good feeling between the parties, and United was experiencing a brief prosperity in the normal boom and bust cycle affecting the entire airline industry. Negotiations were kicked off at a luncheon given by United for the bargaining committees for both sides at which the airline's president pledged his cooperation in bringing about a new and mutually beneficial relationship between the parties.

The contract negotiations lasted for several weeks. My role was a modest one, confined to keeping the parties focused on the task before them, cooling down occasional flare-ups between individual negotiators, and inserting some new ideas to break deadlocks over particularly contentious issues. The results were gratifying. The terms of a new agreement were reached and ratified several months before the expiration of the previous contract—something never before achieved—and the relationship between the parties noticeably improved.

Both parties were so satisfied with the outcome that they adopted the same format for the next round of negotiations several years later, and again asked me to serve as moderator. Unhappily, we were unable to repeat the success of the last experience. The bloom was off the relationship between the parties; the briefly popular president of United was now perceived by ALPA as dictatorial and somewhat hostile. Negotiations did not go well, and I was unable to bring the parties closer together. The sessions ended without reaching agreement on the terms of a new contract, and ALPA threatened to strike. Some time after the expiration of the previous agreement, the parties signed off on a new one, but the era of good feeling had been destroyed by rancor and mutual distrust.

Despite the failure of this second round of negotiations under the auspices of a neutral moderator, I think the experiment was worthwhile. The requisites for success were, first, a genuine desire by both sides to reach an agreement, even at the cost of making some compromises, and second, a favorable economic environment, which the airline industry has rarely enjoyed in recent times.

I look back on my long association with United and ALPA with great satisfaction and gratitude for a rewarding experience. The cases I heard were the usual mixed bag characteristic of arbitration in general: some were routine and not very interesting; others, of which the Ramey case was by no means the only example, were extremely challenging. These and other cases in which I served as arbitrator for other airlines—including American Airlines, Continental Airlines, Delta Air Lines, Eastern Air Lines, Hawaiian Airlines, National Airlines, Northwest Airlines, Pan American World Airways, and Trans World Airlines, as well as for other unions, including the IAM, the Transport Workers, and the Teamsters, and various associations of flight attendants—provided me with a valuable familiarity with the airline industry. My closest personal ties were with Flynn and Bernstein, the leading members of the United system board. Flynn died some years ago, and I seldom see Bernstein anymore, but I cherish the memories of their friendship and of the good times we shared.

Reflecting on my experiences as an umpire or sole arbitrator in a substantial number of cases for the same parties, I am struck by the protean nature of the arbitrator's authority under different collective bargaining agreements. In some, the parties expect the arbitrator—even one designated as an umpire—to behave very much like a judge or ad hoc arbitrator, confining his decision and opinion to a parsing and application of the relevant term(s) to the facts presented at the hearing. In others, the parties seek a closer relationship with the arbitrator and expect him to expand his role to include discussion with either or both parties, on or off the record, designed to bring about a solution that will be satisfactory to both. Most collective bargaining agreements treat the introduction of new jobs and the setting of wage rates as a management prerogative, although they may permit those actions to be challenged, on limited grounds, by individual grievants. But other agreements entrust the arbitrator with final authority to make such decisions. One of the great strengths of labor-management arbitration, I think, is that it permits the parties to design a system of grievance adjudication that best suits their needs and to dismiss the arbitrator whenever he no longer retains the confidence of either or both.

During the 1980s, I served as the sole arbitrator for the U.S. Postal Service and the two major unions representing its employees: the National Association of Letter Carriers (NALC) and the American Postal Workers Union (APWU). Two other unions—the Mail Handlers and the Rural Mail Carriers—were also covered by the national agreement, but only a few of their cases came before me. I started out as a regional arbitrator; later, I served as the national arbitrator designated to hear cases of major importance. All hearings in those cases were held in Washington D.C.

I hesitated to accept the appointment as national arbitrator. It didn't make much sense, in my view, for the parties to select an arbitrator based in Los Angeles when all the hearings were in Washington. But the parties insisted that they wanted an arbitrator of national standing, for whom they were willing to pay the extra transportation costs. I finally agreed to serve because the regional cases I had been hearing were, on the whole, poorly prepared and presented and most of the issues that were raised did not interest me very much.

Almost all of the national cases submitted to me were challenging, especially those arising from the introduction of new technology, such as the multi-position letter-sorting machine (MPLSM) and the optical character reader (OCR) system—including the channel sorter (OCR-CS) and the bar code reader (BCR)—and the establishment of new positions, such as OCR operator and mail processor. Disagreements between the parties arose over the right of the postal service unilaterally to introduce new systems and to create new job classifications during the term of the existing collective bargaining agreement and to assign the work to a particular national craft. The rates of pay set by the postal service for the new classifications were also challenged by one or more of its unions. To the difficulty of resolving these questions by reference to agreements that provided clues but not specific and definitive answers was added the necessity of understanding how the new machines worked: for example, the OCR-I was 60 feet long and was staffed by seven to nine employees, whose duties included loading, sweep-tiering, and feeding two mail transport units (MTUs), each of which handled approximately 20,000 pieces of mail per hour.

The most notable of these cases was brought by the APWU in April 1984. The specific issues were (1) whether the creation and implementation by the postal service of the new standard position, mail processor, at pay levels 3 constituted an impermissible unilateral midterm modification of the 1981–1984 national agreement, in violation of either that agreement or the National Labor Relations Act; (2) whether the change in the postal service's personnel handbook to include the new standard position effected changes that were "fair, reasonable, and equitable" within the meaning of the 1981–1984 national agreement; and (3) if the ranking of the new standard position was unfair, unreasonable, and inequitable, what was the appropriate remedy?

The dispute originated in June 1982 in a letter sent to the APWU, the NALC, and the mail handlers union by the assistant postmaster general advising them of the new bargaining unit position, mail processor, at pay level 3. The letter also expressed the view that the new position should be assigned to the clerk craft, but offered to consult with the three unions prior to making a craft assignment determination. After such consultations had been held, the postal service did assign the new position to the clerk craft, and the mail handlers filed a grievance protesting that assignment. Meetings between the APWU and the postal service were held in August and September 1982; in October, the union appealed its case to arbitration. In December, APWU filed an unfair labor practice charge against the postal service with the NLRB, accusing the service of refusing to bargain in good faith and of unilaterally taking actions that would downgrade up to 44,000 existing clerk craft positions. In accordance with existing practices, the NLRB regional director advised the parties in February 1983 that he would not issue a complaint because of his determination that further proceedings should be administratively deferred for arbitration. He also advised that if the case went to arbitration, the union could obtain a board review of the arbitrator's award.

Noting in my opinion accompanying the award that the NLRB's policy was not to defer to an arbitrator's decision unless it purports to deal with the unfair labor practice issues as well as with the contract violation issues, I reluctantly ruled on the former despite my belief that it is an unwise policy to require arbitrators to pass upon statutory rights in a private proceeding over which the NLRB has primary jurisdiction. On the basis of my analysis of the relevant provisions of the collective agreement, I held that the postal service's bargaining obligations in respect of the introduction of new mechanization or equipment or the establishment of new positions were limited to giving the union advance notice of its decision, subject to the union's right to challenge that decision by filing a grievance appealable to arbitration; prior union consent was not required. It followed that the postal service was not guilty of an unlawful refusal to bargain in good faith.

Apart from the procedural issues, I found that the dispute was over the pay level assigned to the new standard position. OCR-1 operators were rated at pay level 5; mail processors were rated at pay level 3.

APWU argued that the pay rate for mail processor should also be pay level 5. After a lengthy analysis of the parties' conflicting arguments and of the applicable provisions of the collective agreement, I concluded that the ranking of the mail processor position at pay level 3 was patently unfair, but that the postal service's judgment that level 5 was too high a ranking should not be overturned unless it was equally unfair; and that although the choice between levels 5 and 4 was a close one, the appropriate pay level for the mail processor position was level 4. Accordingly, I held that all employees assigned to work as mail processors at pay level 3 must be reimbursed the difference between pay level 3 and 4 for all time spent in that position.

It was a pleasure for me to arbitrate cases such as that involving the mail processors, not only because of their complexity but also because of the excellence of the presentation and arguments by counsel for all the parties involved. This was in marked contrast to the situation in most of the regional cases I had handled, in which the representatives arguing the cases, particularly those on the union side, were simply unequal to the task. Nevertheless, I became increasingly frustrated by the growing number of situations in which I flew to Washington only to be told on my arrival that the hearing had been cancelled. My remonstrances against the lack of sufficient notice of these cancellations and the consequential loss of a day spent in traveling from the West Coast, for which I did not charge the parties, were in vain. At length I resorted to a threat to resign if the situation did not improve, but the parties, after promising to do better, failed to do so. Finally, I had enough and tendered my resignation, which was accepted. Shortly thereafter, I received a telephone call from a high-ranking member of the postal service management asking if I would take just one more case. This was a hot potato involving the discharge of 14 employees at the Anson Jones postal station in Houston, Texas, in August 1983, allegedly for (1) engaging in an unlawful walkout and work stoppage against the postal service in violation of federal law; (2) violating a provision in the 1981–1984 national agreement stating that APWU and NALC, on behalf of their members, agreed not to sanction a strike or slowdown; and (3) being absent without leave. My caller explained that the discharges were so controversial that, in all likelihood, the arbitrator would be discharged by the losing party. For that reason, he said, all parties were reluctant to ask my replacement to handle this case, and inasmuch as I was leaving anyway, they would be grateful if I would take on the thankless assignment. Although I disliked the role of designated cat's-paw, I did appreciate the refreshing candor of the request, so I grudgingly agreed to accept the assignment.

I held a two-day hearing in March 1984 in Houston. The events precipitating the mass dismissal of the employees at the Anson Jones station were as follows. On the morning of 18 August 1983, Hurricane Alicia hit Houston, bringing with it massive destruction and interrupting normal services such as light and power. The Houston post office was effectively shut down that day, and employees were granted administrative leave. On Friday, 19 August, the post office management attempted to resume normal postal operations. All of the almost 50 stations in the Houston post office had employees delivering mail, but most were without power and water. To deal with the loss of power, the postal service moved a few portable generators in and out of stations deemed to be critical points. Efforts to secure additional generators were unsuccessful.

All of the 14 grievants worked at the Anson Jones station. There was considerable divergence between their accounts and the accounts of management personnel of conditions at the station on Friday, 19 August, and Monday, 22 August. Grievants testified in part that, when they reported for work on Monday, they had smelled gas fumes and sewage odors, that there had been barely enough light to see where they were going, that it was very hot and the humidity was almost as high as the temperature, that there was no electricity and no water pressure in the water fountains, and that there was only one generator for the entire station. A number of grievants reported that they had become ill or dizzy and had gone outside to keep from passing out. Management witnesses testified in part that the toilets were "kind of smelly" on Friday because of urine on the floor, but that conditions were not so bad on Monday. One testified that he had brought a gallon of ice water from home.

All 14 grievants reported that conditions in the station were so bad that they became ill and had to leave. Each of them made that decision independently and did not urge anyone else to leave. Some filed out forms used for leave requests and left them on the supervisor's desk before leaving, but some left without doing so. None of them received express permission to leave. All of them eventually returned voluntarily when conditions in the station improved.

The principal issue in the case was whether the grievants had engaged in an unlawful strike. My discussion of this issue was in part as follows:

> A strike is commonly understood to be a concerted withholding of labor by employees in order to protest against working conditions, to enforce compliance with specific demands, or both....One may assume that if there was concerted activity, it was to protest against working conditions, rather than to enforce specific demands, because the conditions at the Anson Jones station that caused the 14 grievants temporarily to leave were mostly beyond the control of management. Moreover, as soon as those conditions were even slightly ameliorated, the grievants voluntarily returned to work.
>
> A common incident of a strike is the concerted activity of the strikers to urge fellow employees to walk off the job, and to attempt to persuade others, by setting up a picket line or resort to some other means, not to enter the struck establishment. It is conceded in this case that the grievants sought neither to persuade other carriers at the Anson Jones station to walk out, nor to dissuade the substitutes called in from other stations to help out from entering the premises. No picket line was established.

My conclusion, on the basis of the entire record, was that the postal service had failed to prove, even by a mere preponderance of the evidence, the charge of a concerted walkout by the grievants. I also agreed with the union that the postal service's procedures, both during and subsequent to the events of 22 August, were seriously deficient. At no time during the morning hours on 22 August did a management representative expressly forbid any of the grievants to leave or warn any of them that he or she might subsequently be accused of engaging in a concerted walkout. It was clear from their testimony that management witnesses suspected at the time that the grievants were acting in concert and that their individual claims of illness were a sham, yet they did nothing more than to advise some of them to "think for themselves" and to urge a few others to remain on the job because they were sorely needed.

Subsequently, the postal service treated each of the grievants exactly the same, without attempting to differentiate between them on the basis of their actual physical conditions or other relevant circumstances, such as the fact that several returned to work only a few hours after leaving. In a matter as serious as this, I declared, the postal service was required to review the cases of the 14 grievants individually, instead of treating them as so many fungible units.

For all the foregoing reasons, which I set forth in considerably greater detail than is feasible in this account, I held that the discharge of each of the 14 grievants was without just cause. Accordingly, I ruled that each must be reinstated with full back pay and seniority. I also directed that all time not worked by any of them on 22 August be charged to sick leave.

The union had requested that the grievants be awarded damages in addition to back pay, and that they be paid interest on all monies due to them. It also asked for reimbursement for costs and attorneys' fees. I denied the request for costs and attorneys' fees, but retained jurisdiction over the interest claim until I had ruled on that issue in another case then pending before me. That case involved the postal service and NALC and APWU.

The case involving payment of interest arose in the postal service's Denver regional office, but it was removed by the postal service to the national level, where the issue was one of first impression. The case was heard in December 1983. The stipulated issue was as follows: "Whether the arbitrator is authorized by the [1981–1984] National Agreement to award interest as part of a back-pay award when sustaining a disciplinary grievance."

The grievant had protested a five-day disciplinary suspension. At all stages of the grievance procedure the union had asked that the grievant be made whole for all the wages and benefits lost due to the suspension, plus interest at the rate of one and one-half percent per month from the date wages were withheld until the date lost wages were paid. No settlement of the dispute was reached, and it was eventually referred to arbitration at the national level. The merits of the grievance were not involved: following my decision on the interest issue, the grievance was to be remanded to the regional level for disposition. The unions did not seek a ruling that an arbitrator *must* award interest in this or any other discipline case; they sought only a decision that arbitrators in national, regional, and expedited discipline cases had the authority to *consider* a request for interest. The postal service insisted that arbitrators had no such authority in postal service cases. My decision in this case, therefore, was in the nature of a declaratory judgment.

All parties in this case claimed that the national agreement and the employee manual supported their respective positions: Article 16 (Discipline) provided in pertinent part that any discipline or discharge alleged to be for just cause should be subject to the grievance arbitration process "which could result in reinstatement and restitution, including back pay." The postal service's principal argument was based on this language. It asserted that the substance of Article 16 had been in every agreement since the 1970 Postal Reorganization Act and that it made no provision for an award of interest on back pay. The unions countered with the argument that nothing in Article 16 prohibited an award of interest on back pay in appropriate cases. They also maintained that the word "restitution" in that article was broad enough to encompass interest on back pay.

The postal service found it significant that the unions had three times previously sought, unsuccessfully, to include language in the national agreement that back pay awards must always include interest at a predetermined rate. The unions asserted, however, that none of their previous attempts to obtain language mandating interest on back pay embodied an admission that the national agreement precluded any and all interest awards.

My decision, handed down in December 1984, was ultimately based on my interpretation of Article 16; I disregarded a number of conflicting arguments by the parties on the basis of irrelevance or nonapplicability. The accompanying opinion read in part:

> A phrase commonly employed in reference to arbitrated remedies for wrongful disciplinary suspensions or terminations is that the grievants should be "made whole" for what they have lost in wages, seniority, and other benefits. When a successful

grievant is forced to wait a long time before recovering back pay he has lost as a result of an unjust disciplinary penalty, denial of interest means he cannot be "made whole." Although … interest on a back-pay award has been neither asked for nor granted in the bulk of disciplinary cases in which the grievances have been sustained, I can see no logical reason why it should not be granted in circumstances in which the penalty was excessive or vindictive, or imposed in bad faith or in violation of an established public policy, particularly when the grievant has had to wait a long time before being paid.…

Postal Service did not challenge interest on back-pay awards until it became alarmed by their increasing frequency. [The unions had cited ten cases since 1982 in which regional arbitrators had awarded interest on back pay in postal cases]… Arbitrators are often called upon to interpret ambiguous language, the meaning of which is disputed by the parties. To do this, they require more leeway in the exercise of their discretion, especially in formulating appropriate types of relief for employees who have been unfairly punished.

My award in this case declared:

An arbitrator is authorized by the National Agreement, in his discretion, to award interest as part of a back-pay award when sustaining a disciplinary grievance.

A few days later, I issued a supplementary decision in the Houston case covering the reserved issue of interest on the back pay awards to the 14 grievants. Noting that my previous findings in this case that the discharges of the 14 grievants constituted excessive and unwarranted punishment and that the procedures followed by the postal service in determining that punishment denied the grievants due process, I held that each of them was entitled to interest on the back pay due. In the absence of a predetermined interest rate in the national agreement, I adopted as appropriate the "adjusted prime rate" used by the NLRB. For the period 1 January to 30 June 1984, the adjusted prime rate was 11 percent. Accordingly, my final award provided:

Postal Service shall pay to…the…grievants interest on their respective back-pay awards in the amount of 11 percent. Interest shall be computed from the date of discharge to the date when back pay was actually paid to the individual grievants.

I never found any reason to my regret my resignation as arbitrator under the postal service national agreement. Nevertheless, in retrospect, I concluded that despite the inability of the parties to hold all the hearings in Washington that had previously been scheduled, resulting in substantial losses of my time, the experience on the whole had been a valuable one.

During the 1950s, I heard quite a few arbitration cases in the motion picture industry. These disputes involved all of the major studios and a number of different unions representing office workers, blue-collar crafts, and professional guilds. I learned a great deal about such matters as the new technology of color films, the rules governing the granting of film credits, the fine distinctions between an added scene and a retake, and the rival claims of jurisdiction over various types of work by the craft unions.

The jurisdictional disputes may seem ridiculous and inexcusably wasteful to the uninitiated. These examples were typical: the costumers and the make-up artists fought over the right to make military uniforms look battle-worn and the fitting of "falsies" for the actresses; the carpenters and the stagehands quarreled over the right to sweep up sawdust on the stages. From the point of view of the participants, however, disputes over the right to do certain types of work made a lot of sense. The motion picture industry, with its relatively high wages and its generous overtime payments (referred to in collective bargaining agreements as "golden hours") attracted a large pool of workers. But many of those in the pool were only sporadically employed. They put great pressure, therefore, on their unions' business agents to fight to secure for their members whatever work was available.

The cold war between the United States and the Soviet Union led to the notorious loyalty security program in this country and to the rise to power of legislative committees such as the House Un-American Activities Committee (HUAC). These bodies soon turned their sights on the motion picture industry, especially actors and directors, and this brought a surge of highly unfavorable publicity. Also, because the industry cooperated completely with HUAC and similar federal and state committees, many actors and directors were dismissed or blacklisted. Those developments, plus the relatively low profitability of the industry, contributed to a pervasive fear among all studio employees that their jobs were in jeopardy.

My very first studio arbitration involved the discharge by MGM of an assistant film editor. It represented not only the lengths to which a studio would go to rid itself of a long-serving employee in order to avoid paying him a pension but also the standard practice of witnesses of lying to protect themselves and preserve their jobs.

Al Sarno, the discharged employee, had worked for MGM for about 25 years and was getting ready to retire with a promised pension. Under the applicable collective bargaining agreement, a discharge for just cause would render him ineligible to receive his pension. The reason given for Sarno's discharge was, incredibly, that he could not get along with his fellow employees. To prove this preposterous charge, the studio called as witnesses a number of his co-workers. One by one, the witnesses took the stand, swore to tell the truth, and then declared that Sarno was ill-tempered and so hostile that no one could get along with him. As this litany was repeated by the string of witnesses, Sarno reacted, first with disbelief, then with sadness. "Sam," he asked one of the witnesses in a tearful voice, "we've been friends for 25 years. Why are you doing this to me?" He received no answer. The witness did not even look in his direction, let alone make eye contact with him.

By the time the hearing was over, Sarno was slumped in his chair, his face a picture of inconsolable sorrow. Finding that MGM's reason for discharging him was obviously spurious and that the testimony given by witnesses against him was not credible, I held that the discharge was not for just cause and reinstated him with back pay. Shortly thereafter, he retired with his pension.

I encountered this pattern of lying to save one's job throughout the industry. In a case I heard at 20th Century Fox involving some employees with relatively high ranking, the witnesses called by the studio were so defensive that their answers to questions about the conduct of others were usually preceded by assertions that they themselves were innocent bystanders.

I once asked George Wasson, head of the studio's legal department, whether he could explain this peculiar conduct. No studio employee, from the highest to the lowest, he replied, ever was thanked or congratulated for anything. The only occasions when they were called in by their superiors involved criticism or discipline for something they had allegedly done or failed to do. Consequently, he continued, anyone called by the studio as a witness in an arbitration case automatically assumed that he was being blamed for something. This attitude was matched by management's suspicion that any request for an interview by an employee was a prelude to making a complaint. Wasson illustrated the intensity of that suspicion with the following anecdote:

> The actress, Celeste Holm, had just finished a picture at 20th Century Fox. Everything had gone well, and she was so pleased with the experience that she decided to thank the studio head, Darryl Zanuck. Accordingly, she telephoned his office and asked for an appointment. For what purpose? his secretary asked. Holm replied that it was a personal matter. After further conversation, she was given an appointment two weeks later. Holm showed up at Zanuck's office at the designated time, but was left to cool her heels for an hour before being ushered into his presence. He sat in a chair with his back to her and waited for five minutes before turning around to face her. As he did so, he asked sternly, "Okay, Celeste, what's the beef?"[5]

My experience as an arbitrator in the motion picture industry included one very interesting case involving an internal dispute in the American Federation of Musicians (AFM), which organized the sizable number of musicians employed by the various studios. Led by its "president for life," the redoubtable James Caesar Petrillo, the AFM was noted for the inelastic rules it imposed on all employers of union musicians. Its West Coast local had, prior to 1947 when the Taft-Hartley Act outlawed the practice, established the closed shop as part of its collective bargaining agreements with the studios. Subsequently, a rival group of musicians, calling themselves the Musicians' Guild, succeeded in wresting representation rights from the AFM at one of the studios. The Guild then demanded that all members of the AFM working at that studio join the Guild as a condition of continuing employment. A number of AFM members, including a majority of the most talented, did in fact join the Guild and were summarily expelled by the AFM. They sued to have that

---

[5] My reference to this story is a violation of my self-imposed rule not to include hearsay accounts in my own recollections, but I have made an exception in this case because it so perfectly illustrates the point being made.

action reversed, and eventually the case was referred to arbitration. I was selected as arbitrator.

The gist of the complaint filed by the expelled musicians was that they had been denied due process of law. They pointed out that if they refused to join the Guild, they would be out of a job. The AFM defense was that by joining the Guild, the complainants had engaged in dual unionism, a crime equivalent to treason, and had thereby forfeited their right to continued membership in the AFM.

I held a series of evening sessions at which most of the individual complainants out of a total of about 50 testified on their own behalf. AFM was represented by an able attorney, Robert Rissman, a member of a prominent Los Angeles law firm specializing in protecting civil liberties. The individual complainants chose to represent themselves. Each of them seemed to share two prominent characteristics: the lack of any ability to stop talking, and an unfounded conviction that he had a thorough understanding of applicable constitutional law principles. In the end, despite the welter of excessive testimony and the constant repetition of incorrect or irrelevant arguments, I concluded that the due process rights of the complainants had, indeed, been violated and that they had been expelled without just cause. Accordingly, I held that they should all be reinstated as members of good standing in the AFM.

When the text of my award and lengthy opinion was received by the AFM general counsel's office in Washington, it responded with a great blast of wrath, including a strong personal attack on me. I do not know what action, if any, it took in response to my award; I assume that AFM eventually complied. In any event, the Guild proved not to be a viable organization and it collapsed shortly thereafter.

Half a century has elapsed since my involvement as an arbitrator in the motion picture industry, which has experienced a number of incarnations since then. I have the impression, which may be wrong, that arbitration of grievances over terms and conditions of employment in that industry is less frequent than it once was. But nothing I have read or heard leads me to believe that the patterns of behavior described in the preceding paragraphs have changed significantly over the years

In 60 years of practice as an arbitrator of labor-management disputes, I have had my share of "big cases." From these I have selected only one to discuss in these recollections, not so much because of the issues involved, although they were of considerable interest to management and workers in the steel industry, but because of the decision of the parties not only to suppress the text of my award and opinion but also to enjoin me from making any public comment or explanation of the reasons underlying my decision.

The parties to the arbitration were the United Steelworkers of America (USWA) and the Coordinating Committee Steel Companies (CCSC).[6] On 28 February 1983, USWA and CCSC entered into an agreement submitting to me, as sole arbitrator, six issues for binding arbitration. The hearing was held in Los Angeles from 27 to 31 July. The parties submitted both pre-hearing and post-hearing briefs. The voluminous record also included verbatim transcript of the testimony and numerous exhibits. Because I was scheduled to leave for England in early August, the hearing was completed in five days, each of which was lengthy, usually extending into the evening hours.

Each party was represented by extremely able counsel: Michael H. Gottesman and Gary Sasso for the union; Leonard L. Scheinholtz, Hollis T. Hurd, and Dominic B. King for the CCSC. The principal witnesses were Lloyd McBride, president, and Bernard Kleiman, general counsel of the USWA, and J. Bruce Johnston, chairman of the CCSC.

The facts of this complicated dispute were unique in the long history of collective bargaining between the two parties. At least since 1981, the steel industry in the United States had been in the grip of an acute economic depression: each of the seven companies making up the CCSC had sustained substantial operating losses, a number of plants had been shut down, employment in the domestic steel industry was at its lowest point since 1933, and the pressure from foreign competition continued to increase. Although the 1980 collective bargaining

---

[6] The CCSC consisted of seven companies: Armco Inc., Bethlehem Steel Corporation, Inland Steel Company, Jones & Laughlin Steel Company, National Steel Corporation, Republic Steel Corporation, and United States Steel Corporation.

agreement between the parties was not due to expire until 31 July 1983, the two sides agreed to an early reopening of the existing agreement, and negotiations commenced at the end of June 1982. These negotiations, which concluded on 30 July 1982 with a meeting of the union's Basic Steel Industry Conference (BSIC), came to be known by the parties as "Round I." It did not result in any agreement. What came to be known as "Round II" began in October 1982 and resulted in a settlement agreement, dated 19 November 1982, that was recommended by the entire union negotiating team. On the same date, however, the agreement was rejected by the BSIC.

On 21 January 1983, McBride became seriously ill, and his place as chief of the union's top negotiating team was taken by Joseph Odorcich, one of the union's vice presidents. Formal bargaining in what came to be known as "Round III" of the contract negotiations commenced on 15 February 1983 and continued almost without a break until 28 February, when the new settlement agreement, to become effective 1 March 1983, was reached and ratified by the BSIC.

The six issues submitted to arbitration involved the application of the settlement agreement of 28 February 1983 to SUB (supplementary unemployment benefits), regular and/or extended vacation pay for some or all employees, a special initial pension amount (referred to as "special payment" under the pension agreement between U.S. Steel and the United Steelworkers), the extent of EV (extended vacation) of employees entitled to a senior EV in 1983, the quarterly income benefits under the earnings protection plan, and incentive pay under the "old" incentives. In respect of each of these issues, the principal dispute was whether it would reflect a wage decrease of $1.25 per hour provided for in the settlement agreement. The settlement agreement also included, as did the previous collective bargaining agreement, an Appendix A—a narrative summary of the contract changes agreed to by the parties— which provided in part that the changes embodied in the new settlement agreement "shall be treated for all purposes, except as provided in the Pension Agreement, as general wage changes or increases."

The submission agreement also included the following provision:

> Both sides agree that any information which either side deems to be of a sensitive nature that is introduced in the proceedings will be subject to an appropriate protective order. Both sides further agree that all such confidential material will be returned to the side which offered the information upon completion of the arbitration proceedings and the decision of the arbitrator.

It was also made clear to me that my decision and opinion would be the property of the parties and that I would be expected to decline to comment or to answer any questions about the case without their prior approval.

It is not feasible for me to set forth in this account, even in the most simplified form, the detailed history of the three "rounds" of bargaining that preceded the settlement agreement of 28 February 1983 or to analyze the arguments advanced by the parties on the six issues submitted to arbitration. My opinion explaining the award, which on most issues supported the position of the CCSC, was 89 pages in length (the longest I have ever written in an arbitration case). What follows are quotations from certain sections of my opinion in which I explain how I reached my decision.

At the outset of my opinion, I sought to clarify the nature of my responsibility as an arbitrator and the difficulties in carrying it out:

> The contract changes embodied in the Settlement Agreement of 28 February 1983 are now in effect; the issues submitted to arbitration involve only their interpretation and application. Whether they appear objectively to be fair or unfair, wise or foolish, is immaterial....Because of certain ambiguities in the language of the 1983 Settlement Agreement, it becomes necessary to determine, if possible, what... [the parties'] intentions were in respect of the six items on which...[they] are in dispute. Not surprisingly, each side has argued that the language in question is clear and admits of only one interpretation. Unfortunately, the interpretation that each party claims must proceed ineluctably from the contract language, construed in the light of surrounding circumstances, differs radically from the interpretation insisted upon by the other....The first necessary task, therefore, is to review in considerable detail the evidence of what actually took place during the three sets of negotiations covering the period from June 1982 through February 1983, as well as earlier relevant bargaining history.

After reviewing the history of events leading to the 1983 settlement agreement, I observed:

> What the preceding recital does establish...is that the parties at no time reached a specific, orally articulated, mutual agreement on the effect of the $1.25 per hour

wage decrease on the various economic benefits that are the subject of this arbitration. CCSC argues that even if the parties did not reach a specific oral agreement on this issue, the arbitrator must infer from the events already recounted that they did in fact arrive at a mutual understanding that the wage decrease was to have the effect on the presently disputed economic benefits now asserted by CCSC, and that this understanding was incorporated in the 1983 Settlement Agreement. The Union flatly rejects that interpretation.

My own conclusion, based on a detailed analysis of the history of negotiations immediately preceding the settlement agreement of 1983, as well as the parties' respective arguments supporting their understandings of what they had agreed to, was that their failure to reach oral agreement on the impact of the wage decrease on economic benefits other than pensionable earnings was not an accident:

> Indeed, the case is a classic example of mutual reliance upon calculated ambiguity. Clearly, both sides desperately wanted to reach an agreement by 1 March 1983 [General Motors had advised that if no settlement was reached by that date, it might start using foreign steel for automobile production]. It is my impression that each believed, in good faith, in the interpretation it has advanced in arbitration, but that each was anxious to avoid any direct confrontation over the effect of the wage decrease on the economic benefits now at issue for fear that an agreement might elude them. The failures in Rounds I and II to produce a settlement that would be approved by BSIC was obviously on their minds....
>
> As often happens in cases in which the agreement executed by the parties is ambiguous, the testimony offered in support of their conflicting interpretations is inconclusive. Moreover, the arguments advanced by counsel for both parties match each other in persuasiveness and ingenuity. Unfortunately, neither set of arguments conveys the thinking of the negotiators while they were negotiating; both strongly support ideas carefully thought out after the fact.

In light of these circumstances, I was forced to determine the disputed language of the settlement agreement on the basis of inferences drawn from the history of the 1982-83 negotiations. Both sides agreed that the key was Appendix A. That agreement raised two principal questions:

> First, because that Appendix has never previously been the means of expressing substantive changes in Settlement Agreements, should it be ignored? Second, if not, how should the words in the fourth paragraph, "shall be treated for all purposes, except as provided in the Pension Agreement, or general wage changes or increases," be construed?

My answer to the first question, based on all the testimony, was that Appendix A could not be ignored and must be given substantive effect. In a very real sense, I pointed out, the 1983 settlement agreement represented a break with the past: no prior agreements had provided for a wage decrease. Both sides argued, however, that each had the duty to explain to the other exactly what interpretation it placed on the critical language in Appendix A. My response was that both sides were represented by experienced and highly competent persons and that none of the negotiators on either side could conceivably have overlooked the key issue of the extent of the impact, if any, of the wage decrease or related economic benefits. I suggested that the use of the phrase "general wage changes or increases" instead of the more specific "general decreases or increases" was a euphemism acceptable to both sides, because both desired to avoid arousing negative reactions by the use of the word "decreases." The duty of disclosure, I concluded, fell equally on both parties, and both were equally culpable in failing to recognize that responsibility.

Turning to the second question, concerning the meaning of the critical words in paragraph four of Appendix A, I conceded that they were not free of ambiguity, but rejected the union's objection that they were "so opaque that…[it] could not reasonably be expected to have understood that the language was to have [the] substantive results" attributed to it by the CCSC. Indeed, I observed that the parties had spent about six months negotiating a new agreement, well before the old one was due to expire, in order to give the steel industry some cost relief, as well as to provide greater financial support for laid-off employees represented by the USWA, and that at no time had any thought been given to a wage increase; so far as wage rates were concerned, the only question had been the amount of the decrease the union was willing to accept. It therefore seemed to me that any ambiguous language bearing directly or indirectly on wages and on benefits based on wage rates had to be construed as applying to wage decreases as well as to wage increases.

Ultimately, I concluded that the disputed language in Appendix A must be given substantive effect, and that the most reasonable interpretation, based upon the words themselves and in light of the bargaining history immediately preceding the execution of the 1983 settlement agreement, was that, with a few exceptions, the wage decrease was to have an immediate "flowthrough" on economic benefits based on wage rates.

My award was confined to three pages, and it was released by the parties without reference to the 89-page opinion that accompanied it. Spokesmen for both parties declined to comment on the award, and I felt bound to follow suit.

Response to the award was typified by an article in the Chicago Sun-Times headed "Arbitration Deals Big Setback to Steel Union." The two authors of the piece correctly identified the reason for the unusual reticence of the parties about the award, reporting in part that "to their mutual embarrassment, both sides left the bargaining table without deciding whether the pay cut would be applied in figuring vacation pay and supplemental employment benefits." The *Wall Street Journal* reported that a labor arbitrator had "handed the United Steelworkers Union a big defeat, ruling it must give up more than expected in its new concessionary contract with major steelmakers." Surprisingly, *Steelabor*, the official organ of the USWA, simply reported without comment that the arbitrator "handed down an arbitration decision which ruled against the union in most issues involving unresolved issues arising from the February 28, 1983, settlement with the Steelworkers and the major steel producers." The reaction of a newspaper published by a union local at Inland Steel was quite different. Its story carried the headline "International to Blame" and went on to report that cuts in vacation pay, SUB, and special payment for retirees had been upheld by an arbitrator and that "any first term steward" could have accurately predicted the arbitrator's decision. The story concluded:

> The headlines in the newspapers read: "Arbitrator Deals USWA Huge Setback." The truth is the Arbitrator could not render any other decision under the language [of the new agreement]. The truth is the International and the local union president who voted for the contract dealt the "USWA a Huge Setback." It's unbelievable that they made an 80 million mistake. They knew exactly what they were doing. Playing games with the membership, trying to shift the blame for their actions, isn't going to convince one steel worker that the International isn't responsible. It's bad enough that they gave those concessions. The least they could do is to own up to it.

These comments in the media did not rely on the explanation of how I arrived at the terms of the award that was set forth in much detail in the accompanying opinion, which, of course, they had not seen. That was regrettable, but what really upset me were a number of letters from individual union members, written more in sorrow than in anger, expressing bewilderment over one or more provisions of the award and asking for reconsideration or an explanation. My reply to one typified my response to all of them:

> First, once an award has been issued, the authority of the arbitrator is terminated. He cannot change it unless jointly requested to do so by the parties in the arbitration....
>
> Second, the arbitrator is limited by the terms of the submission agreement to deciding the meaning of the disputed language in the agreement—in this case the 1983 Settlement Agreement. He cannot substitute his own ideas of what is "fair" in place of what he determines was actually agreed to.
>
> Third, in a lengthy opinion accompanying my award I tried to explain as clearly and as comprehensively as possible the reasoning on which my decision was based. The steel companies and the Union, however, mutually agreed not to publish the opinion; they also told me not to release it. Under the terms of the Code of Professional Responsibility, which is binding on labor arbitrators, I have no right to publish my opinion without the express consent of the parties. Therefore, I regret that I am not at liberty to explain to you why [I treated certain issues differently from others].

The fact is that I was hugely disappointed at not being able to publish my opinion and to benefit from the comments and criticisms, both pro and con, which it would certainly have elicited. The experience reminded me of something Harry Shulman once said: "When the parties mutually wish to save face, the arbitrator's face is available as a substitute."

My long career as an arbitrator has, on the whole, brought me considerable satisfaction. Even when the issues involved in labor-management arbitration cases were boring, the operation of the collective bargaining system, including the varieties of grievance and arbitration procedures, never failed to interest me. I kept no scoreboard and do not know the proportion of my decisions that favored labor or management. Indeed, I have no idea how many cases I have decided; a conservative estimate would be between one and two thousand. Because I was only a part-time arbitrator, the income I derived from my practice was modest when compared with that of my colleagues who were full-time arbitrators. Although my per diem fees were generally uniform, I occasionally lowered them for parties who would otherwise be unable to afford my services. Moreover, I have always kept my charges lower than those set by the majority of arbitrators with similar experience and reputation. Serving as an arbitrator never was for me simply a means of making money. Rather, it was a way to enrich my knowledge of labor-management relations in a wide variety of industries and thereby to benefit my teaching and research. In the chapter on the National Academy of Arbitrators, I referred to my disappointment at the changes that have occurred in the way arbitrators pursue their calling. Nevertheless, I believe there are a sufficient number of well-qualified and scrupulously honest arbitrators still practicing their craft to justify the claim that as a group they make a substantial contribution to the welfare of our polity.